Joe Morgan
12/25/11
GLORY!!

Tennessee

A Political History

Tennessee

A Political History

Phillip Langsdon

Hillsboro Press
Franklin, Tennessee

TENNESSEE HERITAGE LIBRARY
Bicentennial Collection

Printed in the United States of America

04 03 02 01 00 1 2 3 4 5

Library of Congress Catalog Card Number: 98-75681

ISBN: 1-57736-125-3

Cover design by Gary Bozeman

Cover photo acknowledgments: background photo courtesy of Tuck•Hinton Architects, Kem Hinton, photographer; Sam Houston, Andrew Johnson, John Sevier, and Don Sundquist, courtesy of Tennessee State Library and Archives; Davy Crockett, Andrew Jackson, and James K. Polk, courtesy of Tennessee State Museum; Howard H. Baker, courtesy of Law Offices of Baker, Donelson, Bearman & Caldwell; Ned Ray McWherter, courtesy of Tennessee Secretary of State's Office; and Albert Gore Jr., courtesy of Vice President Press Office.

Published by
HILLSBORO PRESS
an imprint of
PROVIDENCE HOUSE PUBLISHERS
238 Seaboard Lane • Franklin, Tennessee 37067
800-321-5692
www.providencehouse.com

To

My Wife, Carol, and Children,
Lindsey, Eva Lora, Sarah, and Phillip

And To

My Late Parents,
Royal and Eva Langsdon

Contents

Foreword

The rich and varied history of Tennessee is understood best by examining what the people who live here have accomplished. While most of them have led quiet, productive lives filled with conventional human activity, some few have achieved a widespread recognition in their home state and, in some instances, have attained national prominence. The areas in which they have won this acclaim reflect the elements of the state's history which reverberate from its very beginning. Tennessee may have produced relatively few nationally recognized philosophers, poets, scientists, or scholars, but it has nourished numerous citizens who became known to the nation in the annals of music, politics, and warfare.

During the two centuries after the first constitutional convention in 1796, politics has been a favored pastime and an honored activity of Tennesseans. Perhaps because of the highly competitive nature of political struggles between the three grand divisions of the state, as well as between political parties and economic interests, Tennessee politicians have found themselves well-prepared for action whenever they entered the national politcal arena. They have excelled in leadership positions in both houses of Congress and in presidential cabinets. Three Tennesseans have served as president of the United States: Andrew Jackson, James K. Polk, and Andrew Johnson. Two of them were elected vice president: Andrew Johnson and Albert Gore Jr. Tennesseans are routinely included in that select group of Americans considered as potential presidential nominees. At present, three Tennesseans have been described as "members" of this select "club": Lamar Alexander, Albert Gore Jr., and Fred Thompson. Accordingly, politics is of great importance to Tennesseans.

Any bibliography of Tennessee history would contain a large number of books, most of which have been written by professional historians. However, some of the most interesting and readable of these works (whether speaking of general accounts or monographs) have been published by authors without previous experience in writing history. Often these books can provide different viewpoints and new perspectives. *Tennessee—A Political History* is thus a notable addition to the history of the state. Dr. Phillip Langsdon is a successful facial plastic surgeon as well as an associate professor at the University of Tennessee at Memphis. In addition, he has acquired practical experience in Tennessee politics while serving as chairman of the Shelby County Republican Party during an important transitional period for city and state politics.

Although Dr. Langsdon covers his subject in detail from the beginning to the close of the twentieth century, his book is much more than just a political history. The reader will be taken through the development of a frontier land with few inhabitants, engaged chiefly in farming and having to rely on a primitive transportation system, to the complex society found in Tennessee today. Many of the colorful individuals who have contributed to the unique character of the state are included. No doubt the reader will find a valuable feature of this book in the collection of biographies inserted in the various chapters. These may well be one of the most useful parts. Appropriate illustrations, maps, and photographs provide a helpful visual aid; indeed, many readers may wish that even more had been included.

Tennessee—A Political History is divided chronologically into four major parts. The first traces the growth of the state's political structure in the establishment of a one-party system during the initial decades of statehood. Conflicts within various factions of the first Republican Party altered the political landscape during the Jacksonian Era. A new alignment pitted Democrats against Whigs. Andrew Jackson and his followers created the Democratic Party, making it one of Tennessee's contributions to the political structure of the United States. The decline of the Whig Party and the appearance of the new Republican Party during the 1850s complete the first part of the book.

The second section deals with the Civil War and Reconstruction years, followed by Tennessee's return to Democratic Party control in 1870. Subsequently, until the gubernatorial election of 1970 that is, Tennessee was generally considered to have joined the other former Confederate states comprising the "Solid South" as a section consistently dominated by the Democratic Party. This generalization conveys much truth, but there was one remarkable difference in Tennessee: it had the largest Republican Party minority of any Southern state. Three Republican governors were elected during this solidly Democratic century, Republicans consistently were elected in a few congressional districts, and Republicans in small numbers were sent by the electorate to both houses of the Tennessee General Assemby.

The third section of the book describes party conflicts and changes occurring from 1908 to the beginning of World War II, but it is in the fourth (and last) part of this study that the most thorough narrative and analysis are found. The concluding part of Dr. Langsdon's history discusses in detail how the reorganization of the Republican Party enabled its membership in 1970 to win the governorship, for the first time in fifty years, and both seats in the U.S. Senate. Following this election, the governor's office has been held alternately by Democrats and Republicans. Once again Tennessee has become a two-party state. The connection between events in state and national party politics is explored effectively here.

The information provided in *Tennessee—A Political History* is encyclopedic. Dr. Langsdon's writing style is direct and clear. Despite a limited use of citations to the sources used, both the inclusive contents of the book and its extensive bibliography indicate that much research was conducted. Dr. Langsdon's enthusiasm for his subject and his love of writing are evident. It is his first such publicatioin; I am sure that many readers will hope for others to follow.

Charles W. Crawford
Professor, Department of History
The University of Memphis

Preface and Acknowledgments

I have always enjoyed reading history and observing politics, but about fourteen years ago I became an active participant. After working in various campaigns in Shelby County, Tennessee, I was eventually elected chairman of the Republican Party of Shelby County, serving from 1991 to 1995.

During my tenure I oversaw the institution of the first Republican primaries for county officeholders (nonstate or federal) in the history of Shelby County, Tennessee, in 1992 and 1994. We achieved an extraordinary victory in 1994, winning fifeen out of seventeen county races: mayor, clerks, county commission seats, etc.

The experience gave me a firsthand education in the nature of politics and man. I also learned considerably more about Tennessee politics. Shortly after completion of two terms as party chairman, I began reviewing Tennessee politics over a period spanning the life of the state. Tennessee's political history is rich with colorful personalities and unusual stories. In my studies I could not find a text which concentrated on Tennessee political history, political party evolution, major movements, and personalities in a chronological fashion. I decided to compose a review, hence this book.

The Democrats have essentially dominated Tennessee politics. Therefore any discussion of Democratic Party activities centers on the officeholders. Republicans, on the other hand, have held relatively few offices in Tennessee history and have maintained only a working minority. As a result a fair amount of Republican description takes the form of intraparty politics.

Understandably, because of space limitations and stylistic considerations, it was impossible to include all historical detail and maintain the intended synoptic format of the book. Additional details may be obtained from the texts and references included in the bibliography or from other sources found in Tennessee libraries.

It is largely because of the fine work of many great Tennessee historians and authors that I have been able to compile the information contained in this book. I have tried to create a chronological consolidated look at Tennessee political history, adding to previous historical information by my own interviews with some of our living Tennessee politicians. I am grateful for the time and information given to me by the many kind individuals who granted me interviews—Alex Dann, Lewis and Jan Donelson, Winfield Dunn, Harlan Mathews, Don Sundquist, Ned Ray McWherter, Jimmy Duncan, Jimmy Quillen, Kyle and Jayne Creson, Aaron Tatum, Fred Marcum, John Farris, Bill Farris, Harold Ford Sr., and many others.

This book could not have been completed without the kindness and assistance of the many librarians, archivists, and editorial assistants who helped me obtain information and illustrations. I thank the staff of the Memphis and Shelby County Library, including Patricia LaPointe, Memphis Room curator; John Dugan, assistant archivist, and Dr. Jim Johnson, head of the History Department, both of the Memphis and Shelby County Library and Archives; the staffs of the Chattanooga and Knox County public libraries; the Tennessee State Library and Archives; the Tennessee State Museum; the University of Tennessee Library, Knoxville, Tennessee.

I want to thank Dr. Charles Crawford and Karen Bradley of the University of Memphis and Dr. Paul Issac, whose manuscript on early twentieth-century Tennessee politics was indispensable.

I gratefully acknowledge the use of illustrations from the following sources: Chattanooga-Hamilton County Bicentennial Library (CHCBL), Chattanooga, Tennessee; Library of Congress (LOC), Washington, D.C.; Lewis Donelson; Tennessee State Library and Archives (TSLA), with thanks to Wayne Moore and a special debt of gratitude to Karina McDaniel for her enthusiastic assistance in procuring photographs, Nashville, Tennessee; Tennessee State Museum (TSM), Nashville, Tennessee; and the United States Senate Historical Office (SHO) with special thanks to Heather Moore, photo historian, Matthew Cook, and Jo Anne Quatannens, Washington, D.C.

It would have been impossible to organize, edit, and refine the text without the able and professional assistance of my publisher, Andrew B. Miller, and his staff at Providence House Publishers. I would like to give special mention to the following: Kelli Allen, Trinda Cole, Lacie Dotson, Marilyn Friedlander, Stephen James, Holly Jones, Wendy May, Debbie Sims, Mary Bray Wheeler, and Elaine Kernea Wilson of the editorial and production departments.

Finally, there is no way I could have worked on this text for the past four years without the love, encouragement, assistance, and tolerance of my family. Thank you all! I can only hope the effort will prove worthwhile.

Tennessee
A Political History

Early Settlement to the Seeds of Sectionalism

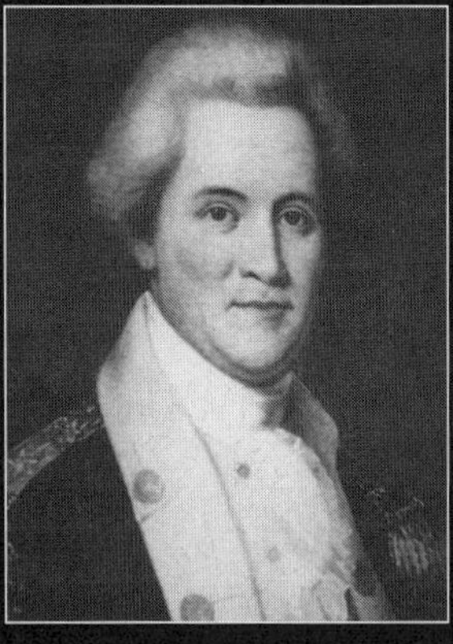

PART I

The Early Lands

Twenty-three thousand years ago and well prior to European migration, Tennessee was a richly diversified wilderness, suitable to the mastodon. Eight thousand years ago, humans began to inhabit the area. These early Native Americans, prehistoric Indians known as Paleolithic Indians, lived in tribes that traveled through the land that would someday become known as Tennessee. They enjoyed an unblemished and fruitful terrain—unspoiled rivers, streams, mountains, and dense forests, plentiful wildlife and incredible varieties of wildflowers. From 1000 B.C. to A.D. 500 civilization had developed to the point that the Archaic Indians, also called Woodland Indians, made pottery, planted crops, and created ceremonial mounds. By A.D. 800, known as the Mississippian period, the natives had improved agriculture and social interaction. They had priests and politicians, and had developed communities which were organized into statelike governments.

As time passed, different tribes came to occupy Tennessee. The Cherokee Indians, thought to be kinsmen of the Iroquois of the north, eventually became the dominant tribe of most of what is today Central and East Tennessee. The Creek Indians lived to the south, in what became North Alabama. The Chickasaw Indians came to occupy what became West Tennessee and parts of Alabama and Mississippi, and remained in this area until they conceded oversight to the Spaniards in the 1780s.

Soon after Europeans discovered the New World, they began to explore the area for financial and strategic advantage. Early Spanish explorers were the first to infringe upon the Indian paradise. They traveled by sea to the coast of Florida, then came inland, or they sailed on to some other part of the southern coast to gain entry. In one of the earliest expeditions recorded (in 1526 or 1527), around three hundred Spaniards left the coast of Florida to explore inland and were caught in rough seas and storms. They may have actually passed their intended destination and landed on the coast of Texas. They suffered from thirst, hunger, and exposure and were soon confronted with Indian attacks. With these trials they would wonder if the gold they sought was worth the personal sacrifice.

Later exploration advanced into the area that would become Tennessee. In May 1539, the Hernando de Soto expedition landed near present-day Tampa, Florida. His troops traveled north through Florida, Georgia, and South Carolina, entering Tennessee near Chattanooga. When the Spaniards first contacted the Indians, they interacted with mutual respect. However, any initial regard shown by the Spaniards toward the Indians was offered to gain trust and provide time for the Spaniards to assess the strength or weakness of the natives. They soon became fairly rough with the Indians, and the Creeks reasoned that it might be wise to motivate de Soto to move on. They told de Soto of copper and gold mined by Indians who lived further west.

De Soto and his men headed southwest into Alabama and then into Mississippi. There they encountered Creeks who had been forewarned of the Spanish party's cruelty. The Indians responded to the threat by teaching the Spanish that future Indian contact could be dangerous.

Nevertheless, Hernando de Soto's search for gold took his expedition to the *Rio del Espiritu Santo*—the Mississippi River—where he stood on the bluffs near the vicinity of what is now Memphis on May 8, 1541. He stayed at the site about six weeks before moving on, and died shortly after crossing the river into Arkansas. After his death, the dwindling band of gold hunters floated down the river, eventually making it to Mexico.

Later Spanish explorer Juan Pardo led another expedition to East Tennessee in 1566 and 1567, again in search of gold. They fought Indians and built forts (one near Chattanooga) but found no gold. When the Spaniards abandoned their posts, the Indians destroyed whatever they left behind, and little evidence remains of these early explorers.

English settlers arrived in Jamestown, Virginia, in 1607. Gradually, the English pioneers began to push inland in search of the better life and riches. In order for England to lay claim to the new land, it had to have English settlers take control of the land. King Charles II of England bequeathed the area south of Virginia and to the west to eight of his friends. By 1673 James Needham and Gabriel Arthur came from Virginia into East Tennessee, where they found some Indian villages. After initial good relations, things turned dangerous, and an Indian shot and killed Needham and cut his heart out. Arthur was nearly burned alive, saved by a chief, and then held prisoner for some time. However, in spite of the dangers, by 1690 the English were moving into the Cherokee country of Tennessee.

While the English came west from Virginia and South Carolina and the Spanish from the south, the French came to Tennessee from the north, from Canada. In 1673 Frenchmen Jacques Marquette and Louis Jolliet explored parts of Tennessee by floating down the Mississippi River. They noted the elevation of the terrain on the east side of the river and visited the Chickasaw bluffs, seeking sites to develop missions and fur trade.

On February 13, 1682 René Robert Cavelier de La Salle started down the great Mississippi River and eventually claimed all the land drained by the Mississippi and its tributaries for France. Unlike Marquette and Jolliet, his goal was national expansion rather than commercial or religious development and whenever possible he worked for peaceful colonization. Later in 1682, his troops landed at the (Chickasaw) bluffs and built a small fort and necessary cabins near the mouth of the river that he named the *Rivière à Mayot* in honor of an Indian who was with him. It later was called the *Margot* (Magpie), which translated means *wolf*. He negotiated a treaty with the Chickasaw Indians and named Fort Prud'homme in honor of the officer he left in charge, Pierre Prud'homme.

La Salle continued to make treaties with the Indians and establish forts. He floated further down the Mississippi to various sites along the banks, including Natchez, where he established a fort. His trip was especially successful in view of the Indian opposition that had confronted his Spanish predecessors. La Salle later traveled up the Arkansas River and established an Arkansas post. After turning back and reaching the mouth of the Mississippi, he traveled back to Fort Prud'homme, where he stayed to recuperate from an illness. Once recovered, he returned to Quebec. Later, he continued his explorations and conquests for France, eventually founding St. Louis and other outposts.

La Salle achieved great fame during his time, but unfortunately, had to deal with the treachery and jealousy of his fellow countrymen. The exploration of the new world created great excitement—and intense competition—in his homeland. Competitors for fame within the French service delayed supplies, detoured convoys, and created as much confusion as possible for the explorer, making wilderness exploration even more difficult for his men, who constantly faced starvation, physical suffering, and confrontations with the Indians. Sadly, infighting within the French service proved to be worse than battling the Indians and the elements of nature. La Salle was assassinated in 1687 by two of his own men, Liotot and Duhunt, at a stop on the Brazos River in what became an area of Texas.

The fort on the Chickasaw Bluffs was abandoned a short time later as the French group went on to make permanent settlements in New Orleans and Mobile. "French officials, traders, missionaries, [passed] to other destinations and [stayed] at the mouth of Wolf only overnight or long enough to kill the buffalo with which the area abounded" (Roper 1970). A treaty between Great Britain and France (1699–1700) made North Carolina an extension of England and expanded its territory west to the Mississippi River. However, the new land was still attractive to the French, and they continued to move into the region. They explored the Ohio and Cumberland River Valleys around 1710 to organize the fur trade. They formed a settlement and a store near a salt spring, where it was thought deer came to "lick." This settlement became known as French Lick and would later become Nashville.

The rapid population increase of English colonists on America's eastern coast caused the French to consolidate their holdings on the Mississippi and its tributaries by developing posts in the West. Indian trade was good, and French and English traders became extremely competitive with each other, just as their mother countries were in Europe over other matters. Both the French and English governments competed for the allegiance of the Indians since neither were successful at conquering them, in spite of repeated efforts.

In 1736 the French government ordered Bienville, governor of the Louisiana Territory, to create resistance in order to protect French domain. To assure total French domination of the region, Bienville ordered forces to meet at Fort Prud'homme on May 10, 1736, to prepare to attack the resisting Chickasaws. These Chickasaw Indians would trade with the French, allow some intermarrying, and cooperate with missionaries. However, they would not be French subjects and would not be conquered. These fierce warriors would prove difficult to overpower.

Bienville, who planned to bring his troops up the Tombigbee, was delayed in Mobile. He had ordered one of his officers, Diron D'Artaguette, to organize the force at Fort Prud'homme and wait for him on May 4, 1736. Evidentially, D'Artaguette, was a bit impatient. Rather than waiting for Bienville, ambition overcame reason, and he advanced on a village of the Chickasaw nation that was occupied by refugees from the Natchez region. On November 20, 131 Canadians and French, along with 366 Indians from the north, attacked the refugees' camp. After a three-hour battle with 500 Chickasaw warriors and thirty Englishmen, only a few French escaped alive. D'Artaguette, his chaplain, Father Senac, and fifteen others were captured and burned to death.

Bienville, who finally left Mobile, went up the Tombigbee River to attack a Chickasaw town. His forces were destroyed, and only he and a handful of his men escaped the massacre. Bienville's plan was in shambles, and it took him the ensuing three years to reorganize. In 1739 he led thirty-five hundred men to the Fourth Bluff (Chickasaw Bluff) and built a new fort, Fort Assumption. Many of his men who were Canadian, unused to the climate and terrain, succumbed to illness. Supplies were limited, exploration was difficult, and Bienville could not determine the exact strength or position of the Chickasaw forces. The French were not in the best of situations, but the size of their forces intimidated the Chickasaws. A battle never took place and after seven months on the bluff, Bienville's forces gave up. He had accomplished nothing, and his men were worn. He burned the fort and returned to New Orleans in disgrace. This meant, of course, that the French did not conquer the Chickasaw Indians and finally understood the difficulties of attempting conquest of so fierce an opponent as a native protecting his home. The French withdrew. The west bank of the Mississippi River, in what would become Tennessee, remained a wilderness for fifty years, until the Spanish returned in the 1780s.

Inevitably, trouble developed with the Cherokee Indians in Middle and East Tennessee who were legitimately concerned over their loss of hunting grounds. The French and the English continued to struggle with each other over fur and other trade as well as the future value of the Indians' lands. Finally, in 1754 when the Indians allied with the French, open warfare between the French and English broke out and the French and Indian War began. In 1759, after five years and many lost lives, the French agreed to halt resistance. But the Indians were uncertain of their future with the loss of their French allies and some of the Cherokee Indians made alliances with the English in order to protect their territory. This cooperation also served the English who wanted to protect their trade relations with the Indians. Meanwhile the French threatened to reinvade, and the Cherokees asked the governor of South Carolina for protection from the French. The English complied with this request for protection by planning a fort in East Tennessee.

The English completed construction of Fort Loudoun, "on the south bank of the Little Tennessee near the mouth of the Tellico, about 30 miles southwest from present day Knoxville" on June 26, 1757 (Corlew 1989). The Cherokees favored construction of the fort in order to protect their land from the French. However, their tolerance of the English weakened because they did not feel they had been well respected or rewarded for the assistance they had provided to the English in the war against the French in Virginia. Trade relations between the Cherokees and the English began to break down.

The Cherokees sent several chiefs to negotiate with Governor William Henry Lyttelton. The fearful English detained (or held hostage) the chiefs. This infuriated the Cherokees. When the English commander of Fort Prince George, Richard Coytmore, came out of the fort to talk with Cherokee Chief Oconostota, Coytmore was ambushed and killed. The English then attempted to chain the detained chiefs. They resisted, and the ensuing fight ended in the killing of the twenty-one Cherokee hostages. This incident escalated hostilities between the Cherokees and English. The Cherokee War had begun.

In 1760 the Cherokees attacked Fort Loudoun, near Knoxville. A stalemate ensued. By August 1760, the fort commander, Captain Paul Demere, surrendered to Chief Oconostota with the understanding that the English could leave without attack and the Indians would take the fort and the supplies. Sadly, after the English surrendered Fort Loudoun, the seven hundred Cherokees killed and scalped their defenseless opponents. They murdered all English officers except one, Captain John Stuart, who escaped. The few other Whites who were taken captive were forced to dance naked. Some were beaten with the scalps of those who had been killed. When English reinforcements heard of the massacre, they burned several Indian villages. Cherokee warriors were slaughtered by English troops from Fort Prince George seeking revenge. Over half of the five thousand Cherokee warriors in the area were killed or maimed in the conflict with the English. Finally, in December 1761 the Indians asked for an end to the war.

English colonists continued to migrate to East Tennessee. In 1762 Spain ceded all the French-claimed territory to the east and west of the Mississippi River. In 1763, the Treaty of Paris ended the French and Indian War and gave Britain claim to all land on the east side of the Mississippi River. England now legally controlled the entire length of Tennessee, from the Chickasaw Bluffs on the Mississippi River to the Cherokee lands of East Tennessee.

Frontier Settlements

By the 1760s Colonel James Smith had explored as far west as the mouth of the Tennessee River. When he returned east, his stories of the rich and fertile lands caused great excitement among the early settlers who were then inspired to move west. Inhabitants of Carolina, Virginia, Pennsylvania, and Maryland began to migrate west. By 1769 a large group had moved into the area of Middle Tennessee, via North Carolina and Virginia.

In order to calm frontier fighting with the Indians, the British issued the Proclamation Line of 1763, which prohibited English settlements beyond the Appalachian Mountains. This allowed some time for the English to negotiate with the Indians. In spite of the prohibition, immigration across the mountains continued, and settlers moved over into the area of what is today East Tennessee. In 1768 Sir William Johnson, superintendent of Indian affairs for the area north of the Ohio River, negotiated the Treaty of Fort Stanwix with the Iroquois. This treaty relinquished Iroquois claims to West Virginia, southwest Virginia, Kentucky, and Tennessee. However the Cherokees also claimed parts of these areas, and conflicts arose over ownership. In 1770, John Stuart, the survivor of the Fort Loudon massacre, and now superintendent of Indian affairs for the area south of the Ohio River, negotiated the Treaty of Lochaber with the Cherokees. This treaty placed the proclamation line east of the Holston River, near present-day Kingsport. The line was surveyed in 1771 by Alexander Cameron and John Donelson, but the expansion of settlers past this line continued.

Some of the earliest settlers were Andrew Greer and Julius Dugger, who came to East Tennessee in 1766. William Bean and other Virginians settled near the Watauga River in 1769 near what became Elizabethton. Other settlers came with James Robertson to escape harsh and unfair treatment and taxation by the English in the North Carolina area. They settled the same area of East Tennessee, as did Virginians Valentine Sevier and his son John. Evan Shelby and his son Isaac came from Maryland and settled an area to the north of the Holston River, called Sapling Grove, now known as Bristol. John Carter and a group of settlers migrated to the area west of the Holston River, northeast of Rogersville in 1770. This became Carter's Valley. Another group came from North Carolina and settled along the Nolichucky River in 1771. In 1772, in order to create some sort of organization, the settlers formed the Watauga Association, a quasi-government body. This was organized into the Washington District in 1775.

The Cherokee Indians resented these settlements in East Tennessee and disputed any land sales to Whites. They brutally attacked and killed many settlers, including

Map of the Watauga Settlements. (Courtesy of TSLA)

women and children, and open warfare raged on the frontier. An army was sent from Virginia and North Carolina, and by 1777 the conflicts with the Indians in East Tennessee again eased. The land disputes were settled with a treaty that was signed at Long Island of the Holston (today Kingsport) in 1777. North Carolina finally acknowledged the need for consecration of the new area, and in 1777 the Washington District (which included all of the new country) became Washington County, North Carolina. Jonesboro became the seat of government for the new North Carolina county. (Spelling changed from *Jonesboro* to *Jonesborough* by Chapter 24 of Private Acts of 1983.)

About 1776, Thomas Sharp Spencer, John Holliday, and Timothy de Monbreun began hunting in the middle portion of the Tennessee country. Spencer stayed in the area and settled near Castalian Springs. De Monbreun built a cabin on the bluffs by the Cumberland River. They were soon to have neighbors.

In 1775, Richard Henderson and the Transylvania Company, for around ten thousand pounds in supplies, had purchased land from the Cherokee Indians that included part of central Tennessee, from Kentucky to the Cumberland River. Virginia refused to acknowledge the portion of his purchase that was deemed to be in Kentucky. In 1779, he convinced John Robertson to lead some of the East Tennessee settlers to the central part of the territory, thought to be in Tennessee. Robertson led eight other settlers into the French Lick area where they surveyed the land, determining that it was not in territory belonging to Virginia, but rather North Carolina. John Rains and Casper Mansker followed with other settlers from Kentucky, all settling in the French Lick area.

After the settlement was in place, Robertson went back to the Watauga area in order to direct his friends and family to French Lick. The party was divided into two groups. In October 1779 his party of two hundred, mostly men, departed the Holston, heading overland with horses and livestock. As they traveled through the Cumberland Gap into Kentucky, they met John Rains and his group which was headed for Harrodsburg. Robertson convinced Rains's party to join his group and move to the Cumberland. They reentered Tennessee near what is today Clarksville. By the last of December they arrived at the Cumberland River, and crossed its frozen waters on Christmas Day, 1779. On December 22, 1779, John Donelson and the second group, predominately women, children, and their possessions, left Fort Patrick Henry, planning to float down the Tennessee River to the Ohio River to the Cumberland River. Their travel was delayed because of the weather and the difficulties of such a journey. Other flatboats joined the group at Cloud Creek and later at the Clinch River. The group suffered extreme hardships. Smallpox broke out on one flatboat, and Indians killed all the passengers on another. Food supplies ran low, and boats ran aground. Disease and the elements made the journey intolerable. Some families left the group and settled in the area of present-day Muscle Shoals, Alabama. Others left for Natchez, while some others headed to settle in the Red River valley near Clarksville. On April 24, 1780, the remainder of the group arrived at the new fort on the bluff overlooking the Cumberland River at French Lick. Henderson arrived about this time. A fort had been completed, and he proposed naming it in honor of General Francis Nash, who died in the Revolutionary War Battle of Germantown in 1777 and had, prior to the war, been a clerk in Judge Henderson's court in Hillsborough, North Carolina. The name of the fort became Nashborough. January 11, 1781, marked the birth of Felix Robertson, the first male child born in Nashborough, to James and Charlotte Robertson.

The new settlers formed a government called the Cumberland Compact. Despite the almost constant fear of Indian attacks, the area continued to grow, and by mid-1780 there were around three hundred people living there. In 1783 the Cumberland group became Davidson County, North Carolina, in order to enjoy some security of additional protection. The government seat of the new county was later to be called Nashville.

Indian fighting would not be the only conflict faced by the settlers of Tennessee. Most Tennesseans supported the Revolutionary War because of British limitations on settlement, oppression, taxation, and unfair treatment. By 1776, the Declaration of Independence had been signed, but the English still viewed the Americans as British subjects. Although the war had little effect on the Tennesseans who lived across the mountains, in 1780 the English demanded that the Watauga people surrender. With this ultimatum, Isaac Shelby and John Sevier recruited about one thousand men who agreed that they should defend their land. They had endured the hardships of British rule, frontier life, and fighting Indians. They were not about to give up their new freedom without a fight. On September 25, 1780, the settlers organized at Sycamore Shoals on the Watauga. The settlers met the British, under the command of Patrick Ferguson, at King's Mountain. When the battle was over, the toughened settlers proved too much for the British soldiers. Ferguson and all the British, except the few that escaped, were killed. The pioneers' losses were twenty-eight killed and sixty-two wounded. This loss demoralized the British and essentially brought to an end the southern part of the Revolutionary conflict. (A year later, Cornwallis surrendered at Yorktown, Virginia, and the battles ended.)

The Treaty of Paris, 1783–1784, which ended the Revolutionary War, ceded all British claims east of the Mississippi River to the colonial government. After the Revolution, North Carolina began selling and granting lands. During a seven-month period of 1783, North Carolina sold or granted seven million acres in what would become Tennessee, and settlers continued to move there. One tract of land along the Chickasaw Bluffs caught the eye of a Nashville land speculator. John Rice was a trader who made trips east to the Appalachian Mountains and as far west as Natchez, Mississippi. Evidently, his travels had shown him some future advantage of the area of the high ground along the Mississippi River. After his return from one trip, he applied for five thousand acres along the bluffs on October 23, 1783. The land was granted by North Carolina on April 25, 1789, for five hundred pounds sterling. The fact that the land still belonged to the Chickasaw Indians evidently did not stop the transaction between Rice and North Carolina, since there were plans to "extinguish" the claims of the Chickasaws at some time in the future.

John Rice was never able to develop his investment. He was killed by Indians in 1791 on the Cumberland River, near Clarksville, while on his way to Nashville. However, his purchase became the foundation of the future city of Memphis.

To protect the interests of the North Carolina settlers in the Nashville area, the North Carolina legislature passed "an Act for the Relief of Sundry Petitioners Inhabitants of Davidson County" on April 19, 1784. This act recognized the claims of the

Flatboat voyage of the Donelson party to Nashville, 1780. (Painting by Peggy Harvill. Courtesy of TSLA)

settlers of Middle Tennessee, granted to those families, requiring they only pay entry and surveying fees. In April and May of 1783, Nashborough was officially recognized by the North Carolina legislature. After July 1, 1784, its name became Nashville. The North Carolina legislature, concerned with the obligation to defend the new settlements, ceded the land that would eventually make up Tennessee to the United States government on June 2, 1784.

The State of Franklin

After the Revolutionary War, many immigrants had bought land from the state of North Carolina and settled in what would later become Tennessee. As immigration continued, the population slowly increased to the point that some settlers wanted to create a new state. When it was anticipated that the land was to be ceded to the United States, representatives of the settlements in the Holston-Watauga region (Greene, Washington, and Sullivan Counties) began meeting in Jonesboro on August 24, 1784. By December the delegates had formed the "state" of Franklin.

The aspirations of the new citizens of Franklin were dashed when in November 1784 the North Carolina legislature repealed its earlier move to grant the land to the United States. The reasons of the repeal were varied. The public reason given for this reversal was the U.S. Congress's failure to repay North Carolina for its expenses incurred during an Indian expedition, which had proceeded at the request of the national government. The change in plans may have also been due to the efforts of Spain and France, who, working with the Indians and some settlers, were planning to challenge domain of the new land. Realistically, there were great profits to be lost by North Carolina land speculators if the legislature relinquished jurisdiction of the territory.

In spite of this setback, Franklin residents did not give up on their plans to become a state. The newly elected legislature met in Jonesboro in March 1785. John Sevier was chosen governor of the new state, though it was not yet recognized by the U.S. Congress. John Carter was elected secretary of state, and Stockley Donelson was made surveyor general. David Kennedy and William Cocke were made brigadier generals.

North Carolina Governor Alexander Martin and the North Carolina legislature were not pleased to hear of the new state's formation. They sent a demand for a written description of the actions taken. A formal reply was prepared by the Franklin legislature and returned to North Carolina describing the state's formation and justifying its creation on the grounds of the need for protection from the Indians. They asked for assistance in being accepted into the Union, but they made their determination to gain independence clear. North Carolina's Governor Martin responded on April 25, 1785, commanding the new state to disband. Governor Sevier in turn issued a proclamation to the inhabitants of the fledgling state asking for loyalty to the state of Franklin. Meanwhile, the request for admission of Franklin was presented to the U.S. Congress by William Cocke. When Congress met in New York, seven states voted in favor of admission and two opposed. But because some states did not vote, Franklin fell short of the nine votes required by the Articles of Confederation. The nonvoting states felt that North Carolina had the right to rescind the land-cession act and did not want to oppose the state's sovereignty. It was, after all, important to maintain the allegiance of North Carolina if the fledgling new nation was to hold its unity. Congress did request that North

Carolina reconsider its repeal of cession of the land, but North Carolina refused and the admission of Franklin was therefore denied.

Although most of the residents of Franklin supported the continued effort for statehood, there were some dissenters. In August 1786, an antistatehood group met in Washington County and elected delegates to the North Carolina legislature. This effort undermined the unity desired by those people supporting Franklin. Revolutionary War hero John Tipton was elected a state senator for North Carolina and led the anti-Franklin effort. A political fracture opened as Tipton and the North Carolina legislature moved to undermine Sevier and his supporters. The North Carolina legislature offered to pardon supporters of the renegade state of Franklin who would agree to forget the Franklin effort and pledge allegiance to North Carolina. North Carolina offered to remit taxes for the preceding two years for those Franklin residents who would cooperate.

To further divide loyalties, North Carolina created Hawkins County and appointed Evan Shelby in place of Sevier as brigadier general of Washington District of North Carolina. (Sevier had been previously offered this appointment.) The disagreement between Franklin and North Carolina was often intense. There were some small skirmishes between the two sides, and some participants were killed. These incidents were infrequent though, because the settlers were unmotivated to shed their friends' blood over the name of their state. The Franklin settlers also had other worries. The continued danger from the Cherokee Indians was their foremost fear. Although the people of Franklin appreciated Sevier, who had valiantly led their defense against the Indians, in an effort to appease North Carolina, they elected Evan Shelby in August 1787 as the next governor of Franklin. However, Shelby refused the position and additionally resigned as brigadier general of the Washington District. He then contacted North Carolina leaders and asked that they appoint Sevier in his place. Shelby knew this was the quickest way to satisfy all involved. However, Tipton held the North Carolina leaders firmly on his side, and they opposed Sevier. North Carolina instead appointed Joseph Martin as brigadier general.

As a result, Sevier continued as leader of the Franklin effort, and the feud between Sevier and John Tipton continued to worsen. Unbeknownst to the participants, the political foundations for a future state were being laid. In essence, this early political struggle sowed the seeds of what were to become the two main political factions in the region: the Tipton faction and the Sevier faction.

The conflict became an out-and-out war between the two groups, with the two leaders, Sevier and Tipton, vying for power. Tipton, acting as colonel of the county militia, organized raids which captured the Franklin court records. By 1788 he urged Washington County Sheriff Jonathan Pugh to capture some of Sevier's slaves in order to pay for a judgment on Sevier, which had been mandated by a court under the jurisdiction of North Carolina. The slaves were removed to Tipton's home. When a force of Sevier's men moved on Tipton's home, to retake Sevier's slaves, they were met by a force of Sheriff Pugh's men. Several men were wounded and captured; one was killed during the battle; and Pugh was mortally wounded, dying a week later. Tipton, in retaliation, planned to hang two of Sevier's sons who had been captured in the battle. Fortunately, Tipton's more reasonable advisors prevailed, and the sons were released.

As the settlers continued to move in and tread upon Indian ground, fighting between the Indians and settlers continued. Even though incremental treaties negotiated settlements between the settlers and the natives, the settlers would later break them and the Indians would attack the settlers. In retaliation the settlers would counterattack Indian villages. The "Franklin" settlement continued to look to forces greater than their own with which to ally themselves for protection and defense against the Indians, but they received little help from the infantile federal government or the state governments of North Carolina and Georgia. The people of Franklin resorted to negotiating with Spain, and they considered separating from the United States if Spain would provide protection and grant free navigation of the Mississippi River. The Spanish who controlled Louisiana had closed the Mississippi in order to discourage settlement east of the river. Louisiana Governor Miró, the Spanish authority, refused to protect the settlers, sensing that they would merely be using the Spanish in order to gain their own independence.

In 1786 the Spanish again tried to take possession of the New World by emerging as a controlling force in the Mississippi Valley. They convinced the Chickasaw Indians of the Chickasaw Bluffs to allow the Spaniards to "watch their possessions" for them from a post across from the east bank of the Mississippi River at Fort Esperanza, which later became Hopeville (or Hopefield), Arkansas. The French fort and trading post established by Marquette and Jolliet in 1673 on the Tennessee side of the river, on the Chickasaw Bluffs, near the mouth of the Margot River still existed. It was here the Spaniards were poised to make an entrance. However, the population increase from settlers after the Revolutionary War and government formations in the new land of Tennessee interfered with Spanish plans.

A New Nation, A New Territory

In 1787 in the city of Philadelphia, the U.S. Constitution was drafted and signed at the Constitutional Convention. (William Blount, a North Carolina delegate to the convention, was present and was one of the signers.) With this, the focus of the federal government changed, as did the aspirations of the state of Franklin. A few months after the signing the Constitution was ratified by the states. However, North Carolina and Rhode Island withheld their approval of the ratification and were not yet part of the United States. It was during this time, on March 1, 1788, that Franklin Governor John Sevier's term ended. Sevier and his group gave up, and the "state" of Franklin collapsed. With the hope that the new nation would provide the area with the protection and direction needed, no new governor was elected to replace Sevier.

In an effort to secure the future of the inhabitants of the Franklin area, Sevier was ready to settle the disputes with North Carolina. By not pursuing another term as governor of Franklin, which he surely would have won, he had demonstrated his resolve for cooperation. Unfortunately, his enemies saw this as a sign of weakness and moved to crush him. Newly elected North Carolina Governor Samuel Johnston ordered Judge David Campbell to arrest Sevier for treason. Campbell would not comply. The governor found a judge in Jonesboro who agreed to issue the order to arrest. John Tipton then received the order to arrest Sevier for trial. Sevier surrendered without a fight on October 10, 1788, and was then "hauled back across the mountains to stand trial for attempting to form a separate state and for refusing to obey the governor who had ordered him to return to pay allegiance to North Carolina" (Phillips 1978).

Although Sevier had made some enemies among the North Carolina loyalists, his efforts in fighting the British and the Indians won him respect and appreciation from many others. General Charles McDowell, who had served as a commander at the Battle of King's Mountain, paid Sevier's bail, and he was released. As the time for the trial neared, a small force was prepared to emancipate their friend, father, and leader, should things get out of hand. In fact they arrived at his place of incarceration, took Sevier without interference, and peaceably rode him home. The trial never occurred, and Sevier took the oath of allegiance to North Carolina. By August 1789 Sevier was elected state senator of North Carolina. He was also made brigadier general of Washington District under the appointment originally made in 1784.

On February 4, 1789, at the electoral college in New York City, George Washington was unanimously elected the first president of the United States. John Adams was elected vice president. The first legislative body consisted of thirty-eight Federalists and twenty-six Anti-Federalists in the House of Representatives, and seventeen Federalists and nine Anti-Federalists in the Senate. Washington was inaugurated on April 30, 1789. The nation's capital temporarily resided in New York City.

When North Carolina delegates sat at a convention for another try to ratify the U.S. Constitution, John Sevier was among the delegates representing the western territory of North Carolina. One of the reasons for North Carolina's delay on ratifying the Constitution was the fear by some delegates that, under the proposed Constitution, a strong government could interfere with their hard-fought liberty and could levy high taxes. Sevier and his friends from the western part of North Carolina wanted to see the state admitted into the Union. Finally, in November 1789, the North

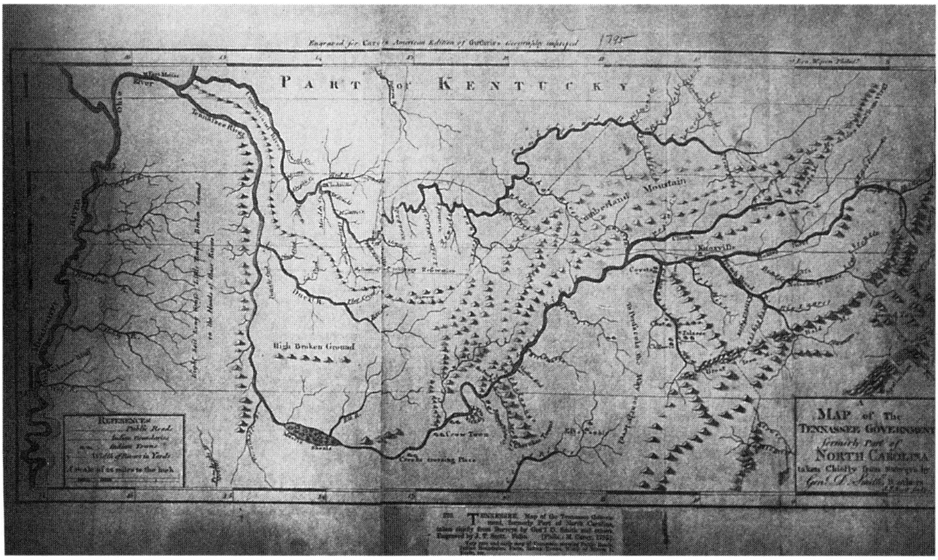

Attributed to Daniel Smith, this map served as a guide for prospective immigrants. (Courtesy of TSLA)

Carolina convention ratified the U.S. Constitution and became the twelfth state in the United States. John Sevier was subsequently elected congressman from the Western District of North Carolina in 1789.

After the United States had admitted North Carolina, the leaders of the new state changed their attitude about their western territory. On December 12, 1789, North Carolina again gave her claim to the western lands, which included the future Tennessee, to the United States. On May 26, 1790, the U.S. government organized this land into the "Territory of the United States South of the Ohio River." These changes were enough to satisfy the Tennessee settlers and they dropped negotiations with the Spanish.

In June 1790 the North Carolina legislature unanimously recommended William Blount to President Washington as territorial governor of the land ceded by that state to the United States. Blount had served in the North Carolina legislature and as North Carolina's representative in Congress, but had lost in a bid for a seat in the U.S. Senate. The appointment as territorial governor carried great prestige as well as opportunity and Blount did not receive it without some political maneuvering. He competed with revolutionary leaders of the likes of George Mason, General George Martin, General Anthony Wayne, and John Sevier. President George Washington appointed forty-one-year-old William Blount, a Federalist from Greenville, North Carolina, as governor of the "Territory South of the River Ohio" on August 7, 1790. Blount also served as superintendent of Indian affairs for the Southern Department.

President Washington also named General Daniel Smith as secretary of the new territory. Joseph Anderson, David Campbell, and John McNairy were named judges in the new territory. Blount, Smith, and the judges constituted the entire government of the territory until the area's population grew

WILLIAM BLOUNT was born on March 26, 1749, in North Carolina. William's grandfather, Thomas Blount, was the son of Sir Walter Blount of Worchestershire, England, who had come to America about 1664. He settled in the Isle of Wright County, Virginia. Thomas Blount was a wealthy landowner, farmer, and shipbuilder. He also owned lumber mills and other businesses. William's father was Jacob Blount and his mother was Mary Gray Blount (they had seven children). His father was also wealthy and well positioned. The Blount family had helped establish the early Virginia Colony and was a prominent part of Virginia and North Carolina landed gentry. William received his early education at home. At age fifteen, he began receiving formal training from a teacher who moved to Craven County.

On February 12, 1778, he married Mary Grainger. During this period of time, the British were becoming intolerably dominant, and like many of his contemporaries, William became involved in the colonial military and local, regional, and state politics. He served as paymaster of several regiments from North Carolina during the Revolutionary War, beginning service in 1776. Between 1780 and 1789 he served four terms as a member of the North Carolina House of Commons, including one term as speaker of the state house and two terms in the North Carolina senate. Blount served as a delegate to the Continental Congress of the United States in 1782–1783 and again in 1786–1787. When he was to the point that a legislature could be elected (in 1894).

Blount appointed his half-brother, Willie (pronounced Wiley) Blount, who later became a governor of Tennessee, private secretary.

When Blount took over as governor of the Southwest Territory, there were two distinct concentrations of settlements. One was at the eastern end of the territory, and the other was in the Cumberland River area. The settlements in present-day Middle Tennessee consisted of Sumner, Davidson, and Tennessee Counties, and the population of this area was only one quarter that of the eastern settlements. Greene, Washington, Hawkins, and Sullivan Counties made up the eastern section. Blount settled in Rocky Mount, Washington County, October 23, 1790, where he established the first capital of the territory, in the forks of the Holston and Watauga Rivers. It was eventually moved to White's Fort, which belonged to James White, and was later renamed Knoxville. Blount built his home in Knoxville, and from there he entertained in the high style of the day. Once in the new territory Blount went about informing the inhabitants of their new leadership and setting up a government. Heading westward, he made a trip to Middle Tennessee, and on December 15, 1790, was a guest of James Robertson in Nashborough for three weeks.

Blount had to deal with the factional disputes between the frontier leaders and the bitterness of the settlers over the lack of protection from the Indians. As superintendent of Indian affairs, he also had to deal with the Indians' complaints over boundary disputes, British and Spanish efforts to stir up hostility among the Indians, and the negative effects of frequent Indian attacks. The new government fought Indians and made treaties with them. However, the people who had lost the lives of family members and homes to the hostile Indians were not patient

---

only thirty-eight, he served as a member of the Convention of 1787, which created the U.S. Constitution. He also served in the 1789 North Carolina Convention, which ratified the Constitution. He later lost an election to represent North Carolina in the U.S. Senate. Having speculated in "western lands" and served as a North Carolina representative, negotiating with the Indians, Blount was knowledgeable about the recently formed Territory of the United States south of the Ohio River. In 1790 the North Carolina legislature recommended him to be governor of the new territory. He was appointed by President Washington in August of 1790. He served until 1796. After the passage of the referendum for statehood, Blount served as president of the state constitutional convention which declared statehood, but when Tennessee was accepted into the Union in 1796, it elected John Sevier as governor. Blount, however, retained a fair amount of popularity and connections and was elected by the first state legislature, along with William Cocke, as one of Tennessee's first U.S. senators. After he went to the senate, Blount was accused of being involved in a plan to take control of Spanish Florida and Louisiana for Great Britain. He was expelled from the senate by a vote of twenty-five to one. There was little proof to substantiate this action, and the House of Representatives dismissed the articles of impeachment in January 1799. Blount returned to Tennessee and was elected to the state senate in 1798 and soon was made speaker of the senate. Unfortunately, an epidemic struck Knoxville in 1800, and William Blount died March 21, 1800. His wife survived him two years. Blount College, now the University of Tennessee, was established in 1794 and was named for him. His son, William Grainger Blount, served as a member of the U.S. House of Representatives from Tennessee. (Photograph courtesy of TSLA) with a government (controlled by the federal government) that urged tolerance, provided little protection, and then taxed them for these services. They demanded action, and of course Blount, as the representative of the federal government, was often blamed for their plight. In response to the issues, he developed a territorial militia and a court system.

Most of Blount's time was spent trying to find peace between the settlers and the Indians. Blount met with Cherokee chiefs at White's Fort (present-day Knoxville) in June 1791, and they agreed on the purchase of disputed land in both the east and Cumberland areas. The payment agreed upon was one thousand dollars per year, tools of husbandry, and protection for the Indians. However, the agreement did not halt hostilities. Many Indians resented giving up their land. Encouraged by northern Indian military success, Spanish instigation and armament, and a federal policy prohibiting White attacks on Indians, some Cherokees and Creeks went on the offensive. By January 1792 Cherokee Indians visited Secretary of War Henry Knox at the nation's capital in an effort to convince him that the settlers should leave. Knox increased the annuity to fifteen hundred dollars and reached another agreement. Still Indian hostilities continued, and settlers were killed. Settlers felt bound in a defenseless and vulnerable position. Their resentment toward the Indians and their own government increased. By the summer of 1793, Blount had a difficult time enforcing federal orders to halt offensives against the Indians. When settlers were slaughtered near Cavet's Station, just east of Knoxville, by Creek and Cherokee raiding parties, the settlers became unrestrained. John Sevier and a few hundred men chased the Indians into Georgia, where they defeated them and demolished several Indian villages. Similar events occurred around Nashville where James Robertson ordered Major James Ore and about 550 men to attack the Indian community of Nickajack, located at the mouth of the Sequatchie River. After these losses, defeat of Indians in the north by General Anthony Wayne at the Battle of Fallen Timbers in the summer of 1794, and decrease of Spanish support for the Indians, the native inhabitants began to lose their fervor for war. Hostilities finally, slowly, began to subside.

Meanwhile, White settlements had continued to increase in population and form official communities. The town of Knoxville, named for Henry Knox, the secretary of war under President Washington, was established in 1792 on land granted to James White (the father of Hugh Lawson White). White had first come to the site where the Holston and French Broad Rivers meet in 1786. When he returned with his family, he settled a little further up near a creek that flowed into the Tennessee River on the land initially bought in 1783 from North Carolina. The log home he built was eventually turned into a fort. The fort became the site of the territorial capital and White, who owned the land around the area, profited very well from his land sales.

Meanwhile, the new national government continued to evolve, but at this point there was little political partisanship yet expressed through party politics. Most of Washington's first term as president dealt with organization of a government. Slowly, however, the factional positioning began as Alexander Hamilton, who was the leader of the Federalist movement, which was mainly interested in the commercial concerns of the north, came into philosophical conflict with Thomas Jefferson. Jefferson led the Anti-Federalist group, which was generally more concerned with the agriculturally based business of the south. By the time Washington's first term was about to end, there was concern that a political battle for the office of president would be destructive to the fragile national government. The new nation was still too unstable to survive a political free-for-all. Many urged Washington to stay for a second term so that the new government would have a better chance of holding together. On February 13, 1793, Washington was unanimously reelected by the electoral college. His inauguration took place in Philadelphia on March 4, 1793. (The capital had moved to Philadelphia from New York.)

During Washington's second term, the demands of the presidency increased, and he came under significant criticism. By this time the French Revolution had occurred and England and other countries were facing an aggressive French Republic. Jefferson wanted to aid the French, while Washington wanted to remain neutral. As issues developed, differing political philosophies began to create factions, and political parties began to crystallize. They became known as the "Federalist" and the "Democrat-Republican."

During the Revolutionary War, the Spanish had prevented the Americans and British from using the Mississippi River. However, by 1794 they officially gave in to free navigation of the river, but this did not prevent them from attempting to make life hard for their national competitors by stirring up trouble.

Sometime prior to 1795, Brigadier General Gayoso, the Spanish governor of Natchez, arrived in Fort Esperanza, which was located on the Arkansas side of the Mississippi River. From there he moved across the river to the Chickasaw Bluffs and established Fort St. Ferdinand on the site of the old Fort Prud'homme. He intended to dispute and prevent not only any other nation's settlement of the area but also the navigation of the river. He was under instructions of his government to do anything and everything possible to prevent the Americans from settling the area. He intended to disrupt the agency and depot of supplies that had been provided for the Chickasaw Indians since 1782, established by Tennessee's James Robertson. Robertson had set this up in the interests of the individuals living in the "Mero" District (Middle Tennessee) of Franklin. On October 27, 1795, the U.S. minister to Great Britain, Thomas Pinckney, signed a treaty with Spain (Pinckney's Treaty), which ended the dispute concerning the western and southern boundaries of the United States as well as the issue over free navigation of the Mississippi River. This was supposed to stop the Spanish from inciting the Indians, but the Spanish were not in any hurry to comply with the agreement, and they actually delayed their departure.

With the Spanish, French, and English supposedly now out of what was official U.S. territory, North Carolina held claim to almost all of what is present-day Tennessee. Georgia held claim to land west to Alabama and Mississippi. Most of the land was granted as payment for military service in the Revolutionary War or for those serving as state militiamen. Unused land warrants were also sold.

Statehood

While the Southwest Territory was regulated by Governor Blount and two judges, the settlers were dissatisfied with their limited protection and input into the government. They wanted protection from the Indians and quickly tired of capitulating their destiny to some far-off government. But, there was hope. The territory was organized such that when the voting population reached five thousand, the people could elect their own legislative body to govern their lives and lands. Blount was in no hurry to give up his control, but pressure from the settlers rapidly increased, and in 1793, he felt that the required population had been reached. He issued a proclamation, and a public vote was held on the third Friday in December 1793. Thirteen men were elected to the first legislature, and they met for the first time in Knoxville (Blount had moved the capital and his family to Knoxville in 1792) on the fourth Monday of February 1794. John Tipton was one of the representatives. He still opposed Blount and Sevier, so from the very earliest times of Tennessee's evolution, political intrigue was part of the deliberations. During the first session, which lasted two days, the issues of the new territorial legislature were mainly concerned with forming a legislative council (a legislative body separate from the elected legislature), the adoption of an address to the governor, a memorial to Congress, a statement of the condition of the territory, and a request to Congress for protection from the Indians. In addition to the publicly elected territorial legislature, the legislative council consisted of five representatives, selected by the U.S. Congress, from among ten names submitted by the new territorial house of representatives. Of the ten names submitted, James Winchester, Parmenas Taylor, Stockley Donelson, Griffith Rutherford, and John Sevier were selected.

While the territory was organizing, some of its future leaders were opening the western frontier of the future state. John Overton, a young lawyer and partner/protégé of Andrew Jackson, came upon the land and estate of the late John Rice. On July 26, 1794, Elisha Rice sold to John Overton, by warranty deed, the five

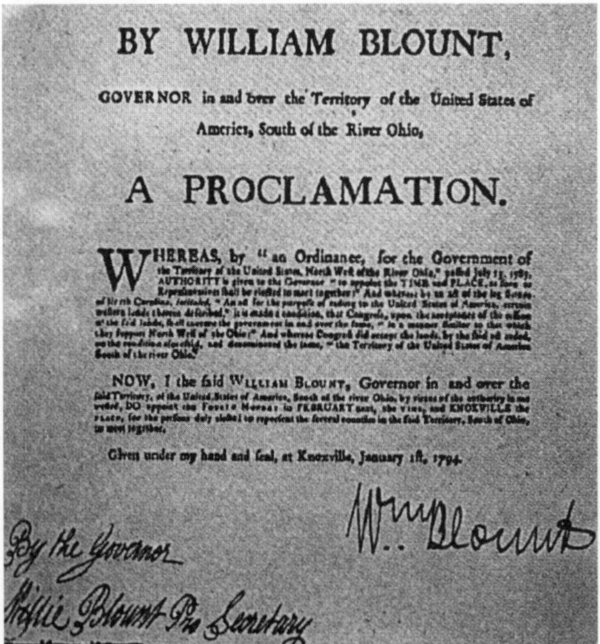
BY WILLIAM BLOUNT,

GOVERNOR in and over the Territory of the United States of America, South of the River Ohio,

A PROCLAMATION.

WHEREAS, by "an Ordinance, for the Government of the Territory of the United States, North West of the River Ohio," passed July 13, 1787, AUTHORITY is given to the Governor "to appoint the TIME and PLACE, [illegible] Representatives shall be elected to meet together;" And whereas by an act of the [illegible] of North Carolina, entitled, "An act for the purpose of ceding to the United States of America, certain western lands therein described," it is made a condition, that Congress, upon the acceptance of the cession of the said lands, shall assume the government in and over the same, "in a manner similar to that which they support North West of the Ohio;" And whereas Congress did accept the lands, by the said act ceded, on the condition [illegible], and denominated the same, "the Territory of the United States of America South of the river Ohio."

NOW, I the said WILLIAM BLOUNT, Governor in and over the said Territory, of the United States of America, South of the river Ohio, by virtue of the authority in me vested, DO appoint the FOURTH MONDAY in FEBRUARY next, the TIME, and KNOXVILLE the PLACE, for the persons duly elected to represent the several counties in the said Territory, South of Ohio, to meet together.

Given under my hand and seal, at Knoxville, January 1st, 1794.

Wm. Blount

By the Governor
Willie Blount Pro Secretary

Governor Blount summons Tennessee's first territorial legislature. (Courtesy of TSLA)

JOHN OVERTON was born in Louisa County, Virginia, in 1766. His father and mother were James and Mary Waller Overton. Overton left Kentucky and arrived in the territory which would become Tennessee, via Nashville, around 1789. He got to know Andrew Jackson when the two roomed at the Widow Donelson's home in Nashville. Their relationship grew as the two lawyers became friends, political allies, and business partners. Overton was married in 1820 at the age of fifty-four. The couple soon had a son, whom they named John. This son married Harriet Maxwell, promoted the Nashville and Chattanooga Railroad, and built the Maxwell House Hotel in Nashville. Overton served on the Tennessee Supreme Court. He was not only a confidant to President Jackson, but a state leader and developer of Memphis. "In 1876, Martha Overton, direct descendant of Judge Overton, married Jacob McGavock Dickinson, whose mother was a granddaughter of Felix Grundy" (Burt 1959). John Overton died on April 12, 1833. (Photograph courtesy of TSLA)

thousand acres along the Chickasaw Bluffs, for only five hundred dollars. Although this was apparently less than John Rice paid in 1783, the money was much more stable. Andrew Jackson and John Overton were business partners and, because of a standing agreement to participate with each other in land purchases, Jackson became one-half owner of the land, at a value listed as one hundred dollars. Because of financial pressures, Jackson would later sell off portions of his land to brothers Stephen and Richard Winchester. The Overton/Jackson land deed would later play a role in extending the Democratic influence of the Jackson political faction from Middle Tennessee to the land development along the Mississippi River.

After receiving the selection of the legislative council from Congress, the territorial legislature reconvened on August 25, 1794, with two legislative bodies. In this term an act to provide relief to those disabled or to the families of those killed in the Indian Wars was passed. Two colleges were chartered: Greeneville College in Greene County, and Blount College in Knoxville. A request was sent to Congress for the relief of families who had settled in Carter County, under the treaty made by the state of Franklin with the Cherokee Indians. James White of Knox County was elected as a delegate to Congress. His political objective was to present the need of the territory for federal protection against the Indians. A list of the more than one hundred persons killed by the Indians in the previous six months was prepared for submission to Congress. A tax of twenty-five cents per one thousand acres was also levied. The session lasted thirty-seven days.

The population of the future state continued to grow, and several new towns began to form. Sevierville, Greeneville, Blountville, and Clarksville were added to a growing list that already included Rogersville, Knoxville, and Nashville. The populace grew impatient over what they considered was a lack of protection by the federal government, and in 1795 territorial Governor William Blount was convinced that he should request admission as a state. Only Vermont and Kentucky had been added to the original thirteen states, but they had not gone through the territorial status prior to admission. There was no clear-cut path for statehood. So Blount took the initiative, calling for the passage of legislation empowering the sheriffs of the eleven counties to determine if the population had yet reached sixty thousand (the threshold the federal government required for statehood). He called the legislature back into session in Knoxville on June 29. The legislation was passed. The census was subsequently taken, and the population was determined to be 36,123 White males, 29,554 females, 10,613 slaves, and 973 others. This represented a total of 77,263.

When the vote was taken seeking public approval for statehood, the eastern section of the territory voted for admission, but the Cumberland area was opposed. The opposition by the Cumberland area could have been from fear of taxes or fear of domination by the higher population and influence of the eastern section. Nonetheless, the vote passed.

On November 28, 1795, Governor Blount issued a proclamation directing the election of representatives to a constitutional convention. The elections were held in each county and the constitutional convention

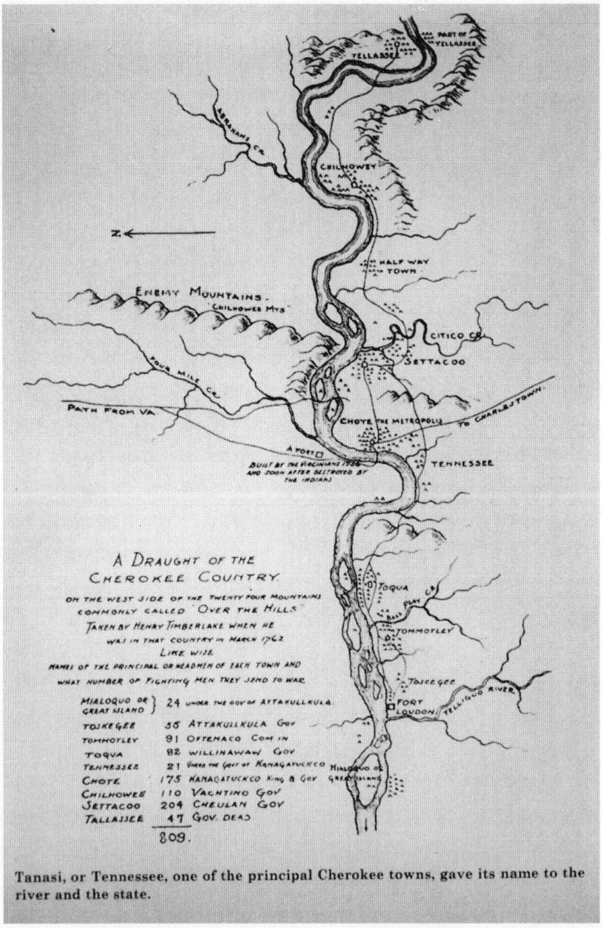

Tanasi, or Tennessee, one of the principal Cherokee towns, gave its name to the river and the state.

Map of Cherokee Country. (Courtesy of TSLA)

convened on January 11, 1796. Blount was elected chairman of the convention.

> The delegates included Territorial Judges Joseph Anderson and John McNairy, Secretary [of State] Daniel Smith, and the congressional delegate and large landholder, James White. James Robertson, Andrew Jackson, and Thomas Hardeman were among those from the Cumberland area. James Houston, father of Sam Houston, represented Blount County. John Tipton and Landon Carter, former speaker of the Franklin legislature, represented Washington County. Men destined to serve later as governor of Tennessee or to represent the state in Congress included William Cocke, Joseph McMinn, John Rhea, and Archibald Roane, in addition to Andrew Jackson. Sixteen members listed their place of birth as Virginia, eight mentioned Pennsylvania, seven North Carolina, four South Carolina, and three Maryland. (Corlew 1989)

A committee drafted the constitution, which was reported to the convention on January 27 and unanimously passed on February 6, 1796. Tennessee County, which was located in the middle of the territory, gave up its name for use by the new state. (The county was subsequently divided up into Robertson and Montgomery Counties.) It is said that this occurred at the suggestion of Andrew Jackson, but that supposition may be purely fictional. By this time *Tennessee* was a well-used name and may have been favored by many. *Tannassee* was said to be the Cherokee name for spoon. A Cherokee town named Tannassee or Tanase sat on the west bank of the Little Tennessee or Tannassee River, which was a few miles above the mouth of the Tellico. The name may have been given due to a "fancied" resemblance of the Tennessee River to a spoon. The name could also mean "old town." Tennessee was a purely American name, rather than European, as was used by other states. The name had likely been popularized by General Daniel Smith's 1793 publication, *Short Description of Tennessee Government.*

The new constitution created by the convention gave the right to vote to freemen over twenty-one, including free Black men who had resided in the state for six months. It provided for a state house of representatives, senate, and governor. All elected officials were to be selected for two-year terms. The judiciary was to be appointed. The Tennessee Constitution was an astonishing product, considering it was the creation of backwoods frontiersmen who struggled to eke out a living, build cabins, and fight Indians and British soldiers. Thomas Jefferson was later quoted saying that the constitution was "the most republican yet framed in America." Once the constitution was passed, territorial Governor Blount instructed the sheriffs of the counties to hold the state of Tennessee's first election for governor and legislators.

The election for the state's first legislature and governor took place prior to its admission to the United States. There were not any real partisan issues or party philosophies to be debated in the new state—there were only personalities. John Sevier was popular and expected to be the first governor. Blount and Sevier were closely related politically at this time. Blount was expected to be chosen U.S. senator and, therefore, did not oppose Sevier becoming governor. Sevier was so popular in East Tennessee that even friends of John Tipton did not bother to oppose him. However, in the Cumberland area Colonel James Winchester, Thomas Hardeman, and Colonel Robert Hayes worked to gain support for Judge Joseph Anderson. John McNairy and James Robertson led the campaign for Sevier in the Cumberland area. Their influence combined with Sevier's strength in the east was overwhelming, and Judge Anderson withdrew from the contest. John Sevier, a Democrat-Republican from Washington County and the most popular man in the new state, soon looked to become elected Tennessee's first governor with no opposition.

The first legislature for the proposed state of Tennessee met in Knoxville on March 28, 1796. James Stewart was elected speaker of the house and James Winchester speaker of the senate. County returns from the gubernatorial election were tabulated on March 29, 1796. Sevier was declared the winner and was inaugurated as Tennessee's first governor on March 30, 1796. William Cocke, Dr. James White, Judge Anderson, and William Blount ran for the two U.S. Senate positions. Blount was easily elected to the Class 2 seat. Then Anderson, White, and Cocke were left as candidates for the remaining seat. Anderson and White withdrew, and Cocke was elected by the new legislature as the other U.S. senator to the Class 1 seat (Class 1 and Class 2 seats were determined by the time frame of the term of office) from Tennessee. Andrew Jackson was elected to the U.S. House of Representatives by the people.

John Sevier enjoyed universal approval during his tenure as Tennessee's first governor. There were not yet political parties

JOHN SEVIER was born on September 23, 1745, in Rockingham County, Virginia. His ancestors were Huguenots and used the name Xavier. In the seventeenth century his paternal grandfather fled France because of religious persecution. Upon arriving in England, his grandfather changed his name to Sevier, married and had two children. Valentine, one of the children, ran away from home and came to the Shenandoah Valley of Virginia. He married Joanna Goade, and they had seven children, one of whom was John.

Sevier attended Augusta Academy, which later became Washington and Lee University. He took Sara Hawkins as his bride and they eventually had ten children. By age nineteen he owned land and was a merchant in New Market, Virginia. A brother had moved beyond the Allegheny Mountains and the stories of opportunity further west pulled at young John Sevier. By 1773, after himself traveling west, he moved his family to a settlement by the Holston River. Later they moved to the Watauga settlement. Once there he, like many of the settlers, found it necessary to protect his family from the hostile Indians. He joined a militia, became a leader, and led thirty-five battles against the Indians (also led the Battle of King's Mountain against the British). Unfortunately, Sara was killed during an Indian attack. Later, he met Catherine Sherrill, who had jumped into his arms while escaping from another Indian battle. They were married, she became stepmother to Sevier's ten children, and together they had eight more.

Sevier's military exploits to protect his fellow man won him respect. After North Carolina's initial release of their Western territory, Sevier and his fellow settlers formed the (never recognized) state of Franklin, to which Sevier was elected governor in 1784. Meanwhile, the North Carolina legislature repealed their previous act of cession of the territory to the United States.

to fight each other. Although sectional and personal differences inevitably developed, there were few political battles during the first few years of the life of the hopeful state. However, Tennessee still had to wait for formal admission into the Union.

Three days after the adjournment of the constitutional convention, the constitution was sent to the U.S. secretary of state (under President George Washington). Another was prepared for the to-be-appointed secretary of the state of the new state. However, there was a federal delay in accepting Tennessee as a new state because 1796 was an election year and the first time there was competition for the office of president. This fostered the development of the two-party system, and as the politicians took sides, they assessed the impact of votes by a proposed new state. Tennessee was a Democrat-Republican state, and the Federalists in the capital of Philadelphia were concerned with the number of electoral votes Tennessee would contribute for or against the Federalist candidate. The approval of the constitution was blocked in the U.S. Senate and voted down. However, friends of Tennessee in the House of Representatives, including Democrat-Republicans James Madison, Albert Gallitin, and Thomas Blount (William Blount's brother, a congressman from North Carolina), managed to keep hopes of statehood alive. The House of Representatives approved admission on May 6, but the Senate was controlled by the Federalists, who held up the admission, refusing to seat

Settlers divided in their loyalty to the wavering state of Franklin.

Sevier and his followers were dedicated to a separate state and formed the "Franklin Party." Opponents, led by John Tipton, were loyal to North Carolina and formed the "North Carolina Party." The effort for statehood soon became futile. After Sevier's term as governor of Franklin ended in 1788, the state of Franklin died and the people returned to the jurisdiction of North Carolina.

Sevier was then charged with treason for forming a separate government and for attempting to defend the State of Franklin against North Carolina. John Tipton was placed in charge of the territory and had Sevier arrested. Sevier was taken back to North Carolina to stand trial. However, just prior to the trial, loyal friends arrived and freed him from custody. North Carolina officials never pursued the issue and soon restored Sevier's privileges.

Sevier was elected to serve as the first U.S. Representative for the Western District of North Carolina in 1789. After Tennessee became a state, he was elected the first governor on March 29, 1796. He served three consecutive two-year terms (1796–1801) as governor. By statute he could not succeed himself. After Archibald Roane served one term as governor, Sevier was reelected for another series of three terms (1803–1809). During this time Tennessee had two major cities, Nashborough (Nashville) in Middle Tennessee and Knoxville in East Tennessee. Andrew Jackson became the chief political rival of Sevier, and their followers were somewhat, though not totally, divided according to the two geographic divisions.

Sevier served six terms as governor, a single term as state senator, then was elected to the U.S. House of Representatives for Tennessee. He remained in Congress until he was sent on a mission to Fort Decatur, Alabama, in the Creek Indian country. During his journey he developed an illness, accompanied by an extremely high fever, and died on September 24, 1815. He was buried in the Alabama wilderness on the east bank of the Tallapoosa River. His remains were returned to Knoxville in 1887. (Photograph courtesy of TSLA)

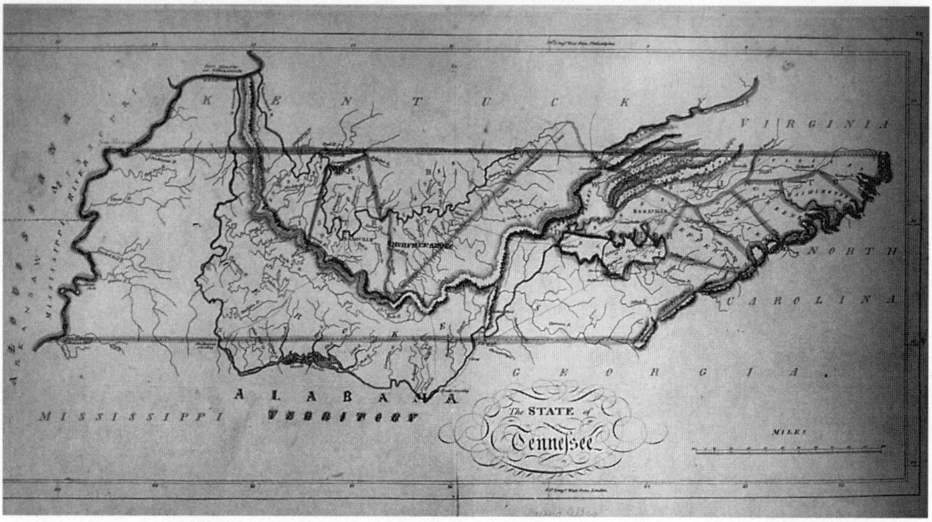

Map of Tennessee, ca. 1796. East and Middle Tennessee is separated by Indian territory. (Courtesy of TSLA)

Cocke and Blount. Finally, a Democrat-Republican compromise was approved, and Tennessee was admitted, but the number of representatives (which equaled the number of electoral votes allotted) would be limited. President Washington signed the legislation making Tennessee the sixteenth state on June 1, 1796. It would have two senators (William Blount and William Cocke) and one representative (Andrew Jackson).

The U.S. Senate did not seat Cocke and Blount until Governor Sevier had the legislature of Tennessee reelect them. Since they had been elected prior to admission, they had been considered elected by the Southwest Territory and therefore unacceptable. Sevier had the legislature meet on July 30, 1796, and the offices were again filled, satisfying the need for authenticity.

In the presidential election of 1796 Federalist John Adams faced Democrat-Republican Thomas Jefferson. The voting was close, and the contest involved a myriad of political maneuvers. Jefferson attacked Adams on grounds that the Federalist candidate intended to set up a hereditary Federalist monarchy. Adams accused Jefferson of wanting to do away with the Constitution. Federalist Alexander Hamilton felt that it would be easier to achieve a Federalist victory with Thomas Pinckney, who he saw as a more palatable choice. Hamilton dangerously set out to switch votes from Adams to Pinckney, almost costing the Federalists the election. Tennessee had three electoral votes and cast all its votes for the Democrat-Republican candidates. The Tennessee electors did exactly what the Federalist suspected they would when the attempt was made to delay Tennessee's admission—they voted for Republicans Thomas Jefferson and Aaron Burr for president and vice president. By a close electoral vote, (seventy-one to sixty-eight), John Adams was elected president. Thomas Jefferson, receiving the second highest number of votes, became vice president. Adams was inaugurated on March 4, 1797.

While the partisanship within the political system of the nation and the state of Tennessee evolved, international politics also played a role in the development of the young state. Even after Tennessee had become a state, the Spanish were still maintaining control of the area of the Chickasaw Bluffs. Without using armed force, Gayoso invaded the Chickasaw lands. The Chickasaws, sensing the dominant attitude of the Spanish, complained to Governor Sevier, who under direction of President Washington, sent Colonel McKee to see Governor Gayoso. He carried a letter from Governor Sevier which informed Gayoso of the congressional resolutions and other treaties declaring free navigation of the Mississippi River. He insisted that Gayoso demolish the fort and leave the area, stating that Gayoso was interfering in the territorial rights of the Indians and the state of Tennessee, as well as of the United States. The activities of Gayoso and the response of Sevier were essentially declarations of war. The treaty of 1795 (between the United States and Spain) had established the boundaries and free navigation of the Mississippi River, two years prior, but Gayoso and the Spanish still remained.

Captain Guion, of the Third United States Infantry, sailed down the Mississippi and took possession of the Chickasaw Bluffs for the United States. Spanish troops destroyed Fort San Ferdinando before leaving Tennessee soil and crossing the river back to Fort Esperanza. Guion first constructed Fort Adams on the bluffs, then Fort Pike, later named Fort Pickering in honor of Thomas Pickering, President Washington's secretary of war. Guion then traveled down the Mississippi to do similar duty for his country in Vicksburg and Natchez.

In 1763 France had ceded New Orleans to Spain. When Spain and England went to war around this same time, many in Tennessee were concerned over what Spain would do with the city since it impacted the prosperity of trade along the Mississippi River. U.S. Senator Blount became involved in a scheme to take New Orleans from Spain so it would not be ceded to an unfriendly nation. Blount had mailed a letter containing statements about his plans. The letter was to be destroyed but fell into the hands of the Federalists, who did not much care for the Democrat-Republican Tennesseans, and began to legally pursue the senator. The U.S. Senate then moved to expel Blount for allegedly carrying on correspondence with a James Carey who was conspiring to set up another government with New Orleans as its capital. However, Blount resigned from the Senate thus avoiding expulsion. He returned to Tennessee where he was immediately elected to the state senate. When the sergeant-at-arms of the U.S. Senate, James Matthews, went to Tennessee to arrest the ex-senator, Blount's fellow citizens escorted the intruder out of town, "politely" assuring the federal representative that Blount would be remaining, with them, in Tennessee. [Blount would have easily been reelected to go back to the U.S. Senate; however, he died in 1800.]

On September 26, 1797, the legislature elected Andrew Jackson to the Senate (Class 1) to replace William Cocke, whose term had ended. Joseph Anderson was elected to the U.S. Senate (Class 2) to succeed William Blount, who had resigned. John Sevier was reelected governor in August. John White was elected speaker of the state senate and James Stewart, of the house. William C. C. Claiborne succeeded Andrew Jackson in the U.S. House of Representatives. (Claiborne was later appointed territorial governor of Mississippi and governor of the territory and state of Louisiana.)

Andrew Jackson

By 1797 Andrew Jackson was already well-known and well-connected in Tennessee. How else would a thirty-year-old man, not born to position, obtain election to the U.S. Senate? He was born on March 15, 1767, in the Lancaster District of South Carolina. His mother named him Andrew in honor of his father, who had died of unknown causes earlier in the same month of Jackson's birth. Jackson's mother struggled to raise her sons and even dreamed of Jackson becoming a Presbyterian minister. However, this young man possessed little patience, was hot-tempered, and could curse with the best. He received little formal schooling but did learn to read and write (in his own error-plagued style). In 1780, when he was thirteen, the British captured Charleston, South Carolina, and moved into the countryside to pillage the inhabitants, massacring 113 and wounding 150. Jackson's oldest brother, Hugh, age sixteen, died from the strain of battle at Stone Ferry. Jackson and his brother Robert participated in the battle of Hanging Rock on August 1, 1780, in which the Americans almost defeated the British. After his brother Robert returned home, both were discovered by the British. Jackson was struck with the sword of a British officer for refusing to shine the officer's boots, and both boys were taken prisoner. Later they were returned in a prisoner swap, but Robert died shortly after from smallpox. Jackson barely survived the disease.

Jackson's mother, Elizabeth, contracted cholera while nursing soldiers in Charleston and died in 1781. At the young age of fifteen years, Jackson was alone. Shortly after the end of the Revolutionary War he went to live with his aunt. Later he was sent to live with Joseph White, an uncle of his mother's sister, Jane Crawford. He completed minimal education before deciding to learn law. He studied with Spruce McCay for two years, beginning at age seventeen, in the town of Salisbury, North Carolina. After being accepted to the bar, he drifted around North Carolina practicing law for a year. He had been a fellow law student and friend of John McNairy, who had been appointed superior court judge for the Western District of North Carolina (which stretched to the Mississippi River). McNairy appointed Jackson as public prosecutor of the district. In 1788, Jackson, Bennett Searcy, John McNairy, Archibald Roane, David Allison, and others moved to Jonesboro, in what became East Tennessee.

Jackson was not there long before he became engaged in his first duel after a disagreement with another lawyer. While arguing a case in a Jonesboro court against fellow attorney Waighstill Avery, Jackson was angered when his opponent resorted to some sarcasm in the rebuttal. Jackson challenged Avery to a duel. Fortunately, cooler heads prevailed, and when the duel took place both he and Avery fired into the air. Shortly after the spring confrontation, Jackson left for Nashville, along with a few of his friends, to take up his duties as prosecutor. They arrived on October 26, 1788; Jackson found lodgings with John Donelson's widowed wife. (Mr. Donelson had been robbed and murdered in Kentucky, near the Tennessee line, while returning from a trip to Washington.) It was about this time that Mrs. Donelson's daughter, Rachel Donelson Robards, returned to Nashville after a stormy short stint at marriage. Soon accusations flew that there was a relationship between Mrs. Robards and Jackson and he sought other lodging.

In Nashville Jackson found a tremendous amount of work to be prosecuted.

Within six months of his move to Nashville, he joined in the defense of the settlers against the Indians, entering service as a private, but distinguishing himself as a determined Indian fighter.

Jackson ingratiated himself to territorial Governor Blount, who at this time held total power and the key to advancement. Willie Blount, his half brother, and Hugh Lawson White were Blount's private secretaries; Archibald Roane, who had traveled to Tennessee with Jackson, became Blount's attorney general of the Washington District; and David Allison, also a friend and traveling companion of Jackson, became the governor's manager of business. James Robertson was brigadier general of the territorial militia, as was John Sevier. Since several of Jackson's friends were closely associated with the governor, Jackson received help in developing his ties to Blount's team. On February 15, 1791, Jackson was made attorney general for the Mero (Middle Tennessee) District, and subsequently his association with the governor continued to grow.

By September 10, 1792, Blount made Jackson judge advocate for Davidson County cavalry regiment. With this came the opportunity to work more directly under Brigadier General James Robertson. After a while Robertson, a very popular and influential man in Middle Tennessee, became fond of young Jackson. It did not hurt Jackson's

JOSEPH ANDERSON was born on November 5, 1757, in Philadelphia, Pennsylvania. Of his early life, we know little. By May 1776 he was an ensign in the Third New Jersey Regiment, Continental Establishment. He subsequently became a second and then a first lieutenant and by October 1777 had become a captain. After achieving this rank, he served as regimental paymaster, participating in battles against the Indians and the British, and in the Battle of Yorktown in October 1783. After the war, he practiced law in Delaware until President Washington appointed him as a judge in the Territory South of the Ohio River on February 25, 1791. He was a delegate to the first constitutional convention of Tennessee in 1796. The following year he married Patience Outlaw (she was fifteen; he was forty) and they had seven sons. The same year, on September 26, he was elected to the U.S. Senate and served until March 3, 1799. For a short while, Anderson served with Andrew Jackson, and the two Tennesseans usually, though not always, voted the same way. Both voted against the proposal in the Senate to have William Blount arrested. On December 12, 1798, Anderson succeeded Daniel Smith, who held the temporary senate seat appointment after Jackson's resignation, and remained in the Senate until 1815. Anderson served as president pro tempore. In 1799 Governor Sevier ran against him for the new Senate term. Although Sevier was extremely popular among the general public, Anderson held strength within the legislature and defeated him, gaining the right to return to the Senate. In 1815 President Madison appointed Anderson as the first comptroller of the U.S. Treasury, an office he held during the 1819 financial panic and again in the early part of the 1837 financial panic.

One of Anderson's sons, Alexander Outlaw Anderson, served Tennessee as a U.S. senator in 1840 to fill the unexpired term created by the resignation of Hugh Lawson White. Joseph Anderson died on April 18, 1837, at almost eighty years of age, while at the Washington home of his son William. He was laid to rest in the Congressional Cemetery (tract 43 or 44). (Photograph courtesy of SHO) ambitions to have direct contact with and the support of Robertson, in addition to territorial Governor William Blount. He also married into a leading family of Tennessee. Rachel Donelson was the daughter of a pioneer family—the Donelsons— who were as well respected in Middle Tennessee as the Robertsons. (John Donelson had surveyed and led settlement.) Rachel had received a divorce from Lewis Robards, and she and Jackson married. When they later discovered that the divorce had not been legally confirmed, Rachel and Andrew Jackson remarried on January 17, 1794. Jackson continued to distinguish himself as an Indian fighter and also as an outspoken critic of the lack of congressional support for the Davidson County defense against Indian attacks. After statehood, with Blount's support and his newly found social standing, twenty-nine-year-old Andrew Jackson ran for and was elected Tennessee's first member of the U.S. House of Representatives during the fall of 1796. The young politician took his leadership post for the new state along with Sevier, Blount, and Cocke.

Jackson wanted to become major general of the Tennessee militia but lost this election in 1796 to George Conway, who had the support of Governor Sevier. The governor would not support Jackson, who was young, rash, and ill prepared to command military operations, and Jackson's temper flared. With the help of General John Robertson's intervention, Jackson was able to improve his damaged relation with Sevier. Shortly thereafter, Senator Blount was forced to resign from the U.S. Senate for his role in the British plot to seize New Orleans from the Spanish. Jackson ran for the open senate seat without as much opposition as he might have encountered. It was under these circumstances when, on September 25, 1797, the Tennessee legislature elected him to a full six-year U.S. Senate seat (Class 1); twenty votes for Jackson and thirteen for William Cocke. Of course, Cocke was none too happy with being displaced from his seat by Jackson and a rift developed between them, which nearly ended in another duel. However, cooler minds again prevailed and settled the dispute between the two. Jackson took office on September 26, 1797.

Jackson now had his Senate position, and all would seem to be well; however, he did not find the Senate to his liking. He was in debt, away from his wife, and likely just too young to gain acceptance. After one session, Jackson resigned in April 1798.

Governor Sevier then appointed Daniel Smith, on October 6, 1798, to fill the Class 1 Senate seat. He was sworn in on December 3, 1798 and served nine days, until the appointment ended on December 12, 1798. Joseph Anderson, who had been previously serving to complete Senator Blount's Class 2 term, which officially ended on March 3, 1799, was elected, taking the Class 1 seat on December 12, 1798. (Anderson completed his Class 1 term for this Senate seat, which officially ended on March 3, 1803, was reelected to serve until March 3, 1809, and reelected again to serve until March 3, 1815.) At the same Tennessee legislative session in which Anderson was elected, William Cocke was returned to the U.S. Senate by being elected to a full term in the other seat (Class 2), which began in spring 1799. (He served from March 4, 1799, until March 3, 1805.) Much of this confusion related to Senate seat switching came as a direct result of Andrew Jackson's ambition and fickle behavior.

It is possible that Jackson resigned from the U.S. Senate because he felt better opportunity and more adventure awaited him back home in Tennessee. The supreme

WILLIAM COCKE was born in Amelia County, Virginia, in 1747. He received his early education in the common school of the day. Later, he studied law and practiced in Virginia. Daniel Boone was his contemporary and companion and the two of them explored the territory of Kentucky and Tennessee. Cocke led four Virginia companies in Indian battles, defeating the Indians in the Battle of Cocke's Fort, Tennessee. In 1776 he came to Tennessee and in 1784, when Tennessee's forebears were trying to form the state of Franklin, Cocke was sent to North Carolina to work for recognition. He was a delegate to the convention that created the state of Tennessee, then he was elected U.S. senator by the 1796 legislature serving from August 2, 1796, until March 3, 1797. Governor Sevier appointed Cocke to succeed himself in the senate, where he served April 22, 1797, until September 26, 1797, when the legislature elected Andrew Jackson. In 1799 Cocke ran for the senate in Tennessee's other seat and was elected to the full term that began on March 4, 1799, serving until March 4, 1805. He lost a race for governor against Willie Blount in 1808 but was then appointed judge in the First Circuit of Tennessee the following year. In 1812, he was impeached as a judge (as occurred often in those days) and convicted, the first judge convicted in Tennessee. (His son, John Cocke, was Speaker of the senate that convicted him.) He served in the War of 1812 under Andrew Jackson and was elected to the Tennessee legislature in 1813. Later he moved to Mississippi and was elected to that state's legislature. President James Madison made him Indian agent to the Chickasaw Nation in 1814. Cocke died in Columbus, Mississippi, on August 22, 1828. (Photograph courtesy of SHO)

court of Tennessee paid six hundred dollars per year and allowed travel throughout Tennessee. This of course, would allow Jackson to do some campaigning among the people who could open the doors for his future ambitions. With the help of the Blount faction in the state legislature and his developing reputation, there was little difficulty in gaining a court appointment. Governor Sevier signed the appointment September 20, 1798. Although Jackson's legal preparation left something to be desired, he would earn a good reputation and make respectable legal decisions. He held court in Nashville, Knoxville, and Jonesboro for the next six years.

In 1799 Governor Sevier, ever popular, was again reelected governor without any significant conflict. However, political battles in Tennessee were increasing. The constitutional limit in the state at the time was three consecutive two-year gubernatorial terms. Therefore, Sevier had to prepare another path for his future political ambitions. Likewise, his upcoming departure from the state's top post would create a void for which other ambitious men could compete. No more would personal and sectional differences be hidden. The clash of ambitions would provide the opportunity for political conflict.

Although Tennessee had not yet divided along party lines, political parties did have some impact in the federal elections of this day. As the presidential election of 1800 neared, the differences between the Democrat-Republican and the Federalist Parties became more clear. The election would strengthen the national two-party system and would further bind Tennesseans against the

Federalist Party which represented "Eastern interests" and what many Tennesseans considered were monarchial attitudes. The controversy over United States involvement in the war between Britain and France was the main topic of federal political debate. The French Republic wanted the United States to join them in their war with England. After all, the English had not been respectful of American independence. The French, however, also treated Americans in a high-handed manner. They refused to see American diplomats, threatened to hang any Americans found on English sea vessels, etc. American political party affiliation and positions on matters such as this war did impact support for presidential candidates. By 1800, the Federalist Party was divided over going to war against France. President Adams wanted to avoid war with France. Alexander Hamilton, a Federalist Party leader, had succeeded Washington (after his death) as commander in chief of the U.S. Army and wanted to lead a war with France. When Hamilton circulated a letter among Federalists which contained information—secret only to members of Adams's treacherous cabinet and critical of Adams's actions—it served to divide support for Adams. The Federalists of the day were autocratic and power-hungry, and showed little regard for a democratic approach to government. As the election approached, it became apparent that Vice President Thomas Jefferson would be the "anti-Federalist" candidate. He wanted no war with France and favored a democratic approach to government. He had secretly written the Kentucky Resolutions which said that the Alien and Sedition Acts passed by the Federalists were unconstitutional and in violation of states rights.

The Alien and Sedition Acts were passed in the Federalist-controlled Congress of 1798 and gave the federal government the right to arrest aliens or opponents of the U.S. government who disagreed with its policies, and to shut down newspapers and arrest critics. The passage of these acts was a dangerous precedent that could have destroyed the very liberty fought for in the Revolution. Jefferson understood this. By supporting the acts, Hamilton destroyed the unity of his own Federalist party, divided Adams's support, and assisted Jefferson's cause. When the electoral votes were counted, it was clear that the Jefferson-Burr Democrat-Republican ticket had defeated the Federalists seventy-three to sixty-five for Adams and sixty-four for Charles Cotesworth Pinckney. However, there was a flaw in the Constitution dealing with the ballot. It was understood that a vote for the Jefferson-Burr ticket was a vote to elect Jefferson president and Burr vice president and the Democrat-Republican electors had clearly intended it that way. However, the outgoing Federalists maneuvered to take the election by claiming the vote was technically a tie between Jefferson and Burr. According to the Constitution, a tie would be decided by the House of Representatives and the House was controlled by the Federalists. In the end the Federalists feared the cunning and perfidious Burr and his own history of questionable maneuvers more than they distrusted Jefferson. Jefferson was elected president of the United States on the thirty-sixth ballot. President Adams had just moved into the new White House (not yet under that title) in November 1800. Thomas Jefferson would move into the new executive mansion when he was inaugurated on March 4, 1801.

Political Factions Take Shape

During this era James Robertson was considered the father of Middle Tennessee and held almost absolute control over this portion of the new state. In East Tennessee, Sevier and Blount were the political leaders. Sevier was re-elected governor twice, in 1797 and 1799 and served three consecutive terms, consolidating his political organization in the process. Because of constitutional prohibition, the very popular governor had to sit out the following term. Jackson's friend Archibald Roane, a Democrat-Republican from Knox County who had served as attorney general as well as a member of the superior court of Tennessee (with Jackson) decided to run for governor. His opponent was John Boyd, the sheriff of Nashville. With the support of the Blount faction, Archibald Roane received 8,432 votes to near none for Boyd. Roane served the gubernatorial term beginning in 1801 until 1803.

When Senator William Blount died suddenly on March 21,1800, Jackson saw his chance to end his dependence on others for high office and take control of politics in Tennessee himself by replacing the deceased Blount as the prominent Tennessee political leader.

ARCHIBALD ROANE was born of 1760 in the area that is now Dauphin County, Pennsylvania. His parents had emigrated from Ireland. His father, Andrew, was a weaver who died after coming to America, leaving four children for his mother, Margaret, to care for. His paternal uncle, John Roane, helped provide security for the children and gave Roane twenty pounds to use for his college education. Roane went to college in Lancaster, but left there to join the Continental army and fight in the Revolutionary War. He crossed the Delaware River with George Washington on December 24, 1776, and was also at Yorktown during the surrender of the British. After the war, Roane taught at Liberty Hall Academy, Rockbridge, Virginia, then undertook the study of law. As a new lawyer, he moved to Tennessee and was appointed district attorney general. In 1788 he married Ann Campbell from Campbell's Station, Knox County, Tennessee. They eventually had nine children. He served as a member of the convention that created the constitution of the state of Tennessee in 1796. Roane succeeded John Sevier as governor of Tennessee in 1801 and served one term which ended in 1803. During his term, the state was divided into three U.S. House of Representative districts (justified by the state's growth)—Washington, Mero, and Hamilton. The Mero district was named after Miró, the Louisiana governor (his name was misspelled).

Roane was a friend and political ally of Andrew Jackson. During his term as governor, the major general of the militia died. Although John Sevier had been governor for six years, had more experience in battle, and was the likely successor for the office, Jackson also wanted the position. There was a seventeen to seventeen tie for the position and Roane broke it in favor of Jackson. While this did not earn Governor Roane any friends among Sevier's allies, it did set Jackson on his way to military fame and eventually the presidency. Roane lost his attempt at reelection to John Sevier in 1803. For a period of time he returned to teaching. One of his pupils was Hugh Lawson White. Roane served as a superior court judge of law and equity in 1811. After his retirement, he returned to his "Grassy Valley" home in Knox County, Tennessee. He died on January 18, 1819. (Photograph courtesy of TSLA)

During Roane's term as governor, the major general of the Tennessee militia, George Conway, died and the spot was to be filled by the legislature on February 5, 1802. Jackson had been cultivating support for the office for years and saw his chance. His supreme court appointment by Governor Sevier in 1798 had provided Jackson with even more exposure around the state. Meanwhile, Sevier was out of office and wanted the major general post for himself. He was shocked to learn that the young man he had helped was challenging him. Sevier had considerable military experience, while Jackson had much less. However, Jackson had the Blount faction support and he would need it against the very popular Sevier. The legislature was a seventeen to seventeen tie. Sevier was dumbfounded when Governor Roane broke the tie in favor of his friend, Jackson. (James Winchester received only three votes.) Jackson was thirty-five years old.

Governor Roane had won Jackson his appointment as leader of the state militia, but in the process he intensified his own opposition for his upcoming reelection campaign in 1803. Sevier was not about to sit idly back while the upstarts usurped power and control. He began a reelection campaign that would put the challengers in their places. Jackson's efforts would cost Roane dearly and set Jackson back for years. For the campaign Sevier used his many contacts and friends. Jackson resorted to throwing mud at Sevier's character.

While Jackson was judge, he learned of a land fraud deal in which speculators were forging land warrants from North Carolina that were used to illegally sell Tennessee land. Jackson gave this evidence to the governor of North Carolina who asked Sevier, while he was governor, to extradite the accused. Sevier refused. The evidence Jackson submitted to North Carolina actually included Sevier himself, but Jackson waited on naming Sevier in the dealings. Now that Archibald Roane was governor, Jackson presented his evidence. Roane, of course, had his eyes set on being more than a caretaker governor, and wanted to run for reelection. Jackson thought the evidence would damage Sevier's reputation and aid Roane's chances for reelection. Jackson had now openly challenged Sevier, the Revolutionary and Indian war hero of Tennessee, for political leadership of the state. With William Blount now dead, Jackson moved into the role of leader of the Blount faction. By mid-1803 Sevier announced his candidacy for reelection as governor.

In 1803, while canvassing the state, Sevier stopped to speak to the people of Jonesboro. Jackson was in the crowd, still angry over Sevier's opposition to his appointment as major general of the militia in 1796 and the nasty fight in the legislature. Jackson had supported Governor Roane's claim of Sevier's involvement in the unproven North Carolina land warrants fraud (which was quite a controversy as well as a real concern due to the financial damage suffered by the many individuals and families injured in the dealings). Jackson had even published a letter in the *Knoxville Gazette* which showed his evidence against Sevier and charged him with fraud. When Sevier saw Jackson standing in the crowd, he could not contain his anger at him for his propagation of the unsubstantiated rumors. He commenced to denounce Jackson in "unmeasured terms." Jackson instantly made reply in kind, and closed by referring to his services to the State. "Services," rejoined Sevier, "I know of no great services you have rendered the country, except taking a trip to Natchez with another man's wife." "Great

God!" exclaimed Jackson, "Do not mention her sacred name" (Keating 1888). They both drew their guns, the crowd scattered, and shots were fired.

It has been recorded that Jackson then pushed through the crowd to chastise the man, once a supporting friend, who had appointed him as supreme judge. There was then apparently a call for a duel, followed by the customary back and forth correspondence required to finalize the terms and location of the proposed confrontation. The duel, however, never materialized since Sevier was very late in coming. When Jackson started back from the designated dueling spot to Knoxville, he met Sevier and his companions on the road. Jackson dismounted and drew two guns. Sevier did the same and the two began to swear at one another. The verbal exchange must have provided some relief between the Tennessee judge and the former governor, and they put their guns back in their carrying cases. At this point Jackson lunged at Sevier and threatened to cane him. When Sevier drew his sword, his horse ran away with his guns. Jackson then drew his gun, and the governor ducked behind the nearest tree. Then Sevier's son drew his gun and Jackson drew his second gun. "Friends then intervened, and a melee was prevented" (Remini 1988). The accuracy of the incident is certainly subject to the variation of the reports as developed by the two adversaries. The two never restored their friendship, and the bitterness as well as the ridiculous humor of insults and threats continued.

Jackson could not control his feelings and felt that everyone should share his views and opinions. This personality flaw would continue to injure his early career. One incident in particular added to Jackson's self-inflicted political damage. In October he had overheard Tennessee Secretary of State William Maclin speak kindly of Sevier. These were fighting words to Jackson, who then proceeded to pummel the secretary of state. The secretary of state returned the charge and a free-for-all ensued between the two. This did nothing to assist Jackson's declining reputation.

Sevier, on the other hand, continued to be held in highest esteem in Tennessee. He had a long record of defending his fellow citizens against the British and the Indians. Those who had witnessed the ravages of war and wilderness hardships could not believe that their beloved leader was capable of committing fraud. Sevier felt some vindication when he was later returned to the governor's seat by a large majority in the election of 1803. On November 5, 1803, the state legislature divided the state militia into an eastern district and a western district, limiting Jackson's command to the west and further cutting his influence and prestige. Sevier was acquitted of any dishonest dealings in the North Carolina land fraud scheme by the Tennessee legislature, and he tightened his hold over Tennessee politics. There were few state administrative controversies for the governor to oversee in those days; he remained very popular and continued to consolidate his power for his future elections of 1805 and 1807. He could not be dethroned by Jackson, but the power stage of the state was nonetheless set by their political competition and the resulting sectional factionalism between East Tennessee under Sevier and West Tennessee under Jackson.

On the national scene in 1803 President Jefferson had consummated the Louisiana Purchase from Napoleon for fifteen million dollars after discovering that Spain had ceded the territory to France in 1802. In 1803 Meriwether Lewis and William Clark began their exploration of the new territory all the way to the Pacific Ocean. Because of the country's general peace and national expansion, Jefferson was easily reelected in 1804. The Democrat-Republican received 162 electoral votes to 14 for Federalist Charles Cotesworth Pinckney. However, Aaron Burr was off the ticket. Burr's maneuvering and constant plotting had caught up with him, and when he killed Alexander Hamilton in a duel in July 1804, he had alienated his remaining allies and damaged his reputation beyond repair.

By 1804 Andrew Jackson had resigned his seat on Tennessee's superior court. Now he worked tirelessly to obtain the appointment of governor of the Louisiana Territory. Sevier's friend W. C. C. Claiborne also sought the position and no doubt Governor Sevier used all his influence to assure Claiborne's victory over Jackson. Claiborne won, leaving Jackson at a political lowpoint. He had challenged the prominent Sevier and lost. He returned to his home outside Nashville to lick his political wounds.

In 1805 Governor Sevier again decided to run for reelection. Astonishingly, Archibald Roane challenged him. Jackson and his band sought in vain to defeat Sevier. Sevier polled 10,730 votes to only 5,909 for Roane, again crushing Jackson and his friends.

Also in 1805 the Tennessee legislature elected Daniel Smith to replace William Cocke in the U.S. Senate (Class 2). Smith took office on March 4, 1805, and served until he resigned on March 31, 1809, before the completion of the full term which ended on March 3, 1811.

Jackson's hair-trigger temper continued to involve him in unfortunate events. Particularly damaging was his duel with Charles Dickinson. Apparently, Dickinson and Jackson exchanged insults over the method of payment of a horse race bet between Jackson and Dickinson's father-in-law, Captain Joseph Ervin. Jackson's friend, Captain Patten Anderson, helped foment the affair by repeating Jackson's interpretation of the Ervin-Jackson horse race payment. Dickinson replied to the slanderous statements, but made an error in attacking and insulting the reactionary Jackson. On Friday, May 30, 1806, they faced off. Dickinson shot first and hit Jackson in the chest. The wound would aggravate Jackson for the remainder of his life, but since it lodged in a rib over the heart, it did not kill him. With Dickinson's intent to kill him very clear, Jackson fired his shot to Dickinson's abdomen, who then bled to death. Jackson's reputation was severely damaged for killing the young man over verbal insults. At the time it would have taken an act of God to relieve Jackson of the scorn of the Nashville community. (It was about this time that the city of Nashville was incorporated in 1806.)

With his reputation damaged, Jackson could not turn down a visit to his home by a former vice president of the United States.

Aaron Burr, anathema in the East for killing Alexander Hamilton, and an outcast among Democrat-Republicans for scheming to take the presidency from Thomas Jefferson during the tie of the 1800 presidential election, left his homeland in 1805 and moved to the West, where people shared some of his political views and remembered his support of Tennessee's acceptance into the Union. Burr visited Jackson in Nashville several times and Jackson held a ball in Burr's honor. Still incensed at losing the 1800 presidential election and the glory that went with it, he wanted Jackson's assistance in putting together an army and the necessary supplies to stand ready in case there was need to attack the Spanish who had remained in

DANIEL SMITH was born in Stafford County, Virginia, on October 29, 1748. A graduate of the College of William and Mary, he became a surveyor by trade and married Sarah Michie from Maryland. In 1773, he was appointed deputy surveyor in Augusta County, Virginia. The following year, he served as a company commander in an Indian battle and on January 20, 1775, participated in the signing of the Fincastle County Resolution, which protested against the British government's unfair treatment of the colonists. Smith organized the Washington County Militia serving as major in 1777 and colonel in 1781, and participating in the Battle of King's Mountain. For a period of time he was sheriff of Washington County, Virginia, and chairman of the commission appointed by Virginia and North Carolina to draw the line between Tennessee and Kentucky. During his surveying trip in 1783, he visited the Cumberland Settlement in Nashborough, and made a home, named Rock Castle, in Sumner County, Tennessee (near Hendersonville). In 1784 he was appointed surveyor by the North Carolina legislature to lay out the town of Nashville. By 1787 the North Carolina legislature made him commissioner of the county of Sumner, and the next year he became brigadier general of the Mero District Militia. Smith was part of the 1789 North Carolina Convention which ratified the U.S. Constitution. Then President Washington made him secretary, under territorial Governor Blount, of the Territory South of the Ohio River. In 1793, he wrote a short history of the new territory and in the following year made the first map of Tennessee. He was secretary of the convention which drafted the Tennessee Constitution in 1796. When Andrew Jackson resigned from the U.S. Senate in 1798, Smith succeeded him, but served only nine days. However, he was elected to the Senate again and served from 1805 until 1809. Smith's daughter Polly married Samuel Donelson and was the mother of Andrew Jackson Donelson. Daniel Smith died at his family home, Rock Castle, Sumner County, Tennessee, on June 16, 1818. (Portrait unavailable)

Florida and held land beyond the ceded Louisiana Territory. The Spanish had refused President Jefferson's two-million-dollar offer to purchase Florida. Jackson liked the idea of expelling the Spanish from Florida, expanding U.S. landholding, and protecting the southern sea border. However, Burr's real purpose, likely unknown to Jackson at this time was to lead his own army to take Mexico. Then he planned to lure the western states and new territories to secede from the United States and become a part of an empire that Burr could control. But for all of his courting of Burr, Jackson's reputation remained tarnished. Still somewhat of an outcast, he was denied the general approval and acceptance required for the supreme political power he so desperately sought in Tennessee.

Jackson continued to cooperate with Burr and in October 1806, began calling his officers to assist him. However, on November 10, 1806, Jackson learned from one of Burr's agents, Captain John Fort, that Burr also planned to take New Orleans, close the port, conquer Mexico, and then join the Mexican territory with the western portion of the United States in a new "southwestern empire." Jackson also learned about General James Wilkinson's involvement in Burr's scheme. Wilkinson, who was later revealed to be a double agent for the Spanish and was paid by them while commanding American troops, became fearful that the attempt might fail. Not wanting to be on the losing side, he told President Jefferson of the plot, who then ordered Jackson to ready his troops to move on the troops of the conspirators. Burr heard of his exposure and disguising himself, fled to Mississippi and almost made it into the Spanish Florida territory before he was caught. He was returned to Richmond and charged with treason. Jackson, loyal to Burr, went to testify in his defense, but the defense did not select him as a witness. Jackson became critical of General Wilkinson for his involvement and trickery in this case, and furious that he would not get his chance to attack him on the witness stand, then became critical of President Jefferson for trusting Wilkinson. The criticism would later come back to haunt him. Burr was eventually acquitted by a Federalist-appointed judge, Chief Justice John Marshall, but Jackson was tainted with his involvement with Burr and was now at odds with the president as well as with Secretary of State James Madison. Although all were Democrat-Republicans, Jackson would become an anti-Jefferson and anti-Madison Democrat-Republican.

In 1807 Governor Sevier ran for reelection to a sixth term as Tennessee's governor. He was opposed this time by William Cocke. Sevier was reelected without difficulty.

The Tennessee legislature met in Nashville for the first time in 1807. It had moved from Knoxville and would later meet in Murfreesboro, Kingston, and Knoxville again, until it was permanently located back in Nashville.

In 1808 Thomas Jefferson, popular as he was, declined to run for a third term as president. His secretary of state and fellow Democrat-Republican, James Madison, ran and received Jefferson's full support. Madison faced Charles Cotesworth Pinckney and won 122 electoral votes to 47 for Pinckney. The Democrat-Republicans in Congress now greatly outnumbered the Federalists. They had first taken the majority (temporarily) during the Third Congress under Washington. When Jefferson was elected, the downfall of the Federalists began in the Seventh Congress; Democrat-Republican control of the House and Senate reached a peak in the Tenth Congress but slightly declined in control by Madison's election for the Eleventh Congress (Democrat-Republican—ninety-four, Federalists—forty-eight in the House; Democrat-Republican—twenty-eight, Federalists—six in the Senate).

The Opposition Gets Its Chance

In 1808 John Sevier was in his sixth term (second set of three two-year terms) as governor. Although he was immensely popular and could have likely remained in office, under the Tennessee Constitution he could not run again for reelection. Since politics was in his blood, he ran for the state senate representing Knox County, in the upcoming election cycle, while waiting for the opportunity for higher office.

When Tennessee was first settled, the population and power rested in East Tennessee. However, over the past decade the population of the western part of the state (Middle Tennessee) had grown considerably and now outnumbered the east. This population shift would play a major role in the gubernatorial election of 1809. Willie Blount (William Blount's half brother), a Democrat-Republican from Montgomery County, ran for governor. He was a friend and political ally of Andrew Jackson. The Jackson faction controlled Middle Tennessee and supported Blount, whose claim to fame was his relation to his deceased half brother. His opponent was former U.S. Senator William Cocke, who had served as a judge and military leader and was known throughout the state. However, the population was now greater in Middle Tennessee and a relatively large voting advantage rested with this region of the state where Andrew Jackson resided and had lingering political influence. Unlike John Sevier's elections, where personality and personal relations played a pivotal role,

Blount's election depended more on sectional and factional loyalties. In this election those loyalties prevailed and Willie Blount was elected with about a three-thousand-vote advantage. The Jackson faction of Middle Tennessee now took control of Tennessee politics. However, Jackson's reputation remain damaged and his future in question.

On April 11, 1809, Jenkins Whiteside was appointed to the U.S. Senate to replace Senator Daniel Smith who had resigned his Class 2 seat on March 31, 1809. (Smith left a vacancy which was to be filled until the term ended on March 3, 1811.) Whiteside served from April 11, 1809, until the completion of the term on March 3, 1811. He was reelected to serve the following term and continued in office until he resigned on October 8, 1811. Whiteside became the colleague of Senator Joseph Anderson, who was reelected by the legislature in 1809 (Class 1 seat) to serve from April 11, 1809, until March 3, 1815. Anderson had been serving in this Senate seat since 1808, also appointed to replace Daniel Smith, but for Smith's Class 1 seat. The two Tennessee U.S. senators generally supported the same cause. Both were for the condemnation of Thomas Pickering for exposing private communications of the president. They were both against the United States Bank Charter Bill, which failed.

After Whiteside resigned and returned to the pracitice of law in Nashville in October 1811 (the unexpired term of his Class 2 seat lasted until March 3, 1817), George Washington Campbell, who had served in Congress and on the Tennessee Supreme Court of Errors and Appeals, worked for the open seat. He was outspoken on the need to go to war with Britain, which was a major issue of the day, and this won him the support that allowed him to be elected by the state legislature to the U.S. Senate (Class 2) in 1811. (He served from October 8, 1811, until he resigned on February 11, 1814, to serve as secretary of the treasury of the United States.) Meanwhile John Sevier was out of

---

JENKINS WHITESIDE was born in 1772 in Lancaster, Pennsylvania. He began life with very little advantage. At eighteen he wanted to become a lawyer, but soon discovered that he did not have the proper education. He then underwent a series of disappointments and difficulties but managed to study at the University of Pennsylvania. The president of the university, seeing a determined and capable young man, helped him secure a teaching position. After saving enough money, Whiteside resigned his teaching job and traveled by foot to Philadelphia. He then took a boat (the cheapest manner of travel) to Richmond, Virginia, where he sought a spot in the office of John Marshall (who was later chief justice of the Supreme Court). Marshall allowed him to study with him and also helped him obtain a teaching position in a local academy in order to earn a living. After a period of time Whiteside asked Marshall to examine him in the law, and it was painful for him to learn he was not yet up to par. Determined, he continued his studies. Months later, he was reexamined and passed. Marshall then gave Whiteside work. Once licensed, Whiteside went to Wytheville, Virginia, to practice law, but later left for Tennessee. He first went to Knoxville about 1795 or 1796, and served as a commissioner in the city in 1801–1802. He later moved to Nashville, where he developed a fine law practice. He served in the U.S. Senate from April 11, 1809, until October 8, 1811 when he resigned. After serving in the Senate, he served in the state legislature and maintained his law practice in Nashville. He was one of the most active lawyers in Tennessee between 1811–1822 and a frequent opponent of Felix Grundy. Whiteside died on September 25, 1822, in Nashville. (Portrait unavailable) office and yearned for political action. He managed election to Congress in 1811.

Willie Blount's relation to his deceased half brother bolstered his prestige throughout Tennessee. However, his association with friends like John Sevier, Archibald Roane, and Andrew Jackson helped him consolidate his influence as governor. Political power was now in the hands of the Middle Tennessee faction and in 1811 Governor Willie Blount was reelected.

During this era the French and English were engaged in the Napoleonic War. Each nation wanted to prevent U.S. trade with the other nation, so American shipping and trade was affected by blockades and seizures by both nations. The British navy was the more powerful and inflicted the most damage to U.S. trade, causing a drop in prices of U.S. goods. American hostility toward the British also grew as England stirred up Indians against White settlers. The Indians from the Great Lakes area, under Shawnee Chief Tecumseh, were agitating the southern Cherokees, Chickasaws, Choctaws, and Creeks into joining a large scale attack on the Americans. It was widely thought that Chief Tecumseh was being assisted by the British with the Indian raids occurring in the northern frontier. As Americans looked to defend their homes, rights, and trade, talk of war against England grew day by day. The biggest challenges facing President Madison were dealing with the harassment and killing of Americans, interference with American trade, and the growing call for war.

The British had not forgotten their loss of the colonies and agitating the Indians was an effective way to weaken the feeble nation. Since the Revolution had ended, the British had never settled on a treaty which actually

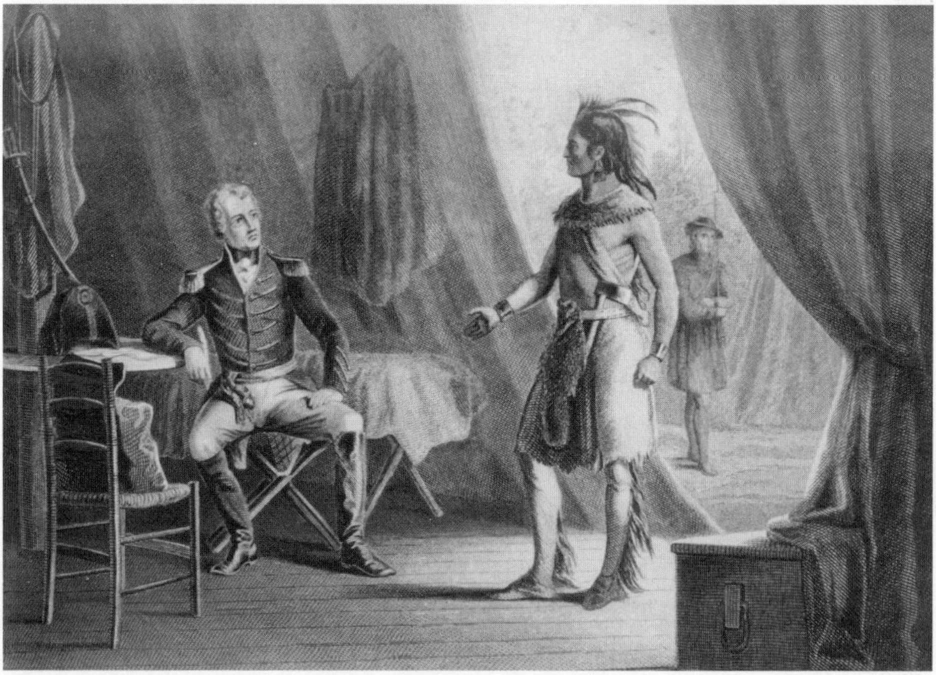

Chief Weatherford of the Creeks surrenders to Jackson. (Courtesy of TSLA)

GEORGE WASHINGTON CAMPBELL was born in the Parish of the Tongue, Shire of Sutherland, Scotland, on February 8, 1769. He came with his family to Mecklenberg County, North Carolina, in 1772. While still young, his father died, and Campbell worked on the family farm. Later he taught school until he entered Princeton as a junior. After two years in college, he graduated in 1794, studied law, then moved to Knoxville, Tennessee, and began practice. By 1802 he was in the U.S. House of Representatives and served three terms. He was a supporter of President Jefferson. John Randolph became an archenemy of Representative Campbell and was quite outspoken in his criticism of him. Campbell was made chairman of the Committee on Ways and Means, on which Randolph also sat. After his third term, Campbell returned to Tennessee, then served on the Tennessee Supreme Court of Errors and Appeals. During 1811 he became outspoken in favor of war with Great Britain. It was on that issue that he was elected by the legislature to the U.S. Senate to fill the vacancy left by Senator Whiteside's resignation. His term began on October 8, 1811. In 1812 he married Harriet Stoddert, the daughter of Benjamin Stoddert, the secretary of navy who served under John Adams. On February 11, 1814, Campbell left the Senate to become secretary of the treasury under President Madison. During this time the nation's financial situation became somewhat distressed because of the War of 1812. The British burned the White House and harrassed the shipping business. Under these difficult conditions, with few resources, Campbell faced great difficulty raising revenue in a young, developing nation. He soon resigned and returned to the U.S. Senate to fill the seat vacated at the end of Senator Joseph Anderson's term. Campbell was elected by the state legislature, beginning his term on October 15, 1815. He then served as chairman of the Finance Committee. He was appointed minister to Russia by President Monroe and resigned his Senate seat again on April 20, 1818. Unfortunately, shortly after arriving in St. Petersburg, one of his four daughters died of typhus, and he resigned this position.

In 1831 Campbell became a commissioner of the United States for effecting the Claims Convention, which was agreed upon with France in that same year. He was a friend and supporter of Andrew Jackson, but returned to private life, after Jackson's election as president, as an extremely successful lawyer. George Washington Campbell died on February 17, 1848. (Photograph courtesy of SHO)

resolved animosities. They even continued to have British troops stationed in the United States. When the people of Tennessee learned that Chief Tecumseh had met with the Cherokees of Middle Tennessee and the Creeks of North Alabama and Georgia, the fear of a deadly Indian war loomed in everyone's mind. If the Indians were to be supplied by the British, then the time had come to do something about this threat as well as the interference with U.S. trade. Tennessee newspapers raised the demand for war with England to a fever pitch. Andrew Jackson wrote to Tennessee U.S. Representative Felix Grundy asking when war would be declared. In this atmosphere young American politicians were clamoring for the opportunity to make names for themselves. Felix Grundy of Tennessee, John C. Calhoun of South Carolina, Richard M. Johnson and Henry Clay of Kentucky, and Peter B. Porter of New York "demanded the restoration of American honor through the chastisement of war." (Remini 1988) (1811 also saw the great earthquake that hit the New Madrid fault along the Mississippi

River and created Reelfoot Lake. Lake County takes its name from the area formed by the earthquake.) Tennessee's U.S. senators, Joseph Anderson and George W. Campbell, felt that war was required to finally put an end to the differences with the mother country. Tennessee's three U.S. representatives, John Sevier, John Rhea, and Felix Grundy, had all joined the "War Hawks" which "plotted and eventually succeeded in forcing President James Madison to ask Congress for a declaration" of war (Remini 1988). It came on June 18, 1812.

In the meantime, Andrew Jackson was floundering in the political wilderness, damaged by his murder of Dickinson as well as his association with Aaron Burr's botched attempt to set up his own nation. Although Jackson maintained his close political friends and connections, he did not have the popular appeal necessary to advance to high political levels. Now, with war declared on England, he saw his chance, or so he thought, to renew his popularity and political prospects. President Madison and his faction of Democrat-Republicans were not fond of Jackson, and Madison remembered Jackson's conduct and criticism during the Burr trial.

Jackson, as the Western District general of the state militia, thought it would be his right to supply an army to challenge the British. He notified President Madison of the availability of twenty-five hundred Tennessee volunteers. The president replied by acknowledging his offer, but he did not call Jackson. After some months without a call for his patriotic services, Jackson finally realized that the administration had not forgotten his role with Burr and his prior criticism of President Jefferson and Vice President Madison. President Madison stood by as General Henry Dearborn was sent to Quebec and General James Winchester was sent to help General William Henry Harrison's troops in the north. The worst insult was that two of Jackson's regiments were sent north with Winchester. Jackson was stunned and rejected.

Andrew Jackson's political achievements resulted from a combination of the force of his personality and fate. Although he was difficult to deal with and had a temper which was unsurpassed, he also had talents. Fate would give him the opportunity to display those talents. When the fighting against the British began, America's forces suffered its first defeat when Brigadier General William Hull had to surrender at Detroit after a failed attempt to invade Canada. Every battle in the North ended in defeat. In October 1812 the federal government asked Tennessee Governor Willie Blount to send fifteen hundred volunteers to help General Wilkinson defend New Orleans, stand off against a possible Southern invasion, and eventually take East Florida. The request also conveyed an interest in excluding Jackson from participating in the military campaigns. Since Blount was allied to Jackson and most of Blount's political support had come from Jackson's faction in West Tennessee, Blount ignored this portion of the federal request. After a brief hesitation and legal consultation, Governor Blount put Jackson's name on the commission form and sent it to Washington, D.C. This single act of loyalty on the part of Governor Blount and his gutsy dismissal of the president's opinion of Jackson would ultimately result in military respect by the British for the Americans and change the course of Tennessee and the nation. Finally, Jackson was in command.

Without Jackson's men who had already gone north with General Winchester, more troops had to be raised. Fifteen hundred were called for, but on January 7, 1813, 2,071 volunteers left Nashville en route to Natchez, Mississippi, and arrived thirty-nine days later. General Wilkinson, who was in

WILLIE BLOUNT was born on April 17, 1768, in Bertie County, North Carolina. His name was pronounced "Wylie." He was the half brother of William Blount. His parents were Jacob Blount and Hannah Salter Baker Blount (the second wife of Jacob). Blount was educated at Columbia and Princeton, he then studied law with a North Carolina judge. In 1790 he moved to the territory which was to become Tennessee in order to serve as one of territorial Governor William Blount's private secretaries. He was accepted into the practice of law in 1794. In 1796, the new state's legislature (the first) elected Blount as one of the state's judges. The following year he was elected a state legislator from Montgomery County, and served for one term. In 1802 he married Lucinda Baker of Bertie County. They had two daughters, but they also raised the younger children of his half brother William and Mary Blount. (William died in 1800 and Mary in 1802.)

After John Sevier had completed his sixth term, Blount ran for governor of Tennessee, defeating William Cocke, and was reelected in 1811 and 1813. During his terms the state opened new roads and worked to develop commerce. The State Bank of Tennessee was also established in Knoxville with branches in Columbia, Jonesboro, Nashville, and Clarksville.

Blount supported Andrew Jackson during the Creek War and the War of 1812, supplying funding and two thousand Tennessee volunteers to help General Jackson in the war's 1815 Battle of New Orleans, in which the Americans defeated the British and Jackson won premier national fame.

After Blount's three terms, in 1815 he returned to his plantation home in Montgomery County. In 1827, he again sought the governor's chair, but lost to Sam Houston. In 1834 he represented Montgomery County in the constitutional convention of that year. Blount's wife died around 1829, and he passed away on September 10, 1835. (Photograph courtesy of TSLA)

New Orleans, did not want Jackson in his command, but he did want his troops. He sent orders for Jackson to halt in Natchez and, on March 15, 1813, Secretary of War John Armstrong sent orders for Jackson to dismiss his troops and disband. This did not sit well with Jackson. Rather than disbanding his troops in dangerous Indian territory and having the survivors end up with Wilkinson, he marched them back to Nashville. It was difficult to keep the ill-fed and poorly clothed troops together and out of harm's way, especially after a depleting trip to Natchez and then back to Nashville during a cold winter, without supplies. Many were sick and had to be carried. However, Andrew Jackson had one talent, above all the rest. He possessed an almost superhuman determination. Defeat or capitulation was unacceptable. One month later, the army was back in Nashville. Because of his determination and dedication toward his men, he won the nickname "Old Hickory" and the undying loyalty of his troops. Andrew Jackson would be known as tough but loyal to those who served under him, and his popularity began to regain ground.

In 1812 Governor Blount called the legislature into session to reapportion districts. With the population advantage clearly resting with Middle Tennessee, he felt that it was time to reapportion districts in order to obtain the advantage in the state house and senate and further strengthen the power of the Jackson-Blount faction. The new majority voted, once again, to move the capital to Nashville. They began meeting there in late 1812.

In the meantime, in the election of 1812, President Madison, a Democrat-Republican, was running for reelection against Federalist De Witt Clinton. Madison won 128 to 89 electoral votes. The Federalists continued to lose ground. The House had 112 Democrat-Republicans to 68 Federalists, while the Senate had 27 Democrat-Republicans to 9 Federalists in the Thirteenth Congress.

In 1813 Governor Willie Blount was reelected to a third term. During his tenure he supported the war effort against the British and the Indians (who were instigated by the British.)

Jackson had been blocked from going to New Orleans, but fate would change Tennessee, the nation, and Jackson forever. Chief Tecumseh was able to motivate a faction of the Alabama Creek Indians, the Red Sticks, to make war on the settlers. Led by Chief William Weatherford, the Red Stick Creeks attacked isolated cabins and larger settlements and murdered innocent men, women, and children. Then, on August 30, 1813, they moved on Fort Mims (present-day Alabama) and massacred 250 White settlers. "The children were seized by the legs, and killed by batting their heads against the stockading. The women were scalped, and those who were pregnant were opened, while they were alive, and the embryo infants let out of the womb" (Remini 1988). When word of the horror reached Tennessee, outrage and anger took the state by storm. Tennesseans had fought Indians before, as well as the British. They had been a state that could be counted on not only to send citizen soldiers into battle, but soldiers who would persevere in battle. Now they would put an end to the horror they had tolerated so long. When the defenseless of Alabama territory called for help, Governor Willie Blount, without federal authorization, immediately ordered Jackson to gather his troops and march. He also called on Major General John Cocke to march his twenty-five hundred East Tennessee volunteers into Alabama. Politically, it was good for Jackson that the popular John Sevier was away in Congress or he would have been the military leader to be called.

Jackson now had his chance, but he had another problem to deal with which could block his opportunity for glory. This time it was not his political enemies, but a physical problem severely limiting his ability to get out of bed. He was weak and almost unable to get around due to loss of blood and damage from a gunshot wound to his arm and shoulder. The ridiculous episode started when one of his junior officers, William Carroll, and a soldier, Littleton Johnston, developed a disagreement during the march from Natchez back to Nashville, and scheduled a duel to resolve it. Johnston retained Jesse Benton as his "second" (to fight for him), since Carroll refused to fight him "on grounds that he was no gentleman" (Remini 1977). Jesse Benton was the brother of Thomas Hart Benton (another Jackson junior officer who would one day become a U.S. senator from Missouri). Carroll was convinced that his enemies were jealous of his favor with Jackson and were trying to get rid of him. Thinking that Jackson could settle the dispute if he were involved, he persuaded him to be his (nonfighting) second. When the duel took place on June 14, 1813, no one was killed, but it made matters worse for Jackson, or rather, Jackson made things worse for himself. Apparently, Benton was shot in the buttocks as he wheeled around to shoot, and he hit Carroll in the thumb. Benton became the focus of great ridicule around Nashville. Consequently, Thomas Hart Benton, furious that Jackson had involved himself in something that caused such embarrassment to his family, flew into a rage and criticized Jackson. Jackson had only just begun to reobtain popularity and was not about to allow the Bentons to damage his status with their charges and insults. He promised to "horsewhip Thomas the first time he saw him" (Remini 1977).

In September 1813 Jackson, John Coffee, and Stockley Hays (Jackson's nephew) went into Nashville and stayed at the Old Nashville Inn. On a trip to pick up the mail at the post office, they saw the Benton brothers standing in front of the hotel. Jackson and company calmly walked back to the hotel. As they approached, the Bentons, waiting there with pistols loaded (two shots each), Jackson suddenly "brandished his whip, and cried, 'Now, you d_____d rascal, I am going to punish you. Defend yourself'" (Remini 1977). Guns were drawn and Thomas Benton backed into the hotel. Jesse Benton ducked through the barroom, into a hallway, from which he fired at Jackson, hitting him in the arm and shoulder. Jackson fell, fired, and missed. Thomas fired twice at Jackson who was now lying severely injured on the floor. Jesse moved to shoot again but was blocked by another man, James Sitler, who happened to be in the room. Coffee rushed in, and then came Stockley Hays with two more men. Hays forced Jesse to the ground and stabbed him multiple times in the arms with a dirk. Coffee fired at Thomas Benton, missed, then attempted to club Benton with his pistol. As Benton stepped away, he fell backwards down the stairs going to the back of the hotel. The fight thus ended, with Jackson severely injured. Doctors considered amputation, but Jackson refused.

The Bentons, with great glee, recounted their defeat of Jackson. Jesse "paraded back and forth across the plaza" (Remini 1977), defiantly took Jackson's sword, and broke it in half. Soon, though, the Bentons realized that Jackson had many loyal friends who did not like the fact that Jackson had been injured, insulted, and ridiculed by them. Nor did Jackson's friends appreciate their "accompanying theatrics" (Remini 1977). They soon left town out of fear for their lives. Thomas Hart Benton returned to Franklin, Tennessee. (After the War of 1812 he moved to Missouri to make his fame in the new state. He would not see Jackson again until 1823, when both were in the U.S. Senate.) Meanwhile, Jackson had suffered serious blood loss and his recovery was slow. He was still weak when his friend, Governor Willie Blount, called him to ready his troops to take on the Creek Indians. He faced a dilemma created by his involvement in the ridiculous Benton fiasco. He wanted to lead his troops, but his injury and debilitated condition nearly prevented him from getting out of bed.

The Creek War

By October 7, 1813, with arm in sling and very weak, Jackson took command of the West Tennessee army at Fayetteville. On November 3, 1813, he moved upon his first group of Red Sticks. He sent Colonel John Coffee and a thousand men to the Indian village of Tallushatchee. Not one warrior escaped. Jackson had tried to spare women and children and the army did as good a job of it as possible. But, the battle was vicious. Young David (Davy) Crockett, who was with the army, was later quoted as saying, "We shot them like dogs" (Remini 1988). The Creeks were no match against the angry Tennessee army and their determined leader.

Shortly after this victory a friendly Creek Indian (after news of Jackson's army began to spread, many Creeks felt that the fighting must stop) came to Jackson's camp and told the general that Chief Weatherford's Red Stick Creeks were about to attack the town of Talladega. The town, thirty miles south of Fort Strother, was comprised of about 154 friendly Creek Indians. Weatherford was trying to force them to join his rebellion against the Whites or else be killed themselves, and they were fearful of doing anything. Weatherford was poised to attack, but on November 9, 1813, Jackson struck first, killing 300 Red Sticks, and losing only fifteen men. However, a hole in the Volunteer line allowed a few hundred Red Sticks to escape. The tide against the warring Indians was turning, but it was not yet over while Chief Weatherford was still leading the war. At this point Jackson's men were tired and hungry and many of their enlistments were up. Then General John Cocke arrived with his East Tennessee militia. This additional 1,500 soldiers would help, but many of their terms of enlistment ended as quickly as they had arrived. True to its reputation, the Volunteer State would not be long in sending fresh troops. By March 14, 1814, Jackson would have about 2,000 Tennessee volunteers and 500 friendly Cherokee and Creek Indians.

Jackson then moved on Chief Weatherford's army. By January 21, 1814, he was within three miles of the Red Stick fortification at Tohopeka, which was a one-hundred-acre peninsula within the curve of the Tallapoosa River. Because of its shape, the site was called "Horseshoe Bend." The next day the Indians attacked. The fighting cost

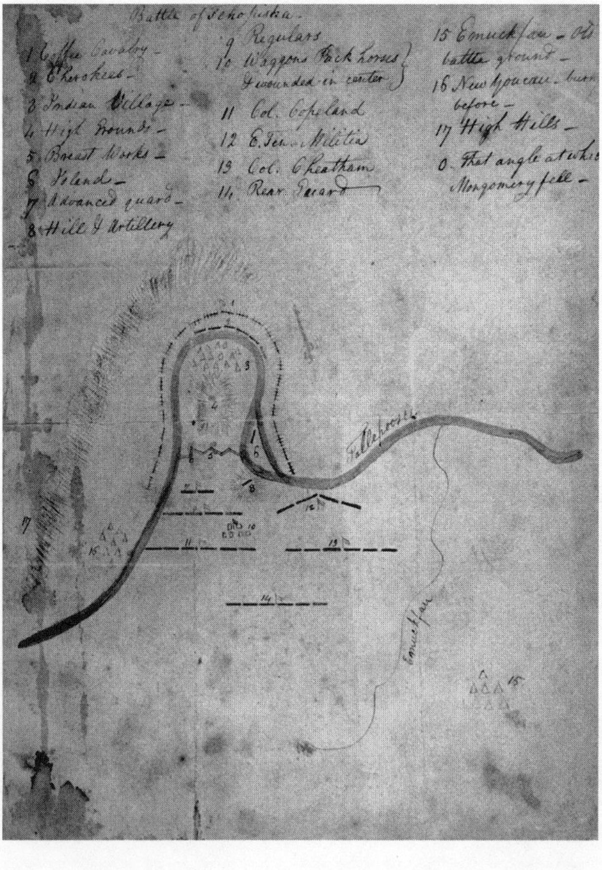

Map from the Battle of Horseshoe Bend from a report by Andrew Jackson. (Courtesy of TSLA)

200 Red Stick and over twenty American lives. Jackson withdrew to Fort Strother. On February 6, 1814, Colonel John Williams of the Thirty-ninth Regiment of the U.S. Infantry arrived. An additional 2,000 East Tennesseans also came in early February. Now Jackson had around 5,000 men. On March 27, 1814, he returned to Horseshoe Bend with 4,000 men and completely encircled the Red Sticks. At 10:30 A.M. Jackson opened fire. The Indians had built a breastwork of large tree limbs and trunks which the troops had to charge over. Major Lemuel Montgomery was the first to reach the top of the breastwork, leading his men. He was shot in the head and died instantly. Young Sam Houston took the lead and motivated the men, but was soon hit in the thigh with an arrow. The fighting was ferocious. The Americans continued into late afternoon with persistent attack, until the Red Sticks were nearly all slaughtered. A few escaped in the dark, after hours of bloody killing. Five hundred fifty-seven Indians lay dead on the ground. Colonel Coffee, who defended the only escape route via the river, had blocked that path and 300 more Red Sticks lay dead in the river. Three hundred were taken prisoner, all but four of those women and children. Jackson lost forty-seven Americans and twenty-three friendly Cherokees and Creeks. However, Chief Weatherford had escaped. On April 5 Jackson moved out, destroying Indian villages along the way. By April 18 he reached the old Toulhouse French Fort and had the American flag hoisted. The fort was renamed Fort Jackson. William Carroll, Davy Crockett, and John Williams were among the many who fought during this conflict. They, like Jackson and Houston, would go on to political careers.

Many Creek Indians surrendered to Jackson at the fort. They wanted no more to do with him. Old Hickory had shown what many other U.S. generals had not shown in the War of 1812—that the Americans could win the war and that the Indians could not help the British in their plan to conquer America. Shortly after April 18, 1814, Chief Weatherford surrendered and placed himself at Jackson's mercy. The chief agreed to urge any Indian holdouts to surrender. (He retired to farm, and he later visited Jackson at the Hermitage on several occasions.)

Meanwhile during the Creek Indian War, U.S. Senator George Campbell resigned on February 11, 1814 to accept appointment as secretary of the treasury under President Madison. The financial condition of the nation was difficult at best when Campbell was called to raise U.S. revenues. Foreign trade was limited due to British and French efforts to restrict U.S. shipping. All the while the costs of war increased demand for revenues. Frustrated, Campbell later resigned this position and returned to his political home in Tennessee. Governor Blount appointed Jesse Wharton to take the Senate seat (Class 2) vacated by Campbell. Senator Wharton took office on March 17, 1814, and would serve until October 10, 1815.

Jackson and Fate

With the Creek War over and the troops clearing any resistance that remained, Jackson's reputation was not only restored, it was greater than ever before. The Creek War had made him a hero of the common man. The national government "begrudgingly awarded him the rank of major general in the United States Army" (Remini 1988). He would now command the Seventh Military District, to which New Orleans belonged. His enemies found his advance distasteful; nonetheless, Jackson had done what others had not. He accepted the appointment on June 18, 1814. Tennessee and the nation would never be the same. The appointment

JESSE WHARTON was born on July 29, 1782, in Covesville, Albemarle County, Virginia. He received some primary education and later studied law, beginning his practice in Albemarle County. Later he moved to Tennessee, became involved in politics, and was elected to the Tenth Congress as a U.S. representative. He served from March 4, 1807, until March 17, 1814. He was appointed by Governor Willie Blount to fill the U.S. Senate seat vacated by George Campbell and took office on March 17, 1814. During his time in the Senate he supported U.S. efforts to continue the pressure on the British in the War of 1812. When Governor Blount's three terms were about to end on August 1, 1815, Wharton resigned his Senate seat to run for governor against Robert C. Foster, Robert Weakley, Thomas Johnson, and Joseph McMinn. He lost to McMinn and returned to Nashville to resume his law practice. Wharton died in Nashville on July 22, 1833. (Portrait unavailable)

would mark a change in destiny and in the power and stature of the United States. William Carroll was appointed to take Jackson's place as major general of the Tennessee Militia for Middle Tennessee.

On August 22, 1814, Jackson moved his men to Mobile in order to block British troops from using the Gulf Coast city as their entry point. The Spanish governor then invited the British troops to enter at Pensacola. When this plan became apparent, on November 6, 1814, Jackson moved his troops to confront the Spanish and demanded possession of Fort Barrancas. In response to his demand, the Spanish shot his flag of truce. The attitude of the Spanish appeared clear to him, and in character with his personality, Jackson did not take long to react. His troops immediately attacked and swiftly took the town. Within a few moments Spanish Governor Gonzalez Manrique began to understand the consequences of dealing with Jackson and surrendered. The British and their Indian allies returned to their ships and sailed off. Jackson then estimated that the British would move to New Orleans. He allowed the Spanish governor to resume control of the fort, and turned command of Mobile over to Brigadier General James Winchester. He sent Colonel Coffee with his 2,000 men to New Orleans by way of Baton Rouge. By December 1, 1814, Jackson was in New Orleans with around 2,000 men who traveled with him.

Once in New Orleans, Jackson met with W. C. C. Claiborne (former Tennessee U.S. representative and political competitor of Jackson's), who had been appointed governor of the Louisiana Territory. On December 14 the British armada was spotted near New Orleans. After a small skirmish near Cat Island between American gunboats and the British armada, the American ships were forced to surrender. Six Americans were killed and eighty-six captured. The captured Americans claimed that Jackson's troops were much larger than they really were. This caused the British commanders to pause and rethink their attack plans, giving the Americans more time. Jackson's army was only around 3,500 to 4,000 strong, but the delay by the British gave Jackson time to increase his numbers. Coffee made it to New Orleans by December 20 with his now 2,800 men; William Carroll arrived December 21 with around 2,500 to 3,000 recruits; and Colonel Thomas Hinds arrived with "a regiment of Mississippi dragoons" (Remini 1977).

On December 22, 1814, the British landed and began the move to take New Orleans. Jackson set up his defenses behind Rodriguez Canal. On New Year's Day, 1815, the British fired rockets at the Americans. American ships countered by knocking out British batteries mounted on the levee. Then, on January 8, 1815, with William Carroll and John Coffee leading the defense, Andrew Jackson's Americans met the British assault under the command of thirty-seven-year-old Lieutenant General Sir Edward Michael Pakenham. Other opponents might have fled out of fear of British numbers and reputation, but Jackson's men stood firm. As the British marched in traditional upright formation toward the American breastworks, the frontier soldiers could barely contain their trigger fingers. However, they followed their command and at the given time began their volley of fire. Jackson's men crushed the British advance. In only two hours there were 291 British dead, 1,262 wounded, and 484 captured or missing. The Americans lost 13, had 39 wounded, and 19 missing. It was a magnificent victory for the United States. Ironically, the peace agreement between the English and Americans had been signed already, on December 24, 1814, but word had not yet arrived. In any event, British conduct toward the Americans had belied a sincere willingness to honor independence. After Jackson's victory, there was nevermore a question in the mind of the British of the resiliency of the Americans. The British could have gained a temporary peace, regrouped, and reattacked the Americans. After all, they had reneged before. It was not until this victory at New Orleans that the British finally accepted the fact that they had permanently lost control of the United States.

While the Battle of New Orleans shocked the British and provided freedom to the United States, it also guaranteed lasting fame for Andrew Jackson. When the news of the victory reached Washington, D.C., on February 4, there was great celebration. Newspaper printers worked overtime to get out the story of the battle. Andrew Jackson became the "Hero of New Orleans" to the grateful nation. He was awarded a gold medal of appreciation from Congress.

After the war with Britain, attentions returned to politics at home. With Jackson now a national hero, his thoughts were of the presidency. Tennessee was excited about the future. State politics would now be influenced not only by Jackson's ambition and national plans, but also by the ambition of others who sought state office, particularly the governorship. Governor Willie Blount had served three consecutive terms and was ineligible to run for reelection in 1815. Robert Weakley, who served as U.S. representative and state senator; Jesse Wharton who served as U.S. representative and U.S. senator; Thomas Johnson, who helped write the Tennessee Constitution, and later served in the state legislature; Joseph McMinn, who served in the constitutional convention and three terms as speaker of the state senate; and Robert C. Foster, who had served as speaker of the state house, all declared themselves candidates. Most of these men were from Middle Tennessee and voting patterns tended to divide along sectional lines. However, even though the population advantage had shifted to Middle Tennessee, McMinn, who was from East Tennessee (Hawkins County) was in a favorable political position. His opponents in the race spread publications implying that McMinn was running merely because he wanted to be governor, while they were running at the request of "their fellow citizens" (Phillips 1978). McMinn received 15,600 votes. The remainder of the field, from Middle Tennessee, divided up

22,000 votes, giving McMinn the victory. In 1815, Joseph McMinn, a Democrat-Republican from Rogersville, Tennessee, began serving as governor and served until 1821. He would be the last East Tennessean to serve as governor until 1853 when Andrew Johnson was elected.

John Sevier was reelected to a third term in Congress in 1815, but the old war horse never received the news. He was on his way to Alabama with U.S. Army troops to settle a boundary dispute with the Creek Indians, when he died of "fever" on September 24, 1815, and was buried by his men at Fort Decatur, Alabama.

Governor McMinn began his tenure as governor, in 1815, during a period of rapid growth and economic stability. The outlook for Tennesseans was bright and the new governor took the reins of power with much optimism. There were Indian treaties to be settled and land to be acquired. Tennessee would begin a great expansion from Middle Tennessee toward the Mississippi River and the population would expand with the opening of the new territory. Along with the land and population growth would come farms, stores, and banks. This rapid expansion would eventually strain the economic stability of Tennessee.

The vacancy in the Tennessee U.S. Senate seat (Class 2), caused when Jesse Wharton resigned to run for governor against McMinn, was filled by appointment of John Williams, who officially took office on October 10, 1815. [This seat was originally filled by Jenkins Whiteside, who was replaced by George Campbell, who was replaced by Jesse Wharton on March 17, 1814.] Williams would serve in this Senate

JOSEPH McMINN was born on June 27, 1758, in Chester County, Pennsylvania, into a family of ten children, with Quaker parents. His education was limited to what was available in the backwoods. He was a member of the Friends' Church, which taught against violence or war. However, the church allowed each man to decide for himself if he should participate in war, and McMinn served in the Revolutionary War, working his way up to sergeant and later becoming commander general of the militia. Afterwards he moved into the frontier of Tennessee, finally making a home in Sullivan County (which later became Hawkins County). He married Hannah Cooper, who had come with her parents from Virginia. They bought a farm, where he and Hannah both worked the fields. They had one child, a daughter named Jane. McMinn was a "strong-willed, rustic frontiersman whose controversial private life set its own precedent" (Phillips 1978).

McMinn became a merchant and was named to a county office by Territorial Governor William Blount. He served in the territorial legislature in 1794, and in 1796 helped write the constitution of Tennessee. He was elected to the state senate in 1807 and served as speaker of the senate until 1809. Hannah died in 1811, and in 1812 he married Rebecca Kinkead. Rebecca died on January 11, 1815, having had no children. McMinn's daughter, Jane McMinn Gains, died two weeks later.

In 1815 he ran for governor against Thomas Johnson, Jesse Wharton, Robert Weakley, and Robert C. Foster. In spite of the negative campaigning against him by his opponents, McMinn won.

In 1816 he married for a third time, to Nancy Glasgow Williams. Nancy had four sons by a prior marriage. She was the daughter of the secretary of state of North Carolina (1777–1778), seat until the completion of the term on March 3, 1817. He was reappointed by the governor during a recess of the legislature to serve from March 4, 1817, until October 1, 1817, and then reelected to serve from October 2, 1817, until March 3, 1823.

The population of Tennessee grew dramatically as settlers left the East Coast during the war with the English and the Indians. With the population growth came more trade and city organization. During this time, in spring 1815, Andrew Jackson had been given the command of the Southern Division of the United States Army. He was allowed command from his home, the Hermitage, just outside of Nashville, Tennessee. Thus, he could serve his country and maintain his plantation. He was also paid $2,400 per year and had $1,652 in expenses. He surrounded himself with loyalists, including Sam Houston, whom he had come to know well since the Creek War. His general staff lived at his Hermitage. Sam Houston, Richard Keith Call, Andrew Jackson Donelson, Robert Butler, James Gadsden, John Overton, Sam Overton, Dr. James C. Bronaugh, and James H. Eaton were all with him. An irritant to Jackson was Article IX in the Ghent Treaty from the War of 1812 which agreed to return twenty-three million acres, which he had taken, to the Creek Indians. Jackson ignored this until the new secretary of war, William H. Crawford, signed a treaty with the Indians on March 22, 1816, which returned four million acres, including Fort Jackson. Jackson raged and let Crawford know how he felt. Then Crawford appointed a commission to look into the situation and work out a settlement with the Indians. Jackson was appointed to the

---

James Glasgow. The marriage was ill-fated and created quite a controversy. Nancy accused McMinn of leaving her family alone for long periods of time while he lived with the Indians. Divorce was a rarity in those days, but when Nancy left, McMinn filed a petition before the Tennessee house of representatives. Felix Grundy represented Nancy. There was no better lawyer of the day. The house vote ended in nineteen for divorce and twenty against. The two eventually separated. In any event, McMinn lost little support over the unhappy union with Nancy.

McMinn remained a popular governor who was known for fairness. He successfully negotiated with the Indians, thereby obtaining acres of land for White pioneers. This allowed expansion of Tennessee westward and the addition of peaceful parcels of land, which provided some security from hostilities for the settlers. East and Middle Tennessee had been taken by fighting and death, while West Tennessee, under McMinn, was obtained through negotiation with the Chickasaws. Without the hostilities, West Tennessee expanded more rapidly than the East or Middle sections had. The settlers moved into the area with zeal, creating roads and bridges, and setting up a primitive commercial base. McMinn's popularity allowed him to be reelected in 1817, defeating Robert C. Foster. He was again reelected in 1819, defeating Enoch Parsons.

During McMinn's six years as governor of Tennessee (1815 to 1821), fifteen counties were formed: Shelby, Fayette, Hardin, McNairy, Hardeman, Henderson, Haywood, Madison, Tipton, Carroll, Gibson, Obion, Henry, Weakley, and Dyer—all in West Tennessee. The state capital was moved from Knoxville to Murfreesboro during his tenure.

After Governor McMinn's separation from Nancy, he bought a farm which was about ten miles from Cleveland, Tennessee, on the Hiwassee River. From 1822 until 1824 he served as an agent for the Cherokee Indians. He died at the Indian agency on November 17, 1824. (Photograph courtesy of TSLA)

JOHN WILLIAMS was born on January 29, 1778, in Surry County, North Carolina. He received a good early education in his home county. Sometime later he moved to Knoxville, Tennessee. In 1799 he became captain of the Sixth U.S. Infantry. He studied law, was admitted to the bar, and began practice in Knoxville about 1803. He married Malinda White, from Knoxville, the daughter of General James White and the sister of Hugh Lawson White, who later became an enemy of Andrew Jackson. In 1812 Williams raised a company of volunteer troops, becoming the company's colonel. They fought against the Seminole Indians. He then became colonel of the Thirty-ninth U.S. Infantry and fought under General Jackson in the Creek War. His troops played a significant role in the Battle of Horseshoe Bend. When Jesse Wharton resigned his Senate seat in 1815 to run for governor, John Williams was appointed to fill the vacancy (from March 4, 1815 until October 1, 1817). He was elected to the full term beginning October 2, 1817, through March 3, 1823. When he ran for a second full term, he opposed Andrew Jackson, who wanted to move into the Senate to position himself to run for president. Williams was closely associated with Jackson's political enemies such as William H. Crawford and his friends. This set the stage for a nasty political fight with long-lasting consequences. Jackson won, essentially ending Williams's political career, since Jackson was the political power in Tennessee at that time. President Adams, who had beaten Jackson through the "corrupt bargain" in 1824, appointed Williams as chargé d'affaires to the Federation of Central America in 1825. He went to Guatemala, returning in 1827, and was elected to the state senate. John Williams died in Knoxville in 1837. His and Hugh Lawson Whites's split with Jackson helped initiate Whig political opposition to Jackson in Tennessee. In fact Williams's son was elected to Congress as a Whig.. (Photograph courtesy of SHO)

commission, along with General David Meriwether from Georgia and Jesse Franklin from North Carolina. During the next several months the group negotiated with the Indians until Jackson was satisfied. Jackson's time between 1816 and 1818 was spent on maintaining his plantation and making treaties with various Indian tribes.

During the worst times of the War of 1812 when Americans were suffering defeat after defeat, President Madison was forced to reassess his approach to the war. After Washington, D.C., was conquered and the presidential mansion was burned on August 24, 1814, the president appointed his secretary of state, James Monroe, as secretary of war. Victory, the war's end, and general national expansion provided a great deal of popular support for both President Madison and Secretary of War James Monroe. Monroe ran for the presidency in 1816 as the Democrat-Republican candidate. He won the nomination over Secretary of the Treasury William H. Crawford, in a congressional caucus, 65 to 54. Jackson was pleased since he was still angered with Crawford for returning land that Jackson had seen his men die for.

As the nation grew westward, the Federalist Party grew weaker by the year. Monroe was elected president in 1816 with 183 electoral votes to 34 for Rufus King, the Federalist candidate. The Senate was now comprised of 34 Democrat-Republicans and 10 Federalists, and the House had 141 Democrat-Republicans and 42 Federalists.

In the 1817 gubernatorial race, Robert C. Foster challenged incumbent Governor

McMinn. However, McMinn, who was considered to be a fair administrator and was well liked, had played the political game smartly by temporarily satisfying the two major political factions in Tennessee, and was reelected.

George Campbell had resigned from his Class 2 Senate seat on February 11, 1814, to serve as secretary of the treasury. Once back in Tennessee after leaving the Treasury Department he wanted to return to the political arena. The opportunity presented itself again through the U.S. Senate. His friends in the state legislature supported him when Joseph Anderson's seat became available. (Anderson received an appointment as the first comptroller of the U.S. Treasury.) Campbell again became U.S. senator (Class 1) on October 10, 1815. His term was to last until March 3, 1821, but again he resigned, on September 5, 1818, when President Monroe appointed him Minister to Russia. By 1818, Jackson and his band of political friends were on the road to power, and they were able to put their friend John Eaton in office. Eaton was appointed by Governor McMinn to fill the seat vacated by Campbell. He served by appointment from September 5, 1818, until October 8, 1819, when he was elected. He served from October 9, 1819, until he later resigned on March 9, 1829. Governor McMinn could easily see the advantages of cooperating with the rising political faction composed of famous, popular, and influential men. It would have been disastrous to create enemies by ignoring the opportunity to cooperate.

After the War of 1812, the Spanish control of Florida was uncertain. The British were gone, and without them, the Spanish knew they stood alone against American expansionist fervor. With the likes of Andrew Jackson among the American expansionists, it would only be a matter of time before trouble came for the Spaniards. Although the United States had won claim to land, the Indians still had their own right of domain to be dealt with. During 1817 a misunderstanding arose between the Creek Indians, supported by the Spanish government, and the United States over the boundaries agreed upon in a prior treaty consummated with Andrew Jackson. Some Seminole and Creek Indians then initiated war by massacring families in Georgia.

Major General Andrew Jackson was now in command of the Army of the Department of the South and was ordered by the secretary of war to respond. President Monroe wrote a carefully worded letter to him on December 28, 1817, and urged him to take Florida if the opportunity arose. In the letter the president did not actually come out and tell Jackson to conquer the territory. He simply mentioned "other services" which might be undertaken. Jackson invaded Spanish Florida on March 15, 1818, and one of the bloodiest and costliest Indian wars ensued—the Seminole War. Jackson "punished" the cooperating "Spanish, terrorized the Indians, and put a gross insult upon the British by hanging Arbuthnot and shooting Ambrister" (Keating 1888).

Arbuthnot and Ambrister were British subjects who traded with the Indians. Jackson thought that Ambrister had counseled the Seminoles to make war with the Americans, a situation which he considered intolerable. As he saw it, families had been murdered because of the instigation and assistance of these men. Arbuthnot was found guilty of fomenting war and acting as a spy. Ambrister was found guilty of aiding the enemy and assuming command of the Seminoles. On April 29, 1818, they were put to death. Jackson then captured

Pensacola, the center of the Spanish Florida government, on May 24, 1818. By June 2, 1818, the Seminole War was over.

President Monroe had thought that Jackson was the man to solve the Indian problem and apply enough pressure to convince Spain to simply give up any further claim to Florida. However, while Jackson achieved the president's goals, he created a potential international crisis. He had executed two British subjects, openly conquered Florida, and forcibly removed the Spanish governor. His actions could have justified declarations of war from Spain and England, and in response, the Spanish minister came to Washington and registered formal protest.

Here was a man who had been orphaned as a child and grew to become a national hero by conquering the British, the Spanish, and the Indians. His popularity was becoming so great that jealousies arose among those concerned with their own political rise. John Quincy Adams accused Jackson of procrastination in the face of the international "storm" his actions had created. John C. Calhoun argued for censure and an official investigation into Jackson's actions in Florida. Secretary of Treasury William H. Crawford urged the return of Florida to Spain. As Jackson's reputation and heroic stature grew, political competitors felt that he must be removed from the national spotlight. In late 1818 and early 1819, Crawford and Henry Clay began a campaign to injure Jackson's reputation over the Florida affair. For a variety of reasons, other congressmen clamored for punishment or some recourse against Jackson. In January 1819, Clay rose in the House of Representatives and began to cut Jackson to the core. He condemned his taking of Fort Jackson, stated that this had started the Seminole War, condemned him for executing Arbuthnot, and criticized his

JOHN EATON was born on June 18, 1790, in Scotland Neck, North Carolina. He was educated at the University of North Carolina. He studied law and began practice in Franklin, Tennessee. Eaton's first wife was the daughter of William B. Lewis, who was a close friend of Andrew Jackson. This relationship certainly provided the opportunity for him to get to know Andrew Jackson. Eaton served in the state legislature, receiving the appointment by Governor Joseph McMinn to fill the empty U.S. Senate seat of September 5, 1818. He was only twenty-eight years, although the constitutional age required to serve in the U.S. Senate is thirty years. Henry Clay was also younger than thirty, but John Eaton was the youngest to have ever entered the Senate. He was rightfully elected to fill the seat to which he had been appointed, beginning the term on October 9, 1819. He won a total of three elections to the Senate, staying until March 9, 1829, when he resigned to become secretary of war under President Andrew Jackson. Eaton had been a campaign manager for Jackson and a close ally. He served as secretary of war until June 18, 1831, when he resigned to avoid further damage to Jackson, brought on by a controversy over Eaton's second wife, Peggy. During Eaton's service on President Jackson's cabinet, a furor of jealous fighting began with attacks against Eaton's wife, the former Peggy O'Neal Timberlake, involving her in an alleged affair with Eaton while she was still married to her first husband. John Timberlake was in the navy, and Peggy and Eaton were rumored to have had some social interaction during his absence. When Timberlake died while he was away, the relationship between Peggy and Senator Eaton blossomed and they were public popularity as a misunderstanding by the public of Jackson's insubordination of the government and Constitution. (In future presidential competition, Clay would be Jackson's rival for Western votes while Crawford would rival him for Southern votes.) His enemies may have tried to discredit him, but it was all for naught. Even with the best politicians in the nation trying to destroy him, the people would not accept it and in fact, these politicians jeopardized their own reputations by continuing to attack him. On February 8, 1819, four resolutions intended to condemn Jackson failed in the House of Representatives.

Tennessee Moves West

In 1818, within an environment of cooperation with the Indians, Andrew Jackson and Isaac Shelby were appointed cocommissioners by President Monroe to negotiate a treaty and the release of lands which later became West Tennessee and western Kentucky. Isaac Shelby had become well-known, as had his father, by defending his country against the Indians and the British in the Revolutionary War. The Shelbys, who were early pioneers of Tennessee, had fought at King's Mountain alongside John Sevier. Isaac Shelby became a friend and associate of Sevier, and also of Robertson and Jackson. He moved to Kentucky, and when it became a state, he became its first governor.

The governor and the general completed the treaty on October 19, 1818, but only after some difficult negotiation with the Indians, as well as some disagreement between themselves. During negotiations, Jackson was apparently fairly rough in his dealing with the Indians. Shelby became distressed over Jackson's less than "forthright" bargaining and his insinuation to the Indians that the United States might just take the lands if the Indians did not accept what was

---

married. (John Eaton helped rear Peggy's two daughters; a son had died early in life.) Accusations were used to discredit Eaton and disrupt Jackson's cabinet. To quote Senator McKellar's account, "Their marriage made the tongues of gossip wag but the faster. In this life there are always to be found a large number of 'better-than-thou' people" (McKellar 1942). A bitter intracabinet war developed over the acceptance or denial of Peggy Eaton's social status. Apparently, Vice President and Mrs. Calhoun, the Branch couple, the Inghams, Judge Berrien, and the Andrew Jackson Donelsons were against Mrs. Eaton; President Jackson, Martin Van Buren, Postmaster General Barry and his wife supported her. Although Andrew Jackson Donelson was not a cabinet member (he was personal secretary to the president), the dispute was so bad that his wife left the White House and returned to Tennessee; Andrew Donelson left at the end of the term. The infighting spread to the newspapers, and the cabinet became seriously damaged. Ingham, Berrien, and Branch were asked to resign. Eaton and Van Buren also resigned in order to help the president out of the political/social dilemma.

John Eaton then became governor of the Florida territory from 1834 until 1836. He was an envoy to Spain from 1836 until 1840. After Jackson's two terms as president, Eaton supported Martin Van Buren in 1836. However, he declined to support him in 1840 and slipped out of the political arena. He made his home in Washington, D.C., and was very successful financially. His wife inherited a fair amount from her father and was well off in her own right. John Eaton died in Washington on November 17, 1856. Peggy remained a leader in the Washington social scene until her later years, when she married a twenty-year-old man. He wasted a great deal of her finances and was also, simultaneously, married to Peggy's granddaughter, Emily. Peggy Eaton died in 1879. (Photograph courtesy of SHO) offered. Shelby and Jackson had been very close, but as the negotiations became difficult, a moment of tension almost clouded the relationship. The two men not only had different philosophies concerning the manner of negotiations with the Indians, but Shelby also knew that Jackson had purchased a portion of the Rice grant from Overton and was in fact working in his own behalf (Sigafoos 1979, Remini 1988).

The Western Purchase (Chickasaw Cession) was signed on January 7, 1819. The United States gained all of Tennessee and Kentucky west of the Tennessee River for twenty thousand dollars per year for fifteen years to be paid to the chiefs. This was a paltry four and one-half cents per acre. (Actually, North Carolina had granted lands near the Chickasaw Bluffs some time prior to this. In fact, by 1819 there were daily emigrants from Middle and East Tennessee, as well as North Carolina, South Carolina, and Virginia. However, no final settlement had been made with the Indians until this treaty.)

Jackson, who was half owner with John Overton in the five thousand acres of the Chickasaw Bluffs, was noted to officially take possession, by quitclaim deed, on December 12, 1818. However in 1797, he had sold half of his interest to Stephen and Richard Winchester for six hundred twenty-five dollars. Soon after the Chickasaw Cession Jackson sold one-eighth of his interest in the five-thousand-acre Rice tract to General James Winchester for five thousand dollars.

The new western land, freed from Indian control, was brought into the state of Tennessee. In 1819 Hardin County was organized. It was large and contained what eventually became Hardin, Fayette, Hardeman, McNairy, and Shelby Counties, several of which were formed the same year.

Eighteen nineteen was also an election year in Tennessee. Governor McMinn was

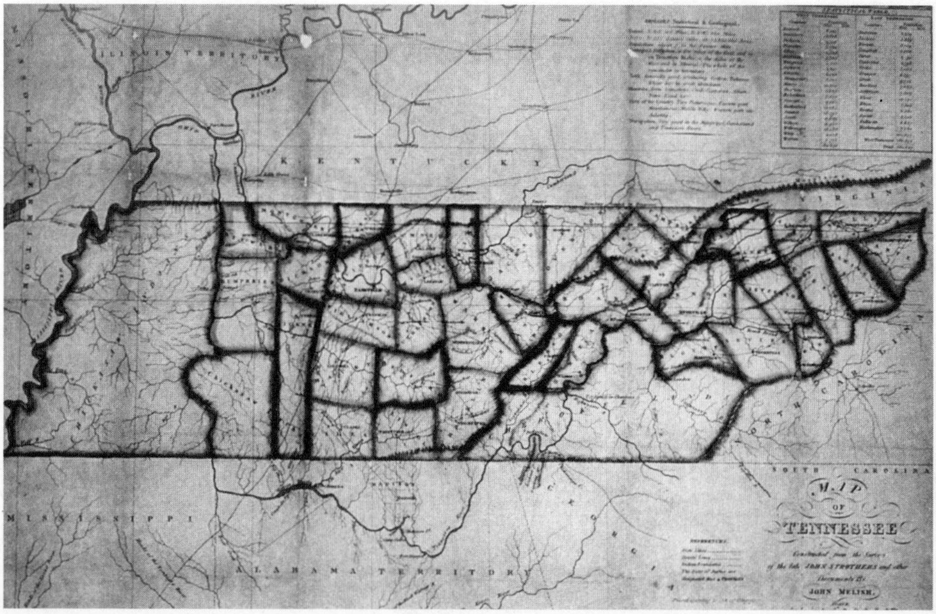

Tennessee in 1818, drawn by John Melish. Indian lands remain in southeast corner and west of the Tennessee River. (Courtesy of TSLA)

challenged by Enoch Parsons. The state enjoyed financial stability and was now rapidly expanding. McMinn had again covered his political bases and was reelected.

Migration into West Tennessee was slow initially because there was still little to attract settlers to the area. Most of the growth in Tennessee had occurred in the east and middle part of the state, and Memphis was little more than an Indian trading post. If the land were to have value to its investors, it had to have people. The question to Jackson and his fellow investors was how to attract settlers.

Shortly after the Chickasaw Cession was ratified, Jackson, Overton, and Winchester hired surveyor William Lawrence to lay out 362 town lots next to the river. They sent Winchester's son, Marcus B. Winchester, to the town to serve as its first real estate agent. (He would become a politician, civic and business leader, and remain a leading citizen for the following twenty years.) The group advertised to stir interest. One ad in the *Nashville Whig* encouraged the "prudent and discreet adventurer of all classes to settle and improve the place" (Sigafoos 1979).

In 1819 Memphis had only fifty-three residents, far fewer than Nashville, Knoxville, and the other towns located further east in Tennessee. Yet the town's developers thought that it would be the next major community of the state. However, soon after the great western migration began, it started to slow down. The national economy suddenly turned. The demand for land and products slowed, prices dropped, and a financial panic gripped the nation. Leaders felt that something must be done to stimulate commerce and development. Governor McMinn called a special session of the state legislature in Murfreesboro in June 1820. Felix Grundy led the plan to establish a state bank. It was thought that by establishing a bank with paper money, low interest loans could be made and commerce could be rejuvenated. Branches were established in Nashville and Knoxville.

Banks sprang up around the state. In those days, however, banks lent for speculation with little collateral and no financial reserves available for hard times. As a result of the great growth and business speculation of the preceding several years, the risks these banks took were high. When the foreclosures began, the banks had little or no reserves to protect the depositors. They halted payment with gold and silver (specie) and paid only with paper money, in which the people had little confidence. This of course caused a run on the banks. Many investors lost all their holdings; those who had deposited their savings were unable to pay for their own needs.

The financial panic of 1819 and the plight of the debtor class set the stage for a revolution in the judicial, representative, and taxation structures of government. Until this time the taxation system was somewhat unfair. Land was taxed equally, whether the farm was large or small. This unfairly disadvantaged the small farmer by forcing him to pay the same taxes as the large landholder. Political leaders were generally members of the aristocracy and controlled both state and local government. The legislature selected the members of a county court, who then held office for life. These appointed representatives of the community thus held sole power to select the county sheriff, trustee, etc. This was hardly a representative form of government. At the least, it was distantly representative. The need for change—for better representation and fairer treatment of the poorer classes—set the Tennessee political stage for the elections of 1821.

By 1820, Andrew Jackson did not need much urging to run for the presidency, and he carefully analyzed his opportunity. The Democrat-Republicans were strong and had elected the last three Presidents (Jefferson, Madison, and Monroe), and Jackson was certainly no Federalist. He was extraordinarily popular with the people, but in those days it was the politicians who elected presidents. Monroe was a sitting president who planned to run for reelection. Jackson decided to wait.

During his first term, President Monroe had tried to end national sectionalism by naming John Quincy Adams, from Massachusetts, his secretary of state and John C. Calhoun, from South Carolina, his secretary of war. When he began his run for reelection in 1820, opposition was nonexistent. Monroe received 232 electoral votes to 1 for Secretary of State John Quincy Adams. This one dissenting vote was allegedly cast to preserve the honor bestowed on George Washington as the only president elected without dissent. The recurring election of Democrat-Republicans to the presidency and Congress continued to erode the Federalist Party base; the party was now almost dead. The Seventeenth Congress had only twenty-five Federalists to 158 Democrat-Republicans in the House and only four Federalists to forty-four Democrat-Republicans in the Senate. The Washington inner circle perpetuated power and controlled the nation. The people had little voice. The presidential elections were essentially inner-circle decisions. This was quite a good deal for those already in power. However, there were many outside of the circle who intended to break the hold on power. The old political parties and the niceties of presidential elections were about to change. In four short years the issue would become a national debate.

It was around this period, in 1818 that Missouri applied for statehood. Prior to its application, the issue of slavery had not yet become a great national debate. But when Missouri requested admission as a slave state, great public discord over the issue began. The question now was whether slavery should be restricted in the new state. In the Missouri Compromise, passed by Congress in 1820, Maine was separated from Massachusetts and admitted as a free state. It was also decided that other than Missouri there would be no more slave states above 36°30' parallel, in any new territory within the Louisiana Purchase. The troubling issue of slavery was temporarily put to rest.

William Carroll and Early Reform

Andrew Jackson quietly made his plans for the election of 1824. To prepare, he needed to do some political organizing in Tennessee. In order to ensure solid backing from his home state, he needed his friends in office. This would make it more likely that the state legislature would support his run for president. The next important issue for Jackson was the upcoming gubernatorial race and the election of a friendly governor.

Jackson was popular throughout the nation, as well as in his home state of Tennessee. After his eventual election as president, the island off the Chickasaw Bluffs near Memphis became referred to as President's Island in his honor (Keating 1888).

As Andrew Jackson had enjoyed public popularity due to his military exploits, so had some of his lieutenants. William (Billy) Carroll had gained much popularity via his role as Jackson protégé in the Battle of New Orleans. After all, he had served as second in command to Jackson in the battle. Carroll had commanded the men who had sustained the strongest attack by the British at New Orleans, and he had successfully repulsed them. If he had fallen, the battle might have been lost. Carroll, in fact, was deserving of a large part of the credit for the victory. However, his fame was overshadowed by that of Jackson, who was the general in charge of the battle, and since 1815, a hero of national stature. So Carroll was well-known and respected, but he was a political and military second to Jackson.

After the war, Carroll worked in business and civic affairs and prospered to the point of owning a steamboat and a general store in Nashville. However, for whatever reason, he was not politically anointed by the political/aristocratic elite of Tennessee. Jackson held the cards with them. Then, Carroll, along with many others, suffered a setback in the financial panic of 1819. By 1820 he had taken some hard social knocks and came to understand what the common Tennessean faced in everyday life. He may have been down financially, and he may have been an outsider to the political aristocratic mainstream, but that did not stop Billy Carroll. A self-made man and a greatly determined individual, Carroll would not allow his destiny to be determined by the elite. He decided to run for governor.

On the other hand, Andrew Jackson, also a man of common origins, had close ties with the elite of Tennessee. Marrying a Donelson had given him immediate entree into Tennessee aristocracy. His friend, John Overton, was a wealthy banker, land speculator, and a powerful political operative. Overton's brother-in-law, Hugh Lawson White, whose father had founded Knoxville, owned most of the land around the community and was also a banker in Knoxville. The Blounts were also wealthy and influential friends of Jackson's. Pleasant M. Miller, married to a daughter of William Blount, the deceased territorial governor, was another successful Knoxville businessman politically tied to White, Overton, and Jackson.

Even though the common man could identify with Andrew Jackson, he was not the leader who brought fairness and democracy to Tennessee—this would be William Carroll. Jackson did not support Carroll, nor did his inner circle of Tennessee aristocrats. They pondered Jackson's options, one of which was the gubernatorial race. However, there were real risks in running against William Carroll. What if Jackson lost? His career opportunities might be seriously injured. Jackson, instead, decided to support his neighbor Edward Ward. Ward was a wealthy farmer with holdings on the outskirts of Nashville. He had served as speaker of the Tennessee senate from 1815 until 1819. Overton, White, and Miller, all supported Ward, as did Senator John Eaton and Governor Joseph McMinn.

Carroll, on the other hand, had the support of those who resented the Jackson/Overton group and their power. U.S. Senator John Williams, from East Tennessee, was on the "outs" with them. State Senator Theoderick F. Bradford and Davy Crockett from West Tennessee, and Andrew Erwin and Congressman Newton Cannon from Middle Tennessee were also enemies of the Jackson/Overton coalition. They all supported Carroll.

Carroll needed the votes of the people to win the governorship. Therefore, he championed the little man and the downtrodden, and he very carefully criticized banks and their treatment of debtors. He campaigned for judicial, legal, and tax reform in Tennessee.

On the other hand, to most people Carroll's opponent, Edward Ward, represented the elite. He was closely associated with bank owners, and during this day of financial hardship, there was no love lost for these lienholders. Banks held stringent and unbending policies on loans. They continued payment of dividends to bank stockholders during the financial panic of 1819, while the poor debtors went under. The voters turned against the bank policies, bank owners, and those associated with them, blaming much of their hardships on them.

During the preparations for this gubernatorial election, Jackson not only faced opposition to his candidate but also faced a threat to his job as U.S. major general. By 1821 Congress had reduced the size of the U.S. Army, thereby necessitating a reduction in officers. Major General Jacob Brown commanded the Northern District while Andrew Jackson commanded the Southern District. President Monroe did not relish the thought of dismissing one of his generals. Each had powerful political friends and could cause the president some serious unpleasantries, and each had tempers and could stir the public. Secretary of Treasury William H. Crawford wanted to preserve the military position for his friend General Brown.

Meanwhile, President Monroe received information that the Spanish had accepted the treaty with the United States and that Florida was finally in America's hands.

WILLIAM CARROLL was born on March 3, 1788, near Pittsburgh, Pennsylvania, the oldest of nine children. When he was about eighteen, his family moved to Davidson County, Tennessee. He had a limited education but obtained a job with a merchant who allowed him to develop his business acumen. When he was twenty-two, he borrowed money and opened the state's first nail store in Nashville (at the time the population of Nashville was only about eleven hundred). After success with his nail business, he went into the state militia to serve under Andrew Jackson. He became a dedicated military politician, and in 1812 became captain of the Nashville Uniform Volunteers. When Carroll was twenty-five years of age he married Cecelia Bradford from Fauquier County, Virginia. It was not long before General Jackson appointed Carroll as brigadier-inspector. Shortly, he was made a major in the state militia.

Carroll was smart, motivated, and brave in battle. He had to defend himself in a gunfight, wounding Jesse Benton, and subsequently had differences, along with Jackson, with Thomas Hart Benton. He and Jackson also had some differences through the years, but Carroll held firm to Jackson, who provided him with the opportunity for public popularity. He fought under Jackson in the Creek War and later in the Battle of New Orleans. Carroll's conduct in these battles earned him a respected place in the public mind.

After the 1815 Battle of New Orleans, Carroll brought the first steamboat to Nashville, and named it the *Andrew Jackson*. Carroll was popular, and his association with Andrew Jackson did not hurt. Carroll ran for governor in 1821 against Edward Ward. The race was marked by the entry of newspapers into the gubernatorial campaign. William Brownlow's East Tennessee *Whig* supported Carroll, while a Nashville paper, the *Clarion*, supported Ward. Even though Jackson supported Ward, Carroll won 31,290 to 7,294.

Monroe asked Jackson to take the post of territorial governor of Florida and organize the territory. This move allowed Monroe to eliminate a general, remove Jackson from the military, and avoid a backlash from Jackson's circle of friends. It also avoided the appearance of a rebuke toward Jackson; in fact, it appeared as an honor to him. John Quincy Adams said that appointing Jackson would allow "a fortunate occasion to save the nation from the disgrace of even the appearing to discard without compunction a man to whom they were so deeply indebted" (Remini, *American Empire,* 1977).

After considering his options, Jackson resigned his commission in the U.S. Army and accepted the appointment as territorial governor of Florida. He accepted in February, was commissioned in March, and assumed his post in June 1821, staying just long enough to organize the territory, which was not an easy task. Monroe never gave Jackson complete freedom, and the Spanish procrastinated in relinquishing Florida. Nevertheless, Jackson quickly completed his task. After eleven weeks of service, the Florida territory was organized and Jackson's job was done. He was back in Nashville by November 7, 1821; his official resignation was dated November 13, 1821. It was officially accepted by President Monroe on December 1, 1821.

In the election of 1821, gubernatorial candidate William Carroll dominated the

Carroll was reelected as governor in 1823 and for a third term in 1825. The state capital was moved from Murfreesboro to Nashville in 1826. In 1827, state law prevented him from succeeding himself for a fourth term. Sam Houston was elected governor in 1827, but did not complete his term, and William Hall served the remainder of the term. Carroll sought a U.S. Senate seat (Class 1), but was denied this by John Eaton, who was reelected in December 1826, and by Felix Grundy, who replaced Eaton when he resigned to become secretary of war in 1829. Hugh Lawson White, who served as U.S. Senator (Class 2), demonstrated no inclination to give up his seat, to which Carroll had initially appointed him. Carroll served three more consecutive terms as governor, from 1829 until 1835. During his twelve years as governor, Tennessee made great strides. The population increased, commerce and agriculture expanded, communities grew, homes were beginning to be modernized from log cabins to frame structures, and numerous counties were created. During Carroll's last term, a constitutional convention was held in 1834. The new constitution allowed land to be taxed according to its value (rather than an equal taxation regardless of the worth of the land) and allowed voters the right to elect county officials. (Under the old system, county court members were elected by the legislature for life and the court members chose the sheriffs, etc.) Governor Hall had begun a plan for a state prison, and during Carroll's fourth term he completed the plan. Carroll pushed the closure of the Bank of Tennessee and continued to work for internal improvements.

Carroll wanted a fourth consecutive and seventh term as governor, arguing that he could run for another three consecutive terms under the laws of the new constitution adopted in 1834. His dominance of state politics and association with Andrew Jackson (who was now president) created a fair amount of resentment by the other politicians and the populous and mobilized the anti-Jackson forces against him. He was defeated in the election of 1835 by Newton Cannon (Whig). He was denied appointment to the U.S. Senate when Governor Cannon appointed Ephraim Foster in 1838 to replace Felix Grundy (who was named U.S. attorney general). He also lost the legislative election to fill this U.S. Senate seat for the next term. William Carroll died on March 22, 1844, and was buried in Nashville. (Photograph courtesy of TSLA) scene. He ran as a Democrat-Republican, a war hero, and a common man's man, and thus was able to take political control from the elite political establishment of the state. The political word spread that Ward was an educated man of wealth. The voters, now fed up with the aristocratic and unfair government, responded with a natural feeling of resentment toward those in power. This election was the first in Tennessee in which the newspapers took sides and played a role in the campaign. Carroll won by a landslide. He took 31,290 votes to 7,294 for Ward. The Blount faction, of which Jackson was part, was slammed at the polls. The Sevier faction, now led by Colonel Andrew Erwin and U.S. Senator John Williams, took political control of the state.

Carroll had enjoyed the unique advantage to observe Jackson, the master general and politician, from his personal experience. Even though he did not have the support of Jackson in this election, he had learned very well from him in the past. Carroll would use this political knowledge to consolidate his own power. He was determined to bring fairer conditions to the people of Tennessee. Elected without the help of Jackson and his compatriots, he would position himself to become the most powerful politician within the boundaries of Tennessee.

Governor Carroll took office in 1821 and began a program of reforms. He first moved for a constitutional convention (a move for a convention had been defeated under his predecessor in 1819), hoping to address the small farmer's desire for a more equitable land tax. But the move for a convention was defeated again in 1821. The financial hardships brought on by the panic of 1819 began to ease during Carroll's first term and the citizens of Tennessee began to see an improvement in the general economy. This was more due to the natural economic cycle than to anything any politician had done. Nonetheless, it did not hurt Governor Carroll's political standing since he continued to push for improvements for the common man.

Meanwhile Andrew Jackson prepared to run for the presidency. He and his supporters knew that the congressional caucus would never nominate him. Therefore, they reasoned that if they could have the Tennessee legislature nominate him, other states might follow, leading to not only his nomination but a revolt against the congressional caucus nominating system. In July 1822, Felix Grundy, Pleasant M. Miller, John H. Eaton and William B. Lewis pushed a resolution in the state legislature to propose Jackson for president. The Tennessee legislature adopted the resolution and also condemned the congressional caucus as a method to nominate a candidate for president. (Up until this time, congressmen would hold a caucus in order to agree upon a presidential nominee. The nominee would be voted upon by state electors. The entire process was carried out by elected officials.) The legislature felt that the current nomination process removed the popular choice for president from the people and left it in the hands of politicians. They also urged Tennessee's congressmen to boycott the congressional caucus. Then there came word that Tennessee U.S. Senator John Williams, who had succeeded to head the Sevier political faction in East Tennessee, opposed Jackson.

Jackson then piqued political curiosity by declining President Monroe's offer to become minister to Mexico. Many felt that Monroe was trying to remove Jackson from a potential Washington position, which would carry more visibility, by tempting him with a lesser office. The Jackson/Overton political faction felt that Jackson needed to hold office in order to reappear on the political stage prior to his campaign for president. They resented the setback dealt by the Carroll defeat in 1821 and considered running Jackson for governor against Carroll in 1823. However, Carroll was strong and a loss could kill Jackson's presidential chances. They needed a smoother path, and a seat in the U.S. Senate seemed easier to engineer, although this plan was not without serious political risk. It would be difficult for U.S. Senator John Williams to hold his seat if the legislature was faced with the opportunity to honor Tennessee's leading citizen and assist his presidential chances. Pleasant M. Miller, with political ambitions of his own, tried to convince his friends that Jackson should run for governor and rid the state of Carroll's political friends. Part of Miller's plan included his own move to take John Williams's place in the Senate. However, the Jackson/Overton team finally concluded that they had more influence and possibilities on a national level. In Tennessee the power was with Governor Carroll and the possibilities were limited and politically dangerous. The decision was made; Jackson would run for the U.S. Senate.

The legislature met in Murfreesboro in 1823. Jackson left the Hermitage and rode through the night to reach Murfreesboro in time for the vote. The personal appearance of Jackson, who was by now legendary, was enough to secure his victory. No doubt part of the tact to secure Jackson's election was to remind members of the legislature that incumbent U.S. Senator John Williams had voted to censure Jackson over the Florida affair. This vote was an issue of Tennessee honor. Besides, Jackson had a chance to become president. With this in mind, the legislature turned out Williams, and Jackson was elected to the U.S. Senate (Class 2) October 1, 1823, by a vote of thirty-five to twenty-five. The term was scheduled to officially begin on March 4, 1823, but the election took place later. Once elected, Jackson packed and left for Washington, D.C., arriving on December 3, 1823. The first session of the 18th Congress did not open until December 1823 (Remini 1981).

With Jackson now in a visible position and not wishing to endure the defeat of another political ally, he did little to oppose Governor Carroll. In fact Carroll was so powerful that no one challenged him. The state was in reasonably good shape. The common man could identify with Carroll, who was acting to change laws which would result in more equitable treatment of the average Tennessean. William Carroll, unopposed, was reelected governor of Tennessee in 1823. In April 1824, Governor Carroll and the legislature created legislation requiring banks to pay in specie, relieving some of the effects of the financial crisis of 1819.

While Governor Carroll worked to improve Tennessee, Jackson's eyes were sharply focused on the presidency. President Monroe would soon end two terms. He had run unopposed for reelection in 1820. His tenure has been called the "era of good feeling" because the young nation was not involved in any major conflict, and was enjoying incredible expansion, and a recovering economy. He had moved into the new White House, which had been destroyed during the War of 1812. Under his administration the British agreed to halt fortifications along the Canadian border; Florida was bought from Spain; the Monroe Doctrine was established; and the Missouri Compromise, which admitted Missouri as a slave state in order to calm differences between abolitionists and slaveholders, had been approved. Most of all, President Monroe was a peacemaker and avoided conflict in national affairs and interfering in the debates of Congress. He also avoided anointing a successor. However, his reluctance to be involved in the process of selection of the next president set off a monstrous political battle.

As Monroe's second term neared an end, ambitious politicians began feeling out their chances for the presidency. Previous presidents had come from the East. Meanwhile the nation continued to grow in the West, and Westerners began to resent the political dominance of the East Coast politicians. Andrew Jackson, the most popular man in the nation, was from the West (Tennessee was considered west in those days) and many felt that it was time for a president from the West. Jackson had defended the settlers against Indian hostilities, crushed the British, defeated the Spanish, and nearly conquered his political enemies. He was just the type of hero the people of the West could enthusiastically support. If he was to take advantage of his popularity, now was the time. However, there was one serious problem. Prior to this time, all presidential candidates received their party nomination by congressional caucus. Many jealous politicians in Congress wanted to be president themselves. Since Jackson could not manipulate the political strings of these congressmen, something else had to be done in order for him to obtain the nomination.

There were interests other than Jackson's own for him to run for president. Members of the Tennessee Junto, the old William Blount political faction which included Grundy, Lewis, Overton, Eaton, and others, needed to regain political control. Many in this group were bank owners. Jackson was their ticket to power. They saw that the congressional caucus form of nominating a president had to be challenged. Otherwise, Jackson had no chance with the Washington politicians. His power and the potential power of his friends lay with the people.

When the first session of the Eighteenth Congress opened in Washington in December 1823, the biggest topic of conversation was the presidential election. The stalwarts of the Democrat-Republican faction, controlled mostly by East Coast politicians, wanted to continue the congressional caucus nomination process. There was no better way to maintain power. They pushed for William H. Crawford to obtain the nomination.

When Jackson went to Washington to take his seat in the Senate, he found his old subordinate, now his enemy, Thomas Hart Benton. Benton, after his 1813 gunfight with Jackson, had moved to Missouri where he was subsequently elected to the U.S. Senate. When Jackson arrived, he found he was assigned to a seat adjacent to Benton's, since both were placed on the Committee on Military Affairs because of their military experience. Because they were constantly forced to be together, they eventually began to speak to each other, though for a while, all conversation was limited. However, after a time Jackson decided to breach the years of enmity and inquired about the well-being of Benton's wife. The conversation finally eked past the perfunctory. A few days after, Jackson visited Benton at his Washington abode. At their next encounter, Benton walked up to Jackson and bowed. With that Jackson extended the hand of friendship. Benton did likewise, and they shook hands. The two had finally made amends with each other after the gunfight in Nashville ten years before. This was fortunate since Benton would become a tremendous supporter of Jackson in the years ahead. Benton was an intelligent man with great legislative and political awareness and ability. He was not only someone Jackson did not need as an enemy in the Senate but someone who had the potential of being an enormous asset as a political ally.

There were other issues which needed to be resolved if Jackson wanted to run for president. He had suffered some criticism over his alleged fraud involving the Chickasaw Cession deal. By ridding himself of ownership of the Memphis property, he could end any lingering controversy. In 1823 he traded his remaining interests in the property to John C. McLemore, protégé and assistant to Jackson, for rural land in what is now Madison County.

When the Democrat-Republican Party called for the congressional caucus to nominate its candidate for president in 1824, it would be for the last time. When the caucus met on February 14, 1824, only 68 of 261 party members showed up. The weak attendance exemplified the feelings of those congressmen who were now opposed to the caucus form of nomination. Even so, the caucus took place. Astonishingly, 48 of the 68 were representatives of Georgia, New York, Virginia, and North Carolina. William Crawford of Georgia received sixty-four votes, John Quincy Adams two, Jackson one, and Nathaniel Macon from North Carolina one. Jackson was disgusted and told his friend John Coffee, "Everything is carried by intrigue and management" (Remini 1988). What Jackson said was true. The Democrat-Republicans were trying to maintain power, but as the nation grew West and the party grew, competition among its members began tearing the party apart. The caucus had served to hold the party together, but by necessity it thrust the power in the hands of a few men. The congressional caucus form of nomination essentially passed the presidency on to those who had worked their way into a clan of power brokers. The few could not hold back the ambition of the many, and the fracture occurred. The caucus may have nominated, but it could be seen by the meager attendance that an uprising was not only coming, it had already begun. The general populous had turned against the caucus, and many congressmen agreed with their constituency. Change was coming, and Jackson was just the man to lead the charge.

The events about to occur not only created the modern political party system, but also provided the vehicle for regional party factionalism in the state of Tennessee. Up until now, politics in Tennessee was based mainly on personalities and sectionalism. As the political parties organized, the party would become the focus of political allegiance.

Several states ignored the congressional caucus nomination of Crawford and instead held state caucuses to nominate candidates. Kentucky nominated Clay, Tennessee nominated Jackson, and Massachusetts nominated Adams. By rejecting the congressional caucus system, these states set in motion a political struggle to find a way to bring the nomination closer to the people and to respond to the desire of Westerners to overcome the domination of Eastern politicians. Certainly a state legislative nomination provided more input from a state than the anointment of a new president by the power elite of Washington.

In 1824 the political convention in Pennsylvania, an important state in the electoral process during this period, also nominated Jackson for president. As the election procedure progressed, Adams, who was from Massachusetts, came to represent New England. Jackson and Clay were the Western candidates. Secretary of Treasury William H. Crawford, who was from Georgia and had been nominated by the congressional caucus, was the Southern candidate. Although the election would be decided by electors, this was to be the first election in which the popular vote had a major impact on the outcome.

Secretary of War John C. Calhoun from South Carolina was also in the race and had support, but he could clearly see that the votes would be divided. He reasonably let the others fight it out and quickly dropped out of the race for president. Instead he ran as vice president for both Jackson and Adams.

This divided election marked the end of the congressional caucus system of electing presidents. Democracy would grow as a more fair selection process evolved. Here was the beginning of a real party system for electing presidents, the end of East Coast political domination (which up until this point had total control of the federal government), and a demonstration of the will of the populous to participate in selecting leaders. There was no doubt about the outcome and the message of the voters. When the votes were counted, Jackson had won the largest number of popular votes, but not a majority. He received 152,901 popular votes (99 electoral votes) to 114,023 (84) for Adams, 47,217 (37) for Clay, and 46,979 (41) for Crawford. Jackson needed 131 electoral votes to be elected, but he was short by 32 votes.

The Twelfth Amendment to the Constitution provided that if no candidate received a majority of electoral votes, the House of Representatives would decide who should be elected. Since Clay had the lowest number of electoral votes, he had to drop out

HUGH LAWSON WHITE was born on October 30, 1773, in Iredell County, North Carolina. General James White, Hugh's father, came to the territory that would become Tennessee and settled. His father was largely responsible for the founding of Knoxville, Tennessee. There was little if any education available when the Whites settled in Tennessee. Hugh received the basics from his local Presbyterian minister, the Reverend Samuel Carrick, and was further educated by Judge Archibald Roane (who later became governor). Territorial Governor Blount made White one of his private secretaries. White fought Indians under General John Sevier, then went to Philadelphia, Pennsylvania, to study math and later to Lancaster, Pennsylvania, to study law. He returned to Tennessee and set up his law practice around 1796. In 1798 he married Elizabeth Moore Carrick, the daughter of his former teacher, Reverend Carrick. (Reverend Carrick became the first president of Blount College—later the University of Tennessee. The Carrick and the Heiskell family of Tennessee were related.) They had twelve children but two died in infancy and the other ten died at young ages of tuberculosis. In 1801 Hugh Lawson White was placed on the supreme court of Tennessee. He resigned in 1807 to run successfully for the state senate. He stayed only a short while, subsequently becoming U.S. district attorney for the Eastern Tennessee District. He resigned this office and went back to the legislature, helping pass a bill outlawing dueling in Tennessee. By 1809 he was back in the court system, serving as presiding judge, Supreme Court of Errors and Appeals. In 1811, he became president of the Bank of Tennessee and served in this capacity until 1827. During the Creek Indian War, he served with his brother-in-law, Colonel John Williams of the Thirty-ninth U.S. Infantry, under Andrew Jackson. White later served on a commission to decide claims against Spain according to the Florida Treaty, helping to assess Kentucky and Virginia claims. In 1825 he was elected by the state legislature to the U.S. Senate where he remained for fifteen years. President Jackson offered him a cabinet position in 1829 and the position of secretary of war in 1831, but he of the running, but he had powerful influence in the House of Representatives. Intrigue engulfed the House, and Jackson could see what was coming. After a meeting between Clay and Adams on the night of January 9, 1825, Clay's friends moved their votes to Adams. This included some votes from states whose U.S. representatives had been instructed by their state legislatures to vote for Jackson. For example, the Kentucky delegation had been instructed by its legislature to vote for Jackson (since Adams had not received any popular votes of the people during the general election). Instead, their representatives listened to Henry Clay. When Clay's intention to support Adams and the intentions of some of Kentucky's representatives were announced, a great outcry of disbelief was heard. It was hard to believe that some of the Western delegations were not going to vote for Jackson in spite of the fact that he had received 90 percent of the popular vote in the West. Accusations erupted, charging Clay and Adams of making a deal. On February 9, 1825, the House of Representatives voted for president. Each state had one vote. Adams received thirteen votes, to seven for Jackson, and four for Crawford. John Quincy Adams was elected president.

When Adams selected Clay as his secretary of state, many clearly believed a deal must have been struck. Jackson and his friends were outraged, and they complained

declined. He became president pro tempore of the Senate in 1832, but by this time there was a clear breach between White and Jackson. White had his own presidential ambitions, and Jackson had begun to make known his support for Martin Van Buren. Jackson recommended that White become Van Buren's vice president. He declined. White was also offered a position on the U.S. Supreme Court, but he refused all offers. By this period of time, White was the second most powerful man in Tennessee—next to Jackson.

White's fatal political mistake may have been voting against the expungement resolution, proposed by Senator Thomas Hart Benton, which was designed to protect the character of President Jackson. Previously, Vice President Calhoun had cast the deciding vote denying Van Buren Senate confirmation as ambassador to Great Britain. This was embarrassing to the president and to Van Buren, who had already been in London for a year. For this act of disloyalty on the part of Calhoun, the president set up Van Buren to become his vice president in the election of 1832. Together they soundly defeated Clay and Sergeant. Then Clay proposed a resolution condemning the president. It passed, but Senator Thomas Hart Benton proposed an expunging resolution to protect the integrity of the president. In fact, he persisted until it passed just before Jackson's second term ended. However, White voted against it. Jackson had offered the vice presidential spot on Van Buren's ticket to White, with the understanding that White could then have their support to run for president at a later date, but White refused. White's refusal to overtures and his voting against the president's expunging eliminated Jackson's support of him for president in any future elections. Van Buren had stuck with Jackson and Jackson's loyalty was with Van Buren.

When White ran for president in 1836, with John Bell of Tennessee as his campaign manager, he won only Tennessee and Georgia. His break with Jackson created the opportunity for Jackson's enemies to build an organization, resulting in the development of a national and Tennessee opposition (to Jackson) party, which became the Whig Party. White resigned from the Senate in 1840. He lent his name to support William Henry Harrison (Whig) in 1840. Mrs. White died in 1831 of tuberculosis. White died from the same infection on April 10, 1840. (Photograph courtesy of SHO) bitterly about the "corrupt bargain" between Adams and Clay. In view of the fact that over 90 percent of the Western popular vote had gone for Jackson, it was unthinkable that Henry Clay could overrule such a mandate and cause a state's U.S. representatives to succumb to his wishes rather than to those of the Western constituency. Adams had been elected, not by competition between Democrat-Republicans and Federalists, but rather by a "coalition" of politicians, intent on maintaining power.

The entire 1824 election escapade clarified the need for political reform, of placing the government in the hands of the people, rather than the politicians. The congressional caucus was gone. The old Democrat-Republicans and the Federalists were gone. What evolved was the coalition required to defeat Andrew Jackson and Jackson's supporters for political reform. The makeup of the House and Senate, reflecting the beginnings of the modern two-party system, was officially listed as Coalition Party, formed to defeat Jackson, and Jackson Party, those opposed to the old order. In the House, the Coalition Party had 105 seats to the Jackson Party's 97; in the Senate, the Coalition had 26 seats to Jackson's 20.

With Adams's election as president, Jackson's campaign for 1828 immediately began. Jackson would not be manipulated out of office over trades for positions and jobs. He was determined to carry his case to the people. Shortly after Adams's election, the president himself "unwittingly" (Remini 1988) assisted with the initial development of the Democratic Party. When he gave his December 6, 1825, "State of the Union" message, Adams implied that the U.S. government must not be limited to the will of the voters, that the elite must do what is best for the country, saying ". . . we are palsied by the will of our constituents." His speech did more to define for politicians and the voters the differences between aristocracy and democracy than anything ever clarified for public understanding before. After his message, those politicians who favored the autonomy of states over the federal government and who were against the centralization of power in the hands of a few men, broke with Adams. Jackson's movement gained support from those who favored democracy, and the support was not limited to the Western states. Senator Martin Van Buren of New York would not only join with the "Democrats" but he would help lead the charge for Jackson.

With the power of the old political order somewhat broken, many came to the aid of Jackson and his new party which set its sights on reforming the system. In December 1826, Vice President John Calhoun, from South Carolina, met with Van Buren to develop a new system of nominating their candidate and a new party to do the job.

When Andrew Jackson resigned his U.S. Senate seat on October 14, 1825, Hugh Lawson White, who at that time was a Jeffersonian or Jacksonian Democrat and generally opposed to President John Quincy Adams, was nominated to fill the seat. Ironically, White's brother-in-law, Senator John Williams, had lost his Senate seat to Jackson in 1823 and opposed Jackson in his presidential run, siding with Adams. But Hugh Lawson White, and his father too, were quite good friends with Jackson. Although White had served in the state senate and on the state supreme court and was well-known and respected throughout Tennessee, he would have found it difficult to be elected to the U.S. Senate by this Tennessee legislature were it not for Jackson. Fortunately, he had assisted Jackson in his presidential campaign of 1824, and with his support was appointed by Governor Carroll to succeed Jackson to the U.S. Senate (Class 2). He took his seat on October 28, 1825.

After the presidential election, Jackson returned to Tennessee and remained fairly quiet on the political front. His friends John Overton and John Eaton led the political preparation for the next contest for the presidency, which would occur in 1828. Others such as John Coffee, Sam Houston, and William B. Lewis joined in the preparation. Missouri U.S. Senator Thomas Hart Benton worked to shore up support for Jackson in the Senate and the state of Missouri. Martin Van Buren of New York also joined in to organize support from New York. John Calhoun used not only his national influence but his influence in South Carolina for Jackson. The momentum of the organization, already strong because of Jackson's great popularity, was only heightened by

DAVID (DAVY) CROCKETT was born on August 17, 1786, near present day Rogersville, Tennessee, near the junction of the Limestone Creek and the Nolichuckey River (later this became Greene County, now Hawkins County). His parents were John and Rebecca (Hawkins) Crockett. His mother was born in Maryland. His father was born either in Ireland or on the boat over from Ireland, and fought in the Battle of King's Mountain in the Revolutionary War. His parents moved from Lincoln County, North Carolina, to Tennessee around 1783, and his father became a tavern keeper. Crockett attended some common school, then ran away at age thirteen to escape a whipping. Three years later he returned home and worked for two years to pay off family debt. He worked the tavern, cared for horses, and helped at his father's mill. He later worked for cattlemen and eventually became bound to a Virginia hatter for eighteen months.

On August 14, 1806, Crockett married Mary Polly Findley. He hunted and farmed, but did poorly as a farmer. In 1811 the Crocketts and their two sons moved to Lincoln County and in 1813 to Franklin County. Crockett left home to serve in the Creek Indian War and commanded a battalion of riflemen under Andrew Jackson in 1813–1814. After his return, Polly gave birth to a daughter, but died soon afterward. A year later, Crockett married Elizabeth Patton, a soldier's widow with two children.

After the Creek War, Crockett served as a magistrate in the Shoal Creek area. He moved there and became a colonel in the militia. In 1821 he began serving in the Tennessee state legislature and served until 1823. He became a public speaker with a colorful wit and sense of humor and won fame for his abilities with his rifle. He lost his home to fire and moved to the Obion River area surviving by hunting. While living in Gibson County he was reelected to the state legislature in 1822. An unsuccessful run for Congress in 1824 (Nineteenth Congress) was followed by election to Congress in 1826 and reelection in 1828 (from March 4, 1827, until March 3, 1831, in the Twentieth and Twenty-first Congresses). Crockett was defeated in his congressional campaign of 1830 but was reelected by a narrow margin as an anti-Jackson candidate in 1832 (serving from March 4, 1833, until March 3, 1835, in the Twenty-third Congress). By this time he had made many enemies among Andrew Jackson's allies in Tennessee. In 1834, he went on a public tour of the North displaying his homespun wit, humor, and talent as a public speaker. Crockett was defeated for reelection in the campaign of that year.

By fifty years of age Crockett was out of Congress. He left Tennessee for Texas and made it to the Alamo in February 1836. He died in the siege on the fort shortly after his arrival. (Portrait painting by Lorine Goodwin courtesy of TSM)

their message to supporters that the "corrupt bargain" between Clay and Adams had removed the selection of president from the hands of the people.

In 1824 Davy Crockett, who had served three terms in the state legislature, lost his first race for the U.S. House of Representatives to Colonel Adam Alexander, the first congressman from West Tennessee. Crockett was popular and well-known for his folk stories of the pioneer country. However, he was also a bit erratic and politically volatile, occasionally tending to stray from the political fold. Crockett had angered

SAM HOUSTON was born in Rockingham County, Virginia, on March 2, 1793. His father, Sam Houston Sr., served in the Revolutionary War and as an inspector with the Virginia Militia. He died in 1807, leaving his wife, Elizabeth Paxton Houston, to care for their nine children. Sam Jr. came with his widowed mother and family to Baker's Creek, near Maryville, when Houston was fourteen. The move was made to land that had been purchased by Sam's late father, and the family moved west in hopes of a better life.

He had learned to read and write prior to coming to Tennessee, but his education amounted to little. Once in Tennessee, he tried formal education at Maryville Academy, but this did not last more than a few months. He developed a liking for literature and especially a fondness for Pope's translation of *The Iliad*. Sam did not take much to farm work, and this created some resentment among his brothers. He preferred relaxing and reading rather than manual labor, but his family pushed him into taking a job as a clerk in a store. After a while, the restless youth left home and went to live with the Cherokee Indians, becoming good friends with them. He developed a close relationship with Cherokee Chief John Jolly. For a period of time he delved deeply into Indian ways and acquired an understanding of the way they lived and thought. When he returned home, he was in great need of finding a way to earn a living, and his life with the Indians did little to prepare for this. He tried teaching and opened a school, charging eight dollars per child per year. This went well for a while, and he earned enough to pay his debts, but the role as a school teacher did not satisfy this restless and ambitious young man. He set his sights on greater glory and decided to enter the military. The young glory seeker joined the Thirty-ninth U.S. Infantry, where he advanced to sergeant and later to ensign. His regiment fought in the Creek War, under the command of Andrew Jackson, and during the height of the Battle of Horseshoe Bend in 1814, Houston was wounded in the thigh by an arrow. Near the end of the battle, when one area of the enemy continued to hold out, the wounded Houston volunteered to participate in the charge. Once begun, his comrades hesitated, and Houston took the lead, rallying the group to continue their charge. He was hit in his right arm and his left shoulder by musket fire before collapsing. Because of his heroism, Houston won the respect of Jackson. After the Creek War, Houston tied himself closely to Jackson and his friends. His wounds prevented him from fighting with Jackson in the Battle of New Orleans. However, after the war, he rejoined the Thirty-ninth Regiment in New Orleans.

Upon returning to Nashville, the twenty-five-year-old Houston was made an Indian agent with responsibilities that included negotiating with the Cherokee Indians. He escorted a delegation of Indians to Washington, and once there, was charged with violating U.S. law by preventing the smuggling of "Negroes" from Florida (under Spanish domain at this time) to the West.

many West Tennessee citizens by supporting the addition of an East Tennessee brigade to the militia of the Western District. This was insulting to the people of the area who felt every bit as capable and important as those in East Tennessee. His enmity with Judge John Overton did not help him either. Even though Andrew Jackson, the "king" of Tennessee politics at this time, had supported Crockett in the past, he could not help him out of this blunder regarding the militia.

The next Tennessee campaign was the gubernatorial race of 1825. William Carroll had little trouble. He was politically

---

Houston, who denied any such wrongdoing on his part, became incensed by such charges against his national loyalty and resigned his position as Indian agent.

Houston again returned to Nashville, where he studied law with James Trimble. Although he did not study the required eighteen months, Houston passed the bar after only six months and opened his own law office in Lebanon, Tennessee. Soon he became adjutant general of Tennessee. In 1819 he took over as district attorney for Nashville, serving in this position for one year, and then returning to the private practice of law. In 1821 he was elected major general of the Tennessee Militia. In August 1822 he was elected to the U.S. House of Representatives (the term began in 1823). He was reelected to the term beginning in 1825. By 1827 he was an extremely popular and colorful figure in Tennessee. He was a flamboyant and sometimes outlandish dresser, standing over six feet tall, and held a prominent bearing. All this, combined with his close friendship with Andrew Jackson positioned him well to run for governor.

He was elected governor of Tennessee in 1827. He enjoyed his tenure and his popularity continued to grow. He began to seek reelection in 1829, facing former Governor William Carroll, who announced his reelection bid the day before Houston's marriage. On January 22, 1829, Eliza Allen and Houston were married. By April 16, 1829, about three months into his marriage, they were separated and Eliza returned home. Houston, embarrassed and unable to face social and political fallout, resigned as governor of Tennessee on April 16, 1829, five and a half months early. He then left Tennessee and traveled west into the region of what is now northwest Arkansas and Oklahoma to live with the Cherokees. He built a log home, lived with an Indian wife named Tiana Rogers, and accumulated cattle, horses, and a couple of slaves. However, Houston, who was forever spirited, left behind his Indian home, family, and ways when he heard of the Texas war. He went to Texas in 1833 and eventually became commander in chief of the Texas army, leading and winning the Texas Revolution against the Mexicans. He was married a third time, in 1840, to Margaret Moffatt Lea, of Marion, Alabama. They eventually had eight children. Houston served two terms as president of Texas. He served as U.S. senator from Texas for thirteen years (from 1846 when Texas was admitted into the Union until 1859). In 1848 he sought the nomination for president, but the Democrat National Convention nominated Lewis Cass. In 1852 Houston again sought the Democrat nomination for president, but this time he lost the nomination to Franklin Pierce. While still in the U.S. Senate, he again sought the nomination for president in 1856 as a Know-Nothing candidate. (Houston had previously fought to win Texas's independence and admission into the Union. He became separated from his Democrat colleagues because of the issue of slavery and the desire by some Democrats to secede from the Union.) However, Millard Fillmore was nominated as the presidential candidate, and Andrew Jackson Donelson was nominated for vice president. In 1859 Houston was elected governor of Texas. When the Texas legislature met to secede from the Union, Houston left office in 1861 by refusing to become a Confederate. He died on July 26, 1863, in Huntsville, Texas. His wife died in 1867 in the yellow fever epidemic. (Portrait painting by Washington B. Cooper courtesy of TSM) unbeatable as he continued to work for democratic reforms. He was also a smart politician, taking great care to maintain cordial relations with as many politicians as possible. Carroll was reelected governor of Tennessee in 1825.

Crockett's 1824 unsuccessful congressional campaign had not dissuaded him. In the federal elections of 1826 he ran again. He managed to recover from the 1824 fiasco and was elected to the U.S. House of Representatives representing West Tennessee.

Andrew Jackson may have been the leader of the national politics of Tennessee and a favorite son, but by 1827 Governor William Carroll dominated most state politics. In 1827 Carroll could not run to succeed himself—the Tennessee constitutional limit for governor was three consecutive two-year terms—without sitting out one term. Since Sam Houston was a Jackson loyalist, there was talk that he might be allowed to stand in for the governor. Carroll would not necessarily oppose this, as long as Houston stayed only one term and did not get in the way of Carroll's own political ambition. Carroll had hopes of becoming the next U.S. senator from Tennessee. However, the popular vote and the vote in the legislature were two different things. If Carroll were to win the Senate seat he would have to obtain the support of Andrew Jackson and there was no way Jackson would support Carroll over incumbent John Eaton. (Eaton had filled the unexpired (Class 1) term of Senator George W. Campbell via appointment by Governor McMinn in 1818. He was later officially elected by the legislature in 1819 to complete the term scheduled to end on March 3, 1821.) Carroll may have wanted the Senate seat, but he was viewed as an outsider to Jackson's inner circle. When John Eaton was reelected by the Tennessee legislature for a second full term in the November 1826 vote, Carroll's suspicions of Jackson were reinforced.

In spite of his distrust, Governor Carroll was concerned about his political viability, and cooperated with Jackson to a certain extent. Now the Jackson faction wanted him to support Sam Houston for governor. Houston had remained loyal to the Jackson clan, had served in the U.S. House of Representatives for Tennessee, and appeared to be the kind of supporter Jackson would like to have in the governor's chair while he ran for president. An arrangement was discussed for Houston to serve as governor from 1827 until 1829, then bow out again for Carroll. Carroll would have to wait to see if Houston would keep his agreement to run only one term.

But, Carroll was not a man to allow another to control his destiny, not even Andrew Jackson. His concern over the Jackson faction's strength and his own loss of autonomy led to the encouragement of Newton Cannon, who was tied to the old Sevier faction (and a known enemy of Jackson's), to run against Houston.

In the gubernatorial election of 1827, Sam Houston faced not only Colonel Newton Cannon, but former Governor Willie Blount, John C. McLemore, R. C. Foster, Felix Grundy, and John Rhea. With the increase in candidates for the office came an increase in tension and rancor.

Sam Houston was a bit unusual. He had run away from home as a teen to live and learn with the Indians. This experience had an impact upon him, and he adapted some of the ways and dress of the Indians. Restlessness, unusual clothing, and a driving ambition combined to create a unique and likable personality and flamboyant style that was well accepted in this campaign and that had helped put him in

Sam Houston was well aware of the importance of image. He flamboyantly fostered the self-image of a larger-than-life figure throughout his life. Above, Houston is depicted as Marius, the noblest Roman, in both cartoon and classical form. (Courtesy of TSLA)

Congress. He had been serving in the House of Representatives since his election in August 1822.

Houston had a long history of allegiance to Jackson. He had served him during the Creek War and in many of Jackson's political maneuvers and elections, and Jackson in turn helped him. Jackson was usually strong in Middle and West Tennessee, but Cannon did better than expected in these regions of the state. East Tennessee was not Jackson's stronghold since the transfer of the state capital from Knoxville to Nashville. However, Sam Houston was from East Tennessee and the idea of electing a favorite son prevailed over factional affiliation. Houston, only thirty-four years old, won 44,426 votes to 33,410 for Cannon. He was inaugurated governor of Tennessee on October 1, 1827.

Tennessee's First President

In 1825, Andrew Jackson resigned from the U.S. Senate in order to campaign full-time for president. He felt, along with others, that he had been cheated in the election of 1824. The Tennessee legislature nominated him again for president as quickly as 1825, and by 1827 the campaign was under way for the 1828 presidential election. The disparagement in this campaign sank to new lows. The Clay/Adams-controlled newspapers reviewed the questionable details of Jackson's courtship and marriage to his wife, Rachel Donelson Jackson, claiming that Jackson had "seen" Rachel while she was still married to her former husband. Then Jackson counterattacked with "corrupt bargain" charges referring to the Adams and Clay trade off of cabinet posts in exchange for engineering the House of Representatives' vote for Adams in 1824.

Jackson's campaign helped redefine American politics. The old political organizations began to change as Jackson's popularity gained strength. He was the candidate of the common man who opposed the power structure of Washington politicians. As his campaign gained momentum, his large popular base of support created a "Jacksonian" political party which opposed the old order, the congressional caucus, and the "corrupt bargain." The opposition to Jackson faced growing odds. This was not a battle between the old Federalist and Democrat-Republican orders, but rather between the Washington elite and the people. A division in the ranks of the old

ANDREW JACKSON was born in Waxhaw, South Carolina, on March 15, 1767, to Andrew and Elizabeth Hutchinson Jackson. Jackson's father died before his birth. When he was only a young boy, between 1780–1781, he and his brother Robert fought in the Battle of Hanging Rock and were captured by the British. While imprisoned, the brothers contracted smallpox and Robert died. After Jackson was released, in 1781, he learned the saddler's trade. A few months later, when Jackson was only fourteen his mother died of cholera and he went to live with relatives. He received very little early education, attending school conducted by Robert McCulloch for a short while. He worked from 1783 to 1784 as a teacher in Waxhaw. When he was seventeen, in 1785, he began to read law with Spruce McCay, in the town of Salisbury, North Carolina. He also studied with John Stokes. Completing his studies in 1787, he was admitted to the bar in North Carolina on September 26. He drifted around North Carolina practicing law for a year, and for a period of time, tended a store in Martinsville. In 1788 John McNairy, who had been appointed superior court judge for the Western District of North Carolina (which stretched to the Mississippi River), appointed Jackson as public prosecutor for the district. In 1788 Jackson moved to Jonesboro, Tennessee, and began practicing law. That same year, he fought his first duel, with Waightstill Avery; however, no one was injured since both men fired into the air following a pre-duel agreement.

In 1788 Jackson moved to the settlement of Nashville and continued to practice law. On February 15, 1791, he was made attorney general for the Mero (Middle Tennessee) District of North Carolina. He married Rachel Donelson Robards in August 1791, but on January 17, 1794, a second ceremony was performed after Rachel clarified her divorce from her previous husband. They had no children.

Jackson became Tennessee's first member of the U.S. House of Representatives in 1796, when Tennessee was admitted to the Union, and served from 1796 until 1797. In September, 1797, the legislature elected Andrew Jackson to the U.S. Senate for a term that was to last from September 26, 1797, until March 3, 1803; however, he resigned in April 1798, returned to Tennessee, and was elected to the state superior court of Tennessee on December 20, 1798. In February 1802, he was elected major general of the Tennessee Militia.

On May 30, 1806, Jackson fought a duel in which he killed Charles Dickinson. Several years later, in September 1813, he was injured in a gunfight with Jesse and Thomas Hart Benton in order would not be able to overcome Jackson's support; therefore, a "coalition" developed in order to oppose Jackson. President Adams was part of this coalition, and the House of Representatives was comprised of "Jacksonian" and "Coalition" representatives. In the midterm elections, under President Adams, the Jackson Democrats took control. The Twentieth Congress which would serve from 1827 until 1829 would be made up of 119 Jackson Democrats to 94 Coalition members in the House and 28 Jackson Democrats to 20 Coalition members in the Senate. By now public sentiment was moving solidly in favor of Jackson.

By 1828 the campaign was in full swing, and the entire nation knew about the "corrupt bargain" and the slanderous attacks on Jackson and his wife. Jackson's enemies alleged improprieties in the courtship and marriage of the Jacksons, and they attacked

---

Nashville. Under his leadership of the Tennessee Militia between 1812 and 1815, his troops defeated the Creek Indians at Horseshoe Bend in March 1814, establishing his military reputation. He was made major general in the U.S. Army and commanded the Seventh Military District, soundly defeating the British at New Orleans on January 8, 1815. In March 1818, he invaded Spanish Florida, capturing St. Marks on April 6 and Pensacola on May 24. Because of some questionable methods used in his Florida invasion, and the jealousy of political competitors, Jackson's congressional enemies attempted to censure him, but this was rejected on February 8, 1819. He was made governor of Florida Territory in March 1821, accepted the land transfer from the Spanish on July 17, and resigned his post on November 13.

Returning to Tennessee, Jackson was nominated for president by the Tennessee legislature, on July 20, 1822, then reelected by the legislature as U.S. senator. The term ran from March 4, 1823, until March 3, 1829; however he again resigned, on October 14, 1825, to prepare to run for president. He lost this election for president to John Quincy Adams in 1824, but ran again the next race and was elected president in November 1828. His wife, Rachel, died shortly after his election. He ran for reelection in 1832 against Henry Clay and won. During his presidency Jackson worked successfully to reduce the national debt. He forcibly removed the Indians from the eastern region of the continent, exercised his veto power, fought the Bank of the United States, worked for the western expansion of the United States, and survived physical and political assassination attempts. He dealt with the nullification issue, in which South Carolina attempted to avoid federal tariff laws and planned to secede from the Union. Jackson demanded that France pay for damages to American shipping during the Napoleonic Wars and ignited a diplomatic crisis. In 1836 the French paid four past due installments and the disagreement was resolved. On March 3, 1837, he recognized Texas's independence and on March 4, 1837, he completed his terms as president.

Jackson was the first president to dominate Congress. He altered the balance of accepted power between the presidency and Congress, making the presidency much more powerful. His determination to maintain the Union and his impact on the power of the presidency set the stage for later efforts to preserve the Union.

After retiring from the presidency he returned to his home, the Hermitage, outside Nashville, Tennessee. He joined the Presbyterian Church on July 15, 1838. He continued to support the Democratic Party, the annexation of Texas, and in 1844, he endorsed James K. Polk for president. Jackson died on June 8, 1845, and was buried in the gardens of the Hermitage beside his wife. (Portrait painting by Otis Bass courtesy of TSM)

Rachel's dignity. Jackson was incensed. Journalists throughout the young nation got into the act. The character and integrity of Jackson and the political processes which elected Adams were put on trial in newspapers throughout the country. Charges and slander kept the media alert, the public attentive, and tension high. Communication might have been slower in those days, but the process of attack and counterattack was the same as modern day, and helped to shape the philosophies of the candidates and their followers. The now clearly defined political division was set forth for the public, and this division developed into a new political system with parties representing the differing philosophies.

Jackson was also attacked by his opponents for executing six deserters from the Creek Indian War days. He was criticized for his duels, his short association with Aaron Burr, and his aggression in Florida, including the hanging of two British men for complicity with the Spanish during his military movements in Florida. Jackson's supporters kept up their campaign against the "corrupt bargain" and accused Adams of being nothing more than an old Federalist maintaining aristocratic power.

During this period of time, balloting methods varied between states and was spread out over a period of weeks. Voting began in September and ended in November. Unlike the election of 1824, in the election of 1828 the voters were not only voting for a president, they were sending a message—a demand for fair representation. When all the votes were tallied, Jackson (Democrat) received 647,276 popular votes to 508,064 for Adams (National Republican); and 178 to 83 electoral votes. Jackson carried the West, the South, and Pennsylvania, part of New York, Maine, and Maryland. His vote in Tennessee was a resounding 44,193 to only 2,240 for Adams. By early December, Jackson knew he had been elected the seventh president of the United States. The glory of victory was diminished on December 22, 1828, when Rachel Jackson died from what was probably heart disease. Her husband charged that her death had been hastened by the campaign slanders. He was still grieving when he was inaugurated in March 1829.

As a result of the political battle of this election, newly defined political parties emerged. The party of Jackson would be called the Democratic Party. The opposition to Jackson and his supporters would no longer be called the Coalition Party. They would become the National Republicans. (This party would last until the mid-1830s when the Whig Party would develop.) The election of 1828 placed 139 Democrats and 74 National Republicans in the U.S. House and 26 Democrats and 22 National Republicans in the U.S. Senate. Democrats increased strength in the House, but they declined by two seats in the Senate. The Senate decline was not directly representative of public sentiment since Senate seats were still filled by state legislatures. This election demonstrated a steady trend toward Jackson, the new Democratic Party, and an out-and-out revolt against the old way (the congressional caucus system) of electing a president.

In 1828 the Tennessee state legislature faced an election to fill the U.S. Senate seat held by Hugh Lawson White. White had been appointed by Governor Carroll in 1825 to fill the unexpired term of Andrew Jackson's seat (Class 2). Former Governor Carroll had put White in office but fully expected to be elected himself upon the next vacancy. Again, as with the reelection of John Eaton in November 1826, Carroll faced a situation in which an incumbent, who was a

Andrew Jackson, seventh president of the United States, on his horse, Sam Patch. (Courtesy of TSLA)

close associate of Andrew Jackson, held office and again Carroll lost. White was elected to a full term which began on March 4, 1829, and ended on March 3, 1835.

While Jackson was campaigning for president, Sam Houston enjoyed his time as governor and gained considerable fame and popularity. When Jackson was elected president, Houston contemplated using his own influence and that of his mentor to continue furthering his goals. As governor, he had been careful in his decisions and left little to be criticized. He slowly moved away from the Carroll wing of Jackson followers and left no indication that he planned to give up his new office. With Jackson as president and so much national prominence coming from so illustrious a state, Governor Houston appeared to be headed for national fame, possibly even the presidency.

However, his popularity began to suffer when it became apparent he might not step aside for the upcoming gubernatorial race. He had been a member of the Masonic Lodge in Nashville, and in 1828 his past participation in dueling became an issue with the lodge, which then expelled him. Additionally, former Governor Carroll was incensed that he had once again been overlooked for the U.S. Senate in the 1828 Tennessee legislative election, which favored Hugh Lawson White. Carroll needed no more convincing that being nice to Jackson's political power brokers would not serve his own career. He had no intention of allowing the upstart Houston to retake the governor's seat without a fight. In addition, Carroll was still irritated that Houston had the audacity to seek his support when he ran in 1827, while he rode into office on the support of the Jackson power brokers. Carroll knew that Houston was simply trying to placate him while the Jackson political coalition further undercut his hold in Tennessee.

The ambitious Houston was now near thirty-six years of age. If he were to go any further he knew it was time to settle down. His eyes were set on eighteen-year-old Eliza Allen of Gallatin, Tennessee. Her family was prominent in Middle Tennessee. John Allen, her father, was a friend of Andrew Jackson, and her uncles Robert and Campbell Allen had fought in the War of 1812 under Jackson. Robert had served in Congress and there met Sam Houston, who was introduced to Eliza when she was only thirteen years old during a visit to the Allen home (which Jackson had visited many times). Although twice Eliza's age, Houston was a war hero, leading political figure, and a gallant, mysterious, charming gentleman. Soon, Eliza and her family decided that Houston would be a fine and suitable husband.

On January 22, 1829, they were married in a candlelight ceremony at the Allen home, in Sumner County. Although Andrew Jackson could not attend this glittering social event since he was on his way to Washington to be inaugurated as president of the United States, he gave the couple a silver service that belonged to his late wife Rachel. The day after the wedding, the couple set out for Nashville, spent a night on the way at the home of Robert Martin in Locust Grove, and then stayed for a few days at the home of Houston's cousin, Robert McEwen, on the Gallatin Pike. After arriving in Nashville, they moved into the Nashville Inn.

The day before Houston's wedding, William Carroll announced that he would run for the governor's seat. He knew that Houston planned to run for reelection and that President Jackson was likely to have encouraged it. Carroll, not one to be pushed around, began planning his attack before Houston's wedding.

Eight days after the wedding Houston formerly announced he would stand for reelection. Under ordinary circumstances, this is what one might expect. However, former Governor Carroll had other ideas and expected Houston to vacate the position and throw his support his way. After all, Carroll was the mentor and Houston the subordinate. But Houston had too much to gain and dared to challenge the chief. The question on everyone's mind was who the president would side with. Houston was soon openly telling folks in Tennessee that he had the president's support. The campaign began in earnest, with each intent on victory. By April the candidates were on the stump, and Houston immediately saw proof of his popularity.

A Governor Resigns; Destiny Altered

Houston's aspirations were quickly dampened as personal tragedy altered all of his plans. Something had happened in the new marriage. It is not clearly known, but it is possible that the glamour of the marriage of a young lady to a governor quickly melted into the reality of marriage to an older man. In any event the physical attraction normally present in the early stages of marriage may not have been strong enough. By April 16, 1829, only three months into the marriage, they were separated and Eliza returned

WILLIAM HALL was born on February 1, 1775, in Surry County, North Carolina. His parents moved from Mecklenburg, North Carolina, about 1779 and eventually settled near Bledsoe Lick, which is today known as Castalian Springs (near Gallatin, Tennessee), in Sumner County. When William was twelve years old, during the Indian Wars he saw his family ambushed by Indians. His father, Major William Hall, was scalped; two brothers, two brothers-in-law, a sister, and her child were all killed by the Indian hatchet. Young William quickly became a man and tilled the land that Major Hall had bought and settled. He did well as a farmer and married Polly Alexander, whose parents had migrated from Iredell County, North Carolina. They eventually had eight children. Her father, William Locke Alexander, like Major Hall, had served in the military, fighting in the Revolutionary War. Also of note, six members of the Alexander family signed the 1775 Mecklenburg Declaration of Independence.

William Hall served as a county sheriff and as brigadier general in the Creek War. He was well positioned in the Jackson political coalition through his friendship with Jackson, as well as William Carroll. In 1797 Hall was elected to the Tennessee house, and he remained in the legislature for six years. Then in 1821 he was elected to the state senate, where he later served as speaker. When Governor Sam Houston resigned, Hall, according to state statute, became governor ad interim.

Hall served as governor of Tennessee for five and a half months. He essentially continued the programs of Sam Houston and his predecessor, William Carroll. These included revising the penal codes, setting up prisons, and improving education, currency, and interest rate laws. Hall retired from the governor's seat, allowing William Carroll to be reelected, and returned to his home and farm, Locust Acres. In 1831, he ran for Congress and was elected. However, he served only one term and again retired to his home in 1833. He lived the remainder of his life there and died on October 7, 1856. (Photograph courtesy of TSLA) home. Word spread quickly, with Carroll, of course, fueling the spread. The Allen family was embarrassed. Houston, refusing explanations, would not defile his wife's character and willingly accepted all blame rather than defend himself possibly at her expense. Gossip took all forms. "The tongues of scandal hesitated at nothing. Tales of the marriage-bed were bawled from the roof-trees and Sam Houston was burned in effigy before a howling crowd in the court-house yard at Gallatin" (James 1929). Houston, embarrassed and unable to face social and political fallout, resigned as governor of Tennessee on April 16, 1829. (He served from 1827 until April 1829, resigning five and a half months early.) Speaker of the Tennessee senate, William Hall, a Democrat-Republican from Sumner County, completed Houston's unexpired term as governor. After his resignation, Sam Houston left Tennessee and traveled west into the region of what is now northwest Arkansas and Oklahoma to live with the Cherokees.

In the midst of Houston's problems, Senator John Eaton resigned his Senate seat on March 9, 1829, to become secretary of war under President Andrew Jackson (Eaton held this post until he resigned on June 18, 1831). Felix Grundy was appointed by the governor to take the U.S. Senate seat (Class 1) and was subsequently elected to hold the seat. (He took office on October 19, 1829, completed the term of office, was elected to a full term beginning March 4, 1833, and resigned July, 4, 1838, when appointed U.S. attorney general by President Martin Van Buren.)

With Houston out of the way, the infighting for power subsided within the Andrew Jackson political coalition. Eaton's resigned Senate seat was filled and the governor's seat was essentially a foregone conclusion. Governor Hall would have an uphill battle if he were to run against former Governor Carroll in the 1829 gubernatorial contest. Carroll had little standing in his way and he was elected for a fourth term as governor of Tennessee. The Democrat-Republican from Nashville would serve another three consecutive two-year terms as governor of Tennessee (from 1829 to 1835).

In Carroll's fourth term, he was finally able to obtain legislation for penal reform. Up until this time horse thieves were hung. Lesser crimes might result in the perpetrators having their ears nailed or cut off, or being publicly whipped or branded. Governor Carroll worked to halt the physical abuse and give lesser criminals less harsh punishment. The 1829 laws halted criminal whipping and the nailing or severing of body parts. He also worked to reform debtors' laws, but it took several more years before much could be accomplished.

Although there was no governor's race or U.S. Senate seat to fill in 1830, Tennessee's U.S. representative positions were up for election. One election was particularly tumultuous. Davy Crockett, who had been an early friend and follower of Andrew Jackson, was running for reelection. He had previously had the support of Jackson's friends in Memphis. Unfortunately for Crockett, he refused to vote for a bill, favored by Jackson, which he felt was unfair to the Indians. When Crockett returned to his district, he quickly found that:

> a storm had raised against me sure enough; and it was echoed from side to side, and from end to end of my district, that I had turned against Jackson. This was considered an unpardonable sin. I was hunted down like a wild varment, and in this hunt every little newspaper in the district, and every little pin-hook lawyer, was engaged (Crockett)

Crockett quickly understood the consequences of failing to cooperate. Angered, he denounced Jackson as a tyrant and "worse than the Caesars" (Keating 1888). His comments did not please Jackson's friends, although they sounded good to the old Federalists of Boston who dreamed of seizing national control from Jackson and the Democrats. Jackson's supporters were already preparing for the 1832 presidential contest and were in no mood to tolerate the dissenter. Some West Tennessee Jackson supporters began to turn against Crockett.

Judge John Overton and M. B. Winchester went to work to defeat Crockett. Jackson made sure that Memphis received some federal assistance, a stage route through town, and some United States public printing for its newspaper. Overton and Winchester reminded the public of Jackson's loyalty to them and the fact that Jackson would soon stand for reelection in 1832. Their efforts produced results. Crockett was defeated in his campaign of 1830. However, this was not the last that Overton would see of Crockett. Crockett knew that Overton had been responsible for narrowing his margin of victory in the previous election of 1828, and he was none too pleased that Overton helped defeat him in 1830. He remained determined to run again.

With short, two-year gubernatorial terms, no sooner had William Carroll taken back the position than it was time to run for reelection. The gubernatorial race of 1831 was relatively easy for the incumbent governor. He who worked to improve the plight of the common man still received his vote of confidence. Once Carroll was reelected, Tennesseans focused on the presidential contest of 1832.

Andrew Jackson was politically strong, not only in Tennessee, but throughout the nation. However, those outside his political inner circle within the state of Tennessee began to form a strong base of opposition. The opposition was led by Andrew Erwin, and Jackson's supporters were led by John Overton. Jackson's major political supporters in Tennessee beside Overton were John Eaton and William B. Lewis. Tennessee's U.S. Senators Hugh Lawson White and Felix Grundy and U.S. Representatives James K. Polk (Columbia) and Cave Johnson (Clarksville) were supporters of Overton's political network and therefore of Jackson. They squared off against anti-Jackson leaders Newton Cannon, Theoderick F. Bradford, and Andrew Erwin of Middle Tennessee; John Williams and William B. Carter of East Tennessee; and Davy Crockett of West Tennessee. Crockett would in fact run to regain his former seat to represent the Western District of Tennessee in the U.S. House in the 1832 campaign as an anti-Jackson candidate. Governor Carroll, U.S. Representative John Bell, and state Senator Theoderick Bradford had played both sides of the political fence up until now. (The governor would later support Jackson's man for president in 1836 while providing patronage for the Erwin faction. State Senator Bradford, Representative Bell, and Senator White would later become more overt in their opposition to Jackson.)

The major issue of the 1832 presidential election centered on the rechartering of the Bank of the United States. Jackson had witnessed the power, influence, and maneuvering of the bank and its head, Nicholas Biddle. He felt that the bank had become so powerful that it not only had too much control over the national economy, but it had too much political and public influence, overriding the power bestowed on public officials by the electorate. Because of

FELIX GRUNDY was born in Berkeley County, Virginia, on September 11, 1777, to English parents. He had six older brothers. His family moved to Brownsville, Pennsylvania, while he was very young. Around 1780 they moved to Kentucky. There he received his education at the Academy of Bardstown, Kentucky. He was orphaned at an early age. His mother had wanted him to become a physician, but he studied law under George Nicholas and also developed a remarkable public-speaking ability. Grundy was a member of the Kentucky constitutional convention in 1799 (which revised the constitution), representing Washington County, and also served in the Kentucky legislature from 1802 to 1806. In 1806 he was appointed as judge of the Supreme Court of Errors and Appeals. Grundy, at twenty-nine, became chief justice of the Kentucky Supreme Court when Judge Todd created the vacancy by accepting an appointment to the Supreme Court of the United States. He moved to Nashville from Kentucky in 1807. Nashville had by now become a very attractive community for frontier America, and it would prove to be a good move for Grundy. He served as a member of the U.S. House of Representatives, representing the Nashville region, from 1811 until 1814. In Congress, he was appointed to the Committee on Foreign Affairs and pushed for America to declare war against England in 1812. He became a political leader and staunch supporter of Andrew Jackson. After his first couple of tours in the U.S. Congress, he decided not to run for reelection, and returned to Tennessee to practice law. He served in the Tennessee state legislature from 1814 to 1819, and as a U.S. senator from 1829 (replacing John Eaton, who was appointed secretary of war) until 1833. He was reelected and served until 1838 when he was appointed U.S. attorney general by President Van Buren. He served one year and then resigned to go back to the U.S. Senate when he was again elected in 1839. Grundy died on December 19, 1840, while home in Nashville. (Photograph courtesy of SHO)

this, Jackson had vetoed the bank rechartering bill. His opponents tried to use this against him, but he took his case to the people, who loved and trusted him. Jackson was probably the only politician of the day who was strong enough to challenge the Bank of the United States and veto the bill.

In 1832 Jackson and his Democrats were reelected by a substantial margin. Jackson received 688,242 popular votes to 473,462 for Clay, who ran as a National Republican; and 101,051 for William Wirt (219 to 49 to 7 electoral votes). The House stood at 147 Democrats to 53 anti-Masonics and 60 other; the Senate was now composed of 20 Democrats to 20 National Republicans and 8 other. Davy Crockett had run for his old seat as an anti-Jackson candidate and was narrowly reelected to Congress in 1832. However, all of Jackson's Tennessee friends were against him and since Jackson had been reelected, Crockett knew he faced serious political adversity.

Birth of the Whigs

A fracture which began in the Tennessee political dynasty would rupture throughout the nation. The break was a natural one and occurred among some of the leading men of Tennessee. There were many Jackson supporters who were capable of holding office, and there were many who felt that they deserved Jackson's support for advancement. However, not everyone could obtain recognition or office, no matter how deserving. Additionally, the Jackson team expected cooperation. To go against Jackson's wishes on nearly any matter meant risking rejection from the team or political reprisal. This struggle for position by Tennessee politicians and the dictatorial nature of the Jackson political faction played major roles in the development of the two-party system in Tennessee and the nation.

Jackson maintained popularity for a while after his reelection by standing for the preservation of the Union. This was hardly an issue that anyone could disagree with—except John Calhoun. In 1832 Vice President John Calhoun forwarded the cause of "states' rights" over nationalistic mandates. Calhoun felt that a state had the right to nullify federal legislation it did not agree with. He proposed that if a state held a convention to nullify a federal law and three-fourths of the other states failed to uphold the federal law in a ratification process, then the state could void the law within its borders. He also felt that if the complaining state was overridden by a three-fourths ratification process, then the state could still avoid the law by withdrawing from the Union.

In the latter part of 1832 the concept of nullification was put to the test when Calhoun's home state of South Carolina decided to nullify the tariffs imposed by federal legislation in 1828 and 1832. The theoretical controversy was now real. Preservation of the Union was a strong political ideal to President Andrew Jackson who had fought for independence and lost family and friends in the bloody struggle. He had little tolerance for the idea of a state's right to leave the Union and issued a Nullification Proclamation on December 10, 1832. In the proclamation he forewarned military intervention in South Carolina to enforce the perpetuation of the Union and the tariff. Jackson received support in Tennessee, Washington, D.C., and around the nation for his stance. The popularity of Jackson's positions and programs were now at a high point.

When it came to his Indian removal policy, Jackson did not support the rights of the federal government as he had in the nullification crisis. When the Cherokees won a Supreme Court case in 1832, protecting Cherokee autonomy, Jackson refused to comply. Instead, he ordered the U.S. Army to begin preparation for forced removal, resulting in the 1938 "Trail of Tears." By the end of Jackson's administration, almost all Indians in the East—Creek, Cherokee, Choctaw, and Chickasaw—had been moved west of the Mississippi.

By the time of the 1833 gubernatorial race, the reelection of William Carroll was essentially a foregone conclusion. The state had grown out of the depression he inherited when he went into office in 1821, and he had successfully achieved democratic reform. He still planned on pushing a constitutional convention. He had twice, during his first six years in office, tried to hold a convention, but the vote had failed the test of the people. When he returned to the governor's office after his two-year hiatus, he tried again in 1831, but it again failed. However, in 1833 a democratic zeal had gripped the populous. Most of the support for a more democratic constitution came from the rural areas of western and Middle Tennessee. Opposition came from East Tennessee and Davidson County in Middle Tennessee. Tennessee voted by over eight thousand votes in favor of holding a constitutional convention, which was scheduled to take place in 1834.

Eighteen thirty-three was also the year for the state legislature to select a U.S. senator (Class 1). Felix Grundy had been serving in this position (after the resignation of John

Eaton), but now John Eaton, along with John Bell and Ephraim Hubbard Foster, all wanted to go to the Senate. Eaton had resigned from Jackson's cabinet in 1831 because of a controversy over the social acceptance of his wife. The competition was fierce, and endless rounds of ballots were cast in the legislature. Foster, who had served as Jackson's personal secretary during the Creek War (between 1813–1815), had developed a fair amount of animosity toward his old boss over the years. Once he determined he could not win, he marshaled his support against John Eaton, who was very close to Jackson. Although Grundy was also a Jackson supporter, Foster felt more of a kinship toward Grundy than toward Eaton. By bolstering Grundy's support with his, Grundy was able to be elected on the fifty-fifth ballot of the legislature. After the election, Foster completely broke with Jackson and became a leading member of a new political group forming in Tennessee—the Whigs. (Grundy was elected to continue in office, serving in the term from March 4, 1833, until March 4, 1839; however, he resigned on July 4, 1838, to become attorney general under President Martin Van Buren. Ephraim Foster was then elected to fill Grundy's spot in the Senate, but by then Foster was a solid Whig.)

When the Tennessee state constitutional convention met on May 19, 1834, in Nashville, many of the participants were less known politically. However, Adam Huntsman (who would defeat Davy Crockett for the U.S. House election in 1834), Newton Cannon (U.S. representative and future governor), Willie Blount (former governor), Terry H. Cahal, Francis B. Fogg, John A. McKinney, and William B. Carter were some of the better known political leaders who did attend. Prior to this meeting, taxes had been equal, no matter the size or value of a holding, an inequitable advantage for the large landowner. County officials served for life and were selected by the state legislature. The county court members then appointed the sheriffs, trustees, and other county officials. This system unfairly empowered lifetime control of county government to a select few individuals.

Under the new constitution, land taxes would be more fairly proportioned according to the land's value. In addition, the number of state representatives would be made to coincide with the population of a particular area. The people would be given the right to elect county officials. Free Negroes would be denied the right to vote under the new code. Any man found guilty of dueling would be denied the right to hold office. Judges would have to run for office rather than enjoy lifetime appointments. Ministers would be prohibited from holding office. A provision designed to exclude alcoholics was defeated. The members of the convention voted to submit their proposals to the public for approval. In March 1835, the proposals passed 42,666 to 17,691. Governor Carroll's push for democratic reform in Tennessee paralleled Andrew Jackson's rise in national popularity, the growing desire for national democratic reform, and the enthusiasm for more equitable representation of the West in the politics of the nation's capital.

By the time of Davy Crockett's 1832 reelection, his popularity had waned and he had won only narrowly. By 1834, he was deeply allied with Jackson's enemies. His opponent for the U.S. representative election was Adam Huntsman, who had lost a leg in an Indian battle. Crockett had great confidence in his own popularity, nurtured by his backwoodsman humor and style. He bragged that "he had great hopes of writing one more book, and that shall be the second fall of Adam, for he is on the eve of an almighty thrashing" (Crockett n.d.). But Congressman Crockett had several factors coalescing against him. He had to fight against the power of Jackson and his friends. Governor Carroll, the consummate politician and part-time enemy of Jackson, was expert at knowing when to help his own cause. He also opposed Crockett's reelection in 1834. The financially influential men from Jackson, Tennessee, the leading city of his district, were supporting Huntsman. President Jackson's men were appointed as poll judges and officers, allowing a distinct advantage for Huntsman (these were the days of numerous opportunities to control poll counts in elections). Jackson also had Congressman Crockett's pay and mileage reimbursement sent to his constituents in the district. When the results were finally all in, Crockett lost to Huntsman by 230 votes. He wrote about the election in his autobiography on August 11, 1835, from his home in Weakley County, expressing his view that the election had been stolen. Though obviously not in good humor, he attended a constituent meeting and warned his old friends that in their victory for Huntsman, they would pay the price. He reminded them that he had lost because he had spoken his mind and the truth against despotic politicians. By not standing up to this kind of politics, they would ultimately be damaged. He reminded them of his service and that he had been "knocked down and dragged out, and that I did not consider it a fair fight any how they could fix it." He concluded by "telling them that I was done with politics for the present, and that they might all go to hell, and I would go to Texas" (Crockett n.d.).

Jackson's power and popularity may have been at an all-time high, but his opposition was growing. Tennessee U.S. Representative John Bell had rebelled against Old Hickory ever since Jackson had opposed him for Speaker of the House in favor of James K. Polk. In 1834, Jackson supported Polk for Speaker, but, Bell maneuvered his own victory on the tenth ballot, using the anti-Jackson forces in Congress to pull it off. From then on, Jackson and Polk became open in their criticism of Bell. Two of Jackson's old friends, Hugh Lawson White and Davy Crockett, had supported the mutiny against him. To make matters worse, Bell and Crockett were among those urging White to run for president in 1836, against the wishes of Jackson who supported Van Buren. This shift had essentially allied them with Jackson's enemies in the North as well as with those who supported the U.S. Bank. This was mutiny to Jackson. He had put all his efforts into dismantling the bank and knew which politicians had sold out to the supporters of the bank in exchange for self-advancement. Not all of Jackson's old friends could see the danger of the political power of the U.S. Bank, and some opposed him on the issue. Jackson's dictatorial nature only served to undermine his intentions.

Actually, several events occurred between 1831 and 1837 which would change Jackson's total dominance of Tennessee and national politics. For one thing, the nation's economy was in poor shape, and people were suffering financially. Other issues weighed heavily on the minds of the politicians and voters. Jackson's fight to end the U. S. Bank was used by his enemies to injure him. The system of national conventions, which Jackson had pushed for, created some controversy. These challenges to his national political stature occurred simultaneously with the growing political animosity within his home state. The number of politicians outside Jackson's inner circle, within Tennessee, began to grow in size and influence.

Hugh Lawson White had been friends with Jackson for almost forty years. Their philosophies were nearly the same, and White had succeeded Jackson to the U.S. Senate when Jackson resigned in 1825. Tennessee was becoming a rich and politically powerful state, and its leaders were often regarded as national figures. White was such a figure, and it was reasonable to assume he was a viable candidate for president in 1836. However, Jackson had allegiances outside Tennessee, having had help from other sectors of the nation to win the presidency in 1828 and 1832. Jackson had offered White a cabinet position in 1831, and had urged him to accept a spot as the 1836 vice presidential candidate under Martin Van Buren. White refused all offers. Influential, financially well-off, and politically powerful himself in Tennessee, he was not a man to be dominated by Jackson, and by all rights he did not have any reason to accept second best. He had gained great respect in the U.S. Senate and had advised and helped Jackson on his way to the presidency. Now White wanted to succeed Jackson to the highest office in the land, and to many around the nation he looked to be a likely candidate. However, Jackson had obligations to Van Buren who was also well positioned in his own right. White did not accept Jackson' s lack of support and began

JOHN BELL was born near Nashville on February 15, 1797. He completed studies at the University of Nashville at age seventeen, was admitted to the bar by 1816, and began his practice in Franklin, Tennessee. He was elected to the state senate in 1817, but did not run for reelection and returned to Nashville to practice law. He married Sally Dickenson in 1818. Together they had four children. In 1826 he ran for U.S. representative as a Democrat and defeated Felix Grundy, serving in Congress from 1827 until 1841. Bell became an enemy of Andrew Jackson by disagreeing over the removal of funds from the U.S. Bank, which Jackson thought was dangerous because of its concentration of financial power. After this break, Bell was no longer a Democrat in good standing. However, it was his support in 1836 of Hugh Lawson White for president against Democrat Martin Van Buren, whom Jackson supported, that forced him to seek other official political affiliation. Even though Bell was for low tariffs and was a Democrat in philosophy, the only party left to him was the Whig Party. After this, the political enmity between him and Jackson continued until Jackson's death.

While in Congress, in 1834 Bell ran against James K. Polk for Speaker of the House in the second session of the Twenty-third Congress and defeated him. He lost the speakership in the next two races. Bell's wife, Sally, died (date uncertain), and around 1835 he married Jane Yeatmen (maiden name Ervin, from Bedford County). In 1840 he supported the Whig candidate for president, William Henry Harrison, and was subsequently appointed by him as secretary of war on March 5, 1841. However, when Harrison died, Tyler, who was a tenuous Whig at best, broke ties with the Whigs. Bell was out of his cabinet position by September 12, 1841, when Tyler replaced the hostile cabinet with his own conservative Democrats. Bell supported James C. Jones over James K. Polk for governor in both 1841 and 1843 and helped carry Tennessee for Whig Henry Clay over James Polk for president in 1844. Then he became a candidate before the state legislature for a U.S.

to formalize his break with Jackson.

Many of Tennessee's leading politicians, who were friends with White, were repulsed by Jackson's support of Van Buren over White as well as by Jackson's dominance of state politics. White and Nashville Congressman John Bell became leaders of the opposition to Jackson in Tennessee. Jackson felt that Bell was too independent and was risking the political influence of Tennessee by failing to go along with him on all the issues before Congress. Bell made it known that he could not support Jackson's plan to assist Van Buren in the presidential election of 1836.

Politicians were not only splitting from Jackson in Tennessee but throughout the nation. He had developed so much animosity by early 1834 that a resolution was passed in the U.S. Senate "censuring" him for taking action not authorized to the president, specifically when he mandated the removal of federal money from the U. S. Bank. Jackson's friends in the Tennessee legislature then proposed a resolution that would in effect enjoin Tennessee's U.S. senators to vote to expunge (to remove the written condemnation of Jackson from the congressional record) the president when the votes were counted in Washington. Senator Grundy was a friend to Jackson and could be expected to support him. Senator White, however, had by now split with Jackson. The Tennessee legislature

---

Senate seat. His main competitor was Spencer Jarnagin, who had fallen from grace within the Whig Party for opposing high tariffs. John Bell was elected U.S. senator on November 22, 1847, after forty-eight ballots. He would serve from 1847 until 1859 (being reelected in 1853).

As a Whig Tennessee U.S. senator, Bell had opposed the annexation of Texas and the Mexican War. Although he was a slave owner, he was opposed to the spread of slavery because of the controversy created each time the United States formed a new state. He felt that the best way to protect the Southern way of life was to stop exacerbating the national issue and allow the reoccurring controversy to subside.

In later years Bell supported Whigs for president and governor. He helped Neill S. Brown become governor in 1847. He also helped carry Tennessee in the Whig column for Winfield Scott for president when nearly the entire nation went Democrat for Franklin Pierce. Bell added significant strength to the Whig Party, but after 1852 the Whig Party disintegrated and Bell was without a party. By the time he was out of the Senate, in 1859, the controversy over slavery had become a national crisis. In 1860 he was nominated as a candidate for president by the Constitutional Union Party. He won the nomination on the second ballot of the convention, defeating former Tennessee Governor Sam Houston. Bell, along with Northern Democrat Stephen Douglas and Southern Democrat John Breckinridge, lost to Republican Abraham Lincoln. After completing his Senate term and the 1860 presidential campaign, Bell returned to his home, near Cumberland Furnace, Tennessee.

After Lincoln was elected president, a Tennessee vote was called for secession; Bell opposed this. He spoke to Lincoln and reassured the people of Tennessee that the federal government would do nothing rash. He led the effort to defeat the call for a secession convention, and it was defeated on February 9, 1861. However, after Lincoln called for troops and made it known that he intended to use force against the South, Bell changed his mind, along with the majority of Tennesseans. Tennessee voted for secession on June 8, 1861. Bell lived the remainder of his life at home until he died on September 10, 1869. He was survived by his wife, who lived until 1876. (Photograph courtesy of SHO) believed White would be bound by honor to follow the dictate or resign his seat from the Senate. The legislative battle over the Tennessee resolution crystallized the resentment developing toward Jackson and showed that the split went to even a local representative level. State Senator James L. Totten (from West Tennessee) and State Representative Joseph C. Guild (from Middle Tennessee) sponsored the Tennessee legislative resolution to instruct to expunge. However state Representative Addison A. Anderson (from East Tennessee) led the effort to table the proposed resolution and went on to commend the resistance of Senator White to vote to expunge.

In order for Jackson's Tennessee enemies to protect their ally Senator White and his future candidacy for president, they moved to reelect him to the U.S. Senate. They made sure to accomplish this prior to the vote on the resolution to expunge. White was reelected to his second full term to the U.S. Senate. (White was first appointed by Governor Carroll to fill the vacancy, then elected in 1825 to fill Jackson's unexpired term and reelected in 1829 to a first full term ending on March 3, 1835. His term was to run from 1835 until March 3, 1841. There was a vacancy from March 4, 1835, until October 5, 1835; he took office on October 6, 1835, and resigned on January 13, 1840.) Then the legislature proceeded to endorse White for president and to criticize Jackson for his dictatorial conduct. The tabled resolution for the instruction to expunge the president could not be removed. No doubt Jackson was furious with the mutineering Tennessee legislature.

The pressure for a Hugh Lawson White presidential candidacy continued. Plans were formalized by a meeting of Tennessee's congressmen in December 1834, at the Washington home of Congressman Balie Peyton. When the endorsement of White was made public, the fracture between the Jackson and anti-Jackson politicians in Tennessee became complete.

There had been no party directly controlled by the public, before Jackson. The congressional caucus nomination system, composed of Washington insiders, had previously held control of the government. Andrew Jackson broke that power. His election, by popular mandate, had helped destroy the weak party system that preceded it, and in its place created a stronger party system supported by a broader base of politicians outside of Washington. However, the power shift was swift and startling and Jackson was left with nearly absolute dominance since there was no other strongly organized competing party. (An example of Jackson's power was reflected by some of those he defeated. In 1832, defeated third party candidate for president, William Wirt, said, ". . . he may be President for life if he chooses" (Remini 1997) However, around 1835 there was finally enough opposition to Jackson that a new party was created. The organizers called themselves the Whigs, the name of the British Party opposed to the king in the eighteenth and nineteenth centuries. It took the form of the liberal party or the party opposed to autocratic rule. The use of the name "Whig" in America was begun by those needing a party label to oppose the "autocratic" rule of Andrew Jackson.

On May 23, 1835, Congressman Bell made the revolt against Jackson public in a speech at stylish Vauxhall Gardens in Nashville. There, Bell began recruiting support for White and antagonism for Jackson. His cause was helped by Jackson's support of Van Buren over the fellow Tennessean. Many Tennesseans resented Jackson for this, but Jackson owed Martin Van

Buren a great deal of political debt—Van Buren's deliverance of the New York delegation helped Jackson win the 1828 election—and Van Buren was both very strong politically and the most likely Democrat to receive the nomination in 1836. Bell showed no consideration to Jackson's debt or the power created for the Tennessee political establishment by virtue of Van Buren's support of Jackson. Additionally, Jackson did not feel that White had a chance, even if he were nominated, to win the presidency. He felt that White's ambition had led him to listen to Bell (whom Jackson considered a jealous troublemaker) and expressed hope that White would come to his senses. But White was surrounded by troublemakers for Jackson. Rather than lose all that had been created, Jackson felt that Van Buren could best hold the coalition together, and Van Buren received Jackson's support. This caused a split among Tennessee politicians based on loyalties to Jackson or loyalties to White. This split would foster stronger, more defined political parties in Tennessee and would also align the parties somewhat along the geographically based political affiliations which lasted into the late twentieth century.

By 1835 the national political parties would be aligned as Democrats and Whigs (the House had 145 Democrats and 98 Whigs; the Senate had 27 Democrats and 25 Whigs). The Whig Party was essentially made up of any politicians opposed to the power of the Jacksonian Democrats. (It would later disintegrate and evolve into the Republican Party.)

In 1835 Congressman James K. Polk again challenged Congressman John Bell for the speakership of the U.S. House of Representatives. President Jackson was open in his support for Polk, and Bell was defeated. James K. Polk became Speaker of the U.S. House of Representatives (as he did when again challenged by Bell in 1837). This open political warfare between Tennesseans on the national scene only served to further alienate political factions within the state toward Jackson.

The vehicle for opposition to Andrew Jackson came through Senator Hugh Lawson White. He was an independent-minded senator and Tennessee politician—too independent as far as Jackson was concerned. Even though he had supported Jackson in the past, he was not closely affiliated with the Jackson faction of Tennessee politics. White was from John Sevier's old territory in East Tennessee and had the support of many descendants of that coalition. His father was a founder of Knoxville, Tennessee. Hugh White was a lawyer, landowner, and banker, as well as U.S. senator. He had also been a judge, state legislator, and a prominent name in Tennessee for years. Many Tennessee Democrats felt that White should become a candidate for president in 1836 and that Jackson should support him. Jackson's loyalty to Van Buren, rather than White, aggravated the split among Tennessee politicians. John Bell led the Tennessee coalition for White, while James K. Polk, Felix Grundy, and others supported Jackson's man for the Democratic presidential nomination, Martin Van Buren.

In dealing with the split among his Democratic friends in Tennessee, Jackson tried to find a solution that would unify everyone in support of one Democratic presidential candidate and therefore preserve the fragile integrity of the new political party. He suggested that a national Democratic convention be organized to nominate one Democratic candidate. (This was the second national Democratic presidential nomination convention. The first national presidential nominating conventions were held for the 1832 election. The Anti-Masonic Party nominated William Wirt in September 1831; the National Republicans nominated Henry Clay in December 1831; and the Democrats nominated Andrew Jackson in May 1832.) However, White's supporters knew that the convention would be controlled by Jackson and that Van Buren would ultimately obtain the nomination. Therefore, the White organization did not send any delegates to the Baltimore Democratic National Convention in 1835. This left the Democratic National Convention, founded by Tennessean Jackson, without any delegates from his own home state. Ever determined to make the convention official, Jackson's supporters found a man from Murfreesboro, Tennessee, who happened to be in Baltimore on personal business, one Edmund Rucker. Rucker was brought into the convention and made the Democratic delegate representing Tennessee. Rucker cast Tennessee's fifteen votes for Van Buren. All of White's and Bell's friends ridiculed the way in which Edmund Rucker was allowed to cast all of Tennessee's votes. The criticism leveled at the Jackson and Van Buren coalition only served to widen the breach. The Tennessee legislature proceeded to defy Jackson by nominating White and ignoring the Democratic convention nomination. White's candidacy continued to consolidate Jackson' s opposition and solidify the new Whig Party of Tennessee, along with all those who were determined to oppose Van Buren. Meanwhile, the Massachusetts legislature nominated Daniel Webster. The Whigs from Ohio nominated William Henry Harrison. Nationally, the Whig Party evolved from politicians left over from the defunct Federalist Party, after Jacksonian Democracy helped to dismantle it, and those left over from Henry Clay's short-lived National Republican Party.

While the uproar began over the presidential nomination, the political shift away from Jackson's men could begin to be felt within Tennessee state politics in 1835. In the Tennessee gubernatorial election there was so much animosity against Jackson for not supporting White, that the Tennessee Whig Party solidified. Governor William Carroll was running for an unprecedented seventh term as governor (his fourth consecutive term). The constitution had been changed in 1834 and Carroll argued that another three consecutive terms would be legal. At least for the present, he was a friend and ally of Andrew Jackson. The president even came to Tennessee to support Van Buren and the governor. Carroll may well have won this election had it occurred two years earlier, before the new Whig party system developed.

But the animosity against Jackson's control of Tennessee politics turned the public tide against Carroll. The Tennessee Whigs' candidate, Newton Cannon, had no easy task taking on Jackson's political power. Throughout Jackson's presidential campaigns, both the loss and victories, his influence reigned supreme in Tennessee. He appointed scores to offices and held the great power of patronage. However, he had made enemies too, and one of those was Hugh Lawson White, arguably the second most powerful politician in Tennessee. Jackson's opposition to him in the upcoming presidential election divided Jackson's base and cost him many political allies.

Newton Cannon had been a longtime enemy of Jackson. He had supported Jackson's opponent in the presidential elections of 1824 and 1828. He had also run against Jackson's protégé, Sam Houston, in the gubernatorial race of 1827. When Jackson helped create the Democratic Party, Cannon broke with many Tennesseans, becoming a National Republican instead. By the time of the Tennessee political revolt

NEWTON CANNON was born on May 22, 1781, in Guilford County, North Carolina. When his family first attempted to migrate to Tennessee, they, along with several other families, were halted by an Indian attack at the Cumberland Gap. Later, they ventured into the dangerous country again and made it to Nashborough (later Nashville). It was here that the Cannons settled.

Cannon received little early education and became a saddler. However, he was ambitious and became a surveyor and a merchant and eventually studied law. He was elected to the state legislature in 1811 as a representative from Williamson County. He and Leah Prior Perkins married in 1813, and had one son, but Leah died after two years of marriage. After serving as a colonel in the Creek War, Cannon was elected to Congress, succeeding Felix Grundy. About 1818 he married Rachel Starnes Welborn and they had eight children. Early in the course of his legal career, he had offended Andrew Jackson during a lawsuit dispute. Jackson "pointed his finger in the young lawyer's direction and warned, 'Young man, I will mark you'" (Phillips 1978). Cannon became Jackson's enemy and opposed him whenever the opportunity arose.

Cannon became governor in 1835 by defeating incumbent Governor William Carroll. His two terms as the state's first Whig governor, from 1835 until 1839, occurred while the Jackson Democrats held control. (Van Buren was elected president in 1836). Middle Tennesseans favored Cannon, but West Tennesseans (politically dominated by the Jackson coalition) generally opposed him. The Memphis *Enquirer* ridiculed him, calling him a "farm boy and saddler" (Phillips 1978). East Tennesseans were perturbed over the lack of internal improvements taking place. However, his four years were peaceful, reforms were taking place, and the state continued to grow in population and commerce. Authorities put an end to a group of outlaws who had been terrorizing the populous by wrecking havoc, stealing, and killing. John A. Murrell, of Madison County, the leader of this notorious gang of bandits, was finally captured and imprisoned for stealing slaves from a neighbor. The remainder of the group was captured in Vicksburg, Mississippi. Mississippi citizens had little tolerance for this group and hung them, without a trial, on July 4, 1835. Cannon lost reelection to James K. Polk in 1839. He retired to his Harpeth River farm near Franklin, Tennessee, and died on September 16, 1841. (Photograph courtesy of TSLA)

over Jackson's support of Van Buren, Cannon had a coalition of ready-made Jackson enemies to help his campaign for governor. He proceeded to closely align his campaign with support for White's campaign for president. William Carroll, now needing all the support he could muster, was forced to tie his future to Jackson's and, therefore, support Van Buren.

Jackson was furious over his opposition and used all his political power against anyone supporting White for president or Cannon for governor. Nevertheless, all the presidential power could not overcome the tide of revolt against Jackson's domination in Tennessee. Governor Carroll was swamped by the tide. He polled only 31,205 votes to Cannon's 41,970, and Parry W. Humpherys's 8,054. In 1837 Newton Cannon became the first Whig governor of Tennessee. Control of the Tennessee legislature elected for 1835 went to the Cannon, White, Bell coalition, a turn of events which mortified and embarrassed Andrew Jackson. The coalition would soon elect one of their own to the U.S. Senate—Ephraim H. Foster, who was now a close supporter of White and now firmly anti-Jackson.

Tennessee Whigs joined with the Northern anti-Jackson politicians to oppose the Democrats. The anti-Jackson politicians now began to congeal into a National Whig Party. Old National Republicans, once stung by Jackson's defeat of Adams in 1828, also joined the Whigs. The Masonic organization was a powerful political tool of the day and one that Jackson had benefited from. There were many who saw dark danger in the organization and the "anti-Masons" developed to oppose them. They also joined in the Whig Party, as did those who broke with Jackson by supporting the U. S. Bank. States' rights politicians, stung by Jackson's actions over the South Carolina nullification attempt, joined in the Whigs' anti-Jackson battle. Essentially, Andrew Jackson had been the catalyst which sparked the creation of the Democratic Party. As a result of his pervasive political success, the opposition had collapsed. When it returned, it did so in the form of the Whig Party. Jackson had played a role in forming his own party as well as the opposition to it, both nationally and in Tennessee.

As the Whig organizations crystallized in other states, Hugh Lawson White became their anti-Jackson candidate. But, everyone knew that the new party would not be strong enough to defeat Jackson's Democrats. It was soon realized that other candidates nominated for the presidency—Daniel Webster, nominated by the Massachusetts legislature, and William Henry Harrison, nominated by the Ohio Whigs—might split the vote and hopefully throw the contest into the House of Representatives.

The White campaign did not run as an overt Whig organization. In Tennessee, White's supporters campaigned against the New Yorker, Van Buren, while trying not to direct the public attack toward Jackson. They tried to portray White in the mold of a Jackson Democrat in order to win the votes sympathetic to the old hero. White was presented as the new torch carrier of the common-man Democrat.

Jackson's men in Tennessee who supported Van Buren simply campaigned that White had no chance and that it would be better for Tennesseans to have a Democrat in the White House who was loyal to Andrew Jackson and Tennessee than to lose out to the Northeastern political establishment. This was a potent message in view of the fact that Jackson, a Tennessean and thus a westerner, had moved the political balance of power away from the East Coast. Moreover, many Tennessee politicians had received national prominence through this transition. Nevertheless, Tennessee held strong loyalty and many ties to the well-respected White.

When the votes were counted in the presidential election of 1836, White managed to carry Tennessee 35,962 votes to Van Buren's 26,120. He did so by winning East and West Tennessee. Jackson's team was still strong in Middle Tennessee, but they managed only to split the vote there. Jackson's own Hermitage precinct went 61 to 20 in favor of White. The only other state won by White was Georgia. Van Buren won the presidency in 1836, receiving a majority of votes—765,483 to 739,795 for the entire field including White, William Henry Harrison (closest with 549,567), and Daniel Webster. There were 170 electoral votes for Van Buren to 73 for the three other candidates. Although the Jackson coaliton was weaker in Tennessee because of the split between Old Hickory and many of Tennessee's future power politicians, it was still powerful on a national level. Democrats controlled the presidency as well as the House and Senate. The margin had narrowed in the House to 108 Democrats to 107 Whigs and 24 other (from 145

Democrats and 98 Whigs two years earlier), but in the Senate the Democrats widened the margin to 30 Democrats to 18 Whigs and 4 other (up from 27 Democrats to 25 Whigs two years earlier).

White's campaign and subsequent loss led to a revolution in state politics by those not wanting to submit to the old Jacksonian order any longer. After this election, the Whig Party became a power in Tennessee gubernatorial elections, alternating the seat with the Democrats until the Civil War. (In presidential elections, Tennessee would not go Democratic for a president for the next twenty years.) White (who was still a senator at this time), Governor Cannon, John Bell, Ephraim H. Foster, and Balie Peyton pulled their political organizations over to the Whigs. By 1837 the Tennessee Whigs were well motivated to continue their defiant revolt against Jackson. Their organization gained strength, and when Governor Newton Cannon ran for reelection in 1837, he was reelected.

However, on a national level, the Democrats still had control, and Jackson's men were still in power. When Congressman Bell challenged Speaker James K. Polk in 1837, he was again defeated, and Polk maintained control of Congress.

President Van Buren appointed Felix Grundy as U.S. attorney general, who then resigned his Senate seat on July 4, 1838. Whig Governor Cannon appointed Ephraim Hubbard Foster to fill the Senate seat (Class 1) on September 17, 1838. Foster had to compete with former Governor William Carroll, now supported by Jackson, for this Senate seat. Carroll had long sought a seat in the Senate. Although he had been a dominant political figure from 1821 to 1827 and from 1829 until 1835, all his past accomplishments in reformation of the old feudal system in Tennessee made little difference now. All that mattered was his party affiliation. With the Whigs now maintaining a majority in the legislature, they elected Foster. He would only serve from September 17, 1838, until March 3, 1839, resigning before the March 4, 1839, term began.

Shortly after Whig Governor Cannon was reelected in 1837, Tennessee Democrats began meeting to plan for a comeback. The leading officeholding Democrat left in Tennessee was Congressman James K. Polk. He served as Speaker of the U.S. House and had plans to run as vice president on Van Buren's ticket in the next presidential election and possibly later as president. The Democrats needed a strong and popular leader to run for governor if they wanted to take back control of Tennessee government. The governor's office was considered high enough profile for a presidential or vice presidential aspirant. Polk was perfect. By August 30, 1838, Democrats were beginning their comeback. At a rally in Murfreesboro, two thousand people gathered for a lively celebration that included barbecue, liquor, and speeches. Polk inspired his followers, and he received endorsements, including one from former Governor William Carroll, thought by some to be seeking reelection himself.

Many old Democratic warriors could not understand how so many people could turn on Andrew Jackson and dishonor all that he had done for the Democratic Party and Tennessee. The Democrats in Tennessee were badly damaged as the Whigs gained power and defeated their candidates. However, James K. Polk remained an untarnished Democrat in the midst of all the political bickering between the two parties.

Polk had lost an election as Speaker of the U.S. House of Representatives to Whig John Bell in 1834, but Polk, with President Jackson's help, took the position in 1835. He was reelected Speaker in 1837 and served during Van Buren's term as president. However in 1839 he received his party's nomination for governor to oppose incumbent Governor Cannon and therefore did not return to Congress. Cannon was running for a third term as governor and was politically strong. However, Democrats felt that Polk's notoriety would help them retake the governor's seat. For Polk, the visibility would not hurt should he later run for president.

Cannon and Polk traveled the state to campaign in a series of joint debates. The first debate opened on April 11, 1839, in Murfreesboro, Tennessee. The two candidates stayed in rooming houses and private homes, many times staying in the same room and the same bed. Even though there was a great deal of rancorous stumping between the two, it

JAMES KNOX POLK was born in Mecklenburg, North Carolina, on November 2, 1795. His father's family changed their name from Pollok, to Polk, sometime after they had settled in Maryland in 1680. They then migrated to North Carolina. Polk's family moved to Maury County (Columbia) Tennessee when he was ten years old. His father, Samuel Polk had married Jane Knox, the great-grandniece of the great Scotsman John Knox. James Knox Polk was a sickly youth. His weakness disappointed his father, who wanted James to take up surveying and farming. When James was fourteen, his father took him to Danville, Kentucky, to see Dr. Ephraim McDowell. Dr. McDowell decided that young Polk had gallstones and operated on James. The anesthesia was brandy.

Since Polk could not take up the normal duties of a pioneer, his mother, who was a strong Presbyterian, wanted him to become a minister. Polk had other ideas and looked to law. He studied for a while at Murfreesboro College, then returned to North Carolina at age nineteen to study at the University of North Carolina. After college, he returned to Tennessee to study law under Felix Grundy in Nashville, was accepted to the bar at twenty-four, and began practice in Columbia, Tennessee.

Polk married Sara Childress on January 21, 1824. Sara was the daughter of Joel and Elizabeth Whitsett Childress, who had come from North Carolina, settled in Sumner County, and built the first home there. Joel Childress was the first postmaster in Murfreesboro. Sara received a good education, was well attuned to the realities of position, and encouraged her husband to seek public office. He was elected to the state legislature in 1823, and in 1825, when he was thirty, he was elected to Andrew Jackson's old seat in Congress. He remained in the U.S. House of Representatives until 1839, serving as chairman of the Ways and Means Committee and as majority leader for the Democrats. He was elected Speaker of the House during the last years of Jackson's presidency and the first two years of Van Buren's presidency (1836 to 1838). Polk was a staunch supporter of Jackson and his Democrats. At forty-three years of age, in 1839, he returned to Tennessee to run for governor and was elected, the first college graduate to serve as Tennessee's governor. He was defeated for reelection in 1841 and then again in 1843. In 1844 he was elected president of the United States. He served one term and did not run for reelection. Polk led the nation's efforts during the Mexican War, which expanded the United States, but increased Northerners' fear of a rising number of slaveholding states. Polk was a hardworking president and remained true to his stated purposes. After completing his term as president he returned to Tennessee. Polk died of cholera on June 15, 1849. His wife lived until 1891. (Painting by an unknown artist courtesy of TSM) must not have been too intolerable since they actually lived together during the campaign. Cannon was a good speaker, but he was slow, deliberate, and cautious. Polk was "clever and witty" (Keating 1888, Phillips 1978), and he used this talent to occasionally cut into Cannon. He became sarcastic, even sometimes belligerent toward Governor Cannon, attacking him as a Whig tool of the likes of Henry Clay. This was an obvious attempt to remind voters that Cannon was anti-Jackson and by inference, somewhat anti-Tennessee. Cannon insisted that Polk was a tool of Andrew Jackson. He attempted to stir up animosity toward Jackson for his heavy-handed political tactics and blame him for anything negative that occurred on a national level, such as the depression of 1837. Even though the candidates ostensibly got along during their campaigns, fights between Whigs and Democrats turned angry and violent. Many candidates and voters carried pistols and knives during the contests of this era.

When the votes were counted, Democrat Polk was elected governor in 1839, but by a slim majority, receiving 54,680 votes to 52,114 for Cannon. His strong vote in Middle Tennessee won the election, for he lost both West and East Tennessee. The election was a setback for Tennessee Whigs. The Democrats controlled the state house, but the state senate still had a Whig majority (by one vote). Democrats also gained Tennessee U.S. House of Representatives seats, now holding six with the Whigs holding four.

The Tennessee Democrats now had enough votes in the legislature to control the state, but both sitting U.S. senators (Foster and White) were Whigs. The Democrats soon planned to change that. Shortly after the August gubernatorial victory, the legislature met in October 1839 and immediately passed a resolution which put forth James K. Polk's name for vice president in the upcoming 1840 contest. After this, they addressed some state issues, then turned their attention to the important political issue of Tennessee's U.S. senators.

During this period, it was an accepted fact that U.S. senators (who were elected by the legislature) would do the legislature's bidding on the Senate floor. Both Senators Foster and White were of the mind that there was no way to really cooperate with their political enemies, and the Democrats knew it. The Democratic legislature therefore passed resolutions which mandated that both Foster and White support Democrat President Martin Van Buren's programs which came before them. However, Foster refused the Democratic dictation that he support the annexation of Texas. (This was a stormy issue of the day. Foster's misjudgment of Tennessee public opinion over the matter would one day cost him election as governor.) Foster and White, being men of honor, both resigned, planning to run again with the Whig candidates for state legislature in the 1840 election cycle. Foster resigned forthwith on November 15, 1839, after seven months in office, giving up a full term which would have run until 1845. Senator White resigned his term, scheduled to end in 1841, on January 13, 1840. He returned to his home in Knoxville and died soon afterward of tuberculosis, as had nearly his entire family. White had been exceedingly popular in East Tennessee. His forced resignation alienated any potential support that the Democrats might gain from this area of the state.

Since the legislature elected the U.S. senators, it was important for any aspiring senator to campaign for legislative candidates, hoping to earn their support in future contests for U.S. Senate seats. However, the legislature rejected Whig Foster by electing

ALEXANDER OUTLAW ANDERSON was born at Soldiers Rest, Jefferson County, Tennessee, on November 10, 1794. His father was Senator Joseph Anderson. His early education was obtained from preparatory schools and his higher education from Washington College, in Greeneville, Tennessee. He served in the War of 1812 and fought under Andrew Jackson at the Battle of New Orleans. He then studied law in the nation's capital city and was subsequently admitted to the Tennessee Bar, and began practice in Dandridge, Tennessee, later moving to Knoxville. He served as superintendent of the United States Land Office, located in Alabama, in 1836, and as a government agent in the removal of the Indians from Alabama and Florida in 1838. When Hugh Lawson White resigned from the U.S. Senate, Anderson was elected to fill the vacancy, serving only slightly over a year, from February 26, 1840 until March 3, 1841, and did not run for reelection. He then practiced law in Washington for twenty years and became a personal friend of John C. Calhoun. The gold rush in 1849 inspired him to move to California as leader of an overland company. He helped draft the constitution for the state of California, sat in the California state senate from 1850 until 1851, and served as a supreme court judge of California from 1851 until 1853. He returned to Tennessee in 1853, also practicing law in Washington, D.C. At the time of the Civil War, Anderson moved to Alabama, working as a lawyer in Mobile and Camden, Alabama. After the war he returned to Knoxville, Tennessee, and died on May 23, 1869. He was buried at Old Gray Cemetery. (Photograph courtesy of SHO)

Democrat Felix Grundy, his former political ally, to fill his resigned Class 1 Senate seat. (John Bell had defeated Felix Grundy for Congress in 1826.) Grundy took office on December 14, 1839, and was to serve until March 3, 1845. However, he died on December 19, 1840. To replace him Governor Polk appointed Alfred O. Pope Nicholson on December 25, 1840. Alexander Anderson was elected to fill the other U.S. Senate seat (Class 2) vacated by the resignation of Senator White. Anderson began serving on February 26, 1840 (although the term actually commenced on January 27, 1840), to serve until March 3, 1841. Even though Anderson was from Knox County, the Democrats gained little sympathy in the east section of Tennessee from his election. Senator White's death, following his politically forced resignation from the Senate, only served to hoist him into martyrdom.

In 1840 the nation was still in the midst of the financial panic begun in 1837. William Henry Harrison had lost to Van Buren in 1836, but was still the strongest Whig positioned for his party's nomination again in 1840. Harrison had defeated the Shawnee Indians in the Battle of Tippecanoe and served as a general in the War of 1812. He, like Jackson, was a national war hero, and had served in the House of Representatives and the U.S. Senate. He had also served in the Ohio state senate. Although Tennessee Whigs supported General Winfield Scott and Henry Clay at the Whig National Convention in Harrisburg, Pennsylvania, in December of 1839, Harrison was nominated for president. His running mate was John Tyler from Virginia.

John Tyler had previously been a Democrat. While serving as U.S. senator, he split with the Democrats because of

President Andrew Jackson's tough stand against the nullification by South Carolina in 1832. At that time Tyler did not think it was right for the federal government to interfere in the state's affairs. (Jackson had essentially threatened South Carolina with war if they tried to secede from the Union.) Tyler, a slaveholding Virginia planter, was the only U.S. senator to vote against the "Force Bill" which gave the president the right to collect taxes by military force if necessary. This bill had been created because of South Carolina's refusal to cooperate with federal authority. In spite of pressure that Jackson put on Senator Tyler via his friends in Virginia, Tyler refused to follow the instructions of the Virginia legislature to vote for a Senate resolution expunging a censure that had been placed on President Jackson. Tyler resigned his Senate seat rather than support Jackson. After his resignation, the Whigs took him in, and he ran as their vice presidential nominee (White was the presidential candidate) in the losing race of 1836. He then was elected as a Whig to the Virginia legislature in 1838 and was chosen as speaker of the Virginia house of representatives. He tried to gain reelection to the U.S. Senate as a Whig by the Virginia General Assembly, but the vote deadlocked and no one was chosen. In 1839 he was chosen as the Whig candidate for vice president again, running with William Henry Harrison. Tennessee Whigs readily supported Harrison and Tyler once they received the nomination.

As 1840 appeared on the horizon, Governor James K. Polk pressed ahead with plans to run on the national Democratic ticket. National friendships were renewed and new contacts were made in order to maneuver for a position on the ticket at the upcoming Democratic National Convention. The convention took place in Baltimore, Maryland, in May 1840. Tennessee Democrats Aaron Brown, Cave Johnson, William Carroll, Samuel Laughlin, and Felix Grundy were all there prepared to campaign for the nomination of Polk as the vice presidential nominee. Although President Van Buren was renominated, the convention did not nominate a vice presidential candidate, deciding instead to leave the position vacant for the electors of each state to decide who that should be. Without his party's endorsement, Governor Polk declined to run in a mixed field and declined the Tennessee legislature's nomination.

The campaign of 1840 marked the advent of the activities that were to characterize elections for the following one hundred years. Tennessee Whig campaigners cooperated with national campaign efforts to create public excitement and bring people out to the festivities as well as to the polls. Harrison's campaign ran with the slogan of "Tippecanoe and Tyler Too." "Tippecanoe clubs" were organized, parades were held, and uniforms were made and worn for the activities. Small log cabins were built and placed on wheels as a symbol to remind voters of Harrison's humble beginnings (coon skins were placed on the little cabins). Large festivals were held in which the Whig candidates generally refused to debate the Democrats; they would only "sing." Songbooks were distributed, and Tennesseans generally had fun with this election. At a Clarksville, Tennessee, rally in May 1840, over seven thousand people came out for the activities, fanfare, food, barbecue, liquor, and political ballyhoo. The Democrats campaigned the same way, but with a unique disadvantage—President Van Buren had not selected a vice presidential candidate, who could then

James K. Polk speaking to a political rally, Knoxville, 1840. (Courtesy of TSM)

campaign for the Democratic ticket. Another disadvantage for the Democrats was that the people generally blamed the Jackson and Van Buren administrations for the financial panic which began in 1837. As a consequence the voters felt the Democrats were "responsible" for their hardships, and decided to give the Whigs a chance.

On election day Harrison received 1,274,624 votes nationally to 1,127,781 for Van Buren (234 to 60 electoral votes). It was the first presidential election in which any candidate received over a million votes. The excitement generated by this election was illustrated by the additional fact that more than a million more voters went to the polls in 1840 than in 1836. Since the last presidential election the national mood had changed and so had the makeup of Congress. For the first and only time the Whigs gained control of both the U.S. House and Senate. Tennessee voted Whig for Harrison in 1840 by over 12,000 votes. This was a devastating loss for Tennessee Democrats.

Meanwhile Governor Polk lost the support of some of his friends. He and fellow Democrat Felix Grundy became at odds with each other over a disagreement. (Polk was a man who stuck to his decisions and would not be swayed.) By the time of the 1841 reelection for the governor's seat, he was in a difficult political position. Whigs had enjoyed a resurgence of support in 1840 not only nationally; the Harrison presidential campaign had created a lot of excitement and had shored up support for the Whig Party in Tennessee. Polk's narrow margin in 1839 would be tough to hold in 1841. Since Polk and his supporters still wanted him available for the Democratic ticket in 1844, they felt he needed to stay visible by running for reelection as governor.

Democrats Decline

With the Whigs on the rebound, they had no intention of allowing Polk to stay in office, but they needed a campaigner who could equal Polk's satirical eloquence. At first David W. Dickinson (John Bell's brother-in-law) sought the Whig gubernatorial nomination of 1841. However, there was another candidate who possessed some unusual talents, and the Whigs took a hard look at the young man. James C. Jones, a tall and very thin state legislator, was better known as "Lean Jimmy" Jones. Jones could talk. He owned a folksy twang and was a fine imitator. He was also a good storyteller and possessed a cutting wit. However talented this young man was, though, he was still an unknown. The Memphis *Appeal* even asked, "Who is James C. Jones?"

The campaign began in Murfreesboro, Tennessee, on March 27, 1841, with the first of a series of joint debates held across the state. In the nineteenth century, opposing candidates would commonly travel to the same campaign sites and speak from the same stump. During campaign stumps, Jones was quick to show his talents as an entertaining comedian, and created quite a spectacle. Polk discussed the issues, while Jones, "master of hilarity and mimicry." (McKellar 1942), put Polk, ever the dignified statesman, on the defensive and made fun of him and his position. But he was never mean. He spoke to the common man and kept the crowds mesmerized with his manner. The Democrats tried to downplay the contrast between the hilarious Jones and the solemn Polk.

Other factors that influenced the 1841 gubernatorial race included public support for the State Bank, the state of the economy, and political patronage. It may not be an insignificant fact that when President William Henry Harrison, a Whig, was elected in 1840, he appointed Tennessee Congressman John Bell, from the Franklin-Nashville area, as secretary of war. Other federal officials in Tennessee were replaced with Whig supporters and this garnered some cooperation among patronage seekers.

When Polk and the Democrats repealed the internal improvement act in order to save the credit of the State Bank and to help ensure solvency by reducing the amount of issuance of risk, the amount of capital in the bank was reduced. The State Bank had served its intended purposes of standardizing the currency and providing the bonds necessary for turnpike and railroad companies. Though Polk's repeal of the act was well meaning, the immediate reaction of the public did not take into account the long-term benefits.

Also, the financial panic of 1837 affected many elections, including those involving President Van Buren and Polk. The public eased their financial pain by punishing elected officials who stood as easy targets for the blame. Polk, a Democrat, was defeated for reelection as governor in 1841. He had been elected in 1839 by a 2,500-vote margin. In 1841 he lost by 3,243 out of 103,929 votes cast to the relatively unknown James C. Jones. Jones, a Whig from Wilson County, Tennessee, was the first native Tennessean to be elected governor. His contests with Polk, in 1841 and 1843 were "two of the most remarkable contests for governor ever waged in Tennessee" (Mckellar 1942).

The results of this race, when compared to the results of 1839, showed that Tennessee's two political parties, the Whigs and the Democrats, were in a delicate political balance. In 1841 the state house was controlled by the Whigs, and the state senate was controlled, narrowly, by the Democrats (twelve Whigs, twelve Democrats, and one Independent, Samuel Turney, in the state senate.) As a result, there was a difficult struggle in electing U.S. senators. When Governor Jones and the legislature first met in 1841, this was a primary issue to be dealt with. After the death of U.S. Senator Felix Grundy in 1840, a portion of the term was filled by Alfred Osborne Pope Nicholson, who had been temporarily appointed to the seat by Governor Polk. However, after the appointment term ran out, the position remained vacant for about two full years. This was because the legislature of 1840–1841 fought so much for control that no compromise could be obtained. The term of the other U.S. Senate seat, held by Alexander Anderson, who took the seat after the death of Hugh Lawson White, expired on March 3, 1841. Therefore, it also became vacant.

The political struggle for the Senate seats was a test of dominance by each party and exemplified the height of political activity of the time, as well as the near equality of power between the Whigs and the Democrats. The Democrats offered to divide the U.S. Senate seats so that each party would have one seat. However, the Whigs, with control of the state house and the governor's seat, felt that they should have both seats. It was customary, up to this time, for the election to occur in a joint session of the Tennessee state house and state senate, although this was not mandated by law. However, because a joint session would favor the Whigs, they demanded it. The twelve Democrats, including state Senator Andrew Johnson, and the Independent Samuel Turney, felt that if they could prevent the joint session they could take one seat, leaving the Whigs the other. They held that the election of U.S. senators

JAMES CHAMBERLAYNE JONES was born on June 7, 1809, in Davidson County, Tennessee, near the Hermitage. His parents, Peter and Catherine Chapell Jones, died when Jones was a young boy, and he was raised by an uncle. He grew tall and skinny and was nicknamed "Lean Jimmy" Jones. Jones received very little education compared to some of his colleagues in later life. He did attend the Old Field Schools. By 1829 he married Sarah Munford, the daughter of William and Letitia Ball Munford. They eventually had nine children. They settled in Wilson County, Tennessee, and Jones became a farmer.

In 1837 he was elected to the state legislature and reelected in 1839. During his early political years he studied law and polished his speaking abilities. He was a very talented, comical, entertaining speaker, and well liked by his fellow Whigs, though known as a rabble-rouser in the political debates in the state house. By 1840, he was a Harrison (Whig) elector during the presidential election and helped with the Whig effort to carry the state. He evidently impressed many Whigs through his efforts on Harrison's behalf.

In 1841, the Whigs needed someone with great speaking ability to challenge Governor Polk, and Jones was nominated as the Whig candidate. Jones was disadvantaged by not having a college education, not being a lawyer (he was a farmer), and not having any strong family, political, or business connections. By contrast, Polk had served as U.S. representative and Speaker of the House, was the incumbent governor, and was also tightly tied to Andrew Jackson and his powerful political network. Jones, however, had as good an intellect as Polk and the thirty-two-year-old made the by joint session was unconstitutional and would only agree to the election by the concurrent separate action of the state house and the state senate. The Whigs held fast for their cause and would not compromise with the Democrats. They wanted both seats or nothing. The Democrats refused to meet in a joint session with the Whig-controlled state house and therefore blocked the election by using their thirteen votes to defeat the twelve votes of the Whigs. The leader of the Democratic state senators was Andrew Johnson and they became known as the "Immortal Thirteen."

In an effort to break the deadlock, Turney proposed the election of his brother Hopkins L. Turney, who was a Democrat, in separate session, but the Whigs refused. The twelve Whig senators became known as the "Twelve Destructives." Since the Whigs would not allow the Democrats to elect their one seat, the "Immortal Thirteen" successfully blocked the election of a Whig to the other seat. As a result, no one was elected, and Tennessee went without any U.S. senators between 1841 and 1843. Governor Jones called a special session of the legislature in 1842, but the "Immortal Thirteen" held out. Governor Jones and the Whigs then began to plan for redistricting.

The deadlocked Tennessee General Assembly tried to address other controversial issues, such as the election of directors of the Bank of Tennessee. However, because of this gridlock no progress could be made on this or other matters before the body.

Meanwhile, in March of 1841 Mexican General Antonio Lopez de Santa Anna moved fifteen thousand troops into Texas in response to the threat of the growing American migration. Santa Anna feared that the continued migration of settlers would eventually threaten

---

forty-six-year-old Polk look to be the weaker debater. Jones made a comical mockery of Polk and the public turned out in large numbers for the entertainment provided by their joint appearances. He defeated Polk and became the first elected native-born Tennessee governor. He was reelected in 1843, defeating Polk a second time.

During his administrations, Tennessee, as well as the rest of the nation, enjoyed great commercial and social progress. The first railroad in Tennessee, the LaGrange and Memphis line, began operation. Religious denominations underwent rapid growth. The state capital permanently moved to Nashville, and the cornerstone of the new capitol building was laid in 1845 (it was completed in 1856). The School for the Blind in Nashville and the School for the Deaf in Knoxville were established.

After his terms ended in 1845, he temporarily retired from politics. In 1848, he campaigned as a Whig elector for the Taylor-Fillmore ticket, and in 1850 he moved to Memphis to become president of the Memphis and Charleston Railroad Co. However, he could not get politics out of his system, and he later ran for the U.S. Senate. The legislature elected him to the seat, and he served from March 4, 1851, to March 3, 1857. On August 9, 1856, while serving as a U.S. senator, Jones quit the Whig Party saying, "The Democratic Party affords the best, if not the last hope of safety and security for the South" (McKellar 1942). Even though he had held office as a Whig, his philosophy was Democrat, so he turned to that party. He retired from the Senate after one term, and returned to Memphis to continue his work with railroad development, becoming a leader and supporter of Memphis development. He worked for the Democrat presidential candidate James Buchanan in 1856. Jones died October 29, 1859, when only fifty years old, and was buried in Elmwood Cemetery in Memphis. (Photograph courtesy of SHO)

Mexico's control of the territory. His move caused a real stir among the patriots of the new nation, including those in the Volunteer State. Public meetings were held to rally support and raise troops to assist the Texans. Though divided over state politics, both political parties were represented at these meetings as Tennessee prepared to aid the cause of Texas independence.

President William Henry Harrison was inaugurated on March 4, 1841. The sixty-eight-year-old president gave a long speech on a cold and wet day and subsequently developed what was thought to be a lingering cold. During his short tenure as president, he removed Senator Henry Clay from the White House for demanding jobs for his friends; the president wrote Clay telling him that he was "too impetuous" (Whitney 1982). The president's cold worsened, developing into pneumonia, and he died on April 4, 1841. Harrison was the first U.S. president to die in office. Vice President John Tyler was sworn in as president.

President Tyler had a mind of his own and he, like Harrison before him, would not be directed by Henry Clay and other leading Whigs. By September 1841, he had vetoed two bills supported by the Whigs. Tyler had only quit the Democratic party because of his disagreement with Andrew Jackson. Philosophically he was not a Whig and would not tolerate their domination. In retaliation, on September 13, 1841, he was officially expelled from the Whig Party. The cabinet he had inherited from Harrison (other than Daniel Webster) resigned. Relieved, he then appointed conservative Democrats to the cabinet positions.

President Tyler followed his own feelings. He did not agree with the Whig plans to raise tariffs, so he vetoed the bills they submitted for that purpose. In response, the Whigs tried to impeach Tyler. The impeachment attempt actually came to a vote in January 1843, but it was defeated twenty-seven to eighty-three.

By 1844 there was a fair amount of national tension because of the possibilities of war. Britain and the United States were in a dispute over the Oregon Territory, and Mexico was gravely concerned over settlements in the southwest. The United States had a relatively well-fortified eastern coast, but the west was undefended. Thirty-eight-year-old Lieutenant Matthew Fontaine Maury, of the U.S. Navy, formerly of Williamson County, Tennessee, saw this as an opportunity for Memphis. He petitioned Congress to create an inland naval depot and dock at Memphis in order to prevent any blockade of the Mississippi River by a foreign enemy. When in 1844 the Memphis Naval Yard plan was approved

Lieutenant Matthew Fontaine Maury. (Courtesy of TSLA)

by Congress, there was celebration in the city. Ironically, the yard ultimately contributed little to the nation's navy, and the plan was given up in 1854.

During all the political fighting within Tennessee, Governor Jones and the Tennessee legislature were finally able to make limited progress in revising the laws. Previously, a person could be imprisoned for a debt. However, in 1842 the law was changed, and imprisonment as punishment for debt was outlawed.

Meanwhile the ousted James K. Polk and Democratic leaders were still stung by their loss of the gubernatorial race to the Whigs in 1841. If Polk was to be taken seriously as a vice presidential contender in 1844, they thought he had no choice but to force a comeback. Certainly, they thought, the public would see by now a clear comparison between the "stately" patriot Polk and the "foolish" Jimmy Jones. Polk decided to run the most grueling speaking campaign ever known to Tennessee in his 1843 comeback try. No other Democrat even considered challenging Polk for his party's nomination for Tennessee's leading seat. Whigs, however, were not sure that Jones would not be a liability in 1843 and considered other Whig leaders as their nominee. However, Ephraim H. Foster was in charge of the Whig organization and felt that Jones should receive the full support of the party.

In the campaign one of the main issues was the legislative deadlock over the election of the state's two U.S. senators. Neither the Whigs nor the Democrats had capitulated. The state assembly was unable to send Tennessee senators to Washington. One seat had been vacant since February 8, 1842 (remaining so until October 16, 1843), while the other seat had been vacant since March 4, 1841 (remaining so until October 16, 1843). Jones favored legislative maneuvering which would elect two Whigs. Polk favored a plan to end the deadlock and elect one Whig and one Democrat. Jones, however, tied the responsibility of the deadlock to the Democrats. Polk again tried to tie the Tennessee governor's Whig Party to Henry Clay and his national positions, but this did not inflict a political wound deep enough to injure Jones. Polk lost again and Jones was reelected. The Whigs also picked up legislative seats, taking a five-seat lead in the Tennessee house and a two-seat lead in the state senate. The Whigs had succeeded in blocking the appointment of senators and preventing a Democrat from taking office, thereby holding both seats open until they were in a position to control them.

The Whig increase in the state legislature (aided by redistricting in the 1840–1841 session) ended the deadlock over the election of U.S. senators. In 1843 the state legislative battle resumed with Ephraim Foster vying with former Governor William Carroll again for the U.S. Senate seat. Ephraim Foster (Whig) was elected to complete the term begun by Grundy (the Class 1 seat had been temporarily filled by Alfred O. P. Nicholson upon the 1840 death of Grundy) and Spencer Jarnagin (Whig) was elected to succeed the seat (Class 2) originally vacated by White's resignation in 1840 (temporarily filled by Alexander Anderson until the completion of the term on March 3, 1841). Foster served from October 17, 1843, until the remainder of Grundy's original term expired on March 3, 1845. Jarnagin served for four years from October 17, 1843, until the completion of the term on March 3, 1847.

At this point the Tennessee legislature put an end to the tradition of split-body elections (Senate and House) of U.S. senators. The Whig-controlled General Assembly passed a law mandating a joint session for

SPENCER JARNAGIN was born in Grainger County, Tennessee, in 1792. His grandfather was a captain in the Revolutionary War and fought under Isaac Shelby. His grandparents, Thomas and Mary Witt Jarnagin, moved from the region of Danville, Virginia, around 1780, to Tennessee, finally settling in Hamblen County. His parents, Chesley and Martha Barton Jarnagin, settled in Grainger County. Jarnagin received his early education from his mother. He studied at Greeneville College and graduated in 1813. He studied law under Hugh Lawson White, was admitted to the bar in 1817, and began practice in Knoxville. He was elected to the state senate in 1833 and served two years. He was an elector for President Harrison in 1840. He received much notoriety for his campaign on behalf of Harrison and was thought to be the Whig choice for U.S. senator by the legislators. However, the legislative deadlock of 1841 prevented any election. The Whigs elected him in 1843 to serve the remaining three and one-half years of the term. As senator, he worked to obtain approval for a navy yard for Memphis. Later in his Senate term, in 1846, he voted with the Democrats to reduce tariffs. He received criticism for voting for low tariffs, even though Tennessee had historically been a low-tariff state. This alienated Henry Clay, who at that time still opposed Polk after being defeated by him for the presidency. This also alienated Jarnagin's fellow Whigs in Tennessee and made it impossible for him to be reelected to his Senate seat. "At heart he was not really a Whig, but the exigencies of politics put him in that Party" (McKellar 1942). By being a Whig, but not agreeing with their philosophy, he lost their support. By voting against the annexation of Texas he acted against the wishes of the Democrats and the feelings of most Tennesseans, and could not get reelected to the Senate. He was a trustee of East Tennessee College from 1836–1851. Later in life Jarnagin moved to Memphis. He was a man of high intellect who played a part in the colorful evolution of the Tennessee two-party system. He died on June 25, 1853, in Memphis. (Photograph courtesy of SHO)

U.S. senatorial elections. Another important issue facing the General Assembly was the permanent location of the state capital. Since 1796 the capital had been located in four different cities and had moved six times. When Tennessee was just a territory under the command of territorial Governor William Blount, the capital was located in Knoxville. In 1796, upon statehood, Knoxville continued as the site of the capital. In 1807 the General Assembly moved to Kingston for one day. After a treaty was completed with the Cherokee Indians, the capital was instantly moved back to Knoxville. In 1812 it moved to Nashville and remained there until 1817, when it relocated to Knoxville. It remained there until 1818, when it moved to Murfreesboro. There the capital remained until 1826, when it moved back to Nashville. The constitutional convention of 1834 mandated that the 1843 legislature would select a permanent site. After much negotiation and political maneuvering, Nashville was selected.

Meanwhile James K. Polk was suffering a deep political dejection. His old friend and mentor Felix Grundy had been dead since 1840. After serving as Speaker of the U.S. House of Representatives, being a close ally of former President Andrew Jackson, and serving as governor of Tennessee, he had suffered two straight defeats at the hands of his own people in Tennessee. After his losses in 1841 and 1843 he returned to Columbia to practice law. However, he did not give up and continued to keep in touch with Democratic leaders.

By the time Whig Governor Jimmy Jones started his second term, the public began to look forward to the 1844 presidential election campaign. Politics had become a social sport of sorts, great entertainment which made for interesting discussions on street corners, in stores, and during social visits in communities throughout Tennessee. By 1843 the Volunteer State had made substantial contributions to national politics and held a prominent place in the national spotlight because of its many colorful and influential political personalities.

President Tyler, a Whig, would have liked to have been nominated for president for the 1844 campaign. However, the Whigs were irritated with him since he would not cave in to the demands of the Whig leaders. It was apparent that he was Democrat by philosophy and Whig in party name only. He had broken with the Democrats a few years earlier because of his disagreement with President Jackson over the nullification and secession issue. But Tyler agreed with the Democrats on most issues and when president, he appointed many Democrats to cabinet and other positions. By nomination time he had been totally cast out by the Whig leaders. He tried to organize a new Democrat-Republican Party and was nominated for president by them. The Whigs favored Henry Clay. The Democrats favored Martin Van Buren. Tyler began campaigning on the issues of states' rights and the annexation of Texas, but his agenda would eventually be adopted by the Democrats.

A Second President

After James K. Polk's great political career in Washington and one two-year term as governor of Tennessee, his losses to Jimmy Jones for governor in 1841 and 1843 had many thinking his career was over. By 1844 it looked as if Martin Van Buren would get the Democratic nod for president. Van Buren had served as president, was one of the great Democratic leaders of the day, and maintained the support of Andrew Jackson. Jackson's dominance of the Democratic Party was legendary. Even in his decline, his network of friends and old associates from the military and halls of political power was so strong that his support was mandatory. It was in fact because of this power and influence that politicians in his home state of Tennessee had revolted and played a key role in the formation of the Whig Party. Therefore, Van Buren was in an excellent position to again take the Democratic nomination for president. However, by April of 1844, Van Buren had changed one of his key policy positions.

Van Buren had made a terrible political blunder through an agreement with the Whig nominee Henry Clay. They both agreed that they would oppose the annexation of Texas. They even went so far as to make public announcements to that effect on April 27, 1844. Van Buren's agreement with Henry Clay enraged Jackson, who had always favored American expansion and strongly supported annexation. To Jackson, Van Buren had overstepped the bounds of loyalty. He then shifted all his political influence to his friend and fellow Tennessean, James K. Polk, who, along with many other Tennesseans, supported the annexation of Texas and remembered the many former Tennesseans, including Sam Houston and Davy Crockett, who had fought for the independence of Texas.

After Houston's resignation as governor of Tennessee in April 1829 and a period of time living with the Cherokees, he had gone to Texas to fight for independence. Under his military leadership, Texas had defeated Santa Anna and his ruthless army in April 1836. The territory had gained its independence and become a nation, with Houston serving as president of the Republic of Texas. He and Jackson maintained communication regarding their plans for Texas. After recognition as an independent nation, the ultimate goal was Texas annexation into the United States. By 1842 the legislatures of many states, Tennessee included, recommended annexation. Tennessee was especially enthusiastic since so many of its residents had gone to live there or fight for its independence. In 1843 U.S. Representative Aaron V. Brown, upon Jackson's advice, lobbied in Washington for annexation. However, there were many who feared that the acceptance of another Southern slave state might tip the political balance between the North and South.

When the May 1844 Baltimore Democratic National Convention met, it deadlocked between Michigan's Lewis Cass and New York's Van Buren. If they were still split coming out of the convention, then it would be unlikely that the Democrats could regain the presidency. They did not like being out of power and sought a solution to their lack of unity. After several convention votes did not produce a nominee, Tennessee's Gideon J. Pillow circled Polk's name as the choice of Jackson (Old Hickory) for the nomination. The feeling was that Polk (Young Hickory) could bring the Democratic Party back to power. As a result of the nomination and some lobbying, Polk was made the Democratic nominee on the ninth ballot. The news of his nomination was unexpected to many. The first official use of Samuel F. B. Morse's telegraph was to transmit the Polk nomination from Baltimore to Washington and many thought the new communication device had failed to operate properly since they could not believe the transmission.

The Whigs nominated Henry Clay of Kentucky. During the campaign Clay became sarcastic toward Polk, commenting, "Who is James K. Polk?" However, Clay found out soon enough that the Democrat's pulse on public opinion was more accurate than his own, particularly regarding the Texas annexation issue.

In 1844 Andrew Jackson publicly announced his support for James K. Polk, and agressively pursued victory for his friend and longtime supporter. Both candidates, Democrat Polk and Democrat-Republican Tyler, supported the annexation of Texas. So Jackson intervened and convinced Tyler to withdraw, leaving the election between Polk and Clay. As the presidential campaign progressed, accusations flew both ways.

Polk spoke of national expansion and annexation of Texas and Oregon. Clay talked about the Whig principles such as supporting the National Bank (which Jackson ardently opposed), supporting tariffs (theoretically intended to protect Americans), and opposing the annexation of Texas. Clay shortly realized that a majority of Americans felt a patriotic duty to protect Texas and support the Americans, many of them friends and relatives, who lived there and had died there. Clay's sudden change of position in favor of annexation came too late. Polk's messages of "Reannexation for Texas and Oregon!" and "54°40' or Fight" (referring to the northern geographic mark for America's claim in Oregon) had solidified his position in the minds of the voting public. The vote was closer than any since 1824, but Polk's five-thousand-vote victory in New York gave him the edge he needed. If Polk had lost there, Clay would have had the electoral votes to win.

Polk was elected by 1,338,464 popular votes to 1,300,097 for Clay (170 to 105

Political cartoon from the presidential campaign of 1844. (Courtesy of TSLA)

electoral votes). Ironically, Whig candidate Clay carried Tennessee by 267 votes. The election, although close, brought great pride to Democrats of Tennessee, especially Andrew Jackson. However, there was still a strong anti-Jackson Whig force in Tennessee. Clay's reversal on his Texas position allowed them to vote against Polk without having to vote against annexation. The loss of the Tennessee vote was an embarrassment and certainly a low point in an otherwise great victory for Tennessee Democrats.

With Polk's victory, Texas, the Democrats, and Andrew Jackson were now assured of continued support for the annexation of Texas. Many of Jackson's enemies had fought against annexation. The American Anti-slavery Society opposed annexation for fear that it might add slave votes in Congress. The society actually stated that there would be no condition in which Texas could be admitted. During the campaign annexation became such a prominent issue that Northern Whig newspapers began a public campaign against the possibility. They opposed the possible extension of slavery through the admission of another Southern state. The continued inflammation of the issue by the newspapers fueled public sentiment over abolition and began to sow the seeds of war. Tennesseans strongly favored annexation of Texas as part of an expansionist fervor, rather than as an effort to support the concept of slavery.

In 1844 and early 1845, Texas's annexation into the United States and admission as a state was the biggest issue of the day. The debate held expansionist, social, military, and national psychological importance. Both Whig senators from Tennessee, Ephraim

James K. Polk, eleventh president of the United States. (Courtesy of TSLA)

Foster and Spencer Jarnagin, voted against annexation, but the measure passed in spite of the Whigs' negative votes. Since the people of Tennessee overwhelmingly favored bringing Texas into the Union, those state legislators who had opposed it and had elected Foster and Jarnagin to uphold their opposition, would have to answer to the voters. This would initiate a power shift, and in the next election of the General Assembly the Democrats would gain control.

The people of Texas felt revived confidence with the election of Polk. In December 1844, Dr. Anson Jones, who succeeded Sam Houston as president of Texas, renewed the proposals for annexation with the federal government. President John Tyler, who was still in office (Polk's inauguration would not take place until March 1845), supported the annexation. Sam Houston was not sure that Congress would approve the treaty between the United States and Texas that had been signed April 12, 1844. Tyler had sent it to the Senate, and it looked as if it would fail approval by a small number. However, after Polk's election (prior to his inauguration), foreign attitudes changed. The British eyed Texas and the leaders of Texas held discussions with them. The threat of war with Britain incensed the American people to the point that they placed sectional and philosophical jealousies behind considerations of national honor. The opposition from Northern antislavery political forces slowed. Jackson, though now physically very weak, wielded his remaining political influence, as did Houston, Polk, and Tyler. Texas's annexation was finally approved by joint resolution of the U.S. House and Senate a few weeks prior to Polk's inauguration. Tyler signed legislation which officially annexed Texas, as a territory, into the Union two days before his term ended, on March 1, 1845. On March 3, 1845, Tyler signed legislation to admit Florida as the twenty-seventh state.

Whig Senator Ephraim Foster's term ended on March 3, 1845. He decided to run for governor and did not enter the battle for reelection to the U.S. Senate (Class 1). General William Trousdale, Hopkins Turney, W. C. Dunlap, and A. O. P. Nicholson all vied for the Senate seat. The Democrats met in caucus and decided to elect Nicholson. The Whigs wanted to elect Whig leader John Bell. However, the Whigs were hopelessly outnumbered at the time of this election. Their only hope was to possibly block Nicholson. For two weeks a deadlock ensued and Nicholson finally withdrew in order to break it. Hopkins Turney met with the Whigs and agreed that if elected to the Senate, he would hold certain positions against President Polk in exchange for their support. Turney was subsequently elected with the support of the Whigs and six Democrats. When it became apparent that he was closely aligned with the Whigs, he garnered a great deal of animosity. Finally, when the Democrats were made aware of Turney's agreement to work against and denounce Polk, they kicked him out of the party.

James K. Polk was inaugurated as the eleventh president of the United States on March 4, 1845. At forty-nine years of age, he was, at that time, the youngest man to become president. Shortly after he took office, the U.S. minister from Mexico protested the American annexation of Texas, and Polk was faced with his first foreign affairs crisis. To help deal with the Mexican situation, Jackson persuaded President Polk to appoint Andrew Jackson Donelson as minister plenipotentiary.

Andrew Jackson (Jack) Donelson, nephew of Rachel Jackson. (Courtesy of Lewis Donelson)

On the same day that Polk took office, Hopkins Lacy Turney began serving as a Tennessee U.S. senator. He would serve until March 3, 1851.

Meanwhile at the Hermitage, Andrew Jackson relished the victory of the decision of Congress and President Tyler to annex Texas. It was important to him that Texas become part of the Union, believing as he did in the expansion and dominance of America. His family had died in the cause of the American Revolution. He had been part of Tennessee's marriage to the young nation in 1896. He had driven off the British in the Battle of New Orleans in the War of 1812. He had helped take Florida from the Spanish. He had played a major role in driving the Indians off new territories in Alabama and Tennessee. To Jackson, annexing Texas was the culmination of a lifetime of struggle. Before, during, and after his presidency he had worked for this cause. He had swung his support to Polk for president for several reasons, not the least of which was that his fellow Tennessean supported the Texas expansion effort.

Sam Houston, the Texas leader, was twice spurned by the United States in his Texas annexation efforts. Although many times the recipient of slanderous accusations by jealous men when he championed a public cause, Houston had once again responded to Jackson's wish that Texas apply for acceptance into the Union. He could not turn away from his old friend and political mentor.

Houston, whose career was so closely tied to Jackson, wanted to see his aging teacher. In a letter to Jackson he wrote: "Mrs. H. and myself . . . It is our ardent desire to see the day when you can lay your hand on our little boy's head, and bestow upon him your benediction" (Marques 1929). He began a journey back to Tennessee to see Jackson. On June 3, 1845, he stopped in Memphis on his way to the Hermitage. Houston, recently retired president of Texas (he could not run for reelection in 1844), had achieved national fame for his military and political exploits there, and his company was sought by many. He was invited to stay for an extended period of time by an esteemed committee of Memphis citizens, including both Democrats and Whigs. In truth, the group was also interested in hearing the gossip concerning Texas's negotiations with other nations—specifically Britain. That, however, was in the past, before the action of the House and Senate and President Tyler's signature. There was no use wasting time in Memphis. Declining that invitation but assuring them of the speedy admission of Texas, Houston, along with his wife, Margaret, and son, Sam, hurried to

Nashville to see his old mentor and friend Andrew Jackson.

Andrew Jackson had carried the remnants of injuries from gunfights and battles throughout his life. He also had contracted malaria years before. He suffered from recurrent episodes of hemoptysis (coughing up blood)—perhaps from a lung disease or an abscess from an old gunshot wound to the chest. He also suffered from an intestinal disturbance which resulted in intermittent diarrhea. Many did not think he would make it home from Washington after completing his second term as president in 1837. In spite of all his health problems, however, he lived on for many years. On Sunday, June 8, 1845, Jackson, propped up in his bed, called his family and servants. Knowing he was breathing his last few breaths, he said, "I want to meet you all, white and black, in heaven" (Marques 1929). He died at 6 P.M. Unfortunately, Houston and his family did not make it to the Hermitage until about 9 P.M. Houston, upon entering the room with his dead mentor lying lifeless on his bed, fell to his knees and embraced the man who had been so much like a father to him. He pulled his own son close and said, "My son, try to remember that you have looked upon the face of Andrew Jackson" (Marques 1929). Sam Houston and all the state of Tennessee mourned.

Memorials were held around Tennessee and the nation. Flags were dropped to half-mast. Jackson had been a force that had molded the new nation beyond what the founders had ever thought possible. He had

HOPKINS LACY TURNEY was born in Dixon Springs (Smith County), Tennessee, on October 3, 1797. He learned the tailor's trade, unable to read or write until later in life. He served in the war against the Seminole Indians in 1818. Becoming literate after he was grown, he learned law and began to practice in Jasper, Tennessee, later moving to practice in Winchester, Tennessee. He was elected to the state house in 1828, and kept that seat until being elected to Congress in 1837, serving there until 1843. His election to the U.S. Senate required some difficult negotiation. The Democrats who controlled the General Assembly in 1845 had met in caucus and decided to elect A. O. P. Nicholson to the Senate seat. The Whigs wanted to elect the Whig leader in Tennessee, John Bell. However, Nicholson could not get all the Democrats to support him. To become elected, Turney met with the Whigs and agreed to certain stands (including the denunciation of the administration of President Polk). Democrats were enraged; however, Turney received forty-seven Whig votes and six Democrat votes providing him enough support to be elected. The Democrats accused him of being a turncoat. He served from March 4, 1845, until March 3, 1851.

Senator Turney was "a vigorous and sometimes violent supporter of extreme doctrines and measures for the South, but his methods were not pleasing to the people of Tennessee" (McKellar 1942). When the Whigs eventually regained control in Tennessee of not only the governor's seat, but also of the legislature, they eventually elected a Whig to the U.S. Senate in place of Turney. After leaving office, Turney was defeated in an attempt to be elected to the state legislature. He returned to his law practice and died in Winchester, Tennessee, on August 1, 1857. His son, Peter Turney, was later elected governor of Tennessee and served from 1893 until 1897. (Photograph courtesy SHO) led the battle that defeated the British at New Orleans, a victory that left no sovereignty to doubt the resolve of the young nation. Although many concerns linger regarding his treatment of the Indians, Jackson did add strength and dignity to the infant nation and was responsible both directly and indirectly for enlarging the landmass to nearly what we know today.

Jackson had played the central role in ending the congressional caucus process of nominating a president, the formation of the opposition to old aristocratic control of American government, and the creation of the Democratic Party. Jackson created great power for the Democrats. But from the midst of great political movements eventually comes opposition. Thus was born the anti-Jackson Whig Party and the resultant competiveness of the two Tennessee parties. From 1839 until 1853, the Whigs and the Democrats were evenly balanced as their power rocked back and forth. Whig governors alternated with Democratic governors. So close were statewide elections that usually few votes separated the winners from the losers. No governor of either party could count on being able to win reelection and stay longer than one two-year term. After Newton Cannon (Whig) served two terms, 1835–1839, the subsequent governors, from James K. Polk, 1839–1841, to William Campbell, 1851–1853, served just one term. The exception was James C. "Lean Jimmy" Jones who won two terms, 1841–1845. Neither party was strong enough to control Tennessee during this period. It would be 1853, with the inauguration of Andrew Johnson, before the pendulum of power swung enough for the Democrats to grasp a more permanent hold. To say the least, Andrew Jackson had a dominant impact on the evolution of Tennessee and the United States.

Alfred Osborne Pope Nicholson, a Tennessee U.S. senator from 1840 to 1842 and later from 1859 to 1861, like many prominent as well as common Tennesseans, attended Jackson's funeral. He was later quoted (mistaking the summer of 1844 for the summer of 1845) as saying:

> During the summer of 1844 Jackson died. I attended his burial at the "Hermitage." The throng of visitors was immense; the ceremonies most simple. As I stood near his open coffin where I could see his stony face, looking up my attention was reverted by the bearing of General Sam Houston, who stood at the head of the bier, holding in his arms his baby and on his arm his fond wife. I have never forgotten the look of intense devotion which he cast on his child. The dead and living heroes are a vivid picture in my memory as I then saw them. (McKellar 1942)

During 1845 political contests were hotly debated and occasionally ugly. In a U.S. representative campaign in West Tennessee, the Democratic candidate, P. F. Stanton, was a Catholic. At this time, religious affiliation fomented some prejudice in society. A man named J. R. Christian apparently did not accept the idea of a Catholic being his representative and made his opinions known to the Democratic Party. Some members decided they, too, could not support a Catholic and instead supported P. T. Scruggs, the Whig candidate, who evidently had acceptable religious credentials. The Whigs, of course, tried to use the religious issue to their advantage. Disparaging articles were written in the Sommerville *Reporter*. The bitterness continued to arouse Christian's anger to the point that he shot Stanton at Germantown. Stanton survived the shooting and the Whigs' attempt to discredit him because of his religious affiliation, and went on to win the election.

Governor Jones decided not to run for reelection in 1845. Instead he took a job as president of the Memphis and Charleston Railroad. The Whigs planned to retain the governor's chair and looked at several candidates who might carry their torch. Gustavus A. Henry, Neill S. Brown, and Ephraim Foster were all considered. At the April 20, 1845, Whig state convention, U.S. Senator Ephraim Foster was selected to become the Whig nominee for governor of Tennessee. (He did not run for reelection to the Senate; Hopkins Turney replaced him on

EPHRAIM HUBBARD FOSTER was born near Bardstown, Nelson County, Kentucky, on September 17, 1794. At three years of age his family moved near Nashville, Tennessee. He graduated from Cumberland College (later the University of Nashville) in 1813. He served as private secretary to Andrew Jackson during the Creek Indian War and participated in several battles from 1813 to 1815. He apprenticed law under John Dickinson, a well known lawyer in Nashville, was admitted to the bar in 1820, and eventually developed an outstanding law practice. He married the widow of John Dickinson. He was "quick-tempered, but he had very winning ways" (McKellar 1942). Foster served in the state legislature from 1829 to 1831 and from 1835 to 1837, during which time he served as speaker of the Tennessee house. In view of his earlier stint under Andrew Jackson, it is curious as to why Foster broke with the Democrats and became a Whig, since the Whigs existence was based on opposition to Jackson. The distance between them widened after Foster's animosity toward Jackson fully surfaced in 1833 when he supported Felix Grundy for the U.S. Senate, over Jackson's choice at the time, John Eaton. In the 1836 presidential campaign Foster worked against Democrat Martin Van Buren (Jackson's choice) in favor of fellow Tennessean (Whig) Hugh Lawson White. In 1838 Grundy resigned his Senate seat to take President Van Buren's appointment as attorney general of the United States. Foster was then appointed to the U.S. Senate seat, serving from September 17, 1838, until March 3, 1839. During his partial term, in 1838, he competed with former Governor William Carroll for the full-term election and won. He refused to vote, as instructed by the Tennessee legislature, for the annexation of Texas and resigned his full-term seat on November 15, 1839, to campaign with the Whig electoral ticket in the 1840 Tennessee elections in which William Henry Harrison ran for president. When Foster tried to reclaim his Senate seat, he was defeated in 1840 by Grundy. After Grundy died in 1840, the state legislature deadlocked and went without any U.S. senator from Tennessee for two years. After the deadlock ended in 1843, Foster was elected, again defeating William Carroll, to serve the unexpired term from October 17, 1843, until March 3, 1845. During his later term as senator, he worked for (Whig) Henry Clay and opposed his fellow Tennessean, James K. Polk. As senator he opposed the annexation of Texas, misreading the public's attitude, and subsequently paid the political price to his fellow Tennesseans. He was defeated in a bid for governor of Tennessee in 1845. Foster's political weakness began when he changed parties and opposed Andrew Jackson. However, the success of his law practice may have given him the courage to act his mind and bolt both party and Jackson. After his defeat, he returned to the practice of law in Nashville. He died in Nashville on September 6, 1854, and was buried in City Cemetery. (Photograph courtesy of SHO)

March 4, 1845.) Foster had served under Andrew Jackson in the Creek Indian War and had remained a supporter of Old Hickory for several years. Eventually, he split with Jackson and became a Whig. Democrat Congressman Aaron V. "Fat" Brown, who had served in the state house and senate and had been serving in the U.S. House since 1839, decided to retire from office in order to devote himself to his personal business. However, Tennessee Democrats nominated the retiring congressman from Pulaski, Tennessee, to carry the Democratic torch for the governor's race.

Aaron Vail Brown and Ephraim Foster fought it out on the campaign trail, beginning in Clarksville, Tennessee, in spring 1845. The race was exciting, contentious,

AARON VAIL BROWN was born in Brunswick County, Virginia, on August 15, 1795. His father was a Methodist minister. There were eleven children in his family. In 1813, his family moved to Giles County, Tennessee, but Brown stayed in the East to study law at the University of North Carolina, graduating from the university as valedictorian in 1814. After completing school, he came to Tennessee and studied law with James Trimble of Nashville. He then entered practice with James K. Polk (the practice included Giles County). After Polk became congressman, the business association was dissolved, but Brown made a good name for his practice. Brown's first wife was Sarah Woodford Burrus, who died when she was thirty-five. The couple had six children. (One daughter eventually married a grandson of Governor Willie Blount. A granddaughter was later the mother of Hill McAlister, who became governor in 1933.)

In 1821 Brown was elected to the state senate and except for 1825 served until 1827. He then served in the state house from 1831 until 1835. By 1839 he was elected to Congress and remained there until 1845. He ran for governor as a Democrat against Whig candidate former U.S. Senator Ephraim Foster and was elected and inaugurated in 1845. He married his second wife, Cynthia Pillow Sanders (widow of John W. Sanders), after one month in office. The couple had one son.

Texas was admitted into the Union about the time Brown took office, and his term saw Tennessee's involvement in the Mexican War, a dispute over the boundary between Texas and Mexico. Governor Brown again proved that Tennessee was the Volunteer State. He called for twenty-eight hundred soldiers, but thirty thousand volunteered. The United States won, and the war ended in 1847 with the acquisition of an enormous landmass reaching to the West Coast.

When the governor ran for reelection, the Whig/Democrat tide had reversed again. President Polk had appointed enough Tennessee Democrats to ignite the Whigs into action. With Polk's expansion of the United States via the victory of the Mexican War, politicians became concerned over whether the territories would tip the balance of power toward the free or slave states. The slavery issue was causing turmoil, and the Democrats took the blame for stirring up the discontent. This may have been enough to cause Governor Brown to lose to the Whig candidate Neill S. Brown, who was also from Giles County, by only a few hundred votes in the gubernatorial race of 1847. Brown was appointed as postmaster general of the United States by President Buchanan, and his family moved to Washington. Mrs. Brown served as first lady of the White House for the unmarried Buchanan until Brown died of pneumonia on March 8, 1859. The former governor was buried at Mount Olivet Cemetery, Nashville, and his wife and children returned to Nashville. (Photograph courtesy of TSLA) and very close. Whig Foster took East and West Tennessee but not by enough to outpoll Brown's Middle Tennessee advantage. As with recent Democratic victories during this era in Tennessee, the election was won by the Democratic majority in Middle Tennessee. Brown was elected governor, defeating the former senator by 1,400 votes out of 115,000. He served from 1845 to 1847. Democrats also won control of the state legislature in 1845. This was not a good campaign season for the Whigs.

Since the Democrats now controlled the state legislature as well as the governor's seat, the Memphis *Appeal* suggested that a Democrat from West Tennessee should receive one of the U.S. Senate seats. These usually went to men from Middle and East Tennessee. The paper also suggested that slavery was acceptable in Tennessee (Keating 1888).

On November 12, 1845, Memphis was host to the great Commercial Convention, presided over by the legendary John C. Calhoun. The purpose of the convention was to discuss ideas that would assist with the development of the western and southwestern portions of the nation. It was hoped that proposals such as the construction of a ship canal between the Great Lakes and the Mississippi River and the completion of the Memphis and Charleston Railroad would assist the Mid-south and the surrounding states with socioeconomic progress. The convention was of interest throughout the United States and the fact that it was held in Memphis was a point of pride to Memphians as well as to all Tennesseans. There were dreams of Memphis one day competing with the likes of Chicago and Cincinnati. John Calhoun was given a hero's welcome to the city, and he lent credibility to the convention. For this happy, festive, and hopeful occasion, Whigs and Democrats joined together in the proceedings for the good of Memphis.

During 1845 the biggest topic of conversation among Tennesseans continued to be Texas. The debate centered on its admission into the Union as a slave state. Opinions varied somewhat between those held in West and those in East Tennessee. The West Tennessee attitude was printed in the Memphis *Appeal* and suggested that slavery was acceptable in Tennessee. Even though many Tennesseans were opposed to slavery, they did not necessarily feel that slaveholders should be forced to give up their property—property that was necessary to help support the cotton crops, the commercial base of the area. West Tennessee Democrats favored supporting the Union's defense of Texas, while the Whigs were split in their support. Whig hesitancy was based mostly on the issue of Texas's admission as a slave state. However, overall, West Tennesseans did not support abolition and felt little reluctance to support Texas. In East Tennessee, where there was no agricultural base requiring slaves and a greater percentage of Whigs, the people did not hold as much fervor over Texas. Nonetheless, many still felt it was their patriotic duty to support fellow Tennesseans now in Texas.

By December 1845 Texas had accepted the United States proposal for annexation and drafted a new state constitution. On December 29, 1845, U.S. Congress officially admitted Texas as the twenty-eighth state. After Texas was annexed into the Union, the Mexicans decided to put an end to what they considered was an infringement on their territory. The talk of war with Mexico now became the greatest topic of discourse throughout the state. President Polk continued with plans to purchase New Mexico and California from Mexico. However, nothing could be worked out with the Mexicans over Texas. When a dispute developed over the boundaries of the Texas-Mexico border, the Mexicans crossed the border of the Rio Grande on May 9, 1846, and attacked U.S. Army troops. On May 13 the United States declared war on Mexico.

Tennessee, always the "Volunteer State," was ready to assist in the war effort with troops and moral support. Meetings were held and resolutions adopted to publicize support, as well as to organize enlistments of volunteers for the army. Tennessee would come through with volunteers, as it always had since the War of 1812. However, politicians throughout the country were uncertain that there would be enough troops for a war that was still controversial. Because of the issue of slavery, not everyone had been in favor of Texas statehood. However, when Tennessee was asked to supply twenty-eight hundred soldiers, thirty thousand volunteered. Newspapers had already begun to refer to Tennessee as the Volunteer State, but after this war, the nickname stuck. Men actually paid those already inducted into the army for the right to take their place in the fight against the Mexicans.

In the meanwhile, Oregon Territory issues brewed. For over thirty years the British and Americans had discussed the issue of ownership rights. Since 1818 the two nations had enjoyed joint occupation, but as more Americans migrated into the territory, many felt that all of the territory should belong to the United States. Some even talked of war, with slogans like "54°40' or Fight," during the 1844 presidential campaign. After Polk's election as president, some Democrats demanded the United States go to war with Britain rather than settle for less than all of the Oregon Territory. Polk, after conferences with party leaders, wondered if a compromise might be preferable to another war, and put the question to the U.S. Senate. They voted thirty-seven to twelve recommending a compromise at the forty-ninth parallel. Polk accepted the Senate's plan—the only time in his presidency that Polk asked the advice of the U.S. Senate and followed it. A treaty was signed June 15, 1846, designating Canadian-United States boundaries.

The Mexican War began on the nation's southern frontier. Zachary Taylor was sent to command the troops of the Rio Grande. He was soon made a major general and allowed to invade Mexico. He enjoyed numerous victories and won great popularity for his military successes. When Taylor, a known Whig, had become a little too popular, President Polk had his troops reduced to cut down his chances of winning any more headlines. When Santa Anna's twenty thousand troops attacked Taylor's at Buena Vista in February 1847, Taylor had only about five thousand men. Nevertheless, they held off the Mexican force, achieved a great victory, and Taylor became a hero. The effort to block Taylor from fame actually helped him.

Many Tennesseans went to Texas to lead in its defense. Colonel William B. Campbell, Brigadier General Gideon J. Pillow, Colonel William Trousdale, Colonel John H. Savage, Colonel B. F. Cheatham, and Colonel William Haskell all received distinction in the Mexican War.

The cotton trade continued to increase to the point that much of the South became a one-crop region of the nation. Cotton required a huge labor force in order to harvest and maintain growth. The cotton gin, invented in 1793, was by now used throughout the South, greatly aiding in the development of cotton commerce. The South became noted for its large amounts of cotton which were shipped throughout the nation and exported to England. In a few short years consumption reached 588,200,000 pounds of cotton from a low 51,000,000 recorded in 1800.

In the nation's capital, John Calhoun introduced a resolution in the U.S. Senate that was intended to clarify a state's right over the federal government's interference. The resolution stated that the federal government had no right to interfere with personal property, including slaves. There were opposing views, and the resolution only inflamed the national debate. The growth of the controversy was temporarily overshadowed, however, by several U.S. victories against the Mexican forces in the latter part of March 1847. In April, at the Tennessee Democratic Convention, Aaron V. "Fat" Brown was renominated as the Democratic candidate for governor of Tennessee. His opponent was Neill S. "Lean" Brown, a Whig (both Browns, unrelated, were from Giles County). This was a busy and exciting time for Tennessee. The Memphis *Appeal* said, "We are feeding Ireland, whipping the Mexicans, electing a governor, and doing a thriving business at that; still we can well spare the time and means to get up a good public library" (Keating 1888).

The gubernatorial race of 1847 was an interesting campaign. The issues concerned topics facing the nation rather than the state. Once again, the campaign was based on the philosophical differences between the Democrats and the Whigs.

NEILL S. BROWN was born in Giles County, Tennessee, in 1810. His father, Duncan Brown, was a farmer and a Whig. The family was Presbyterian and of Scotch-Irish descent. His grandfather, Angus Brown, had served in the Revolutionary War and was also a farmer. Brown received little education as a child and taught himself to read. Later, he taught school in Giles County and received some college education. He began studying law under Judge James Trimble of Nashville and in Pulaski, Tennessee, in 1833, and was admitted to the bar in 1834. He went to Texas to develop a law practice but found the opportunity limited. He married the judge's daughter, Mary Ann Trimble. The couple had eight children and survived the deaths of four sons.

After Brown returned to Tennessee, in 1836, he participated in the Seminole War. He was nominated as a Whig elector-at-large for Hugh Lawson White's candidacy for president in 1836, and in 1840 he campaigned for William Henry Harrison (Whig) for president. In 1844 he worked for Henry Clay (Whig). An excellent speaker, he served three terms in the state house of representatives, and in 1847, was nominated as the Whig candidate for governor, defeating incumbent Governor Aaron Brown.

Governor Brown worked for the development of a public education system. When he ran for reelection in 1848, he was defeated by the Whig candidate, William Trousdale. In 1850 President Taylor appointed Brown as minister to Russia. In 1853 he returned to Nashville and was elected as a state representative in 1855, and then speaker of the state house. Brown took no part in the Civil War; however, Union forces burned his home. He served in the Tennessee constitutional convention of 1879. Brown died on January 30, 1886, and was buried in Mount Olivet Cemetery in Nashville. His wife died in 1895. (Photograph courtesy of TSLA)

The Whigs opposed President Polk and his policies—national expansion, the Mexican War, Oregon expansion. By now the Mexican War was beginning to take its toll on the people, and the former fervor for war was losing its pitch. At first the nation had been enthusiastic about fighting the Mexicans, but as dysentery and other diseases claimed as many lives as the death tolls from battles, Americans and Tennesseans began to abandon their enthusiasm for war and blamed President Polk for their hardships. As the pendulum of opinion swung, the electorate turned slightly back toward the Whigs. Whig candidate Neill S. "Lean" Brown defeated the incumbent but only by a thousand votes. The legislature also moved back to a Whig majority.

In 1847 the Class 2 U.S. Senate seat was up for election, and now the Whigs controlled the state legislature. U.S. Senator Spencer Jarnagin was a Whig, but he had been criticized by his colleagues for supporting the Walker Tariff Bill, which was a Democrat-sponsored bill designed to reduce tariffs. Former Governor Jones, Congressman John Bell, Memphis businessman Robert Topp, John Netherland, and several others wanted the Senate seat. There was some serious competition, handshaking, and lobbying in this very exciting month-long intralegislative campaign to elect the next U.S. senator from Tennessee. Finally, after forty-eight ballots, Whig John Bell was elected to the U.S. Senate, assuming his seat November 22, 1847 (the seat had been vacant from the scheduled beginning of the term on March 4, 1847).

Later in 1847 General Winfield Scott captured Mexico City and the end of the Mexican War was at hand. The successes in the war only heightened the slavery issue. Organizations opposing slavery began to strengthen. A newly formed Abolitionist Party held a presidential nominating convention in Buffalo, New York. John P. Hale of New Hampshire was nominated for president, and Licester King of Ohio was nominated for vice president.

With the news of the end of the Mexican War came the United States's claims to the conquered and acquired territories which would make up California, Utah, Nevada, part of Arizona, and New Mexico. This great increase in landmass was good for American expansion capabilities, but it worsened the crisis over whether or not these areas would be slaveholding or free.

A Pennsylvania congressman, David Wilmot, had his own ideas as to how the new territories should impact slavery. He added a measure to an appropriation's bill in Congress which excluded slavery from any of the land bought from Mexico. Most of the soldiers who had fought in the Mexican War were from Southern slave states. When Southerners found out about the Wilmot Proviso, there was a great outcry. They felt that they were being excluded from the land that they had helped win for the United States. President Polk, U.S. Representative Andrew Johnson, and Tennessee's state senators all saw the proviso as an attempt to create trouble, and denounced it. In Tennessee people were appalled. There was general opposition to the proviso among all political persuasions. In the nation's capital there was a legislative firestorm over it. The provision passed in the House but failed in the Senate. In the process, it focused national attention on the issue of slavery. The subject was now a political lightning rod.

The treaty between the Americans and Mexicans was signed on February 2, 1848. The Senate approved the treaty with Senators Bell (Whig) and Turney (elected as a Democrat but renounced by his party) both voting for it. Senator Bell actually was opposed to the expansion into California and New Mexico because of the slavery issue. However, he felt that it had to be done in order to stop the Mexican War.

President Polk, who during his tenure had overseen an incredible western expansion of the United States, also signed a treaty that allowed American right of passage over the Isthmus of Panama and reduced tariffs. He came to the presidency with clear goals, and he worked for them. He was a president who carried out his campaign promises. Even though the Whigs won a majority of the seats in the U.S. House during the midterm elections (due mainly to Northern opposition to the Mexican War and American expansionism), Polk worked with them for the nation's best interest. (The makeup of Congress changed from 143 Democrats and 77 Whigs and 6 other to 115 Whigs and 108 Democrats and 4 other in the House and from 31 Democrats and 25 Whigs to 36 Democrats and 21 Whigs and 1 other in the Senate.)

Many urged Polk to run for reelection, but true to his campaign pledge, he declined to do so. Because of this, Senator Lewis Cass from Michigan was selected as the Democratic candidate for president. Martin Van Buren attempted to run as the Free-Soil, antislavery candidate. The Whig National Convention in Philadelphia in June 1848 nominated Zachary Taylor, now a popular war hero, as their candidate for president and Millard Fillmore of New York as vice president.

General Zachary Taylor had gained distinction during the Mexican War. Whig leaders felt that he was popular enough to win the election even though they did not know his positions on any important issues. Taylor himself, being a military man, did not really have a grasp of the intricacies of the issues that would confront a candidate, or an elected official, in his day.

The election was very close. Van Buren did little except split the New York Democratic Party into disarray. The state's thirty-six electoral votes went to Taylor, which provided his margin of victory. Zachary Taylor was elected president receiving 1,360,967 popular votes to 1,222,342 for Cass. The electoral vote count was 163 to 127. This exciting election dominated the news of the day and was the central topic of conversation throughout Tennessee. The first official transmission of the recently installed telegraph line in Tennessee was the news of the election of Zachary Taylor as president in 1848.

After the Mexican War, the New Mexico and California Territories became part of the United States. With America's landmass now stretching to the Pacific Ocean, interest in Pacific coastal migration and westward trade development heightened. When gold was discovered in California in 1849, excitement and speculation over Memphis becoming a major trade route to the West Coast captured the imagination of the people from West Tennessee. St. Louis, Vicksburg, New Orleans, and other cities also saw the opportunity. The revolution of travel by railroad was on the verge of changing America in the late 1840s.

A Commercial Convention was held in Memphis on October 23, 1849, to promote the site as a terminus for a proposed transcontinental railway. The advantages were clear. Memphis had the Mississippi River to connect to the north and south. The location was far enough south to avoid harsh winter snowfall and was about equal distance from the Gulf of Mexico and Lake Michigan. Tennessean Lieutenant Matthew Maury, who was well-known and respected for his expertise in transportation, championed the cause of Memphis during congressional discussion of the proposed site for the rail terminus. Sectional competition for the site was strong, and over the next decade Memphis could not seal its selection. Finally, during the Civil War, when there was no Southern representation in Congress, a Northern site was selected.

By 1848 the apprehension over states' rights had reached the point that many people felt a need for formal discussions of common concerns among Southern states. In December 1848 several political leaders met to discuss the organization of such a conference. John C. Calhoun organized a meeting in Washington to discuss available options for Southern states to oppose the Wilmot Proviso and confront the growing discrimination of Southern states. Tennessee U.S. Senator Hopkins L. Turney was one of the Southern leaders who attended the meeting, which produced an "Address to the People of the Southern States" (Corlew 1989). Essentially, the December meeting solidified plans for a Convention of Southern States in which they could organize and formalize their position and make plans to defend against Northern intrusions on their sovereign way of life, which the North did not understand or care to understand.

Early in 1849 President-elect Zachary Taylor visited Memphis on his way to Washington to assume office. His visit to the Volunteer State, which frequently supported Whig candidates, was marked as a special occasion, and he was received with great honor and admiration.

After Taylor's inauguration on March 5, 1849, former President Polk left Washington and returned to his home in Tennessee. Polk had completed a successful term and was honored as a man true to his word. His tenure as president had been marked by great successes. He had completed the annexation of Texas and Oregon, took control of California and New Mexico, reintroduced an independent treasury, cut tariffs, and served only one term as president. Under James K. Polk, the United States doubled in size. Before his presidency, the Mississippi River was the western border of our nation's settled frontier. At his term's end, the Pacific Ocean was the western boundary of this great experiment in government.

On his trip home after leaving Washington, former President Polk visited Memphis on March 27, 1849, and was enthusiastically received. Unfortunately, he contracted cholera sometime during the trip and died on June 15 after returning to Nashville. (In January 1849, the Asiatic cholera hit Tennessee and spread rampantly throughout the state.)

After Polk's death, Tennessee politics soon began to heat up once again as the next gubernatorial campaign neared. The Whigs renominated Governor Neill S. Brown. The Democratic state convention met in the summer of 1849 and nominated General William Trousdale. Trousdale was a Democrat from Sumner County with a record of military service. He first served while just a boy in the Creek Indian War and recently had earned distinction in the Mexican War serving as a colonel. The Democratic state convention also declared that they supported a joint meeting with other Southern states to discuss ways to unite against the aggression of the North, if in fact, the Wilmot Proviso were passed in Congress.

The Seeds of Discontent

The issues of the 1849 gubernatorial campaign were the Wilmot Proviso and the consequences of the U.S. victory in the Mexican War. Governor Brown campaigned hard, but Trousdale's reputation as a hero in

WILLIAM TROUSDALE was born in 1790 in Orange County, North Carolina. His father, James Trousdale, had served as a captain in the Revolutionary War. As payment for his service, in 1784 he received a land grant in the Territory South of the Ohio River, which eventually became Sumner County, Tennessee. The family moved to the area when William was six years old. In 1801, commissioners were selected by the legislature to choose a site for a county seat in Sumner County. They selected the home farm of the Trousdales. The area became Gallatin, Tennessee.

William received only a little education at the local school before his mind drifted to adventure. He quickly traded the schoolhouse for the battlefield and fought in the Creek War and in Pensacola with Andrew Jackson. After serving as a soldier, he married Mary Ann Bugg. In 1835 he was elected to the state senate. Then, it was back to the military. He served in the Mexican War, was wounded twice, and ended up a hero and a brigadier general in the U.S. Army. He was elected governor in 1849 as a Democrat, and it was during his term that the Southern Convention was held in Nashville. The voters took a dim and suspicious view of the Democrats' readiness to oppose the Union, and the Whig gubernatorial candidate, William Campbell, defeated Trousdale in 1851. President Pierce appointed Trousdale as minister to Brazil in 1852. He lived until March 27, 1872, and was buried in Gallatin, Tennessee. (Photograph courtesy of TSLA)

the Mexican War overcame incumbency. The Democrat Trousdale won by fourteen hundred votes. He was elected to serve from 1849 to 1851. Brown then was appointed as minister to Russia by fellow Whig President Zachary Taylor.

The concern over California admission prompted Southern leaders to consider a Nashville convention to discuss the implications and options. Senators Jefferson Davis and H. S. Foote and Representatives Jacob Thompson, W. S. Featherstone, W. McWillie, and A. G. Brown of Mississippi supported a request for legislative opinion over the matter. Mississippi Governor Quitman promoted the Nashville convention. Delegates to the convention were to be elected by joint session of each state's legislature. Mississippi leaders urged other states to consider a meeting.

The close of the Mexican War brought with it peace, but the vast new territories gained by the victory brought on another national crisis. Concern now developed over whether these new regions would become slave or free states and which section of the nation would gain in the balance of power. The North feared more slave states, while the South feared more free states. Southerners were concerned that if the Northerners gained the advantage of the federal votes in Congress, they would overpower the South and force mandates on a culture they did not support. Late in 1849, after President Taylor assumed office, the territory of California made it known that it wanted admission to the Union. Former Tennessee Democratic Senator Alexander Outlaw Anderson helped write the California Constitution which complicated the national crisis over slavery by mandating California a free state. This was not only a moral issue, it was also an economic issue. In the 1850s Southern culture and slavery were inseparable. The American economy was evolving within a budding industrial revolution in which the North was far ahead. Northerners, in general, did not understand the agriculturally based South which was dependent on intensive labor to bring in crops.

The proposed admission of California threatened Southern state leaders since the addition of votes in Congress would tilt the national balance of power in favor of the North. Although President Taylor was a Southerner (from Louisiana), he supported the admission of California. In response, the state of Texas tried to claim New Mexico in an attempt to prevent this territory from eventually being admitted to the United States as a free state. The United States, however, claimed that New Mexico was part of the purchase from Mexico. A national controversy erupted. Congress held off on the admission of California as a state.

In December 1849 Henry Clay proposed a "compromise" and in January 1850 introduced several bills known as the Compromise of 1850. He proposed to admit California as a free state, leaving the remainder of the territory given up by the Mexicans without restriction to slavery. He also proposed to allow slavery in Washington, D.C., but not slave sales. An important point in his proposals was the creation of a tougher law regarding fugitive slaves. Clay's ideas were extensively debated in Congress, and Tennessee leaders participated in the action. Tennessee Senator John Bell thought the best solution would be to make Texas a slave state to counter California's free state votes in Washington. Bell ended up agreeing with most of Clay's ideas but opposed the cessation of slave sales in Washington, D.C. Andrew Johnson, a Tennessee U.S. representative, was recorded in opposition to Northern violation of Southern sovereignty. When the votes were counted, only four out of eleven of Tennessee's congressmen voted against the admission of California and only one voted in favor of the District of Columbia bill. Senator Bell supported all but the District of Columbia bill. The only point supported by Senator Turney was the fugitive slave code.

Tennessee Democrat Governor Trousdale opposed the abolitionist attitudes of some of the federal officeholders. He endorsed the proposal submitted in October 1849 by political leaders from the state of Mississippi calling for a Southern Convention to be held in Nashville, Tennessee, in June 1850 to adopt proposals of resistance and formally protest the intrusion upon their states' rights. The Whigs in Tennessee did not want the convention on Tennessee soil; nonetheless the convention was set to be held in Nashville. Even though the Whig-controlled legislature prevented Tennessee from sending official delegates to the convention, one hundred or so Tennesseans attended.

About this time in the Senate, Henry Clay, Daniel Webster, and John C. Calhoun attempted to work for compromise. In his speech on March 4, Calhoun, a Democrat, said that since the balance of influence had been tipped in favor of those in Congress who supported free states, the people of slave states should have their rights protected. Webster foresaw the eventual breakup of the Union over the issue and in his speech on March 7 expounded on the protection of the rights of the individual. Even though he was a Whig and an opponent of slavery, he wanted to protect the nation and offer leniency toward the South. Northern abolitionists felt betrayed by Webster, but he had made friends in the South. Both speeches were published in

Tennessee papers. While the issues were approaching a crisis level, Calhoun died on March 31.

The eyes of the nation were now fixed upon the actions of Congress. Every man with any knowledge of political matters knew that the issues at stake were political power, the balance of representation on the floor of Congress, and the future course of the nation.

While the compromise was being debated, the Southern Convention opened in Nashville on June 3, 1850, despite the opposition of the Whigs. The purpose of the convention was to investigate how best to protect the rights and property of Southern people in a manner that would preserve the Union. Andrew Jackson Donelson and Alfred O. P. Nicholson were two of the principle organizers of the convention and spoke for opposing sides. Donelson had returned to Tennessee from Prussia and Germany where he had served as ambassador, and from Washington, where he had edited the *Washington Globe*—the official Democratic Party newspaper. Nicholson was a former and future U.S. senator from Tennessee. Donelson opposed secession, while Nicholson supported states' rights.

Many Southerners came to Nashville for the convention, which demanded that the Mexican territory, annexed after the war, be divided along the line of the Missouri Compromise. It also stated that the Wilmot Proviso was unconstitutional, asked for better fugitive slave laws, and demanded that all states have the same rights in the new territories (without restrictions placed on the Southern states). Essentially, the resolutions of the Southern Convention said that the rights of the individual and the states should be preserved and protected and that Congress had no right to interfere in the rights given to an individual by his state. The resolutions also warned against Congress using a territory's future statehood to alter the protection of slaveholders who might move to the new area. The convention elected to withhold any other action until the U.S. Congress finalized its action. The convention eventually adjourned without really achieving its mission. Nicholson and Donelson then toured the South, debating states' rights and secession in several cities, including Charleston, Mobile, and New Orleans.

While participating in the laying of the cornerstone of the Washington Monument on July 4, 1850, sixty-five-year-old President Zachary Taylor suffered from heat exposure (it is supposed). He died five days later on July 9. President Taylor had been opposed to the Compromise of 1850 and very likely may have vetoed the bill. Later, Daniel Webster was convinced that Taylor's death may have prevented the beginning of civil war. Vice President Millard Fillmore now became president. Fillmore was more approving of the efforts of the compromise.

In August and September of 1850 the Compromise of 1850 was finally passed. Earlier, in July, the bill had been reduced to address the territory of Utah. The negative public sentiment and preparation of Texas to raise troops to defend New Mexico caused the Senate to address the other issues, but this was done in separate bills. The Whigs accepted the parameters of the compromise, while the Democrats pressed toward separation. Local attitudes were reflected in newspaper articles like one which said, "Can a State Secede from the Union?" (Keating 1888). The final form of the Compromise of 1850 was a series of measures which included the admission of California as a free state; the establishment of the territories of Utah and New Mexico under the provisions that neither could pass laws dealing with slavery; the disclaimer of the right of Texas to claim New Mexico (and the payment of ten million dollars to Texas for the land); continuance of slavery in the District of Columbia with a halt to slave sales there; and a new fugitive slave law (which required federal assistance in returning runaway slaves.) When President Fillmore signed the compromise, he lost the support of his abolitionist Whigs. The Whig Party was now destined to become weakened since they failed to satisfy ardent antislavery political forces with the compromise bill. As a result, Fillmore would be the last Whig ever to serve as president.

The leaders of the June 1849 Southern Convention went ahead with plans for the next meeting since the compromise bill did not satisfy all concerns. Many Southerners felt that the bill did about as much as anyone could expect and wanted to give it a chance to settle differences with Northern abolitionists. However, there were still many Southerners who did not feel that the bill would solve the differences between the South and the abolitionists. The Southern Convention met again, on November 19, 1850, and expressed its wish to preserve the Union. Tennesseans Aaron V. Brown and Gideon J. Pillow prepared the Tennessee resolution to the convention. In their resolution they pressed for the convention to accept the Compromise of 1850 and work to preserve the Union. Their desires may have been based upon their unique understanding of the Whigs in Tennessee. With upper East Tennessee strongly Whig, they may have felt the need for compromise more than those from the other states attending the convention. The other states clearly did not agree with the Tennessee delegation. The vote was six states for stronger recommendations and one state, Tennessee, against. The participants then went ahead and expressed their disappointment that the Missouri Compromise did not extend the line to the Pacific Ocean or protect the rights of slaveholders in the District of Columbia, Utah, or New Mexico. The convention also expressed concern that the rights and wishes of Texas in regard to the New Mexico Territory were being ignored.

The resolutions of the 1850 Southern Convention stated that until their rights were restored, the South would not take part in the conventions for nomination of presidential candidates and that they would hold another convention to make plans to restore their rights and oppose any more aggression. Tennessee was the only Southern state to vote against the resolutions.

The agitation continued to intensify. In the North, slavery was an evil to be ended. In the South, their property had been violated and they were being politically and economically dominated.

While the national debate over slavery raged, Tennessee continued its progress. By 1850 it was the fifth most populous state in the nation and held a prominent position among the states. Railroad systems continued to be developed. Efforts were made to create a public education system. The population growth was exemplified in the two largest communities: Memphis increased from 1,700 in 1840 to 8,841 in 1850; Nashville increased from 6,629 in 1840 to 10,165 in 1850.

During 1851 the issue of slavery dominated social discourse and local political battles between Whig and Democratic candidates. The next presidential contest was also drawing significant attention because of the issues of slavery, the fugitive slave law, and the Compromise of 1850. The Tennessee governor's race was set between two leaders in the Mexican War. Incumbent Democrat Governor William Trousdale was renominated by his party. The Whigs nominated William B. Campbell. Campbell was a circuit judge and, like Trousdale, a hero of the Mexican War. Governor Trousdale was tied to the Democrats who had talked and acted against the Union via the Southern Convention. The Southern Convention of Nashville did not help Trousdale's cause. The general populous was suspicious of the Democrats' ready consideration of action against the Union. Even though the Whigs, nationally, were beginning to weaken, in Tennessee they were a reasonable alternative to the Democrats whose ideas many people considered to be treasonous.

In 1851, voting was beginning to become sectional on the basis of the slavery issue, rather than simple party preference. For example, in agriculturally based West Tennessee, Democrat Stanton was elected to Congress, but in the gubernatorial race, the Whig challenger Campbell beat the incumbent, Democrat Trousdale. The two conducted a campaign that was different from previous Tennessee gubernatorial contests. Campbell had served as a captain in the Seminole War under General Trousdale and had run against his commander before, in 1837, for Congress, defeating him then. Trousdale, well respected, was known as the "War Horse" for his brave and successful fighting. Campbell had come a long way from his father's unsuccessful farm—all the way to Congress—and he too was well thought of. When these two men met on the campaign trail for governor, they were both respectful of the other. There was none of the sniping and criticism which was normally seen. They were gentlemen, kind and committed to a dignified campaign. Campbell won by fifteen hundred votes and was inaugurated on October 19, 1851. He served until 1853 and he was the last Whig governor ever elected in Tennessee. Along with winning the governor's seat in 1851, the Whig Party took control of both the state senate and house.

When Hopkins Turney's Class 1 U.S. Senate term ended in 1851, it was time again for the legislature to go through the selection process. Since the Whigs had control of the legislature, they would have their preference. Former Democrat Governor Trousdale wanted the seat but so did former Whig Governor Jimmy Jones. James Chamberlayne Jones was elected. On December 15, 1851, Tennessee's other U.S. senator, John Bell, presented the credentials of the Honorable Mr. Jones to the Senate. His term officially began on March 4, 1851, and he served until March 3, 1857. Now both Tennessee U.S. senators were authentic Whigs.

The General Assembly of 1851 performed gerrymandering antics by forming a committee comprised of ten Whigs and five Democrats which would reapportion districts according to the census of 1850. The assembly made it as certain as possible that the party in power could maintain its control. The legislature also passed a resolution of determination to maintain the Union and disregard any idea of secession.

On January 2, 1852, the Democratic state convention was held, and delegates to the Democratic National Convention and state electors were elected. When the Democratic National Convention took place in Baltimore, the delegates' votes for president were divided between James Buchanan and Lewis Cass. On the thirty-fifth ballot, the name of New Hampshire's Franklin Pierce was entered, and he was finally nominated on the forty-ninth ballot.

The Whig candidates for president included Tennessean John Bell, Daniel Webster, Henry Clay, President Millard Fillmore, and General Winfield Scott. President Fillmore was essentially without a party since he had signed the Compromise of 1850, attempting to pacify the South regarding slavery, and thus alienated abolitionist Whigs. Webster had gone out on a limb for Southern slaveholding interests during his speeches on the compromise, but Southern Whigs did not support him. After fifty-three ballots, the 1852 Baltimore Whig National Convention could not decide on a candidate. Fillmore was finally removed and General Winfield Scott was nominated; however, the convention forced Scott to endorse the Compromise of 1850. This only further alienated the ardent antislavery constituents who would no longer tolerate the Whig Party's scurrying of the issue. The South was Democrat; the North had to be something, and it was not going to be Whig if the party did not represent the antislavery interests.

With both the Democrat and Whig candidates embracing the Compromise of 1850, the campaign took on a life of its own as it rocked with the public emotions of the day. Scott's support for the Compromise of 1850 cost his candidacy votes. Many Whigs did not want to compromise anything, and there was a difference of opinion over how to deal with the South. The abolitionists wanted a party that was against slavery, but the Whigs were not providing that solid

WILLIAM BOWEN CAMPBELL was born on the banks of Mansker's Creek, Sumner County, Tennessee, on February 1, 1807. His family's farm was unsuccessful and young Campbell (who was the oldest of six children) went to his uncle's home to obtain an education. His uncle, the governor of Virginia, was a man of influence. Campbell studied law with him, and after completing his course in the governor's law office, returned home to Tennessee. He set up his own practice in Carthage, Tennessee, around 1829 and soon became an attorney for the state of Tennessee. In 1835 he married Frances Isabella Owen from Smith County, Tennessee. They eventually had nine children. That same year, he was elected to represent Smith County in the state legislature, but he soon took leave to serve in the army. He became a captain of volunteers in the Seminole War, serving under General William Trousdale and distinguishing himself. In 1837 he defeated Trousdale for a U.S. Representative seat. He served three terms in Congress and then returned to his law practice.

When Governor Aaron Brown called for troops to fight the Mexican War in 1846, Campbell volunteered and became a colonel for the First Regiment of Tennessee Volunteers (from Middle Tennessee). Colonel Campbell's men served valiantly in the Battle of Monterey in September 1846. The "Tennessee First" was then sent to assist General Taylor in storming a Mexican city, against a force that was twice their size. The "Tennessee First" was the first regiment to make it inside the city, and they raised the American flag, but one-third of the men in the battalion died position. The Whig Party was trying to have it both ways. As the disagreements between the abolitionist Whigs and compromise-favoring Whigs grew, the Party split. Clay and Webster had been the leaders who had held the Whigs together. However, shortly after the convention, Webster died on October 24, 1852. Clay had already died on June 29. Their deaths left a void in the strength of the party. A defeat for Whig candidate Scott would spell an end to the viability of the Whig Party.

Scott's endorsement of the Compromise of 1850 also divided Tennessee's Whigs. Some of those who favored slavery did not accept any compromise, while others, from agriculturally dependent parts of the state, did. Both of Tennessee's Whig U.S. senators, John Bell and Jimmy Jones, supported Whig candidate Scott. Others, such as abolitionist Whig William G. Brownlow, ardently withdrew their support.

Although Tennessee went Whig in the 1852 presidential election by 1,679 votes, the Democrats won the national election. Franklin Pierce won with 1,601,117 to Scott's 1,385,453 popular votes (254 to 42 electoral votes). This was the last presidential election in which the Whigs would carry Tennessee. Pierce was inaugurated on March 4, 1853.

Pierce's wife, however, did not attend the ceremony or participate in White House social functions for the next two years. Their only son, eleven years old at the time (they had lost two other children as infants) died when the railroad car in which the Pierces traveled from Boston to Concord prior to the inauguration came off the tracks. The president-elect and Mrs. Pierce were only slightly injured, but they saw their only son die before their eyes.

---

in the assault. Tennessee soldiers already had a reputation for volunteering and fighting, but the "First Tennessee Regiment" solidified this reputation. They became known throughout the army as the "Bloody First." They were then sent to assist General Scott at Vera Cruz, where Campbell had the opportunity to work with Robert E. Lee. The "Bloody First" participated in several battles the next year before they were finally sent home.

Now famous, Campbell ran for governor in 1851. Even though the Whigs were weakening nationally, he was elected governor. After a single term, he declined to run again. In 1853, he moved to Lebanon, Tennessee, and became president of the Bank of Middle Tennessee. During the crisis of impending civil war in 1861, he traveled the state to oppose secession. He worked to prevent Tennessee from leaving the Union, and after it seceded, he worked to have it return. By July 23, 1862, he became a brigadier general in the federal army, not to fight but to serve as a negotiator. He resigned a month after the appointment, finding it impossible to participate in a situation where he had to oppose his friends and neighbors. He eventually became a Democrat as a result of the political changes caused by the Civil War. By the time Andrew Johnson was military governor of Tennessee, Campbell worked against the election regulations that were enforced. This caused somewhat of a split between Johnson and Campbell, but it was later mended. Campbell's wife died in 1864. A year later, he was elected to the U.S. House of Representatives and supported and defended President Andrew Johnson against the impeachment proceedings. He retired after serving this term in Congress, returned to his home in Lebanon, Tennessee, and died on August 19, 1867. He was buried in Cedar Grove Cemetery in Lebanon. (Photograph courtesy of TSLA)

With Pierce's election the Democrats made gains. The count in the House was now 159 Democrats to 71 Whigs and 4 other and the Senate was 38 Democrats to 22 Whigs and 2 other. However, Northern Democrats were sorely divided with Southern Democrats over the same issues that had split the Whig Party. President Pierce had little control over them.

Democrats Return

By the spring of 1853 political divisiveness had worsened within the ranks of the Tennessee Whigs. The party had been victorious in six of the last nine gubernatorial contests and six straight Tennessee presidential contests. But now the tide began to turn. At the April 1853 Whig state convention, the disagreement over slavery reigned. No matter how much the convention leaders reflected on past successes, they could not forestall an intraparty division. They nominated Clarksville attorney Gustavus A. Henry as their candidate for governor.

When the Tennessee Democrats met, they knew they had an opportunity to win back control from the Whigs. However, they needed a strong Democratic leader. They could find none better to consider than Andrew Johnson, a four-term East Tennessee Democratic congressman. In spite of living in Whig territory, he was popular enough that he won his congressional seat as a Democrat. Several Whigs had tried to defeat him but were unsuccessful. For whatever reason, the Whigs could not be rid of this Democrat. Finally, the Whig-controlled state legislature, acting in desperation, redrew Johnson's congressional district lines in order to ensure his defeat. (This act by the Tennessee legislature may have changed the course of the nation considering the role Andrew Johnson would ultimately play.) Johnson then decided he would consider the gubernatorial contest. He received his party's nomination in 1853, and the campaign began.

Campaign activity was heightened in Tennessee during the summer and fall of 1853. The gubernatorial campaign began with a joint appearance in Sparta, Tennessee, on June 1, 1853. Johnson was the candidate of the common man. He spoke of his support of the Homestead Bill in Congress and his work for an amendment mandating the direct election of U.S. senators, Supreme Court justices, and the president. He compared his humble beginnings to his opponent's princely origins. Gustavus Henry countered by attacking Johnson's work in the "Immortal Thirteen" which years before had locked up the state legislature, blocking Tennessee from having U.S. senators in Washington for two years. Henry also defamed Johnson by accusing him of being antislavery. The issues of the campaign and the vigor of the candidates created an acrimonious climate. The voter turnout was at an all-time high and at first the results were too close to call, just as many of Tennessee's recent gubernatorial races had been.

In the end Johnson defeated Henry by 2,261 votes. Johnson lost Whig East Tennessee and Whig West Tennessee but won a high enough majority in the Democratic stronghold of Middle Tennessee to win the election. He would become the leader of the Democratic Party. (He would serve this term and be reelected, serving from 1853 until 1857 during his first tour in office. He would later return as military governor.) The Whigs suffered a devastating loss of the governor's seat but held on to five of the ten U.S. Representative seats and maintained control of the state legislature. The great Whig leader Senator John Bell was discouraged over the gubernatorial loss, but the Whig power in the state legislature eased his concern over his upcoming legislative U.S. Senate contest. He was reelected. His Class 2 U.S. Senate seat was vacant from March 4, 1853, until he officially commenced his term on October 29, 1853.

In 1853 railroad development continued with the chartering of new companies. Those spearheading the drive to raise the money for a West Tennessee rail line, which was to cross into Arkansas, were Colonel John T. Trezevant, Robert C. Brinkley, who had come from Nashville in the early 1840s, and Robertson Topp. Topp was a flamboyant businessman who had moved from Nashville to Memphis. He was a speculator and invested in real estate and railroads. He used creative financing to raise the capital for his many projects and was a leading developer of the time. He was also a leading figure in the Whig Party. (During the Civil War, Topp would continue to trade with Northern businessmen.)

In 1854 a law was passed by the legislature authorizing counties to levy taxes of twenty-five cents on each poll and half a cent on each one hundred dollars of property to help pay for education. Deaths due to "consumption" and "inflammation of the brain" had decreased since the highs of 1851–1852.

The Democrats controlled both houses of Congress during Pierce's first two years as president. In spite of having the numbers required to control legislation, they were divided over many issues. In May 1854, President Pierce, a Democrat, assisted Stephen A. Douglas in passing the proslavery Kansas-Nebraska Act of 1854. This act effectively repealed the Missouri Compromise of 1820. Tennessee U.S. Senator John Bell opposed the bill (he was the only Southern senator to do so), while Senator Jimmy Jones supported it. Jones harshly denounced Northern senators during the debate and effectively resigned from the Whig Party over the issue, becoming a Democrat. In the House of Representatives, six congressmen from Tennessee supported the bill while four opposed it. Tennessee Whig Congressman William Cullom, from Scott County, castigated the supporters of the bill and claimed that they were stirring up disharmony among the nation's people and leaders. As harsh statements flowed from the House chamber, he and Congressman William M. Churchwell, a Democrat from Knoxville, became involved in fisticuffs on the House floor.

Under the Kansas-Nebraska Act, Kansas would become a slave state if the citizens voted for it. The environment became more volatile as proslavery individuals migrated from the slave state of Missouri and began a proslavery government in Kansas. A struggle for control ensued between those opposed to and those supporting slavery. The bill and the resulting crisis created a revolt among antislavery forces which climaxed with the development of a stronger movement.

There was disagreement among politicians as well as average citizens over the morality of slavery, a state's right to determine the legality of the issue, and the federal government's role. Opinions regarding slavery varied by region, economic circumstances, and personal ideology. Political chaos took hold as members of each party, Whig and Democrat, began to question philosophical platforms.

Out of the divisiveness grew the need for a new party which would better represent the views of the growing number of people dissatisfied with the alternatives available. In Crawfordsville, Iowa, in February 1854, a group of dissatisfied Whigs met and decided to create a new political party that coincided more with their views—the views of the North and the abolition of slavery. A second

ANDREW JOHNSON was born December 29, 1808, in Raleigh, North Carolina. His father, Jacob Johnson, was illiterate and died when Johnson was only four years old. His mother, Mary McDonough Johnson, married Turner Dougherty. The family was poor. Mary earned what she could by taking in washing and sewing, and apprenticing her two sons to a tailor named James Shelby. Johnson was then ten and stayed until he was sixteen, learning very little except tailoring. He and his brother ran away from their obligation to the tailor; his brother kept going, but Johnson, feeling guilty, returned. When he got back, he found that Shelby had quit the business. So, Johnson opened his own shop in Raleigh, and by the time he was seventeen years old, was the head of the family. When he was eighteen he took his mother and his family's belongings to Greeneville, Tennessee, by horse-drawn cart. There he set up a tailor's shop and was married at age nineteen, in 1827, to Eliza McCardle. They had two daughters and three sons. He was unable to read very well, but Eliza taught him math, reading, and writing.

Johnson began to read, joined a debate group at the college in Greeneville, and soon realized he had a speaking talent. He formed a common-man's opinion about many of the issues of the day, and his shop became a gathering spot for some of the issue-minded citizens. They elected him alderman at age nineteen, and at twenty-one he was elected mayor of Greeneville. Later, in 1835, at age twenty-seven, he was elected to the state house of representatives, where he worked against waste in government.

While in the state house, Johnson put forth a bill opposing opening the legislature with prayer. He also opposed a bill for internal improvements because of the corruption he knew existed in dispersing the profits from the projects the bill would fund. Likely for these two reasons, he was defeated for reelection to the state legislature in the depression year of 1837. However, things turned around when the public realized that he was correct in predicting graft in the internal improvement appropriation's bill, and he was reelected in 1839.

In 1841 he was elected to the state senate. He ran for Congress in 1843, at age thirty-four, against Colonel John A. Aiken, a lawyer from Jonesboro. Although the district was a Whig stronghold, Johnson, a Democrat, won. He was reelected four times to Congress and became the undisputed political leader in East Tennessee. His other opponents for Congress during successive reelections included William G. Brownlow, Oliver P. Temple, Nathaniel G. Taylor (the father of Alf and Bob Taylor), and Landon C. Haynes. Some of his races for Congress were fairly rough. William G. Brownlow owned a newspaper called *The Whig,* in which Brownlow stated that, "Andrew Johnson is a VILE CALUMNIATOR, AN INFAMOUS DEMAGOGUE, A COMMON AND PUBLIC LIAR, AN IMPIOUS INFIDEL, AND AN UNMITIGATED VILLAN" (McKellar 1942). From the beginning of his political career, Johnson developed a reputation of supporting the common man and the downtrodden. The people did not take Brownlow too seriously and Johnson was reelected.

During his congressional tenure, Johnson proposed the "Homestead Act" in which a family could be given 160 acres if they moved to and used their land for five years. (It would take twenty years, until 1862, for legislature to pass.) After Polk was elected president in 1844, Johnson assisted him in his efforts to declare war on Mexico. However, Polk's more aristocratic ideals clashed with Johnson's approach, resulting in political and personal differences between the two men. Polk did not care too much for Johnson and would not make any appointments sought by him, essentially denying him the federal power of patronage. Johnson later supported the Compromise of 1850 in an effort to solve the crisis over slavery.

In 1853 the Whigs controlled the state redistricting and redrew Johnson's district's lines, making it impossible for him to be reelected to Congress. At this, he returned to Tennessee to run for governor. His opponent was Whig Gustavus A. Henry. The Whigs ridiculed Johnson because of his background, but the common man identified with his clear view of right and wrong. He was elected as a Democrat governor of Tennessee in 1853.

The snub-nosed aristocrats in Nashville ridiculed the tailor governor, saying he did not belong in so high a position. Disadvantage had never stopped Andrew Johnson and neither did the words of his opponents. He worked for improvements in education of the masses and road construction, and against using prison labor which competed with the working-class laborers' opportunity to earn a living. He proposed an amendment to the Constitution that would limit the term of federal judges to twelve years instead of lifetime appointments. He proposed that presidents and U.S. senators be elected by a vote of the people, rather than by electors and the state legislature. The popular election of senators was eventually enacted. In many ways Johnson was ahead of his time.

By 1854 Johnson faced both Whig and Know-Nothing candidates for governor. In the 1855 campaign he was threatened with assassination at one stop. He refused to cancel the engagement. He went to the arranged place for the speeches to be given, walked up to the crowd, laid a hand on the gun on his hip, and in a most straightforward manner reminded the crowd of the right to free speech. The dare, once placed, received no reply. He gave his speech and was reelected governor. He served until 1857 when the Democrats of Tennessee nominated Isham Harris because Johnson was recovering from injuries suffered in a train accident. By October 1857 he had recovered, and the legislature elected him U.S. senator.

While in the U.S. Senate, Johnson stood squarely with the Union. He opposed secession and remained in the Senate after Tennessee left the Union. He was the only senator to refuse to leave. This made him a hero to the North, and President Lincoln appointed him military governor of Tennessee, serving from 1862 until 1865. He worked to bring Tennessee back into the Union and planned to hold free elections for those who remained loyal to the Union. By March 1864 he was arranging to send Tennessee representatives to Washington. His loyalty and efforts to hold the nation together won him a place in the hearts of many, and he was made vice president on the 1864 ticket with President Lincoln. Only six weeks after the inauguration Johnson became president. He continued to work the plan he and Lincoln had agreed to, which would return the Southern states into the Union, but the Northern power brokers would not agree to it since it would threaten their monopoly of Congress. The Northern power mongers tried to impeach Johnson, but they narrowly failed. He completed the term, but was not renominated in 1868.

Johnson guided the nation through the dangerous turmoil of early Reconstruction, stood up to the radicals in Congress, and saved the country in the process. After serving his term as president, he returned to Greeneville, Tennessee. In 1875, Tennessee sent him back to the U.S. Senate. He died of a stroke on July 31, 1875, and was buried in Greeneville. His wife died within a year of his death. Three sons preceded him and his wife in death. (Photograph courtesy of TSLA) meeting was called in a church in Ripon, Wisconsin. At that meeting Alan Bovay rallied a group in the antislavery cause and adopted a resolution against the Kansas-Nebraska Act. Another meeting followed on March 20, 1854, in a schoolhouse in Ripon. Fifty-four citizens met and dissolved their local political organizations to form the core of a new party. Alan Bovay, Jebediah Bowen, Amos Loper, Abram Thomas, and Jacob Woodruff were elected to lead the new party. The committee that was formed would alter the political direction of the nation for generations. It was said by Alan Earl Bovay, "We went into the little meeting Whigs, Free Soilers, and Democrats. We came out Republicans and . . . were the first Republicans in the Union" (Murdock 1993). Years before, Thomas Jefferson had given credence to the word "Republican," which is synonymous with equality. It was selected as the name of the new party. •

The numbers of the new party grew along with the intensity of the crisis. By July 1854 the "Anti-Nebraska Convention" group was so large that it met in an oak tree grove rather than in a building, in Jackson, Michigan. There, a national platform was written. Strategy was planned to counter the Democrats who were set on extending slavery to the new territories coming into the Union. Resolutions were adopted, and candidates were nominated for state offices. One of the resolutions said, "in view of the necessity of battling against the schemes of an aristocracy, the most revolting and oppressive with which the Earth was ever cursed or man debased, we will cooperate and be known as Republican" (Murdock 1993).

The Kansas-Nebraska Act resulted in the annihilation of the Whig Party. There would be no more pretense of having it both ways. Most Whigs from the North did not feel their party represented their views and became Republicans, while those of the South became Democrats. This solidified the Northerners, generally opposed to slavery, into more of a geographical party of Republicans. By the midterm congressional elections of 1854, several Northern Democrats lost to Republicans and Know-Nothings. All of a sudden, this new party of Republicans had control of the House of Representatives (108 Republicans to 83 Democrats and 43 other) and took a toehold in the Senate (42 Democrats to 15 Republicans and 5 other).

The disagreement over slavery in Kansas had escalated from talk to sword. Zealots on both sides of the issue of slavery became violent in the name of their cause. The fighting and bloodshed in the new territories would become the issue of the 1856 presidential election.

The controversy over the Kansas-Nebraska Act had divided and destroyed the Whigs. Many had become Republicans, but there was now a political void for those who were not Democrats and who could not agree with the Northern Republicans. The radical tone that Northern Republicans arrogantly conveyed demonstrated a lack of sensitivity for the people of the South and their agricultural economic realities. These people with no political home needed a party to represent their views. During the Kansas-Nebraska controversy, a supposedly secret political organization called the "Know-Nothing Party" was formed in Boston. Formed in opposition to Catholics and foreigners, the Know-Nothing Party had grown out of the Star Spangled Banner Society and was organized to protect the interests of "Native Americans." The party was supposed to be secret, and in fact, several Know-Nothing lodges had already been formed in Tennessee by this time.

During this period of American history, the Irish made up a substantial portion of not only Tennessee's but the nation's population. Irish immigrants had come to America since its early history, particularly during and after the potato famine of 1845–1846. The Irish were viewed as laborers, a common class of people. (In fact, they performed a significant portion of the labor in the United States, including a large portion of the work on Tennessee's state capitol, which was completed in 1859.) Catholics were viewed with inordinate suspicion because of fear that the pope was somehow behind a plan to take control of U.S. government, much in the way that the Church had interfered in past European governments. Part of the reason that Andrew Jackson had drawn such opposition from the Eastern U.S. aristocracy was that he was viewed as an underclass Irish commoner who was expected to taint the dignity of the presidency and surround himself with common ruffians.

With the Whig Party now destroyed in Tennessee, the Know-Nothing Party was, for a small time, their substitute. Some Tennesseans would not become Republicans (which was almost an exclusively Northern abolitionist party) and they would not accept the Know-Nothings. U.S. Senator Jimmy Jones was one of many Southerners who became a Democrat during the controversy. However, whatever party an individual chose, the Whigs were no longer an option. An instantaneous political void was created by the dissolution of the Whigs. The Democrats, solid in their views to protect the South, were propelled into the political power of the region.

The Know-Nothings experienced a growth spurt, which complicated the upcoming elections in Tennessee as it did across the nation. Although Middle Tennessee was still strongly Democratic and East Tennessee was more Whig (Republican), West Tennessee had a particularly strong mix of Democrats and Know-Nothings. Newspapers took sides. In Memphis, the *Appeal* was the paper for the Democrats, *The Whig* was the organ for the remaining Whigs, and the *Eagle and Enquirer* represented the Know-Nothing views. The politics of the nation was changing and the campaigns sometimes became volatile. However, Tennessee did not suffer the riotous destruction some other areas of the country experienced. In the campaign of 1855 the main party contenders were the Democrats and the Know-Nothings.

In this 1855 election Governor Andrew Johnson was renominated by the Democrats. Since the Know-Nothing Party was a secret organization, there is no record of a state nominating convention. However, Meredith P. Gentry, from Bedford County, made his Know-Nothing candidacy known. Gentry campaigned on an anti-Catholic and protemperance platform. The campaign began on May 1, 1855, in Murfreesboro, Tennessee, and Governor Johnson minced no words comparing the Know-Nothings to the famous Tennessee criminal gang of John A. Murrell. This campaign stop quickly became rowdy and dangerous. Opponents in the crowd allowed their feelings to heighten until tempers flared and guns were drawn. Fortunately, the crowd cooled, quiet resumed, and Johnson completed his speech. Throughout the campaign Meredith Gentry campaigned hard, but did not refute the charges against the Know-Nothing Party. Johnson once received word that he would be killed while speaking at a certain engagement. Johnson took his own weapon to the gathering and dared the perpetrator of the threat to challenge his right to free speech. There were no shots fired, and Johnson was able to continue his campaign.

Overall, the people of Tennessee still favored Governor Andrew Johnson. He was reelected by 2,157 votes (out of a total of 232,841 cast), but again he lost East and West Tennessee. His victory came, as it had in 1853, by his strong following in Middle Tennessee.

Although they lost the governor's race, the Know-Nothings won several posts in Tennessee. They had enough strength in the state legislature to elect Dr. F. N. W. Benton, secretary of state, and James C. Luttrell, comptroller. But the Democrats managed to elect G. C. Torbitt as treasurer. The Know-Nothings took control of the state legislature and made Edward S. Cheatham speaker of the state senate and Neill S. Brown (the former governor) speaker of the state house. The Know-Nothings also elected six of the ten Tennessee U.S. representatives.

During the time of these tumultuous campaigns of 1855, yellow fever hit the Mid-south, killing 220 people.

Slavery, Abe Lincoln, and the Emergence of the Republican Party

By 1854, forty-five-year-old Abraham Lincoln had been out of any office for five years after serving one term in the U.S. House (1847–1849). Previously, he had served in the Illinois house of representatives. During his U.S. House term he had been an outspoken critic of President James K. Polk for his support of the Mexican War. The Whig Party leaders were not happy with Lincoln's conduct. The war, which freed Texas to eventually become a part of the United States, was a great point of pride to many Americans. Lincoln supported the bills that were required to finance supplies to the army, and as a delegate to the Whig National Convention in 1848, he voted for the nomination of war hero Zachary Taylor for president, but his compliance was too late. He had alienated his supporters by criticizing the president. Whig leaders did not renominate him for Congress, and Lincoln was soon out of office. He returned to the practice of law.

Lincoln sorely wanted back into politics and knew that Illinois Senator Stephen Douglas would have to accept some criticism for sponsoring the Kansas-Nebraska Act, which had inflamed the abolitionists. Lincoln used Douglas's position as a vehicle for his return and blamed him for trying to earn Southern delegate votes by passing an act that they favored in order to win the upcoming Democratic nomination for president in 1856. When Douglas tried to defend his actions at the fall 1854 state fair in Springfield, Lincoln overwhelmed him in their debate and thereafter became the leader of the anti-Kansas-Nebraska Act forces in Illinois. After their debate a few days later in Peoria, Douglas quit speaking on the subject. The publicity generated from these debates hurt Douglas during the Democratic National Convention of 1854, leaving the nomination to James Buchanan. On the other hand, the publicity hoisted Lincoln out of political oblivion. Regaining popularity, he was elected to the Illinois state legislature in 1854. He resigned shortly thereafter to run for U.S. Senate. The Democrats had controlled the state legislature, and there was no way they would allow the abolitionists and the dwindling number of Whigs to wrest their control. Douglas was influential with his friends in the Illinois legislature and the political hierarchy of the state to win enough support to return to the U.S. Senate. However, his proslavery actions would haunt him on the national level.

After the passage of the Kansas-Nebraska Act, it was alleged that proslavery activists migrated from Missouri to Kansas and added enough votes to elect the first legislature as proslavery. They first met on July 2, 1855, and made Kansas a slave territory. However, the antislavery citizens refused to be bound by the acts of a new legislature. They felt that the move toward slavery did not result from a vote by the territory's true citizens, but rather by immigrants who had seized control, and whose votes were falsely representative of the true attitude of Kansans.

Support was gathered for an antislavery convention. It met on September 19, 1855, in Topeka. The convention decided to call for the election of delegates to a constitutional convention. The delegates elected met at Topeka on October 23, 1855, and wrote the antislavery Topeka Constitution. At election on January 15, 1856, the Topeka Constitution was approved and C. Robinson was elected the state's first governor. A legislature was also elected which then met on July 3, 1856. Kansas now had two legislatures, causing more confusion and dissension among the citizens and destabilizing the government. President Pierce intervened. The second legislature that met on July 3 was disbursed on orders of President Pierce. This was the beginning of armed conflict in Kansas. The fiasco aroused antislavery forces throughout the nation and polarized the North and South into sectional opponents. The people of the North, who were generally antislavery, began joining the Republican Party. In the South, the proslavery supporters could not agree with the Republicans and generally sided with the Democratic Party.

On June 17, 1856, the first Republican National Convention was held in Philadelphia. John C. Freemont was nominated as the Republican candidate for president. Abraham Lincoln, who had helped organize the Republican Party in Illinois, was proposed for the nomination of vice president by the Illinois delegation (Lincoln was not present at the Convention), but Senator William L. Dayton received the nomination as the Republican candidate for vice president.

By 1856 Democrats felt that there was sufficient national divisiveness among their political opposition to dominate the presidential election. The Democratic National Convention convened in Cincinnati, Ohio, in June 1856. A Democratic contender for his party's presidential nomination in 1856, James Buchanan, gained support from Southerners because of his association with two proslavery Southern U.S. diplomats to France and Spain. Together they wrote the "Ostend Manifesto" which pushed "manifest destiny" to the limit in calling for Spain to turn Cuba over to the United States. Although associated with these proslavery diplomats, Buchanan did not espouse the proslavery cause as had his chief rivals for the nomination, Senator Stephen A. Douglas and President Pierce. By this time Douglas had already debated Lincoln twice regarding the issue of slavery and the Kansas-Nebraska Act, and Douglas was forced to carry the baggage of his statements into the Democratic National Convention. President Pierce counted on renomination, but political damage from his support of the Kansas-Nebraska Act cost him the backing of Northern Democrats. By "possessing the indispensable attribute of being acceptable (to the South), yet untainted" (Whitney 1982) to Northern Democrats, Buchanan won the nomination. President Pierce had tried to find a way to prevent civil war, but his effort to save lives cost him the presidency.

Tennessee's delegation to the Democratic convention worked for the nomination of either Aaron V. Brown or Governor Andrew Johnson for vice president. However, John C. Breckinridge of Kentucky was nominated.

The Know-Nothing Party was badly fragmented because of the desertions to the new Republican Party. Nevertheless they nominated former President Millard Fillmore. Andrew Jackson Donelson of Tennessee, the nephew, foster son, and personal secretary of Andrew Jackson, was nominated for vice president.

Most Tennesseans evidently felt Democrat Buchanan was tolerant of slavery and that they had no choice but to support his candidacy. The Democratic Party won the state in the presidential election (for the first time since Andrew Jackson was reelected president in 1832), marking the return of Democratic dominance in Tennessee over the Whigs. The Whigs had carried Tennessee in every presidential election since 1832. (Tennessee had gone Whig for Hugh Lawson White in 1836, for William Henry Harrison in 1840, for Henry Clay in 1844, even though James K. Polk was running, for Zachary Taylor in 1848, and for Winfield Scott in 1852.) But now the Whigs were split over slavery, while Southern Democrats generally agreed on their position. The Know-Nothings had significant support during the election cycle, but only as an alternative party. The anti-Catholic, antiforeigner position could not compete with the emotional tug of the Democratic Party and its promise to preserve a way of life and economic stability for Tennesseans. Further, there was no national strength of substance to the Know-Nothings. After this election cycle, there was nothing left of the Whigs or the Know-Nothings. Since the time that the Whigs had first appeared in Tennessee, West Tennessee had voted almost as a block with East Tennessee. However, in 1856 that coalition was broken. West Tennessee joined Middle Tennessee Democrats to dominate the political field. In Tennessee, Democrat Buchanan received 73,638 votes to 66,178 for Know-Nothing Fillmore, and no votes for Freemont, the Republican. The Republicans were essentially powerless in Tennessee during this election, but they had organized their first national ticket. The Democrats of Tennessee were once again in control.

Nationally, Democrat Buchanan polled 1,832,955 popular votes, Republican Freemont received 1,339,932, and Know-Nothing Fillmore captured only 871,731 (174 to 114 to 8 electoral votes). Although they lost the election, the new Republican Party now had national prominence. The Democrats had their victory, but with it came the divisive issue of slavery. With the Whig and Know-Nothing Parties all but dead, Tennesseans who could not identify with the Democrats but were slaveholders who would never become Republicans, needed political representation through a party. Therefore the isolated activists coalesced into a weak organization simply called the Opposition Party.

With the return of Democratic strength in the state legislature came the opportunity to elect a Democrat for the 1857 U.S. Senate seat (Class 1). Since the Whigs had more or less controlled the state for the past two decades, there was no one else possessing the stature of Andrew Johnson in the Democratic Party of Tennessee. The other power brokers had all been Whigs. Johnson had served in elective office in his home community as well as in the state house, state senate, U.S. House of

Representatives, and as governor. With Andrew Jackson's death in 1845 and James K. Polk's in 1849, Andrew Johnson was now the leading Democrat in Tennessee. Therefore, in 1856, he eyed becoming the Democratic candidate for the U.S. Senate seat now occupied by Senator Jimmy Jones. The other U.S. Senate (Class 2) seat was midterm and was held by John Bell, a Whig.

By January 1857 the conflict between proslavery and abolitionist forces in Kansas had escalated to sad consequences. Federal officials had prevented the meeting of the Topeka legislature and arrested some members. Territory Governor John White Geary resigned, and Mississippian Robert Walker, former secretary of the treasury under President James K. Polk (1845–1849) took over administrative duties of the territory in an effort to establish peace.

Another issue stoked the firestorm in Kansas. Years earlier, just prior to 1848, a slave named Dred Scott was the property of a John Emerson of the U.S. Army. Emerson took Scott with him from Missouri to Illinois, where slavery was prohibited. He afterwards went to Fort Snelling in upper Louisiana (present-day Minnesota), where slavery was also prohibited by the Missouri Compromise. When they returned to Missouri, Scott reasoned that his removal to areas where slavery was illegal had made him a freeman and he sued to gain his and his family's freedom in the state circuit court in St. Louis, obtaining a judgment in his favor. The decision was appealed, and a great national controversy boiled over the question of constitutional law. Some felt that Congress should have power over slavery in the territories. Others felt that the judiciary had the power to overrule Congress. The U.S. Supreme Court decision in the Dred Scott case was finally ready for delivery by December 1856, but it was delayed because of the intensity of the conflict in Kansas. On March 6, 1857, the Supreme Court declared that because slaves were property, Congress did not have the right to stop slavery in territories. This was a proslavery decision, nullifying the Missouri Compromise of 1820, and leading the nation a step closer to civil war.

Impending Civil War to the Election of 1908

PART II

States' Rights Issues

President Buchanan sought to place himself above intraparty conflict by announcing, during his inaugural address, that he would not be a candidate for reelection in 1860. In an attempt to side-step the slavery issue, Buchanan said that the question should be decided by the Supreme Court and that he would go along with whatever the Court decided. This attempt at neutrality accomplished little except to prematurely pass the Democratic Party leadership to Senator Stephen A. Douglas, who was proslavery.

In March of 1857 the Supreme Court announced its decision, which reversed the dictate of the Missouri Compromise. In its ruling on the Dred Scott case, the Supreme Court essentially decided that Congress did not have final authority over the territories. In general, the people of the North rallied to oppose the decision. In the South, and in most of Tennessee, the media and the people felt relief and joy over the Supreme Court's decision. Northerners who had voted Democratic for Buchanan felt that he had betrayed their vote and had skirted the issue by taking a neutral position. To Northern abolitionists the Democratic Party no longer represented their views. Their determination to end slavery coalesced into a movement. But for any movement to have an impact upon law, representatives would have to be elected who agreed with the views of the members of such an effort. In this instance the movement developed into the Republican Party.

During the time that the Supreme Court handed down its proslavery decision in the Dred Scott case, Democrats had held a majority in both houses. Tempers flared over the admission of Kansas. President Buchanan tried to end the conflict by submitting legislation to admit Kansas as a slave state. When he submitted the Lecompton Constitution to the House, outraged Northern Democrat congressmen revolted and joined the Republicans to defeat the bill. Stephen Douglas led the fight against the Lecompton Constitution in the Senate, and Buchanan became enraged over Douglas's maneuvers to place himself center stage. Many felt that Buchanan had betrayed them, and the Democratic Party continued to weaken as the issue of slavery became more volatile. Proslavery and antislavery candidates took the forefront as traditional party lines faded.

By 1857 the short-lived Know-Nothing Party had begun to disintegrate. In Tennessee, they had met with minimal success. East Tennesseans were abolitionists and were heavily Whig. West Tennesseans, once evenly Whig and Democrat, were now clearly proslavery and pro-states' rights and were becoming politically bonded to Middle Tennessee, which was traditionally strongly Democratic. The only way for Tennessee Whigs and Know-Nothings to survive was to form a coalition strong enough to counteract the once again powerful Democrats. This coalition nominated Wilson Countian Robert Hatton for the race for governor in 1857. Although they knew they had little hope that year, Hatton, a great leader of their cause, was chosen to carry their banner.

Democrat Governor Andrew Johnson, recovering from injuries suffered in a train accident, was unable to run in 1857. Because of the slavery controversy, there were many politicians who rethought their party affiliation. Tennessee Democrats were in a much stronger position in 1857, and they chose Isham G. Harris of Memphis to run for governor. Harris had lived in several places in Tennessee. He had been elected to the state senate from Henry County in

1847. In 1849 and 1851 he was elected as U.S. representative from that area. After he served his second term in Congress, he moved to Memphis and continued to practice law. Having good political ties, being a Democrat, and living in the reconverted (from a Whig and Democrat area) Democratic West Tennessee made him a good candidate to hold the Middle and West sections of the state together for the 1857 gubernatorial match.

The campaign began in Camden, Tennessee, on May 25, 1857. June and July were active months for Democrat Isham G. Harris and Know-Nothing/Whig coalition candidate Robert Hatton as they made their positions known to the people of Tennessee. The slavery/states' rights issue was a hot and sometimes violent topic. The more the North fought slavery, the more the South defended its independence. Democrats were gaining popularity and strength in the South as the Southern people began to resent Northern domination. Northern congressmen worked to prevent any legislative advantage that could assist with the South's self-determination within the federal structure. Southerners began to see that the Northerners were determined to dominate legislation whether dealing with commerce, transportation, or practically any issue. Northern senators and congressmen opposed the selection of a path from Memphis to Little Rock to be included in the Pacific Railroad route. Instead they selected one along the thirty-fifth parallel. Because West and Middle Tennessee commerce depended so heavily on agriculture, there was much at stake. Many people could not accept the high-handed attitude of Northern politicians toward the way Tennesseans made a living. This impacted the gubernatorial campaign as well as Democratic Party affiliations. Many times during the campaign stops, fights would develop in the crowds as differences of opinions turned to violence. On one occasion the candidates themselves became involved in fisticuffs.

The attitude of Tennesseans was reflected in the results of the August 1857 election in which Democrat Harris was elected governor of Tennessee by defeating Hatton, 71,178 to 59,807. Harris had defeated a popular Hatton with the help of Governor Johnson's political strength as well as the growing Southern sentiment toward the Democratic Party's states' rights base. The election represented a sudden, not yet complete, shift in the popularity of the Democratic Party in Tennessee compared to the relative close results of similar contests of the past two decades.

As a result of the growing sentiment of the South toward the Northerners, Middle and West Tennessee elected many "states' rights" men and gave the new Democrat governor power to express their states' rights views, solidifying West and Middle Tennessee as a Democratic Party political power base.

Democrat Andrew Johnson's election as governor in 1853 had foreshadowed the decline of the Whigs in Tennessee. Johnson was elected without the political superiority of Democratic dominance in West Tennessee (or Whig East Tennessee for that matter). It was the strength of Democrats of Middle Tennessee that had positioned the Democrats. Johnson was reelected in 1855, doing what the Democrats had not been able to do for years—keep themselves in power for two consecutive terms. He had been reelected without Democratic dominance in the West section of the state. By the time Democrat Isham Harris ran in 1857, it had become apparent that West Tennessee depended on the proslavery/states' rights Democrats for survival. The people in this section of the state now saw that it was to their advantage to bind their political future with the Democrat power base in Middle Tennessee. This West/Middle Tennessee Democratic Party base of support would last well beyond the next one hundred years. Harris's election solidified the new political realities in Tennessee while also delivering the final blow to the state's Know-Nothing Party.

Democrats also won control of the Tennessee house and senate. They planned to take both U.S. Senate seats as soon as they were open. Whig U.S. Senator "Lean" Jimmy Jones's term had expired. Governor Andrew Johnson, leader of the Tennessee Democrats, wanted the spot and so did former Governor Neill S. Brown. However, Johnson was elected. On October 8, 1857, Andrew Johnson became U.S. senator (Class 1); there had been a vacancy in Senator Jimmy Jones's Senate seat from March 4, 1857, until Johnson's election. Johnson served until he became military governor on March 4, 1862.

Perhaps due to party rivalry or personal jealousies, John Bell, originally elected as a Whig and senior U.S. senator from Tennessee (Class 2), and Johnson did not get along. Sometime after Johnson was sworn in, in 1857, they actually "had an altercation on the floor" of the U.S. Senate that looked as if it might "lead to bloodshed; but each apologized to the other, and nothing came of it, except that they were never friends" (Keating 1888).

By 1858, a relatively unknown Illinois politician began a meteoric rise on the national scene. Abraham Lincoln was virtually unknown nationally and was politically weak in his own home state of Illinois. Because of his work in organizing the Republican Party and his outspoken position regarding slavery, the 1858 Illinois Republican State Convention again nominated Lincoln to run against Douglas for U.S. Senate. Lincoln's acceptance speech gained national attention because of the growing crisis over slavery. His "A house divided against itself cannot stand" was repeated many times over the next few years (Thomas 1982).

Even though, in 1858, U.S. senators were elected by their state legislature, Lincoln and Douglas campaigned in Illinois for support. Each Senate candidate needed the allegiance of the legislators to become elected or reelected, as the case may be, by the state legislature.

During the campaign, Lincoln followed immediately behind Douglas in order to take advantage of the crowds Douglas created and to seize the opportunity to campaign for himself. First at Bloomington, Lincoln simply sized up Douglas's speaking points. Then at Springfield, Lincoln followed Douglas's afternoon speech with his own stumper later in the evening. Since Douglas had already published his list of stops in order to gather the crowds, Lincoln challenged him to out-and-out debates and let it be known to the communities to be toured. Douglas had little to gain by debating him, but now, he also had little choice. He agreed.

The Lincoln-Douglas debates ensued at Ottawa, Freeport, Jonesboro, Charleston, Galesburg, Quinch, and Alton. The candidates campaigned and spoke to crowds in between debates, nearly every day, for four months. In the formal debates as well as the speeches in between, Douglas stated that Lincoln's "house divided" doctrine, given in Lincoln's nomination acceptance speech, invited a war of sections. Douglas said that our nation could continue to exist part-slave and part-free, avoiding a nasty national clash

ISHAM GREEN HARRIS was born on February 10, 1818, near Tullahoma, Tennessee, and was the youngest of nine children. He was the third generation to have the same name. His forebears had originally come from North Carolina and had participated in the Revolutionary War. He received the standard education of the day until he was about fifteen. His father's health was then poor, and as a result their farm was not sufficiently productive or profitable and could not support his son's educational ambitions. Harris moved to Paris, Tennessee, in order to live with an older brother who was a successful lawyer there, and he worked as a clerk in a store. He then went to Ripley, Mississippi, and started a business for himself which was backed by his brother. It did not do well, so he sold it and returned to Middle Tennessee. He paid off his parents' farm, sold it, and bought a home for them in Paris, Tennessee. Later, he opened another business that did fairly well. By 1841 he had studied and begun the practice of law, and in 1843 he married Martha Travis, from Henry County. He was elected state senator in 1847, serving Henry, Weakley, and Obion Counties. He served as an elector for Lewis Cass in 1848. In 1849 he was elected to the U.S. House and was reelected in 1851. Two years later, he moved to Memphis and went into law practice, staying with his practice and out of the public limelight until 1856, when he became a state elector-at-large for Buchanan. In 1857 he was the Democrat candidate for governor of Tennessee, running against Robert Hatton, who was the "Coalition" candidate (representing the Whigs and Know-Nothings). Harris was elected governor by an 11,000 vote majority. In 1859 he ran again, against the "opposition" (representing the Whigs, remaining Know-Nothings, and disgruntled Democrats) candidate John Netherland, from East Tennessee. (Netherland was a forebear of the Heiskell family and a noted lawyer.) Harris was easily reelected. He was the first governor to come from West Tennessee.

By 1861 Harris was a leading figure in Tennessee. An ardent states' rights man, he favored secession and was defiant when Lincoln tried to get Tennessee to send troops to support the Union's retaliation toward the other Southern states. After Tennessee seceded from the Union, Harris called for troops for the Confederacy. He was reelected in 1861. During the Civil War, Robert L. Caruthers was elected governor in 1863, but he never took office and Harris continued to serve until Andrew Johnson was appointed military governor. When Middle and West Tennessee were taken by the Union forces, Harris was forced to leave the state. After the war Governor Brownlow put a five-thousand-dollar bounty on Harris's capture, and he left for Mexico and then England. In 1867 he returned to Memphis and went back into the practice of law in the firm of Harris, McKissick, and Turley. Harris remained popular throughout Tennessee and was elected to the U.S. Senate in 1877, serving until he died in Washington, D.C., in 1897. He was buried in Elmwood Cemetery in Memphis. (Photograph courtesy of SHO)

over a federally mandated position on slavery.[6] He said Lincoln supported uniformity of domestic laws and eventual war that would result over such a position. (History proved Douglas correct on this point.) Lincoln denied Douglas's charges and claimed no interest in forced uniformity. Lincoln stated he wanted the ultimate extinction of slavery to be achieved only by confining it to where it existed. After denying the inflammatory charges, Lincoln would then go on to speak against the issue of slavery itself. This identified him as opposed to slavery while he ducked the volatility of the issue.

The debates attracted so much attention that both men, especially Lincoln,

"The Tailor and Rail-Splitter Mending the Union"

Political cartoon from the gubernatorial campaign of 1853. Andrew Johnson was the Democratic nominee running on a Reconstruction platform. (Courtesy of TSLA)

gained national visibility. Holding his own against the nationally known Douglas put Lincoln on equal standing and gave him enough prominence in the minds of men to qualify him as a candidate for president. By gaining greater publicity of his proslavery position, Douglas helped secure Southern support for his nomination for president at the 1860 Democratic National Convention. This would become a double-edged sword since the division in the Democratic Party between the Northern and Southern Democrats, pro-and antislavery, would ultimately cost him the election.

Senator Douglas, or the "Little Giant" as he was known, faced a tough political challenge. He had earned the wrath of President Buchanan for opposing the president's proslavery Lecompton Constitution. The Lecompton Bill was an attempt to end the Kansas fiasco by admitting it as a slave state. Democrats from the North opposed the bill. Stephen Douglas had worked with the anti-Lecompton forces to defeat the bill. Buchanan was determined to destroy Douglas and set up a rival organization in Illinois which recruited Democratic legislative candidates pledged to oppose Douglas in the state legislative U.S. Senate election of 1858. The fight did not stop with that. All of Douglas's friends who served in federal jobs as postmasters and U.S. marshals were removed from office. Buchanan moved money into the campaign, and editors of Democratic newspapers joined in to destroy Douglas.

However, the public and supporters of Douglas were incensed at the thought of the president using such a heavy hand on their elected official and in their own home state. As a result, Douglas gained sympathetic support and additional popularity within his home state. His organization reformed and gained strength just as the antislavery Lincoln gained momentum.

Election day 1858 favored Douglas. Even though Republicans outpolled their opponents by four thousand votes, redistricting had favored the Democrats in Illinois, winning fifty-four seats, with forty-six for Republicans. Douglas retained enough support for the Illinois state legislature to return him to the U.S. Senate. The Memphis *Appeal* reported on September 28, 1858, of the "hearty rejoicings by the Democrats over the defeat of Lincoln, in Illinois, by Senator Douglas" (Keating 1888). On October 29, 1858, Senator Douglas was received by thousands from Memphis and the surrounding areas during an enthusiastic gathering at the Exchange Building.

After Lincoln lost the Senate election, he knew his political career was in jeopardy, but he did not lose hope. He maintained communication with Republicans in other states such as Kansas, Indiana, and Ohio concerning such issues as planks in the Republican platform. In the late summer and fall of 1859 he spoke in Iowa, Missouri, Ohio, Indiana, and Wisconsin. The Lincoln-Douglas debates had given him great national exposure, and some Republican newspaper editors indicated they might support a Lincoln presidential bid. However, there were others with great national prominence who were running for president.

Meanwhile, Tennessee Senator John Bell's term ended in 1859 and Alfred Osborne Pope Nicholson was the Democrat elected to take the Class 2 Senate seat. He was sworn into office on March 4, 1859. (Nicholson had served as U.S. senator by appointment of Governor Polk, upon the death of Senator Felix Grundy, in 1840, but was not reelected at that time due to a Democratic split in Tennessee. Nicholson's present term was scheduled to run until March 3, 1865, but he would retire on March 3, 1861, and be officially expelled by the Union politicians on July 11, 1861. The seat would then remain vacant because of the Civil War until May 4, 1865.)

By 1859 the Know-Nothings were essentially nonexistent, and the Whigs were in the obvious minority in Tennessee. Looking for a way to take control back from the Democrats, the supporters of these two parties combined their efforts along with those of disenchanted Democrats who had split with the Tennessee and Washington Democratic leaders. Some of the disenfranchised Democrats had become disgruntled over Senator Andrew Johnson's recent speech which dwelt on the costs of several Pacific Railroad routes (there being much competition among cities along the Mississippi River for the site of the rail) and his opposition to national party conventions. It was thought that his position regarding the rail crossing at Memphis was not loyal to Tennessee and that his attitude toward national party conventions was heresy (since his success had come from state convention nominations). They formed a coalition, called simply the Opposition Party, and nominated Hawkins County resident John Netherland. Democrats again nominated Isham Harris.

The summer campaign of 1859 centered on the great national controversy. The many campaign stops were boisterous and exciting. Netherland suffered a backlash because of his Whig support, and spent most of his time defending his candidacy against Harris's charges that he had sold out to the North. It was not a good time to be even distantly associated with Northern Whigs. Netherland defended his candidacy by claiming support for states' rights and slavery for Tennessee. The national controversy over states' rights played well into Harris's hands. Harris successfully turned the unsettling fear of Northern domination into a negative for Netherland's campaign.

The combination of Whigs, Know-Nothings, and disgruntled Democrats proved to be a strong force against the Democrats, but they were not strong enough. At this point in time, Southern fear of Northern domination had not yet

ALFRED OSBORNE POPE NICHOLSON was born in Williamson County, Tennessee, on August 31, 1808. He was educated in common schools of the day, completing his early education in Columbia at fourteen years of age. He then left on horseback for the University of North Carolina and graduated by age eighteen. He later went to Philadelphia to study medicine but did not complete this course. When he returned home from Philadelphia, he traveled through Washington and saw the inauguration of Andrew Jackson in 1829. On June 17, 1829, he married Caroline O'Reilly. He studied law, and was licensed to practice in October 1829. He established a newspaper, the *Western Mercury*. Soon afterward Nicholson was defeated for the state legislature by Colonel Dobbins in 1831. However, he was elected in 1833, and served for many years in the Tennessee house and Tennessee senate. In 1836 he was appointed as chancellor for the Middle Division of Tennessee. He temporarily supported Hugh Lawson White for president during 1835, but switched to Jackson's candidate, Van Buren. When U.S. Senator Felix Grundy died in office in 1840, Nicholson was appointed by Governor James K. Polk as senator. He served from December 25, 1840, until February 7, 1842, being defeated for the right to continue in office by a one-vote margin because of a split among Democrats. He returned to the state legislature and his law practice. He supported his friend James K. Polk for president and was actively involved in his presidential campaign of 1844. Nicholson also served as a director of the Nashville and Chattanooga Railroad, and became president of the Bank of Tennessee in 1847. In 1848 he supported the Democrat presidential candidate Lewis Cass. Nicholson declined an appointment to the cabinet of President Pierce in 1853, instead becoming the editor of the *Washington Daily Union* (the administration's publicity organ). He was also selected as public printer for the U.S. House of Representatives. He was elected to the U.S. Senate in 1859 as a Democrat replacing Whig John Bell and supported Senator Johnson and the Homestead Bill. Serving from March 4, 1859, until he resigned on March 3, 1861, he was officially expelled by the Republicans on July 11, 1861. Nicholson died on March 23, 1876. (Photograph courtesy of Lewis Donelson)

reached its crescendo, and there was still a generous reception to some of the Whig ideals if not the party itself. Therefore, the election was not a foregone conclusion. However, when the votes were counted, the August 1859 elections were again a victory for the Democrats over the Oppositionists. Governor Isham G. Harris was reelected over John Netherland, 70,273 to 68,042. The election was close, but West Tennessee held with the hometown candidate and the Democrats. Tennessee Democrats won majorities in the state house and senate. However, Opposition candidates for U.S. representative seats won seven races in Tennessee. The opposition to Democratic dominance in Tennessee was still alive.

Up until about 1859 most Tennesseans did not consider secession a real possibility. Most felt that as long as the Compromise of 1850 was followed, the North would not dictate another state's future. However, New York Senator William H. Seward held that no state or territory had a right to allow slavery. He ignored the economic realities of the Southern agricultural states and made remarks over the inevitability of war between the states which were viewed as inflammatory and fanatical by Southerners. Seward caused the word

"Republican" to be equated with abolition. Republicans began to be thought of as Radicals, bent on destroying livelihoods and fomenting war.

On October 17, 1859, a wild, fanatical, and illogical John Brown, with a band of five "colored" and seventeen White men, "by the authority of the Almighty God," seized the United States' arsenal at Harper's Ferry (Keating 1888). His purpose was to initiate guerrilla war upon the people of the South. Brown had a reputation for being cold-blooded and a bit insane. The terror he inflicted on Kansas, his attack at Harper's Ferry, and the subsequent publicity only helped polarize the growing distrust between the North and South and to identify the Republican Party and the Northern people, in the minds of Southerners, as violent agressors (Keating 1888).

When Brown and several of his men were captured by a group of soldiers led by a Colonel R. E. Lee, and subsequently hung (in December at Charlestown, Virginia), the North and the South held very different views of the incident. The South generally felt that a criminal had been stopped. In the North, Brown's hanging made him a martyr. Church services were held and funeral bells rang in Boston. This acceptance of his criminal conduct convinced Southerners that Northerners would go to great lengths to dominate and invade the sanctity of Southern communities and Southern ways of life.

Tennessee Democrat U.S. Senator Andrew Johnson condemned Republicans, especially Senator William Seward, for fomenting hatred and agitating Brown to his actions. In Tennessee, tensions mounted. Already, the Republican Party had been tainted in Tennessee as the party of Northern oppression over the South. In December, Senator Andrew Johnson gave a speech which partially redeemed him from his previous speech (which had caused some of his fellow Tennesseans to believe he had lost his loyalty to the state). In his December speech, he stated that some Northerners planned on enforcing their own ideas on the South and that Congress would bend its laws to allow this enforcement. Johnson said that he was opposed to slavery, but he did not agree with the conduct of the likes of John Brown. However, he did not rescind his prediction regarding slavery. He stated that slavery would be abolished eventually and that "Whether it shall be done peaceable or by blood, God only knows; but it will be accomplished, I have no doubt; and by whatever way, I say, let it come. If it is to come by blood, let it come" (Keating 1888).

The Southern populous slowly withdrew into a unified quest for self-preservation, for the protection of their property and their rights—the rights of every citizen, not just the rights of Northern citizens. The antiabolitionist feeling was particularly strong in Memphis, the heart of the mid-South and a central point of Southern agricultural commerce. To be sure, there were many who were against the concept of slavery. But, just as sure, some of these same Southern people who favored freedom for every man were horrified at the thought of Northern domination and the misunderstanding of regional economic realities. Middle and West Tennessee mirrored the thoughts, hopes, and fears of the South.

During all the turmoil over slavery, Memphis continued to grow and prosper. By 1860 the population had reached 22,643. The rapid increase in population was assisted by railroad and river commerce along with the cotton business and the related industry and community support services. Cotton commerce through Memphis had reached about 400,000 bales. In 1860 the population of Nashville was 16,988 including "719 free colored . . . 3,266 Negro slaves . . . 1,360 Irish" (Burt 1959). Nashville was a thriving city years prior to 1860 and had a diversified economic base. However, its agricultural economic base, although smaller than that of Memphis (in 1860 25,000 bales of cotton went through Nashville), was still substantial. Nashville citizens were nearly unanimously pro-Union until Northern Republicans began to show disdain and disrespect for the Southern way of life (the realities of the agriculturally based economy). By 1860 there were good roads connecting Franklin, Columbia, Murfreesboro, Charlotte, Gallatin, and Nolensville to Nashville. One could reach New Orleans from Nashville in six days by boat.

East Tennessee, although mostly Republican, was repulsed by the insensitive actions and statements of Northern Republicans. Although East Tennessee did not have the agricultural base requiring significant slave labor, many of the area Republicans rejected the Republican Party because of the recent conduct of their Northern counterparts.

Nationally, the Republican Party had grown to proportions nearly equivalent to the Democratic Party. Along with this growth came the confidence for Republicans to openly speak out against slavery and the admission of any more slaveholding territories. Because Lincoln had been so outspoken in his opposition to slavery and therefore helped define the new Republican Party, he became their new leader.

> Out of comparative obscurity he had reached the center of national life, by a bound. His antagonism of the ablest of the leading Democrats in an unlimited discussion of the great question at issue had made him the figure head of the Republican column, and he was beginning to be made the target for abuse by the Democratic newspapers, as he was the object of the eulogies and panegyrics of the Republicans everywhere. (Keating 1888)

Tennessee Democrats, with great concern over the national growth of the Republican Party, met in various county meetings around the state to prepare for the upcoming presidential election. They elected delegates to the Democratic state convention which met on January 18, 1860. Andrew Johnson was selected as Tennessee's Democratic nominee for president. The convention also passed resolutions supporting the Supreme Court's Dred Scott decision as well as states' rights positions.

On February 27, 1860, Lincoln spoke at Cooper Union, in New York City. Fifteen hundred of New York's intellectual and cultural elite weathered a snowstorm to hear this political enigma. Although the publicity over the 1858 Lincoln-Douglas debates had given Lincoln considerable notoriety, the people of the East were not quite sure what to think of this Mid-western backwoodsman politician. Lincoln had been invited back in October 1859 for this date and had well researched and prepared his speech in which he would tie his attitude against slavery to the Constitution. In his speech he defended Northern antislavery feelings and essentially ended his talk with a call to arms, politically speaking: "Let us have faith that right makes might, and in that faith let us, to the end, dare to do our duty as we understand it" (Thomas 1982). Lincoln also used this trip east to visit his son who was at Phillips Exeter Academy in New Hampshire. Robert Lincoln had failed fifteen out of sixteen entrance examinations to Harvard and was in New Hampshire for a year of repreparation. During Lincoln's trip he spoke at Providence, Concord, Dover, Exeter, Manchester, Hartford, New Haven, Meriden, Woonsocket, Norwich, and Bridgeport. Most of these communities put on spontaneous, or hastily planned, receptions, at which he was received with great honor.

Lincoln's reputation in the East was substantially enhanced by this trip. There was no doubt now; he was a presidential contender. He represented the views of the North and of Republicans. Being the politician he was, he made sure to agree with unions and other interest groups which would be necessary to hold the North together for electoral victory.

When the Democrats met in Charleston, South Carolina, on April 23, 1860, for the Democratic National Convention, the convention split over resolutions on slavery. Northern and Southern Democrats could not agree on a consensus. Tennessee's Andrew Johnson was a candidate for the Democratic nomination for president at that convention. A consensus could not be obtained for an agreeable platform, and most Southern Democrats walked out. The Tennessee delegation remained, but nothing was settled and the convention ended without nominating a candidate.

During the suspension of the Democratic National Convention, the fragments of the old Whig Party and Know-Nothings, some Democrats, and others met in Baltimore on May 11, 1860. This new "Constitutional Union Party" felt that the best way to handle the growing crisis was to stop talking about it. The continued publicity was dangerously inflaming the crisis. The party platform simply stated that the Constitution should be upheld and the laws enforced. It avoided mention of slavery. This group wanted to preserve the Union by avoiding conflict. Senator John Bell of Tennessee was nominated for president and Edward Everett of Massachusetts was nominated for vice president. The aging Sam Houston, the leader of the Texas revolution and former Tennessee governor, was Bell's strongest rival for the presidential nomination, but Bell won.

Lincoln received the support and encouragement of the Illinois Republican State Convention in May 1860. Later, on May 18, the Republican National Convention convened in Chicago. Since Lincoln had not held high national office, such as the U.S. Senate, his views, other than on slavery, were not known. Likewise, he did not carry the customary baggage and built-in opposition one normally acquires from holding high office. In essence he did not have much of a record to defend. New York Senator William Seward led the first ballot of the convention. However, Lincoln's supporters bargained cabinet posts to prominent Midwestern Republicans, and Lincoln passed Seward on the third ballot. He was then elected by acclimation as the Republican nominee for president. Maine's Hannibal Hamlin was chosen as Republican nominee for vice president. There were no Tennesseans at the Republican National Convention.

The badly split Democrats convened for a second time on June 18, 1860, in Baltimore. Southern Democrats had hoped that the delay since the last attempted convention would allow time for an agreement to be reached among Democrats. When they appeared at Baltimore to participate in the Democratic National Convention they found that some of their states had elected other delegates to the convention. Battles commenced for the seating of delegates. After four days of contention, and much publicity, part or all of the delegates from Tennessee, Virginia, North Carolina, Delaware, Maryland, Kentucky, and California withdrew. The "succeeder" Democrats moved to the Maryland Institute, held convention, and nominated the current vice president John Breckinridge of Kentucky for president and Joseph Lane of Oregon for vice president.

The Northern Democrats, including four remaining from Tennessee and a few from other areas of the South, nominated Senator Stephen Douglas of Illinois for president and Benjamin Fitzpatrick of Alabama for vice president.

Several campaigners passed through Tennessee. Presidential nominee Stephen Douglas, Yancey of Alabama, and Senator Wigfall of Texas were some of the few campaigners who made it to the Volunteer State in the fall of 1860. Senator Andrew Johnson spoke in Memphis on October 16 and claimed that he would never secede from the Union. He did give support (although inconsistent) to the Breckinridge ticket, most probably because it represented Southern Democrats. His support came with the caveat, of course, that he opposed secession.

Most of Douglas's Tennessee support came from West Tennessee and the Memphis *Appeal*. William H. Polk, the brother of the former president, was the leader of the Douglas campaign in Tennessee. Henry S. Foote, V. K. Stevenson, and Harvey M. Watterson were some of Douglas's most ardent supporters.

John Bell, the Constitutional Union Party candidate, found support from many of his Tennessee friends from Middle and East Tennessee. Those included Andrew Jackson Donelson, Edwin H. Ewing, and Neill S. Brown from Nashville; Balie Peyton from Gallatin; and William G. Brownlow, Horace Maynard, Oliver P. Temple, Nathaniel G. Taylor, and Thomas A. R. Nelson from East Tennessee. The Bell campaign was conducted with all the excitement of the Harrison campaign of 1840. Celebrations and parades were held, but the candidate remained at home, as did most candidates during this era. However, in September, Bell participated in a festive affair in Nashville. A parade was held which traversed from Public Square to College Street to Watkins Park. Other parades and activities were held in Knoxville and Memphis. It was exciting anytime a Tennessean campaigned for president; however, many felt that Bell could not win and urged him to withdraw in favor of a major party candidate, specifically the Southern Democrat nominee, John Breckinridge of Kentucky. Breckinridge received support from Tennessee Governor Isham G. Harris, Landon C. Haynes, Gideon J. Pillow, and U.S. Senators Alfred O. P. Nicholson and Andrew Johnson.

On election day, November 6, 1860, Bell carried East and West Tennessee. He lost Middle Tennessee to Breckinridge, but carried his home county of Davidson. Bell received 69,176 votes; Breckinridge received 64,809; Douglas received 11,330; and Lincoln received 0 votes in Tennessee.

On the national level, all Northern States went for Lincoln. Bell carried only Tennessee, Virginia, and Kentucky. Missouri went for Douglas. Alabama, Florida, Georgia, Arkansas, Louisiana, Maryland, Mississippi, North Carolina, South Carolina, Texas, and Delaware went for Breckinridge. New Jersey split between Lincoln and Douglas. Lincoln won 1,866,452 votes; Douglas 1,376,957; Breckinridge 849,781; and Bell 588,879. Lincoln won 173 electors, Breckinridge 72,

Bell 39, and Douglas 12. Lincoln received only a minority of the popular vote. He would have needed almost an additional million votes to equal the number of total votes cast for the other candidates. Douglas and Bell alone totaled 100,000 more votes than Lincoln. Lincoln did not poll a single vote in the South, except for a few votes in the Virginia Panhandle and the border states. However, he managed to win a majority of the electoral vote. The House of Representatives had returned slightly Republican under Buchanan during the midterm elections (113 Republican to 101 Democrat to 23 other), while the Senate had remained Democrat (38 Democrat to 26 Republican to 2 other). With Lincoln's election, the Republicans retained firm control in the House (106 Republican to 42 Democrat to 28 other) and took control of the Senate (31 Republican to 11 Democrat to 7 other). It would not help the balance of political power in Washington when Southern states began to secede and remove their representatives from the U.S. Congress.

In six short years the Republican Party had grown from a small group, meeting in churches and schools, to electing the sixteenth president of the United States. A party was born, but it had won the presidency with less than a majority. There was significant opposition to Lincoln and Republican positions.

Immediately after the election, on November 9, 1860, South Carolina Governor Gist issued a proclamation calling the South Carolina legislature into session. On November 13, their U.S. senator, James Chestnut, resigned his post. South Carolina's militia began to drill in preparation to defend the state against federal intervention. The federal government sent a company of United States artillery to Fayetteville, North Carolina, to protect the grounds and ammunition there. This was viewed as an aggressive act by South Carolina, which was preparing for secession. Other Southern states were preparing to follow suit and were sending their assurances of mutual cooperation to the leaders of South Carolina.

Most Southerners viewed the election of Lincoln as a guarantee of Northern control of the political process. The North elected him by a minority of the total vote and to the South, this was not representation; this was Northern dominance. A crisis loomed and Lincoln's election created additional apprehension because of his abolitionist reputation. Around December 9, President-elect Lincoln wrote to Mississippi Senator Jefferson Davis stating that he was preparing a letter that would prove satisfactory to the South and allay their fears. In spite of the communication, Southerners who were federal office-holders began to resign.

On December 20, 1860, the South Carolina legislature passed an ordinance of secession. Other states soon followed. Attempting to halt the tide of secession, Senator Andrew Johnson gave a speech on December 22 in which he denied the right of secession of the Southern states. He was censured by the Memphis *Appeal* and roundly denounced in Memphis, being burned in effigy as a traitor. The state that had elected Johnson felt threatened by the new federal leaders. Tennessee citizens held meetings across the state to discuss the crisis and their options. Would it be secession or compromise?

Lincoln had gained fame and the presidency on an antislavery platform. Now elected, the South had little doubt that Lincoln and the North intended to ignore their rights and would fail to demonstrate any sensitivity to regional realities. For a short period of time some effort was made, by each side, to hold the tide of war. But, tensions were strong. Lincoln had won an office, but at the cost of plunging the nation toward disaster. As Northern attitudes and the new president-elect continued to demonstrate inadequate consideration toward the South, Georgia and the Southern states along the Gulf of Mexico soon followed South Carolina. Mississippi seceded on January 9, 1861. On February 4, 1861, delegates of the seceding Southern states met in Montgomery, Alabama, to form the Confederate States of America. Jefferson Davis, from Mississippi, was elected president and Alexander Stephens of Georgia was elected vice president.

Secession and War

At this point in time only seven states were in the Confederacy. Tennessee and seven other slave states had not yet joined. Governor Isham Harris called the legislature into session on January 7, 1861, to consider a secession referendum. John Bell, however, knew Lincoln, felt that he was a reasonable man, and thought that the states were overreacting. Bell urged caution and accused Governor Harris of misjudging Lincoln and being unfair to him. He urged that Tennesseans give Lincoln a chance, and indeed most of Tennessee and its press agreed. Many believed that the new president would be reasonable in his approach and respond appropriately to the financial repercussions of abolition. On February 9, 1861, the people of Tennessee voted against a convention for secession. The vote was 68,000 against and 59,000 in favor. In February, Bell went to Washington to confer with Lincoln, who apparently reassured him. Bell returned to Tennessee and tried to calm the growing storm by communicating Lincoln's reassurances. Unfortunately, it was not long before Bell's efforts proved futile.

On March 4, 1861, Lincoln was inaugurated as the sixteenth president of the United States. In April, South Carolina waited for the federal government to turn over Fort Sumpter, which was in the Charleston harbor. Instead of "surrendering" the fort, Lincoln attempted to send supplies. To Lincoln's defiant act, South Carolina replied with an attack on the fort, which surrendered the following day, on April 12, 1861. After the Fort Sumpter incident, most Southern people gave up all hope of peace.

Lincoln called for recruits to quell the rebellion of the seceding states. Tennessee's Governor Harris replied that, "Tennessee will not furnish a single man for purposes of coercion, but 50,000, if necessary for the defense of our rights and those of our Southern brothers" (McKellar 1942). John Bell and other men who had urged compromise realized that Lincoln had forced them to stand with their neighbors. Bell had owned slaves but supported the Union. He had hoped that something could be worked out to prevent disaster. In spite of Lincoln's reassurances to Bell, the president now believed that peace would come through submission.

The state legislature met on April 25, 1861. The attitudes of Tennesseans had changed substantially since the Fort Sumpter incident. By May 1, it authorized Governor Harris to enter into a military compact with the seceding states. On May 6 the legislature passed the ordinance of secession to be submitted to the people on June 8. On May 7, the legislature approved joining the Confederacy. When the public referendum was held on June 8, the people of Tennessee approved the ordinance of separation 104,913 to 47,238. (The vote was recorded by the secretary of state as 108,418 for and 53,336 against, but different numbers are given by other sources.)

East Tennessee, along with Andrew Johnson, opposed secession. About 33,000 of the total vote of 47,238 against secession came from there. However, Middle and West Tennessee voted overwhelmingly in favor of separation. East Tennessee was mostly mountains, with little of the plantation life found in West Tennessee, Arkansas, and Mississippi. The need for labor was not the same for an East Tennessee farmer as it was for the West Tennessee cotton planter. East Tennesseans and their leaders like Andrew Johnson, William G. "Parson" Brownlow, Thomas Nelson, Oliver Temple, and Horace Maynard could not accept the decision of the rest of the state. These East Tennesseeans, mostly from Knox County, were Union sympathizers. Some of these men actually owned a few slaves. The difference was that in East Tennessee slaves were used mostly in homes as domestic help since there was little or no farm activity compared to West Tennessee and other areas of the South. The East Tennessee slaves were, in many instances, like family members because of their domestic role. Total agreement in this area of the state over separation did not exist. Knoxville voted for it, but Knox County voted against.

Judge Thomas Nelson called an East Tennessee Convention on June 17, 1861, shortly after the public referendum for separation, at the Greeneville home of Andrew Johnson. A meeting of representatives of all East Tennessee counties, except Rhea County, was held in Greeneville, Tennessee, June 17–20, 1861. A rapid progression of events soon took place. The convention adopted a proposal to send to the state legislature, ". . . asking its consent that the counties composing East Tennessee . . . may form and erect a separate state" (Creekmore 1958). They wanted to secede from Tennessee. Since the legislature was controlled by Democrats, the petition was not accepted. (The legislature never acted on this resolution.) This was not unlike the request from the people in the western part of Virginia, which did result in the formation of a new state—West Virginia. Though unable to separate, some East Tennesseans held with the Union and retained some representatives in the U.S. House.

With the threat of war looming on the horizon, the request had gone out for the tools of war and the men to use them. Ammunition, cannons, swords, uniforms, tents, etc. were all needed. Contracts were made and fund-raising was begun to pay for the necessities of a military defense. Memphis and other communities in West Tennessee quickly assisted. Middle Tennessee was somewhat slower in its preparations for defense.

Four armies were called for in order to defend the South. One of these was organized in Tennessee, upon the call of Governor Harris, under the command of Gideon J. Pillow. The "Provisional Army of Tennessee" was organized in Memphis and on July 31, 1861, was commissioned by President Davis as a part of the Confederate army. General Leonidas Polk was officially assigned command by President Davis a few days earlier on July 4, 1861. Felix Zollicoffer, a former newspaper editor, was given command of Confederate troops in East Tennessee and the rank of brigadier general. Prior to General Polk's arrival, the citizens, under their own initiative, had begun organizing troops. Governor Harris had also, prior to the official Confederate call, sent General S. R. Anderson to organize militia in Memphis. Many of the major cities of Tennessee had made war preparations the priority of their daily lives. Excitement and activity were at a height. People of the state found new talents in manufacturing the tools of war. Tennessee, by war's end, had contributed 187,000 men to the Confederate army and 31,000 to the Union army, most of the latter coming from East Tennessee.

Meanwhile, William Brownlow had decided to represent East Tennessee as the pro-Union candidate in the gubernatorial election, but by April he withdrew in favor of William H. Polk. Polk was from Middle Tennessee and was thought to have a much better chance against the incumbent governor (who was from Memphis and had a solid West and Middle Tennessee base of support) than an East Tennessee Radical. As the campaign geared up, Polk blamed Democrat Governor Isham Harris for Tennessee's leaving the Union and stated that Harris's Confederate tendencies would continue to worsen the alienation of Tennesseans in the east section of the state, thus driving them toward the Union. However, Harris, stating that he was defending his state, only had to point to the aggression shown by the Northerners and their obvious lack of concern for the rights of Southern states. The majority of Tennesseans agreed with Harris's view. In the August 1861 elections, Governor Harris (Democrat) was reelected over W. H. Polk (Unionist), from Columbia, by 30,000 votes (75,300 to 43,495). The sentiment of the majority of the citizens of the state was obvious. Confederate candidates won majorities in the state house and senate. Meanwhile, East Tennessee Union supporters proceeded to elect U.S. representatives in the August election. Of those elected, Dr. A. J. Clements, George W. Bridges, and Horace Maynard were seated by the Northern-controlled Congress. Thomas A. R. Nelson was arrested by Confederates as he traveled through Virginia. He never made it to Congress; instead, he changed his mind and returned to Tennessee.

All the Southern U.S. senators from the Confederate States had resigned from the U.S. Senate except Andrew Johnson. Senator Alfred Nicholson "retired" from the Senate on March 3, 1861, because of the Civil War (the term was scheduled to run until March 3, 1865), only to be officially expelled by the Republican majority on July 11. Even though Senator Johnson had supported Breckinridge for president, when Lincoln was elected, Johnson began to support him in the U.S. Senate. Johnson was in full agreement that preservation of the Union was of utmost importance.

The new Tennessee legislature met in October 1861. They elected two Confederate senators—Gustavus A. Henry and Landon C. Haynes. They also created eleven Confederate congressional districts. By November 6, the general election was held in which the eleven Confederate congressmen were selected. (This would be the final session before the war began. Once Grant moved toward Tennessee, the legislature feared capture. They eventually left Nashville for Memphis to hold session in January 1862.)

As the Union and Confederate armies prepared for war, the Union army gathered along the Ohio River in Kentucky, intending to move into Tennessee by way of the Tennessee, Mississippi, and Cumberland Rivers. Ulysses Grant was given command of the Union forces at the

GUSTAVUS ADOLPHUS HENRY was born in Scott County, Kentucky, on October 8, 1804, to General William and Elizabeth Julia (Flournoy) Henry. He received a classical primary education. He then went to college, graduating with first honors from Transylvania University in Lexington, Kentucky, in 1825. He then studied law in Hopkinsville, Kentucky and passed the bar. He served in the Kentucky house of representatives, representing Christian County, from 1831 until 1833. He married Marion McClure, daughter of Hugh and Susan (Gibson) McClure of Clarksville, Montgomery County, Tennessee, on February 17, 1833. They had seven children—Marion, Benjamin, Thomas Flournoy, John Flournoy, Susan, Gustavus Adolphus Jr., and Patrick Henry.

Henry began practicing law in Hopkinsville, Kentucky, but moved his practice to Clarksville, Tennessee, in 1833. He helped found the Marine Fire Insurance, Life and Trust Company in Clarksville in 1839 and the Clarksville Insurance Company in 1858. He served as a Whig presidential elector three times, supporting William Henry Harrison in 1840, Henry Clay, in 1844, and Winfield Scott in 1852. As the Whig party disintegrated, Henry and others supported former Whig John Bell, who was the Constitutional Union party candidate in 1860.

Henry was unsuccessful in an attempt to win a seat in the U.S. House of Representatives in 1842, but he served in the Tennessee house of representatives from 1851 to 1853. He ran as the Whig nominee for governor against Democrat Andrew Johnson in 1853 but narrowly lost by 2,261 votes out of 124,000 cast. On May 1, 1861, Henry was appointed by Governor Isham Harris as one of the Southern Confederacy military league commissioners. In October 1861 he was elected by the legislature as senator to the Confederate States. He continued to support the Confederacy and its military struggle until the end of the Civil War. After the conflict ended, he returned to his law practice in Clarksville. He served as chairman of the Democratic State Convention in 1874. He was a member of the Episcopal Church, and one of the original trustees (1848) of Masonic University and Montgomery Academy.

Henry died at his home of "Emerald Hill" in Clarksville on September 10, 1880, and was buried at Greenwood Cemetery. (Portrait painting by Cornelius Hankins courtesy of TSM)

Tennessee (Paducah, Kentucky) and Cumberland (Smithland, Kentucky) River outposts on September 1, 1861.

Shortly thereafter, on September 10, 1861, General Albert Sidney Johnston was given command of the Confederate forces of Department Number Two which included Tennessee, Arkansas, portions of Kansas, Missouri, areas of the Indian Territory, which were of military importance, and Kentucky, which was officially neutral. Johnston's title was general commanding the Western Department of the Confederate States of America. Johnston spread his troops along a thin line from Columbus, Kentucky, to Bowling Green, Kentucky, to Cumberland Gap. This was called the "Line of the Cumberland" and was an important barrier against Union invasion of the South. Just south of this line, Fort Henry was built where the Tennessee River entered Tennessee, and Fort Donelson was built where the Cumberland River entered Tennessee. The left part of the "Line" was commanded by General Polk, the center by General Simon B. Buckner, and the right by General George B. Crittenden.

Grant decided to attack both the left and right sides of the Confederate defense prepared by General Johnston. The first engagement of conflict for the Confederate army, which was headed by General Polk, took place at Carthage and Wilson's Creek, Missouri. Next came the Battle of Belmont, which was in Missouri, on the west bank of the Mississippi River, across from Columbus, Kentucky. Here, the Union forces were defeated and thrown back.

While Tennesseans were fighting the Union advance on the west end of the front, East Tennesseans loyal to the Union began burning railroad bridges, assisting the Union forces' effort to disrupt Confederate movements. On November 8, 1861, five strategic bridges were destroyed. Tennessee Confederates captured six of the conspirators and hung five of them. The war quickly began to cause serious hardships on the citizens of Knoxville. Food stock dwindled. Coffee, tea, and spices all disappeared and salt became a rare and rationed item. East Tennessee University, the Tennessee School for the Deaf, and the courthouse buildings were used as hospitals for the Confederacy. By January 1862, Union General George Thomas felt the East Tennessee railroad had been disrupted enough for his troop advancement and he moved to attack Confederate General George Crittenden, who was charged with defending the east end of the Tennessee fortification line. Crittenden moved his troops out of the Cumberland Gap to meet the Union advance. Brigadier General Felix Zollicoffer was ordered along the south bank of the Cumberland River to watch General Thomas's troops. On January 19, 1862, close to Mill Springs, Kentucky, Zollicoffer prematurely moved to attack a superior Union force. He was killed and his troops defeated. The east end of Johnston's line was now open to Yankee advancement.

General Albert Sidney Johnston was duly concerned with the lack of preparation at Forts Henry and Donelson on the west end of the line. In an attempt to shore up his forts, he sent Brigadier General Lloyd Tilghman, a Kentuckian who held command at Hopkinsville, to prepare the forts. In February 1862, before the forts could be completed, Grant ordered an advance on Fort Henry, initiating the first battle fought in Tennessee. Captain Andrew Hull Foote moved Union gunboats within firing range of Fort Henry and began pounding the uncompleted fort with sixty-five cannons. There were only twenty-eight hundred Confederates and twelve cannons in the fort. The Confederates, under Tilghman, surrendered on February 4, 1862, even before Grant's ground troops arrived.

Grant picked up additional troops, bringing his command to thirty thousand soldiers, and wasted no time in heading straight for nearby Fort Donelson, which was only a few miles from Fort Henry. General John B. Floyd was in command of the Confederates, overseeing Generals Pillow, Buckner, Bushrod Rust Johnson, and Colonel Nathan Bedford Forrest. By now, Grant's forces were nearly double that of the Confederate troops. On February 13, 1862, Union forces attacked. At first, the Northerners were repulsed from the perimeter of the fort. On February 14, Foote's gunboats were also driven back. The next day, Pillow's troops, who had driven the Union assault back, returned to the fort with nearly depleted supplies. Grant continued his assault. After five days of fighting, a disagreement arose between

Floyd and the other Confederate generals over which course to follow. Their escape route was now held by the enemy and they had little left with which to fight. Surrender was discussed. Generals Floyd, Pillow, and Johnson marched their troops out of the fort and escaped, leaving General Buckner. The fort was surrendered on February 16, but Forrest's cavalry made their way out and vanished from the Union's grasp just prior to the surrender.

With the two forts along the Confederate's western defensive line gone, Middle Tennessee was helpless. With little opposition, Union General Don Carlos Buell moved his troops into Nashville on February 24, 1862. Tennesseans were dumbfounded that their state could be so easily taken. Confidence had been high, no doubt ignoring the fact that the Union army was well equipped and better trained, even with many new recruits. Nashville, the capital of Tennessee, was regarded as one of the finest aristocratic cities of the South. With the position lost, Tennessee citizens, especially those in Nashville, were in a hysterical frenzy, as the state lay open to Yankee advance.

Now that Middle and West Tennessee were occupied, General Grant declared martial law. The conquered state would no longer be used to Southern advantage.

U.S. Senator Andrew Johnson had remained loyal to the United States, refused secession, and remained in the U.S. Senate. Now that Middle and West Tennessee were essentially under Union control, President Lincoln wanted to appoint a military governor whose job it would be to oversee control of Tennessee until the state rejoined the Union. His choice was Senator Johnson. However, Johnson was viewed as a traitor to his fellow Tennesseans. (Both times Johnson had been elected governor, he lost East

---

LANDON CARTER HAYNES was born on December 2, 1816, in Elizabethton, Carter County, Tennessee, to David and Rhonda (Taylor) Haynes. He was a descendent of South Carolina Governor Robert Y. Haynes. Haynes studied at Washington College in Washington County, became a Methodist minister, and then studied law with T. A. R. Nelson. Admitted to the bar in Jonesboro, Washington County, Tennessee, in 1841, he practiced law and farmed near Johnson City (at the present-day Tipton-Haynes Place). He married Eleanor Powell, the daughter of Joseph and Eleanor (Wheeler) Powell. They had seven children—Joseph E., Mary A., James, Ann Helen, Landon, David, and Robert W. Haynes.

Haynes served as a presidential elector in 1844 and 1860. He served as a Democrat in the Tennessee house of representatives, representing Washington County from 1845 to 1847, then the Tennessee state senate from 1847 to 1849, representing Washington, Johnson, Carter, and Sullivan Counties, and again in the Tennessee house from 1849 to 1851, representing Washington, Greene, and Hawkins Counties and serving as speaker. He was elected a senator to the Confederate States by the Tennessee legislature in 1861 and remained a strong and active supporter of the confederate cause. After the war Haynes was arrested by federal authorities, but was pardoned by President Johnson. He left his East Tennessee home because of vindictive post-Civil War Union radicals. He moved to Memphis and practiced law. He was unsuccessful in a race for the U.S. House of Representatives in 1872.

Haynes died on February 17, 1875. He was buried in Elmwood Cemetery in Memphis. In 1902 his remains were moved to Jackson, Madison County, Tennessee. (Portrait unavailable)

Tennessee, now pro-Union, and won only by his Democratic support in the rest of the state, mostly Middle Tennessee, now strongly Confederate.) Both General Buell and Assistant Secretary of War Thomas A. Scott opposed Johnson's appointment on the grounds that it would create a violent uproar among the agitated Tennesseans. Nevertheless Lincoln supported the loyal U.S. senator and ignored their reservations. On March 3, 1862, President Abraham Lincoln appointed Andrew Johnson military governor of Tennessee.

Upon appointment Johnson was indeed treated as a traitor by the citizens of Middle and West Tennessee. He tried to argue his point with the citizens in a statement issued on March 18, 1862, in which he offered pardons to those who would take the Union oath, but this effort was to no avail. He existed under a threat and resentment that he clearly understood. He removed the Nashville mayor and city council from office and put Union loyalists in their place. Eventually, he put Nashville Mayor Richard B. Cheatham in jail, along with dissenting doctors, ministers, and other leaders. Former Governor Neill S. Brown was also jailed. Newspapers were shut down. Johnson sent some Tennesseans to Northern prisons. This was an unprecedented act upon those who had previously given him the Middle Tennessee vote advantage required to achieve his election as governor, for two terms, and the legislative support to become a U.S. senator in the peaceful times prior to the war. Johnson was hated. Cotton bails were used to barricade him in the capitol building in Nashville. He was thus fairly isolated and had little he could do outside of the immediate vicinity of the capitol.

During its Union occupation, Nashville developed into a medical center for the Union army. Life in the city became radically different. The Union army marched through the streets in the middle of the night. Citizens were required to sign loyalty oaths to the Union, but there was espionage and counterespionage. Homes were entered and searched at all hours of the night by Union soldiers. Women, as well as men, were arrested as Confederate sympathizers and sent to local prison or north to prison camps. Blacks were rewarded for providing information against Nashville's citizens. Houses were stoned and old trees were cut down, at will, by the Union army for firewood. Horses were confiscated. Nashvillians were sometimes denied the right to bury dead Confederates. Churches were taken and used by the Union army. Heavy assessments were levied on the citizens. Most of the hardships occurred after General Buell left and General Rosecrans was put in charge of forces, which outnumbered the population threefold.

After General A. S. Johnston ordered his troops to withdraw from Middle Tennessee, Confederate General Leonidas Polk, who was now in Columbus, Kentucky, moved some of his troops south to Island Number Ten on the Mississippi River and the remainder on to Corinth, Mississippi.

General Grant continued to move south in pursuit of the Confederates. By the middle of March 1862 he had arrived at Savannah, Tennessee. He then continued down the Tennessee River to Shiloh, following General Johnston's forty thousand Confederates who were by now in the area of Corinth. The Confederate forces had all gathered by April 4, 1862. Johnston's

Hospital laundry yard in Nashville, July 1863. There were twenty-four military hospitals in wartime Nashville. (Courtesy of TSLA)

forces included his own, General Beauregard's, General Polk's, General Braxton Bragg's, General William Hardee's, and General John Breckinridge's (former vice president in the Buchanan administration and Southern Democratic presidential candidate in 1860). Although Grant's troops were close behind the Confederates, the general, not anticipating anything other than being the aggressor, was holding behind, at Savannah (over eight miles from Shiloh). Johnston surprised Grant's Union forces when he reversed his retreat and turned to attack at Shiloh, instead of being chased. While the Union soldiers were leisurely taking breakfast and preparing for another day, the Confederate soldiers overran many of their campsites. The Confederates badly defeated the Union forces on Sunday, April 6, 1862, but the cost was high. General Johnston had taken a bullet in the thigh (it likely hit the femoral vessels, the main blood vessels supplying the leg) and bled profusely. Governor Isham G. Harris was with Johnston and helped him from his horse to a place to rest. He could not stop the bleeding and Johnston died. During Sunday evening the Union forces received twenty to thirty thousand reinforcements. On Monday, with Confederate General Johnston now dead, General Pierre Gustave Toutant Beauregard took command. The Union forces counterattacked and forced the Confederates to retreat to Corinth. Over twenty thousand Union and Confederate soldiers were killed or wounded in the bloody battle of Shiloh. The Union forces lost more than the Confederates, but for a fragile Confederacy the cost was more damaging. Now the entire South and West lay open to the Union forces.

With most of Memphis's able-bodied and willing men off at war, her only defense was a few Confederate gunboats. The city was not in the Confederate plan as a strategic defense site. This determination was made because planners felt that the town was too forward a position and difficult to supply. Also, the South did not want to risk Memphis's destruction by making it a target for battle. Aside from these considerations, the fortification at Fort Pillow, which was a short distance north of the city, was thought to be an adequate defense.

On June 6, 1862, the Union fleet of gunboats and rams, attacked the Memphis fleet on the Mississippi River adjacent to the city. Five thousand Memphians watched from the banks of the Mississippi River as nearly the entire Confederate fleet was destroyed. One Confederate boat, the *Van Dorn*, escaped downriver. Mayor John Park had no choice but to surrender the city, but the citizens remained defiant. Stores closed and refused to open. Now under Union control, citizens were prohibited from moving in and out of the city at will. Newspapers were not allowed to be published unless editors took an oath of allegiance to the Union and followed expected conduct. Since Middle and West Tennessee were now under Union control, the Memphis *Appeal* presses were hurried out of town on a rail car to escape into Mississippi. From then on, during the war, the *Appeal* would attack the North from wherever it could set up its presses.

On June 26 the federal government allowed the city to hold an election. Mayor John Park was reelected. Since citizens were required to take the federal oath of allegiance in order to vote, only seven hundred votes were cast.

On July 4, 1862, President Lincoln signed the Pacific Railroad Act, authorizing the transcontinental railroad. Instead of Memphis, the eastern terminus would be on the Missouri River, at Omaha, Nebraska. By using this route the Union could guarantee control of Western expansion as well as troop supplies. (The rail system was not completed until 1869.)

In July 1862 General Grant expelled all Memphis citizens who had any relationship with the Confederate government. Men were forced to take the oath of allegiance or leave the city. It was prohibited to pay gold, silver, or treasury notes to planters for their cotton. On July 21, 1862, Major General William Tecumseh Sherman assumed command of Memphis. The Union forces then instituted strict business guidelines and sought out Confederate sympathizers. Cotton was an important crop to Northern merchants, who wanted the fiber to sell to U.S. and European manufacturers. Cotton and corn harvesting was assured by recruiting Blacks to assist with the continued flow of agricultural products. All cotton purchased after July 23, 1862, was seized and sent north, with the only hope of payment being proof of claim by the planter. Tennessee "paper" could be used for payment, or the value could be deposited with the federal quartermaster to be held in trust. "This of course led to evasion, perjury, the corruption of officials and the open and shameless robbery from the planters who had been induced by Sherman's first order to enter the city and offer cotton for sale" (Keating 1888).

Since cotton was in short supply in the North, prices rose from 13¢ in 1860 to $1.44 per pound in 1864. Most of the cotton trade was illegal, and market speculators resorted to smuggling. This was tolerated somewhat since the North needed the fiber. Yankee officials, Southern officials, and corrupt military officials "were making fortunes in contraband goods." General Grant even commented on the "disloyalty of some Memphians to their own cause" (Sigafoos 1979).

Businessman Robertson Topp, because of his Union ties, was permitted to move about as an agent for Memphis business interests. However, most other businessmen were restricted. Topp played a significant role in preventing total stagnation of the wartime economy of Memphis, West Tennessee, and the surrounding areas.

Federal troops took over vacant houses and stores and confiscated property. They ordered the families of Confederate volunteers who were off at war to leave their homes and their city. Sherman was a terror to the people of Memphis. Their only recourse was the organization of a defiant, though quiet, resistance.

Governor Johnson and President Lincoln wanted Tennesseans to feel that they had some input into the Union government in hopes of making them less resistant. They felt that if Tennesseans would elect representatives in Congress, this would serve as a sign of loyalty to the Union, which would then move Tennessee closer to restoration. East Tennessee posed no problem to this plan since the area contained a majority of Unionists. Western and Middle Tennessee would have to be won over, though, with the west end of the state being the biggest challenge. On order from Military Governor Andrew Johnson, an election was to be held for U.S. representatives in the solidly Confederate West Tennessee. But, to the embarrassment of the president and governor, the effort was of little avail. General Forrest took his troops and rode through the area, successfully preventing the polls from opening. West Tennesseans resisted the election of congressmen from the Ninth and Tenth Districts.

In November 1862 Tennessee Confederate soldiers elected Judge Robert L. Caruthers as governor, but the Union occupation of Nashville prevented his inauguration. Meanwhile, Governor Isham Harris continued to act as Confederate governor of Tennessee, working with Southern commanders in planning to retake the state. When Union forces took Middle and West Tennessee, Harris was forced to leave the state. After his departure, he served as a volunteer member of the staffs of Generals Albert Sidney Johnston, Braxton Bragg, and Joseph E. Johnston, and he fought in many important battles of the war.

After Shiloh, the Tennessee army retreated to Corinth, and General Braxton Bragg took command. In the meantime General Kirby Smith had taken command of the Rebel troops in East Tennessee. Searching for a way to make a counteroffensive, General Bragg and General Smith planned to join forces and move into Kentucky against the Yankees. Bragg moved thirty thousand troops to Chattanooga. Smith had taken charge of Crittenden's forces in East Tennessee and moved from Knoxville into Kentucky, winning a victory at Richmond on August 16, 1862. Then he took Lexington and Frankfort. Bragg, shortly thereafter, moved out of Chattanooga on August 28 and into Kentucky near Glasgow. Meanwhile, General Buell's forces followed him up from Corinth, Mississippi. On October 8, 1862, near Perryville, Kentucky, a fierce battle was fought between Union troops and some of Bragg's forces. The move to invade Kentucky, in light of the damage to their troops and conditions back in Tennessee, seemed secondary to Bragg. Additionally, he had not picked up Kentucky recruits as he had anticipated. Bragg subsequently moved his troops back into the state, heading for Murfreesboro and hoping to join forces with Generals Breckinridge and Forrest who planned to retake Nashville.

Meanwhile General William S. Rosecrans had taken command of Union forces in Nashville. He knew of Bragg's position and planned to head him off at Murfreesboro. He moved his troops in Bragg's direction. In the early morning hours of December 31, 1862, a portion of Bragg's men came upon some of Rosecrans's Yankees, holding just on the west side of Murfreesboro. The Rebels held the advantage that day and pushed the Yankees back. However, Rosecrans's troops did not flee and made camp a few miles from the battle site. Rosecrans received reinforcements. On January 2, 1863, Breckinridge's forces tried to take the Yankees in their position, west of Murfreesboro. The battle at Stone's River was a draw. Each side suffered heavy casualties and withdrew after three days of bloodshed. Bragg withdrew to Shelbyville and Tullahoma, while Rosecrans retreated to Murfreesboro. Rosecrans's army was torn apart by this battle.

General Grant traveled to Nashville to reorganize the army. He occupied the

ROBERT LOONEY CARUTHERS was born to one of the oldest families in Tennessee. His forebears were originally from Scotland. They settled in Virginia and then North Carolina. Later, they came to Tennessee, moving near Columbia in Maury County. Robert was the youngest of seven children of Samuel and Elizabeth (Looney) Caruthers and was born in Smith County, near Carthage, on July 31, 1800. He received his early education near Columbia, Tennessee, at Woodward's Academy, then later attended Greeneville College, in Greene County, and Washington College, near Jonesboro, in Washington County. He then studied law with Judge Samuel Powel in Greeneville and began his practice in Carthage, Tennessee, in 1823.

Caruthers married Sarah Sanders, the daughter of James and Mary (Smith) Donelson Sanders, from Sumner County. From 1823 to 1824, he served as a clerk in the state house of representatives when it met in Murfreesboro. He served as clerk of chancery court and was editor of the *Tennessee Republican* in Carthage. In 1826 he moved to Lebanon, Wilson County, Tennessee. The following year Governor Sam Houston appointed Caruthers state attorney general for Lebanon (Sixth Judicial District), a position he served in until 1832. He became brigadier general of the Tennessee Militia in 1834 and was then elected to the Tennessee house of representatives, serving Wilson County, from 1835 until 1837, on the House Judiciary Committee. He succeeded John Bell as congressman, serving from March 4, 1841, until March 3, 1843, but did not run for reelection. He served as a state elector-at-large for the Whigs in 1844, supporting Henry Clay and opposing James K. Polk. In 1842, Caruthers founded

Carter home at Sixth and Union Streets. When, on February 28, 1864, Grant's wife arrived, he moved from the Carter home, returned the front door key, offered to pay for his lodging, and "offered to provide protection for the family against the drunken soldiers, who at this time were terrorizing the city" (Creekmore 1958).

The next six months went by without a major battle in Tennessee. However, the cavalry of Forrest and Joseph Wheeler spent this time raiding Union posts. (Wheeler, originally from Georgia, commanded the Nineteenth Alabama Infantry.) In April 1863, the adjutant general's office of the War Department issued general orders Number One Hundred, which suspended the authority of any elected government in Tennessee. It forbade any official act by Tennessee citizens, nullified all elections, and authorized the military to run communities.

In June 1863 Bragg withdrew from Middle Tennessee, fighting skirmishes along the way, while Union soldiers under General Rosecrans followed. Simultaneously, Confederate General Simon B. Buckner withdrew from East Tennessee. In September 1863 Unionist East Tennessee was freed from Confederate control when Union General A. E. Burnside moved south from Kentucky with his ten thousand troops into Knoxville. Union headquarters established on Gay Street. Forts were built south of Knoxville in order to protect the city from Confederate General Longstreet's forces, which were moving north from Chattanooga.

Bragg's troops had retreated to Chattanooga, with General Rosecrans and reinforcements of close to seventy

---

Cumberland University in Lebanon, Tennessee and cofounded Cumberland University Law School, along with his brother, Abraham Caruthers, in 1847. He served on the college's board of trustees from 1842 until 1862 and was the board's first president. In 1852 Governor William B. Campbell appointed him to the state supreme court. He was elected to the court by the legislature in 1853 and by public vote in 1854. (An amendment to the state constitution changed the position to one elected by the public rather than the legislature.) He remained on the court until it ceased to function during the Civil War.

Caruthers was elected by the General Assembly on January 24, 1861, to serve as a delegate from the Fifth Congressional District to the Washington Peace Convention, which was created to resolve the differences between the North and the South. In 1863 he was elected to succeed three-term Governor Isham Harris. However, the Union occupation encompassed most of the state, including the capital, which was occupied by Military Governor Andrew Johnson. Therefore, Caruthers was never inaugurated, and Isham Harris continued in what little gubernatorial capacity remained for the Confederate Tennesseans. Caruthers married, in 1862, Sarah Vaughn Lawrence, whose family owned a large plantation in Davidson County which was burned a short time later. Sarah had one son from her previous marriage—Vaughn. He served with General Forrest and was for a time a prisoner of war. Caruthers also served in the Confederate secret service.

In 1868 Caruthers became professor of law at Cumberland and continued in this capacity for the remainder of his life. He was active in the Cumberland Presbyterian Church in Lebanon and was a Grand Master of the Grand Lodge of Tennessee Free and Accepted Masons. Robert Looney Caruthers died on October 2, 1882, and was buried in Lebanon, Tennessee, at Cedar Grove Cemetery. (Photograph courtesy of TSLA) thousand men in pursuit. Bragg crossed the Tennessee line into North Georgia. Soon they had enough of retreating, and with reinforcements from General John Bell Hood and General James Longstreet who had come from the Virginia battlefields to help, on September 18 they turned to fight. Rosecrans was startled when he found Bragg had reversed his retreat. Bragg halted in an area about twenty miles south of Chattanooga and prepared to fight. On September 19, 1863, the forty thousand Confederate troops engaged sixty thousand Union soldiers in the battle of Chickamauga Creek. When the Confederates attacked, the Union forces were nearly overcome by the violent determination of the Rebels. The veteran Union soldiers were devastated by this volunteer Southern army. It looked as if Chattanooga would have to be bypassed by Union forces, and therefore the remainder of Rosecrans's troops retreated. Shortly thereafter, however, General Grant took over and brought in reinforcements to face the Confederates.

Because of the fear that the last of Tennessee might be lost, Bragg sent some of his troops to Knoxville, under General Longstreet, to help drive General Ambrose Burnside's Union troops out of East Tennessee. Burnside had brought liberation for the many Union loyalists. One Unionist became particularly vocal, after liberation. William G. "Parson" Brownlow's paper printed his pro-Union messages. Brownlow had been a caged tiger in a literary manner of speaking. When he was finally freed to his own designs, he went on a journalistic crusade against his fellow (Confederate) Tennesseans.

The Confederates planned to drive the Yankees out of Knoxville. On November 18, 1863, Confederate Major General Lafayette McLaws, a subordinate of Longstreet, met

General Ulysses S. Grant on Lookout Mountain. (Courtesy of TSLA)

Union Brigadier General William Sanders's forces at Kingston's Pike near the home of Robert H. Armstrong. The battle was extremely difficult. At the point of stalemate, General Sanders rode up front in order to "rally his men and to organize their retreat" (Creekmore 1958). The sight of a general on his white horse made an easy target. Sanders was shot and died the following day.

The city of Knoxville seemed close to coming under Confederate control again. General Longstreet was determined to reseize the community by blocking incoming supplies. Knoxville had only recently been placed under Union command, but the seizure of its facilities and occupation was temporary and friendly. East Tennessee had thousands of Union sympathizers, and the citizens in the surrounding countryside brought in supplies to the Union army. This resupply allowed Union forces to survive. Finally, on November 25, 1863, Longstreet received word that General Bragg needed his troops back at Chattanooga and he gave up the Battle of Fort Sanders. Longstreet delayed leaving until November 29, 1863, and then retreated. But by then it was too late to help Bragg, and now that he had withdrawn, East Tennessee was completely and permanently under Union control. Citizens of Knoxville and the surrounding area were relieved and enthused over the Union triumph.

General Grant, now at Chattanooga, began to remove the Confederates from their Chattanooga stronghold. General William T. Sherman was ordered to bring Union forces from Mississippi to join Grant. Bragg, rather than pursuing Rosecrans and ending the battle, had dispersed his troops in an effort to address many problems, such as the Union occupation of Knoxville. Spread too thin and allowing the Yankees time to gain reinforcements put victory out of reach for Bragg. Grant's forces met Bragg's at the Battles of Lookout Mountain and Missionary Ridge on November 23. By November 25, Chattanooga was under Union control, and the Confederates, soundly defeated, left in a hasty retreat with a tattered residual force.

General Joseph Johnston replaced Bragg and retreated to Atlanta in December 1863. Union forces under General Sherman followed Johnston to Atlanta. No battles were fought for several months as forces took a winter rest. President Davis, somewhat irritated with Confederate losses, replaced Johnston with General John Bell Hood.

By spring 1864 it began to look as if it were time for the Union to provide avenues of reinstatement for Southern citizens who had finally come to reckon with Union domination. Lincoln issued a "Proclamation of Amnesty and Reconstruction." It said that when one-tenth of a state swore loyalty to the Union, the state government would be readopted in Washington. Military Governor Johnson was cautious in allowing Tennesseans to vote. After all, some determined Confederates might take a nonbinding oath, take over the government, and then cause serious damage to the progress thus far accomplished. Therefore, Johnson created an even more stringent oath to be used for the election planned for county officials on March 5, 1864. East Tennesseans, who were mostly Union sympathizers, were insulted by having to take the oath. Many Middle and West Tennesseans still resisted domination and refused to submit to the oath. Election participation was pitiful. Johnson was trying to maintain order and control, but he instead suffered more

Detail from the "Battle of Lookout Mountain" by James Walker. (Courtesy of TSLA)

hatred. The statewide election of local officials drew mixed results. Only half of Tennessee's counties elected officials. Boycotts, irregularities, and a Union Party now divided over the loyalty oath nearly ruined the elections.

By the summer of 1864, even in the midst of war, it was time for another presidential election. In spite of the division among Union supporters in Tennessee, they elected delegates to the upcoming national convention, and the convention accepted the Tennessee delegation. The June 1864 Baltimore convention for the renomination of Lincoln called its party the National Union Party rather than the Republican Party, reflective of a nation still split in war. It was hoped that Republicans could attract Democrats by using the National Union Party name to bridge the similarities of purpose. Andrew Johnson had endeared himself to the North for his loyalty and efforts on behalf of saving the Union. Although hated by his fellow Tennesseans for his philosophy and compulsive effort to maintain control while military governor, he had significant political experience and had served the Union well. The Tennessee delegation endorsed Johnson as the vice presidential nominee.

Andrew Johnson, like Lincoln, wanted the Southern states back in the Union as states, rather than conquered territories. However, many Northern politicians were more radical in their views and wanted to punish the South. Supreme Court Justice Salmon P. Chase, Massachusetts Senator Charles Sumner, Ohio Senator Benjamin F. Wade, Congressman Thad Stevens, and Congressman H. Winter Davis were a few of the more outspoken extremists. "They wanted to disfranchise the White people and enfranchise the negroes" (McKellar 1942). This would have guaranteed that Northern Republicans, who had nominal control of federal power in 1860, had control of Southern votes and, therefore, control of the entire country. "They wanted to put control of all this territory under the absolute domination of the negroes" (McKellar 1942). These leaders opposed Lincoln's more reasonable view of returning the Southern states. They abused him in public and opposed his renomination. However, after the tide of war turned in favor of the North, Lincoln was too strong politically for his nomination to be stopped. Even with the nomination locked up, Lincoln desperately needed political support for his views. He felt that a vice president who would be loyal to him and assist in fending off the more radical legislators who constantly opposed him would be an asset to his administration and the nation.

The June 1864 National Union Convention renominated Lincoln. The larger fight was for vice president. Since the Democratic Party had recruited General George McClellan, there was an obvious need to attract loyal Democrats' votes for the National Union ticket. Lincoln felt that a "Jackson Democrat" as his running mate would help counter McClellan. A slaveholding Democrat transformed into a loyal Unionist would be even better. A war Democrat who supported the North should win the hearts of Northern Democrats. Andrew Johnson fit the bill. Johnson and Lincoln had the same, less harsh views of returning the Southern states to the Union. To the South, Johnson was considered a traitor. To the North, he was a patriot.

At the convention, infighting among the New York delegation ended in the exit of Vice President Hannibal Hamlin and, after a few ballots, the nomination of Andrew Johnson of Tennessee. Johnson's nomination as vice president helped restore some credibility to his reputation with his former friends in Tennessee.

At this time in the war, the South and their troops were discouraged. However, Nathan Bedford Forrest provided a source for some cheering. He regrouped Southern soldiers and continued to raid Northern outposts in defiant antagonism of their military domination. He befuddled and confused the Union soldiers with his continued surprise raids on their encampments. They just could not stop this Tennessee Confederate. During the night of August 21, 1864, Forrest moved fifteen hundred men into Memphis and took Union security by surprise. He wanted to capture Union Major General Stephen A. Hurlbut. It has been conjectured that his troops rode directly into the quarters where Yankee officers were thought to be sleeping, but the general was elsewhere that night. Forrest's men wrecked havoc on Union supplies. In spite of penetrating the heart of Union command, he evaded capture and continued to irritate and embarrass Union forces. Forrest's surprise raids upon Union troops also unnerved them. They never knew when he would strike next. This gave Tennessee Confederates hope. As a result, the Union powers in Tennessee could never gain the forced cooperation of the remaining Tennessee citizens.

When Forrest was not around, the impugnable Union-enforced government continued to oppress the people. The citizens of Tennessee were degraded and swindled by those in control or by those friendly with those in control. The citizens had been conquered and were treated as such. If they remained in their homes, they only did so with permission of the authorities. Their lives were controlled, and they were denied the normal rights of citizenship that were previously taken for granted.

During the war, many Tennessee communities were left helpless while the men were away at war. Conniving bandits plundered and robbed helpless families. The underhanded blatantly robbed and used legal maneuvering to take advantage of the naive and helpless. These were particularly difficult problems and a sad reflection of human nature.

Their plight was unfathomable for the citizens of the Volunteer State. They could not begin to comprehend their new position of subjugation. Tennessee had supplied volunteers for the making of the new nation at Heaton's Station, King's Mountain, and Nickajack; in the War of 1812 at Emuckfaw, Horseshoe, and New Orleans; and at Florida, the Alamo, and in Mexico. It was a heroic state that had played a victorious role in the destiny of America. If it were not for Tennessee, its volunteers, and its leaders, the "nation" might be under British or Spanish rule. This last armed effort to defend Tennessee rights, as seen by the citizens of the day, had all the spirit and enterprise ever known by its people. The loss of their freedom, incomprehensible to many, was painful to accept.

In the nation at large, the people despaired over the war, the bloodshed, and the hopelessness of finality to the conflict. Their desire to end the war gave impetus not only to the Democrats but also to the conniving and ambitious Republicans, who plotted the presidency for themselves. Even during the depths of despair of the war, selfishness prevailed. Those politicians who had not received their desired appointments (or election) connived with devious individuals, who at one time Lincoln had actually helped, in order to maneuver for themselves. They conspired to force Lincoln to step aside and held secret meetings in a grand attempt to force him to withdraw. When he would not cooperate, some Republicans actually tried to plan another convention prior to the election in order to have themselves nominated.

Meanwhile, in Chicago, on August 29, 1864, the Democrats met in national convention. General George McClellan was nominated for president and George H. Pendleton was nominated for vice president. In their platform, the Democrats called the war a failure and stated the need for immediate peace. It was the hope of Southerners that the Democratic "Peace Party" could defeat Lincoln. The nation was in agony and exhausted from war. The Democrats only had to convince the people of the North of the futility of it all. Then, hopefully, they would turn from Lincoln.

The Democratic strategy seemed promising, but suddenly the fate of the war took an immediate turn. Confederate General John B. Hood and Union General William T. Sherman met on the battlefield, resulting in a Confederate loss and retreat from Atlanta on September 1, 1864. Before the end of the Democratic convention, everyone knew the war's end was in sight, and would mean victory for the North and Lincoln's leadership. This turn had the usual effect on many of the conniving politicians who began positioning themselves for the spoils of political victory. Many who were ready to turn on Lincoln now stampeded to support his campaign.

In Tennessee, Johnson's political allies supported the Lincoln-Johnson ticket, but there was Confederate opposition. Fortunately for the Republicans, these Confederates were not allowed to vote in

NATHAN BEDFORD FORREST was born on July 13, 1821, in Chapel Hill, Tennessee, the eldest son of William and Marian (Beck) Forrest. William moved to Tennessee in 1806 and worked as a blacksmith. The family later moved to Hernando, Mississippi. Forrest had little formal schooling. By the time he was sixteen, his father died, leaving him the breadwinner for a large family. He worked as a farm laborer, horse trader, real estate broker, farmer, and slave dealer. In 1845 he married Mary Ann Montgomery and later moved to Memphis.

When the Civil War began in 1861, Forrest went into the service as a private in the Seventh Tennessee Calvary but by war's end was a lieutenant general. He organized and funded a battalion of mounted troops. After escaping with some troops from the Fort Donelson defeat, he organized a raiding cavalry. He was promoted from lieutenant colonel to colonel. He fought and was seriously wounded at Shiloh, and by July 1862 he was made a brigadier general. For the remainder of the war, he wrecked havoc on Union camps, supplies, communication, and paths of transportation. He was in and out so quickly that he confounded Union defenses. He was an asset to the South and a constant source of confusion and embarrassment to Union leaders. His actions kept the Union forces off balance and delayed total submission of Tennessee to the North. He was promoted to major general in 1863 and lieutenant general in 1865.

After the war Forrest returned to his farm but soon sold it and returned to Memphis in 1867. He failed in the insurance business and then served as president of a railroad. The yellow fever epidemic and the financial panic of 1873 damaged the economy of Memphis to the point that he was bankrupt again. He then moved to President's Island, on the Mississippi River, and ran a plantation through the use of paid convict labor. He paid off his creditors and was recovering financially when the scalawags and carpetbaggers took control of the economy. In response to the violence and oppression of Governor Parson Brownlow's radical Reconstruction government, Forrest became the Grand Wizard of the newly organized Ku Klux Klan. When peace returned, he resigned. Twenty thousand people attended Forrest's funeral when he died in Memphis on October 29, 1877. (Photograph courtesy of TSLA)

the election. Those who did favor the Union but opposed the Lincoln-Johnson ticket were mostly supportive of the Peace Party and General George McClellan, the Democratic candidate. Many Tennesseans just could not accept Lincoln. Those who were allowed to vote accepted the fact that Tennessee would remain in the Union. They now simply wanted the war to end. McClellan based his campaign on peace, justice, public welfare, and the end of the war. General William Campbell, Emerson Etheridge, Thomas A. R. Nelson, and others supported McClellan.

Because only Union loyalists could vote in Tennessee, there was little question that the Lincoln-Johnson ticket would win the Tennessee vote. Likewise, there is little question that in an open election they would have overwhelmingly lost that contest. The lack of fair electoral representation raised tensions. Tempers ran high, and the campaign took a violent tone. Johnson won some support among Tennesseans by playing to human nature. He proposed to seize the estates of well-to-do farmers and divide the land among Union sympathizers. The envious rejoiced, while other Union supporters could not understand Johnson's campaign of vengeance. Violence broke out throughout the state as the campaign heightened anxiety. Tennessee was in shambles. Many businesses, farms, roads, orchards, and homes lay in waste. Northern and Southern troops had confiscated cattle, crops, and supplies. Many volunteers had died wearing the colors of either the Union or the Confederacy. Now, at war's end, scores of survivors were weak or dying from amputations and other war injuries. When these soldiers returned, many found that their homes had been taken for back taxes or were literally in ashes. Feelings, whether for Lincoln or McClellan, ran high. In the end it did not matter. Congress threw out the Tennessee electoral vote. On election day, November 8, 1864, Lincoln polled 2,203,831 to 1,797,019 for McClellan (212 electoral votes to 21).

While the election raged, the war eked to a close. General John Bell Hood had lost one leg and the use of one arm. Nevertheless, his determination never waned. He continued his campaign and sought to break from Georgia. Nashville was a major supply source for the Union forces fighting in the South. If Hood could break the Yankee supply line, he might break the Yankee forces located South of the supply route. Hood headed north to Nashville.

By the time Hood made it back to Tennessee, the Union forces were prepared. Union General John M. Schofield had just returned from the western part of the state. He met Hood's Confederates in the Battle of Franklin on the afternoon of November 30,

The Battle of Franklin, November 30, 1864. (Courtesy of Chicamauga Chattanooga National Military Park and Eastern National)

1864. The confrontation was brutal. Union forces quickly retreated to Nashville. Hood had won the battle but suffered three times the loss of the Yankees. He advanced to Nashville. On December 15, 1864, Union forces overcame Hood's Confederates at the Battle of Nashville. Hood pulled back about two miles. The next day, Schofield's men again defeated the Confederates. Nashville was the last significant battle fought in the beleaguered state of Tennessee. Hood marched what was left of his army south, to Mississippi. From there they went to North Carolina. Hood was relieved of command (at his request) and General Joseph E. Johnston replaced him. Only about five thousand Confederate soldiers remained with the move to North Carolina. Final surrender for Tennessee's Confederate volunteers would come to General Sherman at Durham, North Carolina.

A Third President; Reconstruction Begins

After Lincoln's reelection and Johnson's election as vice president, a convention of Union supporters was held in Nashville on January 9, 1865. They called themselves the East Tennessee Central Committee. Their essential purpose was to implement a method to maintain total control of the state. The group of Union men held what amounted to a constitutional convention and drafted an amendment to the state constitution which abolished slavery and set up a schedule of plans to nullify the secession of Tennessee, repudiate the war debt, and establish a test for voters (which would disqualify three-fourths of the populous). This effectively limited who could vote and run for office. They set the date to elect a new governor and legislature for March 4, 1865. The convention nominated William Gannaway "Parson" Brownlow as candidate for governor and essentially selected the complete legislative body. The convention proposals passed a popular vote on February 22, 1865, with 21,104 voting for and 40 against the proposals. The new legislature limited political participation to unconditional Union men, those who had come of age since the war, persons of proven loyalty from other states, federal soldiers, loyal men who had been forced into the Confederate army, and persons known to the election judges to have been true friends of the United States. Ex-Confederates of high rank were excluded for fifteen years and other Confederates for five years.

Another bill was passed which declared that all Black men had the right to vote. The Tennessee Constitution of 1796 had provided this right to any free man. However, this right had been restricted in the 1820s.

With Andrew Johnson's election as vice president, the way was paved for a new governor for Tennessee. In this election all former Confederates and anyone closely affiliated with them were "barred from the polls." On March 4, 1865, the same day as the presidential and vice presidential inauguration, W. G. Brownlow was elected by the Union people of Tennessee as a Whig-Republican governor. They also elected the entire state legislative slate which had been proposed along with Brownlow. Many viewed Brownlow as a "preposterous" choice for governor and a "dangerous psychopath" (Corlew 1989, Burt 1959).

Brownlow was from Knoxville and possessed the East Tennessee antisecession fever. He disliked Nashville and Nashvillians, and no doubt from his actions, the people of Nashville knew of his resentment. Few women would even speak to him. The citizens showed their "tender feelings" for the governor by sending him boxes of used bandages from recent victims of smallpox, which was epidemic in Nashville in 1865. Technically, Brownlow could not be inaugurated until the legislature met in April. However, he essentially "declared himself king" and took over. He demanded reports from the sheriffs in all counties. He organized his own "personal militia, some 1,500 strong, including colored troops, and assigned them to occupation of Nashville and Middle Tennessee." He arrogantly helped elect A. E. Alden as mayor of Nashville, though Alden did not even live in Nashville. Alden "and his ring (subsequently) looted the city of hundreds of thousands of dollars" (Burt 1959).

On April 5, 1865, the Tennessee legislature ratified the Thirteenth Amendment, abolishing slavery. Soon Governor Brownlow pushed for legislation designed to punish former Confederates. Much of the legislation was designed to keep power in the hands of former Whigs and subjugate the former Confederates. Brownlow's attitude in Tennessee was not any different from that which prevailed on the national political scene. Washington, D.C., legislators, who believed in harsh treatment of Southerners, were called "Radicals." On the other hand, there were those in power

WILLIAM GANNAWAY BROWNLOW was born on August 29, 1805, near Wytheville, Wythe County, Virginia. His parents were Scotch-Irish of origin and both were dead by the time he was eleven years old. He was raised on his uncle's farm until he was eighteen. He learned carpentry at age eighteen and went to work, but after a while gave up building to become a circuit rider in the Methodist Episcopal Church. He came to Tennessee in 1828 and became minister in a church in Jonesboro, Tennessee. Thus he became known as "Parson" Brownlow. He married Eliza Ann O'Brien from Carter County and they had seven children. As a circuit-riding preacher, he showed his tendency toward bias by preaching against the Presbyterians and Baptists. In 1838 or 1839 Brownlow moved to Elizabethton and established a newspaper called the *Elizabethton Whig.* He moved it to Jonesboro the next year and then on to Knoxville, where he printed *Brownlow's Knoxville Whig.* Brownlow used his paper to abuse anyone his disliked. An agitator who would battle with anyone, he was called a "master of vituperation" and a "psychopath" (Burt 1959, Corlew 1990). In 1843 he ran for Congress against Andrew Johnson and lost, but he abused Johnson severely through his newspaper. He owned slaves and advocated slavery, but was devoted to the Union and opposed secession. After the Civil War started, his newspaper continued to print pro-Union editorials, and Brownlow flew the United States flag above his home in Knoxville. He was accused of bridge burning in East Tennessee, and when soldiers were sent to arrest him, he left for the Smoky Mountains. After several months in hiding, he gave up and was arrested and jailed by Confederate sympathizers, but later freed after he agreed to move North. His story spread, and he became somewhat of a national hero as the "Fighting Parson." People in the North paid to hear him speak (in such places as Cincinnati, Dayton, Indianapolis, Chicago, and Philadelphia) and purchase a book he wrote. His profits allowed him to restart the *Knoxville Whig* in 1864 after who felt that a less Radical Reconstruction course should be followed. They wanted to normalize Southern states with an inclusive attitude designed to avoid lasting hostilities. These "conservatives" generally agreed with President Lincoln. (Johnson had agreed with and would in fact perpetuate the Lincoln-Johnson plan for normalizing [reconstructing] the South after the war.)

On April 9, 1865, General Robert E. Lee surrendered to General Ulysses S. Grant at Appomattox Court House. The remainder of Hood's former troops, now in North Carolina, surrendered shortly thereafter. On April 14, 1865, Lincoln was shot by John Wilkes Booth. The mortally wounded president was carried across the street from the Ford Theater to the home of a tailor, William Peterson, and placed upon a bed in a small bedroom. Doctors and national officials crowded the small abode and held vigil for the critically wounded president. Word arrived that Secretary of State William Seward had been critically stabbed and his two sons, Augustus and Frederick, had been possibly critically wounded. The plot also included a plan to kill Vice President Andrew Johnson, but this part never transpired. On the morning of the fifteenth Lincoln died, and Andrew Johnson became the seventeenth president of the United States.

Union forces had taken Knoxville. He was a member of the convention that changed the state constitution to the advantage of Reconstructionists. That convention nominated him to run for governor to succeed Andrew Johnson. He received only twenty-three thousand votes, since most of the voters were either officially disenfranchised or in the army; therefore, only a fraction of the citizenry actually elected him. He assumed the power but was greatly opposed and had little sympathy for those who had opposed him. He needed only a majority of the votes of "his chosen minority" to maintain power. Brownlow was intent to maintain political control.

Some of Brownlow's antics were memorable in a humorous sort of way. When Governor Andrew Johnson announced in Nashville on August 8, 1864, that he was freeing his personal slaves, "he called himself the hope of the colored people of the South . . . and . . . likened himself to Moses, who would lead them out of the house of bondage" (Creekmore 1958). When Brownlow heard this, he called his own announcement and said (paraphrased) that if Andrew Johnson proposed to be their Moses to lead them to the Promised Land, he, Brownlow, would be their Pharaoh to drive them right back again. After Andrew Johnson became president, Brownlow continued to attack him, embarking on a northern speaking tour in which he continuously berated his political archenemy, Johnson, classifying him as a disloyal traitor.

Tennessee was the first state to come back into the Union (July 2, 1866). The legislature, under Brownlow, created "separate schools for Negroes." Fisk (Negro) University soon opened in Nashville. Brownlow, who controlled the franchise of voting, was reelected governor in 1867. Many despised him. His actions hardened the resiliency of many former Confederates. Just before the beginning of his second term as governor, the state had horrible problems with "crimes, carpetbaggers, and the unstable Negroes" (Phillips 1978), and turmoil and chaos raged. Finally, calm began to return to Tennessee when Brownlow was elevated to the U.S. Senate on March 4, 1869. He remained in the Senate until March 3, 1875. He died at his home in Knoxville on April 29, 1877, and was buried in Gray Cemetery, Knoxville. (Photograph courtesy of TSLA)

Seldom thought of because of the greater issues of the day were other accomplishments that occurred during Lincoln's tenure. The Department of Agriculture, the national banking system, and the Bureau of Internal Revenue were created. The Homestead Act was passed (Andrew Johnson had worked for its passage since his days in the House of Representatives), which opened the American frontier to settlement, and the Land Grant College Act was passed, which donated land to the states for colleges. In 1865, Lincoln pushed the Thirteenth Amendment. This, along with the Emancipation Proclamation, began the end of slavery. His great list of accomplishments ended on April 14, 1865, when he was murdered.

General Joseph E. Johnston surrendered on April 26, 1865, as did General E. Kirby Smith. On April 29, President Johnson issued a proclamation of the end of the war. In the proclamation, he offered amnesty, with certain conditions, to all except former civil, political, or military leaders of the United States who sided with the Confederacy.

The Civil War was over. The great Volunteer State lay in waste. Homes, fences, barns, crops, trees, and much else had been destroyed by the torch of war. Tennessee had lost many sons. Those who survived faced financial devastation and disease. Some had lost legs and arms to the destructive path of gun slugs or the infection brought about by the wounds of war. Additionally, Tennessee had many newly freed slaves who did not know where to turn or how to survive in a free world. As the state lay destroyed, the opportunists tried to steal from the weak.

In East Tennessee hostilities continued among the citizens. The protracted war took the form of shoot-outs on the streets of communities. One group would attack another as the fighting sporadically continued. Peace did not come with the official end of the war, and Tennessee remained in turmoil.

The war had brought on many changes throughout the state. In Knoxville, business activity was disrupted. Banks had been forced to close, and its citizens set out to establish a new sound bank. Homes, occupied by first the Confederates and later the Union forces, had to be renovated. Nashville, Chattanooga, and other communities throughout Tennessee had to face similar issues.

The Tennessee legislature had taken the necessary steps to return to the Union (Tennessee would be the first, and for a while, the only Southern state returned to the Union) and awaited readmission. In 1865 David T. Patterson, Horace Maynard, A. A. Kyle, and Nathaniel G. Taylor became candidates for the U.S. Senate (Class 1 would be a partial term, since the full term would have begun on March 4, 1863) from Tennessee. The legislature elected Patterson by a twelve-vote margin over his competitors. The other Tennessee senator (Class 2 was a full term) elected on May 4, 1865, was Joseph Smith Fowler. (Once Tennessee was back in the Union in 1866, the state's federal representatives were viewed with suspicion and their approval by the Senate required some debate.) Senator Charles Sumner and Congressman Thaddeus Stevens were "Radical" leaders who felt that Southern states were conquered territories whose future lay at the mercy of a master Congress. They did not want any votes from Southern states which could dilute their "Radical" oppressive control over the former Confederacy. Sumner opposed admitting Fowler, but with a positive report on his Union loyalties, he was finally approved. Patterson was President Johnson's son-in-law and understandably received an easier approval. However, before any other senators from the South could be reinstated in the Senate under the more reasonable Lincoln-Johnson method, the Radicals took control and changed the Reconstruction requirements, in effect stopping the admission of Southern senators.

The Tennessee delegation was denied seating by the Radical Congress on December 4, 1865. There was a furious congressional debate over what should be done with the defeated states. Should they be considered a conquered land at Congress's mercy? Should they be admitted into the Union? A joint committee consisting of nine U.S. representatives and six senators presented a plan on April 30, 1866, which stated that when a state ratified the Fourteenth Amendment (granting Blacks the right to vote) it should be readmitted into the Union.

DAVID TROTTER PATTERSON was born in Cedar Creek, near Greeneville, Greene County, Tennessee, February 28, 1819. Both parents were descendants of Irish ancestry and Presbyterian. His mother was Susan Trotter. After a common school education, he went to Greeneville College for two years, and then worked as a papermaker, laborer, and miller. He studied law under the Honorable Robert J. McKinney (who was later a Tennessee Supreme Court judge) and began practicing law in Greeneville in 1841. He served as judge of the first circuit court from 1854 until 1863, and married the daughter of Andrew Johnson.

Although he was originally a Democrat, Patterson supported the Union and the Union ticket. He was elected a delegate to the Baltimore (Republican) Union National Convention in 1864, which nominated Lincoln and his father-in-law, Andrew Johnson, but did not attend. He called for Reconstruction of the state and in 1865 ran for the U.S. Senate against Nathaniel G. Taylor (father of Alf and Bob Taylor), A. A. Kyle, and Horace Maynard. All of the candidates supported the Union but being the son-in-law of the president was an advantage for Patterson and he was elected for the term from March 4, 1865, to March 3, 1869. However, because of Reconstruction, he was not seated. Movement was made to restore Tennessee under the Lincoln-Johnson plan that assumed that Southern states had never left the Union and could be returned after they cooperated. Although radicals in Congress were alarmed that Tennessee would be reinstated, the House and Senate passed a resolution restoring the state to the Union. However, an amendment stipulated that no other Southern state could return to the Union without the consent of Congress in order to prevent Southern states from obtaining advantage in congressional control. The fact that Patterson was Johnson's son-in-law may have saved the South. After the Fourteenth Amendment was passed by Tennessee and the state was readmitted to the Union, his credentials were presented to the Senate on July 26, 1866, and he was sworn in on July 28, 1866. Soon there was tremendous pressure in the Senate to impeach Johnson. Patterson's most important vote in the Senate, along with the vote of fellow Tennessee Senator Joseph Fowler, was to prevent the impeachment of his father-in-law. (Johnson was saved by only one vote.)

Patterson was not a candidate for reelection to the Senate. After his term ended on March 3, 1869, he returned to Tennessee and to his wool-goods and flour-manufacturing businesses and farming. He died in Afton, near Greeneville, Tennessee, on November 3, 1891, and was buried in the Andrew Johnson National Cemetery in Greeneville. (Photograph courtesy of SHO)

On July 3, 1865, the military authorities, in order number 170, revoked the previous order and turned the Memphis city government back over to Mayor Park and those elected on that day. Although Memphis did not suffer great destructive ravages of war, it and the region of the Mid-south had suffered enough damage to slow economic recovery. Railroads were destroyed, municipal governments bankrupt, and the agricultural economy was seriously paralyzed. Without its prewar labor force and with the interruption of the transportation system, the region could not get products to market.

Governor Brownlow put out a call for federal troops, not only to maintain order, but to "oversee" elections. He made many enemies by, among other things, throwing out votes through the power of his control over elections. If he did not want them to count, they were discarded and declared invalid. He maintained control by force, and the public opposition against him grew. He empowered himself with loyal White votes, "new Negro votes," and his own state militia "to do the counting" (McKellar 1942).

With Johnson as president and Brownlow as governor, the old Confederates in Tennessee were fearful of retribution. Brownlow and the new Radical legislature put up a five-thousand-dollar reward for the capture of former Governor Isham G. Harris, who had escaped to Mexico and later to England (returning in 1867). Brownlow proclaimed in the bounty:

> His complexion is sallow. His eyes are dark and penetrating—a perfect index to a heart of a traitor—with the scowl and frown of a demon resting upon his brow. His study of mischief and the practice of crime have brought upon him premature baldness and a gray beard. . . . He chews tobacco rapidly and is inordinately fond of liquor. In his moral structure he is an unscrupulous man, steeped to the chin in personal and political profligacy—now about lost to all sense of shame, honor, with a heart reckless of social duty and fatally bent upon mischief . . . (McKellar 1942).

Those who wanted the power of the government on their side hurried to convert and take oath. They were labeled "scalawags." Those who were Unionists all along had no interest in allowing Confederate participation in government, but instead wanted to punish ex-Confederates and maintain total political control of the state. In Middle and West Tennessee the anger subsided within a short period of time. However, in East Tennessee some ex-Confederates were beaten, murdered, hung by mobs, and run from their homes. Ex-Union soldiers were allowed to carry weapons for self-defense, but this privilege was not extended to ex-Confederate soldiers. Some Unionists sued and received judgments against ex-Confederates for suffering and losses due to the war. Civil order was not yet totally restored, and in areas without Union troops, outlaws terrorized the citizens. The only recourse for some citizens was to arm and defend themselves against this violence.

The power of Radicals like Governor Brownlow came from the federal government. At first the Radicals in the U.S. House and U.S. Senate tried to win President Johnson over to their punitive approach toward the South. His popularity in the North for holding with the Union before and during the war, of course, had propelled his nomination as vice president. However, when the Radicals realized they could not force him to cooperate, they turned on him. Johnson, however, thought for himself. No one made him; he was self-made. He owed no one and would make his own decisions.

JOSEPH SMITH FOWLER was born in Steubenville, Jefferson County, Ohio, on August 31, 1820. His parents were from Maryland. He was educated in the common schools and Grove Academy, in Steubenville, Ohio. He completed college at Franklin College in New Athens, Ohio, in 1843. In 1844, he taught school in Shelby County, Kentucky, then served as mathematics professor at Franklin College in Davidson County, Tennessee, from 1845 until 1849. On November 12, 1846, he married Maria Louisa Embry. He studied law in Bowling Green, Kentucky, and was admitted to the bar. He practiced in Tennessee until 1861 and served as president of Howard Female Institute in Gallatin, Tennessee, from 1856 until 1861. When the Civil War broke out he moved to Springfield, Illinois, with his family.

When Andrew Johnson became military governor in 1862, Fowler returned to Tennessee and became state comptroller until 1865. He was elected as a Unionist to the U.S. Senate. He was initially to take his seat on May 4, 1865, but was delayed because of Reconstruction until July 24, 1866. An active senator, he, like Senator Patterson, voted against the impeachment of President Johnson. The Radicals threatened and tried to intimidate Fowler with investigation and expulsion from the Senate in order to pressure him to vote for impeachment, but the threat did not stop Fowler. He was a man who stood firm for what was right and just. He, along with the few others who opposed impeachment, prevented chaos and further pillage of the South. In 1868, he supported U. S. Grant for president. He completed his Senate term on March 3, 1871, and was not a candidate for reelection. In 1872 he supported Democrat Horace Greeley for president, instead of Grant. Fowler practiced law in Washington, D.C., until he died on April 1, 1902. He was buried at Lexington Cemetery, Lexington, Kentucky. (Photograph courtesy of SHO)

He was tough, but honest, in his quest for what he believed to be right. The Northern Radicals soon learned to despise this Tennessean. After defeating the South, the North found itself having to deal with a Southern president.

Prior to his death, the Great Emancipator had announced a plan to allow the Confederate States to return to the Union. It was a reasonable plan. The ciitizens of a state were to take an oath to the United States. If 10 percent should do so, the state would be readmitted. However, the Radicals in Congress did not care for so forgiving a plan. They wanted to maintain power by limiting the admission of Southern congressmen and senators. After Lincoln's death, President Johnson supported Lincoln's plan. When the Radicals could not change Johnson, they revolted against him.

In Congress, the Radicals tried to pass laws with more severe consequences, thereby getting around President Johnson's more reasonable approach. The task for President Johnson was the "Reconstruction" (return into the Union) of the ex-Confederate states under an intolerant Radical-controlled Congress that was out for revenge against the South. Johnson had the immense task of holding the nation together, while preventing the pillage of the South by selfish politicians who grabbed at the opportunity of limiting the right to vote in order to hold and gain power for themselves.

Back in Tennessee, Governor Brownlow spewed hatred against President Johnson. He had never liked him and certainly did not appreciate this Tennessean being president. As far as Brownlow was concerned, Johnson was simply too reasonable and lenient on former Confederates. He wanted a peaceful return of the Southern states, while Brownlow wanted to subjugate them and maintain power. Brownlow went so far as to develop a plan to deal with a possible second Southern uprising, which he expected would occur when the people retaliated against the abuses of Reconstruction. According to him, the revolt would be led by President Johnson, who would become the new Jefferson Davis. Brownlow said that once his plan had defeated the new revolt and Johnson had been executed, things would be as they should (Corlew 1990). As one of his first acts as governor, Brownlow even tried to pass an additionally restrictive voting law in Tennessee. The legislature was determined to prevent those who had assisted the Confederacy from voting. In this way the Radicals would totally control the Tennessee vote and maintain power.

Those Tennessee Radicals who had a conscience, and many leaders, both former Unionists and Confederates, who were well respected in the state, took a stand against Brownlow's harsh actions. Indignant citizens, leaders, and members of the Tennessee house of representatives felt that Brownlow was becoming dictatorial. They spoke to crowds and newspapers denouncing the Radical despotic governor. Brownlow was determined and still wanted to have all things his way. He needed more votes to stay in power. In April 1866 the U.S. Congress had proposed the Fourteenth Amendment for Black rights and privileges. The approval of three-fourths of the states was needed for federal acceptance, and Tennessee had to gain approval, under the current climate at the nation's capital, if it were to have its representatives seated in Washington. Browlow called a special session of the General Assembly to seat on July 4, 1866. However, there were several legislators who opposed Black suffrage, and in order to resist the vote, and prevent a quorum, several refused to attend the session. (A two-thirds attendance was required.) Arrest warrants were issued for Representatives Pleasant Williams from Carter County and A. J. Martin from Jackson County. Black troops were sent to arrest and bring the two men to the capital. However, Davidson County Judge Thomas N. Frazier granted them writs of habeas corpus, but the legislature denied cooperation with the judge's order. On July 19 the county sheriff accompanied by "posse comitatus . . . stormed the capitol" (Corlew 1989) and set the two prisoners free. However, it was a futile act. The legislature had held its vote on July 18. Representatives Martin and Williams were recorded as present but having "'failed and refused' to vote" (Corlew 1989). With Brownlow's heavy hand, the vote passed the Tennessee house and he immediately sent word to the secretary of the Senate via telegram: "We have fought the battle and won it. We have ratified the Constitutional amendment in the House, forty-three voting for it and eleven against it. Two of Andrew Johnson's tools not voting. Give my respects to the dead dog of the White House" (McKellar 1942). On July 23, 1866, President Johnson signed the congressional resolution which placed Tennessee back in the Union.

With Tennessee back in the Union, the state's congressional delegation was seated. Fowler and Patterson were finally seated in the U.S. Senate in July 1866. These two seats alone would prove important in the coming great federal storm over Reconstruction and essential to the survival of democracy.

Male freedmen were now assured the right to vote, but many Tennesseans (former

Confederates) were still denied the privilege. In Memphis, "Partisan zeal, bias and prejudice prevailed in every department, even in the criminal court, and much depended upon the political color of a criminal's coat whether he was to suffer or not" (Keating 1888). Murders went without justice, as did every other criminal act one could imagine.

Meanwhile, Governor Brownlow traveled north on a speaking tour denouncing President Johnson. His actions only served to undermine a president who was trying to reconstruct the South, while preventing thievery and pillage by Northern carpetbaggers and Southern scalawags. Johnson was already dealing with a Radical Congress and his political vulnerability was high. Brownlow's criticism could accomplish little other than further stall the peace which eluded the people of Tennessee.

Discontent, unfairness, and danger loomed over the people of Tennessee. Crime and political oppression were destroying communities. With freedom, many Blacks left the plantation life and moved to urban areas throughout the state, unsure of how to survive as freedmen. Now on their own, many were literally without basic necessities. In Memphis, the Black population grew to fifteen thousand but without a means of subsistence or social order. Some Black population growth also occurred in Nashville and other communities (Coppock, 10 March 1974).

In Memphis four thousand Black troops were placed at Fort Pickering by the Freedmen's Bureau, established in 1865 to assist in the transition from slavery to freedom. Bureau commanders took control of the freed slaves and distributed food, shelter, and clothing. The bureau also distributed land to freed Blacks and set up a system of labor contracts to support the plantations which now needed workers to replace the slaves. Orphanages, hospitals, and schools were also organized.

Most Southern Whites were happy to see something done to help the former slaves lift themselves out of the destitution and danger brought on by their new freedom, and they were especially happy over education efforts. However, the Freedmen's Bureau recruited Northern teachers as educators, and this ultimately created a great deal of tension. Many of the teachers recruited from the North came to teach more as intellectual conquerors of the Southern mind than to provide a basic education. Many fomented hate instead of peace and improvement in their students' lives. Additionally, the bureau was used to propagate Republican candidates for office, and became a political machine designed to maintain Radical Republican control of government. The bureau created Black armies to "maintain order" in Tennessee communities. This only heightened tensions and enraged ex-Confederates.

The Freedmen's Bureau was headquartered in Memphis, Knoxville, Nashville, Chattanooga, and Pulaski. It was viewed as a tool of oppression wielded by Northern congressmen and caused tremendous resentment. As a federal agency created to assist the four million former slaves, the bureau had significant autonomy, and some of the designers used it as a method of intimidation for citizens who lived in the ex-Confederate states. At Fort Pickering some of the troops formed gangs that became involved in assaults. The citizens of Memphis demanded that the gangs be removed, and they petitioned President Johnson to help.

The placement of the Black troops was viewed by the former Confederates as a scheme of the Radicals in Congress to punish Southerners. President Johnson vetoed a bill which perpetuated the subsidy of the "troops." He took on the entire Radical Congress in an attempt to bring peace and order back to the South. By April 1866 Congress had enough votes to override his vetoes. The Radicals depended upon the Black voters for political survival and continued to do everything possible to maintain their cooperation, including maintaining support for the Freedmen's Bureau troops. With little duty and a lot of time, the troops became more aggressive.

When, in Memphis, a Black soldier killed a White citizen on May 2, 1866, a dreadful riot developed. Several individuals were killed, Blacks and Whites. The riot raged for hours until Mayor Park and Sheriff Winters intervened. Sheriff Winters called together a posse, while Mayor Park called for General Stoneman's troops to protect the city from the gangs. The next day the Black troops attacked Memphis. The Sixteenth Regulars were called and confronted the rioters and quelled the hostilities. But since the federal authorities would not disband the riotous group, peace was not achieved. Congress quickly sent a Select Committee to investigate. On May 22, the committee examined 170 witnesses and found that both Black and White were at fault. It pointed out that once provoked, the Irish policemen in Memphis worsened the situation by their harsh treatment of the Blacks. During the investigation Mayor Park was criticized for being drunk during the riots.

Another conflict occurred in October on the Burgett plantation, near Cat Island. Forty-eight people were killed in the riots. After it was quelled, the arms were taken from the survivors. Similar political/military bureaus were posted throughout the South. Northerners controlled Southern communities through the Freedmen's Bureau and denied suffrage to the "former" citizens. New Orleans had riots similar to those in Memphis three months later, but the results were much worse. In both the Memphis and New Orleans riots, the Freedmen's Bureau was blamed by the citizenry.

Carpetbaggers and scalawags used the Blacks' newfound voting privilege to legally and sometimes illegally take control of Southern municipal governments. They spent communities into indebtedness by exploiting their power to create government contracts and business opportunities for themselves and their friends. They siphoned communities' assets. An enraged population began to fight back.

Johnson Clubs were formed in Tennessee communities to show support for the president who was, by now, being severely abused by the Northern Radicals in Congress. The Johnson Clubs, along with the "conservatives" (these were essentially any Tennessee citizen who opposed the Radicals), nominated candidates for the legislature in an election controlled and dominated by Governor Brownlow and the Radicals. In spite of the domination, Tennessee's citizens began to retaliate. Although the Radicals won the next judicial elections, conservatives including Dan Able and W. W. Coleman were actually elected to the state legislature. But the Radicals refused to seat them. Another election was held on November 28, 1866, and both were reelected. Again, the legislature refused to seat Able.

The overlap of city, county, military, and federal control created a chaotic environment in which no one knew what authority was actually in control. Generally the city and county governments were secondary in authority to state, military, and federal authorities. The Black troops were under the jurisdiction of the federal government via the Freedmen's Bureau. Governor Brownlow controlled the police within Tennessee communities. They were viewed as his personal militia and were detested. Charges were trumped up against citizens or elected officials who tried to enforce some sense of fairness in the criminal justice system. In November, the Tennessee legislature went so far as to pass an act prohibiting ex-Confederate soldiers and sympathizers from serving on juries.

In January 1867 Brownlow made preparations for his planned August reelection. County conventions were held, but the Radicals maintained tight control. At the Republican state convention the Radicals renominated Brownlow. The convention also took the opportunity to formally condemn President Johnson.

Brownlow knew that he needed secure votes. Just after the end of the Civil War he had favored the idea of colonizing Blacks in Texas or other Western states. Some of his Radical sympathizers and the Radical newspapers castigated him on such an opinion. By 1867 Brownlow had made so many enemies that, in spite of his domination of the Radical vote, he knew that he would need additional support to ensure his political dominance, and moved to gain Black support. Thus, the Radical Tennessee legislature passed a bill which gave Blacks the right to vote but denied them the right to hold office or to serve on juries. Brownlow signed the bill on February 26, 1867.

Meanwhile, President Johnson endured attack from the Radical Congress and the Radical Republicans in Tennessee state government. The populous, however, agreed with Johnson's more reasonable approach to Reconstruction. The conservatives held their own state convention to nominate a candidate for governor. They supported the Black right to vote, but they also wanted immediate return of their own voting rights and full privileges as Tennessee citizens. The convention showed their support for President Johnson and said that martial law should end in Tennessee. They nominated a former state legislator and congressman from Dresden, Tennessee, Emerson Etheridge, as their candidate for governor. Etheridge had been supportive of the Union during the war but was not a Radical and wanted Tennessee restored in a reasonable fashion.

During the gubernatorial campaign, Governor Brownlow made additional moves to ensure his return to office. On February 20, 1867, the Radical legislature and Brownlow enacted a Tennessee State Guard (military force) to oppose acts by those disloyal to the Radicals. Of course, its purpose was shrouded in acceptable legal jargon. Brownlow also oversaw the passage of another bill which allowed the governor to simply cast out voter registrations in any county. Brownlow used the legislature to simply set himself up as a dictator.

Not only had Congress ignored the right of the people to vote and work for their own political benefit, but they showed little concern for the division of powers between the legislative, judicial, and executive branches. They dictated control of the legislative branch via voting rights. They dictated control of the courts by limiting the jury selection process and controlling judicial appointments. Now, the impugnable Radicals tried to control the executive branch by manipulating the president's cabinet. Never had the ambition of men ignored the will of the people and the

Constitution any more than during Reconstruction.

The 1867 gubernatorial campaign between Republican Brownlow and conservative candidate Emerson Etheridge was nasty and violent. Etheridge ran a strong campaign and verbalized the feelings of the conservatives toward the oppressive government. He was physically attacked and his life was threatened, particularly in East Tennessee. Incidents occurred at Elizabethton, Greeneville, Rogersville, Knoxville, Columbia, Franklin, Gallatin, Fayetteville, Lewisburg, and Pulaski. The election of 1867 in Tennessee was the first in which the "newly enfranchised Negroes were permitted to vote" (Parks et al. 1973). They voted with the Republicans. The Radicals even organized them into "Loyal Leagues" which marched to the polls.

The league vote, combined with the rigid enforcement by Brownlow of the disfranchising law, delivered a Republican victory. Most Tennesseans were denied the right to vote, so the Radicals and Blacks controlled election day. Brownlow received 74,034 votes with 22,550 for Etheridge. Brownlow had won reelection, but Etheridge had voiced what most Tennesseans thought—Tennessee was under a dictatorship. The election heightened resentment toward Brownlow, the Radicals, the carpetbaggers, and the scalawags. The resultant animosity became so strong that an unstoppable retaliation of the populous was now in motion.

(During all the civil and political turmoil, the attraction of infectious mosquitoes resulted in the arrival of yellow fever—the third onslaught of the century—in Memphis. The first deaths were reported on September 29, 1867; the last deaths attributable to the fever occurred on December 1, 1867. During the two months of the disease, 550 citizens of 2,500 who contracted the infection died.)

Only three conservatives were elected to the state legislature; the rest were Radicals. The entire Tennessee U.S. congressional delegation was composed of Radicals. Even though the state legislature was mostly made of Radicals, in November 1867 it repealed its previous reward for capture of former Governor Isham Harris. After the reward was repealed, Harris returned to Nashville.

The reelection of Brownlow as governor brought the promise of more abuse for Tennessee citizens. Furthermore, Brownlow's reelection proved that Tennessee citizens could not obtain fair representation. Most could not vote, and there was no likelihood of fairness from the Radical government. Governor Brownlow's metropolitan police controlled the populous. The governor had also created politico-military organizations like the "Loyal League," "The Constitutional Alliance," and the "Grand Army of the Republic." The purpose of these groups was to keep the power of office strictly in Brownlow's hands. They, along with the governor, controlled every aspect of life. As a result of the oppression, the people began to seek ways to overcome it.

In December 1865 a group of young men in Pulaski, Tennessee, had formed a secret organization, the Ku Klux Klan. Their purpose was to dress in ghostlike costumes to scare the Negroes and White Radicals who they felt ignored their rights. At first the group was small and a mere social organization. However, as the oppression continued, the group evolved into more of a political organization that spread throughout the South. The Radicals, who maintained power through martial law, had such a stranglehold upon the South that the citizens felt helpless and vulnerable. "Many saw in the Klan a way to do in secret what could not be done openly. 'Dens' of the Klan were organized throughout Tennessee and the other Southern states. The Klan was especially powerful in all the ex-Confederate counties of Middle and West Tennessee. Thousands of veterans joined the secret 'dens'" (Parks et al. 1973). Since they had little or no protection or rights, the members used the Ku Klux Klan to defend themselves against their oppressors. The numbers grew as their rights were ignored. The more Tennesseans were abused by the military government, the more attractive the Klan looked to the defenseless.

By 1867 the Klan had developed in West Tennessee. They were led by Civil War hero General Nathan Bedford Forrest. Under his leadership, the Klan carried out a campaign to frighten ex-slaves from cooperating with the scalawags and carpetbaggers and to prevent them from voting. Union League members were also intimidated and literally frightened out of their arrogant domination of a defeated people. The Radicals discovered that even though they controlled the government the Klan controlled the element of fear. Because of its identity-hiding costumes and nighttime raids, it instilled a terrible fear in Blacks. It had its effect. The Loyal Leagues and Constitutional Alliances "were shortly confined to their lodge-rooms, forays upon the farmers ceased, and there was comparable peace where before people were living in a state of siege or of war" (Sigafoos 1979). Brownlow had wanted absolute control of everything, no matter the cost or toll on the citizens of Tennessee. Now many Tennesseans found their protection through the Klan. By 1867 the Klan became strong enough to threaten Brownlow's hold on power through its potential to overthrow the government.

In April 1867 a national meeting of the Klan took place at the Maxwell House Hotel in Nashville. It proceeded to formally organize into a political counter-active body to protect the people of the South against the abuses of the Radicals. The sentiment spread like wildfire throughout the counties of Tennessee. The Klan became even more aggressive. Their actions now were not only directed at the Union zealot. Those in elective office who had participated in Reconstructionist abuse of Tennesseans were also subjected to their intimidation. For two years the organization was active throughout West and Middle Tennessee.

In reaction to the threat of the Klan, Brownlow called a special session of the legislature and planned to reenact the state militia and give himself the right to declare martial law. With government aggression apparently escalating, a group of former Confederate leaders, including Nathan Bedford Forrest, John C. Brown, William Bate, and others, met in Nashville at the time that the legislature was investigating the Klan (and before the new anti-Klan laws were enacted). They denied that any of them were antagonistic to the government and indictated that if the government treated the people of Tennessee fairly, they believed the Klan's countermeasures would halt.

The Radical legislature passed its laws. The state militia was reactivated and Governor Brownlow was given the power to declare martial law. A Ku Klux Klan Act was passed which provided strenuous penalties, including fine and imprisonment, for members of the Klan. The law also gave every citizen the right to arrest alleged members of the Klan. However, after many months there were no arrests. Brownlow had assumed that average citizens would turn in members of the Klan, but it was the ordinary citizens who were being abused by the Radical government. Nearly every Tennessean came to hate Brownlow and his Radicals. Only those empowered by the abusive control of Tennessee approved of his plan.

Therefore, with no satisfaction from his legislation, in late 1868 Brownlow hired Captain Seymour Barmore, a famous detective from Cincinnati, to spy on the Klan. After his arrival in Tennessee he was warned by the Klan to return home. Undeterred, Barmore went directly to Pulaski, disguised himself as a member of the Klan, attended meetings, and began to compile a list of names. When he took the train back to Nashville in January 1869, he was taken captive and kidnapped from the train in Columbia, Tennessee. By February 20, 1869, he was found dead in the Duck River—hung and shot in the head. Brownlow immediately declared martial law in several Tennessee counties, but to enforce it he needed a state militia. He soon discovered that fewer and fewer people wanted to cooperate with him. Initially he could not find enough men willing to join his army. After a time, he was able to round up enough bodies to outfit his troops. However, his efforts to enforce the martial law that he declared were largely unsuccessful.

The Radicals Turn against the President

Meanwhile the congressional Radicals had flattered, cajoled, and threatened President Andrew Johnson, at first to curry favor and then later to persuade him to side with their Radical plan to maintain power through exclusion of Southern representation. The Radicals misjudged Johnson as a weak man who would easily bend to their will. They quickly found a strength of character far beyond their initial impression. When they discovered that he was determined to carry out Lincoln's more reasonable plan for bringing the Southern states back into the Union, they quickly turned on him. Since he would not cooperate, they decided to remove the president's power. In March 1968 over Johnson's vetoes, they passed the second Freedmen's Bureau Bill, a Radical Reconstruction Act, divided the Southern states into military districts under control of military commanders, and passed the Tenure of Office Act, which was intended to remove the president's powers of controlling the appointment of some federal officials, including cabinet members.

Essentially, Congress was removing the president's powers and giving them to General Ulysses S. Grant. Grant was reasonable, and not radical, and got along well with Johnson in spite of the power struggle. When Johnson finally figured out that Secretary of War Edwin M. Stanton considered it his duty to disrupt the president's cabinet and prevent it from carrying out his goals, he fired him and appointed Grant. It was then that Congress tried to return Stanton under the questionable auspices of Tenure of Office Act. But, Grant, after having promised Johnson he would not give up the office while allowing the courts to decide, surprised Johnson and let Stanton take over the office in February 1868. President Johnson felt betrayed by Grant, who was clearly the subordinate. The president demanded Stanton leave on February 21. Stanton then barricaded himself in his office. Johnson subsequently appointed Major General Lorenzo Thomas.

President Andrew Johnson, seventeenth president of the United States. (Portrait painting by George Dury courtesy of TSM)

It was just after the Tennessee elections that Congress moved to impeach President Johnson. In October 1867 the Radical Tennessee legislature sent a statement to their congressional delegation in Washington urging them to vote for impeachment of Johnson. Isaac R. Hawkins would be the only Tennessee congressman to refuse to vote for impeachment.

On February 24, 1868, the House of Representatives voted to impeach President Johnson for ignoring the Tenure of Office Act (which ultimately proved unconstitutional) and firing Stanton. On March 13, 1868, the trial began in the Senate. Senator Benjamin F. Wade of Ohio had personal plans to succeed Johnson and be named president. However, Wade was one vote shy of taking over the government. Senator Edmund Ross of Kansas would not tell Wade how he planned to vote. The fiasco of Johnson's impeachment demonstrates the extent to which a Radical Congress would go in order to obtain conviction. The Radicals' determined efforts to eliminate President Johnson could be viewed as unethical and an abuse of political privilege. The rules of Congress, the judiciary, and the law were subordinate to whatever tact was required to impeach and convict. Tennessee

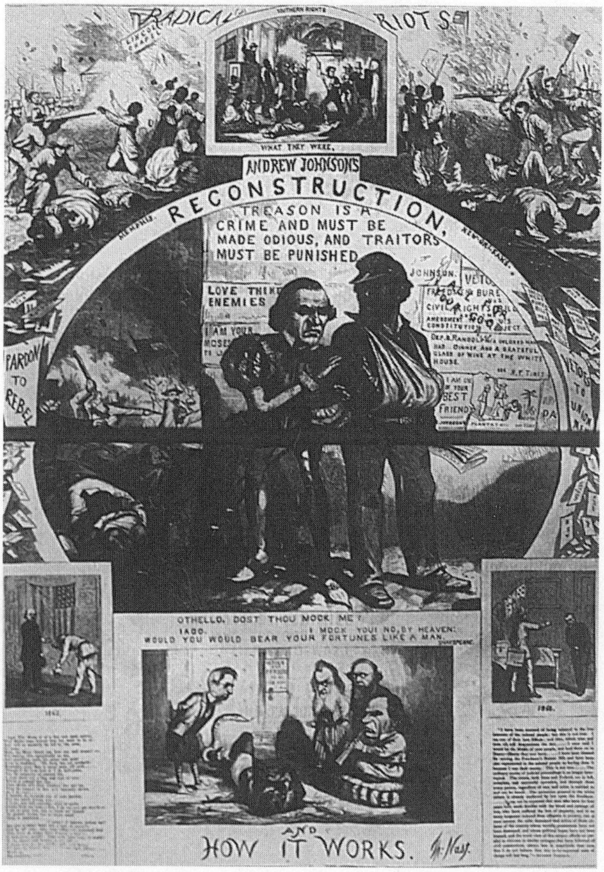

Andrew Johnson branded as a traitor. (Courtesy of TSLA)

Senator David T. Patterson, the president's son-in-law, as expected voted against the impeachment conviction. Senator Joseph S. Fowler, on the other hand, was another question. No one knew for sure how he would vote. The Radicals pressured him hard and even demanded that he resign unless he vote for conviction. Hundreds visited and wrote him urging that he vote for impeachment. However, he kept everyone in doubt. When the roll was called, both of Tennessee's senators voted for acquittal. On May 16, 1868, Senator Edmund G. Ross of Kansas, jeopardizing his political career, stopped the ridiculous spectacle and stunned Wade by casting his decisive vote as not guilty. Two further attempts, on May 26, to convict Johnson on other charges also fell short by one vote. In all, twelve Democrats and seven Republicans in the Senate voted against conviction. Senator Fowler subsequently suffered a fair amount of castigation by the Radicals, who had clung by a hair to their plan to dominate, pillage, and destroy the southern portion of the United States.

Throughout the entire ordeal, President Johnson stood firm. It would have been easy for him to cooperate and make plans for his election as president in 1868. Many men would have taken this course. Instead, Johnson sought reason and the protection of the Constitution. He did so at his own political expense. He had borne the burden and served his nation well, even in the face of overwhelming circumstances. He also proposed the Fifteenth Amendment, which guaranteed voting rights to the freedmen and oversaw America's expansion by purchasing Alaska from Russia for $7.2 million.

For opposing the Radicals and attempting to protect the people of the South, the man who was the Jackson Democrat and who was nominated for vice president on the National Union (Republican) ticket in 1864, was denied the nomination for president in 1868. At the May 1868 Republican National Convention Ulysses S. Grant was nominated as the Republican candidate for president.

The recent domination by the Radical Republicans motivated the Democrats to reconsider their prior divisiveness. In New York, in June 1868, Northern and Southern Democrats finally united again for the Democratic National Convention. They nominated Horatio Seymour, former governor of New York, for president and Frank P. Blair for vice president. During the convention, the Honorable T. W. Blair, of Memphis, spoke and described the condition of the South. The speech helped the nation understand what atrocities were being committed by the Republicans who held power.

The united participation of all the states in the Democratic National Convention gave renewed enthusiasm and hope to the people of Tennessee. Rallies were held, torchlight processions took place, and resolutions were adopted at mass meetings. The Democrats had hope. In West Tennessee, Mayor John W. Leftwich (who was also a former congressman) was elected to Congress. W. W. Vaughn from Brownsville was elected as an at-large elector for the state. However, the Republicans won almost everything else in Tennessee since they controlled who could vote.

During the campaign, the people were reminded of Grant's nomination acceptance speech in which he called for peace. Many voters felt that he favored a less radical approach to Reconstruction. Grant was elected the eighteenth president with a national vote of 3,013,421 to 2,706,829 for Seymour (214 electoral votes to 80).

The Civil War and its aftermath left horrible destruction for Tennessee farmers. Buildings, equipment, and livestock losses were heavy. In many cases, all that was left was the land itself. The freed slaves had little knowledge of self-sufficiency. Many Blacks returned to the homes of their former owners. Things, however, were different. The farmers, whose businesses and homes had been destroyed and pilfered by the Union soldiers, the postwar Radical government, and thieves, had little with which to pay for farm labor. Many farmers had to resort to sharecropping and became heavily mortgaged to their suppliers.

During this time "[theft] and robbery were as continuous as the corruption of the state government, and for their own preservation the farmers were compelled to band together" (Keating 1888). Their animals were stolen and butchered, their crops were burned, and they lived in fear. They could expect no protection from a government controlled by the Radicals. Additionally, the government instituted high taxes in order to fund their schemes. The situation became intolerable. The combination of high taxes, political oppression, and unfairness brought the people close to revolution (Keating 1888).

The railroad system had also suffered heavy losses not only due to the war but also to the postwar Radical government. Although most railroads were in decent financial shape prior to the war, some of the systems were losing money. In spite of

The Nashville and Chattanooga rail yard. Nashville was a railroad center for Union forces in the West. (Courtesy of TSLA)

this, the prewar railroad system was making progress. However, during the war there were no profits from which railroad companies could pay the interest on their bond debts. After the war, Tennessee railroads nearly collapsed. The federal government assisted in rebuilding a small portion of the system, but most destruction was left for the state to deal with.

Governor Brownlow, who possessed little administrative experience, decided that he could rebuild the system and proceeded to institute his own ideas. The railroads turned to the legislature to issue bonds to pay not only the interest on the previous bonds, but also to help rebuild the war-ravaged systems. Brownlow's legislature showed little restraint in the issuance of railroad bonds. The problem was that little of the money actually went to reconstruct the rail system. Most went in the form of political payoffs to legislators or railroad officials. The public soon became aware of the schemes. Accusations flew. There was talk of bribery in the form of liquor, money, clothes, and other gifts. The legislature was viewed as out of the control of the voting public. It had appropriated over $13 million to the rail companies by 1869; the debt eventually grew to over $43 million. The bonds that had been issued for this debt would later come back to destabilize Tennessee's financial and political system, but for now there was nothing Tennesseans could do. They did not control the government.

Grant was inaugurated president on March 4, 1869. Age, conflict of interest, and lack of interest plagued his cabinet. He pledged strict enforcement of the laws. Unfortunately, these included the Reconstruction Acts previously designed by the Radicals. With little hope of relief from the abuse of a Radical government, Southerners continued to turn to the Klan, and, as a result, it continued to grow.

President Grant, brought to office by the Radical Republicans, was treated as a puppet who should do their bidding. He tried to institute a milder form of Reconstruction for the South, but those in control had no intention of giving up power by allowing Southerners to vote and achieve representation. They were willing to subjugate an entire sector of a nation, force it to wallow in destitution, while they padded their own pockets and egos.

In 1868 Governor Brownlow had enlisted a "guard" of "loyal" men to be stationed in Middle and West Tennessee to capture and imprison members of the Klan. Brownlow's hold on the state was firm, but by now Tennesseans had tolerated about all the oppression they were willing to accept. Revolt was inevitable. Anyone associated with Brownlow had become the enemy of oppressed citizens. In early 1869 Brownlow had declared martial law in Overton, Jackson, Maury, Giles, Marshall, Lawrence, Gibson, Madison, and Haywood Counties. Brownlow sent out his state guard of "freedmen" and stationed this armed militia throughout the state. The tension mounted between the populous and Brownlow's Radicals. As conflict neared, the rational politicians searched for a way to provide relief.

The opportunity came with the U.S. Senate seat election. U.S. Senator David Patterson's term (in the Class 1 seat) would officially end on March 4, 1869. There was no doubt that in the current political climate of Radical Republican control of Tennessee, Patterson or any non-Radical would not be returning to the Senate. In October 1868, William G. Brownlow was elected U.S. senator by the legislature.

Many saw this as an opportunity to get Brownlow out of the state. When he was finally sworn in to the U.S. Senate, his empire and the turmoil that he brought to Tennessee made a remarkable reversal. He resigned as Tennessee's governor on February 25, 1869. (His term in the Senate would run from March 4, 1869, until March 3, 1875.) With Brownlow's removal from Tennessee state government, a sigh of relief overtook the populous. General Nathan Bedford Forrest, commander of the Klan, immediately ordered that the Klan destroy its costumes and cease hostilities. The crisis halted now that Brownlow was out of power.

Speaker of the state senate Republican Dewitt C. Senter became governor of Tennessee, assuming office on February 25, 1869. Senter understood the crisis which existed in Tennessee and followed a more reasonable approach. A Union man before and during the war, he had served in the Tennessee legislature prior to the war and had worked and voted against Tennessee's secession from the Union. Once the state had seceded, Senter was taken captive by Confederate soldiers. Later he was literally run out of his home by Confederate sympathizers. He then went to live in Louisville, Kentucky, for the remainder of the war. Once the war was over, he returned to Tennessee and was elected to the state senate in 1867, supporting Brownlow and his plans. Over time, Senter came to realize that Brownlow's radical acts could not heal a war-torn state. He worked to elect Brownlow to the U.S. Senate and then developed a more reasonable approach toward mending the state. Now that Brownlow was out, it was up to him to deal with the many problems facing the Volunteer State.

Governor Senter had only a short time in office until the term begun by Brownlow was complete. Soon he would have to stand for election as governor. He quickly made his more reasonable approach to the crisis of Reconstruction known. He declared that the state militia be under the control of civil authority. He then disbanded the militia. These acts helped give hope of relief to the dominated "former citizens" of Tennessee, but Senter was still viewed with suspicion. After all, he was a Republican. Complicating his task was the fact that all the Radicals in government did not go to Washington with Brownlow. The Radical Republican legislators still wanted to hold power and turned against Senter as he weakened their political dominance. Other less radical Republicans saw the logic in a more equitable treatment of all citizens, and they supported him.

Republicans fell into an intraparty battle. Some wanted to continue the Radical course, while others wanted to take a more reasonable course of Reconstruction. The dispute escalated and the Tennessee Republican Party split. On May 20, 1869, a gubernatorial convention was held in Nashville. Tempers flared and chaos engulfed the meeting when three different men tried to seat themselves as chairman. The convention became so rowdy that it broke up after a few days of melee. Later, two separate Radical Republican meetings were held. Senter was nominated by the more tolerant group of Radicals. The actual conservatives did not nominate anyone. The Radicals, who declined to accept enfranchisement of Confederates, also chose their own candidate, William B. Stokes, who was from Middle Tennessee. Stokes had served as congressman from the Third District and was a former general.

Stokes had previously lost a gubernatorial race to Brownlow. But in 1869 he had substantial support. In addition to his personal alliances, he had support within the Radical ranks from those who felt that Senter was far too tolerant of the former rebels. When the campaign began in Nashville on June 5, 1869, it looked as if Stokes would win, given the restrictive voting laws of Tennessee. Senter then enacted a plan which allowed former Confederates to vote and began to talk about immediate enfranchisement. Disenfranchised Tennesseans approved of his plan and support for him swelled. When Stokes realized that conservative voters would favor Senter as the more lenient candidate, he adopted a public position favoring "gradual" enfranchisement of Confederates. Senter then proposed that all voting restrictions be immediately removed for former Confederates and promised that if reelected he would work for total enfranchisement of Confederates. Stokes and the Radicals were not happy, but there was little they could do. It was Brownlow and the Radicals who had given the

DEWITT CLINTON SENTER was born in 1834 in McMinn County, Tennessee. He studied law on his own. In 1859, he married a third cousin, Harriet T. Senter, who was eleven years younger than him. They had no children. Senter was a strong Union man, but he did own slaves. He was elected to three terms in the state legislature before the Civil War, voting against secession. During the war he was jailed by the Confederates, then driven from his home in East Tennessee by guerrillas. He moved to Louisville, Kentucky, until after the war. In 1865 he returned to Tennessee and was elected to the state senate representing Anderson, Grainger, Union, Claiborne, and Campbell Counties. After he was elected to his second term as state senator, he was elected speaker. Initially he sided with Governor Brownlow and the Radicals, voting for disfranchisement of any Confederates. Then on February 25, 1868, Brownlow, who had been elected by the legislature to the U.S. Senate, resigned to become senator on March 4. As speaker of the senate, Senter became governor. Shortly afterward, he was elected in his own right when he changed the radical-controlled political system of the day and allowed ex-Confederates to vote. He won by a great majority, which was not unexpected with the enfranchisement of former voters in 1869.

Senter's administration had to face the postwar problems left over from the Brownlow administration. He had to deal with the abusive carpetbaggers, who were using their influence to plunder the state, and the lawless Ku Klux Klan, which had arisen to counteract the abuses of the carpetbaggers and the Radical government. Governor Senter also had to deal with the state debt due to the railroads. The previous governor's extraordinary powers were normalized during Senter's term; the right to vote was restored to male citizens; and a constitutional convention was set to be held in Nashville in January 1870. The convention was made up of future leaders of the state, a past governor, and Tennessee leaders from both the Northern and Southern armies. Radical leaders closely watched the meeting. Along with other more important decisions of the convention was the selection of November in even-numbered years as the time for state elections. Senter was governor during a difficult time, but he provided the much needed guidance to normalize life in Tennessee. He was committed to saving his state from civil disorder. After his term ended in 1871, he returned home to Morristown, Tennessee. He died on June 14, 1898, and was buried in Jarnagin Cemetery. (Photograph courtesy of TSLA) governor the power to appoint the county registrars. The registrars decided who was eligible to vote.

Senter campaigned on the right of all men to vote and the restoration of peace and prosperity to the state. He fired most of Brownlow's Radical registrars (who would have helped elect Stokes) and appointed his own. They, of course, planned to allow ex-Confederates to vote. By the time the campaign reached Memphis, Stokes knew that Senter had won the Confederate support. He then stated he also favored total enfranchisement. But, it was too late. Even former Governor Brownlow supported Senter and his policies. Brownlow knew the state was changing and in order to have a chance of being reelected to the Senate by the legislature, he had to be on the side of the majority of the voters. Senter smashed Stokes 120,333 to 55,036. In addition, the people of Tennessee elected twenty conservatives and only five Radicals to the state senate and sixty-six conservatives and seventeen Radicals to the house.

The vote was also influenced by the ruling of the state supreme court in the case of a Gibson County man. William Staten, who had voted in county elections on March 7, 1868, had been arrested and tried for "illegal voting" under former Governor Brownlow's Reconstructionist government. However, Staten had a certificate as a legally qualified voter. The supreme court was clear in its repudiation of Brownlow's actions (he had passed a law that allowed the governor to essentially disregard the vote in a county if the governor simply gave reason for possible fraud), clearing Staten and declaring that the actions of Brownlow were not only against the law but repugnant.

Governor Senter quickly returned the right to vote to many Tennesseans. It was about this time that the supreme court ruled that voting restrictions were illegal. Even the judges, placed by a Radical government, had seen madness in the dictatorial control of Tennessee's people. The election of 1869 was the beginning of the end of Reconstruction in Tennessee.

After Senter's election, Stokes and the Radicals protested the results of the election to the U.S. Congress. They appealed to Congress to reinstitute military law in Tennessee and remove Senter from power. But by this time the Radical Reconstruction attitude that had prevailed in Washington was finally beginning to soften. Stokes could not obtain the support for the dictatorial response he needed. It was too late.

As the voting privilege was returned to the Tennesseans, the political power structure began to change. The ex-Confederates, who had been abused by Brownlow and the Radical Republicans, did not easily forget this harsh treatment, and their reaction to the abuse would ultimately worsen the disenfranchisement for Blacks. The White Southerners had no intention of letting carpetbaggers and Radical Republicans remove their freedom and possessions again. It was the Republicans who had manipulated the law and held the state hostage. The present and future resentment toward Republicans would be long lasting. Even though it was a Republican from Grainger County, Governor Senter, who finally recognized the damage done to the state and helped return the right to vote to the ex-Confederates, the party would not be forgiven. The 1869 Tennessee Republican victory would be a unique event in Tennessee history. The Republican Party could not, for the foreseeable future, be associated in the minds and hearts of

Tennesseans or Southerners as their party.

Democrats immediately took power in Middle and West Tennessee. Former Whigs, Know-Nothings, and Democrats would not be associated with the Republican Party, a haven for Radical extremists during the war and the early postwar period. Thereafter, Democrats would dominate Tennessee. Blacks, wherever they lived in Tennessee, voted Republican from 1870 until 1890 when Black voting slowed. In the coming years, Republicans would be elected in the First and Second U.S. Representative Districts on a regular basis and occasionally elected in the Third and Tenth Districts. However, most of the state would remain under Democratic political control.

After Governor Senter was inaugurated, he soon began to repair the damage to the state. The State Guard Act (which provided Brownlow's military control of the state) was repealed. The requirement of loyalty oaths in order to hold office was removed. The legislature proposed a constitutional convention in 1870. Tennesseans sorely wanted to salvage their state and approved the proposed convention by a margin of five to one.

On May 10, 1869, the transcontinental railroad crews from the West and East met at Promontory, Utah. There the last spike was driven to complete the line from Omaha to California. The path for future western migration was set, and Memphis, which had competed as a locale for a rail station, and Tennessee were left out of the running and lost some of the industrial development that occurred in other communities during the coming decades. Tennessee had played a prominent role in the development of America by serving as an important migration path, and it is likely that the transcontinental railroad might have run through this state if not for the Civil War.

In 1870 the United States altered its Constitution with the Fifteenth Amendment, giving Blacks across the United States the right to vote. The state of Tennessee also altered its state constitution in 1870. The constitutional convention began in Nashville on January 10. A former Confederate general and prewar Whig, John C. Brown, was elected chairman of the convention. The constitution of 1835 was revamped. It upheld the right to vote, but a voters' poll tax was added. The Tennessee Constitution of 1870 also separated Whites and Blacks in schools, and it set the date for state elections on the second Tuesday in November.

The new state constitution was approved by the voters on March 26, 1870—98,128 votes in favor and 33,972 against. One of the most important accomplishments of the constitution was the prevention of the state legislature from granting money to corporations. This was done in response to the actions of the legislature under Governor Brownlow, which issued bonds pouring millions of dollars into the railroads (a substantial portion of which was pilfered), leaving the state with millions in debt—a debt to be dealt with by the Tennessee taxpayer. The new constitution essentially reenfranchised ex-Confederates. The power of political domination in Tennessee now firmly shifted back to the Democrats.

After the voters had approved the constitution, the Radicals made one last attempt to hold power. They appealed to President Grant to ignore the new Tennessee Constitution and to send military forces to place Tennessee under the 1867 Reconstruction guidelines. Grant refused. This denial assured the right to vote to ordinary Tennessee citizens. It solidified political affiliations for the next century.

Middle and West Tennessee now began to return to their political base, the Democratic Party, begun by the politics of Andrew Jackson. The roots of East Tennessee politics, on the other hand, were decidedly different. Standing on the political foundation laid by John Sevier, East Tennesseans became Whigs in the 1830s, Unionists during the Civil War, and were now Republicans.

With the Democrats now dominant in Tennessee again, John C. Brown, who had chaired the 1870 constitutional convention, became the party nominee for governor. Brown was a lawyer from Pulaski, Tennessee (Giles County), and the brother of former Governor Neill S. Brown. He had been a Whig before the Civil War, but he was a conservative postwar Democrat who opposed the Radicals and their abusive dominance of Tennesseans. His supporters wanted to put an end to Reconstruction policies and bury the idea, forever.

Republicans nominated William Wisener for governor. Wisener was from Shelbyville, Tennessee, and had been a Whig before the Civil War. He had served as speaker of the Tennessee house and was also a member of the constitutional convention of 1870. Wisener represented a party that was now considered reprehensible to Tennesseans. It would take unusual circumstances for the Republicans to be considered acceptable. In November 1870, the voters elected Democrat John C. Brown governor of Tennessee. He received nearly double the votes of Republican Wisener—78,979 to 41,500. During this campaign cycle the Democrats dominated the legislative elections. They won sixty seats in the state house, while Republicans held fifteen. They took twenty seats in the state senate, while Republicans held only five. The Civil War, the treatment suffered at the hands of the North, and Reconstruction had taught Tennesseans that Republicans represented war, death, confiscation, and destruction of property. The narrow balance between prewar Whigs and Democrats was over. The election marked the end of Republican dominance and any remote semblance of a two-party system in Tennessee. (Brown would hold office from 1871 until 1875.)

Andrew Johnson returned to Tennessee after completing his duty as president. He had suffered under the abuse of Northern Radicals who wanted a free hand to take advantage of a defeated people and had held off the debacle as best he could. Still, Tennesseans resented him for working to preserve a Union that they felt had ignored their sovereignty. He was hated by the Radicals and by his own people. He longed for the opportunity to clear his political name. A Senate term was coming up, and Johnson sought it, hoping for vindication. In spite of having a great number of enemies, he still had many friends. Indeed the vote in the legislature of 1870 for the U.S. Senate seat was very close. His secretary, Edmund Cooper, worked hard for Johnson as did his brother, state Senator Henry Cooper, but as he came within one vote of victory, the election stalled. The Coopers switched paths, jockeying for Henry Cooper's election as a compromise. They managed to find another vote, and Henry Cooper was elected U.S. senator by that one vote. The Coopers had certainly benefited from their prior association with Andrew Johnson—the absolute leader of the prewar Tennessee Democratic Party, the source of federal power during the war, and the president of the United States after the war. But they saw their chance and took it. With

JOHN CALVIN BROWN was born in 1827 in Giles County, Tennessee, of Scot descent, to Duncan and Margaret Smith Brown. He was the younger brother of Neill Brown, who served as governor from 1847 until 1849. After an early education at Old Field Schools, he went to Jackson College in Columbia, Tennessee. He took his legal studies with his Uncle Hugh Brown in Spring Hill, Tennessee, and began practice in Pulaski in 1848 at age twenty-one. He married Anne Pointer, who died in 1858; they had no children together. Although a solid Union man when the discussion of secession came up, he was loyal to his Tennessee friends and joined the Confederates. He was soon elected captain and served in many battles, being wounded at Perryville and Chickamauga. He was also wounded at Franklin on November 30, 1864. He eventually achieved the rank of major general. In 1864 he married Elizabeth Childress, from Murfreesboro, who was living in exile in Griffin, Georgia, during the war. Together they had four children. (The oldest daughter would become the wife of Benton McMillin, who later served as governor of Tennessee from 1899 until 1903.)

When the war was over, Brown went back to practicing law in Pulaski. When the 1870 constitutional convention met, he served as its president and held a steady and respectful hand at guiding the state through different times. He was elected governor in 1870 and was reelected in 1872, serving 1871–1875. Although a former Whig, he was the first Democrat elected governor after the Civil War. During his terms he faced the issues of the state debt and a weak school system. Governor Brown was defeated for reelection to a third term in 1874 by James D. Porter. He later ran for the U.S. Senate but was defeated by former President Andrew Johnson in the legislative election. After his public service, he continued his legal practice in Pulaski. He served as receiver of the Texas Pacific Railway Company in Texas and became president of the company in 1888. He served as president of the Tennessee Coal and Iron Company in 1889. Brown died in 1889 at Red Boiling Springs, in Macon County, Tennessee, and was buried in Pulaski, Tennessee. (Photograph courtesy of TSLA)

their personal victory came the end of the opportunity for a great leader, a bulwark of the Union, and an unselfish guardian of the Southern people. Johnson had lost his chance for election as president by defiantly denying the Radicals the cooperation they needed in order to dictatorially rule the Southern people. To this man, exoneration of his reputation was denied and with it went the friendship between Johnson and the Coopers.

By 1870 peace was finally restored as justice was returned. There was no more militia, control of the votes, or control of the courts as had been present during Reconstruction policies under Governor Brownlow. Once again the people had more reasonable control of their lives. With this return of self-determination came local reinvestment and the early stages of economic progress. Even though Tennessee communities were in poor financial and physical condition, recovery slowly took root. Ahead of some surrounding states, life began its transition to normalcy in Tennessee. The state and its communities set out to tackle the debt and unstable economy.

Eighteen seventy was the year of the great Chicago fire. Tennesseans gathered contributions to send to Chicago for relief.

Democrat John C. Brown, the first governor elected after the approval of the new state constitution, was inaugurated in January 1871. Democrats were placed in all

HENRY COOPER was born in Columbia, Tennessee, on August 22, 1827. He went to Dixon Academy in Shelbyville and then to Jackson College, finishing in 1847. Admitted to the bar in 1849, he began practicing law in Shelbyville. In 1851 he married Ann Eliza Stickler. When Governor Andrew Johnson held the state house in 1853, Cooper was elected as Whig to the house of representatives, and they became close friends. He was reelected in 1857 when Isham Harris was governor. He opposed secession, and though a Whig in Tennessee, attended the Democrat National Convention in Baltimore in 1860. During the Civil War, President Johnson appointed him judge of the Seventh Judicial Circuit in Tennessee. He resigned in 1866 and later taught law in Lebanon, Tennessee. After a year, he moved to Nashville and practiced law. He was elected a state senator in 1869 and served until 1870, when the legislature elected him U.S. senator. He served from March 4, 1871, until March 4, 1877. His brothers Edmund Cooper, William Cooper, and Duncan B. Cooper all were politically minded. Duncan Cooper later played a conspicuous and controversial role in Tennessee politics and was involved in the shooting and death of Edward Carmack.

After Cooper's single term in the U.S. Senate, he did not run for reelection. His term marked a sad chapter in his life—his wife, daughter, and two sons all died. After his U.S. Senate term, Cooper was involved in mining operations in Mexico. There, in Tierra Blanca, Guadelupe y Calvo, Mexico, he was killed by bandits on February 3, 1884. (Photograph courtesy of SHO)

appointed offices, and party legislators planned to gerrymander elective districts favoring their party. Some particularly enthusiastic Democrats planned to make it impossible to elect Republicans to any seats in the state legislature or Congress. Governor Brown worked diligently to restore the order and finances of the state. He felt that Tennessee had an obligation to repay the state debt accumulated under Brownlow's administration even though many Tennesseans felt that the debt had been unethically incurred. Many people felt that bonds had been issued because some legislators had been bribed. A great debate thus began over the state's obligations—the manner and amount that would be repaid. Meanwhile, some of the railroads were sold and the debt was reduced to around $31 million.

In addition to the state's railroad debt, communities were also burdened with a great war debt, sometimes having been incurred under questionable circumstances. In 1871 the city of Memphis had a debt of $3.8 million. Mayor John Johnson made a plea for reduced spending and lowering taxes, but the effort was not enough to stop the spiral of debt.

The next election cycle was in 1872 and campaigns were rife with discord. It was in this year that an additional congressional seat was awarded to Tennessee (just prior to the elections). Since there was little time to prepare, the Tennessee legislature decreed that the seat should be initially filled by a statewide election. Horace Maynard became the Republican nominee.

Maynard had been a congressman from the First District before the Civil War. He had opposed the return of former Confederates to normalized life, favoring Radical control of Tennessee. Former

President Andrew Johnson although still viewed by many in Tennessee as a traitor, could not allow himself to remain relegated to the reputation unfairly assigned him. Some of his friends urged him back into the arena by taking on the race for the new congressional seat. He initially declined since it was so soon after losing the Senate seat. But in Nashville, with all his friends around, he became inspired to make this race and to do so as an Independent. His opponents were General B. F. Cheatham, the Democratic nominee and Maynard, the Republican nominee. Cheatham had served as a general for the Confederates in the Civil War. Johnson's entrance into the race risked dividing Democratic support.

In 1872, the liberal (non-Radical) Republicans opposed Grant for reelection and nominated New York newspaper editor Horace Greeley for president. The Democrats endorsed the nomination, and Greeley became the Democratic candidate. Grant was renominated by the regular Republicans. In the election, Grant polled 3,596,745 to Greeley's 2,843,446 popular votes (286 to 66 electoral votes). As it turned out, Greeley died November 29, 1872. Republicans had dominated the House and Senate during Grant's first years of the presidency, but the pendulum was beginning to swing as attitudes began to change.

In the Tennessee gubernatorial race Haywood Countian Alfred A. Freeman ran well against Governor Brown, but the Democratic governor was reelected in 1872 and returned to office for the 1873–1875 term. Andrew Johnson divided the Democratic vote in the statewide race for the new congressional seat between Cheatham and himself, allowing Republican Horace Maynard to be elected. Democrats maintained a majority in the state legislature. However, the Democratic ranks were divided, and a coalition formed between the few Republicans and some of the Democrats. This coalition controlled the legislature. However, West Tennessee politics remained under solid Democratic control.

In 1872, the first Black state house representative was elected. Sampson W. Keeble, a barber from Nashville, became the first Black to serve either in the state house or senate. (Twelve Black men were elected to the state legislature from 1872 until 1900.)

The year 1873 began as a prosperous one for Tennessee. However, it was also the year in which yellow fever once again struck Memphis. Occurring between September 17, 1873, and the first week in November 1873, the disease sent panic through the streets of Memphis. Quickly the population declined to 25,000 via a mass exodus as well as death. This same year, 1873, Nashville experienced another cholera epidemic. Cholera had previously struck the city in 1833, 1835, 1850, and 1855. A total of 20,248 people had died in Nashville between 1822 and 1866; 10 percent of the deaths were thought to be from cholera.

By 1873 there was peace in Tennessee. Black and White relations were improved, and the Ku Klux Klan ceased activity, existing mainly in name. Conditions for Blacks began to improve. They were provided with schools and invited by the Democrats to hold office in Shelby and other counties.

By the time of the 1874 elections, public opinion of President Grant's administration was beginning to change, and it was not for the better. His administration was racked with scandal. During his first term, his brother-in-law had tried to help financier Jay Gould obtain inside government information in an attempt to "corner the gold market." It was during Grant's second administration, though, that the trouble escalated. Congressmen, senators, and others involved in government were participating in illegal stock activity relating to the Union Pacific Railroad, which received federal assistance. Five federal judges and two of Grant's cabinet members resigned to prevent impeachment for fraud, bribery, and other charges. Grant's secretary was put on trial for defrauding the government of millions in excise tax. In addition to the scandals, the financial panic of 1873 affected public opinion of Grant.

Back in Tennessee James D. Porter was nominated by Democrats to run for governor in 1874. He was from Henry County and had served in the legislature as a Whig prior to the Civil War. During the war he had served as lieutenant colonel under the command of General Benjamin F. Cheatham (who had lost the 1872 congressional race against Maynard and Johnson). Porter had served in the 1870 constitutional convention and was the Twelfth Judicial Circuit judge. His opponent was Republican Congressman Horace Maynard.

When the 1874 midterm congressional elections rolled around, the country was fed up with the Republicans, and they lost ninety-six seats in the House and eight seats in the Senate. The Democrats took control of the House of Representatives (Democrats 181 to Republicans 107), while the Republicans held on to the Senate (Republicans 46 to Democrats 29). This was the first time since the Civil War that the Democrats had control of the House. After this, President Grant thought it would be better to quit rather than risk defeat and refused to run for reelection in 1876.

In the 1874 state elections, Porter was elected governor, defeating Maynard by nearly double the vote. Porter received 105,061 to Maynard's 55,847. He took office in 1875. The financial panic of 1873 had slowed Tennessee's economy along with that of the nation's. As a result, there was less revenue available for the railroad bond debt. This exacerbated the debate over the debt payment, making it a major political issue. During Porter's years as governor, elected officials debated whether to pay off the bonds at 50 percent or 60 percent of face value. This question would not be resolved during Governor Porter's tenure.

Ex-President Andrew Johnson, refusing to be rendered politically irrelevant, had campaigned for the Democratic candidates for the state legislature, as was the custom in those days if one wished to compete for a U.S. Senate seat. The Democrats were victorious in the state's elections of 1874 and again took the legislature. When the new legislature convened, it took fifty-five ballots to elect a U.S. senator. Johnson had twelve competitors. His chief opponent was former Confederate William Bate. Nathan Bedford Forrest traveled to East Tennessee to campaign for Bate. Johnson commented that "if Tennessee wanted a Confederate general in the Senate, she might as well send Forrest himself, rather than a 'one-horse general'" (Sefton 1980). Even President Grant worked against Johnson's election, stating that it would be taken as a personal offense if Johnson were elected. But Andrew Johnson was elected as a Democrat to the Class 1 seat. He succeeded the seat held by his old enemy, "Parson" Brownlow, and took some satisfaction in that. More important to him

JAMES DAVIS PORTER was born on December 7, 1828, in Paris, Tennessee. His parents were Irish-English descendants. Educated in local schools, he began attending the University of Nashville at age fifteen, and by eighteen held a B.S. degree. He continued his education obtaining an L.L.D. degree from the same institution. He studied law under John Dunlap and married his daughter Susannah Dunlap in 1851. They had six children; three died at a young age. He started a law practice in Paris, Tennessee, and by 1859 was elected to the state legislature. He served as adjutant general to General Pillow and later as chief of staff to General Cheatham in the Civil War. When the war was over, Porter returned to his law practice until 1870. He then became a district judge of circuit court. In 1874 he ran for governor and was selected as the Democrat nominee, running against Republican Horace Maynard. Porter was elected and took office in 1875. He had to deal with the great state debt and the disagreement among the voters and legislators over the payment of the debt. Porter worked for public education and the Meharry Medical College was founded during his term. The "four mile" law was passed, which prohibited the sale of alcohol within four miles of any rural school.

After Porter completed two terms as governor in 1879, he became president of the Nashville, Chattanooga, and St. Louis Railroad. In 1885 Democrat President Grover Cleveland appointed him secretary of state. After two years he returned to Tennessee and served as president of the Peabody Educational Fund and helped establish the George Peabody College for Teachers in Nashville. He served as its president for four years. Later he served as President Cleveland's minister to Chile and continued until 1896. There was consideration of his running for president against William Jennings Bryan, but he declined to run. Porter died on May 18, 1912, and was buried in Old Dunlap Cemetery in Paris, Tennessee. His wife, Susannah, died two years later. (Photograph courtesy of TSLA)

however, was the larger meaning of his election—his redemption and vindication in the eyes of the public in Tennessee and the nation.

Former President Andrew Johnson, along with former Vice President and fellow freshman Senator Hannibal Hamlin, was sworn in as U.S. Senator on March 4, 1875. The oath was administered by Vice President Henry Wilson, one of Johnson's impeachment convictors. In fact, among the crowd in the packed Senate Chambers that day were thirteen of the original thirty-five convicting Republicans, now confronted with the prospect of having to face Johnson. His return to the very body that had tried his impeachment was the result of a monumental effort to survive and was a remarkable achievement.

Soon after his inauguration, Johnson roundly denounced Grant, who had once betrayed his trust during the ordeal over the Tenure of Office Act and again disappointed him by working against his Senate election. Grant had called for troops to support the government of Louisiana, which was made up of a Radical Republican coalition. Reconstruction governments were falling all over the South, and many viewed Grant's call as a desperate attempt to assure himself votes for election to a third term. On March 22, Johnson called the action in Louisiana "monstrous" and reminded the Senate that Grant was "mendacious, cunning, and treacherous" and "totally inept at government" (Sefton 1980). Johnson reaffirmed his belief in the milder forms of Reconstruction he had fought for as president. In the very chamber in which he had been tried, the senators responded with a satisfying ovation. However, Johnson, with his reputation restored, did not live long to enjoy his personal victory. He died on July 31, 1875, of a stroke while visiting his daughter in Carter Station, Tennessee. Governor Porter appointed D. M. Key to fill the U.S. Senate seat. Key took office on August 18, 1875, and served until January 19, 1877.

In 1876 Democrat Governor James D. Porter was opposed in the gubernatorial race by Dorsey Thomas, an Independent Democrat. On election day Thomas received most of the Republican vote, but it was not enough to defeat the incumbent Democrat. Porter was reelected governor and inaugurated in 1877. The period of Reconstruction for the South lasted from about 1863 until the last of 1876, during which the wealth of the South had been plundered by the Radicals, carpetbaggers, and scalawags. During Porter's terms as governor, the people of Tennessee rebuilt their homes and businesses and put many of the old disagreements to rest. Governor Porter worked to build a public education system while dealing with many other problems confronting the Volunteer State. The burden of Reconstruction had lasted well over a decade. Perhaps a new president would end the oppression of the South once and for all.

By 1876, Senator James G. Blaine of Maine, who had been Speaker of the House during Grant's administration, appeared to have the Republican nomination cinched. However, at the 1876 Republican National Convention in Cincinnati, Ohio, Republicans put the name of their favorite son, Governor Rutherford B. Hayes, in the ring. Hayes had been a general for the Union in the Civil War, a congressman, and a three-time governor of Ohio. He had a clean reputation, which was an attribute needed by the Republicans in 1876. Blaine had been involved in controversy and associated with some questions of corruption. Additionally, and important to Tennesseans, Blaine had participated in the attempt to impeach President Andrew Johnson. Blaine went through several ballots at the convention, but could not pull off the nomination. On the seventh ballot, the Republicans nominated Hayes. The Democratic National Convention of 1876 nominated the governor of New York, Samuel Jones Tilden, who had a reputation for reforming corrupt government.

The presidential campaign of 1876 was a dirty battle. Charges of corruption flew both ways. The Republicans had suffered severely, losing ninety-six seats and control of the House, during the last midterm congressional elections. It did not appear to Hayes, or his fellow Republicans, that he could win. In fact, when the votes were counted, Democrat Tilden polled 4,284,020 popular votes to 4,036,572 for Hayes. The electoral vote was 203 for Tilden and 166 for Hayes. Apparently, Democrat Tilden was president, and the newspapers across the country printed this result. Hayes was sure he had lost. However, he had not reckoned with the determination of the Northern Radical Republicans to maintain power. They were about to make the election of 1876 the most bitterly disputed election in history.

Republicans created charges and questioned the results of enough states to challenge the election. They claimed that

Blacks had been denied the right to vote in Louisiana, Florida, and South Carolina. They also took issue with the vote count from Oregon. With the electoral vote changes of these four states, Hayes would win by one electoral vote, 185 to 184. The challenge was particularly incredible considering the Republicans controlled only the Senate while the Democrats had the House. The challenge ended in a deadlock and forced negotiations. Over a three-month period party leaders passed special legislation which set up an "Electoral Commission" composed of five Democratic congressmen, five Republican senators, and five members of the Supreme Court (three of whom were Republicans). The commission was supposed to be nonpartisan and impartial, but this was merely an attempt to feign fairness to the American people. The votes had been carefully counted before the commission was appointed, and the result was a foregone conclusion.

Something positive did come out of this blatant display of power mongering. During the negotiations, the Republicans had to give something to the Democrats in return for their manuevering for the presidency. Even Tennessee Senator David Key, who had supported Tilden during the election, swung his support to Hayes with the understanding that the wounds between the North and South would finally be healed. Senator Key spoke to that effect on the Senate floor on December 18, 1876. The quid pro quo was Southern relief by ending Reconstruction. Hayes pledged to finally withdraw federal troops from the Southern states. The deal was done and then approved

DAVID MCKENDREE KEY was born on January 27, 1824, in Greene County, Tennessee. His ancestors were Scottish and came to Chester County, Pennsylvania, from England about 1700. His father, John Key, was born January 18, 1798, in Greene County, Tennessee. His mother, Margaret Armitage, was also born in Greene County, on April 12, 1804. His parents were farmers in Monroe County, where Key received his early education. He completed college at Hiwassee College in 1850, then studied law, was admitted to the bar, and began practice in Kingston, Roane County, Tennessee. In 1853 he moved to Chattanooga, where he kept his home for the remainder of his life, and served as a Democrat presidential elector for Buchanan in the 1856 election. He married Elizabeth Lenoir, from Roane County, Tennessee, on July 1, 1857. They had nine children. Key was an elector for Breckinridge in 1860. He served in the Civil War as a Confederate lieutenant colonel in the Forty-third Regiment of the Tennessee Infantry and was captured at Vicksburg. After the war he returned to Chattanooga and the practice of law. He participated in the state constitutional convention of 1870 and was chancellor of the Third Division of Chancery between 1870 and 1875. He lost a bid for Congress in 1874, but was appointed U.S. senator on August 18, 1875, by Governor Porter, upon the death of Andrew Johnson. Key served until January 19, 1877, after he was defeated in his bid to hold the seat by James E. Bailey. President Hayes later appointed him as postmaster general in May 1877, and he served until 1880. He resigned in 1880 to become U.S. district judge for the Eastern and Middle Districts of Tennessee. Key remained in that post until he retired on January 26, 1894. He died in Chattanooga on February 3, 1900. (Photograph courtesy of SHO)

by the House of Representatives fifty-six hours prior to the scheduled inauguration. Hayes was elected the nineteenth president of the United States. The inauguration took place on March 5, 1877.

During Hayes's term federal troops were finally removed from the South. The president upheld his end of the bargain. Even so, the Democrats remained resentful over the election scandal. They controlled the House of Representatives, and rarely cooperated with the president.

In 1876 two U.S. senators had to be elected by the Tennessee legislature. One election was held to complete the unexpired term for the late Andrew Johnson, which had been temporarily filled by David Key upon appointment by Governor Porter. This was a very difficult legislative election cycle. Former Whig James Edmund Bailey, from Clarksville, Tennessee, defeated Senator Key and General William B. Bate. Key served until January 19, 1877, when Bailey took his Class 1 Senate seat, serving until March 3, 1881.

Eighteen seventy-six was also the year for the regular election of the other (Class 2) Senate seat. This election was for a full-term seat vacated by retiring Senator Henry Cooper. The legislature elected former Governor Isham G. Harris on the first ballot. Harris took office on March 4, 1877, serving until July 8, 1897, when he died in office.

David M. Key of Chattanooga served as "a leader of Tennessee Democrats during the Reconstruction" (Isaac n.d.) and after the loss of his U.S. Senate seat. He had supported part of the Compromise of 1877 and Hayes's election as president during the congressional debate. He became a close ally and friend of President Hayes. The president returned the kind feelings and respect, in May 1877, by appointing Key as postmaster general of the United States.

JAMES EDMUND BAILEY was born August 15, 1822, in Montgomery County, Tennessee, of Scotch ancestry. His grandfather emigrated to North Carolina. His father, Charles Bailey, was born in Simpson County, North Carolina, moved to Montgomery County, Tennessee, at an early age, and worked for forty years as clerk of the circuit court. Bailey's mother was Mary Bryan, from Robertson County, Tennessee, the daughter of Colonel James H. Bryan. Bailey was educated at Clarksville Academy and the University of Nashville. He studied law and was admitted to the bar in 1842. He married Elizabeth Margaret Lust, of Nashville, on November 7, 1849, and they had five children—four sons and one daughter. Although he was elected as a Whig to the state house in 1853, he served as a Confederate colonel in the Civil War, with the Forty-ninth Tennessee Infantry. He supported the preservation of the Union but could not betray his homeland. Captured at Fort Donelson during the war, he was later freed in a prisoner exchange with the North. He returned to his law practice in Clarksville after the war. After losing a bid for governor in 1874 to Democrat James D. Porter, he served twice as special judge to the state supreme court. He served only four years in the U.S. Senate, from January 19, 1877, until March 3, 1881, losing a bid for reelection in a three-man contest, during the era of Democrat division over the state debt, to Howell Jackson. He died of cancer in Clarksville, Tennessee, on December 29, 1885. (Photograph courtesy of SHO)

During this era Tennessee's major cities struggled to recover from the lasting effects of the Civil War. By 1877 Memphis was recovering its old spirit. After suffering from the devastation of war and yellow fever epidemics, the community held a Mardi Gras, concerts, and balls. Memphis Mayor John R. Flippin worked diligently to repay the bond debts of the city. He went to New York, Baltimore, and Charleston seeking assistance with the debt burden.

Nashville, with a population of around 37,000 in 1877, was well on the way to reestablishing commerce and manufacturing businesses. In 1877 the first telephone call in Nashville's history was made from the home of A. G. Adams, on Vine Street, to Mrs. James K. Polk, on Polk Street. Agriculture had taken a lesser role and the number of steamboats coming through the city had failed to return to the prewar level. But by now the railroads were being built again. Sanitation improvements in Nashville were still behind the times, as they were in Memphis and other cities in Tennessee. Garbage was tossed from windows or just thrown onto the ground. Diphtheria and cholera took many lives. Records of 1876 indicated that Nashville had the fifth highest death rate in the United States.

In Knoxville, once divided by a clash of Union and Confederate feelings, the people began to learn to live together in peace again. Supper clubs appeared and plans developed for the improvement of community enterprises such as expansion of the community library. Wholesale business increased and economic recovery was well under way.

At a state level, the debate over the use of alcohol and the repayment of state debt created a great deal of political and social friction. By 1878 Governor Porter decided not to run for reelection, opening up the race to several nonincumbents. E. M. Wright, a doctor from Chattanooga, Tennessee, became the Republican nominee. Albert S. Marks, from Winchester, Tennessee, became the Democratic nominee. Marks, a chancellor of the Fourth District, had lost his right lower leg from a wound received while serving as a Confederate colonel during the Civil War. As a result of the heightened political bickering over the settlement of the state debt, a third party developed. They called their gubernatorial candidate, R. M. Edwards, from Cleveland, Tennessee, the "Greenbacker."

The problems with the state debt were exacerbated by the national economic depression, which began to impact Tennessee in 1873. The state defaulted in 1875. Because of the enormity of the debt, it would take the next decade to effectively deal with it. Each party and candidate took a position on how this should be done. Even though Democrats blamed Republicans and former Governor Brownlow for the debt, they believed it should be repaid; they were split, however, over how to pay it. The "low tax" group favored reducing the amount repaid to a certain percentage of each dollar owed. The "state credit" group favored full repayment in order to maintain the good credit of the state. Governor Brown, and subsequently Governor Porter, attempted to oversee full repayment of the debt. However, taxes were required to pay the debt, and tax revenue became an increasing problem during the economic downturn. By 1877, it became apparent that full repayment was impossible and due to the economic downturn, taxes had to be reduced. Democrat Albert Marks, after noting the failure of full repayment by his predecessors, favored repayment at less than par value. Republicans generally

ALBERT SMITH MARKS was born on October 16, 1836, in Daviess County, Kentucky. His forebears had come to Kentucky from Virginia. Marks lost his father when he was only fourteen and quickly took on the responsibility of managing the family's large landholdings. He received a good education and then studied law, much of it on his own. In 1859 he was admitted to the bar in Winchester, Tennessee. He had supported the unity of the nation, but he could not turn on his neighbors and served in the Confederate army during the Civil War. He became a captain and then colonel of the Seventeenth Tennessee Regiment. He was wounded in the December 1862 Battle of Murfreesboro and lost a leg to amputation. He was engaged to Novella Davis at the time of his amputation, and he offered to release her. However, she refused, and they were married two years later when she was only nineteen years of age. They had two sons. He remained in the Confederate army after the amputation, serving as judge advocate on General Forrest's staff. He was placed on the Confederate roll of honor.

After the war, Marks returned to Winchester and resumed the practice of law. He was elected chancellor of the Fourth Chancery Division in 1870. He worked diligently to clear the dockets and accomplished this goal. In 1879 he was elected governor and had to face the state debt. The issue was extremely controversial and could not be solved. He did not run for reelection in 1880. Instead he ran for the U.S. Senate; however, he was defeated by William B. Bate and he returned to his law practice. Marks died on November 4, 1891, and was buried in Winchester Cemetery in his hometown. His wife died in 1906. (Photograph courtesy of TSLA)

agreed that the debt should be paid at a reduced rate, but only with permission of the creditors. The Greenback Party favored inflating currency through the use of paper money.

Pre-Civil War Southern Democrat Marks, unlike his two predecessors who had been Whigs, was elected governor in 1878, and most of the legislature elected was also Democrat. He received 89,958 votes to Wright's 42,284 and Edwards's 14,155 and took office in 1879. Marks felt, as did his predecessor, that the state should maintain its honor and good credit by trying to settle the debt. However, a partial repayment began to appear to be the only realistic course. The debate was badly dividing Tennessee Democrats throughout Tennessee. Even in smaller communities, mayoral candidates ran for office with the support of competing factions within the Democratic Party, each espousing a different view of how to repay the state debt.

The midterm congressional elections of 1878 again went badly for the Republicans on a national level. Tainted with the scandal of a corrupt bargain for the presidency in 1876, the Democrats pounded the Republicans, taking the U.S. Senate forty-three Democrats to thirty-three Republicans. (It had been Republicans thirty-nine; Democrats thirty-six; and other, one.) The Democrats now controlled both the Senate and the House (Democrats, 150; Republicans, 128; other, 15).

The pressing disturbances in Tennessee life of disease, debt, and a weak economy would profoundly impact the state and its communities. No better example of the times can be described than with the situation in Memphis. What occurred there would alter politics of the day and create the environment for a future political dynasty.

Memphis, like many other cities in the war-ravaged South, had been lax in developing adequate sanitation procedures to keep the city and its streets clean. Because of the high debt, there was not enough revenue for such projects, however important. There was no organized sewer disposal process and no program for the disposal of ashes and garbage. Bodily excretions from privies either went into the ground or were diverted into a bayou which divided the city. Worse, the bayou was not well drained. The situation amounted to years of accumulated filth. When the first sign of yellow fever appeared again in 1878, the quarantine, which was promoted throughout the city, did little good. The efforts to normalize life in Memphis with Mardi Gras, concerts, theater, and other social activities were forgotten, as the city valiantly focused on preventing decimation by the disease.

To escape the disease, whose cause was unknown at the time, an estimated 20,000 residents fled the city by August 24, 1878. Most fled north or west. Many who had already been bitten by infected mosquitoes died on their trip or shortly after arrival at the point of refuge. In Memphis, death was everywhere. By September 14 the epidemic reached its peak. It touched everyone. It took entire families. Decaying bodies of families were found in their homes. Those who nursed and treated the sick were not immune from the disease. The scene of dead mothers holding their dead infants and children was commonplace. Out of the 20,000 people who remained in Memphis, it is estimated that 17,600 became ill. Of about 14,000 Blacks who remained, in town, 960 died. Of the approximately 6,000 White residents who remained, 4,204 died (a 70 percent mortality rate). Only 200 Whites escaped infection. Most of those who did not become infected had contracted the disease in a previous epidemic and survived. Epidemics had occurred in Memphis in 1828, 1855, 1867, and 1873.

As if the tragedy of disease were not enough, criminals preyed upon the desperate city. Anything unguarded was stolen. Thieves even stole "Howard Nurse" badges from the relief corp that aided the city during this horrendous epidemic. They then went to the doors of the ill and weak posing as members of the health team, entered the homes, and pilfered at will. This went on a short time until the citizens formed companies for defense. After a couple of thieves were shot, the criminals departed. By October 29, 1878, the epidemic was over, but the loss of life put all regular activity on hold. Memphis was now severely damaged, and it would be decades before normalcy returned.

The nationwide financial depression of 1873, combined with the yellow fever outbreaks of 1873 and 1878, fractured the economy of Memphis. Previous railroad financing made the economy that much more uncorrectable. Taxes were not paid, and the city was unable to meet its obligations. Much of the debt may have been due to waste and mismanagement. "The line between corruption and incompetence was obscure during the late 1860s and through the 1870s. . . . Good management controls simply did not exist . . ." (Sigafoos 1979).

The city of Memphis surrendered its charter on January 31, 1879. The bankrupt city was reorganized into a taxing district council type of government. This was done in order to change the political structure in hopes of better and fairer government. The city had made only little progress with the sanitation issues when in April 1879 another yellow fever outbreak occurred. The population, which had returned to around 40,000, dropped to 16,110 by July 29. Thirty-six percent of the White population died, and 16 percent of the Black population died. This epidemic continued until about November 10. Memphis, like the rest of the state, needed debt relief in order to clean the community and modernize.

Soon after Albert S. Marks was inaugurated governor in 1879, he appointed a committee of state legislators to examine the state debt problem in order to clear up the facts and make recommendations for a resolution. Their report found that some of the railroads had conspired to defraud the state of Tennessee and had not abided by the agreements made upon initial issuance of funding. Additionally, they found that officials of railroads had given gifts to Brownlow in order to gain protection when violating the trust.

The legislature debated the issue of the debt and its repayment. New York bankers came to the capital and negotiated a 60-percent-on-the-dollar payoff. However, the legislature rejected the 60-percent deal. They countered with an offer to pay fifty cents for every dollar of debt, to be repaid with a 4 percent interest rate. To the bankers, half of the money was better than defaulting on all of it. The legislature approved the deal by the time of their adjournment in March 1879. The proposal was set for a referendum to the people of Tennessee—it was defeated 76,000 to 49,722. Most of the opposition came from rural counties.

Democrats Divide

In June 1880 the Republican National Convention was held in Chicago. President Hayes had served well and had tried to reform government, paying particular attention to the partisan political tradition of handing out civil service jobs. He had authorized the firing of the collector of the port of New York because of questionable proceedings—an act that seemed at the time to be only a small part of an all-out effort to do a good job. This effort left a good public feeling about Republicans and improved Hayes's political image. However, he could not obtain his party's nomination in 1880. By trying to reform the tradition of partisan job appointments, he had infuriated party regulars. They were not interested in his suggestions about reforming government and civil service on his recommendation that presidents be limited to one six-year term received little support.

Nationally, the Republicans were divided, split into the "Stalwarts," who wanted to renominate Ulysses S. Grant, and the "Half-Breeds," who wanted to nominate Maine Senator James G. Blaine. After a long convention stalemate between the two opposing factions (thirty-three ballots), the deadlock was broken and a new trend began when Wisconsin swung its votes to James Garfield. Garfield had served in the House for seventeen years, including a stint as minority leader, and had just been elected a U.S. senator, but never had time to actually serve. On the thirty-sixth ballot Garfield was nominated after trade-offs were made to pacify the various factions. Chester A. Arthur, a Stalwart, was selected as the vice presidential nominee. Senator James Blaine was to be made secretary of state. Ironically, Arthur was the collector for the port of New York who had been ousted by the Hayes administration. Little did anyone know that the ousted collector would become vice president and eventually president.

With Reconstruction over, Tennessee Democrats returned to power, but they began fighting so much among themselves that deep political divisions developed. Middle and West Tennessee represented the traditional Democratic stronghold, and most Democrats from these regions of the state were happy with the nomination of General Winfield Scott Hancock for president at the June 1880 Democratic National Convention. However, national issues were about the only concerns they agreed on. Their main point of contention was the repayment of the state debt on the old bond issues.

When the Tennessee Democratic Convention of 1880 met to nominate a candidate for governor, the control wielded by the "state credit" Democrats' caused some delegates to walk out. The division resulted in the nomination of two Democratic candidates for governor. The "state credit" leaders nominated Judge John V. Wright, a "high tax" Democrat from Maury County, and a former Confederate colonel and congressman. The "low tax" Democrats, who felt that the debt issue should be addressed through a public referendum, nominated S.F. Wilson, also a former Confederate who had previously served in both the state house and the state senate. R. M. Edwards, a former Union officer, ran as the Greenback candidate. The Republican candidate was Alvin Hawkins, from Huntingdon, Tennessee. He was a former Whig who had previously supported the Unionist ticket for President Lincoln's reelection.

ALVIN HAWKINS was born on December 2, 1821, in Bath County, Kentucky. His parents moved to Tennessee when he was four, first to Maury County, and later to Carroll County. Hawkins attended the local schools, and when he was eighteen, went to Bethel College. After his education, he taught school for a short period of time, then left teaching to study law under Benjamin Totton. He was admitted to the bar and went into practice with Isaac Hawkins, his cousin. By 1843 he set up his own practice in Huntingdon, Tennessee. He married Justina Ott of Murfreesboro, Tennessee, and they eventually had six children. After ten years of practice in Huntingdon, the people of Carroll County sent him to the legislature. He was a Whig and remained loyal to the concept of the Union. When the controversy over secession came up, Alvin fought against the idea. After secession and the appointment of Andrew Johnson as military governor, in 1861 Hawkins was appointed by the governor to Congress. However, in the great political and civil chaos of the Civil War, Hawkins never served in the U.S. House. Instead he returned to his legal practice until 1864 when he was appointed U.S. attorney for West Tennessee. He served in that position for a year and then became judge on the supreme court of Tennessee. After three years, the constitution of 1870 prevented him from continuing in that position. He then returned to his legal practice in Huntingdon. In 1880 a controversy over how to settle the state debt divided the Democrats and allowed Hawkins, a Republican, to be elected governor. During his term, his wife and five of their children remained in Huntingdon. Governor Hawkins and his son Ernest, who served as the governor's secretary, lived in the Maxwell House. He served only one term. In the election of 1882 Democrat William Bate ran against Hawkins, and the vote was divided by a Greenback Party candidate, John R. Beasley. Hawkins and Beasley lost to Bate. Hawkins returned to Huntingdon, where he remained for the rest of his life. He died of pneumonia at age eighty-four, on April 27, 1905. His wife preceded him by four years. Both were buried at their family cemetery in Huntingdon, Tennessee. (Photograph courtesy of TSLA)

During the presidential campaign the public feeling was that President Hayes had performed adequately despite the ill will surrounding his election and the continued opposition by the Democrats, who by 1880 controlled both the House and the Senate. Even though Hayes was not nominated as the Republican candidate, he had considerable general support from his party. The election was close, with Garfield receiving 4,453,295 popular votes to 4,414,082 for Hancock (214 to 155 electoral votes). Garfield's win provided the sixth successive presidential election victory for the Republican Party. He became the twentieth president of the United States. This ensured twenty-four years of continual Republican residence in the White House. The Democrats lost the House to Republicans during this election cycle. The Senate was even with 37 Democrats, 37 Republicans, and 2 other.

In the election year of 1880 the crowded field of Tennessee Democratic candidates gave the Republicans a chance. With the Democratic vote split, Republican Hawkins was elected governor. He received 103,964 votes to 78,783 for Wright, the "high tax, state credit Democrat;" 57,080 for Wilson, the "low tax Democrat;" and 3,459 for Edwards, the Greenback candidate. Hawkins won the election, but his vote count was less than the total of the 139,322 for the other three candidates. The newly elected legislature consisted of fifteen Democrats and ten Republicans in the Senate, and thirty-six Democrats, thirty-seven Republicans, and one Greenback in the House. This election showed that the Democrats could be defeated in a governor's race, but only when they were fighting among themselves and badly divided on the issues. It also taught them that they needed to stick together in order to maintain power.

After Republican Alvin Hawkins was inaugurated governor of Tennessee in early 1881, he at once went to work on the state's debt problem. His administration made some progress, although the problem was not totally resolved. The legislature passed a new plan, by only one vote in the state senate, which satisfied New York bondholders by paying a 3 percent interest on the debt.

In 1881 it was time for the state legislature to elect or reelect a U.S. senator. Senator James E. Bailey had been elected to fill the unexpired term created by the death of former president and senator, Andrew Johnson. David McKendree Key had first, via a governor's appointment, taken Johnson's seat; however, in 1877, the legislature elected Bailey to complete the term. Now, in 1881 he stood for reelection. A bitter legislative battle for votes ensued, and Bailey could not obtain the necessary numbers. Republicans, encouraged by the election of a Republican governor, at first considered electing Horace Maynard, who had served as a First District congressman before the Civil War and as a statewide U.S. Representative from the 1872 race. They eventually realized that the Democrats, even though divided among themselves, would not tolerate a Tennessee Republican in the U.S. Senate, under any circumstances. They then supported someone relatively new to state politics, Howell Edmunds Jackson. Jackson was a prewar Whig turned Democrat and a supporter of the "high tax" plan to solve the state debt. This was enough of a common ground to hold Republican legislators in his corner. Although he did not receive all the Democratic votes, Jackson, who had surfaced as a compromise candidate, was elected. He began serving on March 4, 1881. (His term was to continue until March 3, 1887, but he resigned April 14, 1886, to accept a judicial appointment.)

HOWELL EDMUNDS JACKSON was born April 8, 1832, in Paris, Tennessee. When he was about eight years old his parents moved to Jackson, Tennessee. He was educated in the traditional manner of the day and then graduated from West Tennessee College in 1848. He studied at Lebanon Law School in Lebanon, Tennessee, and graduated in 1856. He had developed a good law practice, but moved to Memphis in 1858 and formed a firm with David M. Currin, who had previously served in Congress. During the Civil War, he served as "receiver" for Confederate sequestration. After the war he returned to Memphis to practice in the firm of Estes and Jackson—later Estes, Ellett, and Jackson. (Henry T. Ellett was a former supreme court justice in Mississippi.)

Jackson married twice. His first wife, Sophia Melloy of Memphis, died in 1873. His second wife was Mary E. Harding, whom he married the following year. (Senator Jackson's brother, William H. Jackson, who graduated from West Point Military Academy, married Mary's sister.) He then moved his family back to Jackson, Tennessee, and formed a law partnership with General Alexander W. Campbell. In 1880 Jackson was elected to the state legislature. In 1881, he became the compromise candidate, receiving enough Republican and Democratic votes to become a Tennessee U.S. senator, replacing Senator James E. Bailey. Jackson served as senator until Democrat President Grover Cleveland appointed him federal circuit judge for the Sixth Circuit on April 11, 1886. He remained a federal judge until February 1893, when Republican President Benjamin Harrison appointed him an associate justice of the U.S. Supreme Court when Democrat senators threatened to block all Republican nominees. Jackson served on the Supreme Court of the United States until his death on August 8, 1895. (Photograph courtesy of SHO)

President Garfield was never allowed to leave his mark on the presidency. On July 2, 1881, Charles J. Guiteau, a disappointed office seeker, shot Garfield at the Baltimore and Potomac railroad station. The president clung to life until September 19, 1881. Later, on June 30, 1882, Guiteau was hung.

After Garfield's death, Vice President Chester A. Arthur became the twenty-first president of the United States. During his term, the navy was upgraded. He oversaw the passage of the Pendleton Act, created to develop a bipartisan Civil Service Commission. This commission set up guidelines for government jobs and written examinations for potential government employees. It also protected the employees from discharge for political reasons.

In the midterm elections of 1882, Democrats again took control of the U.S. House with 200 Democrats to 119 Republicans and 6 others. The Republicans regained the Senate with 40 to 36 Democrats.

On the Tennessee political scene the "low tax" leaders in the legislature challenged the new plan to solve the state debt in the supreme court of Tennessee. By early 1882, in a three to two decision, the court declared it unconstitutional.

In 1882, even though Democrats had officially reunified for the purpose of recapturing total power, they were still divided. At the Tennessee Democratic Convention, James E. Bailey and Duncan B. Cooper and their supporters left the state convention with about one-tenth of the delegates.

However, the convention proceeded to nominate a candidate for governor. Senator Isham G. Harris, a "Bourbon Democrat" leader, led the momentum for consolidation of the remaining delegates. William B. Bate, a former Confederate general and Sumner County lawyer, who was known around the state for serving as an elector for Tilden, as well as for his position on the state debt issue, became the Bourbon Democrat nominee for governor.

In the general election of 1882 Democrat Bate faced incumbent Governor Alvin Hawkins. Also in the race was Joseph H. Fussell, the "state credit" Democratic candidate. Fussell was from Columbia, Tennessee, and had the support of Duncan Cooper and James E. Bailey—those Democrats not agreeing with the Bourbons. Also in the race was Greenback candidate John R. Beasley, who was from Franklin County.

Tennessee Democrats had learned from the election of 1880 what a division of vote would do to them in the general election. This time they held together. Bate campaigned on the plan to repay the state debt in full for bonds held on schools, charities, etc., and by the late President Polk's widow, Sarah Childress Polk. His plan called for the repayment of the remainder of the bonds at 50 percent of the debt and 3 percent interest.

On election day 1882, the Democrats reclaimed their prize by over 27,000 votes. General William B. Bate was elected governor receiving 120,637 votes to 93,168 for Hawkins, 9,660 for Beasley, and 4,814 for Fussell. Bate was inaugurated in 1883. The people of Tennessee, the legislators, and the bondholders were all ready for him to resolve the state debt issue. It had been many years since the initial financing of war-torn railroads and the spendthrift radical and hostile military government had turned the state's finances into a fiscal nightmare.

The debt accumulated under Brownlow's administration was finally settled at 50 percent face value for most of the railroad bonds. This was the most Tennessee would tolerate repaying since they were convinced of the fraudulent dealings on the part of the legislators under Brownlow's administration. However, other bonds, created before Brownlow's administration, were thought to be honest encumbrances and Tennesseans agreed they should be paid in full. Some questionable debts were even paid at higher rates of 76 percent and 80 percent, and a few owned by educational institutions, charities, and President Polk's widow were paid at 100 percent. In any event, after years of debate and political battles, the issue was finally resolved.

Also at issue in 1883 were health, sanitation, and economic recovery. The plight of the farmer, however, took the forefront. During this era, there were 165,000 small farms in Tennessee. Farmers were routinely forced to go into debt to produce crops. A good growth year resulted in general overproduction and lower prices. A bad crop year resulted in lower production and lower revenues, although at higher rates. The railroads and steamers controlled shipping rates; manufacturers controlled equipment prices; merchants controlled seed and supply prices; banks controlled mortgage rates; and the government taxed the farmer on the assessed value of his land, even though it might be mortgaged to the bank. Farmers were providing food but were at the mercy of other commercial interests. They needed some relief so that they could compete on an equal playing field, produce their crops, and make a reasonable profit. In 1883 farmers' protests resulted in the establishment of a state Railroad Commission to regulate railroad rates. The commission lasted a mere two years, when the legislature repealed the law that allowed rate control. (The repeal would cause trouble for the Democrats in the 1886 gubernatorial race.)

The debate over state control of rail rates was a demonstration of who held the political power; it was not the farmer. The railroad interests controlled state power. People wondered what security the common man, the independent businessman, could count on from his government. This was the question being asked around the state. Since most farmers were Democrats, a great deal of infighting recurred in the party. Even though the debt question was settled, there was still no peace among them. The plight of the farmer became the plight of the Democrats.

However, the concerns for the farmers had not yet reached a threshold that would again disrupt Democratic control of the governor's seat. Furthermore, the general economy had improved from the conditions brought on by the panic of 1875. Since

WILLIAM BRIMAGE BATE was born on November 7, 1826, in Sumner County, Tennessee. He was raised in Bledsoe Lick (later called Castalian Springs) and received an early rural education in local one- or two-room academy schools. His father died when he was fifteen, and William took on the task of maintaining the family farm. At sixteen, he became a clerk on a steamboat, the *Saladier,* which ran on the Cumberland and Mississippi Rivers between Nashville and New Orleans. At twenty-one he wanted more than what home life offered and joined the army, serving in the Mexican War beginning in 1845. He married Julia Peete, from Huntsville, Alabama, in 1856. They had four daughters, two of whom died at a young age.

After the war Bate went into the newspaper (Democrat) business in Castalian Springs and studied law at Lebanon Law School in Lebanon, Tennessee. He was also elected to the state legislature. He finished law school by age twenty-six and opened an office in Gallatin in 1852. He later became attorney general of the Nashville District in 1856 and an elector for Breckinridge in 1860. He served the Confederate infantry, entering as a private and attaining the rank of major general by war's end. A veteran of many battles, he was wounded three times and had six horses shot from under him. His brother, Captain Humphrey Bate, was killed at Shiloh, and William was severely injured. Two other family members, one cousin and his brother-in-law, were killed there and a cousin, Dr. Humphrey Bate, was wounded. Bate became extremely popular after distinguishing himself as a soldier. In 1863 he was offered the nomination as the Democrat candidate for governor. However, he declined the offer and remained with the army.

After the war Bate returned home to Castalian Springs, set up a law office in Nashville, and became a well-known and respected lawyer. In 1876 he became an elector for Tilden, and in 1882 he ran for governor as the Democrat nominee against Republican Alvin Hawkins, Greenback Party candidate John R. Beasley, and "state credit" Democrat Joseph Fussell. He was elected and reelected in 1884, and he and his fellow Democrats finally found a solution to the state debt issue. In 1886, he was elected by the legislature as U.S. senator and remained in that office until 1905. Five days after sitting in the cold in front of the U.S. Capitol while watching the inauguration of Teddy Roosevelt as president of the United States, Senator Bate died on January 9, 1905. He was buried in Mt. Olivet Cemetery in Nashville. (Photograph courtesy of SHO)

Governor Bate had made good on his promise to present a plan to settle the state debt, he held some advantage in the upcoming election, but winning was not a foregone conclusion. The Republicans nominated Frank T. Reid, a judge from Nashville, to face Bate.

Reid attacked Governor Bate over the manner in which the state debt had been settled. There were many who felt that a debt was an unavoidable obligation and that they had been jilted out of their money by being paid only a portion of the true debt. There was still a fair amount of lingering hostility over the issue. The plan required thirty years for the state to pay off the debt. The two candidates ran neck and neck, but in the end Democratic loyalty was enough to overcome the resentment over how to settle the debt issue. On election day 1884 Bate received 132,201 votes to 125,246 for Reid. William Bate was reelected Democrat governor of Tennessee.

On the national political scene in 1884, Republicans nominated James Blaine for president. Blaine had served as a U.S. senator from Maine as well as a congressman and Speaker of the House under President Grant. He had been involved in the railroad scandals, and a split developed among Republicans over his nomination that would linger into the election. He was also tainted, to Southerners, by the fact that he had worked as a Radical to impeach President Andrew Johnson. Considering the enemies he had made, the factions in the Republican Party, and the enmity of President Arthur, who had been denied the Republican nomination, Blaine faced an uphill battle.

In July 1884, the Democrats met in Cleveland, Ohio, and selected Grover Cleveland on the second ballot. Cleveland enjoyed a reputation for honesty by cleaning up the corruption of the Tammany machine in New York. Rising quickly after being elected sheriff in New York in 1870, he was elected mayor of New York City in 1881, governor of New York in 1882, and now was nominated for president of the United States in 1884. His reputation for honesty would pay off against the corruption-riddled Republicans.

The presidential campaign was nasty. Republicans charged Cleveland with fathering a son with a woman he did not marry. The Democrats charged Blaine with corruption. A Blaine spokesman in New York said that the Democratic Party was a party "of rum, Romanism [meaning Catholics], and rebellion" (Whitney 1982). Blaine was already having a hard time in the state of New York among friends of President Arthur, a New Yorker. Now he suffered more political damage from alienating the Catholics. In November 1884, Blaine lost New York and the election. Democrat Grover Cleveland was elected the twenty-second president of the United States, receiving 4,879,507 popular votes to 4,850,293 for Blaine (219 to 182 electoral votes). He was the first Democrat elected since the Civil War.

President Cleveland was inaugurated March 4, 1885. By 1886 he was facing the growing power of the labor unions. Cleveland's administration oversaw the first federal regulations of business. During this period the railroad industry and its leaders were politically powerful. They could set arbitrary rates, and since they essentially possessed a monopoly on long-range rapid transportation, they could hold companies or communities hostage to their rates. They were becoming more powerful than the government or the people. Cleveland and Congress passed the Interstate Commerce Act in 1887, then reclaimed over eighty million acres of public land grants which were being used to the advantage of the railroads.

In 1886 U.S. Senator Howell Jackson was appointed a federal judge, and he officially resigned his Senate seat on April 14. Governor William Bate then appointed Washington Curran Whitthorne to fill the seat (Class 1), and he began serving on April 16, 1886. The term would be complete on March 3, 1887. There was speculation that Governor Bate selected Whitthorne in order to hold the seat for himself.

The War of the Roses; Continued Democrat Dominance

Governor Bate's great goal was to become a U.S. senator. Indeed, he had spent the last part of his tenure as governor preparing to make his move. Therefore, he did not run for reelection in 1886. The gubernatorial campaign of that year shaped up into a heated spectacle to find a successor and became a memorable period in Tennessee history. Republicans held a slight opportunity in 1886. Farmers, who were mostly Democrats, were angry over the legislature's repeal of state regulations of railroad rates. The high rates were hurting farmers. They felt that the railroads held a monopoly which placed high prices on the transfer of crops to market. In addition, other sectors of the economy held the farmers at their economic mercy. Some of the powerful banks and companies possessed much more organized political influence than did the farmers. Farmers had wanted something done for financial relief, had temporarily seen some improvement with the establishment of the Railroad Commission in 1883, and then had seen rate controls repealed. The reversal

WASHINGTON CURRAN WHITTHORNE was born April 19, 1825, near Petersburg, Lincoln County, Tennessee. His family soon moved to Farmington, in Bedford County, where he received his early education. At age fourteen he went to school in Arrington, Williamson County, for eighteen months, then attended college in Lebanon, Tennessee. He next attended the University of Nashville and then the University of Tennessee at Knoxville. After finishing school at eighteen in 1843, he moved to Columbia and studied law with Polk and Thomas (James K. Polk would be elected president in 1844), and began practicing law in 1845. After Polk became president, Whitthorne became a clerk in the Sixth Auditor's Office. Later, Whitthorne worked in the Post Office Department and the Fourth Auditor's Office. By January 1848 Whitthorne, under Polk's advice, was back in Tennessee with plans to begin a political career.

Whitthorne married June Campbell of Columbia. In 1853 he lost an election for state representative, but was elected to the state senate in 1855 and 1857. In 1859 he was elected to the state house, where he became speaker. He was an elector-at-large for the state for Breckinridge in 1860. He served as assistant adjutant general of the Provisional Army of Tennessee, with the rank of lieutenant colonel, via appointment by Governor Isham Harris. After the Civil War Whitthorne returned to Columbia and resumed his law practice. In 1870, he was elected to Congress and then reelected five times. He was appointed to fill the U.S. Senate seat by Governor Bate when Howell Jackson resigned to become federal judge. He served only a year, until 1887, and then returned to the U.S. House, where he remained until he died on September 21, 1891. (Photograph courtesy of SHO) was blamed on the Democrats. With this kind of animosity toward Democrats, Republicans saw an opportunity. The Republican state convention of 1886 nominated Alfred "Alf" A. Taylor for governor.

The Democrats were divided into the Bourbons, who were the old-line conservative Southern politicians; the New South Group, who were the new industrialists, newspaper owners, leading agricultural leaders, and intellectuals who wanted political participation commensurate with their influence (which outweighed their numbers); and the Wool-Hat Boys, who were the common men and small farmers. Democrat leaders looked to the popular thirty-six-year-old Robert "Bob" Taylor to reunite their forces, though Taylor's nomination would not come without a good old Democratic Party fight. Finally, on the fifteenth ballot, Taylor was nominated by the Democratic state convention.

The unusual thing about this election was that Alf Taylor and Bob Taylor were

Brothers Alf and Bob Taylor campaign for governor, 1886. (Courtesy of TSLA)

brothers. They were from far East Tennessee, Alf now from Washington County and Bob from Carter County. Further exemplifying their lack of family political solidarity was their father. Nat Taylor had been involved in politics for years. He had served an unexpired term in the Thirty-third (1853–1855) Congress as a Whig but was defeated for reelection. In 1860 he was an elector for presidential candidate John Bell, the Constitutional Union candidate. In 1866 he was elected to Congress for a partial term, as a Republican. In 1886 Nat Taylor was a Prohibitionist more than a Democrat or Republican.

Both Taylor brothers were entertaining speakers and good storytellers. Bob had already served in the state legislature and had made many friends. During the campaign, the brothers stumped the state together and spoke from the same platform forty-one times. They both told entertaining stories, joked, and played the fiddle. One story goes that they stayed overnight at the boardinghouse of a Tennessean woman. The next morning she cut two roses and gave Bob a white rose and Alf a red rose. The rose wearing caught on at their next appearance, and their supporters starting sporting red or white roses, when they could get them, depending on which candidate they supported. Another story was told that on one stop Bob stole Alf's written speech from his bag and used it himself. Alf went right along and spoke on Bob's positions on the issues. The campaign was jokingly linked to the war between the Yorks and Lancasters of old European stock. Thus, the campaign was called the "War of the Roses."

Essentially this campaign was pure entertainment and displayed a lighter side of politics, and people enjoyed it. Both brothers were popular, but Alf was a Republican. Tennessee was a Democratic state, and Bob won by a sixteen-thousand-vote margin. He was elected at age thirty-seven, in 1886 and inaugurated in 1887. He served two terms.

Governor William Brimage Bate had long and often sought one of Tennessee's U.S. Senate posts. He was a popular man, but the competition for the U.S. Senate was always stiff. After serving four years as governor, he was well prepared to contend for the seat. When Washington Whitthorne stepped down in 1887, after holding the seat for the one-year hiatus after Senator Jackson's resignation, Bate was finally elected, but only after sixty-eight ballots. He began his Senate (Class 1) term on March 4, 1887. Senator Bate was repeatedly reelected and served until his death on March 9, 1905.

By presidential reelection time in 1888, President Cleveland had alienated a number of special interests groups, especially the railroad companies. Civil War veterans were also unhappy with him since he had vetoed a pension proposal. However, his biggest problem was the Tammany machine in New York. Cleveland had curtailed their power, and they were determined to be rid of him. Nevertheless, the Democrats, at the June 1888 national convention, nominated him by acclamation. Former Ohio Senator Allen G. Thurman was nominated for vice president.

The Republican National Convention met in Chicago in June 1888. The convention deadlocked between Ohio's John Sherman and Indiana's Walter Q. Gresham. Republican leaders, including former presidential nominee James Blaine, who was in Scotland and cabled his preference, sought a compromise candidate. Benjamin Harrison, who had served as governor and U.S. senator from Indiana, was nominated on the eighth ballot. Thomas A. Hendricks was named candidate for vice president. (Blaine was later named secretary of state.)

In November Cleveland received 5,537,857 popular votes to 5,447,129 for Harrison. However, due mainly to Tammany machine efforts, New York closely went for Harrison, giving him the huge electoral vote advantage of New York and, along with it, the victory (Harrison 233, Cleveland 168). Harrison was elected the twenty-third president of the United States. In 1888 Republicans also gained firm control of the House and Senate (House, 173 Republicans to 156 Democrats to 1 other; Senate, 47 Republicans to 37 Democrats).

ROBERT LOVE TAYLOR was born in Happy Valley, Carter County, Tennessee, on July 31, 1850, into a political family. His father was Nathaniel Green Taylor, a leader in early Tennessee who served in the House of Representatives as a Whig in the Thirty-third Congress, as an elector for Bell's Constitutional Union candidacy for president in 1860, and a partial term in Congress as a Republican in 1866. Robert Taylor's mother was Emaline Haynes Taylor, the daughter of Landon C. Haynes (Confederate senator from Tennessee). The Taylors were part of the John Sevier faction, while the Haynes family sided with the John Tipton faction. Robert Love Taylor was named after an ancestor, Robert Love. Taylor attended Pennington Seminary in Pennington, New Jersey, and received some education in Athens, Tennessee, at what was to become Milligan College. He learned to sing and play the fiddle, becoming quite an entertainer. Early in his life he raised tobacco and made bar iron. He studied law in Jonesboro, Tennessee, and then became active in political circles. He married Sarah L. Baird and they had five children.

By 1878 Taylor had begun practicing law. That same year, at age twenty-eight, he ran for Congress, as a Democrat, in the Republican First District. Considered a ridiculous attempt, Taylor ran against Republican incumbent Major A. H. Pettibone. A difficult campaign ensued, but Taylor won the term, which ran from March 4, 1879, to March 3, 1881, the only Democrat to ever serve in that district up to that time. He was defeated for reelection by Pettibone. Taylor's district had "probably brought forth more distinguished men in politics than any other District in the United States—not only distinguished names in Tennessee, but in many other States" (McKellar 1942). From this district came Andrew Johnson, John Sevier, William Blount, and many judges, senators, governors, Supreme Court justices, federal judges, congressmen, diplomats, and military leaders.

Taylor served part-time as editor of the *Johnson City Comet*. He was a presidential elector for Cleveland's Democratic candidacy in 1884. After Cleveland was elected, he rewarded Taylor with the post of pension agent for Knoxville. It was after this, in 1886, that he was involved in the humorous and historic "War of the Roses" in which he ran against his brother, Republican Alfred Taylor, for governor. He won and was reelected in 1888, serving until 1891. After Taylor became governor, the Democrats repealed the state's Prohibition laws, passed legislation to help ensure more honest election laws, and passed a law instituting the poll tax. Taylor became known as the "pardoning governor."

After Taylor's first wife, Sarah, died, their five children went to live with Bob's brother Alf until Bob remarried. His second marriage, to Alice Hill from Tuscaloosa, Alabama, did not last. In 1904, he married Mamie Love St. John, the daughter of a Virginia lawyer. Following Taylor's first tour as governor, he was again presidential elector for Cleveland in 1892, after which he went back into law practice in Chattanooga. In 1896 he was convinced to run again for governor in order to help

Tennessee Governor Bob Taylor had remained fairly popular with the people, but was criticized for his free hand at pardoning prisoners. He received his party's renomination in 1888, but only on the fortieth ballot of the state convention. He then faced Republican Samuel W. Hawkins and Prohibitionist J. C. Johnson. The Democrats were too strong for the Republicans, and Taylor was reelected, receiving 156,799, to Hawkins's 139,041, and Johnson's 6,893. Taylor's brother, Republican Alfred A. Taylor, was first elected to the U.S. House of Representatives in that same year.

---

carry Tennessee for William Jennings Bryan. Tennessee voted for Bryan (who lost to McKinley) and Taylor. Taylor then served as governor again, his third term, from 1897 until 1899.

Kenneth McKellar's memory of Bob Taylor is worth recounting here:

> I first saw Robert Love Taylor at the Lyceum Theater in the old Athletic Building at the corner of Union and Third Streets, Memphis, while a student at the University of Alabama in 1892, but temporarily visiting my mother's family in Memphis. I do not recall what the political meeting was about, but I think it was a rally for Cleveland and Stevenson, who were candidates for President and vice president in that year. I recall that Senator Isham G. Harris was one of the speakers, and he made a very long and able speech; but it was clear that the Tennessee hero of that campaign was former Governor Taylor. At the time he was only 42 years of age, but he had been a member of Congress for one term, had been governor twice, and had voluntarily refused to run for a third term. He was the idol of the occasion; and it was one of the most colorful assemblages I ever saw in Memphis. It seems to have been a social as well as a political event. Apparently, all the leaders of Memphis packed the auditorium to its capacity, and many were turned away.
>
> I recall that the personality of the man was what struck me with the greatest force. He was not only a great speaker, but a great actor, and he had the crowd in the hollow of his hand from the moment he rose. They cheered almost his every sentence. He was a candidate for Elector on Democrat national ticket that year. Of course, I had heard a great deal of Bob Taylor and the War of the Roses in which he and his brother took opposite sides; but that was the first time I had ever seen or heard him, and as a country boy I was carried away. (McKellar 1942)

In 1906 Taylor was elected as the Democratic nominee for U.S. Senate over Senator Carmack in a rare public primary (the legislature usually chose the senators). He was subsequently elected to the U.S. Senate after the primary by the legislature and served from 1907 until he died. Taylor became a delegate to the Democrat National Convention in Denver in 1908 which nominated William Jennings Bryan for the third time. While serving as U.S. senator in 1910, he was convinced by the Democratic Party to run against incumbent Governor Ben Hooper. Even though the Democrats were bitterly divided and the people were angry with their previous Democratic governor, Patterson, the party thought that the populous would forget all logic when it came to the popular Bob Taylor. The Democrats were disappointed, and Taylor was, of course, saddened with the rejection. In any event he remained a U.S. senator. Years earlier, in 1879, he had introduced one of the very first bills proposing an "income tax." He continued to support the plan until the amendment was passed on July 12, 1909, when he was senator. This was later ratified in joint resolution on February 3, 1913. Robert Love Taylor died, while still serving in the U.S. Senate, on March 31, 1912. When his body was returned by train from Washington to Knoxville, large crowds gathered to mourn the famous and very likable Tennessean. He was buried in Monte Vista Cemetery in Johnson City, Tennessee. (Photograph courtesy of SHO)

In 1889, after Bob Taylor was inaugurated governor, another volatile issue came to the forefront. Tension surrounded liquor probition laws to the point that a public referendum was held in Tennessee. On election day the Prohibition movement received 117,504 votes, but those who supported the use of alcohol tallied 135,197.

During Taylor's tenure as governor, the Democrats became somewhat more harmonious. The governor saw legislation passed that helped increase school funding and altered election protocols. The Dortch Law was passed which stated that in high population counties, voters' ballots would be marked in privacy (unless the voter required assistance due to disability or blindness). The Meyer Registration Law required communities of over five hundred to register voters. The Lea Election Law required separate ballot boxes for state and federal elections. A poll tax law was also passed that enforced the constitution of 1870, essentially disenfranchising the poor, especially Black Republicans.

After President Harrison was inaugurated March 4, 1889, the Republican-controlled House and Senate soon passed the Sherman Anti-Trust Act, designed to prevent large business organizations from influencing or controlling commerce. Congress also voted to increase pensions to Civil War veterans. To pay for the expenditures, tariffs were increased to new highs on imported goods via the McKinley Tariff Act of 1890. The Democrats called this Congress the "Billion Dollar Congress." It was not long before the prices of goods sold in the United States increased. With the increased federal expenditures, the resultant tariff, and the ultimate increase in costs of goods to consumers, the nation's cost of living increased, and the mood of the nation changed. The people became furious with the Republicans. Common wage earners, farmers, and laborers went to the polls in 1890 and they "threw the rascals out" (Whitney 1982), enabling the Democrats to take over the House (231 Democrats to 88 Republicans to 14 other). This was an eighty-five-seat loss for Republicans in the House, though they maintained control of the Senate, which was still elected by state legislatures rather than by popular vote (47 Republicans to 39 Democrats to 2 other). By 1890 six new states had been admitted into the Union—South Dakota, North Dakota, Idaho, Washington, Wyoming, and Montana. Electric lights were first placed in the White House during Harrison's tenure.

Although the Democrats controlled Tennessee, the state's political balance would receive a gentle rock. The disruption would come not to the Democrats, but to the small minority of Republicans in Tennessee. One of these Republicans was a man named Henry Clay Evans. Evans was born in Pennsylvania, reared in Wisconsin, and had come to Tennessee during the Civil War as a Union soldier. After the war, Evans became successful in the iron foundry industry. As an active Republican leader in the state party, he served as school commissioner, alderman, mayor of Chattanooga, and congressman for the Third Congressional District from 1888 to 1890. (He had lost his initial race in 1884, and then was again defeated in 1890 and 1892.)

There were two factions of Republicans in East Tennessee during this era: the "pro-administration," "GAR," "carpetbagger" (Northern) Republicans; and the "anti-administration" or "home" (Native) Republicans. Evans's Northern Republican background assisted him in developing a close relationship with President Harrison. Harrison likely appreciated knowing a

Tennessee congressman with a mutual ideology, and possibly viewed Evans as a point man for him in the solid Democratic South. Evans became a source of patronage for Tennesseans because of his relationship with President Harrison. Nevertheless, Republican factional bickering did not help Evans's chances for reelection.

Tennessee Democrats did not like the fact that Evans, whom they viewed as a carpetbagger Republican, had taken a congressional seat in the first place. They traditionally controlled the state except for the First and Second District congressional seats in East Tennessee. Even when there was a Republican in the White House, Tennessee Democrats expected to control that patronage. The close relationship between East Tennessee Republicans and the Democrats in the rest of the state usually supported total Democratic dominance during times of either Republican or Democrat presidents. The East Tennessee Republicans needed only to cooperate with the Democrats during times of a Republican presidency and statewide Democrat gubernatorial contests. For this, the Democrats would ensure that those cooperating East Tennessee Republicans maintained continued access to state power.

The current problem was that Evans did not view the Republican Party as subservient to state Democrats. The Democrats, of course, attacked. The *Nashville American,* a leading Democrat newspaper, was severely critical of Evans, painting him as anti-Southern. Evans and Republican Congressman Houk, from the Second District, supported the Lodge Federal Elections Bill of 1890 (Force Bill), but Evans was the one who was attacked for it. The Force Bill was designed to establish federal control over presidential and congressional elections. The Democrats controlled the Tennessee legislature, and they were determined to maintain their power. The easiest way to get rid of a Republican was to bring Democratic voters into his district, and that was the method with which they attacked Evans. They changed the boundaries of the Third District, injuring Evans's chances for reelection.

They also began creating a series of new election laws, between 1889 and 1901 which included

> separate ballot boxes for state and federal elections, voter registration in districts casting over 500 votes, use of the secret ballot in specified election districts, and the imposition of the poll tax. The effect of these changes was to reduce participation, especially among Blacks and poorer Whites. These people found it difficult to pay the poll tax, were unaccustomed to maintaining voting credentials, and often lacked the education necessary to read and understand the secret ballot. Participation levels among Blacks plummeted to near zero, and the level among poor Whites dropped perceptibly. (Shahan1993)

It also did not help Evans that other Republicans resented his influence with President Harrison. Their jealousy was so intense that they simply did not provide the help necessary to protect him. Republican infighting, Democrat maneuvering, and his support of a bill to safeguard Black suffrage contributed to Evan's defeat for reelection in 1890. However, the determined Evans would remain in the center of Republican efforts in Tennessee for some time to come.

Even though Second District Republican U.S. Representative Leonidas C. Houk had supported the Force Bill, he was reelected in 1890. Houk was the leader of the "Native" or "anti-administration" faction and a long-time boss of the Republican Party in Tennessee. Alfred A. Taylor, who was First District representative and also a "Native"-leaning Tennessee Republican, was also reelected in 1890. It was not that these Republicans did not want more Republicans elected to office, but they wanted to control Republican presidential patronage, which was their source of power.

During the political infighting, the state was dealing with economic upheaval. Since the Civil War, farm product prices had been falling, while the costs for supplies, transportation of products, and related expenses required for the farmer to raise his crops had risen. Various farm organizations began forming, beginning in the 1870s. By 1889 the groups had evolved or merged into an organization called the Farmers Alliance. The group also included teachers, doctors, preachers, and other rural-based businessmen. The members of the alliance worked to have the president of the Farmers' Alliance, John P. Buchanan, from Rutherford County, receive the Democratic nomination for governor. Their effort focused on the economy and the hardships of the small farmer/businessman and pitted the small farmers, called the "Hayseed" Democrats, "Wool-Hat Boys," or the "Alliance" against the "Bourbons," who were the big-business Democrats. Urban newspapers across Tennessee ridiculed Buchanan and his chances for the nomination. They even made light of the idea of a farmer obtaining the nomination. However, when it became apparent that Buchanan had serious support, some editors admitted that Buchanan "was not the buffoon they had earlier represented him to be" (Corlew 1981).

By the time of the Democratic state convention on July 15, 1890, Buchanan was a committed candidate for governor. However, the Bourbon Democrats had their candidate, Memphian Josiah Patterson (father of Malcolm Patterson, a future governor), and had little intention to relinquish power. Another faction, the "Colyar" Democrats, supported Nashville railroad businessman Jere Baxter. John M. Taylor, from West Tennessee, also competed for the nomination. The battle for the Democratic nomination went on for twenty-six ballots and lasted six days. Finally, Buchanan was nominated.

The Republicans nominated Nashville banker Lewis T. Baxter. The Prohibitionists chose a Methodist minister named David Cato Kelley. Because the Democrats kept their disagreements within the Democratic Party and prevented a party split, John Buchanan was elected governor in 1890 and inaugurated in early 1891.

During his term Buchanan oversaw the development of laws designed to help regulate the sale of fertilizer products sold to farmers. Pensions were created for disabled Confederated veterans. The poll tax law was strengthened. A law was passed that prevented restraint of trade. Restrictions were placed on foreign companies in Tennessee. Also, efforts were made to improve education (funding, curricula, school organization).

During this period of Democratic dominance in Tennessee, Republicans continued their infighting. Republican Congressman Houk died in 1891, and his son, John C. Houk, was elected to complete his father's unexpired term in the Second District. John Houk evidently saw Republican Henry Clay Evans as a political adversary (as his father had) and tried to prevent Evans's participation as a delegate to the Republican National Convention scheduled for Minneapolis in June 1892. On this count Evans prevailed, but Houk

JOHN PRICE BUCHANAN was born on October 4, 1847, in Williamson County, Tennessee, to Thomas and Margaret Sample Buchanan. Their forebears were among the friends and fellow pioneers with James Robertson at the time of the early settlement of Nashville in 1779. They settled Buchanan Station in 1782. Buchanan received the common education available to the settlers in this day. When he was sixteen, he served under Nathan Bedford Forrest during the Alabama campaigns of the Civil War. Around 1869 he married Frances McGill of Rutherford County, Tennessee. She was the daughter of James McGill and Amanda Norman McGill.

Buchanan became a successful farmer and a leader within farming organizations. In 1886 he was elected to the state legislature and reelected in 1888. After being elected president of the Farmers Alliance, which took control of the Democrat state convention in 1890, Buchanan was nominated for governor. He became the first full-time farmer, whose sole livelihood was derived from farming, elected governor. His election sprang from the Farmers' Alliance's attempt to even the economic playing field and relieve the oppression of the monopolistic control of transportation by the railroad industry. As governor, Buchanan had to deal with riots by prisoners who were forced to work, and coal miners whose work was threatened by cheap prison labor. The national guard (First, Second, and Third Tennessee Regiments) had to be called out to control the riots. Buchanan helped enact the secondary school law, which among other things, added Tennessee history and civics to the curricula. He also helped provide for Confederate pensions.

While Buchanan was governor, his wife stayed on the farm rearing their eight children, taking care of the livestock, and raising the crops. After the Regular Democrats regained control of the next state convention, Buchanan knew he could not wrestle control of the Democrat nomination again in 1892, so he ran as an Independent. He lost and returned to his farm, where he and his family lived until 1926. Then he and his wife moved to Murfreesboro. She died on November 30, 1927. John Buchanan died on May 14, 1930, and was buried in Murfreesboro. (Photograph courtesy of TSLA)

and his friends did take control of the state Republican Party.

Even though Republicans had been seriously damaged in the 1890 midterm elections, they did not change course. At the June 1892 Minneapolis Republican National Convention, Harrison was again challenged for the nomination by Maine's Blaine, but Harrison was renominated on the first ballot. Whitlaw Reid was chosen as the vice presidential candidate. There were 120 Black delegates seated at the Republican National Convention in 1892.

The Democratic National Convention met in Chicago in June 1892. Grover Cleveland was nominated in spite of the Tammany-controlled delegation from New York which voted against its own resident. Cleveland won the nomination on the first ballot. Former Illinois Congressman Adlai E. Stevenson was nominated for vice president.

During the 1880s, America was undergoing a transition from an agricultural to an industrial society. Although the Sherman Anti-Trust Act had been passed, the high tariffs, spending, and inflation under the Harrison administration made Republicans vulnerable in 1892.

The Populist Party, formed in response to the country's economic situation, nominated Iowan General James B. Weaver for president. Weaver campaigned for silver coinage and an income tax. The party did little except draw votes from Republicans, helping Democrat Cleveland, who won 5,555,426 popular votes to Harrison's 5,182,690 to Weaver's 1,029,846 (277 to 145 to 22 electoral votes). Cleveland was elected the twenty-fourth president of the United States. He became the only president to be reelected after a defeat.

Meanwhile in Tennessee, Henry Clay Evans tried to regain his Third Congressional District seat in 1892. Republican U.S. Representative John C. Houk from the Second District led an effort to damage Evans's chances for election. Evans did lose, but he continued to remain active. In fact, President Harrison appointed Evans the first assistant postmaster general, in the early part of 1893 prior to Cleveland's inauguration.

Hayseed Democrat Governor Buchanan could actually do little to lessen the plight of the farmer. Federal legislation would ultimately be required to assist the small farmer. Buchanan had to deal with irate miners who were upset over the state's policy of leasing convicts to perform mine work. This set off riots and attacks by miners in East Tennessee who were losing their jobs to prisoners.

The Bourbon and Colyar Democratic factions could not accept an outsider as governor and sought to reclaim political dominance. The development of the Populist Party during this time drew some supporters away from the Hayseed Democrats. After the short-lived Hayseed victory in 1890 with the election of Buchanan, the Bourbon Democrats bounced back, choosing the chief justice of the Tennessee Supreme Court, Peter Turney, as the 1892 Democrat gubernatorial candidate. Turney's father, Hopkins L. Turney, was a former U.S. senator from Tennessee. The younger Turney's popularity stemmed from his attempt, along with his friends, to secede Franklin County from Tennessee in 1861, because he did not feel Tennessee had acted quickly enough to secede from the Union.

When Governor Buchanan realized that he had no chance of regaining the Democratic nomination, he withdrew as a Democratic nominee. Turney had little difficulty winning the Democratic nomination at the state convention. The Populists, Farmers Alliance supporters, and some mainstream Democrats supported Buchanan, who now ran as an Independent candidate. So Independent Buchanan and Democrat Turney ran against Republican George W. Winstead of Dresden, Tennessee, and Edward H. East, the Prohibitionist candidate. The Democrats accused Buchanan of a deal with Republicans designed to take votes from Turney in exchange for a fifteen-thousand-dollar payoff and later support for Buchanan for the U.S. Senate. Buchanan denied the accusations, but of course some people wanted to believe them. Peter Turney was elected governor of Tennessee in 1892, but with less than half the votes, and the Bourbon Democrats were now back in power.

On the national scene, President Cleveland knew the first order of business was to restabilize the national economy. The free spending of the Harrison administration, combined with the flow of gold out of the United States, had injured the nation's economy, as well as Tennessee's. By the time Cleveland was inaugurated on March 4, 1893, the Philadelphia and Reading Railroad was bankrupt with $125 million in debt. By May of 1893 the stock market collapsed.

During Cleveland's second term as president, he appointed Tennessee Democrat attorney McGavock Dickinson as assistant U.S. attorney general. Dickinson was the grandson of Felix Grundy. His wife was a former Overton and his mother was

PETER TURNEY was born in 1827 in Marion County, Tennessee. His mother was Teresa Frances Turney, the daughter of Miller Frances and Hannah Henry Frances. His father was Hopkins L. Turney, who had served Tennessee as a U.S. senator (elected by Andrew Johnson and the "Immortal Thirteen"). Turney received his schooling in Winchester and Nashville. He studied law under his father, and in 1848 began practice. He married Casandra Garner, who was fifteen at the time, in June 1851. She was the daughter of Thomas and Elizabeth Wadlington Garner from Franklin County, Tennessee. The Turneys had three children before Casandra died about 1857. His second marriage was to Hannah Graham, the daughter of John Graham and Aletha Roberts Graham from Davidson County, Tennessee. The second Turney union produced nine more children.

Just prior to the Civil War, Turney was a loyal Southerner, eager for battle and determined that his area of Tennessee would secede from the Union. He organized a regiment, and went to fight in Virginia even before Tennessee had seceded. An early injury—a wound to the throat—forced him to return to Tennessee to recover. Later he returned to battle by taking command of a regiment in Florida. His family followed, staying in Monticello, Florida. While they were away, the Yankees burned his home. His First Tennessee Regiment eventually surrendered at Appomattox.

After the war, Turney returned home to practice law. He was elected judge on the supreme court in 1870 and served in that position for twenty-three years. In 1892 he won the Democrat nomination for governor and defeated Governor Buchanan in his try for a second term. The Regular Democrats were now determined to hold power, and Turney was a popular figure the party could rally behind. As governor, he oversaw the end to prison unrest and the prisoner work (lease) program.

In 1894 Turney stood for reelection. However, Republican Henry Clay Evans outpolled him and won the election. Turney and his political supporters claimed that many Evans voters had not paid poll taxes and were therefore disqualified. The Democratic-controlled legislature determined that the counties with the most "fraudulent votes" were counties that had gone for Evans. Therefore, they determined that Turney was the rightful governor. After Evans had already taken the oath, he was removed from office and Turney was inaugurated for his second term on May 8, 1895. During his second term, preparations were begun for the state's centennial celebration. After his two terms as governor (1893–1897), Turney returned to Winchester and the practice of law. He died in Winchester in 1903 and was buried in his hometown. (Photograph courtesy of TSLA)

a McGavock. Dickinson was President Cleveland's Tennessee Democratic confidante of sorts.

In 1893 Walter Preston Brownlow made his bid for the First Congressional District seat official. He was the nephew of William G. Brownlow, the Radical Reconstruction governor of Tennessee from 1856 until 1869. Walter Brownlow had moved to Tennessee from Virginia after his father's death. As a thirteen-year-old applicant, he was turned down for the Union army. He eventually bought the Jonesboro, Tennessee, *Herald and Tribune*, which he maintained for the remainder of his life. He served as doorkeeper of the U.S. House of Representatives beginning in 1881 and later became assistant superintendent of the U.S. Senate folding room in 1886. He advanced to superintendent and remained in that position until the Democrats took control of the Senate in 1893. Tennessee's First District congressman, Alfred A. Taylor, hired him as his personal secretary in 1893. Once in Congressman Taylor's office, Brownlow began creating alliances with his fellow East Tennesseans. He became active in Tennessee Republican Party affairs by serving as a member of the First District, State Executive, and Republican National Committees. Over the years, he also was a delegate to Republican National Conventions. By the time of his announcement for Congress in 1893, Brownlow was an influential Republican leader in the First District.

Because the First District was overwhelmingly Republican, receiving the Republican nomination was tantamount to election. Brownlow had significant competition for the nomination, and the convention fight held all the intensity of an open election. After a deadlock, Brownlow withdrew in favor of W. C. Anderson, who was nominated on the 144th ballot. Although Anderson won, he served under a Democratic president. This meant no patronage from which to build loyalty, and therefore, a tenuous hold on the congressional seat.

A Shameful Election; Republican Minority

For several years prior to 1894, Tennessee Democrats had fought among themselves concerning several issues, including the use of convicts to mine coal in East Tennessee and the farmers' plight in dealing with high costs of operation and low prices for products. These debates created factions within the Tennessee Democratic Party, and no Democratic governor could resolve the issues to everyone's satisfaction. Additionally, the financial panic of 1893 created significant disenchantment among voters, most of whom were Democrats.

The gubernatorial election of 1894 shaped up to be a three-party race. The Democrats renominated Governor Peter Turney. Republican Henry Clay Evans and his colleagues had taken control of the state Republican Party in 1894. Fellow Chattanoogan Newell Sanders, Evans's ally, was elected chairman of the state Republican Party, helping Evans gain the party nomination as the Republican candidate for governor. The Populist Party joined the 1884 gubernatorial contest and nominated Nashville schoolteacher A. L. Mims. The Prohibitionists did not nominate a candidate. Tennessee Democrats were divided over the coal miner issue and the economy. Governor Turney was somewhat ill during the campaign and the sixty-seven-year-old governor had *Commercial Appeal* newspaper editor Edward Ward Carmack stand in for his speaking engagements. Evans, a Chattanooga industrialist, was no stranger to politics. He was much younger than Turney and very active. He had won four terms as a Chattanooga alderman, two terms as mayor of Chattanooga, and a single election as U.S. representative. He criticized President Cleveland for the gold crisis and Turney for his lack of administrative ability. Turney accused Evans of being a carpetbagger and supporting the Force Bill during his one term in Congress. Ohio Governor William McKinley came to Tennessee and spoke on Evans's behalf at a rally in Chattanooga on October 20, 1894.

Turney's support was weak in the Memphis and Nashville areas. This was enough for H. Clay Evans, a Republican, to win the election for governor (105,104 for Evans to 104,356 for Turney and 23,088 for Mims). Evans achieved this win in spite of opposition within his own party. Republicans Houk and Brownlow did not want any competition for Republican power should a Republican regain the White House. Additional trouble for Evans stemmed from the fact that the legislature was controlled by Democrats. When they went into session on January 5, 1895, they formed a committee, comprised of seven Democrats and five Republicans to investigate the election results. The Democratic majority members, claiming twenty-three thousand votes to be fraudulent, declared that Turney actually won the election by two thousand votes. The Republican minority members submitted a report stating that the committee was controlled by the Democrats, who were partisan, and that the election of 1894 was as fair as any election in Tennessee. When the joint session of the legislature met, they voted seventy to fifty-seven for the Democrat majority report. They denied Evans the election and returned incumbent Governor Peter Turney to office.

HENRY CLAY EVANS was born in Juniata County, Pennsylvania, on June 18, 1843, to Col. Jesse B. and Anna Single Evans. His family moved to Plateville, Grant County, Wisconsin in 1844. He attended common schools, worked on his family farm, then attended business school in Madison and later graduated from business school in Chicago in 1861. He worked as a clerk for his brother, who was the county register, and served in the state militia, achieving the rank of colonel.

Evans joined the Union Army May 6, 1864, enlisting as a corporal, Company A, Forty-first Regiment, Wisconsin Volunteer Infantry. He was involved in battles in the area of Chattanooga, Tennessee. In September 1864 he received an honorable discharge, and settled in Chattanooga, taking a job with the quarter-master department. Soon he became involved with the manufacturing of railroad cars and organized the Chattanooga Car and Foundry Company. Two years later he joined the Roane Iron Company, where he remained for ten years. On February 18, 1869, he married Adelaide Durand of Westfield, New York.

Evans served as an alderman in Chattanooga and was elected mayor in 1881 and 1882. He organized the Chattanooga public school system and served as the first school commissioner. A Republican, he lost a contest for the U.S. House of Representatives for the Third Congressional District in 1884, but was elected in 1888 and served one term. He was defeated for reelection in 1890 and in a comeback attempt in 1892. He was appointed first assistant postmaster general by President Harrison, serving from 1891 to 1893. In 1894, he was elected Republican governor of Tennessee, defeating incumbent Democrat governor Peter Turney. However, his election was challenged by Turney and the Democratic-controlled state legislature. Enough votes were declared invalid by the legislature to swing the election to Turney. Many felt that the legislature had violated the will of the electorate in denying Evans the post. President McKinley appointed him U.S. commissioner of pensions on April 1, 1897. He served until May 13, 1902, after he received appointment as consul general to London by President Theodore Roosevelt on May 9, 1902. He served until 1905.

Evans remained active in Tennessee politics and the Tennessee Republican Party. He served as delegate-at-large to the Republican National Convention in 1892, 1896, 1904, and as delegate in 1908. He was selected as commissioner of health and education for Chattanooga in 1911. Evans died in Chattanooga on December 12, 1921, and was buried in Forest Hill Cemetery, St. Elmo, Chattanooga, Tennessee. (Photograph courtesy of CHCBL)

Turney was inaugurated on May 8, 1895. Evans's initial win startled the Tennessee Democrats and threatened their political dominance. The manner in which they manipulated the legislature in order to maintain power stained the honor of the state of Tennessee. "Many Democratic newspapers termed the [Tennessee legislature] action a 'steal' second only to the Tilden-Hayes presidential election of 1876" (Corlew 1981). Furthermore, Evans's denial of the governor's seat by the Democratic legislature created a national controversy. This made his name well-known and Evans became a hero to Republicans across the nation.

There were not many Southern Republicans at this time (except in East Tennessee), and because of his notoriety, Evans became what was likely the best known Southern Republican in the nation. There was even discussion of him being considered for the vice presidential nomination in the upcoming 1896 presidential contest.

In a turn of events, Second District Republican Congressman John C. Houk was defeated for reelection by Henry R. Gibson in 1894. Congressman Houk's reputation had been damaged among his East Tennessee Republican constituents because he had worked against Evans's Third Congressional District campaign in 1892.

Meanwhile, President Cleveland's efforts to stabilize the currency and economy did not solve the national crisis. Companies went bankrupt, unions struck, farm prices collapsed, and many individuals lost their jobs. By 1896 the Democrats had lost confidence in Cleveland's ability to control the economy and searched for someone who could rally the public and save Democratic congressional seats. At the Chicago Democratic National Convention in July 1896, they thought they had found this person in William Jennings Bryan. Bryan was an electrifying speaker, and Democrats selected this Nebraskan as the presidential nominee. President Cleveland was humiliated by the Democratic platform which repudiated his "gold standard" economic approach in favor of a "free silver" policy. Few Democrats possessed the patience to wait out the natural downturn in the economy. After Bryan was nominated, Cleveland refused to support him. To Cleveland's credit, he turned down the opportunity to run for a third term as a Democrat split-party (Gold Democrat or National Democrat) candidate.

In Tennessee, Walter Brownlow decided to run again for the First Congressional District seat. The Republican nominee in 1896 would be selected in an open primary rather than by a nominating convention. Even though he had to suffer the accusations of failing to support Evans's 1894 race for governor, Brownlow won the primary by over two thousand votes. But winning the primary was not Brownlow's only objective. He wanted to dominate Tennessee's Republican Party. In order to do this, he would have to battle Evans for control of the Tennessee delegates to be elected for the upcoming Republican National Convention in St. Louis. Alliances were built around who to support for president. After all, it was the president who controlled federal patronage. Brownlow, E. J. Sanford, Foster V. Brown (former Third District congressman), John C. Houk (former Second District congressman), and John E. McCall (Eighth District congressman) backed Speaker of the U.S. House of Representatives Thomas B. Reed.

Evans, on the other hand, had known William McKinley during his tenure in Washington and supported him. McKinley had served for nearly fifteen years as an Ohio congressman and four years as governor. He had considerable political influence as well as the support of millionaire political kingmaker Marc Hanna and his industrialist friends. McKinley's colleagues organized and financed a ten-thousand-mile campaign, including some four hundred speeches in seventeen states, all in eight weeks. By the time of the June Republican National Convention, McKinley had the nomination sewn up. Even before the Tennessee Republican Convention was set to nominate the delegates to the national convention, it was becoming understood that everyone would turn their support to McKinley.

At the 1896 St. Louis Republican National Convention, William McKinley was nominated for president on the first ballot, so the real issue was who would be nominated for vice president. Henry Clay Evans had many friends in Tennessee and had national name recognition. As the most nationally prominent Southern Republican of the time, there was a strong push for his candidacy. His friend and ally Newell Sanders worked the campaign for him at the St. Louis convention. He stood a good chance for the nomination, but there were some serious obstacles.

Even though a Southern Republican vice president would help build Southern Republican strength, and certainly would help the state of Tennessee, a significant obstacle to Evans's nomination came from the infighting for power and control among Republicans in his own state. Marcus (Marc) Hanna, McKinley's political manager, was opting for another candidate, and a solid Tennessee force could help Evans. This was not to be. Brownlow and Knoxville delegate Richard W. Austin actively worked against Evans. Other Tennessee delegates were concerned that Evans might not support their patronage choices for cabinet positions. Additionally, kingmaker Marc Hanna wanted Garret A. Hobart of New Jersey to be vice president, although he did not make his preference apparent and stood aside while others, including Evans, campaigned for the spot. Apparently New York boss T. C. Platt wanted New York Governor Levi P. Morton to receive the nomination. To prevent his own preference from becoming known and polarizing votes toward another candidate, Hanna played the neutral role while privately setting the stage for Hobart. Hobart and Evans were the two biggest contenders, but in the end Hobart won with 533 votes to 277 votes for Evans.

Hanna was chairman of the Republican National Committee. When at the Republican National Convention Walter Brownlow was selected as Tennessee's Republican National committeeman, the stage was set for Brownlow to develop a relationship with Hanna that could lead to patronage control in Tennessee if McKinley were elected.

At the August 12, 1896, Tennessee Republican state convention, Nashville attorney George N. Tillman was nominated Republican candidate for governor. Incumbent Governor Turney suffered from Democrat divisions. He was accused of not appropriating enough funds for the Tennessee Centennial Exposition, allowing his friends to make profits on bonds, and increased state expenditures. Democrats looked for a new hope to unite their ranks. Bob Taylor, the happy campaigner who had served as governor from 1887–1891, was again the Democratic nominee. He was everyone's friend. If any Democrat could unite the fold, it was thought that Taylor could. The issues were the unlimited coinage of silver, the state's back-tax system (which allowed the state to levy new taxes after original assessments and taxes had been paid), and the state election laws of 1889–1890. The ongoing debate among Democrats over gold versus silver split the Party. Memphis Congressman Josiah Patterson promoted the gold standard, while U.S. Senator Isham Harris led the charge for silver. Republicans hoped that the split, combined with public ill will over the Democrats' recount of the 1894 gubernatorial race vote and the subsequent repeal of Republican Evans's victory, would bring success in 1896.

In the gubernatorial race of 1896 Taylor won with 48.8 percent of the vote to 46.6 percent for Tillman. Populist candidate A. L. Mims, from Nashville, won 3.7 percent of the vote and may have drawn mainly from the Republican vote. Tillman actually outpolled McKinley, who received only 46.3 percent of the Tennessee presidential vote. Again, there were questions over honesty with the vote counts. Republicans claimed that Democrats had stolen votes in West Tennessee, and contested the election. The Democratic-controlled Tennessee legislature, ever determined to maintain power, then passed a law requiring Tillman to post a forfeitable twenty-five-thousand-dollar bond in order for an investigation to take place. With the Democrats controlling all questions, Tillman had no choice but to withdraw.

In the presidential election McKinley campaigned on the gold standard as President Cleveland had. Since the Democrats had deserted Cleveland, he was offered the opportunity to head a factional ticket for president, but he declined. Instead, he supported Republican McKinley and rejoiced when the Republican, "sound money" man won, 7,102,246 popular votes to 6,492,559 for William Jennings Bryan (271 to 176 electoral votes). McKinley was elected the twenty-fifth president of the United States (the twenty-fourth if Grover Cleveland is counted once).

The Republican nomination in the First Congressional District was tantamount to election, and Walter Brownlow was elected U.S. representative by more than a two to one margin over the Democratic candidate in the forty thousand votes cast. The "gold standard" Republican candidate received 950 votes. Republican Henry Gibson was reelected congressman from the Second District.

McKinley was inaugurated president in March 1897. He quickly went to work to reduce the national debt. Since he had served fifteen years in Congress prior to serving as governor of Ohio, he knew well how to gain cooperation with national legislators, and needed to use the presidential veto only fourteen times. With the economy recovering under his economic plan, the nation felt some relief. McKinley's popularity increased. He also fulfilled his 1896 campaign pledges to Black Republicans. His administration appointed several to significant federal positions.

In spite of some political setbacks, Henry Clay Evans did not give up his fight for participation in Republican politics. Walter Brownlow's gain had only worsened Republican infighting. By 1897 there were two distinct factions in the Republican Party in Tennessee—the Evans faction and the Brownlow faction. Evans, who had led the charge for McKinley's delegate effort in Tennessee, had seen his nomination for vice president sabotaged. His candidate, for the national committeeman from Tennessee at the convention, had lost to Brownlow. Evans's stature as a leader in Tennessee Republican circles sank, while Brownlow's rose. In a strange turn of allegiances, John

Houk, Evans's former enemy, decided to help Evans return to some position of influence. Evidently, Houk felt that Brownlow had betrayed his support. When President McKinley looked for a Southern Republican to appoint to his cabinet, he considered Evans for postmaster general. Houk supported and worked for Evans's appointment. Again Brownlow (along with Richard W. Austin, Jack W. Baker, and A. M. Hughes) did everything politically possible to prevent his appointment and supported James A. Gary of Maryland. Even though Evans had the support of the Republican newspapers in Tennessee, the State Republican Executive Committee, Republican state legislators, and four Republican congressmen, Brownlow's man got the appointment. It looked as if Brownlow controlled Republican politics in Tennessee.

No one knows if Brownlow had any real influence in McKinley's decision. In any case, McKinley knew he needed to avoid alienating the other Republican faction in Tennessee and reward Evans for his support. He offered Evans the position of commissioner of pensions. After some hesitation, Evans accepted. Although it would take Evans out of Tennessee, awarding pensions carried significant political influence with East Tennessee politicians. The appointment gave a strong boost to the political stature of the Evans faction and a rebuff of sorts to Brownlow. Later, in June 1897, when the president visited Chattanooga, he stayed at Evans's home.

In June 1897 U.S. Senator and former governor of Tennessee Isham G. Harris died. Governor Taylor appointed Thomas Battle Turley to fill the unexpired Senate seat (Class 2). Turley was Harris's former law partner in their Memphis firm. Turley served by appointment of the governor from July 20, 1897, until February 1, 1898, when the legislature would officially elect a replacement to complete Harris's unexpired term. Turley was ultimately elected, on the forty-fifth ballot, to complete the unexpired term and served from February 2, 1898, until March 3, 1901.

Meanwhile in Memphis, a battle brewed for the U.S. Representative seat, not only between Republicans and Democrats, but between Gold Democrats and Silver Democrats. Edward Carmack, who had run the *Commercial Appeal*, had resigned about 1896. He was a fairly well-known man and was urged to run for Congress in 1897, probably by Kenneth McKellar, a Memphis attorney in the firm of William H. Carroll, among others. Shelby County Democrats, like other Democrats in Tennessee and the country, were divided over the gold standard/silver standard debate, and nominated two different slates of candidates. This division, which had been brewing for sometime, was a setup for political feuding. In an attempt to preserve Democratic Party unity, Colonel William H. Carroll had asked Senator Isham Harris (prior to his June death) to come to Memphis to preside over a Democratic convention. It was hoped that Harris's presence—he was viewed as "The Democrat" in Tennessee and no one disputed his credibility as a Democrat—would resolve the nomination dispute between Democratic factions, foster unity, and prevent the formation of more than one slate of Democratic candidates. At the convention, Carmack and Colonel Josiah Patterson, the incumbent congressman, competed for the Democratic nomination for Congress, and Carmack won. However, Patterson would not give up and later received nominations from both Shelby County Republican factions, the "Lily White" Republicans and the "Black and Tan" Republicans. In any event, Carmack won the general election for U.S. representative by 365 votes. However, the contest was not over yet, since Patterson remained determined. The Republicans controlled the U.S. House of Representatives (246 Republicans to 104 Democrats to 7 others), and Patterson contested the election with the hope that Republicans would wrest the seat away from Carmack. Kenneth McKellar was selected to represent Carmack before the House Elections Committee. William Carroll had his junior partner defend Carmack because he did not want to risk damaging his reputation by taking a case that he was bound to lose. McKellar presented an excellent case to the U.S. House Elections Committee. After Carmack finished his campaigning before the state legislature in Nashville for his friend Tom Turley, who was running against Benton McMillin and Governor Taylor to complete the term of the deceased Isham Harris, he went to Washington and spoke before the U.S. House. Astonishingly, the Republican House seated Democrat Carmack in April 1898.

During this era Walter Brownlow, Republican congressman for the First District; Henry Gibson, Republican congressman for the Second District; and Henry Clay Evans, Republican leader from the Third District dictated presidential patronage in their respective districts. Efforts were made to strike a balance between Evans's and Brownlow's recommendations

THOMAS BATTLE TURLEY was born an only child in Memphis on April 5, 1845. His father, Thomas Jefferson Turley, was of Irish descent and born near Alexandria, Virginia. His mother, Flora Battle, was born near Raleigh, North Carolina, eventually settling with her family as early pioneers in Shelby County, Tennessee. Her future husband, who became a lawyer, moved with his family from Virginia to Clarksville, Tennessee, then to Raleigh, and finally to Memphis in 1835. Turley was reared and educated in Memphis schools until the Civil War, in which he enlisted at fifteen, served as a private, was captured in the Battle of Franklin, and remained in military prison in Columbus, Ohio, until the conflict was over. After the war, he attended law school at the University of Virginia, graduated in 1866, and returned home to practice in Memphis. He married Irene Rayner in 1871 and they had five children. He was part of the firm of Harris, McKissick and Turley until 1877. His partner, Isham G. Harris, had served as governor of Tennessee from 1857 until 1862, and as U.S. senator, beginning in 1877. In 1885 Turley and Luke E. Wright formed a partnership that was maintained for the following twelve years. However, when Senator Harris died in June 1897, Turley was appointed U.S. senator by Democrat Governor Bob Taylor, began serving on July 20, 1897, and was subsequently elected to complete Harris's unexpired term, which ended on March 4, 1901. The 1898 election to complete the term was contested by both future governor Benton McMillin, and sitting Governor Robert Taylor. The battle in the Democratic legislative caucus was long and hard. After forty-five ballots, Governor Taylor agreed to support Turley, who won by one vote. Turley lived his entire life in Memphis, other than the time he spent in the Civil War, law school, and his four years as senator. He died on July 1, 1910. His wife died in 1939. (Photograph courtesy of SHO)

for appointments in other areas of the state in order to maintain peace between the two, but of course this did not always happen. Nashville attorney, businessman, and Black Republican leader James C. Napier, a friend of Evans, received Evans's recommendation and support when register of the treasury Blanch K. Bruce died in 1898, but Napier did not get the position. President McKinley also denied Napier the position of register of wills for the District of Columbia.

While Evans played Tennessee politics at somewhat of a distance, he served as an honest and efficient commissioner of pensions for this nation. Immediately after assuming office, Evans called for reform of a system that was filled with abuse. He set strict guidelines for conduct and behavior of employees of the pension office and worked to rid the system of fraud. He moved to publish the pension lists so that fraudulent cases could be detected. He supported a move to make it illegal for pension attorneys or claim agents to be paid fees. He wanted the claimants to simply file with the Pension Bureau, bypassing middlemen. Evans was convinced that the "fraud on the pension rolls had been planted there by the pension attorneys who convinced veterans they had disabilities and persuaded them to file claims" (Isaac n.d.). He strongly felt that the system needed reform, stating, "They [*sic*] practically are so many drummers—soliciting agents—that do nothing but hunt up claims and claimants for the Pension Bureau" (Isaac n.d.).

Of course the pension attorneys did not appreciate Evans's work to reform the system, and neither did Brownlow, who looked for any opportunity to attack Evans. He, Washington pension attorney James Tanner, who had served briefly as pension commissioner under President Harrison, and other pension lawyers encouraged the Grand Army of the Republic to force President McKinley to remove Evans. However, the press generally supported Evans. McKinley stood behind his commissioner, refusing to dismiss him, and likely became quite irritated with Brownlow's maneuvers and instigation of controversy.

Meanwhile, in 1895 off the southern coast of the United States, a revolution broke out in Cuba against Spanish rule. Unfortunately, there were Americans in Cuba trapped in the midst of the conflict. The United States, under President Cleveland, had attempted to maintain neutrality, but two New York publishers, Joseph Pulitzer and especially William Randolph Hearst, continually hyped the conflict in their newspapers, sometimes insulting American leadership for not intervening. In May 1897 Congress appropriated funds to protect Americans from the rioters. On February 15, 1898, the USS *Maine* was destroyed in Havana Harbor, killling over 260 Americans, and turning national sentiment toward war. Even though the Spanish government contacted the United States on April 10 with wishes to halt all conflict and leave Cuban rule to its natives, it was too late to satisfy a nation thirsting for revenge. Wars create heroes and wanna-be politicians, and in fact this conflict would have significant impact on American politics. The U.S. formally declared War on April 25, 1898. By August 15, 1898, the Spanish-American conflict was over. Spain granted Cuba its freedom and ceded Guam, Puerto Rico, and the Philippines to the U.S.

In Tennessee, Benton McMillin, from Clay County, had been rising on the political scene. After serving ten terms as a U.S. representative, he failed to obtain appointment to the Senate seat left vacant by the death of U.S. Senator Isham Harris in 1897. He then lost the 1898 legislative election to fill the seat for the remainder of the term to Thomas Turley. With hopes for a political career in the Senate blocked, McMillin received the Democratic nomination for governor in 1898. The Brownlow-controlled Republican state convention nominated Knoxville attorney James A. Fowler as the Republican nominee. Although Brownlow at the time could control the state Republican Party, he could not control the people's vote which was overwhelmingly Democratic. Receiving the Democratic nomination was tantamount to being elected, as long as there was no split in the party. Eighteen ninety-eight was a year of Democratic Party cooperation. Brownlow's nominee, Fowler, received 39.8 percent of the vote. Democrat McMillin was elected governor, and the Democrats continued to dominate the state legislature.

After finding fame for his command of the Rough Riders regiment in the battle at San Juan Hill in the Spanish-American War, Theodore Roosevelt positioned himself for selection as the Republican candidate for governor of New York in 1898. Incumbent Republican Governor Frank S. Black's administration had been tainted with

BENTON McMILLIN was born in Monroe County, Kentucky, on September 11, 1845. His parents were John McMillin and Elizabeth Black McMillin. He received his early education in Kentucky schools, later attending Kentucky University. Then he moved to Carthage, Tennessee, and studied law with Judge E. L. Gardenshire. He began practicing law in Celina, Tennessee, by 1871, then married Marie Childress Brown, from Pulaski, Tennessee, the daughter of former Governor John C. and Betty Childress Brown. Marie died shortly after giving birth to a son. McMillin remarried in 1888 to Lucille Foster, who was the daughter of James Foster, a wealthy cotton planter from Louisiana. Lucille's mother was an activist for women's rights and was one of the first suffragettes from the South. Lucille would also become a well-known leader for women's rights and achieve recognition well beyond the borders of Tennessee. She eventually became president of the Tennessee Federation of Women's Clubs and a regional director of Democrat Women for Southern States.

McMillin was elected to Congress in 1879 and was reelected, serving until 1898, when he was elected governor of Tennessee. He began his term in 1899. His administration oversaw finalizing a dispute over the boundary between East Tennessee and Virginia. During his tenure education was improved by authorizing each county to create a high school and hold elections for school directors. Additionally, the state standardized a program for textbooks. To fund the new programs, a property tax was instituted. A corporate tax was also implemented during his tenure and the judiciary system was somewhat reformed. McMillin was reelected in 1900 and served until 1903. He did not run for reelection and went into the insurance business in Nashville. He died on January 8, 1933, and was buried in Mount Olivet Cemetery. His wife, Lucille, lived in Washington, serving as civil service commissioner under President Franklin Roosevelt from 1933 until she retired due to her health in 1946. She died that same year and was buried in Mount Olivet Cemetery. (Photograph courtesy of TSLA) corruption and scandals, and the New York public was becoming intolerant of the party. New York Republican leaders thought that with a fresh untarnished candidate they could win again. They liked Roosevelt's clean image and tapped him for nomination at the Republican state convention in September 1898.

Theodore Roosevelt would ultimately impact the Republican Party in Tennessee. His role in party development and civil rights has direct bearing upon political party evolution. Roosevelt's trials of gaining the nomination and his narrow election as governor of New York placed him further into the public mind and national spotlight.

At the end of the nineteenth century, most Southern states were almost totally Democratic, with the exception of select Republican geographic pockets. Southern Republicans consisted of a few White leaders and Blacks. These politicians took advantage of patronage when there was a Republican in the White House. Otherwise, they had very little power or influence. Nevertheless Republicans in Tennessee impacted state politics in the late nineteenth and early twentieth century. Occasionally they would pass on appointments offered to them by Republican presidents, or they would support or carry a few votes for a friendly, patronage-bearing Democrat who was running for statewide or local office.

Because of Tennessee's unique history of a Republican base in East Tennessee combined with its western base of a large Black population, Republicans were able to maintain a perpetual, though weak, minority. (Republicans in other Southern states had much less success.) At the turn of the century they maintained two out of ten congressional districts (this varied from two to five seats), cast 40 percent of the vote in state elections, held a fair number of legislative seats in the General Assembly, and held offices as district attorneys, judges, and city officers. But they did not have enough voting strength to control the entire state. Most of their efforts centered on obtaining federal patronage jobs, maintaining their control over the Republican state party, and selecting delegates to the national conventions. Tennessee Republicans maintained a respectable organization by holding regular county, district, and state conventions, and county primaries. Also, there was nearly always at least one daily, along with several weekly newspapers in Tennessee, which supported the Republican effort.

Some East Tennessee counties voted as high as 80 percent Republican in elections. Democrats were limited in East Tennessee to controlling Sullivan County on the Virginia border of Tennessee and an occasional victory in Chattanooga and Knoxville. A few other communities might also occasionally elect a Democrat. However, on the whole, East Tennessee was a dominant Republican stronghold. Occasionally two to five counties in Middle and West Tennessee held small concentrations of Republicans. Overall, though, the party was weak to nonexistent in these areas, as was the rural Black vote which essentially had been eliminated through intimidation. The metropolitan areas of Nashville and Memphis had a high enough concentration of Black voters that they could organize and create a voting block to combine with the East Tennessee forces for presidential elections. Black Republicans maintained organizations in the larger communities.

Because there was a small but consistent Republican voting block, presidential candidates and sitting presidents could count on some potential votes in Tennessee. Patronage was used to gain support and to assist with the possible growth of Republican support in the South. Tennessee represented the most likely springboard from which to break the Democratic stranglehold on the South. But the development of Republicanism in Tennessee carried a high price for national figures; they would have to become involved in state Republican internal disputes. Tennessee Republicans, always eyeing the patronage plum, often became an annoyance to presidents, involving them in their factional disputes and intraparty bickering for leadership roles. There seemed to be no limit to the degree of Republican infighting.

Most Tennessee Republican organizational control centered in Districts One and Two, the two dominant Republican congressional districts in East Tennessee, and was limited to county, district (congressional), and state party elections. Therefore, the congressional district Republican nomination process received the most attention and turmoil. The two congressional seats were, after all, the only major offices that Republicans consistently held in Tennessee. Second to electing two U.S. representatives, Republicans fought over who would be local or state leaders in the party. On the other hand, most of the Democratic infighting for power centered on who would be elected governor of Tennessee or U.S. senator. This comparison—Republicans struggling for a title within their party and Democrats competing for statewide office—typified the dominance of Democrats and the relative weakness of Republicans during the late nineteenth and early twentieth century.

The factional disputes over control of the two Republican districts in East Tennessee were intense and ultimately weakened the state Republican Party. Republicans created alliances with Democrats in order to defeat rival Republicans. It is telling of human nature that the leaders in the weakest party would undermine each other for the control of so little, rather than allow a fellow party member to participate in the process. Republicans were at a disadvantage of historical proportions and needed total party cooperation in order to achieve any limited success. Democrats always had the advantage of appealing to the voters' memory of the subjugation of Reconstruction, the carpetbaggers, the Freedmen's Bureau, and Radical Republicanism to keep Republicans on the defensive. The possibility of Black domination if Republicans took power was senseless, but the threat of it nonetheless kept Democrats in power. In reality Blacks played only a small role in the Republican Party. In East Tennessee there were relatively few Black Republicans; Whites dominated. In Middle and West Tennessee there were so few Republican Whites that Blacks did represent the majority in these regions, but the party was small and powerless. However, the Black majority in the Republican Party in these regions lent credence to the propaganda promoted by the Democrats.

On February 28, 1900, Republican district conventions were held throughout the state. Tenth District Republicans met in convention at the Memphis City Court House and elected Robert Church and L.W. Dutro, the postmaster, as delegates to the 1900

Republican National Convention to be held in Philadelphia in June. They were elected to support the nomination and reelection of William McKinley for president. The two were basically supporters of H. Clay Evans. Evans-friendly delegates were elected in the Third and Tenth Districts. Walter Brownlow took delegates in the First, Second, Fourth, Seventh, and Eighth Districts. However, the results of the county convention elections had to pass the scrutiny of the state Republican Party, and all non-Brownlow delegates could be effectively contested (this included district and at-large delegates to the Republican National Convention).

"For several years after the Civil War, the Tennessee Republican Executive Committee consisted of one member from each of Tennessee's ten congressional districts. In 1886 the permanent chairman of the state convention could name six additional members of his choice. However, in 1898, after Walter Brownlow won reelection to Congress and was elected permanent chairman of the convention, the convention passed a rule giving the chairman the power to name nine members" (Isaac n.d.).

By 1900 Brownlow had maneuvered the state Republican Party into his total control and his political use of patronage was becoming common knowledge. Those who wanted to participate in the party realized that they had to submit to Brownlow's dominance or pay the consequences. H. Clay Evans and others would not yield to Brownlow and pressed to compete with him. The Evans wing of the party ran state Judge H. Tyler Campbell, from Sneedville, for Congress in the First District against Brownlow. However, Brownlow was too strong and soundly defeated Judge Campbell in the March 10, 1900, Republican primary. After the election Brownlow was quoted saying, "I will be generous to all my enemies as I always have been" (Isaac n.d.).

After Brownlow's primary victory, he called the Republican state convention for April 19, 1900. At the convention, Brownlow gave himself even more power. First, he refused to seat any contested delegates. Over one-third of the county conventions had split between the two factions. Since he had decreed that the disputes would be settled by a Credentials Committee, he could control the outcome of any contested seats.

The convention named Black Republican Josiah T. Settle, as an alternate delegate to the national convention. Congressman Henry R. Gibson, Foster V. Brown, G. N. Tillman, and John E. McCall were elected as delegates-at-large. Brownlow, had himself recommended for national committeeman, and nominated John E. McCall as Republican candidate for governor. He also gave himself power to name twelve members to the State Republican Executive Committee. With this kind of voting ability, Brownlow could pass whatever he wanted through the State Executive Committee.

Brownlow and his followers hated Clay Evans. Mike Grady, a Brownlow man from Chattanooga, was quoted as saying, "H. Clay Evans is now and has been for years, the representative of the 'nigger' gang in Tennessee . . ." (Isaac n.d.). Despite the apparent dominance of Brownlow, the Evans faction continued undaunted. After Brownlow displayed his dictatorial tendencies at the convention, Evans and his supporters left the convention, marched through Nashville, "led by a Negro drum corps," (Isaac n.d.) and held a separate convention. The Evans convention elected

James C. Napier, a Black Nashvillian, as delegate-at-large to the Republican National Convention. The other delegates-at-large elected were H. Tyler Campbell, James Jefferies, and Horace A. Mann. The convention named W. F. Poston, from Alamo, Tennessee, as the Republican candidate for governor for 1900.

The battle for delegate spots to the 1900 national convention continued well past the district conventions. As a result Tennessee sent two sets of delegates from the Fifth, Sixth, and Ninth Districts along with two sets of at-large delegates, causing a heated exchange at the Republican National Convention. Finally, the convention seated all four of Brownlow's at-large delegates along with his delegates in the Ninth District. Brownlow conceded the delegates in the Third and Tenth Districts, while Evans conceded the delegates in the First, Second, Fourth, Seventh, and Eighth Districts. The final result was sixteen Brownlow delegates and eight Evans delegates. Brownlow was elected national committeeman from Tennessee.

The seating of delegates settled nothing as far as Tennessee Republicans were concerned. Brownlow's dictatorial control of the state Republican Party fostered discontent and ill will within the ranks. Marc Hanna, Republican National chairman, further aggravated the situation by intervening to recognize the Brownlow wing as the official state committee. The dispute continued with both organizations naming candidates for governor and railroad commissioner. Finally, a compromise was reached, although the Evans supporters, not having National Chairman Hanna on their side, accepted less than what they wished. The Brownlow candidate for governor, John McCall, was accepted, and the Evans candidate dropped out. A compromise candidate for railroad commissioner was selected and ten Evans men were folded into the State Party Executive Committee.

By 1900 America was back on the gold standard, and McKinley was enjoying popularity. At the June 1900 Republican National Convention in Philadelphia, he was unanimously renominated for president. New York Governor Theodore Roosevelt was nominated vice president. For the short term, Tennessee Republican factions united for the presidential election of 1900. McKinley's chances for reelection looked good, and cooperation was the only course the combatants could take if they had any desire to benefit from his patronage. Democrats again nominated William Jennings Bryan for president and Adlai E. Stevenson for vice president.

Although cooperating with his rivals for the Republican presidential campaign, Brownlow continued to do everything in his power to get rid of his Republican competitor, Henry Clay Evans. During the presidential campaign, he threatened to withhold support from McKinley unless he fired Evans as commissioner of pensions. President McKinley had not made a career of buckling under pressure, and he refused to fire Evans. It did not hurt McKinley.

Generally speaking, other than intraparty rivalries, Tennessee politics had been without any great conflict in the period just prior to the 1900 election.

Business corruption reform was a state issue, just as it was nationally; however, it did not divide Democrats or create a public outcry for change. Although Brownlow had control of the state's Republican Party, it was a party of limited power and he could not sway voters outside of East Tennessee. The Democrats dominated. Tennessee Democrat Governor Benton McMillin was renominated and reelected in 1900, to serve the 1901–1903 term. John McCall, Brownlow's candidate, received only 44.3 percent of the vote, compared to the 46.6 percent for the Republican gubernatorial candidate in 1896.

During McMillian's tenure as governor, effort was made to improve public schools. Laws were passed which allowed local county school boards to set up high schools. Funds were appropriated to educate teachers, and uniform textbooks were selected.

However much cooperation there might have been in Democratic ranks in 1900, U.S. Senator Thomas Turley's replacement in the Senate (Class 2 seat) set the stage for an eventual political disaster outranked by none in Tennessee history. The replacement process was a routine act of the legislature of 1900, but later, when the elected senator was denied reelection because of Democratic infighting, an explosion of personalities occured which dominated the political landscape. Edward Carmack was the man elected by the Tennessee legislature of 1900 to replace Turley, who was not a candidate for reelection. Carmack was seated on March 4, 1901. His term continued until March 3, 1907.

Interestingly, when Carmack gave up his Memphis congressional seat to become a U.S. senator, Malcolm Patterson won the seat. Patterson, a Memphis lawyer, was the son of Josiah Patterson, who had been defeated for the same seat by Carmack. Malcolm had served as his father's campaign manager when he lost the 1898 campaign with Carmack.

When McKinley was reelected president in 1900, he received 7,218,491 popular votes to 6,356,734 for Bryan (292 to 155 electoral votes). However, he received fewer votes in Tennessee in 1900—274,000 (45 percent)—than the 321,000 (46.3 percent) he received in 1896. Brownlow continued to pressure McKinley for the ouster of Evans as commissioner of pensions. Although Marc Hanna did not support Evans, McKinley stood by him, saying he would move Evans out if Evans opted for a better position.

On September 6, 1901, President McKinley, while holding a reception in the Music Hall of the Pan-American Exposition in Buffalo, New York, was shot twice by Leon F. Czolgosz, an anarchist. McKinley held onto life until September 14. Czolgosz was later electrocuted for the crime. Theodore Roosevelt assumed office on the death of President McKinley and became the twenty-sixth president of the United States.

Most Republicans in the South, with the exception of those from East Tennessee, were Black. Booker T. Washington, a leading Black figure, had considerable influence with President Roosevelt. Because of this, Black Tennesseans who wanted a favor or job, would ask for Booker T. Washington's support. Two of Washington's main Black contacts in Tennessee were James C. Napier, a Nashville businessman and lawyer, and Josiah T. Settle, a leading Black Republican from Memphis. Even though Booker T. Washington had influence with Roosevelt throughout most of the South, Tennessee, because of its strong East Tennessee former Unionist, White Republican base, was unique among Southern states. Washington knew this and often referred requests for jobs to Congressman Brownlow.

After McKinley's death, Evans's political position became tenuous. When political maneuvering to oust him was attempted,

EDWARD WARD CARMACK was born in Sumner County, Tennessee, on November 5, 1858. His father died when he was three years of age. He received an excellent early education, first in Mississippi, then later in Maury County, Tennessee, and went on to study law at Cumberland University. He settled in Columbia, Tennessee, and began law practice at age twenty-one. He was elected to the county court in Maury County and later to the state house by the time he was twenty-eight. He began writing for the *Maury Democrat* and later the *Nashville Union-American*, then started the *Nashville Democrat*. The *Democrat* later merged with the *Nashville Union-American* and became *The American*. Carmack was the paper's editor. In 1890 he married Elizabeth Cobey Dunnington. Around 1893–1894 he became the editor of the failing *Memphis Commercial*. The paper was shortly combined with the *Appeal-Avalanche* to form the *Memphis Commercial-Appeal,* with Carmack as editor. Carmack was a strong Democrat, and the paper reflected that. However, he became involved in a dispute with the owners over the national gold-silver question, and resigned in April 1896. (Carmack favored a silver-based economy and frequently used print to attack Democrats who favored a gold-based system.)

Carmack was elected as U.S. representative from the Memphis district (tenth) in 1898, after a disputed election with Josiah Patterson. He served one additional term until he was elected to succeed his friend, Tom Turley, to the U.S. Senate. He served from March 4, 1901, until March 4, 1907. He was denied reelection in 1906 and was defeated for the Democratic gubernatorial nomination by Governor Malcolm Patterson in 1908. As editor of the *Nashville Tennessean,* he opposed the Patterson Democratic political machine through a barrage of attacks in his newspaper articles. Carmack was killed by Duncan Cooper and his son Robin on November 9, 1908, because of newspaper articles critical of Duncan Cooper and Patterson. A statue of Carmack stands in front of the Tennessee State Capitol. (Photograph courtesy of SHO)

President Roosevelt stood by him as McKinley had. After all, the press had praised Evans's annual commission report. Evans proved to be an honest and efficient public servant who performed his duties in the best interest of the nation in spite of political pressure. In March 1902, the GAR Committee on Pensions demanded Evans's removal. Roosevelt later announced that before he was given the report demanding Evans's removal, he had received a letter of resignation from him dated March 15. However, Roosevelt stated that Evans would remain commissioner of pensions until a new position and a replacement were found for him. Then the press reported that Kansas Senator Joseph R. Burton would block confirmation for any appointment for Evans. At this, Roosevelt took a hard stand and reiterated that he had not officially accepted Evans's resignation and would not until he was successfully repositioned. Shortly thereafter, in April 1902, the consul general in London died and Evans was appointed to this post. With Evans out of the way in Washington, Brownlow continued to increase his political influence.

In 1902 former Second District U.S. Representative John C. Houk backed Nathan W. Hale for Congress in opposition to incumbent Congressman Henry R. Gibson, who was closely aligned with

Brownlow. Hale lost to Gibson. However, when Gibson announced he would not seek reelection, the anti-Brownlow forces swelled.

Nationally, many people wondered what the hotheaded young forty-three-year-old Roosevelt would do as president. He spent a fair amount of time early on in his administration assuring Wall Street and the public that he intended to carry out McKinley's policies. However, there was a great deal of public concern over the lack of accountability for the growing business corporations and the need for standards for corporate conduct. Roosevelt created the position of secretary of commerce to address these issues.

On the state political scene, Governor McMillin did not run for reelection in 1902. Both parties geared up to select a new governor. In 1902 the Evans wing of state Republicans knew that Brownlow controlled the state Republican Party and did not challenge him. Brownlow had his former opponent in the First District Republican primary of 1900, H. Tyler Campbell, selected as the Tennessee Republican candidate for governor.

The Democrats nominated James B. Frazier, an attorney from Chattanooga who had served as a statewide elector for the Bryan/Stevenson campaign in 1900. This 1902 campaign would be the last for governor in Tennessee in which the candidates traveled by horse-drawn coach to their campaign stops. Democrat James B. Frazier was easily elected. His opponent suffered the worst showing by a Republican since 1878, with only 36.8 percent of the vote. The 1902 election also suffered from a low voter turnout.

Meanwhile, President Roosevelt worked at trust-busting and upholding the Sherman Anti-trust Act. In keeping with his expansionist policies, Congress passed an act necessary to help finance construction of the Panama Canal. Roosevelt encouraged a revolt of Panamanians for independence from Columbia. When Panama declared independence, Roosevelt recognized the new government and sent battleships to stand guard off the coasts, securing independence for the small country.

Since Tennessee was not a Republican stronghold, Roosevelt made sure to win over as many Democrats as possible before the 1904 election. When, on March 27, 1903, he asked Philippine Governor William Howard Taft to return to serve as secretary of war, Memphian Luke Wright succeeded Taft as governor of the Philippine Commission. Later, when Taft felt that Wright was having some difficulties with the Philippine situation, Roosevelt removed him and appointed Wright ambassador to Japan. He appointed Democrat James C. McReynolds as assistant attorney general. McReynolds, an attorney and law professor at Vanderbilt University in Nashville, had lost as a "Gold" Democrat candidate for Congress in Middle Tennessee in 1896.

In addition to McReynolds, he appointed a Tennessee Democratic lawyer, McGavock Dickinson, as U.S. counsel before the Alaska Boundary Commission. (In 1906 Roosevelt offered to appoint him minister to Norway; Dickinson declined.)

In 1904 Congressman Brownlow continued to dominate the Republican Party of Tennessee and the Republican state convention. He secured the Republican nomination for governor for Jesse M. Littleton, mayor of Winchester. Governor James Frazier was easily renominated by the

Democrats for a second term.

While Henry Clay Evans was out of the country, his associate and confidant, Newell Sanders, became the leader of the Republican opposition which fought Brownlow's dominance. He had been elected chairman of the Third District Republican Executive Committee in 1902. Now that Congressman Gibson was not seeking reelection in the Second District, the anti-Brownlow activity increased. Nathan Hale ran for the U.S. Representative seat as did Richard W. Austin, who was the U.S. marshal in East Tennessee and a close associate of Brownlow. Hale defeated Austin in the March 1904 primary.

JAMES BERIAH FRAZIER was born in Pikeville, Bledsoe County, Tennessee, on August 18, 1856. His father, Thomas N. Frazier, was a judge in the criminal court of Davidson County. His mother was Rebecca Julien Frazier. After attending the common schools for his early education, he graduated from the University of Tennessee, in Knoxville in 1878 at age twenty-one. He studied law in Nashville under his father. He taught school for a short period, then moved to Washington, Rhea County, Tennessee, to practice law. In 1881 he moved his law practice to Chattanooga where he remained until 1902.

In 1884 Frazier married Louise Douglas Keith, the daughter of Alexander Hume Keith and Sara Foree Keith, from McMinn County. In 1894 he decided to challenge incumbent Democrat Congressman Henry C. Snodgrass from the Third District. At that time the Democrat candidate was chosen by a Democrat convention. Although Frazier had become very popular, he did not yet hold enough political influence to control the convention, and Snodgrass was renominated (though he lost to Republican Foster V. Brown, owing in part to the lingering bitterness from the contested Democratic convention). Frazier served as a presidential elector-at-large, supporting Democrat William Jennings Bryan in 1900. This gave him the opportunity to campaign all across Tennessee. He was a great speaker, and the electoral campaign created tremendous respect for him around the state.

By 1901 Frazier decided to run for governor. During the campaign in 1902, the other Democratic candidates slowly dropped out of the race. Eventually, he had little opposition for the Democratic nomination. In the general election, he ran against H. D. Campbell (Republican) and R. S. Cheves (Prohibitionist). Frazier was elected governor, receiving 98,902 votes to 59,007 for Campbell and 2,193 for Cheves. He was inaugurated on January 20, 1903.

Frazier's administration worked to improve public education. At this time law dictated only six months of school per year; only grammar schools existed since high schools had not yet been built; and less than 50 percent of Tennessee's children attended the schools available. Frazier pushed to fund the improvements needed for a better educational system. Laws were also passed which regulated the mining industry and improved safety. Rioting among miners was still a problem. Governor Frazier talked directly to the miners and their leaders, and attempted to negotiate a halt to the riots.

Frazier was reelected governor in the race of 1904. However, just as his new term began, Senator Bate died on March 9, 1905, and Frazier maneuvered to replace him in the Senate. He resigned the governor's seat and moved to the U.S. Senate, where he remained until 1921. Frazier died in Tennessee in 1937 and was buried in Forest Hill Cemetery in Chattanooga. (Photograph courtesy of SHO)

At the June 1904 Republican National Convention, President Roosevelt was nominated by acclamation. Indiana Senator Charles Fairbanks was nominated to run for vice president. Alton B. Parker of New York was nominated for president by the Democrats, with West Virginian Henry G. Davis selected as the candidate for vice president.

In the Tennessee gubernatorial race, Governor Frazier and his Republican opponent, Jesse Littleton, engaged in a series of joint debates which began in Jackson, Tennessee, on September 5, 1904. The debates, held throughout Tennessee, created a great amount of attention and excitement. Both candidates were accomplished speakers and debaters. Littleton favored the four mile law, which prevented the sale of liquor within four miles of any school. Frazier partially favored the law but promoted the local option, which could prevent Prohibition in the major municipalities of the state. Although the campaign stirred the interest of Tennessee's voters, the Democrats still dominated Tennessee, and Frazier was reelected by a thirty-eight thousand vote plurality.

Brownlow was reelected to Congress in Tennessee's First District, and Hale easily defeated his Democratic opponent for the Second Congressional District seat. These East Tennessee Republicans represented the limited political balance to Democratic dominance.

On the national political scene in 1904, the Democrats had little chance. Roosevelt exuded a heroic image for America, and times were good. In the November 1904 election he received 7,628,461 popular votes to 5,084,223 for Parker (336 to 140 electoral votes). Teddy Roosevelt, who had assumed office after McKinley's assassination, was now elected as president of the United States.

During his second term Roosevelt exercised a bold approach to world police efforts. He increased his determination in dealing with corporate impunity by overseeing the passage of the Hepburn Act, which extended the powers of the Interstate Commerce Commission. He also helped pass the Pure Food Act, which established some guidelines for federal oversight of meatpacking houses.

It was about this time that a new and powerful political figure would begin his climb in Tennessee politics. Although his initial role was minimal, it was the beginning of a powerful force that would influence the outcome of Tennessee elections until the late 1940s. Edward Hull Crump arrived in Memphis in 1894. By 1903 Crump had become involved in a political reform movement that was attempting to improve Memphis government, which was under the influence of a criminal element. Although Crump did not begin the movement or lead the initial charge, his participation allowed him to become elected to the Board of Public Works (which was part of the lower body of the Memphis City Council) in 1905. Another young Democrat destined for prominence, Kenneth McKellar, played a legal and leadership role in this reform movement.

Democratic Disruption

Tennessee state politics had been fairly quiet during this period of time. An occasional skirmish arose among the Republican political hopefuls. The Democratic Party was in control and enjoyed limited internal conflicts. However, political peace and harmony within Democratic ranks would not last much longer. On January 11, 1905, Senator William B. Bate was reelected to a fourth term in the U.S. Senate by the legislature. On March 5, 1905, Senator Bate died, setting off a shuffle for his seat that would create a chaotic free-for-all in the Democratic Party. Governor Frazier, former Governor Benton McMillin, and former Governor Robert L. Taylor all vied with the state legislature for the seat.

Taylor had lost an 1881 U.S. Senate race, unsuccessfully challenged Bate for a Senate seat in 1893, and lost a seat to Tom Turley in 1898. He felt it was understood that he would have the next seat available. But Taylor was out of state at the time of Senator Bate's death and not able to work his political contacts quickly enough. Governor Frazier knew that a quick election would prevent the competition from having enough time to gain political ground and force the legislature into considering other options. He did not waste time. Within a week of Bate's death the Democratic caucus met and agreed to give the seat (Class 1) to Frazier. The formalities were completed during the legislative session on March 22, 1905. Frazier's term in the U.S. Senate had officially commenced on March 21, 1905—the day before. (His term ran until March 3, 1911.) John Isaac Cox, the speaker of the senate, became governor. He was inaugurated on March 27, 1905. Frazier's victory set off a firestorm within the Democratic Party that would ultimately end in murder and the election of a Republican as governor.

Bob Taylor and Benton McMillin were none too pleased with Frazier and Cox. Taylor had been a dedicated Democrat, had served as governor for three terms, and had coveted Senator Carmack's seat ever since Carmack took office in 1901. McMillin had served as governor for four years and also felt that he deserved a chance. Cox, Frazier, and Carmack were political allies. Taylor and McMillin viewed the threesome as comrades in arms against their own political ambitions. Taylor knew that Carmack was the vulnerable member of the threesome. Carmack's term would be up for reelection in 1906, and Taylor, who was exceedingly popular, decided that since he had been denied the chance to compete for Bate's Senate seat, he would go for Carmack's seat. Soon an incredible fight erupted among the Democrats, and they became concerned about a potential party split over the Senate seat. The party chose to take an unusual course and allow the voting public to select the nominee in an open primary. A 1901 state law provided the "option" of a statewide primary to choose a party's nominee. This was to be the first primary election for statewide office in Tennessee's history.

It was not long between the time that Frazier took the Senate seat—March 1905—and the new Democratic primary. Taylor and Carmack subsequently stumped the state together, and Taylor won a narrow victory—74,000 votes to Carmack's 66,000. The nomination was tantamount to victory since the Democratic legislature would certainly elect the nominee over any Republican. Taylor had his seat and began serving in the U.S. Senate (Class 2) on March 4, 1907. His term ran until March 3, 1913, (but he died on March 31, 1912).

Carmack was eminently displeased at his Senate seat loss and certainly blamed the situation on the Frazier-Cox action. He had been an excellent U.S. senator, with a reputation as "an orator and a statesman" (McKellar 1942). Although he

JOHN ISAAC COX was born on November 23, 1857, in Sullivan County, Tennessee. His father's family had pioneered Tennessee. Of the original eleven Cox brothers who had come to Jamestown, Virginia, from England, four moved into Tennessee and signed the original Watauga Compact. Cox's father, Henry W. Cox, was killed in the Civil War, and John and his mother faced poverty. His mother sent Cox to work on a farm at age ten for twenty-five cents per week. By age sixteen he was a rural mail carrier, and at eighteen he obtained an appointment as a road commissioner. He received his early education at the Old Field Schools of Sullivan County, eventually worked his way through Blountville Academy, then studied law under Judge W.V. Deaderick. He opened a law practice in Blountville and became a county judge and later a county attorney. In 1889 he lived in Bristol, Tennessee, and served as city attorney.

In 1890 Cox was elected to the state senate. By 1905 he was speaker of the senate. Around this time he married Lorena Butler, the educated daughter of Dr. Matthew Butler and Mrs. Mary Dulaney Butler, from Blountville, and the cousin of the famous brothers, Alf and Bob Taylor. The couple had one son and one daughter. As speaker of the senate, Cox constitutionally inherited the governor's seat when Governor Frazier resigned to assume the U.S. Senate seat made vacant by the death of Senator Bate. As governor he faced rioting by miners in Tracy City and Whitwell. He implemented Quarantines to help control yellow fever, increased veterans' pensions, and adopted a state flag designed by Lee Roy Reeves. Governor Cox also opposed Prohibition. Cox lost his 1906 quest for the Democrat nomination for governor to Malcolm R. Patterson, but was elected to the state senate in 1906 and served from 1907 until 1911. He then retired from the legislature and returned to Bristol. Cox died on September 5, 1946, and was buried in Sullivan County. Lorena Cox lived until 1951. (Photograph courtesy of TSLA)

fought the Roosevelt administration at every turn and in spite of his "bold expressions of opinion on all subjects before the Senate, notwithstanding his vehement and fighting qualities" (McKellar 1942), he had the highest admiration of his colleagues in the Senate. Now, in spite of his service to Tennessee, Carmack was defeated for reelection—a fate he felt he did not deserve—and became determined to have his own revenge. The split in the Democratic Party now worsened.

East Tennessee Republicans, held no major statewide offices and could only continue the fight for the right to dispense presidential patronage. Congressman Walter P. Brownlow held on to his control of the state organization with H. Clay Evans maintaining a strong following as the leader of the anti-Brownlow forces. Evans had been away from Tennessee several years while serving as U.S. commissioner of pensions from 1897 to 1902 and U.S. consul general in England from 1902 to 1905, but neither man had any intention of giving up his presence in the Republican Party of Tennessee.

Brownlow controlled most of the Tennessee patronage as long as his ally, U.S. Representative Henry Gibson, held the Second Congressional District seat. However, once Nathan Hale was elected, Brownlow encountered some resistance. Hale had little intention of allowing Brownlow to curtail his own right to patronage opportunities. Brownlow pushed President Roosevelt to empower him with the ultimate Tennessee patronage authority, but the president did not encourage Brownlow's dictatorial maneuvers. Roosevelt wanted the support of Congressman Hale as well as Democrat confidants such as McGavock Dickinson and Sixth Circuit Court of Appeals Judge Horace Lurton.

Many rank-and-file Republicans became tired of and resented Brownlow's heavy-handedness with the state party. He was accused of using federal patronage to maintain power and hold his group together. Specific allegations that his group consisted of "thugs, democrats, minors, and niggers, with which Brownlow attempted to pack" (Shahan 1993) county conventions were made by Sam R. Sells, chairman of the Republican Party in the First Congressional District, over the events that occurred at the Sullivan County Republican Convention. East Tennessee Republican John C. Houk also related some of Brownlow's questionable methods to Ohio Republican Senator Joseph B. Foraker in hopes of obtaining his assistance in convincing the Republican National Committee to investigate the affairs of the Tennessee organization.

When President Roosevelt relieved Henry Clay Evans of his consul general position in London in 1905, it at first looked as if Brownlow would become more powerful than ever. However, the move actually strengthened Evans among the growing numbers who were resentful of Brownlow. Evans did not learn of his dismissal and of his successors's appointment until he read about it in the newspapers. Secretary of State F. B. Loomis assured Evans that this was an inadvertent neglect of protocal and not an intentional political slight and that both he and the president felt his work had been of the highest quality. To make up for the potential political injury to Evans, Roosevelt pledged support if he decided to run for governor of Tennessee in 1906. The press was given positive information about his future plans, and they printed speculation that Evans would return to Tennessee and run for governor in the next election. Evans quickly began his campaign.

Brownlow chose T. Asbury Wright of Rockwood, Tennessee, as his candidate, setting the stage for Republican party infighting within Tennessee. In an attempt to avoid damage to Tennessee Republicans and Evans's candidacy, President Roosevelt openly expressed his support for Evans. Newell Sanders, Evans's friend and manager, then publicly stated that the president would support Evans since he was the "strongest candidate for governor" (Isaac n.d.) in Tennessee.

Brownlow could hardly control his tongue and made a series of degrading public comments about Evans and Sanders, angering Tennessee Republicans even in his own home of Washington County. The president asked the chairman of the Republican National Committee, George B. Cortelyou, to try and resolve the feud. Brownlow would agree to allow Evans to run for governor, but only if he were left with control of the State Executive Committee. This was unacceptable to the Evans–Sanders wing. On March 6, 1906, the Brownlow-controlled State Executive Committee voted down the Evans team proposal to drop the old method of choosing committee members, which allowed Brownlow to single-handedly select committee members and thus ensure control of the party.

Resentment and criticism toward Brownlow increased. The state's

Republican patronage machine was alleged to be run and controlled by "political cut throats and thieves headed by Walter P. Brownlow" (Shahan 1993). He was losing influence. Many Republicans were willing to follow Evans as he challenged Brownlow's control of the party. After his return to Tennessee, Evans began actively running for governor. Brownlow's nominee, Wright, who could see the opposition growing against him because of his association with Brownlow, withdrew from the race for governor. He knew that Evans's popularity was increasing with each Brownlow antic.

Republican county conventions were held throughout the state on June 28, 1906. Evans was nearly unanimously endorsed as the Republican candidate for governor by the various county conventions. Many also planned to support the Evans faction for control of the upcoming Republican State Convention on July 11. The day before the state convention, eighteen counties were contested and the Brownlow-controlled state committee ruled in favor of the Brownlow contestants in every case. Evans's supporters contested the rulings, and the ultimate test went before the uncontested delegates at the convention the following day. The uncontested delegates were generally disgusted with Brownlow's maneuvering, and they accepted the Evans report. Evans and his allies gained control of the convention, and Evans was nominated as the Republican candidate for governor.

The convention also passed a rule which denied the state Republican Party chairman the right to name any additional members to the committee. The congressional district delegations then elected fifteen Evans and five Brownlow members of the new State Executive Committee, and the day after the convention, the new committee elected Newell Sanders as state Republican Party chairman.

Brownlow, who had rubbed too many Republicans the wrong way, was even challenged for his congressional seat. Republican Alfred A. Taylor ran as an Independent in order to attract Democrats along with the anti-Brownlow movement. Governor Cox, of Sullivan County, former speaker of the senate and East Tennessee Democratic boss, was friends with Brownlow. It was speculated that Brownlow had all along been aided in his maintenance of power in exchange for his support of Democrats. But in anticipation of his own nomination for reelection as governor he traded off his support for Brownlow in exchange for support in the upcoming race against Evans. Cox had John H. Caldwell of Bristol nominated as the Democratic candidate. With a Democrat in the race, Taylor had little chance to draw enough votes to defeat Brownlow. Second District congressman Nathan Hale also had some concern for his renomination, but the anxiety was only momentary as Evans actively went to work on his behalf.

Governor Cox, of course, wanted to stand for election on his own. Under normal circumstances a sitting governor of the day would receive the nomination, and thus victory, of his party. However, Memphis Congressman Malcolm R. Patterson decided to run and challenged the incumbent governor. Patterson felt that there would be lingering resentment against Cox over his previous support for Governor Frazier taking the late William Bate's vacant Senate seat. Patterson began an assault against the alleged Frazier-Cox machine, combining forces with Bob Taylor and Benton McMillian, and campaigning for "honest, responsible government" (Shahan 1993).

The *Memphis Commercial Appeal* attacked the Cox "machine" and stated "it boldly seeks to deprive the voter of his franchise by launching a contesting delegation whenever it can not force its wishes upon the various counties" (*Commercial Appeal* 21 March 1906). The election for the Democratic nomination was close and was determined by county election of delegates to the Democratic state convention. The issue hinged on the debate over the "unit rule" of delegates applying to each local election district versus the entire county. At the May 29, 1906, Democratic State Convention in Nashville, Patterson's organization fought and won the debate that all of the delegates in Davidson County should go to Patterson. If the district rule had held, each candidate would have won some of the delegates from Davidson County. Since Patterson carried Davidson County, one of the few counties with large blocks of votes, and he was from Shelby County, another county with large blocks of votes, the prospects for the incumbent governor looked dim. Cox's delegates accepted the inevitable, and Patterson was nominated by acclamation. He was officially made the Democratic nominee for governor on June 1, 1906.

Democrats were now badly split in Tennessee. There was irritation over the Frazier U.S. Senate election in March 1906, and now infighting over their choice for governor. Republicans saw a glimmer of hope. They had last successfully placed a governor in office during a Democrat split in 1880. Henry Clay Evans had won in 1894, but the Democratic legislature had "taken" the victory away by alleging "irregularities" (Shahan 1993). Perhaps Republicans could take advantage of the current division with their strongest candidate, Henry Clay Evans.

The Republicans adopted a platform, and the campaign began. Evans campaigned on the issues of dishonest elections, providing details of fraud in Knoxville and Memphis. He exposed the Tennessee laws which guaranteed Democratic control of state and local government. He pointed out that the poll tax "defend[ed] White supremacy" and noted the hypocrisy of the Democrats then "buying Negro votes" (Isaac n.d.). He exposed the Democratic gerrymandering that prevented Republicans from obtaining their seats in the legislature and Congress, and he campaigned in favor of statewide Prohibition.

Patterson stated he was in favor of maintaining the four-mile law on the sale of liquor, but he opposed imposing any restriction on the major cities, where he favored local option. He said if Evans were elected, "In the middle and western portions of the State we would be the unhappy witness to the advent of the Negro in politics, led and organized by men intent on plundering the State and controlling it with Negro votes" (Isaac n.d.). He attacked Evans for supporting the Lodge Federal Elections Bill when he had served in Congress, saying that Evans wanted to give "every Negro of voting age the right to cast a ballot and to carry out their accursed and meretricious ideas of racial equality" (Isaac n.d.).

Newell Sanders did try to organize Black Republican voters in West Tennessee. However, some of his Black contacts told Sanders that they wanted to delay registration as long as possible so as not to alert the Democrats. In truth, some Black voters followed the Brownlow faction's lead, often siding with Democrats in statewide elections and Republicans in national elections. This was because Brownlow used federal patronage to gain the cooperation of some Democrats and West Tennessee Blacks. There were two factions of West Tennessee Republicans—the Lily Whites and the Black and Tans. The Black and Tans seemed to side with state and local Democrats (they supported Patterson) and the national Republicans, while the Lily Whites seemed to side with Republicans at all levels. Sometimes the two factions would agree on a state or local candidate, but not routinely.

Statewide, the majority of the media of the day did not consider Republicans as an acceptable part of political life in state politics. Republicans hoped to add the alienated Democrats from the contested Democrat primary to the column of Republicans on election day. When Governor Cox made it clear that he did not intend to help Patterson's candidacy, the *Commercial Appeal* warned the voting public that Cox's motivations were to form a coalition with Republicans and Independents. However, the hopes of Republicans and the fears of Democrats and a Democrat media turned out to be of little real concern. Patterson put the Democrats in the winning column by polling 111,856 votes to 92,804 for Evans (45.2 percent was only slightly better than Republican candidate Jesse Littleton in 1904). After Evans was defeated, he slipped more into the background as Newell Sanders took control of their faction of the Republican Party in Tennessee.

First District and Second District Republican U.S. Representatives Brownlow and Hale were both easily reelected in the general election of 1906. Republican candidate J. C. R. McCall of the Eighth District lost by a close vote. The Democrats took all the remaining eight congressional seats in Tennessee, as well as control of the state house and senate.

Sanders and Congressman Hale moved to neutralize Brownlow's previous control of patronage during 1907. Sanders was successful in having former Congressman Arch M. Hughes, a Brownlow ally from Columbia, Tennessee, removed as postmaster in Columbia in spite of efforts to the contrary by Secretary of War Taft and leading Democrat politicians. Sanders became as tough with the use of patronage as Brownlow had been. In June 1907, twenty-four of Sanders's friends were appointed as postmasters in various towns around Tennessee.

During Patterson's term as governor a law was passed which prevented gambling on horse races. A pure food and drug act was passed. A governor's mansion was purchased (and used until 1922, when it was demolished and replaced with the War Memorial Building).

Patterson's victory did not put an end to the factionalism among Democrats. The Democrat-controlled state legislature provided strong opposition to the governor's programs during 1907. By 1908 opposition within the legislature and among political activists began to gain momentum. Edward Carmack, still reeling over his defeat for reelection to the U.S. Senate in 1906, became a leader of the anti-Patterson forces.

Corruption in city governments was commonplace during this era, and Memphis was no exception. Events that occurred there eventually impacted politics statewide. In 1905, James H. Malone, attorney and career politician, ran for mayor of Memphis as part of a reform ticket and was elected. After he was sworn in in January 1906, he made some efforts at reform. A Memphis good-government organization was formed with Dr. R. B. Maury as its leader. This evolved into an organization known as the City Club in 1907. It later contracted with the Bureau of Municipal Research to investigate and suggest reform measures for the administration of city government. The reform ticket initiated some improvements. It created a uniform tax rate for the city of Memphis and made progress in construction of sidewalks and streets, telephone and light poles, as well as in other areas, but it was unable to put a halt to gambling, prostitution, and Sunday saloon activity. There were 599 licensed saloons in Memphis in 1906.

City Councilman E. H. Crump resigned his position on the council of Memphis. Within three weeks of his resignation he announced his plans to run for fire and police commissioner—a position as a member of the upper board of the city council. His opponent for the November election was former mayor and old-line political powerhouse, J. J. Williams. Crump won the election by a 909-vote margin. That evening there was a fine celebration held at his campaign office. Later that evening, after Crump had gone home, he was called to the police station. Apparently one of his supporters had become so high-spirited that Police Chief George O'Haver was forced to incarcerate him. O'Haver wanted Crump to reassure him that it was safe to release the gentleman, a Memphis sock and Bible salesman. The gentleman, it turned out, was a man named Huey P. Long. Long liked Crump's positions on the issues and was one of his fervent supporters. Crump was sworn into office on January 2, 1908.

In 1908 Governor Patterson stood for reelection. By this time his enemies had increased within the Democratic Party, not only for his opposition to former Governor Cox but for his support for the liquor industry. Since Edward Carmack had suffered at the hands of the Patterson faction of the Democratic Party, the anti-Patterson and antiliquor Democrats (Prohibitionists) encouraged Carmack to take on Patterson. Carmack was an experienced legislator, had served in the U.S. Senate, and had defeated Patterson's father for Congress in the Memphis District. With anti-Patterson fever building, the opportunity looked promising to Carmack. Kenneth McKellar, who had been a strong supporter of Carmack's, urged the former senator to stay out of the race and bide his time to run again for the U.S. Senate under more favorable conditions. At first Carmack agreed with McKellar, but later he changed his mind. G. T. Fitzhugh and William E. Thompson, a Methodist minister, were two of the leaders who convinced Carmack to make the race.

Initially, the campaign debate of 1908 dealt mainly with the issue of primary elections. Governor Patterson wanted to show some legislative progress in the primary process. He had no intention, however, of throwing control to the free will of the people. Patterson agreed to separate primaries in each county in order to select delegates to the Democratic state convention, which would then choose the nominees. Further, Patterson wanted the unit rule in place so that he could pick up all the votes in the larger populated areas where he held some advantage. Carmack, tired of political machine manipulation, wanted a primary which would take the issues directly to the people. In spite of a great deal of support for a primary, the Democrat committee, controlled by Patterson, rejected Carmack's proposal.

The *Commercial Appeal*, which favored Patterson, "played down the importance of a statewide primary . . . and launched a frontal assault on the challenger" and it warned against "that amalgamated lot composed of Republicans, Independents and mugwumps, with 'isms' in their craniums" (Shahan 1993). The paper defended the Democratic Party and its party-controlled primary selection process.

The sale of alcohol was also debated. Patterson wanted the issue of Prohibition decided in each municipality, while Carmack wanted it decided on a state level. The Prohibitionists, therefore, favored Carmack, while Patterson had the support of the liquor industry. The two candidates stumped the state in joint debates trying to influence the primary election (this was a primary for the democratic gubernatorial nomination but with a county unit rule proviso).

MALCOLM RICE PATTERSON was born on June 7, 1861, in Summerville, Alabama, to Josiah and Josephine Patterson. His grandfather, Alexander Patterson, was a leading figure in the Revolutionary War, and a Scotch-Irish pioneer of Abbeville, South Carolina. Later, he moved into North Alabama and married Mary Deloach (from Birmingham). Their son, Josiah Patterson, married Josephine Rice, the daughter of Judge Greene P. Rice and Mrs. Anne Turner Rice.

Josiah Patterson led the Fifth Alabama Cavalry for the Confederates in the Civil War. After the war Colonel Patterson moved to Memphis to practice law. His son Malcolm Patterson earned his early education at Memphis schools, then attended college at Christian Brothers College and Vanderbilt University. He studied law with his father and in 1884 became attorney general for Shelby County Criminal Court. After six years in this post, he was elected to Congress for the Tenth Congressional District, then reelected in 1902 and 1904. In 1906 he ran for governor and defeated Governor Cox for the Democrat nomination and H. Clay Evans, the Republican candidate, in the general election. Prior to becoming governor, Patterson had married Lucille Coe Johnson, the daughter of Malcolm and Sara Coe Johnson, from Memphis. They had three children. Later Patterson married Sybil Hodges who was from Philadelphia, and they had one daughter. While serving as governor of Tennessee he married Mary Russell Gardner, daughter of William Sutherland and Jenny Sutherland Gardner from Obion County. They had one daughter born while he was governor and one son after his tenure.

Governor Patterson's family was the first to reside in an official governor's residence rather than a rented hotel room or other space. Patterson's administration saw several changes, many of which had been set in motion prior to his term. He oversaw creation of the State Highway Commission. Although he had pledged to support temperance, he reversed his position in 1909 and vetoed Prohibition legislation. When a dispute over land rights around Reelfoot Lake, erupted into violence, he called out the state guard to suppress an uprising by the Night Riders, a West Tennessee vigilante group. The decisive Patterson won reelection in 1908, but his glory was short-lived. Because he pardoned 1,412 convicts, he offended law enforcement officials. Others began opposing him because of his association with a political machine based out of Memphis. A split within the Democratic Party resulted in many Democrats endorsing Republican Ben Hooper in 1910. Patterson, helpless in the revolt, withdrew. He made a futile attempt to revive his organization through an unsuccessful attempt to obtain a U.S. Senate seat and then returned to Memphis. He lived there until he died in 1935. He was buried at Forest Hill Cemetery in Memphis. Mrs. Patterson lived until 1956. (Photograph courtesy of TSLA)

During some of the campaign, Carmack suffered from eye inflammation and was disadvantaged during his public appearances.

On June 28, 1908, Governor Patterson won the primary by 7,000 votes, (52 percent) and captured 732 out of 1,319 delegates to the Democratic state convention. The margin of his victory came mostly from the largest counties—Shelby, Davidson, and Hamilton.

Now defeated by Patterson in the Democratic primary, Carmack contemplated his future. Luke Lea, who owned a new newspaper in Nashville, offered him the editor-in-chief position of the *Nashville Tennessean.* Carmack, with the prestige of a position in the media behind him, assumed another well-respected, prominent, and dominant role in Tennessee leadership. He was incensed over his last race and was convinced that Patterson's machine and the liquor industry were controlling the state. Carmack now had the tool to attack Patterson and his political allies.

In October 1907 Wall Street tumbled. Stock prices fell and several investment companies failed. Economic depression shook the nation. President Roosevelt opted not to run for reelection. The president held a great allegiance to William Howard Taft and decided to promote him as his replacement. Taft left the War Department to run for president. President Roosevelt appointed Memphian Luke Wright, who had replaced Taft on the Philippine Commission, to again replace him as secretary of war.

Taft did not need the South to win the presidency, and since the South was solid Democrat, he did not expect it. However, Taft, like other Republican presidential candidates who preceded him, wanted to end sectional splits over the racial issue and encourage the South to see the virtues of Republicans and a two-party system. The most likely Southern state to go Republican was Tennessee. It had a solid Republican base in East Tennessee and the party could consistently poll at or above 40 percent in statewide votes. Taft had a number of friends and associates in Tennessee and had worked to win over traditional Tennessee Democrats. However, Tennessee Republicans were not necessarily a unified voting block. The Evans-Sanders faction had combined with Second District Congressman Hale's team. Lee Brock of Nashville and Robert S. Sharp of Chattanooga were also members of the Evans-Sanders-Hale coalition. In 1907 Congressman Brownlow, although in weak health, and almost blind, regained some allies. By 1908 former Congressman John C. Houk, wealthy contractor William J. Oliver, Jesse M. Littleton, and Richard W. Austin were all connected with the Brownlow coalition. The two factions battled to maintain control of presidential patronage prior to Taft's formal nomination. As a result, Roosevelt and Taft were drawn into the web of political maneuvering. Without a unified party in Tennessee, it became very difficult for Taft to guarantee Tennessee's delegate votes at the Republican National Convention.

During the Republican county conventions of 1908, Brownlow's men found themselves outvoted and most of the delegate spots for the state convention went to the Evans-Sanders-Hale wing of the Republican Party. Without the guarantee of patronage, it was difficult for Brownlow to motivate anyone. Chairman Sanders made sure that his wing of the State Executive Committee would control the state convention. Two-thirds of all contested seats went to his faction, and the Credentials Committee, controlled by Sanders, approved the decisions.

Even though the Evans-Sanders-Hale coalition now held control of the Republican Party in Tennessee, Congressman Brownlow made every effort to regain his former power. Because of Congressman Brownlow's health, William J. Oliver took over efforts for the impending state convention. Oliver was a tough and determined man. As a wealthy industrialist, he paid for a train to take between five hundred and eight hundred of his men, some armed with "hatchets, knives, and pistols" (Isaac n.d.), from Knoxville to the state convention in Nashville. On March 25, 1908, they arrived three hours before the convention was to open and "overwhelmed the guards posted by the Sanders organization" (Isaac n.d.). One witness said that there were "about 50 men who could not speak English and looked like Hungarians" (Isaac n.d.) with the Oliver crowd. By the time Sanders arrived at the capitol for the convention, it was too late. Oliver had physical control of the building and took control of the Republican state convention. "At one point in the melee, Sanders made it to the rostrum but was soon dragged away, choked, beaten, threatened by a large Black man with an ax, and almost thrown out of the window. Nashville city police finally arrived and stopped the actual fighting but not the general confusion" (Isaac n.d.).

Newell Sanders had no chance to even speak. Brownlow's followers claimed that almost all votes passed in their favor, 455 to 76. Oliver was elected national committeeman, and four of his followers were elected as delegates to the Republican National Convention. They also elected their own State Republican Executive Committee.

The Evans-Sanders-Hale clan had no choice and held their own convention the following day, March 26, 1908. They elected delegates to the national convention pledged to Taft for president and Henry Clay Evans for vice president, and they endorsed Congressman Nathan Hale for Republican national committeeman. Some of the Brownlow supporters who were disgusted with Oliver's antics attended this meeting and joined the Sanders faction.

Thus, in 1908 there were two state Republican Parties, and two different sets of delegates were elected to the Republican National Convention of 1908. Whatever the specific nature of the feud, it was clear to Taft that the Evans-Sanders-Hale coalition had most of the legitimate control of Republicans in Tennessee. It was up to Taft to see that there was some harmony and that he got things settled so he could wrap up all the delegate votes prior to the Republican National Convention.

Taft had his campaign manager, Frank H. Hitchcock, talk to Sanders in order to allow some room for Brownlow's people, in hopes for a unified front at the national convention. However, when the convention began there were contests for twenty-two of the twenty-four delegate seats in Tennessee. Brownlow hoped that the national committee would split the delegates between the two factions as it had done with the two slates presented by the Louisiana delegates. However, the national committee gave nineteen of the contested seats to the Evans-Sanders-Hale group. U.S. Representative Hale was chosen as Republican national committeeman from Tennessee, replacing U.S. Representative Brownlow.

At the June 1908 Republican National Convention in Chicago, Teddy Roosevelt, still popular, could have been renominated. However, on his election night in 1904 he had publicly stated that he would not seek reelection. He may have regretted the statement, but Roosevelt, known for his integrity, stood by his word. His secretary of war, William Howard Taft, who Roosevelt felt would continue his policies of reform, received Roosevelt's support. Many Republicans wanted Roosevelt to run, and in fact there was an anti-Taft movement that was designed to force his nomination. The anti-Taft group included Pennsylvania Senator Philander Knox, New York Governor Charles Evans Hughes, Vice President Charles Fairbanks, and Wisconsin Senator Robert LaFollette. However, the resistance came to nothing, and on the first ballot of the Republican National Convention Taft received 702 votes, to 68 for Knox, 67 for Hughes, 58 for Joseph Cannon, 40 for Fairbanks, 25 for LaFollette, 16 for Ohio Senator Joseph Foraker, and 3 for Roosevelt, who was not running. New York Congressman James S. Sherman was selected as the vice presidential nominee.

The Democrats again nominated William Jennings Bryan as their presidential candidate at the Denver convention in 1908. Bryan had lost twice to McKinley, in 1896 and 1900. Indiana attorney John W. Kern was nominated as the Democratic vice presidential nominee.

Back in Tennessee Brownlow political leaders formed an alliance with Democrat Malcolm Patterson in an attempt to deliver Republican votes for Patterson in exchange for Democratic votes for Republican Richard W. Austin in the Second District U.S. Representative race.

President William Howard Taft (left rear) rides in a parade route to a reception in Chattanooga, 1908. (Courtesy of CHCBL)

Austin was Brownlow's candidate set to defeat Congressman Nathan W. Hale. The Democrats did not field a candidate for the Second Congressional District race against Austin and Hale, who were nominated in separate Republican primaries. With the battle set between two Republicans, the Democrats took sides. Carmack Democrats supported Hale, while Patterson Democrats supported Austin. With both the Democratic and Republican Parties of the Second District divided, a vicious campaign ensued.

Each Republican faction held conventions in August of 1908 and elected its own gubernatorial candidate to face Patterson. The Evan-Sanders-Hale coalition elected George N. Tillman from Nashville. The Brownlow group selected T. Ashbury Wright from Rockwood. Later, Wright withdrew, and both groups compromised with Tillman, in exchange for support for Brownlow supporter F. A. Raht as a candidate for railroad commissioner. There would also be ten new members added to the State Executive Committee who would be selected by Wright. However, the compromise fell apart, and John C. Houk and F. A. Raht resigned from their newly appointed positions on the State Republican Executive Committee. Raht refused the nomination as candidate for railroad commissioner.

As the campaign of 1908 heated up, Taft decided to see if he could rouse Republican support in Tennessee and became the first Republican candidate for president to campaign in the South. In Tennessee, he first spoke in Chattanooga on October 16, 1908. He then went to Knoxville, Bristol, Cleveland, Athens, Sweetwater, Loudon, Lenoir City, Morristown, Greeneville, and Johnson City.

On election day, Taft received 7,675,320 popular votes to 6,412,294 for Bryan (321 to 162 electoral votes). Taft carried more of a percentage of votes in the South than Roosevelt had in 1904. He won 46 percent of the vote in Tennessee, compared to 43 percent for Roosevelt in 1904. After his election, Taft still faced Tennessee appointments and patronage disputes. It was only shortly after his inauguration that he declined to reappoint Memphian Luke Wright as secretary of war. Instead he named another Tennessean, Nashville Democrat Jacob McGavock Dickinson.

Party Conflicts and Reforms to World War II

PART III

Continued Conflict

Malcolm Rice Patterson easily won the general election for Tennessee governor on November 3, 1908, with 133,166 votes (53.7 percent). G. N. Tillman received 113,233 votes (46 percent), which was 2 percent better than Republicans received in 1904 and 1906. Tillman's support of Prohibition, the major issue of the campaign, likely aided in his defeat. Tillman felt that he lost because of the vote of anti-Prohibitionist Republicans, Brownlow's friends throughout the state, and Austin's Republican supporters in the Second District who voted for Patterson in exchange for Democratic votes for Austin. In fact the trade-off was good enough for Austin to defeat incumbent Congressman Nathan Hale for reelection. Brownlow was reelected to Congress in the First District, setting the stage for a patronage battle between the two Republican Tennessee congressmen on one side and Newell Sanders and the recently elected National Committeeman (and defeated congressman) Nathan Hale on the other.

In spite of Governor Patterson's reelection victory, he could not halt the tide of discontent within the Democratic Party. Carmack, now the editor of the *Nashville Tennessean,* attacked Patterson and his political cronies. Colonel Duncan B. Cooper was a railroad lobbyist and an ally of and advisor to Governor Patterson. Carmack resented the role that Cooper had played in various political bargains, specifically those that may have cost him his U.S. Senate seat. The animosity between the two men may have begun when Carmack had previously edited the *Nashville American*, which Cooper had owned. Cooper had supported Malcolm Patterson's father, Josiah Patterson, against Carmack in the Memphis congressional race of 1896. Carmack won the race, but later Cooper again opposed Carmack in his unsuccessful 1906 reelection bid for the U.S. Senate against Bob Taylor. Again Cooper opposed Carmack in the Democratic gubernatorial primary of 1908 and supported Malcolm Patterson. Patterson's victory left Carmack tremendously resentful toward Cooper for the repeated political opposition and aggravation. He had nothing but contempt for the notion which some held that Cooper was a man with political abilities—a man to have in one's corner if one had political aspirations. Carmack saw Cooper as a political parasite who possessed little real ability other than obtaining favoritism from elected officials. Embittered, Carmack went on the assault with the only weapon left at his disposal, the newspaper.

The *Tennessean* and a rival Nashville paper that supported Governor Patterson had exchanged "violent editorials" (McKellar 1942) against the allies of the competing papers. A couple of days after Patterson's reelection, Carmack wrote an article ridiculing Cooper. Cooper, a retired businessman and a former Confederate veteran, was greatly offended by Carmack's printed remarks. He bought a weapon and prepared for a physical encounter. On November 9, 1908, shortly after the publication of a morning article in the *Tennessean* which was again critical of Cooper, the colonel and his son, Robin, a Nashville lawyer, found the editor near Seventh and Union Streets on his way to his boardinghouse. According to Kenneth McKellar, Carmack's friend and supporter, Carmack was "peacefully returning to his home" when he was met on the road by the Coopers. After a verbal confrontation, shots were exchanged.

Colonel Cooper was uninjured, but Robin received a wound to the shoulder and Carmack, mortally wounded, died "in the gutter" (McKellar 1942).

Seven thousand people attended Carmack's funeral. His widow received numerous offers of assistance in the prosecution of the Coopers. His son, only nine years old, received a scholarship to a private school. The personal reaction and support for the Carmack family was far overshadowed by the public and political reaction. The murder shook the entire state. Cooper was a known close associate of Governor Patterson. The governor was a known enemy of Carmack. The Democratic split widened, and the Patterson political machine found the opposition forces quickly gathering momentum. Those who opposed Patterson's campaign rules, favoring open contests, were called "statewiders" (for holding a simultaneous non-unit rule statewide primary). Those loyal to Patterson, who opposed progressive election law changes, were called "Regular" Democrats. When the legislature went into session in January 1909, the "statewiders" formed coalitions with Republicans and called for an immediate election for speakers of the house and senate. The Regular Democrats did not field any candidate for speaker of the house and senate but tried to delay the votes. However, they were outnumbered by the coalition. Statewiders took the leadership positions and control of the legislature. They then moved quickly to act on Prohibition. Patterson had supported the liquor lobby and the statewiders moved, not only out of support for the temperance movement but also to weaken Patterson's organization and money flow. One motion was made to make it illegal to sell liquor within four miles of any school in Tennessee. Another motion was made to make it illegal to manufacture liquor for sale. Both provisions passed.

Time for Reform

Governor Patterson vetoed the Prohibition bills, but the determined legislature overrode the vetoes in late January and early February 1909. The legislature then moved to break Patterson's use of the election laws to perpetuate his power. In spite of general public and media support for the legislature's effort to revise the election laws, some Tennessee newspapers, the *Commercial Appeal* for example, defended Patterson and the election law system. The *Nashville American* said the laws were fair and there to ensure Democratic domination of the political arena since Democrats "are in the majority in the state, they represent the wealth and intelligence of the state, and it is only right that they should dominate in political matters, always being fair in the matter of elections, to the minority" (Shahan 1993). The *Nashville American* also insinuated that the proposed bills were "a Republican threat to White political dominance" (Shahan 1993).

One portion of the bill called for uniform printed ballots. Another part of the bill called for removal of any control of the election by the governor. It gave the legislature the authority to choose three statewide election commissioners (two from the majority party and one from the minority party). These commissioners would have the authority to select county election commissioners, who would then have the authority to choose polling officials. Additional measures were proposed that would force Republicans and Democrats to hold direct primaries to choose their nominees for state offices, other than judicial and attorney general offices. Again, the Regular

Democrats tried to delay, but the coalition passed the measures. On February 19, 1909, Governor Patterson again vetoed the coalition legislation, but again, the legislature overrode his veto.

Republicans felt that fair redistricting and nonfraudulent elections would give them better participation in state government, but they could not agree on the specifics of additional legislation. In fact the Sanders coalition and the Brownlow Republicans viewed any proposal with suspicion that it would advantage the other faction. As a result, Republicans lacked the unity required to advance the cause of a two-party system in Tennessee.

The Democrats wanted some election law reform in order to weaken Governor Patterson's hold on power. As a result, there was enough momentum in the legislature to achieve progress. The election laws passed in 1909 "provided for the appointment of election judges and clerks by the majority and minority county election commissioners, and poll watchers by the election judges" (Isaac n.d.). One notable provision prevented minority election commissioner's selection of election judges and clerks in counties with populations "between 24,950 and 27,075, and between 29,500 and 30,595" (Isaac n.d.) (based on the 1900 census). In these cases the judges and clerks would be selected by the whole commission (majority and minority). This special provision just happened to effectively exclude Blacks in Fayette and Haywood Counties from any oversight or control of the election process. These were majority Black Republican counties and would potentially deliver more votes for Republican candidates if the election machinery were honest, unbiased, and unadulterated by legislative maneuvering.

Not willing to be regulated by a legislative process that they did not control, the Regular Democrats challenged in court the laws passed by their own body. In the Chancery Court of Davidson County, the election commission act was upheld, but the mandatory primary act was overturned. The judgment was later upheld in the Tennessee Supreme Court. Patterson went to extended lengths to preserve the old election laws, but with each attempt to preserve the past, increased animosity built against him, cementing his future. By September 1909 a formal opposition coalition began to take shape.

In October 1909, Supreme Court Justice Rufus W. Peckham died. President Taft appointed Tennessean, Sixth Circuit Court of Appeals Judge Horace H. Lurton to replace him. Lurton was a former colleague of Taft's when Taft sat on the U.S. Appeals Court years before. Reform was taking place on many fronts during this era of Tennessee political history. In 1909, Tennessee adopted a statewide Prohibition law. Along with national and state reforms, local municipal reforms were being championed by Tennessee citizens who had grown tired of the old feudal method of government and power. This push for local reform was sorely needed in many communities, not the least of which was Memphis. In 1909, the City Club contracted with the "Bureau of Municipal Research" to investigate the actions and business practices of the Memphis city administration. The bureau found that the city government had no plan whatsoever to retire the city debt that it so willingly took on. The report stated:

> The City has apparently decided to let the future take care of itself. It has hastened to assume obligations without formulating any definite fiscal

> policy looking to the retirement of the bonds issued, and it is today engaged in piling up debt without reference to consequence. (Sigafoos 1979)

The state had no limitations on the amount of debt a municipality could incur. It only controlled the issuance of bonds.

E. H. Crump, a businessman and commissioner of fire and police, was one of the leaders in this new effort of reform. Crump had come to Memphis in 1892 from Holly Springs, Mississippi. He worked as a clerk in the real estate firm of Galbreath Company and in a cotton brokerage house. Later, in 1896, he became a bookkeeper in a carriage and saddlery business, then became a partner in his own business. In 1906, he bought out his partner and ran the E. H. Crump Buggy and Harness Company. On August 22, 1909, Crump announced that he would run for mayor of Memphis. His opponent was former Mayor J. J. Williams. Crump campaigned for mayor on a platform of supporting a five-person commission-form of government that would have the control necessary to make the city government more efficient, honest, and progressive. He defeated former Mayor Joe Williams by 53 votes (5,894 to 5,819 votes). Williams immediately accused Crump of voter fraud.

> On election day Crump helped with poll watching. In the fifth ward, where the saloonkeepers had registered Black voters in large numbers, he found the Black voters taking official ballots already marked into the polling place and then bringing out a ballot marked for the next man. When one voter started in with a marked ballot, Crump stopped him, but the Black voter objected and was backed in the argument by a White saloonkeeper. When the man insisted on voting, Crump struck him in the face, and then turning to the group, he threatened dire consequences to anyone using marked ballots. He spoke of the fracas later: "I should not have done so, but I was so outraged over the matter that I struck him." (William D. Miller 1964)

Williams demanded a recount and claimed that many of his votes were not counted while Crump's premarked ballots had been counted. He also complained that Crump had broken an agreement not to issue any poll taxes from anywhere but campaign headquarters. Williams alleged that he held up his end of the bargain, but Crump violated their agreement. If Williams had issued poll taxes, he would have likely won. Williams was also irritated over the amount of money that was made available for Crump's campaign. Eleven lawsuits were filed against the new administration, but Crump secured court orders to prevent Williams from stopping his inauguration and was inaugurated January 1, 1910. On the same day, the commission form of government became official with the approval of the state legislature.

As with many politicians, Crump used a cause that was appealing to the electorate, in this case the popular movement for reform, to gain office. Once elected, he soon consolidated his power base, coalescing considerable influence in local and state politics in the process.

On the state scene, Republicans Jesse Littleton and John Houk convinced Democrat Governor Patterson's allies that they would be the best Republicans to work for the governor's efforts in East Tennessee and that Brownlow and Austin would be less dependable in this regard. Littleton and Houk began their political plan by working to run anti-Prohibition Republicans for the state legislature in the First and Second Congressional Districts. Their goal was to help Patterson get friendly Republicans elected who would support efforts to repeal the election and Prohibition laws. Houk thought that if he could help Patterson, the governor would secure him a position on the State Election Board.

Within Democratic ranks, Regular Democrats still held enough power to control the state Democratic Party. When the party met on March 29, 1910, it began a process to mandate Patterson's favored unit rule primary to include judicial posts. This was an intended threat for the judges who feared an open and public nomination process. Usually, a separate convention was held to select judicial nominees by Democratic Party insiders. The threat of a public vote was used in an attempt to gain the political cooperation of the judges. State Democratic Chairman Austin Peay stated that inclusion of judges did not dictate any additional political influence over judges; after all, he said, "there is just as much politics and possibly more in the convention plan, than in the primary before the people" (Shahan 1993).

It is interesting to note that the Regular Democrats did not accept the "courts" decision over the election commissioner law. However, other Democrats were not about to be dominated or intimidated any longer by Patterson and the Regulars. Almost immediately after the Democratic Party actions, Civil Appeals Judges Frank P. Hall, Samuel F. Wilson, and Joseph C. Higgins and Supreme Court Justices W. D. Beard, John K. Shields, and M. M. Neil announced that they would boycott the primary. Other high-ranking elected officials, including U.S. Senator James B. Frazier, also condemned the plan.

Meanwhile the results of the Duncan and Robin Cooper murder trial (both were found guilty of second degree murder and sentenced to twenty years in prison) were being reviewed by the Tennessee Supreme Court. On April 13, 1910, it upheld Duncan Cooper's conviction, while ordering a new trial for Robin Cooper. Hours after the ruling, Governor Patterson pardoned both Coopers and said, "in my opinion, neither of the defendants is guilty, and they have not had a fair and impartial trial, but were convicted contrary to the law and evidence" (Shahan 1993).

All of Tennessee was appalled at Patterson's arrogant act. His pardon of the Coopers unleashed a tidal wave that would sweep him from office and end his political career. Statewide, Democrats were incensed over the pardon and became even more determined not to allow the governor to hold them hostage with his mandated version of the unit rule primary. To them, the governor had shown total disdain for and superiority over the justice system by pardoning his convicted political cronies. Shortly after the pardon, other judges announced plans to boycott the governor's primary and run as Independents. Supreme Court Justices Neil, Shields, and Beard then made public that Governor Patterson had offered to handle the judicial nominations in the standard manner through a convention, but had delayed his decision during the Coopers' trial appeal as inducement for their cooperation. Further, they alleged, the unit rule primary had been chosen by the Regular Democrat-controlled, Democratic Party on March 29 and 30 as a move designed to force the judges' decision.

Even worse were their charges published in the *Nashville Banner* on April 27, 1910. Patterson's aide and secretary of the State Democratic Executive Committee, Thomas D.

Lawler, had allegedly met with the judges to offer the governor's assurances that the traditional separate convention for judicial nominations would be held—with a guarantee of the three judges' renomination to the supreme court—if they were to agree to give up the idea of running as Independents. After this the judges claimed that they decided to make public Governor Patterson's interference in the Cooper murder trial appeal.

Although the *Commercial Appeal* defended the governor, his alleged attempt to pressure the supreme court judges incensed the public and severely interfered with Littleton and Houk's plans to win certain East Tennessee Republican legislative seats. The anti-Patterson feeling continued to gain momentum.

The State Democratic Executive Committee and Patterson soon began to recognize their growing weakness not only with rank-and-file voters but also with party activists. On May 7, 1910, they presented an offer of partial conciliation and agreed to hold a separate judicial convention. They gave the judges until June 7 to decide, with the threat to proceed if they did not buckle under by then. The State Democratic Committee also agreed to allow each county to select its own delegates to the Democratic state convention, rather than have the State Executive Committee choose the delegates. But by now the growing anti-Patterson forces had had enough of the political chicanery. They refused the offer.

An "Independent" (anti-Patterson) convention was held on May 18, 1910, and between five and six thousand Democrats gathered to defy Patterson and his "traditional" or Regular Democrats. They decided to boycott the Regular Democrat primary. President Taft then convinced Congressman Brownlow, Congressman Austin, and Newell Sanders that it would be best for a unified Republican front to support the Independent ticket for the August judicial election. Taft brought them to the White House and had them sign a statement which said, "In view of existing political conditions in Tennessee we believe it inadvisable for the Republican Party to nominate a ticket for the Supreme Court and the Court of Civil Appeals in the coming election, and we hereby agree to use our influence accordingly" (Isaac n.d.). Taft's logic was clear. Republicans would not field candidates and would throw their votes for the Independent ticket. This is exactly what happened. Most of Patterson's candidates, therefore, had no opposition in their primary. When the voter turnout for the primary was less than one-third that of previous primaries, Patterson and his cronies knew that even though he was renominated trouble lay ahead.

Although the Republicans were about to take advantage of the divided Democrats, there were some Republican activists who were irate over not fielding candidates for a primary. Practically though, this was a chance that Republicans sorely needed. They did not have the votes to win statewide elections without additional Democratic crossover votes. Now there was a possibility of working with like minds to throw out some machine Democrats and possibly elect Republicans in the fall general election. Despite this logic, some dissatisfied Republicans demanded a hearing with their State Executive Committee over the issue of fielding candidates. The committee knew, however, that the chances of electing a Republican without Independent help was remote. If Republicans fielded candidates, they would draw votes from the Independents, and Patterson's nominees would certainly win. Logic prevailed, and the State Republican Executive Committee rejected the motion for a separate Republican ticket on June 7, 1910.

The anti-Patterson forces then ran as Independents, with Republicans helping in the attack against Patterson and his candidates. The aura surrounding Patterson's machine had a foul smell to the voters and there were too many facts that backed up their suspicions. Carmack had been murdered. Patterson was a friend and political ally of the alleged murderers, and he pardoned the murderers. The Regular Democrats had a record of cooperating with the liquor industry and manipulating the legislature to stop election reforms. They also had twisted the party nominating process of 1910 so that it could be used as a tool for self-sustaining power and intimidation by Governor Patterson.

Along with the Republicans who campaigned for the Independents, the Tennessee press nearly unanimously supported the Independent ticket. Among these were leading papers such as the *Nashville Tennessean*, the *Nashville Banner*, the *Knoxville Journal and Tribune*, the *Knoxville Sentinel*, the *Chattanooga News*, and the *Chattanooga Times*. Only the *Nashville American* and the *Memphis Commercial Appeal* supported the Regular Democrats.

U.S. Senators Robert Taylor and James B. Frazier refused to campaign for the Regular Democratic ticket. No Democratic congressmen campaigned for Patterson's nominees. However, East Tennessee Republican Jesse M. Littleton campaigned for the Regular Democrats. His stated reasoning was that since Republicans had not fielded a ticket, he preferred Patterson's Regular Democrats to the "Independent" Democrats. It is more likely that Littleton was looking for support for his father-in-law, who was a candidate for state attorney general.

On election day, August 4, 1910, the Independents soundly defeated the Regular Democrats. The five Independent Democratic candidates for the Supreme Court received between 136,000 to 144,000 votes. The Regulars received between 95,000 to 97,000. There is no question that the lack of Republicans in the race prevented a split of the vote. With traditional Republican votes going to the Independents, the election was carried by the fusion of political forces. The large majorities from predominantly Republican East Tennessee sealed the doom of the Patterson forces. Patterson and his team now knew the situation looked desperate for the November general election.

Meanwhile, Republicans who were willing to support the Independent ticket in the judicial races were determined to field a candidate for the gubernatorial race, but they had their own factionalism to deal with. Alfred M. Taylor, brother of Democrat Bob Taylor, began to maneuver for the nomination and apparently had the support of the Brownlow-Littleton faction. The Evans-Sanders coalition threw their support to Ben W. Hooper, of Newport, Tennessee, an ardent Prohibitionist and moral reformer who was viewed as neutral in the factional split. Then Robert Sharp, who controlled certain patronage jobs, seconded Hooper's nomination. Since the Sanders faction controlled the convention, Hooper received about 382 votes to about 201 for Taylor. On August 16, 1910, the Republican state convention nominated Ben Hooper as Republican candidate for governor. The convention then endorsed B. A. Enloe, an Independent Democrat leader, for railroad commissioner, elected a new State Executive Committee, and reelected Newell Sanders as chairman. Republicans won so rarely that most united behind Hooper, unwilling to lose the opportunity. Hooper had reasonable relations with the Brownlow faction, and therefore even Jesse Littleton supported him.

The Independent Democrats also decided to give their support to Hooper and the Republicans rather than allow the Patterson machine the opportunity to regain power. Most Independent Democratic county conventions throughout the state endorsed Hooper. Patterson even faced losing his home base of Shelby County. Mayor Edward H. Crump, sensing a loss of influence by associating with Patterson over the might of his opposition, decided to remain neutral. This spelled the end for Patterson. He had to have Shelby County as well as Davidson County in order to gain reelection. The *Nashville Banner* reported that the *Memphis News-Scimitar* published a poll which showed that forty-eight Tennessee newspapers opposed Patterson and only sixteen still supported him.

On September 11, 1910, Patterson withdrew from the race. With him out of the way, the Regulars thought they could salvage the election and state control for themselves. Regular Democrats met on October 6, 1910, and selected the popular U.S. Senator Bob Taylor, who still had two years left in his Senate term, as the candidate for governor. They hoped to bring the Independent Democrats' influence back to the party. However, the Independents feared reempowering the machine with Patterson's puppet leadership and refused the risk. They were well aware of the lengths that the machine would go to in order to assure their empowerment. They had seen public fairness and responsibility trampled on. The same leadership that was supporting Taylor had supported Patterson. Besides, Independent Democrats had little reason to support Taylor since he had defeated their martyred hero, Edward Ward Carmack, in the 1906 U.S. Senate primary.

With the Regular Democrats in serious trouble, the *Commercial Appeal* continued to support them, printing statements such as this: "Elect Hooper and this state will be redistricted, the machinery of the state government will be taken over by the Republicans and the Republicans themselves will bring in a Negro to their support for every bolter who deserts them and it will take a revolution to drive them out of office" (*Commercial Appeal* 14 October 1910). Three days later the *Commercial Appeal* warned that unless Hooper were defeated, Blacks would gain power, carpetbagging would return, and the White Man's Party (Democrat) and the

---

JAMES CARROLL NAPIER was a member of the Southern "Black aristocracy." His paternal grandfather was a White Middle Tennessean who was a pioneer in the iron industry, and left his heirs, including his Black family, a good inheritance. Napier attended Wilberforce University and Oberlin College. Reconstruction Governor William G. Brownlow appointed him to several political offices. He obtained a law degree at Howard University and practiced law in Nashville. He worked with the Internal Revenue Service, served three terms on the Nashville City Council, and helped create the first Black-owned bank in the state of Tennessee. Napier was active in civic affairs and was on the board of several colleges. He was a leading, if not the leading Black Republican in Tennessee during his era, and as such was the Republican nominee for the Sixth Congressional District in 1898, served on the State Republican Executive Committee for almost twenty years, and was a delegate to four Republican National Conventions. (Portrait unavailable)

Solid South would be at risk. Even in 1910, forty-six years after the Civil War, Democrats were bringing up the Lincoln Republicans and Reconstruction Radicals (Isaac n.d., Shahan 1993).

The *Commercial Appeal's* warnings, of course, were not true. In fact, at the August 1910 Republican state convention, contested seats between White and Black candidates systematically went to the White candidates. Even James C. Napier, a well-known active Black Republican from Nashville, was not reelected to the State Executive Committee. This alienated Blacks, and the rejected Black Republicans and other Black leaders held a meeting in Nashville with about thirty in attendance the following day and formed the "Colored Independent Republican Club." They later endorsed Democrat Bob Taylor for governor. However, Republican leaders moved to stop the disenfranchisement.

Tennessee Republican Party Chairman Newell Sanders got involved in the on-again, off-again effort of Napier to gain a federal appointment. Sanders hoped that assisting Napier would encourage Black Tennesseans to come out for the Republican candidate for governor. On September 30, 1910, President Taft announced the appointment of Napier as register of the treasury.

In the First Congressional District, Sam R. Sells, a Brownlow critic and friend of Newell Sanders, had begun campaigning in February 1910 for the congressman's seat. However, he refused to run in the Brownlow-dominated primary, planning to seek an alternative route for election. After Brownlow's death on July 8, 1910, many candidates began campaigning for the spot. The First District Committee set October 8, 1910, as the date for the election to nominate a candidate for the unexpired term and a full term. As events progressed, most of the candidates dropped out except Sam Sells and J. R. Penland for the full term and Alf Taylor and Z. D. Massey for the unexpired term. Sells and Massey won the nominations and the subsequent November elections put both in office for their respective terms.

With Brownlow gone, the balance of power would be altered only within Republican ranks. The basic Tennessee political power structure of Democratic dominance, with Republican and Democrat-Republican coalitions positioning for patronage under Republican presidents, continued. Only the degree of Republican infighting and the names of the players really changed.

In the Second Congressional District there was still friction among Republicans since Richard Austin had defeated Nathan Hale in 1908. Both the Hale and Austin organizations maintained their own Republican Steering Committee. The Hale organization had tried but failed to prevent Congressman Austin from participating in the Republican caucus in the U.S. House. In 1910 each Republican committee planned to conduct its own primary. Congressman Austin ran only in the primary his committee called, on April 2. Then the Hale organization canceled its primary scheduled for September 3 and nominated Hale in convention on September 12, 1910. The *Knoxville Journal and Tribune*, the Sanders supporters, John Houk, and Jesse Littleton worked for Hale. Houk and Littleton had turned against Austin because they were unhappy that he was not appointing their choices to political offices. Even with many Republicans opposing Austin, President Taft remained loyal and used his power of federal patronage to support him. (Taft knew it was important to keep Austin and Brownlow from supporting Democrat Governor Patterson as they had done in 1908.) In spite of his opposition, Austin prevailed. He was reelected by four thousand votes.

In the midst of all the excitement of the fall campaign, former President Teddy Roosevelt visited the Appalachian Exposition to speak at the October 1910 event. Large crowds greeted the former president not only at the Knoxville exposition, but at every railroad stop from Bristol to Knoxville. This, of course, fueled some covert support for Roosevelt to run in 1912. William J. Oliver, who was president of the Appalachian Exposition, was one of the first political activists in Tennessee to openly support Roosevelt for the 1912 election.

As the gubernatorial campaign moved toward election day, Hooper hammered the Patterson machine. On November 8, 1910, the turnout was as large as the 1908 presidential election. Hooper gained 133,074 votes (51.9 percent of the vote) to 121,694 for Taylor. This was the first Republican elected governor of Tennessee since the election of Alvin Hawkins in 1880, and only the second since Reconstruction Governor Dewitt Senter was elected in 1868. In 1868, Reconstruction Republicans controlled the state and the vote. In 1880, Democrats controlled the state but were bitterly divided over the state debt issue. In 1910, Democrats still controlled the state, but this year their division stemmed from unacceptable political dominance within their own ranks, the pardoning of convicted murderers, and the Prohibition issue.

The results of the November 1910 elections created a new body to set the laws of Tennessee. Apparently, the people's negative feelings toward Governor Patterson flowed over into the legislative races. In counties that normally voted Republican, the Independent Democrats voted for the Republicans. In the counties that normally voted Democratic, the Republicans voted for the Independent Democrats. Therefore, the complexion of the legislature was somewhat, though not totally, altered.

The Regular Democrats had a hard time accepting both rejection by the people and a Republican governor. In 1894 they had denied Republican H. Clay Evans his gubernatorial election by overturning results from several counties. When the legislature met to resume business on January 5, 1911, the Regular Democrats intended to put a stop to Hooper's inauguration. They made it difficult to establish a quorum by boycotting the session. Finally, as sentiment mounted against the Regulars and it looked as if they would be blamed for the hold up, they gave in, and on January 10, 1911, the legislature went into session. However, their animosity had not lessened and they now searched for another way to prevent Hooper from taking office. The thirty-seven Regular Democrats in the state house refused to take their oaths of office in hopes of preventing the session from progressing and finding a way to dominate the Fusionists (Independent Democrats and Republicans), who had a slight majority in the state house. Since the Regular Democrats still had enough votes to control the state senate, they indignantly delayed the governor's inauguration as long as they could. The sitting governor (Patterson) had been inaugurated on the fifteenth of January. Now the state senate put Hooper's inauguration on hold until the twenty-sixth. At this, Hooper threatened to ignore the state senate and the house and have himself sworn in. Once the Regular Democrats realized that Hooper could be as brash as they were, an agreement was reached. Ultimately, the Regulars agreed to halt efforts to prevent Hooper from taking his seat in return for the Fusionists' agreement to stop plans to unseat several Regular Democrats who had won disputed elections. Hooper was finally sworn into office on January 25, 1911. The new governor was committed to education, the prison system, Prohibition, honesty in state government, and the inspection of state banks. He made his concerns and agenda official in his inaugural address.

U.S. Senator James B. Frazier's term was scheduled to end on March 4, 1911, and it was time for the legislature to either renew his term or name a new U.S. senator. Frazier wanted a new term, but his support base had shattered from both the recent political upheaval and from the resentment toward him for his manipulations to gain the seat in 1905. The Regular Democrats wanted former Governor Benton McMillin (he had been nominated through the June 1910 Regular Democrat primary in which he was unopposed), but the Regulars could not put together the necessary sixty-six votes for the election in the Tennessee General Assembly; he was two votes shy. The Fusionists, seeing that McMillin did not have the numbers, put forward one of their group who had recently been elected as railroad commissioner, Benjamin A. Enloe. However, he could only come within three votes of the appointment.

The Shelby County delegation of legislators was holding up the process by continuing to vote for its hometown favorite, Kenneth D. McKellar. These eight members of the legislature were holding firm as a block. Although they were loosely associated with the Regular Democrats, they had an objective of their own, and had learned

BEN W. HOOPER overcame adversity from the beginning of his life. He was born on October 13, 1870, in Newport, Tennessee, the illegitimate son of Dr. L. W. Hooper and Sarah Wade. Dr. Hooper was engaged to another woman at the time of the pregnancy and refused to agree to abortion or marriage. Unable to provide for the child, in 1878 Sarah gave the child to St. John's Orphanage of the Episcopal Church. When in 1879 his father, now married and without children, found that his son was in the orphanage, he took custody of him. Hooper was able to grow in a loving and nurturing home, but living in a small town was a painful experience for the young boy. The social stigma of his birth caused him embarrassment and permanently affected him with a determined will to succeed.

Hooper received his early education at St. John's Orphanage. After graduating from Carson Newman College, he studied law with Judge H. N. Cate, then opened his own law practice. In 1892 he ran for the state legislature and was elected, serving two terms from 1893 until 1895. He entered the Spanish American War and served as a captain with Company C in the Sixth U.S. Volunteer Infantry. When the war was over he was elected assistant district attorney in the Eastern District of Tennessee. He took Anna Belle Jones, daughter of Benjamin Jones and Townsella Randolf Jones from Newport, as his wife in 1901.

Hooper ran for governor in 1910 as a Republican. During this period of time Governor Patterson was the enemy of many Democrats who supported Prohibition and who opposed his control of the state's election machinery. With a split among Democrats, Hooper had the support of Republicans and Independent Democrats. He was elected and began serving in that they could exert control over the entire legislative body by working together. Once the senate nomination process was thus stalled, Luke Lea, a thirty-one-year-old newspaper publisher of the *Nashville Tennessean* and *American*, came forward. Lea knew politics and the media well. He had been the leader of the move to maintain unit rule at the Davidson County convention of 1906. The results of the unit rule debate in the primary gubernatorial delegate selection in 1906 had helped Malcom Patterson win the Democrat nomination for governor. Later, Lea had changed his support and helped promote the Independent Democrat's separate primary and "fusion" with the Republicans. After talking with Mayor Crump of Memphis and asking for his support, he won the commitment of some of the Shelby delegation. In addition, Governor-elect Hooper owed a fair amount to Lea for the role he had played in the fusion of Independent Democrats and Republicans on the 1910 election cycle that resulted in his election. Hooper convinced the newly elected railroad commissioner Enloe to bow out long enough to determine if Lea could pull it off. All the Fusionists and two Regular Democrats from Shelby County, Stanley Trezvant and W. M. Stanton, voted for Lea. After thirteen days and numerous ballots, Luke Lea was elected U.S. senator (Class 1) on January 23, 1911. He took office on March 4, 1911, and served until March 3, 1917.

Once the new legislature was in session and the attempts to block the inauguration of the Republican governor were over, the Regular Democrats immediately moved to wrest back political control. Republican

---

1911. His family was the second to occupy the governor's residence, and their fifth and sixth children were born there. Since Hooper owed his support to many Democrats as well as Republicans, he had to answer to several divergent interests. The coalition that had elected him was difficult to manage and control of the legislature was divided. The state house of representatives was controlled by the Fusionists (Republicans and Independent Democrats) while the state senate was controlled by the Regular Democrats. Because of this division, progress was difficult, and the sessions were marked by overt chaos, quorum breaking, and discord. Nevertheless, counties were authorized to issue bonds to buy school property and set up hospitals. Child labor laws were also passed and the Food and Drug Act was created.

The coalition held together long enough to reelect Hooper in 1912. During his second term, although the political chaos worsened, progress continued. State revenue was increased for education. A law was passed making at least four months a year of school attendance mandatory for those between eight and fourteen years of age. Transportation for students was authorized. A system of bank inspection was organized, and a parole protocol was evaluated for the criminal justice system. Execution was changed from hanging to electrocution. Sanitation laws were created and Prohibition enforcement improved. Hooper fulfilled most of his campaign promises. Since most of the problems which had motivated the Fusionists were solved, the Democrats (with Patterson's machine control supposedly out of the way) had little reason not to work together to regain power. Hooper lost reelection in 1914. He retired from the governor's office (1911–1915) and joined the Railroad Labor Board in Chicago. Later he was elected vice chairman of the Limited Constitutional Convention of 1953. Hooper died in 1957 in Carson Springs, Tennessee, and was buried in Newport, Tennessee. (Photograph courtesy of TSLA)

LUKE LEA was born on April 12, 1879, in Nashville, Tennessee. He was the great-grandson of Luke Lea, who served as secretary of state for Tennessee from 1835 through 1839. He attended public schools for his early education, then the University of the South, at Sewanee, Tennessee, where he graduated in 1899. He finished law school at Columbia University in New York, New York, in 1903, returned to Tennessee, and began practice in Nashville. He also founded, edited, and published the *Nashville Tennessean* newspaper. Elected by the Fusionist legislature of Tennessee as a U.S. senator in 1911, he served until 1917, but was unsuccessful in obtaining the nomination in 1916. While in the U.S. Senate Lea served as chairman of the Committee on the Library and on the Committee to Audit and Control the Contingent Expense. He fought in World War I, serving in Europe, and obtained the rank of colonel in an artillery unit. After the war, he returned to Nashville and his newspaper. When Senator Lawrence D. Tyson died in office, he was appointed to fill the vacancy. However, he declined the offer, instead becoming involved in banking and real estate. Lea died on November 18, 1945, in Nashville, and was buried in Mount Olivet Cemetery in Nashville, Tennessee. (Photograph courtesy of SHO)

State Senator Houk and his friends, in an attempt to position themselves for more influence, decided to help the Democrats. His plan involved enlarging the state election commission from three members (two Fusionist Independent Democrats and one Sanders Republican) to seven members in order to gain control of the state election process. The addition would allow the newly appointed three Regular Democrats and one Brownlow Republican to outnumber the other three and take control of the election process. The Regulars controlled the state senate. The new speaker of the house, Clarksville Democrat A. M. Leach, favored the plan. Although Leach had worked with the Fusionists, once elected speaker, he saw the advantage of combining forces with the Regulars. With his defection came a few others wanting to be on the side of power. Even if the governor vetoed the Regular Democrat proposal, there would now be enough votes to override in view of the defections. It appeared that the Regulars were about to ignore the will of the electorate, which had mandated reform of the old political machine, but the remaining Fusionists were determined to see the will of reform succeed. Therefore, thirty-four members of the house broke quorum and left Nashville, on April 13, 1911, for Decatur, Alabama. Without the necessary two-thirds present, the house would be paralyzed.

State Senator Houk publicly criticized Governor Hooper when he vetoed the bill by accusing the governor of "selling out the Republican Party to Luke Lea and the Independent Democrats" (Isaac n.d.). The truth, though, was that the Fusionists and Governor Hooper were trying to prevent the Patterson organization from taking back control of the election machinery, which had given them the power to totally control the election process. If Houk could not control the election commission himself, he could help the Regulars take control with their promise to pass along some influence to him. When denied this opportunity, Houk, a Republican, then was willing to criticize the second Republican governor since Reconstruction and assist the Regular machine Democrats in taking over again.

Public embarrassment over the machinations of the legislature prompted the Fusionists to finagle a deal with certain Democrats. Again, the Shelby County delegation, which was only loosely associated with the Regulars, was the target. On June 11, 1911, Newell Sanders and E. B. Stahlman negotiated with Mayor Crump of Memphis. They wanted the Shelby County delegation's allegiance and votes. The mayor wanted control over the Shelby County Election Commission and support for local legislation, particularly regarding Prohibition which he opposed. The final deal included the placement of Leslie M. Stratton, a Crump loyalist, on the State Election Board, allowing Crump to determine who would be on the Shelby County Election Commission, and thus control the Shelby County election machinery. Once the Shelby County delegation switched support for the Fusionists, the requisite number of legislative votes to override a veto was denied the Regular Democrats. The crisis over the stall in the legislative session and the Regular Democrats' attempt to take over the election process ended.

The Regular Democrats were bitter toward Crump because of his maneuvering, but he was more concerned with his local control. They made a last attempt to discredit Governor Hooper by increasing state appropriations, above income, in an effort to create a budget shortfall. However, Hooper publicly exposed this ploy, and the representatives were forced to modify their bill. The Regular Democrats also tried to set up their own state election commission, but this was eventually denied in the courts.

On April 28, 1911, the secretary of war, Tennessean Jacob McGavock Dickinson, resigned. His wife and son had been ill, and he conveyed that there were some personal financial concerns dealing with his partial ownership of a coal company that he needed to tend to. However, the real and private reason may have been the developing feud between President Taft and Teddy Roosevelt. Dickinson, a Democrat, thought that his friend Taft ought to have a dynamic Republican to stand on his behalf in the position of secretary of war as the brewing national Republican feud gained momentum.

In 1911 President Taft appointed Knoxville resident and Bedford County native Philander Priestly Claxton, who was head of the Department of Education at the University of Tennessee, as commissioner of education. He also appointed Lee McClung, who was originally from Knoxville but currently living outside the state while serving as treasurer of Yale, as treasurer of the United States. McClung was a nonpolitically active Republican. Claxton was a Democrat who was active mainly with education issues.

A national Republican intraparty political war began to take shape. Taft, who had become president with the help of Roosevelt, allegedly had not lived up to Roosevelt's expectations. Republican Congressmen Payne and Aldrich created a tariff act which passed Congress. Taft had previously pledged to cut tariffs. When the bill passed, Taft did not veto it. An irritated public blamed Taft for the higher priced products partially brought on by the tariff. However, Taft oversaw many solid accomplishments. New Mexico and Arizona became states during his term (now there were forty-eight). His administration continued Roosevelt's policy of prosecuting antitrust suits. Actually, there were almost twice as many prosecuted under Taft as under Roosevelt. Parcel post service and postal savings were created, and the Oval Office was constructed next to the White House.

In West Tennessee, a change in the balance of political control would have a strong impact on statewide elections. Mayor Crump continued to consolidate his power, and by the time of the next Memphis city elections, he had it firmly in his grasp. He had gained significant cooperation in "his" nonpartisan city elections by agreeing to provide the Black community with a park, paved streets, and street lights. The August 22, 1911, *Commercial Appeal* noted that Memphis had recently seen the greatest voter registration drive since 1879 and that most of the registration was of "Negro" votes, registered through an organization within the police department. The paper went on to note on September 20, 1911, that the mayor had "made his commission a one man organization [which] grasped not only the political machinery of the city, but that of the county" (Miller 1964). Black Republican George W. Lee viewed Crump's seemingly enlightened politics in a clearer light.

> Crump bossed a corrupt political machine which bought votes by the thousands. Illicit saloons, gambling dives, and houses of prostitution provided an $80,000 yearly slush fund for the registering and voting working-class Negroes in every ward and precinct of Shelby County. (Tucker 1971)

Joe Williams had been elected mayor of Memphis in 1898 by using the "Negro vote" (W. D. Miller 1964). Now, Crump and his campaign manager, Frank Rice, used the Black vote to defeat Williams in the election.

On election day, November 1911, Crump won by over seven thousand votes. Kenneth McKellar, an ally of Crump's, won the congressional seat by defeating Socialist W. A. Weatherall. Since the state legislature had amended the charter of the city to change the term of office of the mayor of Memphis from two to four years, Crump would now officiate until January 1916.

National Republican turmoil continued. Reform minded Republicans felt that Taft had sided too much with big business. When Roosevelt returned from his tours in Africa and Europe in June 1910, he was met by old supporters who were enthusiastic for his return to the White House. Roosevelt was only fifty-one years old at the time and certainly young enough to run again. He demonstrated his interest in pursuing the presidency during speaking tours of the West and Southwest. By 1912 he declared his candidacy and began campaigning for delegates. Taft could not understand why Roosevelt had turned on him. He knew that Roosevelt's candidacy would fracture the Republican Party on the national level and send reverberations into local politics. A three-way vote split would cause the demise of the Republican domination of the presidency, which had continued unchecked except for Grover Cleveland, since the Civil War. Roosevelt either knew this and chose to ignore it or was too self-confident to believe it.

As the political war clouds of a Roosevelt-Taft battle loomed in late 1911, Newell Sanders, Congressman Austin, and Congressman Sells all came out publicly for President Taft's reelection. The convention to elect Tennessee's at-large delegates for the Republican National Convention was slated for after the state convention to avoid bringing the divisiveness of the presidential nomination into Hooper's renomination.

In February and March 1912, counties throughout Tennessee held their conventions and selected delegates to the state convention to nominate a candidate for governor. At the state convention on March 12, 1912, Ben Hooper was again nominated. Black Memphian Josiah Settle seconded Hooper's nomination at the state convention and "promised that the Negro vote in Shelby County would go to the Republicans in 1912" (Isaac n.d.)

For the Fusionists, the 1912 election was a chance to solidify the mandate of the electorate for reform. For the Regular Democrats, it was a chance to seek revenge and regain control of the state. The presidential election added excitement, but also complicated matters for Tennessee Democrats because both the Regular Democrats and the Independent Democrats were loyal to the national Democratic Party. The infighting among Democrats in Tennessee, which had created the breach that helped elect Governor Hooper, had developed because of the desire to destroy Governor Patterson's political machine. If Democrats could take advantage of national Republican infighting and put a Democrat in the White House, then patronage would flow to the Democrats in Tennessee. However, they were still split over the issue of a general party primary. The Regular Democrats supported the status quo. The Independents, fearful that the Regular Democrats would continue to place the politics of power and self gain above that of the general welfare of the people of Tennessee, wanted to create a primary to select candidates for all state offices, delegates to the state convention, and the party's state committee. They had actually created a proposal for harmony, but the Regulars feared the loss of control with such an open process. Both camps were concerned that any settlement would require a reshuffling of power within Democratic ranks.

If the Democrats did not reunite, they not only risked losing the governor's seat to the Republicans again, but they risked affecting the presidential election. With two Democratic factions, there might be two sets of delegates fighting for seats at the Baltimore Democratic National Convention set for later in the year. Negotiations stalled. However, in February, Memphis Mayor Crump, along with about sixty newspaper editors, scheduled a harmony convention to take place in Nashville in late March 1912. The convention did help assure that a single set of delegates would go to the national convention, but it ultimately failed to settle statewide factional differences.

On March 31, 1912, U.S. Senator Bob Taylor died. Taylor had been extremely popular throughout his life, was liked by Republicans and Democrats alike, and had developed friendships around the nation. Kenneth McKellar later wrote that when Taylor died he witnessed "the largest crowds I ever saw at the funeral of any man, not only in Washington but in Bristol, Johnson City, Greeneville, Morristown, Knoxville, and Chattanooga. There were enormous crowds at every place at which the train stopped between Washington and Nashville" (McKellar 1942).

Taylor's death left the Senate seat vacant until his term officially ended on March 3, 1913. By law the governor could name a replacement until the state legislature scheduled a vote. This situation left a Republican governor with the unique opportunity to appoint a Republican. The Democrats, even the Independent Democrats, did not like the idea of a Republican filling a Senate seat. But, Governor Hooper had a pragmatic mind, along with a sense of loyalty. He appointed Newell Sanders to fill the seat. It was indeed a unique occurrence to see a Republican U.S. senator from Tennessee; there had not been any since Reconstructionist Governor Brownlow was in office. The Democrats, of course, were unhappy, and the governor agreed that the appointment would continue only until the legislature reconvened in 1913. This agreement avoided alienating the Independent Democrats necessary for Hooper's reelection, and appeased the anti-Sanders Republicans. Sanders took office (Senate Class 2) on April 8, 1912, serving until the Democrat legislature elected a replacement to take the seat on January 24, 1913.

When the second Republican state convention convened in 1912 to nominate the delegates-at-large, the convention also elected a new State Republican Executive Committee and a new state party chairman. James S. Beasley was selected to succeed Sanders.

The ten Republican congressional district conventions to select delegates to the Republican National Convention were held about the same time period as the county conventions. An intense battle took place between delegates who supported Taft and those who supported Roosevelt. Some of the district conventions became very high-spirited. In Knox County, the Second District Roosevelt supporters held their convention in the Knox County Court House courtroom. Taft supporters left the courtroom, found another room, and held their own elections. As congressional committees were selected, the Republican division widened, depending not only upon whom a delegate supported for president but also whom a delegate supported for the Republican congressional nomination. There was still a Hale committee (for former Congressman Hale), a Roosevelt-Oliver committee, and a Taft-Austin committee. The presidential delegate selection had disintegrated into competition for the Republican congressional nomination in the Second District. There was also competition for the nomination in the First District, where Congressman Sells and A. D. Massey were opponents. The chaos extended from the county convention level to the district convention level, which in turn would nominate the candidate for Congress and select the delegates to the Republican National Convention.

The First District convention was particularly divisive. "One newspaper called it one of the 'most unruly, obstreperous, militant conventions ever held in the state'" (Isaac n.d.). The temporary convention chairman, Colonel Adam Bowman, was hit on the head with the gavel. Finally, the two opposing groups separated and held separate conventions. Both endorsed Taft for president and Hooper for governor but elected different delegates to the Republican National Convention. One group nominated Sells for Congress, while the other Republican group nominated Massey for Congress. After the convention, both groups appealed to the Republican National Committee, chaired by Congressman William B. McKinley, for recognition.

G. T. Taylor, who became involved in the skirmish for the postmaster appointment in the Tenth District, was intimately involved in the positioning for nomination in the Eighth and Ninth District conventions. He supported Taft and was an ally of Second District Congressman Austin. Taylor was from the Ninth District and was opposed there by the Sanders-Hooper coalition. Two separate conventions were held in the district. The Taylor group met on March 26, 1912, while the anti-Taylor group met on

NEWELL SANDERS was born on July 12, 1850, near Bloomington, Owen County, Indiana. He lost his father when he was only two years old. After a common school education, he went to Indiana University where he graduated in 1873. He married Corinne Dodds on October 28, 1873. A partnership in a bookstore with his brother-in-law lasted until 1877, when he moved his family to Chattanooga. There he went into the plow manufacturing business. He ventured into other areas, but none were as successful as his Chattanooga Plow Company. A politically active Republican, Sanders participated in local, state, and national politics, serving as state Republican Party chairman and as a Tennessee Republican national committeeman. He assisted Henry Clay Evans by managing many of his efforts, including the 1894 governor's race. He also assisted Ben Hooper in his successful gubernatorial races of 1910 and 1912.

When U.S. Senator Bob Taylor died, Governor Hooper appointed Sanders to finish out the term. He served from April 8, 1912 until January 24, 1913, the only Republican U.S. senator from Tennessee since Reconstruction. During his term, he supported the Interstate Bill. Sanders later worked for the passage of the Women's Suffrage Amendment. The amendment, requiring only one more vote for ratification, stood before the Tennessee legislature in 1920. When it looked as though the vote would be lost, Sanders led an effort to persuade legislators to vote for ratification, including Legislator Harry Burn from Athens, McMinn County. Burn's vote ratified the Nineteenth Amendment by one vote—the vote of Tennessee was key to finalizing ratification.

Although Sanders was directly in the middle of Republican factional infighting, he was generally held in high regard among his Republican peers. No one worked more unselfishly or was more dedicated to the Republican cause than Sanders. For years he worked for others to be elected. Senator Kenneth McKellar had this to say about him:

> The Democrats disliked him very greatly. Most of the newspapers in the state were Democrat, and they held Mr. Sanders up to public scorn and ridicule, and claimed there was nothing good about him. Indeed, until 1912, when I first met him, I and most of the people of Tennessee who did not know him had come to the conclusion that he was like the fabled monster of hoof and horn, charging and fighting and destroying everything and everybody in his path—especially Democrats. (McKellar 1942)

In 1922 Sanders ran for the Senate, but was defeated by McKellar. Later McKellar admitted Sanders "was universally respected as a citizen, and was regarded as a good man [who] did not deserve the treatment he received from his party associates" (McKellar 1942). After retiring from the Senate, Sanders returned to the plow manufacturing business and continued to be active in Chattanooga affairs. After succeeding in business, leading the Republicans in Tennessee, twice guiding the election of a Republican governor of Tennessee, and being appointed to the U.S. Senate, he died a respected and accomplished man in Chattanooga on January 26, 1939. (Photograph courtesy of SHO)

April 11, 1912, both electing different delegates to the Republican National Convention but both groups supporting Taft. However, Taft had embarrassed Taylor on April 12 by appointing a Sanders man as postmaster in Dyer, Tennessee, even though the president had agreed not to make any more appointments until after the national convention. At this, Taylor issued a call for another Ninth District convention, claiming that there were irregularities at the March 26 convention. The new convention elected the same delegates, but this time Taft lost a delegate; one was now committed to Roosevelt and one to Taft.

The Eighth District convention did not take place until after Taylor had held the second Ninth District convention. The Eighth District also selected one Taft and one Roosevelt delegate. When all the district delegate selections were completed, five districts (Three, Four, Five, Six, and Seven) had selected one uncontested set of delegates. Districts One and Two had selected two separate sets of delegates for Taft, while Districts Eight and Nine had selected two separate sets of delegates that were split between Taft and Roosevelt.

Part-time Republicans

The Tenth District had a greater number of Black Republicans than any other area of the state. Patronage rather than race was the issue. The convention in Memphis on April 25, 1912, disintegrated into a battle for postmaster between incumbent L. W. Dutro and H. O. True, a paint manufacturer, with charges and countercharges flying between the two factions. True was tied in with the Black and Tans wing of the Republican Party, while Postmaster Dutro was associated with the Lily Whites wing. This competition for the postmaster appointment affected the selection of delegates from the Tenth District to the Republican National Convention.

True formed an alliance with Robert Church Jr., a Memphis Black Republican leader. Church led the Shelby County Black and Tans, which consisted of mostly Blacks, with some White members. The Black and Tans held substantial numbers and could significantly contribute to the support of Republican candidates. The Lily Whites existed mainly to control local and state Republican Party representation and any patronage that might be available. The Lily Whites and Black and Tans battled every four years over delegate selection to the Republican National Conventions.

At the age of twenty-six, Robert Church Jr., whose late father was a wealthy Black business leader in Memphis, was already involved in Republican intraparty bickering, fighting the Lily Whites in order to maintain influence in the Republican Party. His father, Robert Church Sr., died in 1912 and left him a fair amount of wealth in the form of real estate and restaurants. At the age of twenty-seven, with few financial worries and the time to become involved, Church became extremely active politically. His charge was to organize the West Tennessee Black vote for East Tennessee Republicans. Later, his relationship with Second District Congressman and national Committeeman J. Will Taylor granted him some influence when West Tennessee patronage was dispensed. Church was careful to include White candidate recommendations for U.S. postmaster, federal judge, and U.S. attorney. Although his sister and daughter inferred in their biography, *The Robert R. Churches of Memphis,* that his selection of Whites for these high-level jobs was because there were few qualified Blacks, it is also possible that Church saw the practicality in softening his Lily Whites' opposition by working with and assisting Whites who supported his own quest for influence.

At the April 1912 Shelby County Republican Congressional Convention, True and Church's coalition outnumbered the competing contingency led by Dutro. A confusing and boisterous battle ensued. Once the larger delegation was seated as delegates, the Dutro group left the convention, and True, who was White, and Church, who was Black, were selected to attend the 1912 Republican

National Convention as delegates from Shelby County. The Dutro group held their own convention and elected C. H. Trimble and T. C. Phelan (both were White) as delegates.

When the 1912 Republican National Convention took place in Chicago in June, both Shelby County groups appeared and demanded to be seated; the Shelby County battle resumed on the Chicago convention floor. However, the convention was controlled by President Taft, and the leaders of the convention sat Church and True as delegates from the Tenth District of Tennessee (both were pledged to Taft as were nearly all of the other delegates selected from contested situations). There were fifty-eight Black delegates attending this 1912 convention. Taft was the incumbent president, and these votes were already pledged to him. Taft, however, had not appointed enough Blacks to satisfy some in the contingency, and an effort was made by Teddy Roosevelt to win them over. The Black delegate count held the convention in doubt about their ultimate vote. If they stayed united, they might retain some influence on the selection of the Republican nominee for president of the United States.

During Taft's term as president he had alienated the liberal wing of the Republican Party. They felt that he had too close a relationship with "millionaires and corporation lawyers" (Whitney 1982). Teddy Roosevelt was also dissatisfied with Taft and accused him of succumbing to the influence of the business community. Roosevelt promoted his "progressive program," which was theoretically more supportive of the common man over the business community.

Taft was bitter with Roosevelt for turning on him and his supporters at the Republican National Convention and refused to seat many of Roosevelt's delegates. After pledges of increased inclusion of Blacks in the next Taft administration, the Black delegation all voted for Taft as instructed by their constituents. Three hundred thirty-four Roosevelt delegates refused to vote because of those not allowed to be seated. They were obviously outmaneuvered by the Taft-controlled leaders of the convention. Taft received the nomination, but at a tremendous cost. The night of the nomination, the 334 delegates, along with the others refused seating, met and pledged their support for Roosevelt as an Independent candidate.

Tennessee Democrats were also divided about who should receive the Democratic nomination for president. The May 1912 Democratic state convention failed to conclude with a unified front. Independent Democrats generally supported Woodrow Wilson, governor of New Jersey. The hardline Regular Democrats supported a variety of candidates. U.S. Senator Oscar Underwood of Alabama had the support of Nashville Mayor Hilary Howse. Speaker of the U.S. House of Representatives Champ Clark had had the support of the late Tennessee U.S. Senator Bob Taylor. Some Tennessee Regular Democrats supported Ohio's Judson Harmon.

Although Republican Governor Hooper looked to be easily renominated, party infighting threatened his chances in November. Jesse M. Littleton and John C. Houk led the opposition against their Republican governor and former state Republican Party Chairman now U.S. Senator Newell Sanders. Since Republicans in Tennessee, who controlled power also controlled the flow of patronage from President Taft, their support of the incumbent president was unwavering. However, Littleton and Houk had no such loyalty and broke to support Teddy Roosevelt. As they saw it, there was little chance for them to gain any control through Taft.

Republicans G. T. Taylor, state treasurer, and John C. Houk organized the Roosevelt campaign in Tennessee. Taylor made plans for a state Progressive Party convention for August 2, 1912. Supporters of Governor Hooper tried to keep his friends in the Progressive Party from carrying their enthusiasm for Roosevelt so far as to nominate a Progressive candidate for governor. To do so would place reelection for Republican Hooper in jeopardy. Taylor then published a letter from Roosevelt supporting the nomination of a state ticket for the Progressive Party and then communicated to William J. Oliver and H. B. Lindsay that they should not "block the nomination of a candidate for governor" (Isaac n.d.). However, Oliver and Lindsay did not attend the State Progressive Convention and supported Hooper, along with Roosevelt. Oliver wrote Roosevelt saying, that neither Roosevelt or Taft "understood the political situation in Tennessee" (Isaac n.d.).

About two hundred to two hundred and fifty delegates, including twenty-five to thirty Black delegates, attended the Progressive Convention in Nashville. They elected a complete party organization, presidential electors, and delegates to a Progressive National Convention. A very real anti-Sanders-Hooper sentiment emerged. The convention nominated William F. Poston from Alamo, Tennessee, for the Progressive candidate for governor and J. E. Edington from Chattanooga for railroad commissioner. This enraged many dedicated Tennessee Republicans who supported Roosevelt but were unwilling to destroy Hooper's chances for reelection. Thirty or so immediately walked out of the convention and held a rump convention that endorsed Hooper.

No Democrat congressman or former governor participated in the Houk-Taylor convention. However, J. H. McDowell from Buntyn, Tennessee, and Thomas S. Hutchinson from Nashville were reasonably well-known Democrats who did participate. Their presence, however, did not change the character of the organization, which was actually a remnant of the Brownlow—now Taylor-Houk—faction.

At the rump Progressive state convention, Roosevelt was endorsed, but the delegates stood by Hooper. The convention felt that Houk and Taylor were trying to destroy the Republican progress that had been accomplished under Governor Hooper and trying to reinstitute the old system of the First District Republicans, combined with the Democrats, to control the state. Nevertheless, Roosevelt supported the Houk-Taylor nomination of a Progressive candidate to oppose Hooper.

At the July 1912 Democratic National Convention in Baltimore, Tennessee Democrats still disagreed over who should be nominated. After forty-six ballots and six days of convention infighting, the convention finally chose a nominee. New Jersey Governor Woodrow Wilson was nominated after six days of convention infighting.

The Progressive National Convention was held in Chicago in August 1912. Roosevelt was nominated for president. Hiram Johnson was nominated for vice president. Three Roosevelt Progressives were nominated to run for Tennessee congressional seats.

Tennessee Democrats were generally unified in their support of the national ticket. However, intraparty negotiations over the Democratic Party primary failed to satisfy the fears of the Independents. They still felt that the Regulars were positioning to retake power, and would not, even for the sake of party unity give in to this old clan of machine politicians. It also did not help the cause of party unity that ex-Governor Malcolm Patterson had decided to run for U.S. senator. Suspicions immediately arose when Patterson made his intentions known. By late July, the Independent Democrats made their break public and warned, once again, against a machine takeover. They called for boycott of the August Democratic primary. Although a total boycott did not take place, the turnout was low and allowed the Regular Democratic candidate for governor, Benton McMillin, to win an easy victory in the Democratic primary. McMillin, a former congressman and two-term governor, defeated Chattanooga banker Thomas R. Preston for the nomination. After McMillin became the Regular nominee, Independents "fused" once again with Republicans.

Regular Democrats held an agreed-upon state convention on August 15, 1912. The purpose was to establish the Democratic Party platform for the fall statewide election. They called for a return to local option for liquor in the state's largest cities. (Most of Tennessee's cities were dry, though not all.) They chose to select their candidates (who would ultimately be selected by the state legislature) for the U.S. Senate and some other state offices by holding a Democratic primary simultaneously with the November general election. Former Governor Patterson and State Comptroller Frank Dibrell, who was severely attacked with accusations over irregularities of administration of the back-tax system, ran for the U.S. Senate and state comptroller positions. Their presence on the ballot served to alienate Independent-minded Democrats.

On September 18, 1912, the Independent Democrats held a convention to endorse Hooper for governor. They were convinced that since the Regular Democrats were supporting Patterson for senator and McMillin for governor, they were truly not interested in seeking reform. There were two predominant issues that motivated them to join forces with Republicans again: the preservation of the improved election laws and maintenance of the gains in Prohibition legislation. Everyone knew that if Patterson was rewarded with a U.S. Senate seat, his political cronies would be better positioned to manipulate the laws to perpetuate their power. Therefore, the Independent Democrats had no reason to cooperate with the Regulars.

Although Regular Democrats endorsed McMillin's race for governor, they could not drum up enough support. U.S. Senator Luke Lea, Malcolm Patterson, and State Comptroller Frank Dibrell attacked one another in the press, creating a clear picture of Democrat division. Hooper attacked McMillin and stated that if the Regular Democrats retook the governor's seat "old times of liquor-machine domination, of pardon brokerage [referring to freeing prisoners], of fraudulent primaries, of stuffed ballot boxes, of tyrannical conventions, of drunken officials, of licensed crime, of legalized murder" (Isaac n.d.) would return. Hooper pointed out that McMillin was supported by the "lawless elements" that he was campaigning against. He also attacked Dibrell and his oversight of the back-tax program in which corrupt officials made large profits in the collection of "delinquent taxes." McMillin campaigned against Hooper's failure to completely stop the sale of liquor and appealed to Democratic loyalty. On October 25, 1912, McMillin's son, Brown, died suddenly, and the candidate stopped personal campaigning.

What little support there was for Progressive gubernatorial candidate Poston came from anti-Prohibition Republicans and a few "maverick" Democrats. State Treasurer Taylor, who was running for reelection, served as Tennessee's Progressive Party chairman. He knew that Poston had no chance to win. His only hope was that he could pull enough votes to defeat Hooper. Up to the very end of the campaign, Harry B. Anderson of Memphis and John C. Houk continued to campaign and speak throughout the state for Poston. Poston attacked Governor Hooper's administration as "extravagant, incompetent, and inefficient" (Isaac n.d.).

Meanwhile the Republicans consolidated with Independent Democrats. In Memphis, efforts to influence Crump's support were wasted. Hooper supporter Republican H. O. True, had worked for McMillin in the Democrat primary. Evidently he had done this because Crump held disdain for McMillin, and True thought that if McMillin won the Democrat primary, Crump would refuse to support him. However, the Shelby Republican vote had always been small in comparison to the Democratic vote. There was little chance that True's hopes held any foundation. On the day before the election True discovered that Crump intended to bring in "Big Shelby" for McMillin (Isaac n.d.).

Factionalism in Tennessee spread into the congressional campaigns. There was crossover support in many directions with multiple motivations. A few Republicans split over factional conflicts and allegiances in the First and Second Congressional Districts. Some supported Hooper for governor; some were old Brownlow factionalists seeking return to power; and some were Progressive Roosevelt zealots. Z. D. Massey, an old Brownlow Republican from Sevierville who did not feel that the Republicans at the Chicago national convention gave him a fair hearing, saw Sam R. Sells (Sanders faction) gain the official Republican title. So he opted to run as the Progressive congressional candidate in the First District. This race quickly disintegrated into a nasty affair. One published letter from a Massey supporter to Congressman Sells said, "Please do not swear to your replies before a defunct notary public, like you did before, nor use any cuss words, as you usually do, as I want to have your reply printed, and it might fall into the hands of some child." (Isaac n.d.) To which Congressman Sells replied, "I have your inquiry which is without date. Replying thereto, I have no lather to waste in shaving an ass. Permission is given you to publish this reply" (Isaac n.d.).

In the Second Congressional District race, Congressman Austin had the backing of Sanders and Hooper. W. H. Buttram, attorney general of the Second Judicial District, ran as the Progressive candidate, but he supported Hooper for governor. John C. Houk and H. B. Lindsay supported Buttram. J. C. J. Williams ran as the Democrat.

In the Middle Tennessee Seventh Congressional District, Independent and Regular Democrats supported separate U.S. House candidates. Arch M. Hughes entered the race as a Republican, but this threatened Independent Democratic support for Hooper in the gubernatorial race. Newell Sanders then convinced President Taft to let Hughes know that he could not endorse him. At this, Hughes dropped out of the race, easing the danger of losing Independent support for Hooper.

In the Third Congressional District there was a Progressive candidate and a Democratic candidate for the U.S. House seat. Sanders and the Taft Republicans decided to run a Republican candidate in order to split the Republican/Independent vote in favor of reelecting Democrat

Congressman John A. Moon, who supported Hooper.

During the presidential campaign, there was scattered Tennessee support for Roosevelt. Only one big city daily, the *Memphis News-Scimitar*, backed him. Some smaller papers, such as the Lawrenceburg *Lawrence Union*, the Sevierville Montgomery *Vindicator*, the Tazewell *Claiborne Progress*, and the *Greeneville Sun* supported Roosevelt. Most of the major newspapers spent more time on the governor's race attacking Hooper than helping Wilson in the presidential race. The *Memphis Commercial Appeal*, the *Chattanooga Times*, the *Nashville Democrat*, and the *Nashville Tennessean* (which had supported Hooper in 1910) all supported McMillin for governor. With Roosevelt running as the Progressive Party candidate, the Republican vote was split. "Multiple splits and combinations in congressional and legislative races, political activities by temperance organizations, racial conflicts, personal rivalries within party organizations, and vote trading all added to the confusion" (Isaac n.d.) in Tennessee in 1912.

The only presidential candidate to campaign in Tennessee was Roosevelt. He stopped in Memphis to speak at the Tri-State Fair and in Jackson to deliver an address to about twenty-five thousand people at the West Tennessee Fair during late September. After traveling into Mississippi and Louisiana, he came back north to Chattanooga on the twenty-ninth of September. He spoke at the train depot on that day, spent the night, and then spoke at the city auditorium the next day. Then he traveled to Knoxville, making stops at the small towns along his route. At the Knoxville depot he greeted a large crowd. He then spoke at the city auditorium and later to a group of blue-collar workers. During the trip the state leaders in Roosevelt's campaign fought among themselves for a place in the spotlight with Roosevelt, bickering over who would chair a reception or a rally or who would ride in the car with him. The Roosevelt campaign in Tennessee did not help itself by getting into the governor's race. Roosevelt imprudently attacked Governor Hooper while in Tennessee. This only lost him support.

Some Tennessee Blacks supported the Roosevelt ticket and opposed Republican Hooper's ticket. Traditionally the Black vote went to whomever the East Tennessee Brownlow faction supported. Nashvillian James C. Napier, the most well-known Black Republican in Tennessee, did support President Taft and Governor Hooper, and campaigned for them in Middle and West Tennessee.

On election day November 5, 1912, Tennessee gave Woodrow Wilson 52.8 percent, Republican Taft 24 percent, and Progressive Roosevelt 21.5 percent of the state's vote count of 251,933. Nationally, Wilson was elected the twenty-eighth president with 6,296,547 popular votes to 4,118,571 for Roosevelt, and 3,486,720 for Taft (435 to 88 to 8 electoral votes). As Wilson headed for the White House, Republicans in Tennessee prepared to lose federal patronage. Patronage had been the source of most of the Republican factional infighting since the time of Reconstruction. Now, as a result of egotistical personality clashes and state and national Republican bickering, Tennessee Republicans would have much less to fight over.

In the governor's race Hooper polled 124,641 votes to 116,610 for McMillin. Progressive candidate Poston gained only 4,483 votes. Hooper won 50.2 percent to McMillin's 46.9 percent. Almost 3 percent went to other candidates including 1.8 percent for Poston. An analysis of the votes indicates that the margin of victory in this basically Democratic state was provided by about fifteen thousand Democrat defectors. Most of the support for the Republican candidate came from East Tennessee and a few scattered counties in Middle and West Tennessee. Shelby County continued tradition by voting Democratic.

Democrats won the third, fourth, fifth, sixth, seventh, eighth, ninth, and tenth District U.S. House seats in 1912. In the Second District, Congressman Austin easily won reelection over Buttram, a Roosevelt supporter, even though Roosevelt outpolled Taft in this district. However, in the First Congressional District, Congressman Sells just squeaked by former short-term Congressman A. D. Massey by six hundred votes out of over thirty-two thousand.

There was a turnover of twenty-seven seats in the state legislature, but the result did nothing to provide a clear balance of power. The numbers were so closely split between the Fusionists and the Regular Democrats that the balance of power laid with the closely knit Shelby County delegation. Houk, who had deserted the Republican Party to run for reelection as a Progressive candidate for state senate in the Fifth District, faced serious hostility from Republicans as well as some Progressives. Governor Hooper made it a point, when speaking in Knoxville, to state that Houk was "a traitor to his party, to its principles and to the people who elected him to office" (Isaac n.d., Shahan 1993). Houk lost, coming in second to the Republican candidate.

Even though Republican Hooper won, the Democrats in Tennessee still exerted control. The election of a Democrat president would serve to strengthen their hold. Shortly after the Cooper murder trial in 1909, former Congressman Arch M. Hughes, a Brownlow Republican who had previously served as postmaster in Columbia for a time up to 1907, suggested that Mrs. Edward Ward Carmack be appointed postmistress in Columbia. Senator James B. Frazier worked on President Taft for the appointment. She was almost appointed, but the objections of Newell Sanders; Frank H. Hitchcock, postmaster general and Republican National Committee chairman under Taft; and Democratic Congressman Padgett held off the appointment. Mrs. Carmack was subjected to an embarrassing public discussion of her private affairs. Nevertheless, she was finally appointed during the Wilson administration, thanks to the efforts of Senator Luke Lea. There would be no federal patronage for Republicans in Tennessee for the next eight years. No significant alteration in political party affiliation occurred in Tennessee. The state was still Democratic. It was the movement for Prohibition and election law reform, and the opposition to politicians who ignored laws prohibiting illegal saloons that had fueled Hooper's reelection over former Democrat Governor Benton McMillin.

Prior to the 1912 elections, Newell Sanders was chairman of the state Republican Party, a national committeeman, the dispenser of federal patronage for most of the state, a U.S. senator, and a leader in President Taft's reelection effort. Since there was no Republican president to dispense federal patronage in Tennessee and Newell Sanders was now out of the state Republican Party chairmanship, Governor Hooper inherited the state Republican leadership role. In 1913 the legislature elected the next U.S. senator and Sanders, being Republican, naturally was not even considered. However, he remained national Republican committeeman. The two Republican congressmen, Austin and Sells, with no presidential federal patronage to dispense, were almost powerless.

Governor Hooper was the only leading Republican with any jobs to disperse, and he therefore became the most prominent and influential Republican in Tennessee.

Hooper had the cooperation of most Republicans, Independent Democrats, and Crump's Shelby County Democrats, but he needed to keep the wayward Roosevelt Republicans in line in order to maintain control of the legislature. In exchange for cooperation, he traded jobs. He appointed his friend, Dr. A. D. Massey, the physician at the central state prison in Nashville. This satisfied Congressman Sells's allies, who wanted to prevent Massey from contesting the congressional race. He also made J. Will Taylor, who had supported Hooper, state insurance commissioner, at the request of one wayward Republican who promised to hold the line with Hooper if he would help Taylor.

Although Memphis Mayor E. H. Crump was adamantly opposed to Prohibition and differed with Republicans and Independent Democrats—the Fusionists—on this issue, he agreed with them on the need to revise the state constitution, and the back-tax law. He also was particularly determined to be rid of State Comptroller Frank Dibrell and prevent Malcolm Patterson from being elected by the legislature to the U.S. Senate. Republican H. O. True of Memphis told Governor Hooper that the "opportunistic" Crump would "'trade any way' to get an advantage" (Shahan 1993). In exchange for bringing his Shelby County legislative delegation into the Fusionist Independents' camp and allowing them to gain control of the legislature, Crump gained from Governor Hooper assurances that Memphis would be safe from enforcement of the state's Prohibition laws. This left Crump with impunity in dealing with those selling liquor in Memphis, who would now have to cooperate with the mayor if they wished to stay in business.

Shortly after the November election, Crump met with U.S. Senator Lea, a convert to the Independents, and Major Edward B. Stahlman. Their objective was to place their friends in the state offices which were up for reappointment. When the General Assembly convened in January 1913, the combined forces of the Fusionists and the Shelby County legislative delegation elected Newton H. White, of Giles County, speaker of the senate. They elected William M. Stanton, a twenty-three-year-old Memphis lawyer, the youngest speaker of the house in Tennessee history. Seeing the strength of the coalition, Malcolm Patterson withdrew his U.S. Senate bid on January 9, and Frank Dibrell withdrew his bid for reelection to the state comptroller's office. George P. Wollen was made comptroller, R. R. Sneed was made secretary of state, and W. P. Hickerson was chosen state treasurer. All of these men were Independent Democrats. Although Patterson lost his bid to become Senator, the Independents were not totally satisfied concerning the U.S. Senate seats. Republican Newell Sanders, who had been appointed by Governor Hooper as interim senator, would have to be replaced. It would have alienated the Independent Democrats to have a Republican remain in the seat, even for just one month longer. It had caused Governor Hooper a great deal of grief to appoint Sanders in the first place and had taken a significant amount of negotiation to convince the Independent Democrats to allow it. Republican interests were thus set aside. The Fusionists were allowed to appoint the headmaster of the Webb School, William R. Webb, to fill the remainder of the Senate short term in Class 2. His term lasted a little over a month, from January 24, 1913, until March 3, 1913. Years later, Kenneth McKellar wrote,

"Senator Sanders did not deserve the treatment he received from his party associates" (McKellar 1942). After the legislature elected Webb, it turned its attention to the vacant full term for the same U.S. Senate seat which was to begin on March 4, 1913. Even though it was accepted that a Democrat would win this seat, there was a scramble for the position among Chief Justice John K. Shields, former Governor Benton McMillin, Fusionist B. A. Enloe, and former Tennessee Attorney General Charles T. Cates. This was to be the last time a U.S. senator would be regularly elected by the state legislature. On January 23, 1913, after several ballots, Regular Democrat Shields narrowly won the U.S. Senate seat (Class 2). Shields served from March 4, 1913, until March 3, 1925, being reelected once.

On the national scene, Woodrow Wilson was only the second Democrat (Grover Cleveland being the other) to be

WILLIAM ROBERT WEBB was born on November 11, 1842, in Mount Tirzah, Person County, North Carolina. After three years his family moved to Oaks, North Carolina. His father died when he was a small child. Webb received his early education from his sister, who taught in a log cabin. When he was fourteen, in 1856, he went to the Bingham School in Oaks. Four years later, he entered the University of North Carolina, but his education was interrupted in 1861 by the Civil War. He was shot three times in the Battle of Malvern Hill, Virginia, sustaining a severe arm wound. Seventy percent of his company were either injured or killed in the battle. After his injury Webb temporarily returned to the University of North Carolina, then went back into active military service in 1864. He fought in nearly all the Virginia battles until he was captured three days prior to Appomattox and subsequently imprisoned on Hart's Island, New York.

After the war Webb returned to North Carolina and taught at Horner School in Oxford. He completed his college studies by "cooperative work and special examinations" (McKellar 1942), receiving A.B. and A.M. degrees from the University of North Carolina. Afterward, he left North Carolina due to his "disgust with carpetbaggers and reconstruction government" (McKellar 1942). Because Tennessee, under President Andrew Johnson, was able to rejoin the Union with much less turmoil than other Southern states, Webb moved to Culleoka, Tennessee, where he founded the Webb School in 1870 (moving to Bell Buckle in 1886). His excellent educational program developed a widespread reputation. The school provided some unusual flexibility for the students, but also some unusual rules. Webb administered corporal punishment for those boys who broke the rules. If a young man proved to require too much attention regarding his conduct or obedience, he would be expelled. (Edward W. Carmack was one of those expelled.)

Webb was a staunch Prohibitionist and on the national board of the Anti-Saloon League of America. He married Emma Clary, from Unionville, Tennessee, on April 23, 1873. In 1896 Webb worked against Democratic presidential candidate William Jennings Bryan and his free silver philosophy. He could not bring himself to vote or support any Republican; therefore, he campaigned as a delegate for the Gold Democrats. In January 1913 Webb was appointed by the Fusionists to fill the remainder of Newell Sander's Senate seat from January 24 until March 3. Although his level of political participation was limited, Webb was known and respected by many. He died at home in 1926. (Photograph courtesy of SHO) elected president since the Civil War. He was inaugurated on March 4, 1913. Candidate Wilson had been the beneficiary of a very receptive Tennessee press. He had ties to Tennessee and his election inspired Tennessee Democrats. His brother, Joseph, worked as city editor for the *Nashville Banner*. The Wilson brothers' father, Joseph R. Wilson, taught at Southwestern Presbyterian Seminary in Clarksville, Tennessee, during the period 1885–1892.

The coalition of the Fusionists and the Shelby County delegation altered the balance of power in Tennessee. As long as it held together, the Fusionists and E. H. Crump were in command of the state. The only question was, could this unusual constellation of forces continue? The answer would come soon. They had agreed on many things, including an immunity bill which would protect those who testified and cooperated during an investigation into former Comptroller Frank Dibrell's office and his administration of the back-tax law. Apparently, the office was used by the Regular Democrats to manipulate the system to their advantage and they desperately wanted to prevent the investigation. Crump wanted the investigation but not at the expense of losing control of his county.

In February 1913 former Governor Cox surprisingly changed his position, now supporting a proposed law that would help pass Governor Hooper's law enforcement measures designed to force community leaders to enforce Prohibition laws. This was something Crump did not want. Crump had no choice but to desert the Fusionists. If he did not, Hooper would have enough votes to pass the law enforcement bill. With Crump abandoning the Fusionists, the balance of power tilted back to the Regulars. This effectively waylaid the immunity bill and any investigation into Regular Democrat conduct during previous administrations.

In March, U.S. Senator Lea, Crump, and a few Independent Democrats sided with the Regulars, ending Fusionist control of the General Assembly. The Regulars, now in control, set out to stop the Prohibition law enforcement bill, to remove some of the governor's power of appointment, and to change election laws. Apparently they favored the tax system that was in place even though there were calls from throughout the state for reform. They made proposals that would enlarge the state election commission from three to five positions, and give control of the commission to Regulars, who then could control county election commissioners. This could effectively prevent Republicans from being able to assure fair local elections.

It now looked as if the Regulars would reverse everything the Fusionists had worked for. In opposition, the *Banner* printed a story stating that the new coalition of "saloon-elected city bosses allied with the horde of revenue agents and back-tax attorneys who have operated the plunderbund" (*Nashville Banner* 21 March 1913; 5 April 1913; 29 March 1913) would reverse the progress of reform.

Governor Hooper vetoed the bills, and the remaining Independents and Republicans broke quorum and left the state on March 30 and 31, 1913. The legislature was unable to act for the next four months. By late June the state was running out of money, and the Fusionists returned to pass the necessary funding legislation. Once back in session the Regulars immediately overrode the governor's veto. Once again the election law put the power to control the votes back in the hands of Regular Democrats. When Patterson was governor, it took the outrage of Tennesseans to slow

JOHN KNIGHT SHIELDS was born on August 15, 1856, in Clinchdale, Tennessee (Grainger County). He received a private tutor education, and was admitted to the bar in 1879. He was married to Mary Fulkerson in June 1883, but she died four months later. He practiced in Grainger and nearby counties until 1893, when he was appointed chancellor of the Twelfth Chancery Division. In 1894 he went back into law in Morristown, Hamblen County, Tennessee. He served as a delegate to the Chicago Democrat National Convention in 1896 which nominated William Jennings Bryan and to the St. Louis Democratic National Convention in 1904 which nominated Alton B. Parker. He was elected as an associate justice of the supreme court of Tennessee in 1902, served until 1910, was reelected, and continued on the bench until 1913. When the split in the Democratic Party occurred over Governor Patterson's machine and his pardoning of the Coopers for the murder of Carmack, Shields was a leader of the state supreme court move to run an Independent Democratic slate for the judiciary in 1910. This move sealed the end of Governor Patterson's control of the Democratic Party in Tennessee. Shields led the Independent movement to "fuse" with Republicans, resulting in Hooper's election as governor and Shields's eventual election to the Senate. Shield's battle for election to the Senate was a free-for-all fight with former Governor Benton McMillin, Fusionist B. A. Enloe, and former Tennessee Attorney General Charles T. Cates.

Shields was elected to the U.S. Senate on January 23, 1913, to succeed Senator Webb, who finished the uncompleted term of the late Robert Taylor, filled by temporary appointment of Newell Sanders. His election marked the last time a U.S. senator would be regularly elected by the state legislature. Since Luke Lea, the other U.S. senator at the time, had supported Charles Cates over Shields, Shields wanted Lea defeated when his reelection came up in 1915. Kenneth McKellar was eventually elected over Lea. Shields was sworn in the same day that Woodrow Wilson was inaugurated president and served from March 4, 1913, until he was reelected in 1918. During this term he married Mrs. Jeanette Swepson Dodson Cowan, a widow. Shields then served the term from March 4, 1918, until March 3, 1925. He lost renomination in the 1924 Democrat primary to Lawrence Tyson. President Coolidge then appointed Shields assistant attorney general for failed banks, where he remained for the following two years. John Knight Shields died in 1934. (Photograph courtesy of SHO)

the corruption. Now the progress that had been made in election law reform was officially reversed—and all to prevent the enforcement of Prohibition in Memphis. The Fusionists broke quorum again in order to prevent any further changes. Finally, everyone gave up and the session was adjourned.

Shortly after adjournment in late August 1913, the governor called a special session in which he could limit legislation. Once back, the legislature took up appropriations for funding government that had been halted during the previous session. Now a curious change of allegiance took place. Former Governor Patterson had suffered political setbacks not only at the hands of Mayor Crump but also, it seems, from Nashville Mayor Hilary Howse. Patterson blamed Howse for organizing a scheme in July 1913 that had resulted in Patterson's arrest during a "police raid on a

Nashville brothel" (Shahan 1993). The charges were dismissed the following day, but the publicity, which included lewd details, was painful for Patterson, and he resolved to strike back at the metro mayors. It was "assumed" that the metro mayors derived some power from the liquor-saloon interests which needed protection in order to continue operation. Patterson saw his chance. Much to everyone's surprise, he sided with Governor Hooper and the Fusionists in support of their law enforcement proposals regarding Prohibition. If Patterson could swing just a few Regular Democrat votes, Hooper would be back in power.

Crump was apparently very concerned about the possible tilt of power and summoned Congressman Kenneth D. McKellar to Nashville to persuade state Senator W. H. Maxwell not to support the law enforcement bill. On September 27, 1913, with armed representatives of both the Fusionists and the Regulars lingering around the capitol, Speaker Stanton, who was from Memphis, held off passage of the bill through parliamentary maneuvering. The special session then ended.

Governor Hooper immediately called the legislature back in another special session. Crump had won delay, but the people had given the state check-and-balance power when it put a Republican in the governor's chair. Public sentiment favored reform and an end to corruption. Some time had passed since former Governor Patterson had enraged the public with his political antics. Now Crump's maneuvering, and the resultant actions of the legislature, reminded the public that these activities continued. They would have none of it, and it looked as if the Regular Democrats might be setting themselves up for defeat. They wondered what they could do to change their image. Governor Hooper was determined to stop corruption, but with a legislature filled with antireform legislators whose power was derived from the status quo, he could expect little help.

Since public sentiment was again building for change, U.S. Senator John K. Shields suggested that the Democrats help pass the law enforcement measures and then take credit for it. This would break the Fusionist coalition of Independents, who abhorred the Regulars' tactics and actions, and Republicans. With Crump opposing, the Regulars helped Republicans pass the law enforcement bill, known as the Nuisance Bill. Governor Hooper viewed passage as a victory, but this episode of cooperation between Independent and Regular Democrats would end the need for any Republican assistance.

The public's push for reform finally turned into political reality. The legislature of 1913, in one regular and two special sessions, passed more reform measures than any Tennessee General Assembly between 1899–1919, and marked the high point of the era of reform. The legislative considerations, of which a significant portion was proposed by Governor Hooper, dealt with enforcement of the law, food and drug laws, worker protection, loan regulations, safer work environment and on-the-job accident reporting, fire safety, mine disasters rescue, child labor law, milk quality assurance, investment company regulation, and standardization of the commission form of government for communities. That same year, national reforms led to the passage of the Seventeenth Amendment, which mandated the direct election of U.S. senators by the people instead of by state legislatures.

Reform for Tennessee in 1913 represented the result of a culmination of responses of the legislature to public outcry and demand for change. Once the change actually began to occur and the public could see some progress, the pressure subsided. Although the state needed more reform regarding such matters as the state highway system, prison conditions, public education, taxation, and restricting "legislators from representing clients or practicing law before a state agency," (Shahan 1993) public pressure and the Independent Democrats' concern for reform was less than it had been in 1910 and 1912. With the outbreak of the European war in 1914, public attention was deflected to national and international concerns. The Democrats stopped most party infighting, and the coalition between Independent Democrats and Republicans disintegrated, marking the end of the Fusionist force. As a result of all these events, the reform movement ended.

When Nashville Black Republican James C. Napier resigned as register of the treasury, in 1913. Robert Church Jr., of Memphis, began emerging as the leading Black Republican in Tennessee. In 1914, the Shelby County Tenth District Republican convention turned into another chaotic affair. Rival factions elected rival competitors for positions on the State Republican Executive Committee. Church was elected by one of the factions, but was not seated on the State Executive Committee. He fought to be seated, but to no avail. For whatever meaningless influence the Republicans still held, they still fought over it. With a Democratic president, there was no patronage to be expected, yet the Shelby County Republicans were so used to scrimmaging for committee seats, to better position themselves for receiving patronage, that they evidently could not understand that their efforts were now futile.

On a state party level, the Republican environment was more peaceful. The 1914 Republican state convention enjoyed a more cooperative atmosphere than it had for years. Governor Hooper was easily renominated by the Republican Party on April 15, 1914.

Once the Regular Democrats gave up their stance against Prohibition and the enforcement of the laws regulating it, the party's wounds began to heal. This change began about October 1913, but would not be truly tested until the Democrats selected their nominee for governor. If the old machine pushed one of their own, the Independents would bolt again. If the nominee was an Independent-minded Democrat, then the restoration of harmony among Democrats would have a real chance.

At the May 28, 1914, Democratic state convention, Thomas C. Rye was nominated as the Democrat candidate for governor, and he endorsed the Democratic platform. Rye was not very well-known, but he was a Prohibitionist and fulfilled the expectations of the voters. When the Democrats selected this Thirteenth Judicial District attorney general, from Paris, Tennessee, as the Democratic candidate and placed the enforcement of Prohibition in their platform, they finally ended their divisive squabbling. Democratic dominance returned to full force in Tennessee. Finally, the Democrats understood not only that the electorate of the day favored Prohibition but that they had to honor public opinion. When Prohibition became part of the platform, the Republicans lost their key to victory.

Many Independents did not trust the Regular Democrats, and they held a state convention in April 1914 to endorse Republican Hooper for reelection.

However, during the fall campaign between Hooper and Rye, without the cause of Prohibition or the need to reform a wayward legislature, the high moral ground was not there for the Republicans, and there was little reason for the traditional Democratic voters of Tennessee to desert their heritage. Many Independent Democrats stayed with the Fusionist movement, but others defected in hopes of a more optimistic Democratic future. Without former Governor Patterson and his machine to fight against, Democrats began reuniting. Among the Independent defectors was Luke Lea. He and his newspaper supported Rye.

Rye championed the causes that were previously the sole property of Governor Hooper—temperance and law enforcement. Hooper tried to convince the electorate that the Democrats did not really support temperance, but were calling for Prohibition only for the sake of victory and should not be trusted. Since both parties were publicly advocating Prohibition, the leaders of the temperance movements in

THOMAS C. RYE was born into a humble beginning in Camden, Tennessee, in 1863. His father was Wayne Rye; his mother was Elizabeth Atchinson Rye. He was reared on the family farm. He obtained his early education in Benton County public schools, then later studied law in Charlotte, North Carolina. By 1884, at the age of twenty-one, Rye was an attorney and had set up his practice in Camden. Four years later, in 1888, he married Betty Arnold, daughter of Aaron and Josephine Arnold. The couple had two children and moved to Paris, Tennessee. Rye was made district attorney general in 1910. He worked in this capacity until 1915.

As the Tennessee Democrats began to accept the public's will regarding Prohibition, the Republicans lost their campaign issue. Rye had a reputation as a tough attorney general and an enforcer of Prohibition. He, although essentially unknown among the political elite, was acceptable to both factions of the Democratic Party. His reputation would win the hearts of the voters; his occupation as a lawyer would qualify him in their minds. Many Democrats supported him in order to regain the power that Republican Governor Hooper had divided. Rye defeated Hooper 137,656 to 116,667 in the election of 1914.

Governor Rye took office in 1915 and, after reelection, served until 1919. He served during a time when the state was in the midst of change and World War I was raging. Alcoa Aluminum Company came to Maryville, Tennessee. Ammunition began to be manufactured in Tennessee at Hadley's Bend, close to Nashville. When the United States declared war on Germany in 1917, Tennessee sent eighty thousand volunteers. Rye oversaw the institution of the Ouster Law, which could remove from public office any official who proved incompetent (i.e., refused to enforce Prohibition) and in fact, ousted Memphis Mayor Crump and Nashville Mayor Howse. His administration oversaw the development of the State Highway Department, additional organization and oversight of the prison system, enlargement of the State Board of Education, and the levy of a school tax. After his two terms as governor were over, Rye and his family returned to Paris, Tennessee, where he continued to practice law. He died September 12, 1953. His wife died in 1961 in Nashville. Both were buried in Paris, Tennessee. (Photograph courtesy of TSLA)

Tennessee divided their support. Of course, by doing so they deserted the very party that had forced the progress they wanted, a desertion that would eventually set them back. Governor Hooper had to deal with the usual Memphis and East Tennessee Republican infighting. The bickering in the First Congressional District demanded a great deal of attention in order to keep it from injuring Hooper's campaign. U.S. Representative Sells's position as the Republican nominee was challenged, but this came to nothing.

President Woodrow Wilson was dispensing patronage to cooperating Democrats. At the urging of Congressman Cordell Hull and U.S. Senators Lea and Shields, Wilson encouraged Tennessee Democrats to reunite. This combination was too powerful for the Fusion movement, and it disintegrated. With the breakdown went any Republican progress and any further evolution of a statewide two-party system.

The political influence of officeholders played a strong role in the outcome of elections in Tennessee. The August 1914 election of John A. Reichman as sheriff of Shelby County was a preview of what Shelby County would do in November. Reichman was a friend and ally of Crump's. The fact that Crump orchestrated a write-in campaign to elect Reichman over Galen Tate signifies Crump's absolute control of Shelby County votes.

On November 3, 1914, Rye outpolled Hooper (137,656 to 116,667), gaining 53.5 percent of the votes cast. The 20,000-vote gap between the candidates represented a return of the traditional Democratic voter and a decrease in East Tennessee Republican votes. The Republican vote declined in spite of the fact that Governor Hooper "rose above the customary patronage politics of East Tennessee Republicans and became an effective advocate of progressive reform and modernization" (Shahan 1993). As one of Tennessee's most effective leaders, Hooper was more concerned with child labor laws, pure food and drug acts, bank regulation, effective enforcement of the law, and prevention of corruption, while maintaining his advocacy for free enterprise, protection of property, and the protection of the individual from the forces of the industrial-economic changes of the time. He took a determined approach to life and did the same with the need to reform government, placing it above selfish interests.

In the gubernatorial race of 1914, Shelby County polled almost double the number of Democratic votes than it had in the two previous elections (10,907 in 1912 compared to 18,407 in 1914). The elections of 1910 and 1912 had elicited much more public sentiment and excitement, yet in 1914 twice as many Shelby Countians voted. How could that be explained? Governor Hooper had his theories, and the Crump machine and fraud were among them. The Shelby County boss, who once cooperated with Hooper when it served his interests, now influenced Shelby County to vote ten to one for Rye. No doubt, Democratic presidential patronage also had some impact. In any event, the Fusion movement was over, and the Republicans' brief moment in the limelight was gone.

In East Tennessee, Second District Congressman Austin had no Republican competition and was reelected. First District Congressman Sells easily defeated Democrat James B. Cox. With Hooper headed out of office, these two congressmen of East Tennessee would become the Republican leaders.

War broke out in Europe in 1914, but America managed to stay out of the conflict. Then, on May 7, 1915, the

Germans torpedoed the *Lusitania,* killing 124 U.S. citizens. Americans began to discuss the conflict with a more intimate interest, and with great concern over the possibility of being brought into war. President Woodrow Wilson was nearing his reelection campaign and made it clear he wanted to avoid American involvement in the war.

By 1915 the few remaining Roosevelt Progressive Party activists debated the wisdom in continuing the movement of a separate party. The Progressives had divided Republicans in 1912, and some factional lines remained. However, many former Republicans saw the need to return to the Republican fold, including Tennessee Progressive Party Chairman Harry B. Anderson, from Memphis. If they did not return to the Republican Party, he surmised, Tennessee Republicans would be controlled again by Newell Sanders. If they returned, they would at least have some influence in Republican political activities.

In January 1915 the Democratic-controlled legislature, under Governor Rye, created the Ouster Law. This law allowed the removal of elected or appointed officials who did not uphold the law or who participated in questionable conduct. Memphis Mayor E. H. Crump and Nashville Mayor Hilary E. Howse were the main targets of the law because of their adamant refusal to enforce Prohibition and their resistance to interference or change. The law was meant to cripple the political dominance of these mayors. By October 1915, a suit was filed against Crump for not enforcing the laws of Prohibition. Howse was also presented with a court challenge for removal from office for failure to carry out the laws. Crump was removed and Howse resigned. Once Crump was officially out of office, Chief of Police William J. Hayes closed some houses of prostitution and liquor establishments. The effect of this action, however, was less than ideal:

> These major demonstrations of law enforcement by the police, often staged for their publicity value only, did force the various vice operations into a somewhat more clandestine approach to their activities. Often, however, the political pressure being applied by City Hall on vice operators was temporary and lasted only until the uproar of church organizations and other moral forces died down. (Sigafoos 1979)

In late 1915 Democrats held a primary to elect a nominee for U.S. Senate. The Seventeenth Amendment, which passed in 1913, mandated that U.S. senators be elected in the general election by public ballot rather than by the legislature. Several politicians were interested in the Senate seat and the new process for election, and were aware that now it was more important to have support from the voting public than from simply the politicians. Incumbent Senator Luke Lea had to face significant opposition—Congressman Kenneth D. McKellar from West Tennessee. Several other members of Congress expressed interest in the Senate seat—Thetus W. Sims, Finis Garrett, and Cordell Hull. Eventually, George L. Berry, who was later elected to the Senate, and former Governor Malcom Patterson joined McKellar in the race against Lea. During the campaign each candidate tried to outdo the others in his demonstration of opposition to liquor. Lea lost the primary, leaving Patterson and McKellar to fight it out in a runoff.

In the runoff, Prohibition was again the issue. McKellar and Patterson each claimed a more committed stand against the liquor interests. Patterson, as governor, had fought the Prohibition movement. Now he worked as a national spokesman for the Anti-Saloon League. And McKellar, while campaigning on his stand against liquor, enjoyed Crump's backing, the same Crump who was currently being "ousted" from the Memphis mayor's office for allegedly failing to enforce the antiliquor laws. Despite the irony of the situation, what was important was which Democrat wielded the most power and could swing the most votes. The answer was clearly shown when McKellar won the runoff.

Crump had been reelected Memphis mayor in late 1915 and was scheduled to take office on New Year's Day, 1916. However, when he was found guilty of violation of the Ouster Law, the Tennessee Supreme Court issued a stay which prevented him from being sworn in. Some weeks later the supreme court sustained the Chancery Court decision against Crump. After he had been removed, Governor Rye and the legislature began a purge of other officials such as district attorneys, judges, and sheriffs. Attorney General Z. Newton Estes of Memphis, Judge Jesse Edgington of Memphis, Shelby County Sheriff J. A. Reichman, along with other officials in Nashville and around the state, were presented with impeachment charges for violation of the Ouster Law. Sheriff Reichman was cleared, but Edgington and Estes were both convicted and removed from office. Without a doubt the center of the controversy and the main target of the Ouster Law were Shelby County politicians.

Once the court ruled against Crump, he took the oath on February 22, 1916, and

KENNETH DOUGLAS MCKELLAR was born on January 29, 1869, in Richmond, Alabama (Dallas County). He received his early education from his parents and his sister, then attended the University of Alabama in Tuscaloosa, Alabama, graduating in 1891. The following year, after completing law school at Alabama, he moved to Memphis, Tennessee, was admitted to the Tennessee bar, and began practice. In 1904 he served as a presidential elector for the Democratic ticket. When Congressman George W. Gordon died in office, McKellar was elected to complete his term. He was reelected twice and served in Congress from November 9, 1911, until March 3, 1917.

In late 1915 McKellar ran in the Democrat primary for the U.S. Senate. After winning a primary runoff he became the Democratic nominee and won the general election in 1916. He was reelected to the Senate in 1922, 1928, 1934, 1940, and 1946. He served from March 4, 1917, until January 3, 1953, and as president pro tempore of the Senate in the Seventy-ninth, Eighty-first, and Eighty-Second Congresses. McKellar served as chairman of the Committee on Civil Service and Retrenchment in the Sixty-fifth Congress, on the Committee on Post Office and Post Roads in the Seventy-third through Seventy-ninth Congresses, and on the powerful Appropriations Committee in the Seventy-ninth, Eightieth, Eighty-first, and Eighty-second Congresses. Finally, after a long and successful career, he was defeated for reelection in 1952 by Albert Gore Sr. and retired in Memphis. A lifelong bachelor, McKellar died on October 25, 1956, in Memphis, Tennessee, and was buried there in Elmwood Cemetery. (Photograph courtesy of SHO) then resigned from office, though not from power. Vice Mayor Alec Utley immediately took the oath of office and then resigned. Fellow commissioners then elected Crump's choice, Thomas C. Ashcroft, as mayor. (George C. Love served as Memphis mayor from 1915 to 1916.) Crump would soon return to elected office.

Although there was a Shelby County Republican organization in Memphis in 1916, it did not have many supporters and existed in name and committee only. It had no power or influence and was unable to carry West Tennessee in any election.

When T. S. Settle, a Black attorney from Memphis who sat on the State Republican Executive Committee, died in late 1915, Robert Church Jr. assumed he would be appointed by the State Executive Committee to fill the slot during the January 1916 meeting. However, Church did not get the vote of the committee. The position was important to him since it solidified his chances to be a delegate from Shelby County to the Republican National Convention in 1916. He realized that he would have to do something to strengthen his position. After a reasonable period of time trying to organize the Black and Tans to oppose the Lily Whites, Church decided he needed to put forth a strong effort in order to unite the Black Republican vote. Therefore, he founded and financed an organization with which Blacks could identify, the Lincoln League. The League organized voter registration drives and paid poll taxes for Black voters, who were essentially disenfranchised. Church hoped that the League could earn better patronage for Blacks by presenting a show of political force to the state Republican Committee. He also hoped the organization would position him for a delegate-at-large seat at the Republican National Convention.

Church was elected as president of the Lincoln League and held some small preliminary meetings. Then, on February 2, 1916, he held the first large meeting at Church's Park and Auditorium on Beale Street. The following day the *Commercial Appeal* carried a story which noted that "Nearly 1000 Negro voters of the city enthusiastically responded to a called meeting last night at Church's Auditorium. . . .The following men were elected officers: R. R. Church—President; T. H. Hayes—First Vice President . . ." (Church 1974). The Lincoln League was, therefore, officially founded in Memphis in 1916. Its purpose was to register and organize Black voters. From this effort, the organization expanded statewide.

When the April 1916 Shelby County Republican convention took place, Harry B. Anderson, chairman of the Progressive Party of Tennessee, showed up to help his father, who was interested in running as a Roosevelt delegate to the Republican National Convention. After participating in the Shelby County convention, Anderson, G. T. Taylor, who had previously served as state Progressive Party chairman, and others attended the Republican state convention in Nashville in May 1916.

At the Republican state convention on May 3, 1916, John W. Overall of Liberty, Tennessee, sought and received the Republican nomination for governor. Overall had served as U.S. marshal in Middle Tennessee under recent Republican presidents. Hooper was nominated for U.S. senator, and J. Will Taylor was elected chairman of the Republican Party of Tennessee. The convention also approved a plank in its platform which supported women's suffrage by a vote of 387 to 288.

After organizing the Lincoln League in Memphis, Church consolidated his effort with Black political organizations throughout the state. When the state convention took place, Church was ready. On May 4, 1916, he fought with Frank Elgin, a former U.S. marshal, for a delegate-at-large position to the Republican National Convention. Ben Hooper, Newell Sanders, and Congressman Sells supported Church for the delegate-at-large spot. However, Blacks from Hamilton County aligned with the Littleton faction did not support him, and he lost. All of Church's organizational efforts were not wasted. Church, along with Elgin, was elected as an alternate delegate to the 1916 Republican National Convention. Congressman Sells then urged a resolution that created eight delegate spots with only half a vote each. This compromise provided the first opportunity since 1892 for a Black Tennessean to serve as a delegate-at-large to the Republican National Convention. A. N. Johnson, who was also Black, was elected as a delegate from the Sixth Congressional District.

A Progressive state convention was called for June 3, 1916, at the request of the national organization. When the convention took place, only fifty attended. Anderson, who had wanted to resign for some time, was finally able to turn over the chairmanship to John C. Houk. G. T. Taylor was elected national committeeman and delegates were elected for a national convention. This meeting was the last gathering of the Progressive Party of Tennessee. In fact Theodore Roosevelt himself pursued the Republican nomination rather than the Progressive nomination.

At the June 1916 Republican National Convention in Chicago, Tennessee had twenty-one delegate votes. There were eight delegates-at-large with one-half vote each and seventeen congressional district delegates. The Tennessee delegation supported Associate Supreme Court Justice Charles Evans Hughes, a former governor of New York, as the presidential nominee. On the first ballot the Tennessee delegation voted nine for Hughes, five for Roosevelt, and three and one-half for John W. Meeks from Massachusetts. Others receiving the remainder of the Tennessee votes were Coleman DuPont, Charles W. Fairbanks, and Theodore Burton. On the third ballot, eighteen Tennessee votes went for Hughes and three for Roosevelt. Charles E. Hughes received the nomination for president. Charles W. Fairbanks became the nominee for vice president. The party overlooked Roosevelt in favor of new leadership to oppose the incumbent, President Woodrow Wilson.

During the convention, the Tennessee delegation, with little else to fight for, battled over who should be the national committeeman. The Hooper-Sanders coalition supported John J. Gore, while the Austin-Littleton faction supported Jesse M. Littleton. A war of words erupted. Finally, Littleton was confirmed to serve as Tennessee's national committeeman until 1920.

On June 10, 1916, after the Republican National Convention nomination for Hughes, Roosevelt rejected his nomination by the Progressive National Convention and declared he would support Republican Hughes. The Progressive National Convention then voted to hold off on any nomination for a presidential candidate and turn their support to Hughes. Most of Tennessee Progressive Party activists left the movement and threw their support behind Hughes.

Robert Church Jr.'s Lincoln League laid plans to enter a slate in the November 1916 elections. They nominated "colored" candidates for Tenth District congressman, flotorial senator, state senators, and state representatives. Sixteen hundred Black voters attended a mass convention for the candidates in August 1916. Even though the factional infighting between Church's Black and Tans and the Lily Whites continued, the fielding of candidates was designed to strengthen recognition for Black voters by showing their motivation and forcing the statewide Republican candidates to acknowledge their voting power.

E. H. Crump, who had resigned as mayor in February, now ran for county trustee. His political organization put out an all-out effort. Once again he was opposed by J. J. Williams, but the effort by Williams was not worth the time. Crump easily won the August 1916 election and was subsequently reelected in 1918, 1920, and 1922.

Although Shelby County Republicans continued fighting among themselves, 1916 was a year that Tennessee Republicans were generally united in their support of Hughes for president, Hooper for U.S. senator, John W. Overall for governor, and Sam R. Sells and Richard W. Austin for reelection to the First and Second Congressional Districts. Jesse M. Littleton, who ran for Congress in the Third District, also had united support from Republicans, and gave incumbent Democrat John A. Moon a real test.

The presidential campaign centered on the issues of the war in Europe and organized labor. In summer 1916 Wilson had called a joint session of Congress to request legislation for the eight-hour work day in order to avert a strike of the railroad unions. Congress cooperated, and labor remembered. During the presidential campaign, Wilson's support from the unions and organized labor proved to be of help to him, whereas Republican Hughes's antiunion platform was a disadvantage. The most important issue of 1916 was the war in Europe, waging since 1914. Wilson campaigned on the pledge to keep America out of the war. Theodore Roosevelt, even though he was not the Republican nominee, had advocated intervention, and Wilson tagged this prointervention stance onto Hughes. In Tennessee Hughes received only 42.7 percent of the vote. Nationally, the popular vote count was Wilson 9,127,695 to 8,553,507 for Hughes (277 to 254 electoral votes). Tennesseans voted for President Wilson by a greater margin than his national margin of victory.

In the governor's race, the Prohibition issue could not be used to John W. Overall's benefit. Governor Rye had demonstrated to the voters that he supported the cause, and he won reelection. Overall received only 44.7 percent of the Tennessee vote. The count was 146,758 for Rye and 117,817 for Overall. This 1916 election year was the first that U.S. senators were elected by the people rather than the state legislature. In Tennessee, Kenneth D. McKellar was elected to the Senate (Class 1). Hooper had tried to demonstrate McKellar's tie to anti-Prohibitionist Crump, but McKellar countercharged that it was Hooper who was allied with Crump. The fact that McKellar refused face-to-face debates with Hooper did not disturb the voters. Hooper received only 44.8 percent of the Tennessee vote.

John C. Houk returned to the Republican Party in the elections of 1916. There had not been a more vocal Progressive Party activist in Tennessee during the party's existence. Viewed as somewhat of a loner who would stick to his ideals against any odds, he had even verbally attacked Roosevelt for deserting the movement. Finally, Houk's friend Jesse M. Littleton told him, "It seems to me it is about time for you to make an announcement that you are a Republican, and quit your foolishness" (Isaac n.d.). He finally accepted the Republican nomination for state senate in the Sixth District (Knox, Loudon, Monroe, and Polk Counties). Houk, who drank and was previously antiProhibition, campaigned as a Republican who supported Prohibition and was elected.

All the Lincoln League candidates for state legislature and Congress lost in Shelby County, where Democrats won all the seats. Although the Lincoln League increased the vote for its endorsed candidates, who received more than White Republican candidates in the same races, the majority of Blacks registered in Robert Church Jr.'s effort did not vote in the state and national races. Church believed in Lincoln and the human rights advocated by Lincoln. But he could see that many Whites affiliated with the Republican Party were participating only to take advantage of the patronage occasionally available when a Republican president was in office.

Overall, the 1916 Tennessee elections demonstrated that Tennessee was unquestionably back under Democratic dominance. The furor over Prohibition no longer negatively impacted the Democrats since they now embraced the issue. With Republicans again in the minority, with no national or state patronage, Whites in West Tennessee had little interest in the local Republican Party. Robert Church Jr. became the leader of the Shelby County Republican effort. Since he had enough support to influence the West Tennessee vote of Black Republicans and there was no statewide Republican dominating the scene, he became the natural contact of the East Tennessee congressmen who wanted some control in West Tennessee Republican efforts. Thus an alliance was formed between Church and the East Tennessee power brokers, and with it began a new era in Republican politics in Tennessee. The East Tennessee Republicans sustained Church against his foes, the Lily Whites, for some years to come, and he wielded influence in state and national party affairs. The Republican Party, with only 40 percent to 45 percent of the statewide vote, would hold only a weak minority for the foreseeable future.

During the presidential race, Wilson had campaigned against intervention in the war in Europe, while tagging Republicans as the party that wanted war. However, in January 1917, the Germans threatened to sink any U.S. ship engaged in trade with their enemies, and Wilson, at the end of February, went before Congress to request the arming of American merchant ships. The Senate withheld approval until the new Congress took office a few days later. Wilson had received an intercepted note from Germany to Mexico which promised to help Mexico regain Texas, Arizona, and New Mexico if the country would go to war against the United States. Just after Wilson was inaugurated for his second term, the Germans sank three U.S. merchant vessels on March 18, 1917. The United States declared war against Germany on April 6, 1917. Tennessee's congressional delegation unanimously supported President Wilson's request for the declaration of war.

Several legislative acts passed during Governor Rye's terms. Rye had overseen the development of the Ouster Law, the abolishment of the back-tax law, the creation of a highway commission, requirements for automobile registration, and highway taxes. In 1917 Tennessee passed a "comprehensive primary law, created a state highway fund, and abolished the fee system for compensating various county officials" (Shahan 1993). The most impacting political reform legislation was a system of nominating candidates for office by public vote rather than party convention nomination.

The act passed by the legislature required both parties to conduct primaries for statewide offices, U.S. House of Representatives, and U.S. Senate. There still was no requirement to conduct primaries for judicial, state house of representatives, or state senate candidates. Also in 1917, the Women's Suffrage Amendment failed to be approved by the voters of Tennessee.

In 1918 there was little interest on the part of Tennessee Republicans for any state offices, even though nationally Republicans had regained strength and taken control of the U.S. House of Representatives. The Democrats were simply too dominant in Tennessee.

Governor Rye decided not to run for reelection to a third term for governor, but instead ran for the U.S. Senate. He faced incumbent Senator Shields, who had gone to the Senate in 1913 when the legislature still elected Tennessee's senators. Shortly after Shields's election the Seventeenth Amendment mandating that senators be elected by popular vote went into effect and Governor Rye felt that he had enough influence and support to defeat an incumbent seated by the legislature. Senator Shields quickly found that much of Rye's confidence was well placed. For one thing, former Governor Patterson supported Rye, who was also from West Tennessee, and both had considerable support and influence there. In addition, Rye had some support from President Wilson, who felt that Shields had undermined him and would do so again. The president's plan for world peace—the League of Nations—was an important issue in his agenda, and he felt he could not count on Shields's endorsement. However, Shields had some influential support, too. E. H. Crump had no love for Governor Rye, who had forced him from office via the Ouster Law, and he and McKellar, a Crump protégé, worked diligently on behalf of Senator Shields.

McKellar convinced the president not to send an intended letter of support on behalf of Governor Rye's candidacy for the seat. He told the president that he was mistaken about Shields and that he would support his League of Nations plan. With Crump and McKellar working for him, Shields maintained enough support from his home base of East Tennessee and allies in West Tennessee to win reelection by a narrow margin. Without their support, he would have lost West Tennessee. After the win, McKellar asked Shields to visit the president and thank him for not opposing him. According to McKellar, Shields said that he would "see them in Hell first" (McKellar 1942). Shields did in fact go on to oppose the League of Nations, proving McKellar's assurances inacurrate.

On the Republican ticket, H. Clay Evans was the nominee. Senator Shields easily defeated him by over 30,000 votes.

For the Democrat gubernatorial nomination of 1918, Overton County Chancellor Albert H. Roberts and Clarksville, Tennessee, attorney Austin Peay competed. Roberts defeated Peay in the primary and then easily defeated the Republican candidate, Campbell County Judge H. B. Lindsay in the race for governor by about 40,000 votes. Tennessee's Republican candidates did extremely poorly in 1918, gaining only 37.6 percent for Lindsay, and 37.8 percent for U.S. Senate candidate Henry Clay Evans. The Republican showing, which may have been affected by the war and the deadly flu epidemic of 1918, turned out to be the worst for Tennessee Republicans since 1878.

In the First Congressional District election, Congressman Sam R. Sells won his Republican primary. However, Second District Congressman Austin, a leading and

ALBERT H. ROBERTS was born on July 4, 1868, in Overton County, Tennessee, to John Roberts and Sarah Carlook Roberts. He obtained his early education in the schools of Overton County. His family moved to Kansas when he was still a young boy and Roberts completed the remainder of his education and graduated from high school there. He came back to Tennessee to attend college and graduated from Hiwassee College (Madisonville) in 1889. That same year he married Nora Dean Bowden, whose father taught Latin at the college, and they eventually had four children. The couple lived in Madisonville, where Roberts taught at Alpine Private School for the next five years, and Nora taught music. After Roberts was made county public education superintendent, he studied law and then began to practice. This he did for fifteen years until he became chancellor for the Fourth Division, Tennessee. In 1918 he ran for governor and defeated Republican H. B. Lindsay. He served from 1919 until 1921. During his term, Tennessee revised its tax law, passed the State Police Bill, passed a workmen's compensation law, ratified the Nineteenth Amendment to the U.S. Constitution which gave women the vote, and built the State Memorial Building.

The governor and his family stayed in Nashville after he completed his term of office. He lost reelection in 1920 to Republican Alf Taylor. Roberts died June 25, 1946, on his farm near Nashville. His wife preceded him in 1932. They were buried in Good Hope Cemetery in Livingston, Tennessee. (Photograph courtesy of TSLA)

active Republican for several years, lost his primary to J. Will Taylor, who served as mayor of LaFollette, chairman of the Tennessee Republican Party, and former Tennessee state insurance commissioner. Taylor was supported by Newell Sanders, Ben Hooper, and John C. Houk. All of these men were political enemies of Austin, and their combined opposition was too much for Austin to overcome. (Austin died a year later, in 1919.) After Austin's defeat, Congressman Sells and National Committeeman Jesse M. Littleton emerged as leading figures in Tennessee Republican circles.

Tennessee has a long history of supplying troops for America's conflicts. Its people have fought in battles and wars even before the American Revolution, prior to its admission as a state. It sent volunteer soldiers to fight in the Indian Wars, the War of 1812, the Mexican War, the Civil War, and the Spanish American War. After the United States declared war on Germany in 1917, eighty thousand Tennesseans went to war. Among the soldiers from Tennessee was a God-fearing, peaceable man from Fentress County named Alvin C. York. In October 1918, York was stationed in France in the Argonne Forest. Several members of his squad were killed and he became separated from the remainder. Alone, York turned on a large group of Germans and against all odds killed twenty-five, disabled thirty-six machine guns, and captured four officers and 132 soldiers. York became an overnight hero and legend. The French gave him their nation's highest award, the croix de guerre; the United States awarded him the congressional Medal of Honor; and Tennessee awarded him a gold medal of honor. The Rotary Club of Nashville gave him a farm, complete with a home, and later Governor Roberts held York's wedding in the governor's residence (the first to be held there). The state built the

War Memorial Building in Nashville in honor of York and other outstanding Tennessee soldiers.

Albert Roberts was inaugurated as Tennessee's governor in early 1919. One of his first jobs was to deal with the ratification of the Eighteenth Amendment, which prohibited the manufacture, sale, or use of alcohol. Prohibition had been a politically volatile issue in Tennessee for several years. The state had essentially been a Prohibition state since 1909. The issue had helped elect Republican Ben Hooper to two terms as governor and had been the catalyst in the political bickering that resulted in the murder of former Senator Edward Carmack on the streets of Nashville. Democrats, by now, knew the feelings of the populous. When the legislature met to vote on the issue, it passed twenty-eight to two in the state senate and eighty-two to two in the state house. Tennessee was the twenty-third state to ratify the amendment. After other states ratified the Eighteenth Amendment, it became law on January 16, 1920.

During Governor Roberts's term the legislature also faced the issue of mounting state debt. They enacted laws which allowed the State Railroad Commission to tax public utilities and other service companies including telephone, electric, water, and railroad companies. The state also once again faced the women's suffrage issue. In 1913, under Governor Hooper, an amendment to allow women's suffrage was proposed in Tennessee. However, it died in a public vote. In 1917 another amendment was proposed under Governor Rye that would allow women to vote in city and presidential elections, and it too failed, but in 1919 the same amendment was passed. It was considered incidental since the national amendment under consideration offered broader rights for women's suffrage.

The mayoral campaign of Memphis in 1919 highlighted the character of politics of the day. Ever since Crump had been expelled from office in 1915, Memphis had seven elected or acting mayors. Although Crump had been removed from official office by the law, he had not been removed from power, and he still headed up a powerful political organization. Rowlette Paine, a Memphis businessman, was a candidate for mayor in 1919. He was opposed by former mayor John J. Williams. This was the first city election in which women had the right to vote. Paine was elected and continued to serve until 1927, but the Crump organization controlled the city and the largest voting block in West Tennessee.

By mid-1920 thirty-five states had ratified the Nineteenth Amendment. Thirty-six states were required for it to become law. Tennessee was one of three likely states (out of the five states remaining) holding the possibility of providing the thirty-sixth vote. Governor Roberts called a special session of the legislature for August 9, 1920, in order to vote on the controversial issue. Over the next several days, the battle was heated and tense, and tempers flared. Finally, the state senate voted 25 to 4 for ratification. However, the situation was different in the house. Speaker Seth Walker made a motion to table the resolution, which would have effectively killed it in Tennessee. The vote to table failed 48 to 48, and a motion to adopt was proposed. Harry T. Burn, of McMinn County, switched his vote in favor of ratification. (In his pocket Burn carried a letter from his widowed mother urging him to vote for ratification.) Seeing that it would pass, Speaker Walker, who had initially favored passage but then opposed it, switched again and voted in favor of it. It passed 49 to 47. Even after the vote, some thirty antisuffrage legislators moved to obtain a restraining order from a circuit judge in hopes of preventing Governor Roberts from certifying the vote and conveying results to the U.S. secretary of state. The chief justice of the Tennessee Supreme Court blocked the injunction.

The Tennessee legislature of 1920 gave women the right to vote by ratifying the Nineteenth Amendment to the Constitution of the United States. It also passed a workman's compensation law during Governor Roberts's tenure.

In 1920 the national mood of the country was about to turn Republican. The East Tennessee Republican stronghold would, as always, be well positioned to play the patronage game should the nation elect a Republican president. West Tennessee, the traditional Democratic stronghold, began to go through its own unique positioning process. White politicians in Shelby County, sensing the possibility of patronage, wanted to be prepared for the spoils of victory should a Republican become president.

At this time there were three Republican factions in Shelby County—the Robert Church Jr. group, the G. Tom Taylor group, and the Harry O. True/Charles B. Quinn group. In the spring of 1920, Republicans gathered at the court house to reorganize at their Republican county convention. G. Tom Taylor showed up with only thirty or so followers and found himself outnumbered by Church's group, which packed the Shelby County convention with four hundred Black supporters. At this, Taylor called police, ordered Church's group out of the meeting

From the Nashville Tennessean—*the Tennessee General Assembly delivers the thirty-sixth vote to ratify the Nineteenth Amendment, thus guaranteeing women's suffrage. (Courtesy of TSLA)*

room, and locked the door. Church held his convention in the hall outside the meeting room. Black Republican George Lee won one of the positions of the Church delegation to the Chattanooga Republican state convention. When the convention rolled around, Church was determined to be seated. He made his request formal via an appeal that the Black and Tans be seated as delegates to the state convention, but the Contest Committee refused to hear the contest. Following this, Church took his case to the floor of the convention. He knew that he needed more help than he alone could muster and contacted the chairman of the Republican National Committee, Will Hays, of Indianapolis. Church convinced him of the necessity of assisting the Black Republicans, presenting the ultimatum to Republican leaders that his delegation would walk out of the convention. After a night of communication between Church, Hays, and Tennessee Republicans, a plan was created by Congressman Sells, chairman of the convention, and Republican National Committeeman Jesse Littleton to settle the disputes. The next morning, the convention gave Church's delegation one-third of the twenty-three votes allotted Shelby County. However, Church was not happy with the compromise.

The next battle occurred back in Shelby County when the Tenth Congressional District convention took place in Memphis. The tension between White Republicans and Black Republicans actually deteriorated into an out-and-out fistfight. But Church's group outnumbered the others and elected him as a delegate and J.T. Settle Jr. as an alternate delegate to the National Convention. This would not go unchallenged by his opponents when they arrived at the Convention in Chicago. John Farley, a Memphis lawyer, opposed Church's delegate spot. Tennessee was not the only state that had to deal with the fighting between Black and White Republicans. Across the South there were more than one hundred challenges from Lily Whites for the Black and Tan delegate or alternate positions. The Republican National Committee sided with Church and temporarily made him a delegate. However, Farley continued his protest stating that Blacks had ruined the party in Shelby County. He claimed that Whites would not vote Republican because of the Black dominance. The Credentials Committee felt Republicans would get more White votes by agreeing with the challenges at the convention and voted twenty-three to eighteen not to seat Church. There were only twenty-seven Black delegates seated at the 1920 Republican National Convention.

In 1920 Warren G. Harding was an Ohio U.S. senator who had little national exposure except his appearance as keynote speaker of the 1916 Republican National Convention. On the second day of the convention, he polled enough for the Republican nomination. Massachusetts governor, Calvin Coolidge, was chosen as his vice presidential running mate.

The Democrats nominated James M. Cox, governor of Ohio, for president and Franklin Delano Roosevelt, assistant secretary of the navy under Woodrow Wilson, as the vice presidential candidate.

In Tennessee's elections, on the Republican side, National Committeeman Jesse Littleton faced Alfred A. Taylor for the Republican nomination for governor. Littleton was badly beaten by Taylor in the primary and also lost his spot as National Republican committeeman from Tennessee. First District Congressman Sells faced serious opposition in the direct primary. World War I hero B. Carroll Reece, who had backing from the remnants of the Brownlow faction, fought a tough race. The old Brownlow faction had been searching for a vehicle to aid their return to power. In Reece, they found a candidate who was popular enough to oust the opposition. Reece defeated Congressman Sells in the Republican primary of 1920.

Church did not forget his treatment and was pleased at the outcome of the August primaries in Tennessee. Evidently, he either felt Sells had worked against him or did not do enough to help him. Carroll Reece, he thought, might be a better friend. National Republican Chairman Will Hays appointed Bob Church Jr. director of the "Republican Negro Campaign." This restored respect for Church in the eyes of his fellow Black Republicans.

On the Democratic side in the state, Governor Roberts faced a less well-known opponent, real estate broker William Crabtree for the gubernatorial nomination. Crabtree had served as mayor of Chattanooga and state senator from his home county of Hamilton. The incumbent governor won the primary but only by a narrow margin.

At the time of the elections of 1920, the people of the nation were just recovering from the pain, government restrictions, and hardships of World War I. They wanted change. President Wilson had enjoyed Democratic rule in both the House and Senate. The national mood had begun to swing with the last midterm congressional elections when Republicans took back both in 1919. In the presidential election of 1920 people wanted to continue the change. Both Harding and Cox were from Ohio, but Harding was the Republican. Warren G. Harding was elected twenty-ninth president, receiving 16,143,407 popular votes to 9,130,328 for Cox (404 to 127 electoral votes).

Nineteen twenty was a year of anti-Democrat sentiment throughout the nation, including Tennessee. Governor Albert Roberts was the Democratic nominee. He had made some enemies in his own party during his term as governor, particularly over women's suffrage and taxes. Additionally, there was quite a bit of infighting within the Democratic ranks. This only aided Tennessee Republicans, who now enjoyed the advantage of the strong national trend away from the Democrats. Alf Taylor was famous and well thought of throughout the state. He and his Democratic brother Bob had previously fought each other in the gubernatorial race of 1886. Bob won that race, but many Democrats remembered and liked both brothers. Strong sentimental support for Alf existed among Democrats. He was seventy-two years old, much older than when he and Bob had toured the state in 1886. Nevertheless, Alf was still humorous and entertaining as a campaigner. The Taylor clan went all out to support him. His three sons and a friend formed a quartet which accompanied Alf on many campaign stops, and they entertained large crowds of supporters. In 1920 Republican Alf Taylor defeated Governor Roberts 229,143 votes to 185,890.

Nineteen twenty was a rare year in which Tennessee voted Republican. The state had not gone Republican for president since the 1868 election of President Grant, and Alf Taylor and Ben Hooper (elected in 1910 and 1912) were the only Republican governors elected in Tennessee since the election of Alvin Hawkins in 1880. The next Republican governor would not be elected for another fifty years.

It was a great year for the minority party in Tennessee to see the votes go for

Then Senator Warren G. Harding and his wife (front row, center) pose for a picture while visiting Chattanooga on October 13, 1920, during his presidential campaign. (Courtesy of CHCBL)

their candidates for president, governor, and five of ten congressional seats. (Thirty-one-year-old B. Carroll Reece, one of the five Republican U.S. representatives elected in 1920, would go on to become a national Republican leader.) This was their best showing since Reconstruction, but it would be temporary and more of an aberration than a true shift in party strength. According to Paul Isaac, the Republican victory of 1920, "had been made possible by Democrat divisions, disillusionment with the Wilson administration, postwar economic problems, greater success in winning the support of newly enfranchised women, and because of the popularity of their candidate for governor" (Isaac n.d.). For the Republicans, a party that was nonexistent until the time of the Civil War, 1920 was the best year for elections without the assistance of martial law.

The success of the Republicans was temporary and the efforts of Presidents Roosevelt and Taft to draw Democrats in hopes of bringing a permanent shift in strength to Tennessee, the most likely Southern state to emerge from Democratic dominance, met with futility. It has been said many times that all politics is local and local power in Tennessee was still with the Democrats. No major Democrats switched parties and there was little lasting effect from the two Republican presidents' efforts. East Tennessee congressmen maintained the status quo as leaders of the minority party, leaving the Democrats in control of the state. Some East Tennessee Republicans traded with the Democrats so they could

ALFRED A. TAYLOR was born in Happy Valley in East Tennessee on August 6, 1848, the second son of Nathaniel Green Taylor, a politician, and Emaline Haynes Taylor. In 1864 the Taylor family moved to New Jersey when President Andrew Johnson appointed Nathaniel a commissioner of Indian affairs. After beginning his education in New Jersey, then studying at Wesleyan University in Athens, Tennessee, Alf studied law and passed the bar in 1870. When he was thirty-four he married Jennie Anderson who was only fifteen. They eventually had ten children. He went to Congress in 1875 and served one term. In 1886 he ran as a Republican against his brother, Robert, a Democrat, for governor. However, Bob had the advantage as a Democrat and won. Alf was reelected to Congress in 1889 and remained in Congress until 1895. He won the Republican gubernatorial nomination in 1920 and, with the advantage of his name, personality, and the Republican momentum, was elected governor over incumbent Governor Albert Roberts. He was inaugurated on January 15, 1921.

Taylor's administration oversaw creation of a state tax commissioner, strengthening of the Railroad and Public Utilities Commission, preservation of President Andrew Johnson's early tailor shop, establishment of the Tennessee Historical Committee, creation of the Mother's Pension Fund Act, and development of the steps for the equalization of property assessments. One of Taylor's greatest achievements for the people of Tennessee may have been his contribution to save the nitrate manufacturing facility in Muscle Shoals, Alabama. The U.S. government had built Wilson Dam, in Muscle Shoals (on the Tennessee River), as the facility site for the production of nitrate to produce munitions for World War I. After the war ended, the incentive for the development of the site waned. However, it held potential to produce fertilizer for farmers and electric power for the citizens of the region (including Tennessee). He led the delegation to Congress to persuade them to continue development.

During this period there were growing labor disputes in Tennessee. Governor Taylor was able to negotiate some calm and cooperation between growing labor unions and management of developing industries. Despite his accomplishments for his state, Taylor was defeated for reelection by Austin Peay. He returned to his circle of family and friends after retiring from office in 1923. He lived another eight years, dying on November 24, 1931. His wife died in 1934. Both were buried in Johnson City, Tennessee, in Monte Vista Cemetery. (Photograph courtesy of TSLA)

obtain patronage from state or national Democratic sources. In return they provided what influence they had with Republican vote switching in East and West Tennessee and presidential patronage during a Republican presidency.

When Alf Taylor was inaugurated governor in early 1921, he found nothing but difficulty in the office he had sought. The Democratic-controlled legislature had little reason to cooperate with a Republican. Worse, Republicans were fighting among themselves over the spoils of victory. In spite of the turmoil, Governor Alf Taylor worked for better schools and highways. He tried to change the tax structure and save on government waste. The position of tax commissioner was created, and the legislature set aside funds to provide for an historical committee to preserve Tennessee's historical treasures. The governor was effective in dealing with growing labor organizations and preventing many labor disputes. He also worked to preserve the Muscle Shoals nitrate plant which would later be important to the Tennessee Valley Authority project of future President Franklin Roosevelt. For the most part, however, the legislature did not support the Republican governor, and Taylor, who was in his seventies, soon grew tired of the fighting. The Democrats, no matter what he tried to accomplish, showed little tolerance or cooperation for a Republican in the governor's seat.

The campaign for the Democratic nomination for governor in 1922 proved to be a rough contest. Austin Peay was a Clarksville, Tennessee, lawyer who had served as a manager for Governor Patterson's election in 1908. Peay had reduced his political visibility from 1908 until his candidacy in 1918 in which he lost the gubernatorial primary to Albert Roberts. In 1922 he ran again. His opponent, former Governor Benton McMillin, was seventy-seven years old but still active. McMillin had served as ambassador to Peru and lost two U.S. Senate bids. The campaign between McMillin and Peay was an intense contest between factional powers. Boss Crump of Memphis and E. H. Stahlman, publisher of the *Nashville Banner,* backed McMillin, while Luke Lea, publisher of the *Nashville Tennessean,* and Memphian Clarence Saunders, founder of the Piggly Wiggly grocery store company, backed Peay. Saunders had grown wealthy from his business interests and had become a formidable political foe for Crump on his home turf in Memphis. East Tennessee went with McMillin and the Crump team, while Peay won the urban vote, including Crump's home turf—Shelby County. Peay took the Democratic nomination.

Meanwhile seventy-two-year-old Governor Alf Taylor was renominated by the Republicans. In the general election Taylor campaigned as he always had, by entertaining with his wit and fiddle. Peay was not an entertainer and had to simply resort to the old stump speech. The campaign of 1922 was interesting not only because of its rough-and-tumble nature, but because this was the first campaign in which radio was used to communicate to the voters. Clarence Saunders, ever the innovative mass merchant, applied the benefits of the new form of mass communication to Austin Peay's campaign.

Alf Taylor was defeated for reelection in 1922 by Democrat Austin Peay. Peay tallied 141,002 votes; Taylor tallied 102,586. Peay lost East Tennessee but won Middle Tennessee and West Tennessee. Luke Lea and Clarence Saunders consolidated political power in the state as Crump and Stahlman took a bit of a backseat. This intensified the rivalry between Crump and Lea. Lea became a dominant figure in Tennessee politics for the next decade and a constant challenge for the indomitable E. H. Crump.

While Tennessee returned to Democratic control, the national tide was also turning. During the midterm elections of 1922, the Republican majorities were reduced in the House by seventy-five and the Senate by eight. However, Republican President Harding still enjoyed control of both. Tennessee's Democratic contribution to the U.S. Senate did not change. In the 1922 senatorial election, Kenneth McKellar rolled past Republican Newell Sanders. Tennessee Democrats held both Senate seats, the governor's chair, and the legislature.

First District Republican Congressman B. Carroll Reece was reelected in 1922. Second District Congressman J. Will Taylor also became the Republican National committeeman, holding control of the state Republican Party, while cooperating with state Democrats. This seemingly strange conduct of East Tennessee Republican officeholders had always allowed them to maintain power. Additionally, Taylor allowed Black Memphian Robert Church Jr. some limited participation in the dispersion of federal patronage. This significantly empowered Church. By 1922 the Republican Party in Tennessee resembled the party in the 1890s, with a strong Republican block from East Tennessee and a weak organization, with few votes, in the remainder of the state, coming mainly from Black Republicans.

In late 1922 and early 1923 President Harding began to learn of the illegal behavior of his trusted insiders and cabinet members. While on a trip away from Washington on July 27, 1923, the president became ill. At first it was thought to be indigestion but later thought to be a heart attack. Then on July 29 the president developed pneumonia. He felt he was recovering when on August 2, 1923, he died suddenly while resting in bed in San Francisco. Calvin Coolidge assumed office, becoming the thirtieth president of the United States.

When Austin Peay took office as governor of Tennessee on January 16, 1923, he began a process of reorganizing state government. Since Democrats controlled the state house and senate, he enjoyed much more cooperation than his predecessor, Republican Governor Alf Taylor. Peay recognized many of the same problems that Taylor had identified. Up to this point the Tennessee state government had developed into sixty-four separate departments. Many departments duplicated efforts and there was general confusion and little cooperation among agencies. Many of the departments took their needs or ideas directly to the state legislature for approval. Unfortunately, many legislators did not understand enough about the state to simplify its organization or to deal with interdepartmental competition.

> Legislators, many of whom served for only one term, were usually unfamiliar with the operation of state government; indeed many had sought election to the legislature not because they were dedicated lawmakers but primarily because they sought recognition in their respective hometowns in order to develop a law practice or business. (Corlew 1990)

State government was disorganized and weak and the governor was little more than a figurehead with minimal executive authority when it came to leading the mass bureaucracy. Governor Peay set out to change that. On January 17, 1923, he submitted legislation to create better economy, service, coordination, and efficiency in state government. He proposed the creation of eight departments, led by a commissioner who was appointed by and responsible to the governor. The departments consisted of education, finance and taxation, highways and public works, health, insurance and banking, labor, and agriculture. The legislature approved the proposal mainly because the voters had generally supported Peay's campaign promises. The plan went into effect on February 1, 1923. This represented an historic shift in state power from the legislature into the hands of the governor.

Not only was this a time of historic reorganization in state government, it was also a time of change for an entire way of life. Radio provided a means of communication in which the public could be instantly reached with information. It was also a day of change in transportation. Many Tennesseans were beginning to try the horseless carriage. However, Tennessee's

AUSTIN PEAY was born on June 1, 1876, in Christian County, Kentucky, to Austin Peay Sr. and Cornelia Leavell Peay. His father was a successful farmer. Austin learned to farm and then was educated at Washington and Lee College and at Centre College, in Danville, Kentucky. He studied law and then moved to Clarksville, Tennessee. In 1895 he married Sallie Hurst of Clarksville, and the couple eventually had two children. He opened his practice in Clarksville in 1896 and essentially limited his professional activity to law until he ran for the state legislature in 1910. He held this position until he ran for governor. He lost the Democratic gubernatorial primary of 1918 to Albert Roberts.

Peay won the Democratic primary of 1922, defeating former Governor Benton McMillin. He then ran against Republican Governor Alf Taylor and defeated him 141,002 votes to 102,586. He took the oath of office on January 16, 1923. Under a cooperative Democratically controlled legislature, Peay reorganized the sixty-four state departments, replacing them with eight—finance and taxation, agriculture, highways and public works, education, health, institutions, labor, and insurance and banking. Also under his administration the dispute of ownership of Reelfoot Lake was settled. The Great Smoky Mountains National Park was established in 1926. Education was improved during his term when, in 1925, tobacco taxes were set aside to fund a full eight months of school in rural areas. The famous Anti-Evolution Bill was also passed during his tenure. Governor Peay oversaw the paving of more than six thousand miles of Tennessee mud roads, improving transportation more than ever before in the Volunteer State. His highway program continued after his service, creating seventy-five hundred miles of roads for automobile travel.

Peay was a popular governor and was reelected in 1924 and 1926, serving altogether from 1923 until 1927. He developed heart disease and died shortly into his third term as governor on October 2, 1927, the first Tennessee governor to die in office. Peay was buried in Clarksville, Tennessee, in Greenwood Cemetery. (Photograph courtesy of TSLA)

mostly dirt roads were not ready for automobiles. Governor Peay set about to improve roads. As transportation improved, more children could go farther to school. These changes brought on the end of the era of the one-room schoolhouse and the development of larger schools.

Roads had to be paid for as did the improvements in education. Land taxes alone could no longer be depended upon to fund the new developments for the state. Gasoline taxes, auto registration fees, and federal funds helped modernize Tennessee. Peay also worked to create Reelfoot Lake State Park and the Great Smoky Mountains National Park.

As the Democrats held major elective offices, Republicans continued to fight over party control. The Shelby County Republican convention in 1924 spawned another of the continuing battles between the Lily Whites and Black and Tans for control of the Shelby County Republican Party. At the April 1924 county convention, George Lee and the Black Republicans arrived early and took front seats in the room. When Ed Kinney, the Lily White captain, arrived with his troops, he ordered Lee's group to take a seat at the rear. Lee instructed his group to stay put. Kinney threw a chair, and a riotous fight broke out. Each side was bloodied. Deputy sheriffs arrived and broke up the battle. One of Lee's supporters was hospitalized. After order was restored, separate conventions were held. Bob Church held one, and John Farley, a Lily White leader, held another. Lee was elected secretary of the integrated Republican Party.

When the time arrived for the state Republican convention at Knoxville, Farley stated that the 1920 Republican convention had not wanted Robert Church Jr. and he therefore should not be sent to the 1924 Republican National Convention. The Credentials Committee of the state convention did not agree with Farley and gave two-thirds of the Shelby County allotment of seats at the state convention to Church's group and one-third to Farley's. Church went to the June 1924 Republican National Convention in Cleveland as a delegate from Memphis, and his seat was not contested. This was the first Republican National Convention to be broadcast nationally via radio. Calvin Coolidge and budget director, Charles Dawes, were the Republican candidates for president and vice president.

A split occurred at the 1942 Democratic National Convention in New York. Al Smith, governor of New York and former secretary of the treasury under President Woodrow Wilson, vied with William McAdoo for the nomination. McAdoo had the backing of Southerners and anti-Catholics. Some people felt that Governor Smith, being Catholic, should not be president. After more than one hundred ballots, a compromise candidate was finally agreed upon. Virginian John W. Davis, former ambassador to Great Britain, was nominated for president. Some liberals unhappy with the choices revived Roosevelt's Progressive Party and nominated Robert La Follette, from Wisconsin, for president.

In 1924 Clarence Saunders of Memphis suffered from a financial crash that reduced his influence and ability to support his candidates, including Governor Austin Peay. Peay, in an effort to mend fences with E. H. Crump, agreed that Crump could name one person to the election commission and that he could have the new University of Tennessee Medical School located in Memphis.

Meanwhile *Nashville Banner* publisher E. B. Stahlman and his faction continued to look for someone to oppose Peay in the 1924 Democratic primary. Again he tried to get former Governor Benton McMillin, now eighty, to run, but he declined. Former Governor Albert Roberts also declined. Their faction finally found University of Tennessee law professor, John R. Neal, to run, but he handily lost the primary to Peay.

Governor Peay then faced former Commissioner of Agriculture Thomas F. Peck, the Republican in the general election of 1924. E. B. Stahlman continued to oppose the governor through his newspaper. It was a Republican year in the presidential election. However, the national mood did not impact the Volunteer State gubernatorial race. East Tennessee turned out to help Coolidge and Peck, but Peck lost traditionally Democratic Middle and West Tennessee, giving the victory to the incumbent governor by 152,000 to 121,238 votes.

Nineteen twenty-four was also a year for Tennessee to elect a U.S. senator. World War I hero General Lawrence D. Tyson of Knoxville ran for the Senate seat held by Senator John K. Shields. Nathan Bachman also entered the race. President Wilson had previously turned against Shields after the Tennessee senator refused to support the president's plan to create the League of Nations. Tennesseans remembered this touchy issue. With Tyson being a war hero and Shields suffering from the negatives that come with holding office, Shields's situation became tenuous. He had also alienated several politicians by delaying or refusing to support them or their friends for federal appointments. His political enemies quickly took the opportunity to oppose him, aiding Tyson in the primary. This combination of factors helped Tyson obtain the Democratic primary victory. He went on to win the general election for U.S. Senate (Class 2 seat) in November. He began serving March 4, 1925, for a term that was scheduled to run until March 3, 1931.

In the First District, Republican congressman and future national Republican leader B. Carroll Reece was reelected. However, there was no Republican trend for Tennessee in 1924. In spite of the fact that the nation went Republican in the presidential election, Tennessee went Democratic, supporting

LAWRENCE DAVIS TYSON was born on July 4, 1861, near Greenville, Pitt County, North Carolina. He received his early education at county schools and then Greenville Academy. Later he went to West Point Military Academy and graduated in 1883, after which he was commissioned as a second lieutenant. He married Bettie Humes McGhee on February 10, 1886. They had a son, McGhee, and a daughter, Isabella (who married Kenneth Gilpin, lieutenant governor of Virginia). From 1891 until 1895 he taught military science at the University of Tennessee, obtaining his law degree in 1894 while at the university. He practiced law in Knoxville until he was appointed to the rank of colonel by President McKinley during the Spanish-American War in 1898. After the war ended, he served for a few months as military governor of Puerto Rico, returned to Knoxville to practice law, and then later went into the cotton-manufacturing business.

Tyson served as brigadier general and inspector general of the national guard of Tennessee from 1902 until 1908. In 1902 he was elected a state representative and was chosen speaker of the house. He became a delegate-at-large for the 1908 Denver Democratic National Convention, but lost a U.S. Senate bid in 1913. When World War I broke out, President Woodrow Wilson appointed him brigadier general, and he took command of the Fifty-ninth Brigade in the Thirteenth Division, which went to France on May 10, 1918. The division saw nearly continuous action and three thousand of the original eight thousand men were either killed or wounded. Tyson's brigade helped break the Hindenburg Line. General Tyson was decorated for "exceptionally meritorious and distinguished service" (McKellar 1942). His son was killed in the war (in Naval Aviation service while over the North Sea), though he was not in the same brigade as his father. After the war he returned to Knoxville, continued to run his cotton mill, and bought the *Knoxville Sentinel.*

In 1920 the Tennessee Democratic convention endorsed Tyson for the nomination of vice president, but he withdrew his name for Franklin Roosevelt and seconded Roosevelt's nomination. In 1924 he ran for the U.S. Senate against Senator Shields, winning the nomination and then the November general election. His term began in 1925. Tyson served in the U.S. Senate until he died, after a surgical procedure in Philadelphia, on August 24, 1929. A member of the Episcopal Church, he was president of several coal and textile businesses, including the American Cotton Manufacturers' Association. (Photograph courtesy of SHO) the losing candidacy of Democrat John W. Davis, the reelection of Democratic Governor Peay, and the replacement of one Democrat U.S. senator with another.

Coolidge was elected president in 1924 receiving 15,718,211 popular votes to 8,385,283 for Davis, and 4,031,289 for La Follette (382 to 136 to 13 electoral votes). With his election came an increase in Republican control in the House and Senate. However, Democrats and Progressive Republicans made some legislation difficult for Coolidge.

In 1925 the Anti-Evolution Act made it illegal for Tennessee's public school teachers to teach evolution. John T. Scopes, a Dayton, Tennessee, high school teacher and lawyer used a text titled *Civic Biology* (apparently to test the Tennessee law). After it was discovered that he was teaching evolution, he was arrested. When the local drugstore owner called the *Chattanooga News* and reported the arrest, the news spread throughout the country, initiating a national controversy. The state prosecution was led by William Jennings Bryan, who had lost three presidential elections, and the defense was led by Clarence Darrow, a nationally renowned defense lawyer. The famous court battle in Dayton, Tennessee, over teaching evolution—it came to be called the monkey trial—took eight days and received national attention. Bryan was a natural orator and delivered his message as well as he ever had for the trial. Attention turned from Scopes, the accused, to the oratorical warfare between Bryan and Darrow. In the end, Scopes lost and was fined one hundred dollars. Bryan became seriously ill on the last day of the trial and died just days afterward. The trial fomented the interest of journalists, novelists, historians, and playwrights, and created significant worldwide interest. Tourists came from all over the nation to visit the site of the famous monkey trial and see Dayton, Tennessee. The story goes that a traveler was passing through Dayton, Tennessee, sometime after the trial and asked, "Are there any monkeys around here?"

"No," a resident replied, "but a lot of them pass through" (Phillips 1978).

During Peay's second term as governor he continued to work for organization and efficiency in government. However, when he vetoed a bill by legislators to give themselves a bonus for "expenses," he angered a number of them. This courageous act would cost him future cooperation and cause him political hardships in his next election. Running for governor in Tennessee, with its many contentious factions, was always a tenuous act. The alienation of a particular group or the development of too many enemies could guarantee defeat. In contemporary elections, voters are reached by mass media. In 1926, however, political victory was based upon support obtained by word of mouth, political groups, and a little old-fashioned campaigning. Political support by the voters was maintained by more tangible relationships with people. Governor Peay had his sights on running in 1928 for the U.S. Senate seat held by Kenneth McKellar. First, though, Peay had to be reelected governor in 1926.

By 1925 several ambitious contenders lined up to run for governor and were encouraged by the growing opposition to Peay. Support for Peay came from the *Nashville Tennessean* and its publisher Luke Lea, but the governor was still opposed by the *Nashville Banner* and its publisher E. B. Stahlman. When Nashville Mayor Hilary B. Howse began to oppose him, trouble loomed for Peay. Few political bosses had the kind of clout that could neutralize the opposition that mounted against him, and losing Howse's support made Peay more vulnerable. By 1926, E. H. Crump was again opposing him, and Clarence Saunders's name was also added to the list of those against him. So Peay found himself opposed by both the Nashville and Memphis political bosses. Crump, coveting power for himself, was not tolerant of independence on the part of elected officials. He was especially concerned that further victories by Peay would only strengthen the incumbent governor, especially in a future bid against Crump's man, McKellar, for the Senate seat in 1928. Peay's opponents settled upon Nashville lawyer and state treasurer, Hill McAlister, as the candidate to defeat the incumbent governor in 1926.

When the Democratic primary rolled around, the political bosses, ever confident, were stunned. McAlister did win Shelby and Davidson Counties. However, Peay took the rural vote. He lost West Tennessee, split Middle Tennessee, and won Republican East Tennessee by a large majority. Overall, he won the Democratic primary by only seven thousand votes. By the time of the general election, it was a given that he would win reelection. Rhea County School Superintendent Walter White was the Republican nominee. Republican leaders knew it was in their interest to cooperate with the man who would become governor. Peay easily won the general election of 1926, 85,000 to 46,000.

Peay was inaugurated for his third term in January 1927, the first governor of Tennessee since the Civil War to be elected to three consecutive two-year terms. He ran independently of the political bosses and withstood serious opposition. He cooperated when possible but would not be dominated. Nevertheless he served with ability and was a credit to Tennessee. He not only faced constant opposition from the political bosses but also opposition from the 1927 Democratic legislature. Peay had made the friendship of many East Tennessee Republicans legislators, and he used their support, combined with that of some friendly Democrats, to continue to build Tennessee roads and improve education.

In February 1927 the governor developed heart complications. The legislative session recessed for six weeks in February and March while he recovered. However, his health never substantially improved nor did his relationship with the legislature. The political fighting continued, and the governor opposed the legislators' plan for another bonus attempt. On October 2, 1927, Austin Peay died of cardiac arrest, becoming the first governor of Tennessee to die in office. The constitution dictated that the speaker of the state senate should assume office. Democratic state Senator Henry H. Horton became governor of Tennessee. Horton had previously served in the state house, but recently enjoyed a quick rise on the Tennessee political scene. He had just been elected to the state senate in 1926, and the following year the sixty-one-year-old farmer and Lewisburg, Tennessee, lawyer was elected speaker of the senate. Now Horton ascended to the position of governor. He promised to continue Peay's programs and won great popular support for his efforts.

Meanwhile, West Tennessee Black Republicans continued their attempt to participate in Tennessee politics, albeit on the party level. George Lee sold insurance and spoke for civil rights. He developed a close relationship with Bob Church Jr., who opened doors for him through his political organization, the "Elks," a prestigious local Black fraternal organization, and introduced him to Black leaders of the day. In 1926

Black Memphians could not serve as policemen or firemen. Some progress in job opportunities had been achieved for and by Blacks in other parts of the nation but not yet in Memphis. Obtaining jobs in city service was a major goal of Black leaders. Robert Church Jr. tried to organize Black voters into a unit that would be strong enough to gain the appreciation of Crump. He called his lieutenants, men such as Lee, Wayman Wilderson, and Dr. J. B. Martin, to assist in voter registration and a poll tax (two dollars) drive. A mass meeting was held at the Beale Avenue Baptist Church in order to rally support in this effort to get Black voters to the polls. This, Church felt, would effect some change. At this meeting, George Lee was elected the first president of the West Tennessee Civil and Political League.

Memphis Mayor J. Rowlette Paine had alienated Memphis's Black community by not providing the city improvements they wanted and by placing a crematory near a Black residential area. The Black community wanted Paine out of office and so did Boss Crump. Paine was supported by the business community and had not obtained office solely through the efforts of Crump. Therefore, he did not see the need to totally submit to Crump. Additionally, Paine had shown his independence by supporting Governor Peay in the 1926 Democratic gubernatorial primary. This independence did not please the political boss, who wanted a subservient mayor. Crump decided to put his own man in office and went to work gathering the support necessary to defeat Paine. He promised that in exchange for votes against Paine, Blacks would get jobs. Thus, a deal was cut between Boss Crump and Black Republicans.

After the massive voter registration rally at the Beale Avenue Baptist Church on the last day of October 1927, Robert Church Jr. endorsed Watkins Overton, Crump's candidate for mayor. Overton was the great-grandson of John Overton, one of the founders of Memphis. This endorsement caused an immediate negative reaction among those Blacks who saw it as only another effort to benefit Crump. The explanation was given that Overton had agreed to their requests for jobs and other concessions. Once this agreement became public, Crump denied it in order to avoid losing support among the White community. The vote materialized, in any event, and the Crump slate won. In the race for mayor, Overton won by a thirteen-thousand-vote margin. The Crump ticket also won in the commission races.

Manipulation of primary laws and other tactics were used to prevent Blacks from voting throughout the South. In 1927, however, Memphis was a rare major Southern city in which Blacks could vote. Boss Crump enjoyed this peculiarity since it helped guarantee his vote control for a significant block in West Tennessee. A deal cut for the block vote from Blacks only enhanced Crump's political power.

Since Tennessee was heavily Democratic, Republicans had little chance in statewide elections. This made it easy for Bob Church Jr., a Republican, and his lieutenants to justify voting for Crump's choices for mayor, senator, or governor, who were always Democrats. Cooperation with Crump was seen as advantageous for Black leaders. They received jobs and dignity by cooperating with and, thus further empowering, Crump. An additional benefit for Church was police sympathy during local Republican convention battles with the Lily Whites.

In a strange twist, Church aided Boss Crump by continuing his cooperation with Memphis's White Republicans and his control of the local party's flow of patronage from the Republican presidential administration. Second District Tennessee Republican Congressman J. Will Taylor assisted Church in maintaining his influence. When judicial appointments came up, Church was able to input with Harding through Taylor and, after Harding's death, with Coolidge. In addition to judicial positions, Church also had input on appointments for U.S. postmaster and U.S. attorney. Crump benefited from some of Church's influence upon the president's selections for federal appointments. By 1928 Church supplied Boss Crump with some votes and input on some appointments. Church now enjoyed support, although limited, from Crump, the East Tennessee Republicans, and the federal patronage of a Republican president. Crump not only controlled the Democrats, he could get what he wanted out of what few Republicans there were in Tennessee.

Crump provided city jobs and school teaching positions to those who cooperated with his political machine. The machine not only gave out jobs, but it allowed organized vice to thrive. The *Commercial Appeal* wrote that Memphians allowed the operation of the most corrupt political machine in Tennessee history. "Bootleggers, gambling houses, pimps, prostitutes, thrived under the protection of the machine" (Tucker 1971). All of these businesses made money which helped fund the machine, thus enhancing its power.

The state was in the midst of an era of change. The radio and the automobile were forever altering communication, transportation, and in essence, a way of life. Tennessee would now have to adapt. It was also a time of financial ruin for many businessmen. Political upheaval and infighting were at a peak. The late Governor Peay had enjoyed the rural and East Tennessee popularity which was necessary to successfully fight off the Nashville and Memphis bosses. But, Governor Horton, unused to the turmoil and lack of support endured by Peay, was about to inherit all the difficulties that Peay had come to deal with during his terms as governor.

During this period of time *Nashville Tennessean* publisher Luke Lea was a leading political figure in Tennessee. Through his newspaper he could promote his candidates. He had supported Peay, and he immediately supported Horton. Soon after Horton assumed office, the new governor made it clear that he intended to run for his own election when the current term was over. He would need help if he wanted to win the election. The bosses of Nashville and Memphis would naturally want their own man in office. With Peay now gone, it appeared to be an opportune time for them to regain control of Tennessee. However, Horton promised to not only continue Peay's programs, but also to remove the land tax that had hurt Tennessee's farmers. His position on these issues won him overwhelming loyalty from the voters.

Nashville Banner publisher E. H. Stahlman, Memphis political Boss E. H. Crump, Nashville Mayor Hilary B. Howse, and others combined their efforts behind state Treasurer Hill McAlister, who had lost a close race with Governor Peay in 1826. The position of the incumbent governor looked fragile in view of this opposition, but he and Luke Lea had additional support to combat the power of the bosses. Lea had developed a friendship and business relationship with Rogers Caldwell. Caldwell had several brothers and they, along with Lea, had become involved in several businesses. They were investment bankers who owned banks, newspapers, and baseball teams, among other enterprises. They had

HENRY H. HORTON was born on February 17, 1866, to H. H. Horton and Lizzie Moore Horton in Jackson County, Alabama. His father was a Baptist preacher and his mother was a descendent of Thomas Moore, the famous Irish poet. There were six boys and six girls in the Horton household. Henry Horton, reared on his family's farm, received his early education in local schools, then attended Scottsboro (Alabama) Academy when he was eighteen. He later attended Winchester College in Winchester, Tennessee, and graduated in 1888. He thought the future lay to the west and moved to Hillsboro, Texas, to teach in local public schools. However, after one year he returned to Winchester, Tennessee, to teach at Winchester College, where he remained for the following five years. Horton decided to study law and was admitted to the bar in 1894. In 1896 he married Adeline Wilhoite, the daughter of John Benton Wilhoite and Elizabeth Bullock Wilhoite. The couple had one son.

Horton, who practiced law in Chattanooga, Tennessee, was elected to the Tennessee house of representatives in 1907. In 1911 he took residence in Marshall County (twelve miles from Lewisburg, Tennessee), where he owned a farm on the Duck River. He was elected Tennessee state senator for Lincoln and Marshall Counties in 1926, becoming speaker of the senate the same year. When Governor Austin Peay died on October 2, 1927, Horton, by law, became governor. He was elected in his own right in 1928 and reelected in 1930, serving from 1927 until 1933. He oversaw the abolition of the land tax that had disadvantaged Tennessee's farmers, the development of a state parole board, the creation of a state division of aeronautics, the improvement of agricultural education, the creation of a secondary road system, and the placement of statues of Andrew Jackson and John Sevier in the national hall of statues.

In spite of these accomplishments, Horton was charged with conspiracy along with Luke Lea and Rogers Caldwell. Lea and Caldwell owned the banks where some six million dollars of state funds were lost when the depression began. In 1931 impeachment charges brought against Horton failed in the state house of representatives, and Horton was not convicted of any wrongdoing. Nevertheless, his honesty had been questioned. Horton did not run for reelection in 1932, choosing to retire and return to his farm. He died on July 2, 1934, and was buried in Lewisburg, Tennessee, at Lone Oak Cemetery. (Photograph courtesy of TSLA)

the power and influence to counter the political hacks.

At the end of his term President Calvin Coolidge decided not to seek reelection as president. When he made this known, his secretary of commerce, Herbert Hoover, became the leading candidate. Hoover was unusual in many ways, not the least of which was the fact that he had never run for office before and that he was not a retired general. He was born west of the Mississippi to a father who was a blacksmith in West Branch, Iowa. His parents had both died by the time he was eight, leaving him orphaned, but he became a successful engineer and a millionaire by the age of forty. He served as an administrator in the war relief in Europe after World War I, then under President Harding as secretary of commerce. After Harding died, he served under Coolidge.

By the time the June 1928 Republican National Convention in Kansas City had arrived, Hoover already had 400 of the 1,084 delegates pledged. The "old guard" (elected Republicans, party bosses, and machine politicians) attempted a "Stop Hoover" campaign, but it was too late. He won nomination on the first ballot. His vice presidential running mate was Senator Charles Curtis of Kansas, whose nomination helped satisfy the party bosses.

The 1928 Democratic National Convention was held in Houston. Many Tennesseans supported favorite son Cordell Hull for president, but Governor Al Smith of New York was nominated. Most Tennessee Democrats then loyally supported Smith.

When Hoover did not reach out for help from Robert Church, he alienated many Black Republicans. White Republicans resented Black participation, and as a result, special committees were formed in order to segregate efforts. The creation of a special "Executive Committee for Colored Voters Division" and the actions of Chairman John R. Hawkins of Washington, D.C., alienated Church and other Black Republicans. In addition, Hoover chose mostly, if not all, White leaders for the significant positions in the campaign. Memphian Robert Church Jr. was not asked nor given a role to his liking in the Hoover campaign. Only very near election day did the party request an endorsement from him. In response Church quipped, "The Republican Party offers us little, the Democratic Party offers us nothing" (Tucker 1971).

The Democratic primary for governor of 1928 was a battle for power between political bosses and powerful financial and political leaders. Governor Horton and state Treasurer McAlister waged intense political campaigns to see who would have the power of the governor's office for the next two years. Former commissioner of institutions under late Governor Peay, Lewis Polk of Pikeville, Tennessee, was also in the race and had the endorsement of Governor Peay's wife. Governor Horton had been politically pressured to discharge Polk as commissioner and Polk charged that Luke Lea was responsible for the dismissal. McAlister, who owed his own support to the big city bosses, claimed Governor Horton was a front for Luke Lea. In truth, Lea had used his influence to obtain certain state contracts for his friends without going through the required bid process.

The political bosses controlled some of what the newspapers wrote, a difficult obstacle for any seeker of political office to face. Fortunately for Horton, who was in a vulnerable position, Lea controlled the *Memphis Commercial Appeal*, the *Nashville Tennessean*, and the *Knoxville Journal*, and they all supported him. E. H. Stahlman controlled the *Nashville Banner*. Boss Crump managed to have the support of the *Memphis Press-Scimitar*. The *Press-Scimitar* and the *Banner* both supported McAlister's campaign.

The newspaper battle consumed large volumes of ink. The campaign consisted of charges and countercharges with the newspapers firing ridicule and blame back and forth between McAlister and Horton. When the votes were counted, Governor Horton won an overwhelming rural victory. He needed it to counter the massive urban (i.e., Nashville and Memphis) vote for McAlister. Horton's win in East Tennessee combined with the rural vote, narrowly gave him the Democratic primary. Boss Crump did everything he could to bring Shelby County in for McAlister, delivering 24,019 votes for him to 3,723 for Horton. However, even "Big Shelby" could not turn the tide. The incumbent governor won the primary receiving around 97,000 votes compared to 27,000 for Pope and 92,000 for McAlister.

During the 1928 presidential competition, Hoover did little campaigning in his race against New York Governor Al Smith. Hoover favored keeping Prohibition; Smith opposed it. Religious bigotry was a problem for Smith, whose Catholic faith did not help him in the polls. Furthermore, no pressing national crisis motivated the voters to turn from the Republicans. Hoover was elected the thirty-first president of the United States, receiving 21,381,993 popular votes to 15,016,169 for Smith (444 to 87 electoral votes). This was the largest margin of victory since the election of President Grant, taking into account both the percent of popular vote and the electoral vote margin. Hoover received 58.2 percent of the popular vote, coming in second to Warren G. Harding's 60.4 percent in 1920. However, Harding's electoral vote margin was only 404 to 127, which made Hoover's victory one of the most decisive recorded up until this time.

In 1928 there was once again a Republican president, but the Democrats still controlled Tennessee. The gubernatorial race went heavily Democratic. Horton won the general election by the largest majority given any candidate for governor of Tennessee, polling a 71,000-vote margin. Democrat Kenneth McKellar was reelected as a U.S. senator. However, despite the election of these Democrats in statewide elections, Tennessee went Republican in the presidential election. This would be the last election that Tennesseans would support a Republican presidential candidate until 1952. Then it would only occur because of the popularity of Dwight D. Eisenhower, rather than because of any shift of party preference.

After President Hoover took office, he felt that since five of the traditionally Democratic Southern states had gone Republican, he did not need to placate Black Republican voters. He gutted the power of the Black and Tans, giving the Lily Whites all the patronage. Despite protests from Church and other Black Republican leaders in Tennessee, Hoover did not reward them. In Georgia, Louisiana, Texas, Mississippi, and Tennessee patronage was now funneled through the Lily Whites, who, with the power of patronage on their side, sought to oust Church and other Black and Tan Republican leaders.

Tennessee Blacks were not used to being left out of Republican presidential patronage. They continued to struggle to participate and share in the spoils of victory. The battles in West Tennessee among the Lily Whites and the Black and Tans Republicans were never ending and bordered on the absurd, at every level. They became an expected yearly spectacle. Accusations and charges of all kinds were made to the Republican National Committee, as well as to the president.

On August 24, 1929, Senator Lawrence Davis Tyson died after an operation in Philadelphia. Governor Horton appointed William Emerson Brock to fill the vacancy in the Senate. Brock took office (Senate Class 2) on September 2, 1929, and served by gubernatorial appointment until November 3, 1930, when he was elected to complete Tyson's unexpired term. He then served from November 4, 1930, until the completion of the term on March 3, 1931.

The stock market crash in October 1929 altered the political fortunes of many lawmakers. Elected officials, who once reigned in a relatively stable economy, now faced a growing and deep dissatisfaction based upon a dire economic plight that neither the populous nor the elected officials could control.

In 1930 three statewide elections were on the ballot—governor, one unexpired

WILLIAM EMERSON BROCK was born on March 14, 1872, near Mocksville (Davie County), North Carolina, and attended public schools in the area. He worked in farming until 1894 when he moved to Winston-Salem, North Carolina. There he worked as a clerk in a general store, and from 1896 until 1901, as a tobacco salesman. In 1909 he moved to Chattanooga, Tennessee, and began successfully manufacturing candy. He became involved in banking and was a director of a life and accident insurance company. He served as a trustee of the University of Chattanooga, Emory and Henry College, and the Martha Washington College for Girls.

On September 2, 1929, Brock was appointed to the U.S. Senate, filling the unexpired term of the late Lawrence D. Tyson. He served by appointment until November 3, 1930, when he was elected to complete the unexpired term, serving until March 3, 1931. Brock did not run for election to the next full term and returned to his candy business in Chattanooga. He died on August 5, 1950, and was buried in Forest Hills Cemetery in Chattanooga, Tennessee. Brock was the grandfather of Senator William E. Brock III. (Photograph courtesy of SHO)

Senate seat, and one full six-year Senate term. Governor Horton maintained reasonable popularity and was able to calm his adversaries. Although financial strains were occurring, the national economy had not yet fully collapsed, and he did not have to assume responsibility for any economic disasters. In addition the Memphis and Nashville city bosses did not openly oppose him in the 1930 election. His opponent in the Democratic gubernatorial primary was attorney L. E. Gwinn from Shelby County, who was not supported by Boss Crump. In fact, Crump had previously supported the Memphis attorney and incumbent congressman, Hubert Fisher, for the position, but then dropped his support. Fisher and Crump had been friends for over ten years. Many people speculated as to how Crump could turn out an old friend, but Crump had demonstrated before that he would withhold support from a former ally if the situation demanded it.

In addition Crump may not have wanted to become involved in a campaign against Horton because Crump, who was running for Congress, wanted Luke Lea's *Memphis Commercial Appeal* to endorse him. As a result Shelby County, which had voted against Horton by a lopsided margin in 1928, now voted by a lopsided margin for him. He received 27,634 votes to 2,267 for Gwinn in the Shelby County Democratic primary vote.

Two U.S. Senate elections were on the ballot. Since Senator Tyson had died in office and his position had been filled by gubernatorial appointment, the Class 2 seat needed to be filled by public election until its term expired in March 1931. The seat also required an election to fill it for its full term. William E. Brock of Chattanooga had been appointed by Governor Horton to the U.S. Senate until the 1930 election cycle. Senator Brock ran for election to retain his right to complete the term. He was opposed by John R. Neal in the Democratic primary.

Fourth District, seven-term Congressman Cordell Hull from Celina, Tennessee, and the former speaker of the Tennessee house of representatives, Andrew L. Todd, from Murfreesboro,

Tennessee, squared off in the Democratic primary for the full-term seat. Hull won this race; Brock won the short-term seat race. Governor Horton easily won the gubernatorial primary. He had won the state by a narrow 6,000-vote margin in 1928. With the switch in Shelby County support in 1930, he won the state Democratic primary by over 35,000 votes (123,642 for Horton, 88,416 for Gwinn). The magnitude of the vote switch immediately rekindled concerns of Shelby County voter fraud. U.S. Senator Gerald P. Nye, chairman of the Senate Investigating Committee, came to Memphis to hold hearings, charging Crump and his men with voter fraud. It was alleged that the fraud took the form of "herding carloads of Negroes from one Democratic primary polling place to another, expulsion of designated watchers, and wholesale distribution of tax receipts" (Miller 1964). But the charges did not stick. When time came to testify, no one would testify to having seen any activity.

By the time of the 1930 primary, America's economy had begun to deteriorate. Soon, some of the politicians and their backers would be affected by the impending economic instability. Newspaper owner Luke Lea and businessman Rogers C. Caldwell were involved in many enterprises, including banks which held Tennessee state deposits. As the economy worsened, their banks began to falter. When their financial power deteriorated, their political influence weakened.

By the time of the general election, the economic collapse had turned the electorate against President Hoover and the Republicans. Anti-Republican sentiment ran so strong in 1930 that First District Republican Congressman B. Carroll Reece was defeated. This was an unusual and

CORDELL HULL was born on October 2, 1871, in Olympus, Overton County (now Pickett County), Tennessee. He attended public school, and by 1891 graduated from law school at Cumberland University in Lebanon, Tennessee. That same year, he was admitted to the bar and began law practice in Celina, Tennessee. From 1893 until 1897, he served in the Tennessee house of representatives. He also served as a captain in the Spanish American War. Hull sat as judge of the Fifth Judicial Circuit of Tennessee from 1903 until 1906, then was elected as a Democratic U.S. representative in 1906, serving from March 4, 1907, until March 3, 1921, being elected a total of seven times. He failed to be reelected in 1920, but in 1922 again ran for Congress and won. From 1921 until 1924 Hull served as chairman of the National Democratic Executive Committee. Reelected to Congress three more times, he served from March 4, 1923, until March 3, 1931. In 1930 Hull became a U.S. Senator, serving from March 4, 1931, to March 3, 1933, until President Roosevelt appointed him as secretary of state. He took office on March 4, 1933, and served until December 1, 1944. Hull became known as the "Father of the United Nations" and was awarded the Nobel Peace Prize in 1945. He retired and lived the remainder of his life in Washington, D.C. When he died on July 23, 1955, he was buried in the Chapel of St. Joseph of Arimathea in the Washington Cathedral in Washington, D.C. (Photograph courtesy of SHO)

temporary phenomenon for the strongly Republican First District. Democrat E. H. Crump was easily elected to Congress representing the Memphis District—23,756 votes for Crump and 1,500 total for the two other candidates. In the November 1930 governor's race, Horton faced Republican C. Arthur Bruce from Shelby County. Bruce campaigned on the issue of state deposits in the Lea and Caldwell banks and their ties to Governor Horton. He tried in vain to awaken public concern over these business dealings. The Democrats denied any wrongdoing relative to the banks holding state funds or showed any concern over the stability of banks.

Tennesseans reelected Democrat Governor Horton. The vote was 144,995 for Horton and 101,285 for Bruce. Cordell Hull was elected to a full term in the Senate (Class 2), and William Brock returned to the Senate to complete the unexpired term (Class 2) of the late Lawerence Tyson.

Republicans lost control of the U.S. House of Representatives. Hoover had gone into office in 1929 with strong control in the House (Republicans 267 to Democrats 163 to other 5) and Senate (Republicans 56 to Democrats 39 to other 1). Republicans had been riding at the high point of the political wave, but the change in public sentiment moved away from the Republicans; congressional representation swung in the House (Democrats 216 to Republicans 218 to other 1), and Democrats took majority control upon the death of a Republican congressman. In the Senate the margin narrowed to Republicans 48 to Democrats 47 to other 1. Even with this reversal, nationally Republicans had not seen the worst. An economic tidal wave was about to shake the political equilibrium with reverberations that would last the remainder of the century. Tennessee remained solidly Democrat.

Governor Horton, like President Hoover, soon found himself (not necessarily his political party) a victim of something out of his control. The Great Depression now began to shake Tennessee as well as the nation. Several state banks failed, including some that contained state-deposited funds. When the Lea and Caldwell banks failed, some six million dollars of state funds were lost. The connection between Governor Horton and Caldwell seemed even more apparent to the public when they learned that Caldwell had supplied the asphalt for many of Tennessee's road projects. Accusations about the questionable dealings were thrown about and, of course, people were looking for reasons for the catastrophic financial disaster that had befallen the entire nation. Republicans took the blame for most of the country's financial problems, but just four days after the November 1930 elections it was reported that the Bank of Tennessee, which was owned by Lea and Caldwell, staunch Democrats, was insolvent. Suspicions arose, and in 1931 Governor Horton was charged with conspiracy along with Lea and Caldwell.

Congressman Crump had shown his political strength many times by bringing "Big Shelby" in for his friends. Now he wanted more statewide influence. Although he had supported Horton for governor in 1930 (or at least had not opposed him), by January 1931 he was moving to take control of state government for himself. Scott Fitzhugh was a Democratic state senator and member of the Shelby County state legislative delegation, and Crump wanted him elected speaker of the senate. Crump and his perennial campaign manager, Frank Rice, went to Nashville on January 4. Within two days, Fitzhugh was elected speaker, the position next in line to become governor if death or resignation should occur.

A few months later, Crump made a public announcement that the legislature should produce articles of impeachment against Horton as soon as it was back in session in May. By Monday May 25, 1931, Crump, the Shelby County legislative delegation, and all their political allies were in Nashville to wage war against Horton. Simultaneously, Crump was teaching a lesson to the new Speaker of the Senate. Scott Fitzhugh had made the mistake of pushing legislation without first consulting Crump. Fitzhugh had written legislation allowing movie houses to run on Sunday in Memphis. Crump asserted that Fitzhugh should have first consulted Mayor Overton, but his actual meaning was conveyed in his statement, "I think it is an act of discourtesy to the mayor and city administration for any member . . . of the Shelby delegation to have introduced a bill affecting the city of Memphis. . . . Some of the members of the Shelby delegation undoubtedly are permitting a little success to carry them off their feet . . . a dangerous sign for anyone in political business or social life" (Press-Scimitar 1931). The legislation was quickly withdrawn. On Sunday, May 24, Crump had Speaker Fitzhugh dine with him for breakfast and let him know that he would have to resign as speaker. When the legislature was back in session Fitzhugh dutifully resigned saying, "I feel that I have fulfilled my duty to the fullest of my capacity. The smoke screen thrown out over the state that I was anxious to get into the governor's chair or that my political friends were anxious for me to get there to capture control of the state government must be put to rest" (W. D. Miller 1964).

The June 4 house vote during impeachment proceedings against the governor failed by forty-one to fifty-eight and Horton was eventually cleared of any wrongdoing. He stopped Crump and hung onto the governor's seat, but Crump would quickly move again. One week later the Democratic caucus did not renominate Horton's choice for state treasurer and comptroller. This office held the power to deposit state money in various banks. Hill McAlister, Crump's choice, became treasurer. (McAlister had been opposed in the past by Luke Lea and the Caldwell brothers.) Horton was still in office, but the state's money and the legislature were out of his control. With all of this and the burden of the Great Depression, Horton did not seek reelection in 1932.

Shortly thereafter, Luke Lea and Rogers Caldwell were indicted for federal bank law violation. Caldwell was indicted for breach of trust concerning deposits from Hardeman County. In August 1931 Lea was convicted in the Asheville, North Carolina, federal court and sentenced to six to ten years of prison. Crump's political opponents were now all weakened, defeated, or in jail.

While Crump was consolidating his state power, Republicans could only battle over party control. Robert Church Jr. and the Black Republicans were soon to be challenged. C. Arthur Bruce, a white Harvard-educated lawyer who had settled in Tennessee and become active in Memphis politics, had only recently been defeated as the Republican candidate for governor in 1930. As White West Tennesseans became active in the Republican Party, they grew resentful toward Church and his Black

Republicans who had not cast votes for Bruce. They did not feel that Church really represented the Republicans but was, rather, playing both sides of the political fence, in order to recieve patronage. Church cooperated with Boss Crump's machine, but produced little for Republican statewide candidates. As a result, Bruce and John McCall led an opposition movement to Church at the 1932 Shelby County Republican convention. The two groups held simultaneous conventions in the same room, their respective speakers talking from the platform at the same time. The event, chaotic and confused, produced two sets of delegates and alternates. Each group planned to request recognition at the Republican state convention.

The State Republican Executive Committee, which had decided the outcome of many previous conventions in Shelby County, certified and seated both lists. However, Bruce and McCall were not satisfied with the ad hoc appointed subcommittee's recommendation and took their case to the floor of the state convention for a roll call vote. The East Tennessee Republican congressmen maintained their support for Church, (confident the Black vote would go their way whether they wanted support for a Republican presidential candidate or a Democrat in a statewide race). The Bruce-McCall faction then took the fight to the Republican National Convention in Chicago. However, the Convention seated Church's delegates.

At the 1932 Chicago convention, President Hoover and Charles Curtis were nominated as the Republican presidential and vice presidential nominees. At the Democratic National Convention, the party nominated the governor of New York, Franklin Delano Roosevelt. He was the first nominee of his party to deliver an acceptance speech in person. In it he pledged other firsts, one of which was the offer of a "New Deal" for the American people. He effectively contrasted the differences between the two parties. The nation was in the midst of the Great Depression, and the people desperately wanted help. Roosevelt promised it.

Democrats would continue to dominate Tennessee politics. With Governor Horton not seeking reelection, the way was cleared for another Democrat and another faction to gain control. Crump's organization was fully behind Hill McAlister. Nashville lawyer McAlister had served in the legislature and as state treasurer. He had run for governor and lost in 1926 to Austin Peay and in 1928 to Henry Horton. In both those races, he had warned the voters about the impending financial crisis. Now it seemed to the voters that he may have some insight into sound money management. He had to face former Governor Malcolm Patterson and Lewis Pope in the primary. Patterson had the backing of Governor Horton and Luke Lea. Pope ran on a campaign for revising the tax system. McAlister, with the support of Boss Crump, received 31,439 votes in Shelby County to only 6,661 for Patterson and 2,318 for Pope. Once again the Shelby County vote had made the difference.

In the Democratic primary statewide results McAlister won by less than 10,000 votes, totaling 117,400 to Pope's 108,400, to Patterson's 60,520. His narrow margin of victory stirred criticism, since it was obvious that he would have lost the race had it not been for his 25,000-vote margin in Shelby County. Pope's campaign manager, Sam Carmack, cousin of the murdered former U.S. Senator Edward

Carmack, charged fraud. Protests were made to the state Democratic Party, but nothing was done. Even before the election, Idaho Republican U.S. Senator William Edgar Borah had publicly complained that Congressman Crump's machine was using government relief flour as a means to assure cooperation, charging that the unemployed could not procure the flour unless they agreed to support Crump's candidates. Even the Memphis newspapers were expressing exasperation with Crump machine's manipulations.

Tennessee had gone Republican in 1928 for Herbert Hoover, but in 1932 as the Great Depression held the nation in its oppressive grip, the state not only favored the Democrats in the gubernatorial race but in the presidential race as well. Many Tennessee businesses closed and jobs were lost. Many people had no income to purchase even the basic necessities of life.

Democrats Dominate the Nation

The Depression shook the economic well-being of the nation to its core. People looked for change—a change in leadership and a change in action. The Republicans had held the White House for the majority of the time since the Civil War. When financial disaster struck they were the party in power, and they would pay dearly, not with the loss of leadership for one term, but for many terms. They would lose both the presidency and the traditional Republican Black vote.

Hoover was defeated. The vote was Roosevelt 22,809,638 to Hoover 15,758,901 (472 to 59 electoral votes);

HILL McALISTER was born in Nashville to William King McAlister and Laura Dortch McAlister on July 15, 1875. Laura was the great-granddaughter of Governor Willie Blount (who served from 1809 until 1815) and the granddaughter of Governor Aaron Brown (who served from 1845 until 1847). Therefore, Hill's great-great-grandfather was Willie Blount, his great-great-uncle was territorial governor and U.S. Senator William Blount, and his great-grandfather was Aaron Brown. He received his early education in Nashville and then attended Vanderbilt University Law School, starting his law practice in 1899. In November 1901 McAlister married Louise Jackson in what was a noted social event. Louise was the daughter of former Tennessee U.S. Senator and Associate Justice of the Supreme Court Howell E. Jackson, who had been appointed to the Supreme Court by Republican President Benjamin Harrison in 1893. The couple had two daughters.

In 1901 McAlister became assistant city attorney, then four years later was elected city attorney. In 1911 when he became a state senator, he led efforts to enforce education laws and to regulate child and women's labor. He worked for better food and drug inspection and introduced legislation to create a Davidson County tuberculosis hospital. After his term he went back to his law practice. Then in 1919 he was elected state treasurer and served for eight years. McAlister was not a stirring political stump speaker, but a rather serious, mild-mannered campaigner who did not customarily tell jokes during his speeches. When he ran for governor in 1926 and 1928, he lost both times. In 1931 the legislature elected him state treasurer. In 1932 he again ran for governor. This time he defeated four other candidates in the Democratic primary and then defeated

57.4 percent of the popular vote went for Roosevelt. Franklin Delano Roosevelt was elected the thirty-second president of the United States, in an absolute reversal of the political fortunes that Hoover had enjoyed just four years prior. With the Democratic presidential victory also came control of the House and Senate. Democrats picked up ninety-seven seats in the House and twelve in the Senate. Congress would be controlled by the Democrats (Democrats 313 to Republicans 117 to other 5 in the House and Democrats 59 to Republicans 36 to other 1 in the Senate).

From the time the Republican Party elected Lincoln in 1860 until 1932, it had dominated the White House, winning fourteen elections to just four for the Democrats. These two interruptions, only aberrations in the national trend, were provided by Grover Cleveland and Woodrow Wilson. The 1932 presidential election cycle was the end of the era of Republican domination. It would take another twenty years and five more White House victories for the Democrats before the nation would give Republicans another chance.

In the November 1932 general election for governor, McAlister was opposed by Republican John E. McCall from Memphis. Pope, in protest of the outcome of the Democrat primary, ran as an Independent. McAlister won, McCall finished second, followed by Pope. With a sixty-thousand-vote margin in the statewide vote count, McAlister, on his third try, was finally elected governor of Tennessee.

In East Tennessee, some of those who had turned on B. Carroll Reece and

---

Republican John E. McCall of Memphis to become Tennessee's next governor. He was inaugurated in January 1933, in the midst of a nationwide depression and with Tennessee millions of dollars in debt.

Governor McAlister cut costs by encouraging the legislature to trim seven million dollars a year from the state's expenses. Although he received over twenty-five thousand job applications for state positions, he reduced the workforce by 2,380, thereby reducing state overhead. While McAlister was bringing some order into the financial chaos of the state, Roosevelt's programs were beginning to impact the nation. The people of Tennessee reelected McAlister in 1934. He had cut the cost on the governor's mansion from thirty-five thousand dollars per year to one thousand dollars. He worked for financial reform and helped build support for the Tennessee Valley Authority. The Pickwick Landing Dam was begun during his term, and Norris Dam was completed and began producing electricity. The convict-lease law was repealed and an unemployment compensation law passed. The iris was adopted as the state flower and the mockingbird was adopted as the state bird. The governor opposed further reductions of Tennessee's limit on liquor, supported agricultural improvements and organized labor, and granted pardons to convicted criminals. His tenure as governor marked a time in which business leaders prepared for Tennessee economic and transportation development. Municipal airports began construction in Chattanooga, Memphis, and Nashville.

After McAlister's two terms (1933–1937) as governor, he and his family moved back to their home in Nashville. He was then made field counsel for the Bituminous Coal Commission in Washington, D.C. He served in this position for over two years and was then appointed as bankruptcy referee in 1940. His wife died in 1955 and Governor McAlister lived until he was eighty-four, dying on October 30, 1959. Both were buried in Mount Olivet Cemetery in Nashville. (Photograph courtesy of TSLA) defeated the Republican in the First District race in 1930 either forgave him or realized he could not be blamed for the current economic debacle. He retook his seat in the November 1932 race, and was now positioned to become the absolute Republican leader in the state. (He served in Congress from March 4, 1933, until January 3, 1947, retired, then returned in 1951.)

For the average Black voter, the Republican loss of 1932 meant little. Most felt that it did not make any difference who was president or that Republicans had not done enough for them. In fact, the Democratic victory had negative consequences for Bob Church Jr., George W. Lee, and other Black Tennessee Republican party leaders. With no Republican president, East Tennessee Republican leaders had no patronage with which to support West Tennessee Black Republicans. Because of the overwhelming Democratic victory delivered in the election of 1932, E. H. Crump had little need for Church's assistance on a local level, and less on a national level since he would be dealing with a Democratic president. Church, Lee, and other Black Republicans lost prestige and influence and consequently, any future assistance from Crump.

While Church had spent his time working Republican circles, his efforts also cultivated Black adversaries who developed strong Democratic connections. He had refused to help Dr. Joseph E. Walker, a Black physician and businessman in Memphis, gain an alternate position to the 1932 Republican National Convention. Walker's reaction was to organize a Black Democratic club called the Independent Business and Civic Association. He then established relations with Crump, who allowed him to distribute free Red Cross flour to poor Black families. He worked the community, established networks, and became a voice for Black rights. Church had been less vocal about Black rights, following a moderate course to maintain what he thought were good relations with Boss Crump. Walker took over the local NAACP and the local Urban League, molding his image as the champion of Blacks to a level beyond anything Church and Lee had ever achieved. Black voters followed Walker and Roosevelt.

In early 1933 Hill McAlister was inaugurated governor of Tennessee. He, along with President Franklin Roosevelt, came to office in the midst of national financial depression. President Roosevelt's radio addresses reflected the feelings of helplessness of the millions suffering desperate financial hardships. To the unemployed, those with mortgage foreclosures on their farms, those who had lost their savings in failed banks, those with bankrupt businesses, etc., the president said,

> This is preeminently the time to speak the truth, the whole truth, frankly and boldly. . . . First of all, let me assert my firm belief that the only thing we have to fear is fear itself—nameless, unreasoning, unjustified terror which paralyzes needed efforts to convert retreat into advance. . . . Our greatest primary task is to put people to work. . . . (Whitney 1982)

The president pushed through many of his programs in the first one hundred days of office. Some of these programs specifically helped Tennesseans. The Tennessee Valley Authority was developed to produce inexpensive and abundant hydroelectric power for the Tennessee Valley. The Home Owners Loan Corporation helped home owners who faced foreclosure. The Federal Emergency Relief Administration made grants, which provided financial relief for the unemployed, directly to states. The Civilian Conservation Corps offered work to unemployed young people. The Agricultural Adjustment Act helped farmers obtain more purchasing power and limited agricultural surpluses, which in the past had caused price decreases, severely limiting profit. The National Industrial Recovery Act was set up to regulate business. Later in Roosevelt's first term he created the Federal Communications Commission, the Securities and Exchange Commission, the Federal Housing Administration, the Rural Electrification Administration, the National Resources Board, and Social Security programs for the elderly, sick, unemployed, and dependent children. These programs immeasurably helped those in need. They also had a partisan political impact.

President Roosevelt nominated Tennessee's U.S. Senator Cordell Hull, who had served only two years of his Senate term. On February 28, 1933, Nathan Bachman was appointed by Governor McAlister to fill the U.S. Senate seat (Class 2) vacated by Hull. (Bachman took office on March 4, 1933, serving until he stood election for the right to complete Hull's term, which officially ended on January 2, 1937. After the election, he took office again on November 7, 1934, and was reelected in 1936 to a full term.)

The Agriculture Adjustment Act provided relief to many Tennessee farmers, who benefited from farm subsidy payments that paid them for not planting certain crops. They had been caught in the

NATHAN LYNN BACHMAN was born on August 2, 1878, in Chattanooga, Tennessee. After attending public schools and Baylor Preparatory School in Chattanooga, he attended college at Southwestern Presbyterian University in Clarksville, Tennessee; Washington and Lee in Lexington, Virginia; and Centre University College in Danville, Kentucky; eventually graduating with his law degree from the University of Virginia, in Charlottesville, in 1903. The following year, on January 7, 1904, he married Pearl McMannen Duke. Bachman practiced law in Chattanooga, served as city attorney from 1906 until 1908, then served as judge of the Sixth Judicial Circuit of Tennessee (Hamilton County) from 1912 until 1918. In 1918 he was elected an associate justice of the Tennessee Supreme Court and served until he resigned in 1924. After losing a U.S. Senate race to Lawrence Tyson in 1924, he resumed his law practice. When Senator Cordell Hull resigned his seat to become secretary of state, Governor Hill McAlister appointed Bachman U.S. senator on February 28, 1933. Representative Gordon Browning ran against him in the 1934 Democrat primary and was critical of his lack of speechmaking on the Senate floor. However, Bachman beat Browning and was elected to complete the remainder of the term by popular vote in November 1934. He was elected to a full term in November 1936. Bachman served in the U.S. Senate from February 28, 1933, until he died on April 23, 1937. He was buried in Forest Hills Cemetery in Chattanooga, Tennessee. (Photograph courtesy of SHO)

spiral of high operating costs, taxes, and interest rates for their bank loans; and low, often totally unprofitable, crop prices. The Agriculture Adjustment Act saved many cotton, corn, wheat, tobacco, and other types of Tennessee farms.

E. H. Crump retired from Congress in March 1934. He did not need the position. By now he was the boss of Tennessee politics. Former political broker Luke Lea had lost control of the *Nashville Tennessean* in a financial collapse, and was convicted of bank fraud relating to Central Bank and Trust Co. of North Carolina. He and his son, Luke Lea Jr., were jailed in May 1934. Lea Jr. was paroled shortly afterward, but his father remained in jail nearly two years. Both were eventually pardoned in 1937. With the death of Austin Peay in October of 1927 followed by the collapse of the Lea-Caldwell coalition, Crump had no political rivals strong enough to compete with his powerful political machine.

In 1934, Crump again supported Governor McAlister, who was again opposed by Lewis Pope in the Democratic primary. The campaign was dirty. The main issue was Crump's control of the governor's seat. In the Democratic Senate primary for the short (uncompleted) term, Congressman Gordon Browning ran against incumbent U.S. Senator Nathan Bachman, campaigning on the issue that Bachman was merely the governor's relative and was appointed rather than elected by the people. He also criticized Bachman for his lack of speechmaking in the Senate. The other U.S. Senate seat was also up for election in 1934. U.S. Senator Kenneth McKellar was opposed in the Democratic primary by John R. Neal.

Bachman was elected in the Democratic primary for the uncompleted term Senate seat (Class 2), as was McAlister for governor, and McKellar for the regular term Senate seat (Class 1). Pope again lost the Democratic primary to McAlister, who won by a substantial majority of the vote in Shelby County.

Political leaders of both parties knew it was nearly impossible to win a Democratic primary race without Boss Crump's support, and many Democrats were fed up with Crump's domination. Disgruntled Democrats supported a fusion ticket. Former Republican Governor Ben Hooper, who had won his own election under a fusion of Democrats and Republicans, led the effort for a combined ticket. He and other political leaders convinced John McCall, the Republican nominee for governor, that only a coalition could win. The understanding was that Republicans would support Pope, who would again run in the general election as an Independent candidate for governor. In turn, disgruntled Democrats would help Republicans by supporting Hooper in his candidacy as the Republican nominee against Senator Kenneth McKellar. However, the plan failed. McAlister, McKellar, and Bachman—all Crump's candidates—won the general election in 1934. (McKellar was now elected to his fourth term in the U.S. Senate.) Republicans gained nothing in 1934. However, the emerging Tennessee Republican power, Congressman B. Carroll Reece, was again reelected in the First District.

Most candidates appreciated Crump's help in winning elections, but few appreciated his control once in office. Governor McAlister was no different. In 1935 he proposed a sales tax to deal with the state debt and the needs of the floundering public school system. The problem was that he proposed the tax without first gaining Crump's approval. The Shelby County legislative representatives opposed the tax and defeated McAlister's measure. By breaking ranks with Crump and showing some independence, McAlister gained his enmity. It also did not help that the Prohibition Amendment had been repealed, and when Crump demanded that McAlister allow Memphis and other metropolitan areas to sell liquor, the governor refused. Almost immediately, Governor McAlister could see his opposition mounting. In 1936, crippled politically, he chose not to run for reelection. To run without Crump's blessing and support would have been an exercise in futility. Crump's organization was at its peak of political power. William

GORDON BROWNING was born in Carroll County to James and Malissis Brock Browning in 1895. His full name was Gordon Weaver Browning, but he later refused to use the middle name. The Browning family moved to Gibson County. There, James Browning served as justice of the peace. Gordon Browning finished Milan High School in 1908, then taught school and farmed before he went to college. At twenty he began studies at Valparaiso University in Indiana, earning part of his tuition and board by waiting tables. After obtaining his bachelor of science degree and bachelor of pedagogy degree in 1913, he decided to go to law school. By 1915 he had finished Cumberland University School of Law and returned to Huntingdon to practice law.

Browning enlisted in the national guard when World War I broke out. He became a captain and was cited for gallantry for his service with the American infantry in France. After the war he returned to Huntingdon to practice law. He married Ida Leach, daughter of William Leach and Madonna Baird Leach from Huntingdon. In 1920 he received the Democratic nomination for Congress, running against a law school friend, Republican Lon Scott, for the right to represent the Seventh Congressional District of Tennessee. Browning lost to Scott in 1920, but in 1922 he ran against Scott again and won. Browning remained in Congress until 1935, serving six terms.

In 1936 Browning ran for governor against Burgin E. Dossett, who was from Campbell County. Browning easily won the primary and general election and was inaugurated in 1937, serving until 1939. In 1939 he was opposed for the Democratic nomination by Prentice Cooper. Browning was defeated. In 1948, he combined his political organization with Estes Kefauver's, who was the anti-Crump candidate for the U.S. Senate. Together, they defeated the Crump machine and Browning was reelected governor. He served from 1949 until 1953.

As governor, Browning oversaw additional funding for education, the institution of automobile operator license requirements, road improvements, expansion of the Tennessee Valley Authority, state government reorganization, a balanced state budget, refunding of state debt, proposals for utility and chain store taxes, corporate excise taxes, an increase on taxes on securities, implementation of a franchise tax, and implementation of a beer tax. After Browning reclaimed the governor's chair in 1949, he improved rural roads and schools. In 1951, the poll tax requirement for voting was removed. Frank G. Clement defeated him in the Democratic primary for governor in 1952, but he continued his political involvement and leadership in the Democratic Party. Browning died at age eighty-six, on May 23, 1976. He was buried at Oak Cemetery in Huntingdon. (Photograph courtesy of TSLA)

Miller, the author of *Mr. Crump of Memphis,* wrote,

> In the thirties he brought his political organization to the peak of its effectiveness. It ran with well-oiled efficiency, so smoothly balanced that the energizing force behind it could almost stand aside and watch it work from its own momentum. If dissonance developed, the trouble was quickly corrected. A telephone call, a word, a hint from Crump restored the balance. (Miller 1964)

Huntingdon lawyer and twelve-year Democratic Congressman Gordon Browning decided to run for governor. He enjoyed statewide name recognition from his 1934 Democratic primary race for the U.S. Senate against Senator Nathan Bachman. Browning had strong veteran support due to his service commanding an artillery battery in World War I under Regiment Commander Luke Lea. Browning's Democrat primary opponent was Burgin E. Dossett, who was superintendent of schools in Campbell County. He had served as state commander of the American Legion and had been an associate of Hill McAlister. In 1934 he managed the governor's campaign. Indeed McAlister, along with Senator McKellar, supported Dossett. The Democratic primary campaign got under way in June, and it was not long before Browning took the lead. Sensing that Browning, because of his rural support, could win without Shelby County, Crump endorsed him, even though Browning had been close to his political enemy, Luke Lea. Crump had another interest in this race. He wanted to see Leon Jourolmon, who was from Knoxville, elected as a state commissioner of public utility. On primary election day in August 1936, Browning won by nearly double the vote of his opponent and in fact did not need the Shelby County vote. In any event Shelby County went almost totally for Browning in the Democratic primary, logging close to 60,000 votes for Browning with only 600 for Dossett.

In the presidential election of 1936 Republican Alf Landon, governor of Kansas, was nominated for president and Frank Knox was nominated for vice president. The nation was still suffering the hardships of the Depression, but it was the Democrats who had implemented programs which provided relief and hope. Roosevelt overran Landon in the popular and electoral vote (27,252,869 to 16,674,665 popular; 532 to 8 electoral). Only two states, Vermont and Maine, went for Landon. In Tennessee, the vote went strongly for Roosevelt and the Democrats. Even in the staunchly Republican Second District, Republican J. Will Taylor was reelected to Congress only by a very close vote. Republican Congressman Reece was reelected in the First District. Democratic Senator Nathan L. Bachman won reelection to a full term in the U.S. Senate. Democratic Leon Jourolmon was elected a state commissioner of public utilities.

The nation moved even farther away from the Republican Party as Roosevelt solidified his grip and the Democrats picked up twenty more seats in the House and sixteen more seats in the Senate since the last presidential election, some of the gain occurring in the midterm elections. Things looked pretty bleak for the powerless Republican Party. The party's actual existence, considering its numbers in Congress, was in jeopardy (House—Democrats 333, Republicans 89, and

GEORGE LEONARD BERRY was born on September 12, 1882, in Lee Valley, Hawkins County, Tennessee. He attended common schools, then worked as a pressman in various communities from 1891 until 1907. He served in the American Expeditionary Forces in World War I. He attained the rank of major in the Transportation Engineers during his term from 1918 through 1919.

Berry became president of the International Pressmen and Assistants' Union of North America in 1907, serving in this position until 1948, and was also involved in farming and banking. He was a delegate to several national and international labor conventions. Berry was appointed by Governor Browning to fill the seat vacated by the death of Senator Nathan Bachman, serving from May 6, 1937, until November 8, 1938, but was unsuccessful in his bid for the nomination as the Democratic candidate to complete the term in the Senate in 1938. After his service in the Senate, Berry returned to his position as president of the Pressmen and Assistants Union of North America. He also continued farming at Pressmen's Home, Tennessee. He died on December 4, 1948, and was buried at Pressmen's Home Cemetery. (Photograph courtesy of SHO)

Independents 13; Senate—Democrats 75, Republicans 17, and Independents 4).

In the Tennessee gubernatorial general election of 1936 Democrat Gordon Browning easily swamped his opponents. Although he won without Crump's initial support, he won without his opposition. Browning appreciated Crump's cooperation but refused to capitulate to his dominance. Not long after his inauguration, a major split developed between the two politicos which would injure Browning in the next Democratic primary. Crump became irritated with Browning for appointing Luke Lea's old friends to positions in state government. Additionally, Browning did not want to erase the liquor laws, while Crump wanted them eliminated. (Much political power in Shelby County derived from the control of liquor.)

On April 23, 1937, U.S. Senator Nathan Lynn Bachman died in office. Browning had sought this seat in the 1934 election, which was held to elect the successor to complete Cordell Hull's term. Bachman had just been reelected to the seat for a full six-year term in the November 1936 election. After Bachman's death, Browning considered resigning as governor so that the lieutenant governor could appoint him to the Senate seat. He ultimately decided against this and appointed George Leonard Berry to fill the vacancy in the Senate (Class 2). Senator Berry was to serve from May 6, 1937, until November 8, 1938, when a successor would be elected to complete Bachman's term. There is speculation that Crump wanted the seat and that Governor Browning's failure to appoint him finalized the split between the two. However, Crump may not have actually wanted the seat, but only used the issue as an excuse to explain their developing feud.

By the 1938 Democratic primary for governor, Crump withdrew his support for Browning. Governor Browning was likely strong enough to win reelection without Crump. Indeed, Crump had given him his support in the 1936 election only when Browning's lead became apparent. However, Browning went too far to protect his hold on office. Specifically, he called the legislature into special session to change the primary election law in order to create a "county unit vote" which would equalize Shelby County's vote with other counties. His proposal was designed to ensure that the results of the primary in each county would be in proportion to the number of votes cast in preceding elections as well as proportional to other counties in previous elections. With this plan, the victor of a county would win all the votes of that county. In support of this plan, Browning told the legislature that something had to be done, when one man, Crump, could disrupt the entire state. Crump had registered 117,000 voters in Shelby County. The vote in the 1936 Shelby County Democratic primary was only around 60,000 votes. Browning charged that Crump was controlling elections and was essentially a political dictator. In October 1937 the bill passed the Tennessee senate, in spite of the fact that U.S. Senator Kenneth McKellar came to the state capitol to speak against it. Crump's men then filed suit and the supreme court of Tennessee found the bill unconstitutional. This gave Crump the freedom to use his new 117,000 registered voters. Legislation was then passed which enlarged the state election boards, providing Governor Browning the opportunity to control election commissions and thus weaken Crump. Legislation was also passed which removed the requirement for a jury to sit in judgment in "ouster" cases. This would potentially allow the firing of government workers and could also weaken Crump. The governor appointed a crime commission which was charged with investigating political corruption, then ordered the Shelby County voter registration to be purged. Thirteen thousand names were removed for improprieties.

By the beginning of the campaign season in the summer of 1938, Tenth District Democratic Congressman Walter Chandler, of Memphis, announced he was running for governor. When State Senator Prentice Cooper of Shelbyville also announced, Chandler, a close ally of Crump's, withdrew. Crump knew that Chandler, for various reasons, might not carry the state and was unwilling to take the risk. When Crump made it public that he would support Cooper, he sent the Senator a platform made up of pledges designed to repair the political damage inflicted by Browning, mixed with some worthy causes. Cooper kept in close touch with Crump, and although he did not sign the pledge, he became the Crump candidate chosen to oppose Governor Browning. Crump bought advertising and portrayed Governor Browning as a "bigoted boor . . . who would milk his neighbor's cow through a hole in the fence" (Corlew 1990), and likened him to Judas Iscariot. Browning was a sensitive man and was wounded by such gross attacks on his character. His campaign was mainly directed against Crump, and his hold on state government, rather than Cooper. Browning said, "I told him he could ride but that he could not drive" (Corlew 1990), but "no one could receive fair treatment unless he bowed to Crump . . ." (Corlew 1990). U.S. District Judge John Martin enjoined the governor from sending the national guard to Memphis to ensure a fair election in August.

The Tennessee press turned on Governor Browning, portraying him

PRENTICE COOPER was born to W. F. and Argie Shefner Cooper, near Shelbyville, Tennessee, on September 28, 1895. W. F. Cooper was a lawyer and banker in Shelbyville who had served as speaker of the Tennessee house of representatives. Prentice Cooper received his early education in the Bedford County area and later was sent to Bell Buckle, Tennessee, to attend the Webb School. He began college at Vanderbilt, but later transferred to Princeton, where he completed his bachelor of arts degree. After completing college in 1917, Cooper joined the army and went into officer training, but the Armistice was signed before he saw battle. He graduated from Harvard Law School in 1921. In 1922 he returned to Shelbyville and practiced law in an office next door to his father's law office.

In 1925 Cooper was elected to the state legislature. He served one term and then in the same year was elected district attorney general for the Eighth Judicial Circuit. He also served as Shelbyville City attorney. In 1936 he was elected to the Tennessee senate and served from 1937 until 1939. In the 1938 Democrat gubernatorial primary, Cooper defeated incumbent Governor Gordon Browning and following this, won the general election. Cooper took office in January 1939. The Great Depression was just beginning to ease when he became governor, and America was beginning to see signs of another war. Cooper developed a "Tennessee State Defense Council" to prepare for Tennessee's contribution in case of war. While he was governor, the legislature passed a civil service act for state employees, the first in the nation. The legislature overrode his veto to pass a "local option" bill which allowed municipalities to vote whether or not their respective communities could sell liquor. School aid was increased, and state debt was decreased. Free school books were provided for school children in the lower grades. Tuberculosis hospitals were organized into a state system.

Cooper was reelected in 1941 and again in 1943, thus serving three consecutive terms of two years each, from 1939 until 1945. His tenure as governor saw the end of the economic depression and the beginning and end of World War II. After completing his term in 1945, Cooper was appointed U.S. ambassador to Peru, where he served from 1946 until 1948. His mother had served as first lady in the governor's mansion to the bachelor governor, and went to Peru with him. After his tenure in Peru ended, Cooper returned to Shelbyville and practiced law. In 1950 he married Hortense Powell, daughter of Ferdinand and Margaret McGavock Hayes Powell, from Johnson City. They had three sons—one, a future Tennessee congressman. In 1953 Cooper was elected to the constitutional convention. He died on May 18, 1969, at age seventy-four, and was buried in Shelbyville. (Photograph courtesy of TSLA)

negatively. Cooper won the Democratic gubernatorial primary of 1938, defeating Browning 231,852 to 158,854, and winning Shelby County 57,225 to 9,315. Cooper took eight of the congressional districts of the state, losing only the Seventh and Eighth Districts to Browning. He then went on to win the governor's office in the general election, defeating Republican Howard Baker Sr. Many thought that Browning had been politically destroyed by Crump, but this was yet to be proven.

In the 1938 Democratic primary election Arthur Thomas Stewart was Crump's candidate against Senator George Berry,

ARTHUR THOMAS STEWART was born on January 11, 1892, in Dunlap, Sequatchie County, Tennessee. He attended public schools for his early education, then attended Pryor Institute in Jasper, Tennessee, and Emory College in Georgia. He received his legal education at Cumberland University in Lebanon, Tennessee, was admitted to the bar, and began practice in Birmingham, Alabama, in 1913. In 1915, he returned to Jasper, Tennessee, then moved to Winchester, Tennessee, in 1919. Stewart became district attorney general of the Eighteenth Circuit of Tennessee in 1923 and served until 1939. He was elected to the U.S. Senate to fill the unexpired term caused by the death of Senator Nathan Bachman, defeating Senator George Berry (who was appointed) on November 8, 1938. Stewart took office on January 16, 1939. He was reelected in 1942 and served until January 3, 1949. Stewart lost the Democrat primary for renomination in 1948 to Estes Kefauver. While in the Senate he served as chairman of the Committee on Interoceanic Canals in the Seventy-ninth Congress. After leaving the Senate, he resumed his law practice. Stewart died on October 10, 1972, in Nashville, Tennessee. He was buried in Memorial Park Cemetery in Winchester, Tennessee. (Photograph courtesy of SHO)

who had been appointed by Governor Browning to complete the unexpired term (Class 2) caused by the death of Senator Bachman. Stewart won along with Cooper. (He took office on January 16, 1939, and was reelected in 1942, serving until January 2, 1949.)

Crump's political power was beyond challenge in 1939. Indeed he had a firm grip on state politics through Governor Cooper (1939–1945) and later through Governor Jim Nance McCord (1945–1949). His influence stretched across the state, but he did not forget to mind his home turf. For that he needed a loyalist as mayor of Memphis. U.S. Congressman Walter Chandler planned to be the city's next mayor, but the congressman had to remain in office for a vote on "an important bill before Congress" (Sigafoos 1979). Therefore, Crump ran for election himself in order to temporarily hold the office until his selected candidate could make it back to Memphis. He did not campaign, speak, or provide any platform. He ran without opposition and received nearly 32,000 votes.

Crump was to be sworn in on New Year's Day 1940, but he had plans to go to the Sugar Bowl in New Orleans. He handled the conflict by showing up at Central Station in the first minutes of New Year's Day 1940. At 12:15 A.M. January 1, 1940, in the presence of his "formally attired" political entourage, he was sworn in as mayor of Memphis and then immediately handed City Attorney Will Gerber a letter of resignation. The following day it was delivered to the city commission. On January 2, 1940, Walter Chandler was made mayor by the commission. With this act Crump "demonstrated to the citizens his awesome political power and his total command of government in Memphis and Shelby County. Crump decided how local government should be run and who should run it" (Sigafoos 1979).

The Republican National Convention in Philadelphia in 1940 nominated Wendell Wilkie of Indiana for president and Charles McNary for vice president. After eight years of Democratic occupation of the White House and no Republican patronage to dispense, the

Republican Party had become progressively weaker. In Tennessee they were powerless as a party and meaningless in the overall political equation.

By 1940 Robert Church Jr. had come under considerable pressure from Boss Crump. Church's real estate holdings were seized, allegedly for taxes. Having no effective redress, Church moved to Chicago and to Washington, D.C. Nevertheless, he still felt that he controlled the Republican Party in Memphis and prepared to have his lieutenants, Dr. J. B. Martin and George Lee, fight the battle for him. Church felt that his fellow Black Republicans would be so outraged over the way he had been mistreated by Crump that they would rally to his cause. However, Lee was a fence-sitter who wanted to maintain relations with both Church and Crump. Lee had actually lost a great deal of respect among his peers for playing up to Boss Crump. While this ploy was sometimes to his advantage, it was actually a sellout of his community. Martin, on the other hand, stood up for Church. At Republican rallies, he, along with others, openly criticized Crump.

Besides owning a drugstore, Martin was a bail bondsman. He had been given the opportunity to make a fair amount of money as a bondsman, even though he did not have a license. Crump felt Martin was a bit unappreciative for the special privileges he had enjoyed. Police were posted in front of his drugstore and searched everyone who entered the store, allegedly to "look for narcotics." This, of course, made the customers afraid to patronize his store. Since no one could control this kind of intimidation, and any protest would be met with more of the same, no one dared any organized confrontation or objection. Only Martin had the nerve to stand up defiantly against what he felt was illegal and unfair treatment. Even the NAACP only offered advice. C. Arthur Bruce, the Lily White Republicans' leader, suggested that Martin keep up his fight and the pressure on Crump. After all, this kind of problem helped the Republicans in their fight for power. During the presidential campaign, Republicans used Democratic "bossism" as part of their strategy by

> identifying President Roosevelt and the Democratic Party with Pendergast of Kansas City, Hague of Jersey City, and Mr. Crump of Memphis. When the Tennessee Republican Convention met in Nashville it declared there was "a real Hitler and Mussolini in Shelby County." (Tucker 1971)

During this time, the nation witnessed a growing menace to world peace. France was invaded by Nazi Germany just as the Democrats met in convention. The enthusiastic Tennessee delegation supported Cordell Hull as the Democratic nominee for president, but the powerful Franklin Roosevelt owned political loyalty. He was nominated for an unprecedented third term. In the campaign President Roosevelt attacked Republicans for allegedly obstructing his attempts to strengthen the military. He defeated Wilkie 27,307,819 to 22,321,018 popular votes and 449 to 82 electoral votes. This was not as great a margin as his previous victory, but it still demonstrated his stronghold on national politics. Tennessee went solidly for Roosevelt in the 1940 general election.

The national political pendulum was beginning to slow its Democratic

President Franklin D. Roosevelt at the dedication of the Chickamauga Dam in 1940. (Photograph courtesy of CH

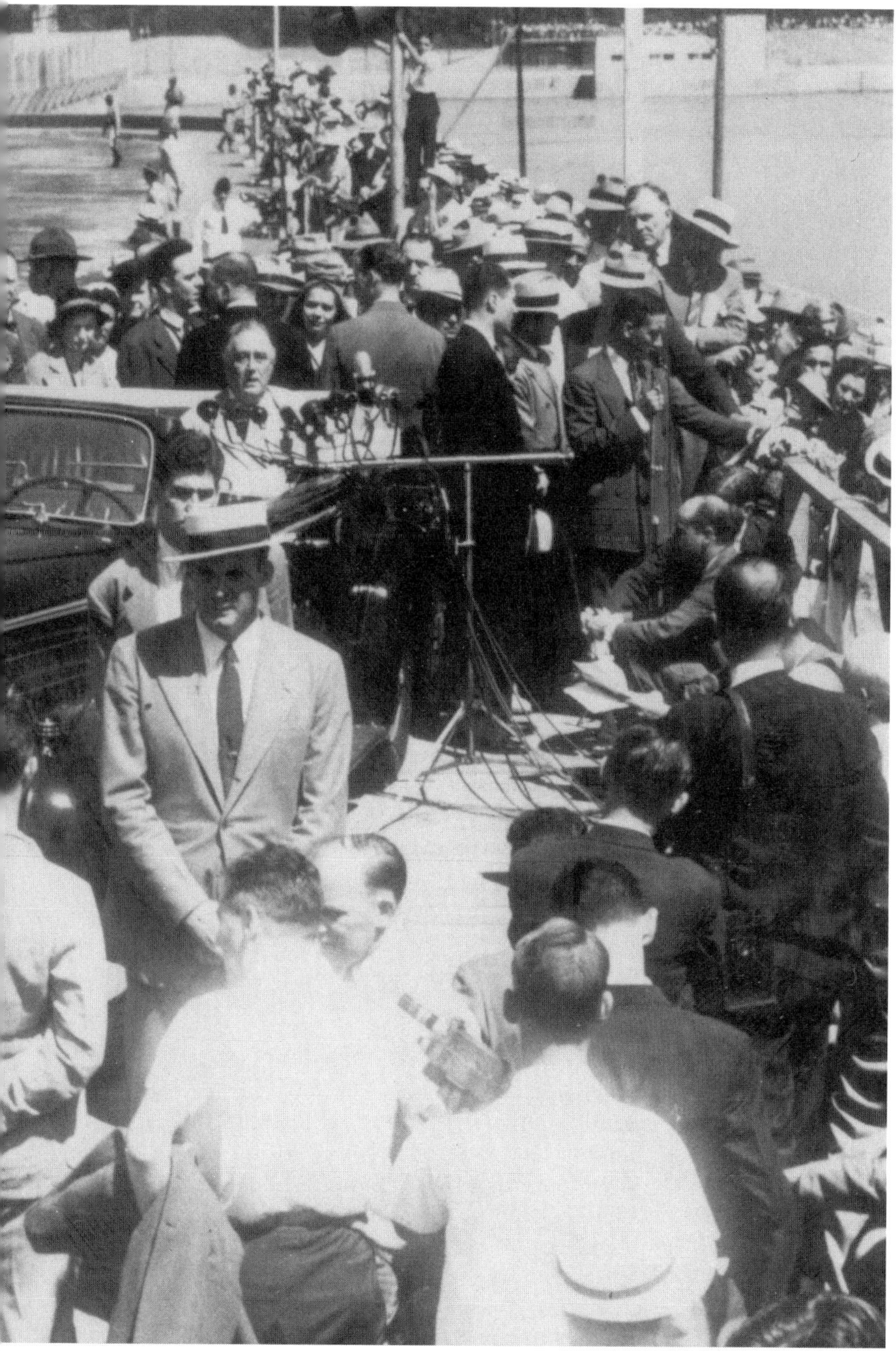

momentum, but there was no doubt that the Democratic party was still dominant. Democrats were down slightly from their high four years prior in the House and Senate and the numbers looked a little better for Republicans (House—Democrats 267, Republicans 162, and Independents 6; Senate—Democrats 66, Republicans 28, and Independents 2).

In Tennessee, Democrats still maintained control. The voters reelected Kenneth McKellar to his fifth term in the U.S. Senate. Governor Prentice Cooper maintained a strong support base, with Boss Crump sticking with him. He won again in 1940 by defeating George Dempster from Knoxville in the primary and won the general election with little effort. The only election aberration occurred because Democratic U.S. Representative Joseph W. Byrns Jr. of Nashville demonstrated a lack of support for the U.S. military at a time of impending worldwide conflict. He had also made snide remarks about the British king and queen. As a result, Independent Percy Priest defeated him.

After the Republicans went down in defeat, Memphis Black Republican Dr. J. B. Martin found himself all alone. Those who had encouraged him to make his stand against the Crump machine either did not have the power or did not have the will to stand up against the establishment. "The Crump organization began building a criminal case against J. B. Martin for making bond without a license" (Tucker 1971). When the charges were filed, Martin left, and moved to Chicago. Some ministers protested Martin's harassment, but this accomplished little, and the threats against Black preachers, doctors, restaurant owners, pharmacists, undertakers, and newspaper writers continued. George Lee was curiously not listed among those whom Police Commissioner Joe Boyle enumerated in his "issued public threat" (Tucker 1971). Lee's peers were suspicious of his apparent good relationship with Boss Crump at a time when many others were being intimidated. His reputation as a political leader suffered.

In the election of 1942, former Fourth District Congressman J. Ridley Mitchell ran in the Democratic primary against Governor Prentice Cooper. By now Cooper's support was weakening and he became somewhat vulnerable, but Crump stuck with him. Gordon Browning and his friends supported Mitchell, who campaigned against Crump's political machine and attempted to ignite the public's antagonism against the Memphis boss. He attacked Crump for his opposition to repealing the poll tax. He attacked Cooper for being a puppet for Crump's control of Tennessee. The *Nashville Tennessean*, now run by Silliman Evans, worked to expose the wrongs associated with the poll tax, and the efforts of the Memphis political machine to continue the perpetuation of the poll tax and the political benefits of such a limit on voting for the Memphis boss.

Crump was still too strong to be defeated. He counterattacked the Nashville paper and Mitchell's accusations, but now the story was out on the poll tax and Crump's machine. Both men suffered political wounds and public scrutiny as a result of the election of 1942 and the campaign against the poll tax. (In 1943, the Tennessee legislature repealed the poll tax, but this was overturned by the state supreme court as unconstitutional.) Governor Cooper won 171,259 votes to 124,037 for Mitchell, winning the Democratic primary by over 47,000 votes, but this was a close victory, especially considering that 45,000 of those votes came from Crump's controlled territory in Shelby County. A reversal of the Shelby County vote would have given the challenger the victory.

In the U.S. Senate Democratic primary, Tom Stewart was challenged by Edward (Ned) Carmack. Carmack won most of the state, but lost Crump-dominated Shelby County. There, Stewart won by 35,000 votes, giving him a surplus of only 20,000 but enough for the victory. Carmack would have won the primary had it not been for Shelby County. This kind of control over elections continued to increase the notoriety of the Memphis boss, and also began to solidify the growing opposition against him.

Cooper was reelected governor in the general election of 1942; Tom Stewart easily won the full six-year Senate term in 1942. The Memphis boss had helped Tom Stewart return to the Senate and Cooper to the state capitol. Cooper managed to remain on good terms with Crump throughout three elections. Six years, or three consecutive terms, was the constitutional limit in Tennessee; therefore, Democrats would have to find another candidate for governor in the next election cycle.

Tennessee did its part to prepare for World War II. The most dramatic contribution was made in a town in Tennessee called Oak Ridge, which held a secret that would change the world. The new city was developed on land purchased by the federal government in 1942. Plants and housing suddenly appeared in the town, but almost no one knew that the atomic bomb was being developed there. Defense plants sprang up all over the state. The city of Millington manufactured powder. Nashville made airplanes for the British. Milan had a plant that loaded shells. Tennessee companies made not only arms, but clothing and food for America's war effort, and employed over two hundred thousand men and women. A total of $1,250 billion in war-related contracts were made in the state. Army camps were organized in Tennessee. Camp Peay, in Tullahoma, was now called Camp Forrest (named for Nathan Bedford Forrest). Clarksville also benefited from the development of Camp Campbell just across the Kentucky border (named for Governor William Campbell).

Many Tennesseans went off to war. Former Governor Gordon Browning, who had achieved significant popularity after his service as an artillery officer in World War I, reclaimed his rank of captain and returned to service in 1942. He rose to colonel, serving with troops in Europe. As the war progressed he was given the job of setting up occupation guidelines in the regions taken by the allied forces, and eventually became military governor of Bavaria.

At the Republican National Convention in Chicago, Thomas Dewey, governor of New York, was nominated for president, and John Bricker, governor of Ohio, was nominated for vice president.

Democrats renominated Roosevelt for president. However, they did not renominate the vice president. By 1944, Vice President Henry A. Wallace proved to be a bit too liberal for Roosevelt, who wanted to replace him with Senator Harry S. Truman from Missouri. Tennessee's Governor Prentice Cooper was also nominated for vice president. He received only favorite son support, and the nomination fell to Truman. Interestingly, Roosevelt had previously withheld support for Truman's reelection to the U.S. Senate in the 1940 Missouri contest.

Fifth District Congressman Jim Nance McCord, from Lewisburg, Tennessee, ran in

JIM NANCE McCORD was born in Bedford County, Tennessee, on March 17, 1879. His parents were Thomas N. and Iva Stelle McCord. Of their eleven children, one, Jim Nance's twin brother, died. McCord learned to work on the family farm and received an education at local schools. He spent a great deal of time in his brother's Shelbyville, Tennessee, bookstore and was generally self-taught. He became an auctioneer, bought the *Marshall County Gazette* and ran the paper for many years. In 1901 he married Vera Kercheval, who was from Lewisburg. They did not have any children. Early in his adult life, Jim was elected mayor of Lewisburg, Tennessee, and served thirteen terms. In 1942 he ran as a Democrat for the U.S. House of Representatives unopposed and took office in 1943. In 1944 he ran for governor and was elected.

McCord began serving as governor in 1945, and soon enacted the state's first sales tax in order to fund additional appropriations for public schools (two cents per dollar). He also helped establish a retirement program for teachers, and oversaw the implementation of a complete, funded school program creating grades one through twelve. New schools were built and new buses were bought for all Tennessee counties. His program raised teachers' pay and added benefits. State colleges also benefited from the additional tax funding and the GI Bill. Twenty thousand teachers were now at work in Tennessee. McCord was reelected in 1946, but the sales tax would hurt him in 1948.

By 1948 people were growing tired of Crump's political domination. Estes Kefauver was running for U.S. Senate on an antimachine platform on a ticket consisting of himself and Gordon Browning, who was running for governor. Crump's machine was defeated in 1948 and along with it, Governor McCord.

McCord returned to Marshall County and continued to remain active in business and community affairs. He ran his newspaper and he and his wife served their church. His wife died in 1953, and in 1954 McCord married Mrs. John Arthur Sheeley, from Paris, Tennessee. She died in 1966. In 1967, McCord, eighty-eight years old, married Mrs. T. Howard Estes from Nashville. Jim Nance McCord died on September 2, 1967. He was buried in Lewisburg, Tennessee, in Lone Oak Cemetery. (Photograph courtesy of TSLA)

the Democratic primary for governor. He had the support of Senator McKellar, Crump, and the *Nashville Tennessean*. Rex Mannin from Nashville and John R. Neal from Knoxville also ran in the primary, but McCord won the race handily.

This election cycle was occurring during the height of America's effort in World War II, and Democrats still dominated the stage. But their hold on the electorate was beginning to weaken. Roosevelt was victorious, but not by as great a margin as in his previous three elections (25,606,585 to 22,014,745 popular votes; 432 to 99 electoral votes). The pendulum had begun to swing toward Republicans in the House and Senate during the midterm races two years before. Republicans had gained 47 seats in the House and 10 seats in the Senate, (Democrats 222, Republicans 209, and Independents 4 in the House; Democrats 57, Republicans 38, and Independents 1 in the Senate), but the trend did not continue in this presidential election cycle. Republicans lost 19 seats in the House and dropped to a total of 190, while holding steady in the Senate at 38.

Many of Tennessee's past governors had been lawyers. This trend was interrupted in 1944 when Democrat Jim Nance McCord, who was an editor from Lewisburg, was elected. He defeated John Wesley Kilgo, from Greeneville, in the general election by a large margin. In the First District, Congressman B. Carroll Reece was reelected to his twelfth term as Republican congressman, remaining the leader of the weak Tennessee minority party.

The presidential election of 1944 was the last political battle that Crump waged for a presidential nominee. He had been a great supporter of Roosevelt's, not only in the first two elections, but also in the third and fourth when the papers and some political leaders began to tire of him. After the round of 1944 elections, on March 13, 1945, the president's secretary telegrammed Crump to request that he come and visit Roosevelt. The visit, on March 21, 1945, was especially long, lasting an hour. Roosevelt's purpose was to ask Crump to withdraw his support from McKellar's 1946 reelection campaign. For whatever reason McKellar no longer served Roosevelt's purposes. Was he too old, too uncooperative, too powerful on the hill? Perhaps there were other reasons. Nevertheless, Crump would not agree to desert McKellar. He was the last person to have an official visit with the president that day. After the visit Crump said, "I went up to the capitol and told Senator McKellar, Senator Barkley, and Senator Hill that the President looked badly" (Miller 1964).

Governor McCord worked to improve Tennessee. Appalled at the poor quality of the schools and the low pay scale for teachers, he made the upgrading of Tennessee's education system one of his chief goals. He was also able to maintain political support from Crump. The two-year gubernatorial term was still in effect in Tennessee, and it was not long before the campaign of 1946 began.

Wartime Leadership to the New Millennium

PART IV

Wartime Leadership

Roosevelt began his fourth term on January 20, 1945. In early February, he attended the Yalta Summit, where the Allied leadership discussed the new world order and plans for peace post–World War II. He spent the next several weeks dealing with the demands of the war as it neared its closing days. On April 12, 1945, the president died.

His vice president, Harry S. Truman, served only twenty-five days as president when Germany surrendered. Truman traveled to Potsdam to discuss the occupation of Germany and the ultimatum to Japan. He authorized the use of the atomic bomb on Japan. World War II soon came to an end.

During the war, Democrats controlled the state and held all the influential positions. Republicans controlled little. Other than the leadership of East Tennessee Republican congressmen, Republican activity was confined to intraparty skirmishes for the right to lead county and state party organizations. If Republicans benefited, to any extent, within the Democrat-controlled state and nation, it was because of cooperation between East Tennessee Republicans and Democratic candidates for statewide office. Candidates had to carry at least two of Tennessee's three grand divisions (East, Middle, West) in order to win a statewide contest.

First District Congressman B. Carroll Reece was by now the leader of Tennessee Republicans. Over the years he became increasingly active in national Republican Party activities, attending the Republican National Conventions as a delegate in 1928, 1932, 1936, 1940, 1944, and 1948. After twelve terms and twenty-four years in Congress, interrupted for two years by a defeat in 1930, he declined reelection in 1946, and instead was elected Republican Party national chairman. He served in this capacity from 1946 until 1948.

Former Governor Gordon Browning and his friends still smarted over being expelled from the political establishment by Crump's machine in the 1938 election. Browning had served in the military during World War II and was still in Germany in 1946. Although he was not able to actively take part in the campaign, he ran for the Democratic gubernatorial nomination against incumbent Governor Jim Nance McCord. His campaign manager, Judge T. L. Coleman, ran the campaign for him in Tennessee. Browning may not have held the advantage of incumbency, but he had achieved significant notoriety from his second tour with the military in World War II. Nevertheless, Governor McCord won the primary, 187,119 to 120,535. In spite of his loss, Browning demonstrated that he still had many supporters.

In the Democratic U.S. Senate primary, incumbent Senator McKellar, still a Crump protégé, was challenged by Ned Carmack, the son of the slain former senator and newspaper editor, Edward Carmack. Memphis Mayor Walter Chandler wanted Crump to ask the aging McKellar to retire with dignity from the U.S. Senate, thereby allowing him to easily move into the seat. But Crump would not desert his friend McKellar. Frustrated and disgruntled, Chandler would soon resign as mayor. President Roosevelt, prior to his death, had supported Carmack, and tried to persuade Crump to abandon McKellar. However, Crump was more concerned with his own coalition than Roosevelt's and refused. Although McKellar's age was becoming an issue, Carmack lost the election by a greater count than Browning had lost the gubernatorial primary.

The Democrats won the governor's seat and U.S. Senate seat in the general election.

After Governor McCord's reelection, he worked to improve education by making capital improvements and increasing teachers' salaries. He led the charge for a 2 percent sales tax, which was opposed by Crump. However, Governor McCord led a caravan of automobiles across the state to Memphis and convinced Crump to support the tax over the opposition of Ned Carmack and Silliman Evans. He won the tax, but the governor's loss of political support over the issue would come back to haunt him in 1948. The political machine that had aided McCord was beginning to face challenges on several fronts.

In Athens, Tennessee, McMinn County State Senator Paul Cantrell, linked to Boss Crump, had for years headed an entrenched political machine, which held an iron grip on local power and policy. On August 1, 1946, a group of World War II veterans in the insurgent GI Non-Partisan League armed themselves by breaking into the local National Guard Armory and laid seige to the jail, where the sheriff and his deputies had absconded with key ballot boxes. The ensuing battle lasted several hours, and a few days later, the veterans were sworn in as duly elected candidates. The political boss system was weakening.

The Machine Falters

In 1948 the political winds of change blew through Tennessee. The change would not necessarily aid Republicans, but it helped break up a Tennessee political machine that had held power in the state since the downfall of Luke Lea. Political leaders, blacks, the middle class, and labor throughout the state had all experienced enough of machine politics. E. H. Crump had been the undisputed chief of politics in Tennessee, regardless of party, since the early 1930s. He had demonstrated his political influence innumerable times over the years by supporting senators, congressmen, mayors, and other elected and appointed officials, then demanding and receiving from them absolute capitulation to his will. The resentment toward his dominance had risen to a crescendo.

By 1948 Gordon Browning had returned from military service in Europe and was back in Tennessee. He had distinguished himself in World War II and had served as military governor of Bavaria. He intended to win the governor's chair in 1948 and to use his popularity as a military hero to aid his political ambitions. The obstacle to his goal was what it had always been—Crump's machine control of the Shelby County vote combined with cooperating factions across the state. Preparing for the race, Browning joined forces with Estes Kefauver, U.S. representative from the Third District, in order to combine their strengths and capitalize on anti-Crump feelings. The poll tax had kept Tennessee voter turnout low, allowing Crump's large Shelby County vote to sway state elections. But the poll tax was repealed in 1943. Together, Browning and Kefauver planned to win the primary and break the Crump machine.

In the 1948 Democratic primary Estes Kefauver ran against Crump's candidate, incumbent U.S. Senator Tom Stewart. Senator McKellar had never liked Congressman Kefauver, a potential future threat as well as a personal and philosophical irritant to the increasingly conservative senator. He had written to Crump in July 1944, from the Chicago Democratic National Convention, that the Tennessee delegation "was very harmonious except for alternate Kefauver. He was present at each meeting of the delegation and . . . objected to everything." The convention "did not pay him a particle of attention. He caused some laughter when he claimed Jefferson as a

CAREY ESTES KEFAUVER was born on July 26, 1903, on a farm close to Madisonville (Monroe County), Tennessee. He was educated in public schools, attended the University of Tennessee, and graduated in 1924. He obtained his law degree from Yale University and was admitted to the bar in 1926. The next year he began his practice in Chattanooga, Tennessee. Politics interested Kefauver early in his career, and in 1936 he ran for the state senate but lost. Kefauver married Nancy Pigott, from Scotland, in 1935. They had three daughters, Linda, Diane, and Gail, and adopted a son, David.

In 1939 Kefauver served as commissioner of finance and taxation for the state of Tennessee. After U.S. Representative Sam D. McReynolds died, Kefauver was elected to fill his seat in 1939. He was reelected four times, serving as a Democrat congressman from September 13, 1939, to January 3, 1949. In 1948 Kefauver ran against the Crump-machine-backed U.S. Senate candidate, won the Democratic primary, then went on to win the general election. He was reelected to the Senate in 1954 and 1960, and gained national notoriety by serving as the chairman of the Special Committee on Organized Crime in Interstate Commerce (Kefauver Committee). In 1952 he ran for the Democratic presidential nomination but was unsuccessful. Again in 1956, he tried for the nomination and failed. Then he tried for the vice presidential nomination in 1956 and was selected to run with the presidential nominee, Adlai Stevenson. However, the Eisenhower/Nixon ticket won. Kefauver continued serving as one of Tennessee's U.S. senators and died midway into his third term at Bethesda Naval Hospital in Maryland on August 10, 1963. He was buried in his family cemetery in Madisonville, Tennessee. (Photograph courtesy of SHO)

Tennessee President. He is about as stupid as they make them" (Miller 1964).

Senator Stewart had defeated U.S. Senator George Berry (who had been appointed by Governor Browning in 1937 upon the death of Senator Nathan Bachman) in the 1938 Democratic primary. Although Crump and McKellar both opposed Kefauver, they feared that Senator Stewart could not beat him. In addition, they were concerned about fighting on two fronts because they also had to face former Governor Gordon Browning, who was taking on incumbent Governor Jim Nance McCord. McCord had Crump's and McKellar's backing, of course, and in the past this would have guaranteed almost certain victory, but it worked against McCord in 1948. He had earned both the enmity of organized labor since signing the right to work (open shop) bill and the public's resentment since enacting the state's first sales tax. These factors combined with anti-Crump feelings were so strong that even Shelby County voters began to revolt. Young Democratic attorney Bill Farris and his friends were active in various community organizations. They represented a new era of West Tennessee Democrats who did not want to be beholden to Boss Crump. In fact they actively campaigned for Gordon Browning. This was a risky tack in 1948, a time in which Crump still dominated Memphis politics. Black voters also revolted against the boss. Memphis Black businessmen, including Dr. J. E. Walker, Taylor C. D. Hays, and Reverend J. A. McDaniel, worked to end the dominance of the Shelby County machine. They publicly campaigned against the Crump machine candidates Stewart and McCord.

As early as September, Crump and McKellar told Senator Stewart that they could not carry him in this race and swung their support to Judge John A. Mitchell from Cookeville. Stewart continued his campaign in spite of Crump's abandonment. This set up a split in the vote between Senator Stewart, Judge Mitchell, and Congressman Kefauver.

Attorney General Will Gerber helped Crump and McKellar design the attack against Kefauver. Crump fought vigorously against him even though his larger reason for being involved in the 1948 statewide election was his abhorrence of Gordon Browning. Nonetheless, he had to oppose all those against his team. He accused Kefauver of communist sympathies. Kefauver countered by tying his opponents to Crump's boss-like domination of Tennessee politics. He wore a coonskin cap and told listeners at campaign stops, including Memphis, that he was not "Mr. Crump's pet coon" and that his cap was "genuine Tennessee coon, whose rings were in its tail, not in its nose" (Dr. Miller, *Crump* 1964). These pronouncements left no doubt that he was an anti-Crump machine candidate.

Crump's anticommunist attacks against Kefauver did not help Senate candidate Mitchell or Governor McCord. Both candidates suffered from their association with Crump and the strong antimachine momentum. However, Crump effectively attacked Browning for allegedly executing excessive pardons of criminals during his previous tenure as governor. The accusations were so destructive that Congressman Albert Gore Sr. returned to Tennessee to campaign for Browning. Newly returned veterans from World War II generally supported Browning in his quest for a return to the governor's chair, and Browning curried this support by at one point comparing Crump to Hitler. In one of his campaign stops in West Tennessee, he told the following story, five days prior to the primary election:

> A fellow from Shelby County was talking to me the other day and told me he lived near the cemetery. He said he saw a light flashing out among the tombstones one night, and E. H. Crump with a notebook and pen, and down on knees was little [attorney general] Willie Gerber, reading off the names. He came to one he couldn't read because the moss had grown up all over it.
>
> "Just put down any name," he said, "I know there's a name here, but I just can't read it."
>
> "No Willie," replied Mr. Crump, "you've got to read it. We've got to have the right name. This has got to be an honest election." (Miller 1964)

In the 1948 Democratic primary in Tennessee, the split vote by Mitchell and Stewart, combined with antimachine fervor and the absence of a poll tax, was enough that Crump lost forty-six precincts in Memphis. This was the first time the Memphis boss had lost an election since 1926. He had recovered from that little setback, but this election broke the absolute invincibility of his machine. Browning defeated the machine-backed incumbent Governor Jim Nance McCord 240,676 to 183,938. (William D. Miller records the vote as 215,000 for Browning and 160,000 for McCord, statewide.) Browning's victory occurred in spite of strong, though not as strong as usual, Shelby County support for McCord via Crump's machine, which managed 48,000 votes for McCord to 20,000 for Browning. However, Browning's lead across Tennessee assured his primary victory. Chattanooga U.S. Representative Estes Kefauver defeated Tom Stewart and John Mitchell for U.S. Senate with only 42 percent of the Democratic primary vote. Kefauver received around 150,000 votes to 79,000 for Mitchell and 118,000 for Stewart. The Shelby County vote was 38,000 for Mitchell, 3,000 for Stewart, and 28,000 for Kefauver. Had Crump stayed with Stewart, Kefauver may have lost.

Boss Crump did not give up after his setback in the 1948 election. In fact, he made it a point to ensure that the revolters understood the potential retribution. Not long after the election results were in he summoned a group of the Shelby County rebels to a meeting. Twenty-five-year-old Democrat Bill Farris was among the assembly. The young budding politicians felt excitement and anticipation as they approached their meeting with the legendary Crump. Perhaps they had finally arrived and would be included in the inner circle of power. Perhaps they would be confidants and heirs to the "Big Shelby" political dynasty. Crump had other ideas. These youngsters had challenged him. In days past, men had lost jobs and been run out of Memphis for much less. Soon after the meeting began, Crump exhorted the young men to "lay off. . . . I run this town. If you don't like it, then, get out of Memphis" (Farris 1997). The meeting quickly ended. This may have shaken them, but they remained defiant. The 1948 election had demonstrated that the boss's domination could now be successfully challenged.

On the national scene, General Douglas McArthur was a phenomenally popular figure in 1948. He had visions of the presidency and wanted to run as the Republican nominee. However, he first had to obtain the nomination, and intraparty politics was an issue distinctly separate from public popularity. McArthur had run a military power, but he had no political organization. Thomas Dewey, however, did and was again nominated as the Republican candidate for president; Earl Warren, from California, was selected as the nominee for vice president. The general feeling was that incumbent President Harry Truman was vulnerable, and after sixteen years of Democratic presidents, it was time for a change. Republicans were confident and felt that whoever received their nomination would win.

When World War II ended, Truman had to face the growth and threat of the communist nations. He oversaw the regular business of the nation, the conversion of the nation to a peacetime economy, and the rise of war heroes as political competitors. This was a controversial time. It would have been tough for any president, and Truman's popularity was at a low, 30 percent, in 1948. Even worse, the Democrats were splintering into factions. They were so concerned about losing the presidency that some hoped to draft General Dwight Eisenhower as the Democratic nominee. Nevertheless, Truman ran for and received the Democratic nomination for president. Senate Majority Leader Alben Barkley, of Kentucky, was nominated for vice president.

When Truman and Dewey squared off in the race, there were two other candidates on the field—Dixiecrat candidate Strom Thurmond, who hoped to capture the anti-civil rights element of the Democratic vote, and Progressive Party candidate Henry Wallace, who had ultra-liberal support. Crump and McKellar initially opposed Truman's nomination. As a result of competition from the left and the right within the Democratic Party as well as dwindling support for the Democratic domination of the White House, Senate, and House of Representatives, Truman looked beatable.

Republicans were excited by the Democratic division in Tennessee and around the nation. Former First District Congressman and (then current) Republican National Chairman B. Carroll Reece was nominated as the Republican candidate for the U.S. Senate. The party also nominated famous country music singer Roy Acuff for governor. Huge crowds gathered throughout the rural areas of Tennessee to see Browning and to hear Acuff perform. Yet, most Democrats could not abandon their roots. Even Crump, painfully stung by his own party, could not turn away from the Democratic ticket. Browning easily defeated Acuff in the general election for governor, and Kefauver went on to be elected to the Senate (Class 2) by defeating Reece. (Kefauver took office on January 3, 1949, was reelected in 1954 and 1960, and died in office on August 10, 1963.)

Truman won the presidential election and in the process made the prognosticators look half-witted. Even the venerable *Chicago Tribune* went to press with the headline, DEWEY DEFEATS TRUMAN. Truman polled 24,105,812 popular votes to 21,970,065 for Dewey (303 to 189 electoral votes). Shelby County gave Thurmond 40 percent of the vote, Truman 37 percent, and Dewey 22 percent. In the statewide vote count, Tennessee gave Truman 49 percent, Dewey 37 percent, and Thurmond 13 percent of the vote.

Although the antimachine Democrats took Tennessee in 1948, Crump still held control of Shelby County and would continue to impact elections.

Once Gordon Browning was inaugurated, January 17, 1949, he immediately began again to work for reform of the election laws that had been used by machine politicians to control election outcomes. Permanent voter registration processes were established in order to maintain some semblance of honesty in the large urban voting areas. Laws were passed which prevented public office holders from serving as election officials. Metal ballot boxes were mandated in instances where there were no voting machines. Election commission meetings were mandated to be held only in circumstances that allowed public attendance. Browning also sought to increase funding for education. He tried to call a constitutional convention to permanently put an end to poll taxes and extend the governor's term to four years. However, the legislature defeated the convention call.

In 1950, after his unsuccessful bid for the U.S. Senate in 1948, former U.S. Representative and Republican National Committee Chairman B. Carroll Reece decided to return to Congress. In the governor's race of 1950, Browning still maintained his momentum and reasonable popularity, but his enemies were mounting. His opponent for reelection was Nashvillian Clifford Allen, who had served a single term in the state legislature. Allen tallied 208,634 votes to 267,855 for Browning in the Democratic primary. The size of the count for Allen showed serious weakness in Browning's support, and encouraged future opponents. Browning was reelected in the November 1950 general election. Reece was elected to the Eighty-second Congress and maintained his position as the Republican leader in Tennessee.

With Browning's return to office came a new crew of young administration officials. One of those was Harlan Mathews, who was hired into the State Planning Office. Browning continued to move Tennessee ahead in the early post-World War II era, and the Democrats remained the dominant party in Tennessee politics.

In 1952 Republicans, who had suffered a twenty-year spell without any presidential patronage, felt there was hope. Since 1933 the Democrats had instituted some very costly federal programs during the severe economic depression and major world conflict. With the national economic condition now stabilized, the public mood was to return to an economy based on more free enterprise and less federal intervention. If the Republicans could find a popular champion, victory was a possibility. With high expectations for victory, Republicans began fighting among themselves for control of their party and the potential spoils of victory.

Robert Taft, the son of the twenty-seventh president, was a U.S. senator from Ohio and the political heir apparent for the Republican nomination in 1952. At first the competition for the nomination was between him, the very popular war hero General Dwight D. Eisenhower, and Thomas Dewey, governor of New York. Dewey held considerable influence within the nomination process, even after losing two presidential elections. Eventually, the competition boiled down to Taft and Eisenhower, and across the nation the Republicans were conflicted. The party needed to undergo a process of maturation and alignment, and nowhere was this process better exemplified than in Tennessee in 1952.

The competition between Taft and Eisenhower for the Republican presidential nomination manifested in Tennessee in the form of a battle between three competing factions. The "old guard" (the Lincoln League) consisted mostly of the Black and Tan Republicans. Eisenhower had created a reason for traditional Democrats to consider becoming Republicans. This was especially enticing to those people who lived in traditionally Democrat-dominated sections of Middle and West Tennessee and had become tired of Democratic machine politics and the philosophy of the Democratic party. A "Citizens for Eisenhower" committee formed which was made up of Republicans and converted Democrats. Another new organization of Republicans formed in response to being locked out of Shelby County convention by the official Republican organization in Memphis (the Lincoln League). It became known as the "New Guard Republican Association" (later the "Republican Association"). This group differed from the Citizens for Eisenhower in that it was a Republican movement more than simply an Eisenhower movement.

The new Republican Association presented candidates for the State Executive Committee in order to break the old guard's control of the state party. But their hold would be difficult to break since they were supported by Congressman Reece. They also had power through the media in some areas of the state. Guy Smith, editor of the *Knoxville Journal*, which was the voice of the party, supported the old guard through his friendship with Reece. So the Republican Association had to fight not only the Lincoln League, but also the power behind the state Republican Party. Since Congressman Reece supported Taft, he ensured that control of the state party remained behind the Lincoln League (which also supported Taft).

Lincoln League leader George Lee gave Reece his cooperative support, and Reece responded in kind. Lee had campaigned for Reece and his Republican friends by traveling to Middle and East Tennessee and soliciting Black votes from Black leaders and churches. Lee also organized the Shelby County Black Republican vote to aid candidates whom Reece supported. In return for his loyalty, Reece saw to it that the Tennessee Republican Executive Committee assisted

Lee in being elected as a delegate to the Republican National presidential Nominating Convention. At the convention in Chicago, Reece arranged for Lee to lead the convention in the Pledge of Allegiance and to give one of the seconding speeches for Taft's nomination for president. Both of Lee's presentations at the convention appeared on national television.

The 1952 convention was essentially a contest between Taft and Eisenhower for the presidential nomination. Whatever support Taft held with rank-and-file Republican politicos and Congressmen was not enough to guarantee the nomination. Many Republicans knew that after two decades of Democratic dominance it would take something more than a simple public mood swing to assure a victory in 1952. They had thought that the mood for change would help them in 1948, but it had not. What was needed was a candidate with paramount popularity, and this was exactly what General Eisenhower possessed. Governor Dewey's endorsement of Eisenhower added to the general's momentum, and he received the nomination. He and vice presidential candidate Senator Richard Nixon of California would face the Democrats in November.

Tennessee Democrat U.S. Senator Estes Kefauver ran for the Democrat presidential nomination in 1952 but was unsuccessful. The Democrats nominated Illinois Governor Adlai Stevenson for president. Alabama Senator John Sparkman was nominated for vice president.

Franklin Roosevelt's dominance of the presidency had strengthened Democrats to the point that any Republican organization had little if any clout in Tennessee. However, in 1952 Eisenhower's campaign for president provided the vehicle for Republican participation and helped to bring a sense of invigoration to a scarcely existent Republican base. Dedicated loyalists went door-to-door in the 1952 Eisenhower campaign in order to organize precinct committees. Grassroots sweat nourished the slow but steady growth of a Republican Party as people flocked to Eisenhower's support.

On the state political front, battle lines were being drawn again, not between Republican and Democrat, but between Democratic coalitions vying for power. In 1952 Governor Gordon Browning faced tough opposition for reelection. As early as September 1950 Frank Clement, a young Dickson, Tennessee, attorney, announced that he was running against Browning in the 1952 Democratic primary. Clement stated that his early announcement was due to his orders to be at Camp Gordon, Georgia, for the army reserves. Commander Brigadier General Hatton Weems was a family friend of the Clements, an advantage which allowed the challenger to return to Tennessee on weekends for speeches and campaign visits. Clement was only thirty-two years old in 1952 and had no legislative or administrative experience. He was involved, however, in organizing the Tennessee Young Democrats and served as state commander of the American Legion. He was a relentless and charismatic campaigner and fought tirelessly against the incumbent governor, along with candidates Clifford Pierce from Memphis and Clifford Allen from Nashville. Browning was accused of fraud in connection with the state purchase of Memorial Apartment Hotel near the Capitol Building in Nashville. Clement charged that Governor Browning was "dishonest, indecent, and immoral" (Corlew 1990).

Television continued to appear in more and more households across the country in the 1950s and was increasingly becoming a valuable campaign tool. Browning did not master the new medium and performed poorly in his television appearances. The televised 1952 Democratic National Convention was viewed by many Tennesseans who saw Governor Browning cast a vote, contrary to the vote of all other Southern states, against a movement requiring a loyalty oath to the eventual Democratic presidential nominee. Browning was viewed as betraying the South at a time when everyone remembered the Dixiecrats of 1948, the traditional Southern Democrats who split from the party in response to the growing civil rights movement, causing Tennessee to cast a split electoral vote in 1948. The fallout from Browning's vote combined with the corruption charges, many unwarranted, damaged his campaign. Additionally, he had to deal with the opposition of his old enemy, E. H. Crump.

In 1952 Crump may have been politically down but he was not out of power. Although Kefauver had defeated Crump's candidate in 1948, Crump's old political ally Senator McKellar was still in office and Crump still had a firm hold on Memphis, in spite of new developments within the election commission. These developments were changing the political landscape, particularly the permanent registration of voters in the Shelby County court house in June 1951, which was arranged by Gilmer Richardson, a solid Browning supporter. With the old poll tax system abolished, Tennesseans no longer had to pay in order to vote. This was the first time in a half century that Tennesseans could vote for free, and it would therefore become more difficult for politicians to control votes. Nevertheless, Crump still held significant loyalty because of the many jobs and assistance he had provided over the years. The fear factor had been diminished since he lost control of the voting apparatus, but patronage was still a powerful influence in gaining support for a candidate. Crump endorsed Clement against Browning.

Crump's endorsement of Clement added strength to another endorsement he had received from a group of Nashville politicians headed by Garner Robinson, Jake Sheridan, and Elkin Garfinkle. Their organization maintained power by holding enough seats on the city council to force a reckoning with them on city issues. They also held county offices, such as sheriff, which gave them control of the county highway patrol and court offices. Mayor Ben West's cooperation translated into city patronage jobs. Thus, this Nashville political organization could sway the voters and pull out some elections much in the same manner as E. H. Crump of Memphis. However, their power in 1952 was on the decline, due to a loss in the sheriff's election in the spring Davidson County Democratic primary. Their candidate, Oscar Capps, lost by a two-to-one margin to Tom Y. Cartwright, and without the sheriff's office, their political stranglehold was weakened. The *Nashville Tennessean* had opposed the coalition and foresaw this loss as the end to the coalition of Nashville machine politicos. To Jake Sheridan and his friends, it meant that they had to make some quick dealings in order to maintain their influence.

The group traveled to Memphis and met with Boss Crump. They needed help, and Crump wanted revenge against his old nemesis, Gordon Browning. If they could pull Davidson County for Clement, while Crump brought in "Big Shelby," they could give Crump access to the governor's mansion once again and assure their patronage from the top of state government. In 1952, because of Tennessee's population distribution and voting patterns, a candidate could win a statewide race by carrying only Davidson and Shelby Counties and picking up a few additional counties. Both Crump and the Nashville group agreed to give their support to Clement, strengthening the list of Browning opponents.

In the 1952 Senate race, Crump's long-time friend Senator McKellar was in trouble. Fourth District Democratic U.S. Representative Albert Gore Sr. had filed to run against the senator and McKellar, who was now eighty-three years old, found himself faced with a tough primary challenge for his Senate seat. Even Crump said, "I told him he hadn't been in the state for 10 years. . . . I thought he had done enough for the people of Tennessee, and could so easily, so gracefully retire" (D. Miller 1964).

New Leaders

Crump's candidates regularly won elections, but by 1952 his machine had less control of the voting apparatus than in days past. The public's will would have much more of an impact than ever before. In 1948 Crump had faced resentment against the machine, the return of veterans from the war, and a national anti-Democratic movement so strong that it almost cost Truman the presidency. In 1952 the political situation was different. This was not an anti-Crump campaign. It was a campaign of a new age of political leaders fighting for the right to lead their party. The Democratic Senate primary presented a problem for almost all Tennessee Democrats who knew that the campaign of 1952 was one for change. The issues were McKellar's age and his contact, or lack thereof, with his constituents. McKellar had served thirty-six years in the U.S. Senate, since 1917, and was eighty-three years old in 1952. Many Tennesseans greatly respected the aging leader. He was a power on Capitol Hill, but he was losing contact with those who had sent him there. Gore was only forty-four years old and a popular man in East Tennessee. The age difference, the sense of a need for change, and Gore's popularity in East Tennessee all worked against McKellar. Senator Kenneth D. McKellar was defeated in the Democratic Senate primary by Congressman Al Gore Sr. of Carthage; the vote was 334,957 to 245,054.

Frank Clement was also a new-breed candidate representing change. Governor Browning was extremely popular, especially for his defeat of the Memphis machine, but in this campaign environment dedicated to the "new" and to "change," he became the victim of the remnants of machine politics and the movement for change. Clement was only thirty-two, but had been groomed by the best, including by Willie Gerber, Crump's legislative liaison, an expedient early ally for Clement. He had learned early in life how to gain the advantage, even convincing the Federal Bureau of Investigation (FBI) to allow his entrance at twenty-two, instead of the required age of twenty-three. As general counsel of the state utilities commission, he gained recognition as a rising Democratic star. Though Clement was gaining political support, he was also viewed as "one-third cop, one-third evangelist, one-third con man, and 100 percent slick" (Squires 1996). Nonetheless, many saw potential in him. Clement was taken under the wing of James Stahlman, the powerful editor of the *Nashville Banner.* In addition, his campaign was supported by the Belle Meade Country Club gang, and benefitted from their financial influence and fund-raising abilities. One trucking company raised over four hundred thousand dollars for his campaign. With a sharp, handsome young governor in office, the Nashville elite could see the White House as a distinct possibility, and with it, influence on a grand scale.

Clement's charges of Browning's failure to keep his campaign promises and his accusations of financial misdealings were too much for the veteran governor. Clement defeated Governor Gordon Browning in the Democratic gubernatorial primary. Shelby and Davidson Counties both went for Clement. He polled 302,491 to 245,166 for Browning, 75,269 for Allen, and 24,191 for Pierce.

In the November election of 1952, Eisenhower won with 33,936,234 national popular votes to 27,314,992 for Stevenson (442 to 89 electoral votes). The Republican trend was strong enough for the party to take control of the U.S. House (221 Republican, 213 Democrat, 1 other) and the U.S. Senate (48 Republican, 46 Democrat, 2 other). Because of the overwhelming popularity of Eisenhower, he became the only Republican presidential candidate to almost evenly split the vote in Shelby County's Black precincts.

In 1952 Frank Clement went on to win the general election and became the nation's youngest governor. He was elected by a large margin, and the victory essentially marked an end to the power of Gordon Browning, as well as the end of the Crump era of power. Even though Clement was supported by Crump, his political strength was not derived from Crump's old-line politics. He was mostly supported by a younger aggressive group. Browning was embittered by his loss and the accusations from the Clement camp that he was dishonest. Victory for Clement came at the expense of Browning's integrity.

Once Clement was in office, he quickly placed his loyal supporters in positions of control. William Snodgrass was made budget director, Eddie Friar became secretary of state, and Jean Bodfish became comptroller; all were part of Clement's inner circle.

Albert Gore took office as U.S. Senator (Class 1) on January 3, 1953 (serving until January 2, 1971). Tennessee was now represented in the Senate by Democrats Gore and Estes Kefauver; neither was part of the Crump team. Tennessee, still a Democratic state, had voted Democratic in the gubernatorial and Senate elections, but Republican in the presidential election. This was the first time a Republican presidential nominee had been carried by Tennessee since 1928.

Tennessee had not held a constitutional convention since 1870. Changing times demanded changes in government. Early in his first term, in 1953, young Governor Clement hosted a convention in Nashville with former Governor Prentice Cooper as chairman and former Governor Ben Hooper as vice chairman. The convention raised the pay for legislators to fifteen dollars per day and lengthened the term for governor from two to four years, while eliminating the eligibility of an incumbent to succeed him or herself. It also complemented previous legislative action abolishing the poll tax, and prohibited legislative action which could interfere with the structure of local governments. It authorized "home rule" and consolidation of county and city governments. The new Tennessee Constitution, with eight new amendments, was ratified that same year.

While Eisenhower led the nation, individuals around the country found new inspiration in the Republican Party. Organizations sprung up as various political groups formed in a quest for a piece of the political action. Tennessee was no different. East Tennessee had been a well-established Republican stronghold for over a century. For the present, the East Tennessee Republican U.S. Representatives B. Carroll Reece (First District) and Howard Baker Sr. (Second District) were the state's Republican point men with Congressman Reece the senior leader. In Middle Tennessee the Democrats

FRANK GOAD CLEMENT was born in Dickson, Tennessee, on June 2, 1920, to Mr. and Mrs. Robert S. Clement. His father was a lawyer. Frank Clement graduated from high school in 1937. He attended Cumberland University in Lebanon, Tennessee, for two years and then completed his law degree at Vanderbilt in Nashville in 1942. When he was twenty-three he began work with the FBI in Chicago, having been accepted at age twenty-two. After the beginning of World War II, Clement left the Bureau, went to Officers Candidate School in 1943, and was made a second lieutenant. He remained in the United States during the war and completed his active tour in two years, being discharged in 1946. He then returned to Dickson to practice law and served as an attorney for the Public Utilities Commission. He married Lucille Christenson, daughter of Houston County Judge and Mrs. Nelson Christenson, and they had three sons. He was only twenty-six when he gained significant notoriety for his efforts to win a controversial telephone rate case. With his new public image and a damaged incumbent governor, Clement ran for governor and was elected in 1952.

Clement's first term as governor was a two-year term (1953–1954). After a state constitutional amendment, he was reelected to a four-year term in 1954 and served from 1955 until 1959. During this term he gave a keynote address at the 1956 Democratic National Convention. His campaign manager, Buford Ellington, succeeded him in 1959. Clement returned to his law practice in Nashville until 1962, when he could run again. Reelected in 1962, he served as governor from 1963 until 1967, then lost two races for the U.S. Senate.

While governor, the Tennessee Constitution was altered for the first time since 1870; a bond issue was authorized to pay for textbooks for all twelve grades of public schools; the state's mental health program was improved; the State Library and Archives Building was opened; consolidated metropolitan governments were authorized; a long-range highway program was started; a hospitalization program for the indigent was begun; a speech and hearing center was opened; a commission for youth guidance and alcoholism was created; and the sales tax was increased.

Clement was a Methodist, a Shriner, and a thirty-second degree Mason. Soon after completing his third term as governor, he died in an automobile accident, at age forty-nine, on November 4, 1969, near Nashville. He was buried at Dickson Memorial Gardens in Dickson, Tennessee. (Photograph courtesy of TSLA)

had dominated since the days of Andrew Jackson, but there was some Republican support even in this area. West Tennessee, influenced by the heavy population in Shelby County, in past decades contained few Republicans in a weak political organization dominated by Black Republicans. The once strong cooperation which existed between the Republican Party and Black voters slowed with the election of Democrat Franklin Roosevelt. After his election, there were simply no Republicans to support—not a president, not a governor, and certainly not a mayor. Additionally, there was no Republican patronage to dispense and thus no cooperation to be found from any political power source. All Tennessee patronage seekers and politicians, Black and White, flocked to the Democratic Party ranks. By 1952, however, a political reversal had begun. There was now a Republican president who could dispense patronage. Black voters in Tennessee still supported state and local Democrats, but they had also provided some assistance in the 1952 election of a Republican president. However, by 1953 there were other Republicans, in the traditionally Democratic divisions in Tennessee, who, inspired by the election of Eisenhower, challenged the Black Republicans for control of the county Republican organizations.

Patronage from Eisenhower flowed to the old guard Lincoln League and George Lee through U.S. Representative B. Carroll Reece of East Tennessee. Both Reece and Lee had supported Taft during the primaries and at the Republican National Convention. This did not sit well with all the new Republican participants who had supported Eisenhower, and they felt somewhat betrayed. Intraparty Republican battles would escalate.

In 1954 Governor Frank Clement completed the last two-year term allowed under Tennessee law and planned to run for a four-year term. However, first the young incumbent governor had to deal with a schism within his own ranks. Apparently, several members of the organization that had helped him to victory in 1950 harbored strong doubts about the young governor's leadership and conduct. Secretary of State Eddie Friar and Comptroller Jean Bodfish had broken with Clement and wanted Clement out of office. They felt that someone else should lead their group to the next victory. In response, Clement and those still loyal to him moved to rid themselves of Friar and Bodfish. Friar had been elected by the General Assembly to a four-year term. Since he was in the middle of his term, there was little Clement could do but limit him to as little influence as possible and keep him on the outside of their plans. Comptroller Jean Bodfish, on the other hand, was elected by the General Assembly for a two-year term. With the help of a cooperative state legislature Bodfish was not reelected. William Snodgrass was then moved into the comptroller's office. Snodgrass hired Edward Boling as budget director, who then hired Harlan Mathews as his assistant.

With internal turmoil controlled, Clement looked to the Democratic primary. He was opposed by former Governor Gordon Browning who still felt injured by the criticism thrown at him during their race in 1952. The former governor felt that the people of Tennessee had been deceived by the young politician and that they would be wiser in 1954. Browning counterattacked in this campaign by accusing Governor Clement's father, Attorney Robert S. Clement of Dickson, Tennessee, of influence peddling his son's power. Browning also pointed out that Crump's organization supported Clement. His charges of Crump's involvement were backed up by the fact that some former Crump men, turned enemies, supported Browning in order to prevent any further Crump influence. The former Memphis mayor and Crump ally, Watkins Overton, even supported Browning. However, Browning could not overcome the strength of Clement's organization. Clement polled 481,808 to 195,156 for Browning in the Democratic primary.

The primary further strengthened Clement's national recognition. Shortly afterward, he was invited to a Democratic rally in Indianapolis, Indiana, where he met Democratic National Chairman Stephen A. Mitchell, Speaker of the House Sam Rayburn, Adlai Stevenson, and other Democratic leaders. This fit in perfectly with his carefully planned political future.

In the 1954 U.S. Senate Democratic primary Estes Kefauver was opposed by Sixth District Democratic Congressman Pat Sutton, from Lawrenceburg, Tennessee. Sutton, a conservative, attacked Senator

Kefauver for his liberal positions. With Sutton in the Senate primary, Pulaski, Tennessee, Postmaster Ross Bass ran for Sutton's U.S. Representative seat. Kefauver easily defeated Sutton in the primary, while Ross Bass won the Democratic U.S. House primary.

In the general election of 1954, Frank Clement was reelected to the first four-year term of a Tennessee governor (under the new constitution he could not succeed himself). Kefauver was easily reelected to the U.S. Senate, and Ross Bass was elected Sixth District U.S. representative. The Democrats continued to dominate the state and took back control of the U.S. House and Senate, while the Republicans continued to grasp for a piece of political power. Clement's future looked bright, but his job as governor was becoming increasingly more difficult. He had to deal with racial integration, now mandated by the *Brown* v. *Topeka* case. While other Southern governors promised to block integration, Clement promoted a moderate civil rights stand and tried to avoid confrontation. (He was the first Southern governor to veto a segregation bill.) He also had to deal with another serious division within his ranks. Some of his closest associates accused him of dishonesty and influence peddling, but he was able to overcome the criticism. He also had to deal with reapportionment of the legislative districts—something ignored since 1901. A battle ensued between Tennessee's rural and urban leaders. Rural areas had a disproportionate amount of influence, which they did not want to give up, while urban areas, underrepresented in terms of their population, fought for equity. Clement had to referee.

E. H. Crump, the Memphis boss, died October 16, 1954. The eighty-year-old politician left many of his friends in power, and they intended to maintain the dynasty as long as possible. However, politicians outside Crump's circle campaigned in 1955 for reformer Edmund Orgill to become mayor. They also campaigned for city government reform and a manager/council form of government as opposed to the old commissioner form of government. The outsiders won the 1955 election and ushered in a more fair form of city government. Effectively, they removed the commission-type government, eliminating one of the Crump organization's sources of power. With Crump now gone and the city under a new system run by a new breed of politician, the path of political power had come full circle. Around the turn of the century, power shifts commonly occurred every few years. Then, with Crump, came the hold which lasted from 1910 until 1954. The state had been held spellbound in the grasp of the Crump machine. Many an election night anxious politicians waited to see what the "Big Shelby" vote was and who would be crowned by the Memphis boss. Now the Crump hold on power was gone; his team was neutralized; and the process was open once again to the ever-changing march of politicians. Of course many politicians would exercise considerable influence on Tennessee politics, but none would likely ever have the influence once held by E. H. Crump.

With the ascendence of Dwight Eisenhower, new guard Republicans felt that they could create a strong and lasting Republican organization which could eventually compete with the Democratic Party on a more equitable basis, and they dreamed of laying the groundwork for the unthinkable in Tennessee politics—a Republican governor and senator. East Tennessee continued to be the traditional Republican stronghold. Alone, the area meant nothing in a statewide race, except to Democrats who held an alliance with Congressman Reece. To win a statewide race a Republican needed the additional support of either Middle or West Tennessee. To convert one of these two areas would be a challenge.

In 1956 Eisenhower was easily renominated by the Republicans. At the Democratic convention, Governor Frank Clement worked for the right to deliver the keynote address. He competed with over twenty political leaders including Massachusetts Senator John Kennedy, Minnesota Senator Hubert Humphrey, Maine Governor Edmund Muskie, Oklahoma Senator Robert Kerr, and Washington Senator Henry Jackson. Clement eventually won the honor. In his forty-minute speech, he attacked President Eisenhower with a long list of criticisms. The speech won Clement added visibility. Tennessee Democratic U.S. Senator Estes Kefauver again ran for the presidential nomination, but was again defeated by Adlai E. Stevenson. Kefauver turned his sights on the vice presidency and became involved in a tight race with Senator John Kennedy, eventually emerging the victor as the Democrats' vice presidential nominee.

Tennessee was impressed with its favorite son but not enough to vote for him. The state went Republican for Eisenhower again in 1956, and he won the national election with a margin even greater than in 1952—35,590,472 to 26,022,752 popular votes (457 to 73 electoral votes). He also won 54 percent of the Black vote in Shelby County. It was the first time in history that Shelby County went Republican in a presidential election. Eisenhower's presidency and the resurgence of Republicans in Middle and West Tennessee marked a change for the Republican Party in Tennessee. Finally, the momentum had begun to move ever so slightly away from the Democrats. Despite the emergence of Republicans, they still had not recovered from their near national political annihilation brought on by Franklin Roosevelt (Democrats still controlled and even made slight gains in the U.S. House and U.S. Senate) nor altered the traditional Democratic voter base in Tennessee. Tennessee reelected Senator Al Gore Sr.

The reelection victory of Eisenhower continued to encourage the few Tennessee Republicans who dreamed of creating their own power base. Their struggles were not necessarily driven by any philosophical grounds, but sometimes by visions of power and control. East Tennessee was already Republican and already had a solid party hierarchy. The internal Republican Party power struggle occurred mainly in the middle and west sections of the state, where the Republicans, small in number as they were, fought among themselves for control of the pittance of the victory spoils.

During the era of the presidency of Dwight Eisenhower, the "conservative" opposition to the oppression and dangers of communism was a call to arms for the Republican Party. Republicans needed a battle cry in order to rally support for their party. Their anticommunism stance was the appeal which helped to rally support for the party's cause. Many recent veterans and everyday citizens began to take a hard look at the party that wanted to protect freedom. With a popular leader—Eisenhower—and a cause—to fight communism—the emerging Republican Party gave the two-party system hope. Grassroots efforts continued to slowly strengthen the party throughout Tennessee.

In the 1958 elections Tennessee was slated to elect a new governor. Although the constitutional convention of 1953 changed the term of office for governor from two to four years, it also mandated that no governor could succeed himself to office. Governor Frank Clement's friend and commissioner of agriculture, Buford Ellington, from Marshall County, was selected to be the candidate of the Clement political coalition. Rural Tennessee strongly supported Ellington. However, he was opposed in the Democratic primary by Edmund Orgill from Memphis. Orgill had run as the reform candidate and won the office of Memphis mayor in 1955 by defeating the Crump organization-backed candidate Watkins Overton. Ellington was also opposed by Clifford Allen from Nashville and Andrew (Tip) Taylor from Jackson, Tennessee. In the 1958 primary elections, the rural vote carried Ellington, who won 213,415 to 204,629 for Taylor, 204,382 for Orgill, and 56,854 for Allen. Usually, carrying Shelby County was a requisite for winning a race in Tennessee, but Ellington carried only 18 percent of the Shelby County vote. His statewide total was only 31 percent of the total vote, to around 30 percent for Orgill and 30 percent for Taylor. The divided vote gave him enough to win.

Meanwhile Senator Albert Gore Sr. faced a tough challenge from former Governor Prentice Cooper. However, Gore

ALBERT ARNOLD GORE was born on December 26, 1907, in Granville (Jackson County), Tennessee. He received his early education in area public schools. Between 1926 and 1930 he taught in the country schools of Smith and Overton Counties. He worked his way through the University of Tennessee at Knoxville and State Teachers College in Murfreesboro, Tennessee. After graduation in 1932, he served as superintendent of education in Smith County from 1932 until 1936. During this time he attended Nashville YMCA night law school and graduated in 1936. He was admitted to the bar and began practice in Carthage, Tennessee, in 1936.

Governor Browning appointed Gore commissioner of labor for Tennessee in 1937, the same year Gore married Pauline LaFon of Jackson, Tennessee, a 1936 Vanderbilt Law School graduate. In 1938 he won election to the Fourth Tennessee District seat in the U.S. House, and was reelected two times, serving from January 3, 1939, until December 4, 1944, when he resigned to enter the U.S. Army. In 1944 he was elected again to Congress, serving that term and three additional terms from January 3, 1945, until January 3, 1953. Gore essentially served seven terms in Congress, from January 3, 1939, until January 3, 1953, with a short hiatus while in the army. In 1952 he successfully challenged Kenneth McKellar, a Crump ally, for his U.S. Senate seat. He entered the Senate on January 3, 1953, and was reelected in 1958 and 1964, serving until January 3, 1971. While in the Senate, he served as chairman of the Special Committee on Attempts to Influence Senators. He lost reelection in 1970 to Republican William Brock III, due to his anti-Vietnam war stance and his support for civil rights. Gore then returned to the practice of law with Occidental Petroleum Co., where he served as vice president and a member of the Board of Directors. He taught law at Vanderbilt University School of Law from 1970 through 1972, and he also served as a member of the Board of Petroleum and Coal Companies. Gore and his wife had two children, Nancy, who died of cancer in 1984, and Albert A. Gore Jr., who was elected vice president of the United States in 1992 and 1996. Gore died on December 5, 1998, on his farm in Carthage, Tennessee. (Photograph courtesy of SHO) won by 375,439 votes to 253,191 in the Democratic primary, losing only the Third and Eighth Congressional Districts. Ellington was easily elected governor of Tennessee in the November general election. Gore was also easily reelected senator in the general election. Democrats again held all major statewide offices.

With Crump dead, the Clement-Ellington coalition dominated Tennessee politics. This political organization was the one to be associated with in order to achieve any kind of political success from the time just prior to Crump's passing for a period of more than eighteen years.

In the west end of Tennessee, Black citizens continued their struggle for political participation. In 1959 a significant effort was launched to register Black voters. In Shelby County alone, 50,164 Blacks were registered. Some ran for office. Although Russell Sugarmon Jr. lost to William Farris for commissioner of public works and Ben Hooks lost to Elizabeth McCain for juvenile court judge, the stage was set for Black political participation on a scale not seen since Reconstruction.

By the time of the July 1960 Los Angeles Democratic National Convention, John F. Kennedy had been campaigning enough to have the nomination nearly cinched. His closest competitor was Senate Majority Leader Lyndon B. Johnson of Texas. Governor Ellington was chairman of the Democratic National Convention and led thirty-three delegates supporting Johnson, while former Governor Clement supported Kennedy. Kennedy won the nomination on the first ballot—Kennedy 806, Johnson 409, Stuart Symington 86, and Stevenson 79.5. Lyndon Johnson became the vice presidential nominee.

At the 1960 Chicago Republican National Convention, Vice President Richard Nixon easily obtained the nomination for president. Henry Cabot Lodge Jr., who had served as one of Massachusetts's senators since 1936 until he was defeated by John Kennedy in 1952, was nominated for vice president.

In Tennessee's Democratic primary of 1960, Senator Estes Kefauver was opposed by Circuit Judge Andrew (Tip) Taylor. Taylor came off his narrow 1958 Democratic gubernatorial primary loss to Ellington with a determination to win. He attacked Kefauver for alleged leniency toward communists and Northern liberals. The charge would not be enough to overcome Kefauver's popularity in the Volunteer State. The senator defeated his challenger by almost twice the number of votes.

Kennedy and Johnson ran on a platform favoring the social security program and the expansion of civil rights. In this era of civil rights movements, Martin Luther King Jr. led marches around the country, preaching nonviolence and championing racial equality. As his movement gained momentum, the opposition to change mounted and animosities developed. On October 24, 1960, during the height of the presidential campaign, King was jailed. Vice President Nixon felt it was safest to sidestep the issue, hoping to avoid alienating White voters. Kennedy, however, took another tact. Without becoming overly involved, he called Coretta Scott King, the leader's wife, and urged King's release. This meaningful gesture, along with his campaign promises on civil rights, won him Black support.

In November 1960 Nixon lost to Kennedy by the narrowest margin in history (34,221,000 to 34,108,000, one-half vote per precinct). Many attributed the margin of victory to the votes delivered by Mayor Richard Daley of Chicago, the

Senator Estes Kefauver with Lyndon Johnson at LBJ's ranch. (Courtesy of the University of Tennessee-Knoxville, Photography Center)

support of the Mob, and the popularity of Kennedy's running mate, Lyndon Johnson of Texas. Two states, Illinois and Texas, were rife with reports of fraud. (Other races in Texas history had evidence of voting fraud. Detailed information can be found in R.A. Caro, *The Years of Lyndon Johnson: The Path to Power*, New York: Alfred A. Knopf, 1982.) In Shelby County, Tennessee, all the Black precincts were carried by Kennedy. Nixon received only 31 percent of the county's Black vote. Lincoln League leader George W. Lee blamed the election result on Nixon's failure to comment on King's imprisonment. The "new guard" Republicans blamed the weak turnout on Lee's failure to deliver and his cooperation with the Democrats.

Tennessee went Republican for Nixon in 1960 as it had in 1952 and 1956 for Eisenhower, but it remained Democratic as far as home state races were concerned. Estes Kefauver was reelected to the U.S. Senate for a third term.

After the 1960 presidential election of John Kennedy, Republicans were even better able to bring their viewpoint into focus for the public. In spite of the Nixon loss, the growing local Republican organizations across Tennessee knew that there would be more Republican opportunities to come. They enthusiastically continued to build at the grassroots level to attract potential voters. Any act of the Kennedy administration that could be construed as radical or nontraditional helped Republicans carry their traditionalist message. These included his effort to establish a cabinet post for urban affairs, his legislative appeals for financial assistance to minorities, and his pressure to prevent a steel price increase. Criticism against him was essentially directed at his administration's attempts at social and economic engineering. Buoyed by the backlash against the new liberalism of the Kennedy administration, and motivated by a cause and a possibility never before seen in Tennessee, Republicans continued to gain momentum in the state. The cause was protection of conservatism and traditionalism. The possibility was derived from the growing dissatisfaction of Southern voters with the Democratic Party's willingness to embrace seemingly radical stances. Republican candidates were motivated to run for offices across Tennessee and began gearing up for the next election cycle in 1962.

In 1961 State Budget Director Edward Boling took an appointment with the University of Tennessee. With his move from the position of commissioner of finance and administration, Governor Ellington appointed Harlan Mathews. On March 19, 1961, longtime East Tennessee Republican power broker, First District Congressman B. Carroll Reece, died in Bethesda, Maryland. (He was buried at Monte Vista Burial Park in Johnson City, Tennessee.) His wife, Louise Goff Reece, was elected in a special election on May 16, 1961, to replace her husband in the Eighty-seventh Congress. She served until January 3, 1963.

In the Democratic primary of 1962, Memphis lawyer Bill Farris and Chattanooga Mayor Ruby Olgiati challenged former Governor Frank Clement for the Democratic gubernatorial nomination. By 1962 significant resentment had grown against Clement within Democrat ranks. Many felt that he had tried to build a political dynasty reminiscent of Crump's. Old antimachine opponents like Senator Kefauver and former Governor Browning were not content to sit idly by while Clement built enough power to control their destinies. They both became involved in the race, each supporting a different candidate. Farris had worked under Browning when he was governor and was therefore supported by the Browning team. Olgiati was supported by Kefauver. This created a split in the Democratic vote. Clement won 309,333 votes to 211,812 for Farris and 202,813 for Olgiati. He won the nomination with only 42 percent of the vote.

The Democrats held all but two congressional seats in Tennessee (the First and Second Districts). However, several Republicans ran for the U.S. House of Representatives in 1962. When Louise Goff Reece did not run for reelection, Jimmy Quillen ran for the First District seat. Howard Baker Sr. ran for reelection in the Second District. Bill Brock ran in the Third District, as did other Republicans across the state, including Bob James in the West Tennessee Ninth District.

In the general election of 1962 Democrat Frank Clement faced Republican William Anderson and Hubert Patty. Clement was again elected governor of Tennessee, but his popularity was declining, apparent in both the "Big Shelby" primary and general election where his margin of victory narrowed considerably.

The Tennessee Republican Party momentum, which started as a grassroots effort in 1952, finally began to bear fruit in the 1962 elections. In the general election Republican James H. Quillen was elected as U.S. representative in the First District. Howard Baker Sr. was reelected as Republican congressman in the Second District. William E. Brock III defeated his

Democratic opponent, picking up the Third District seat for Republicans. Middle Tennessee remained Democrat. In Shelby County, Republican challenger Bob James narrowly lost to Democratic Congressman Clifford Davis by 1,243 votes out of 109,419 votes cast. Republicans now held three congressional seats in Tennessee. The cooperation of the East Tennessee Republican congressmen, especially in the First and Second Districts, remained a requirement for anyone running for statewide office, whether Republican or Democrat.

Voting patterns were slowly beginning to shift in Tennessee. As more people identified with Republican issues, Democratic ballot numbers began to decline. In response to Congressman Davis's close call in Shelby County and the obvious activity of this newly invigorated Republican Party in Shelby County, the Democratic Steering Committee passed an "action" calling for candidates in local elections to declare their party affiliation. The *Commercial Appeal*, a Democratic paper since it was first published a century prior, opposed any move toward party candidate identification in local elections.

Prior to the elections of 1962, the Lincoln League under George Lee dominated the Shelby County Republican Party. This was accomplished by controlling only fifteen or so Shelby County precincts in mostly Black neighborhoods. East Tennessee Republicans ran the state Republican Party and received all the cooperation they needed from the party's West Tennessee portion through Lee's leadership. He was the ally in charge of Shelby County, who held new guard Republican potential threats to their absolute control at bay. The East Tennessee Republican power brokers kept Lee propped up by refusing to hold caucuses outside his fifteen or so precincts. Lee had significant patronage influence with post office jobs via his past relationship with B. Carroll Reece, who had been very close to E. H. Crump of Memphis. This was a very nice deal for Lee since it allied him with the Democrats as well as the Republicans. Between 1953 and 1961 President Eisenhower added to Tennessee Republicans', as well as Lee's, influence through presidential patronage. However, by 1962 things were changing for the Republican Party and Lee. Crump and Reece were dead, and Lee faced a serious challenge to the old system and his control of the Shelby County Republican Party. New Republicans had no intention of tolerating the old feudal political system. In recent Shelby County Republican conventions, Lee was forced to share leadership with a White chairman and steering committees. Up until now, he still played a role and held some influence, but this was all about to change.

The new guard Republican Association was fast becoming a strong influence in Shelby County. They had fought from 1952 to 1960 to gain recognition for precincts outside the fifteen or so controlled by George Lee. By 1962 the Republican Association had successfully fought off the East Tennessee Republican control of Shelby County. However, now Shelby County Republican Party Chairman Bob James had to win support of State Republican Party Executive Committee members. This was necessary in order to prevent future interference in the Shelby County organization by U.S. Representatives Quillen and Baker Sr., the East Tennessee Republican leaders. The new guard foot was in the political door and never again would George Lee and his old guard Republicans monopolize control of Shelby County Republicans. He and his crowd, however, would hold on for the ride, hoping they could share in a future Republican presidential prize.

On August 10, 1963, Tennessee U.S. Senator Estes Kefauver died at Bethesda Naval Hospital in Bethesda, Maryland. He had served fourteen and a half years in the Senate, from January 1949 until his death. Governor Frank Clement appointed Herbert Walters to fill the vacancy (Class 2). Walters was a Democratic power broker from the Republican stronghold of East Tennessee. He had worked in cooperation with East Tennessee Republicans, including J. Will Taylor, in several unified efforts to elect "their" selected Democratic candidates for statewide office. Walters was an important point man when Democrats needed East Tennessee votes for statewide races. His appointment was made with the understanding that he would step aside for Governor Clement who would later run for the office himself. Walters took office on August 20, 1963, and served until November 3, 1964.

On November 22, 1963, President John F. Kennedy was assassinated in Dallas, Texas. Lyndon Johnson assumed the office of president of the United States.

The Purging of the Lincoln League

The last remnants of West Tennessee Black Republicans still struggled to hold on to their political organization. Their only chance was to maintain representation in the Shelby County Republican Party and from that springboard, representation in the state Republican Party. But George Lee was greatly resented for assisting the Democrats and preventing new guard Republican participation. In 1964, thirty-six-year-old Winfield Dunn, a Memphis dentist, was the Republican Association candidate for Shelby County Republican Party chairman. He was opposed by the Gold Ticket candidate, Leo Cole, as well as George Lee from the Lincoln League. When the county convention at Christian Brothers College took place on March 16, 1964, Winfield Dunn was elected chairman by 349 votes to Leo Cole's 78 votes. Lewis Donelson and Bob James were elected as the Shelby County delegates to the Republican National Convention. George Lee lost control of the Shelby County Republican Party. He challenged the results of the convention to the

HERBERT SANFORD WALTERS was born on November 17, 1891, in Jefferson County, Tennessee, in the community of Leadvale. He received his early education in Jefferson County public schools, and also attended Baker-Himmell School in Knoxville, Tennessee, and Castle Heights Military Academy in Lebanon, Tennessee. Later he attended Carson-Newman College in Jefferson City, Tennessee, and the University of Tennessee in Knoxville. He became a prominent banker and chairman of the board of Walters & Prater, Inc. He served in the Tennessee house of representatives from 1933 until 1935, and as commissioner of the State Highway Department from 1934 until 1935. On August 20, 1963, he was appointed as a Democrat to fill the vacancy in the U.S. Senate created by the death of Senator Estes Kefauver. Senator Walters served in the U.S. Senate just over a year and two months and did not run for reelection. He served as a trustee of the University of Tennessee from 1961 until 1973. Walters died in Knoxville on August 17, 1973. He was buried in Jarnagin Cemetery in Morristown, Tennessee. (Photograph courtesy of SHO)

state party but his request to seat his slate of delegates was denied.

The July 1964 Republican National Convention in San Francisco exposed the Tennessee Republican Party's growth pains to all the nation. Lee, a Black World War I infantry veteran who had been a delegate to six previous Republican National Conventions, appealed to the National Credentials Committee, drawing the attention of the national news to his protests and actually delaying the entire convention. Lee's attorney, R. C. Smith of Knoxville, claimed that the Shelby County GOP discriminated against Lee and "rigged party elections to suit itself" (Donelson et al. June 24, 1964). Harry Wellford, attorney for Lewis Donelson and Bob James, countered that "the losers are angry at the winners and the racial and irregularity charges are untrue" (Donelson, et al. June 24, 1964), and prepared a document for the delegates and alternates of the convention to answer the charges. The document countered all of Lee's charges and presented evidence that Lee had in fact supported Democratic candidates and had a very close relationship with Democrat Lester Brenner, who had strong ties to the late E. H. Crump, and was under investigation for questionable payments to allies of the old guard Republicans.

The evidence presented showed this cooperation between Lee and the Democrats was in the form of payment of election commission salaries to part-time employees as election instructors and election machine mechanics, as well as fees for publication notices from the election commission to members of the Lincoln League. The report also showed evidence that there had been little if any support from the Lincoln League for Bob James in his 1962 narrow loss to incumbent Democrat Clifford Davis in the Ninth Congressional District election.

The Credentials Committee, composed of a man and woman delegate from each state, voted sixty-six to nineteen against Lee's attempt to become a delegate, after a four-hour meeting. James and Donelson appeared on national television to respond to questions regarding the incident, and a photo of the two appeared on the AP wire. The battle between Black and White Republicans of West Tennessee, for a moment in time, stood center stage in America. Although the issue was of little consequence to the ultimate outcome of the 1964 presidential election, or the Republican nomination for that matter, it was symptomatic of what was happening to the Republican Party across the nation. Black voters beginning with Roosevelt's election in 1932, had deserted the Republican Party. For a brief period of time they leaned slightly toward the Republican Party when Eisenhower led the nation between 1953 and 1961. However, when the civil rights cause was embraced by Kennedy, and later Johnson, the Democratic Party became the political home for Black Americans. The Lincoln League had been founded so White Tennessee Republicans would recognize and appreciate the support Blacks gave to the party. The only ones left at this moment in time were those resilient troopers like George Lee, who desired to hold on to their once glorious piece of power, influence, and dignity—the remnants of Reconstruction Republicanism.

Senator Barry Goldwater of Arizona carried the 1964 Republican banner as the candidate for president and Representative William Miller of New York was the nominee for vice president.

Lyndon Johnson was nominated at the August 1964 Democratic National Convention in Atlantic City, New Jersey. He chose, and the convention approved, his running mate for vice president, Senator Hubert Humphrey of Minnesota.

After being reelected governor in 1962, Frank Clement decided to allow Herbert Walters to serve out the late Senator Estes Kefauver's term until he felt the public would be receptive toward his own move to the Senate. However, Kefauver's supporters abhorred the idea of this machine politician taking the seat of the man who had fought them. When Clement ran in the Democratic primary for the U.S. Senate, facing M. M. Bullard of Newport, Tennessee, and five-term Sixth District U.S. Representative Ross Bass of Pulaski, Kefauver's old supporters assisted Bass. Clement held state power, but he had supported a state sales tax increase in 1963. The tax increase, along with opposition from the antimachine Democrats injured Clement's chances and gave Bass the Democratic primary win. Bass won fifty-nine counties and 330,213 votes to 233,245 for Governor Clement, and 86,718 for Bullard. For the first time, there was growing evidence of public resentment toward Clement's hold on power. And for the first time in his political career, he lost Shelby County. Since no Republican had ever been elected by the people of Tennessee to the U.S. Senate, this primary win was tantamount to victory for Ross Bass.

Though the Democratic U.S. Senate nominee was likely to win, he still had to go through the motions of facing a Republican in the November general election. Howard Baker Jr., lawyer and the son of Huntsville lawyer and Second District U.S. Representative, the late Howard Baker Sr., considered running as the Republican in the general election. Howard Baker Sr. had served in Congress from 1950 until his sudden death from a heart attack on January 7, 1964. In order to prevent Republican infighting for the seat, his widow Irene Baker, was urged to run. She had experience in her husband's campaigns and had served as a Republican National committeewoman. She won the election with 58 percent of the vote against Democrat Willard Yarbrough, editor of the *Knoxville News-Sentinel*, was seated in Congress in March 1964, and went on to complete her husband's term. Rather than run for his father's seat, Howard Baker Jr. considered other options, while Knoxville Mayor John Duncan Sr., a protégé and part-time field representative for Congressman Baker, ran for the Second District seat.

Howard Baker Jr. had been well prepared for a career in politics. He saw the unexpired Senate seat as an opportunity. By 1964 the mood of the nation was beginning to change. Southern Democratic voters were taking a look at Republicans. Tennessee had, after all, voted Republican for recent presidential candidates. Baker felt that with the right combination of candidates, the change in Tennessee voter viewpoint could elect a Republican to statewide office. He made the run against Democrat Ross Bass.

Also in 1964, Democrat U.S. Senator Albert Gore Sr. had to stand for reelection to the Class 1 seat. Dan Kuykendall, a Republican from Memphis, ran against him.

Meanwhile, President Johnson was seeking election in his own right, after inheriting the presidency upon the death of President Kennedy. Lyndon Johnson did not need any instruction in the maintenance of power. Barry M. Goldwater was no match for his political tactics, and the Arizona senator's conservative views on the issues were too radical for the times. He was the first conservative Republican nominee for president since Calvin Coolidge in 1924. Johnson picked a liberal running mate, and denounced the Ku Klux Klan and the John

Birch Society. As president he had already worked for the downtrodden, developing his "war on poverty" and civil rights agenda. Goldwater had voted against the Civil Rights Act of 1964 and, during the campaign, appealed to social conservatives. Many voters viewed Goldwater supporters as extremists. Certainly, Blacks would not vote for a ticket they perceived as segregationist. As a result, there was little or no Black Republican vote. Lyndon Johnson put an effective end to Black participation in the Republican party. Black voters, liberal and moderate voters, and those influenced by the power of incumbency gave all except six states to Johnson. The national momentum carried Tennessee. The Democratic Party now consisted of a coalition of traditional White Democrat and Black voters, and they held power in Tennessee. The Republicans could not overcome their majority.

Johnson won 61.1 percent of the vote, totaling 43,129,484 popular votes to 27,178,188 for Goldwater (486 to 52 electoral votes). After going Republican in three consecutive presidential elections, Tennessee returned to the Democratic column.

The year of 1964 was not a good year for Republicans in Tennessee. Howard Baker lost to Ross Bass in the short-term Senate seat (Class 2) vacated upon the death of Senator Estes Kefauver. Although he lost, Baker ran the best race of any prior Republican candidate for Senate in Tennessee history, winning 47.4 percent of the vote (568,905 votes for Bass and 517,330 for Baker). Dan Kuykendall lost to Albert Gore Sr. in the full-term Senate race (Class 1), but this race was also surprisingly close for traditionally Democratic Tennessee. Kuykendall came in just shy of Baker's statewide percentage and well ahead of Goldwater's take of 44 percent in the presidential race. Kuykendall earned 493,475 votes to 570,542 for Senator Gore. Kuykendall felt that if the presidential nominee had been stronger, both he and Baker would have won. George Lee, who still smarted over losing control of the Shelby County Republican Party as well as his much-cherished delegate seat for the national convention, successfully worked

ROSS BASS was born on March 17, 1918, on a farm in Giles County, close to Pulaski, Tennessee. He obtained his early education in Tennessee's public schools, and in 1941 graduated from Martin College in Pulaski, where an endowed professorship is named for him. He became an air corps captain in World War II. After the war he owned a soft drink bottling plant and worked as a florist and nurseryman from 1946 through 1947. From 1947 he served as postmaster for Pulaski, Tennessee, until he was elected as a Democrat to the U.S. House of Representatives in 1954. He served from January 3, 1955, until November 3, 1964, when he was elected to complete the unexpired term of Estes Kefauver in the U.S. Senate. He took office in the Senate on November 4, 1964, and served until January 2, 1967. In 1966 he lost renomination in the Democratic primary for the Senate to Frank Clement, who went on to lose to Howard Baker Jr., the Republican candidate. After serving in the Senate, Bass owned a consulting firm in Washington, D.C. In 1976 he attempted to gain election to Congress but lost. He then lived in Miami Shores, Florida, until his death on January 1, 1993. (Photograph courtesy of SHO)

for Bob James's Democratic opponent for the Ninth Congressional District seat and refused to support Goldwater. The only Tennessee Republicans to win congressional seats were those in traditional Republican East Tennessee. In 1964, Jimmy Quillen (First District) and Bill Brock (Third District) both won reelection. John J. Duncan won the Second District, which had been temporarily filled by Irene Baker.

Duncan, former mayor of Knoxville and part-time field representative for Baker, served from January 1965 until his death in June 1988—twenty-three and one-half years. Duncan's district—the Second Congressional District of Tennessee, is the only district in the state to remain Republican since the party was founded.

So once again the Democrats controlled the state with a sitting Democratic governor and two Democratic U.S. senators. With no statewide offices, a Democratic president, most counties controlled by old-time Democrats, and no patronage, Republicans were limited to three Republican East Tennessee congressmen who encouraged a determined, yet weak Republican grassroots organization in Middle and West Tennessee.

This 1964 election demonstrated that Black voter participation, sparked by a voter's registration drive in 1959, began to impact Tennessee elections. Memphian A. W. Willis Jr. was elected the first Black Democrat to serve in the state house in Tennessee history. (In 1885 a Black representative served Shelby County in the Tennessee legislature, but as a Republican.) Willis was elected to represent Shelby County. (At this time, state house and senate seats were voted on by the entire county electorate as opposed to districts.) Civil rights lawyer "H. T. Lockard was elected and became the first Black to serve in Shelby County government" (Sigafoos 1979). This trend did not help Republicans.

Lyndon Johnson emerged from his election as a more powerful president. His adminstration took on the formidable task of balancing the creation of the Great Society and its welfare programs with fighting the increasingly frustrating Vietnam War. Since the Democrats held power, they also were held responsible for the fate of the nation. Suddenly, President Johnson's popularity waned. The Democratic constituency encompassed a huge spectrum of political persuasions. Some people protested the continuation of the war; others the way the war was being fought. Some saw the welfare programs as the redistribution of personal income; others did not agree with Johnson's civil rights positions. Tennessee was Democratic, basically as a response to the carpetbagging Republicans who sided with Union domination during and after the Civil War. Some of these White Southerners did not accept Johnson's civil rights programs.

Republicans took the public pulse and detected a mood for change. While local Democrats throughout Middle and West Tennessee felt secure, Republicans felt defiant, and in some counties they challenged the Democrats for their state legislative seats. Even though the tide was beginning to turn from the Democrats on a national and statewide basis, they still controlled the city and county governments. With this kind of local influence, Republicans would still have a hard time in the state legislative and local elections. Nevertheless, the Republicans made a valiant effort. They defiantly challenged the Democrats up and down the ticket. It was a party-building effort that would set the future stage for a party currently so weak that it had nothing to lose.

Although Republicans made little gains in local races, the federal seats were a different matter. Republicans had the issues on their side. Vietnam, high prices, inflation, and high interest rates hung around the necks of Democrats like political lead balloons.

Howard Baker Jr., who had run a strong statewide race in 1964, a year that was most decidedly a Democrat year, had managed to maintain a great deal of his support and was inclined to try again in 1966. At first Baker held off committing to run. After all, two losses in a row might spell political disaster. When he hesitated, Vanderbilt University law professor, Kenneth L. Roberts, decided to make the run for the Republican Party. Roberts had been statewide volunteer coordinator for Goldwater in 1964. Baker, sensing the mood of the electorate, realized the opportunity and opted to run again. He and Roberts squared off in a cordial statewide Republican Senate primary. Baker maintained most of his 1964 support and easily won with 77 percent of the vote. Roberts quickly conceded the election and endorsed his opponent, who in turn, asked Roberts to be his campaign chairman for the general election.

Republicans Emerge

Buford Ellington was opposed by John J. Hooker Jr. in the Democratic primary for governor in 1966. Hooker was a Nashville lawyer and the son of a friend of former Governor Gordon Browning. He was endorsed by the *Nashville Tennessean* and its publisher, John Seigenthaler. The paper, along with Browning supporters and others, wanted to end the fourteen years of Clement and Ellington office swapping which maintained their control of the state. Hooker also had the support of many of Nashville's social and financial power brokers, but he did not have it all. The *Nashville Banner* and its publisher, Jimmy Stahlman, endorsed Ellington, who also had the support of the Farm Bureau, Governor Clement, and President Johnson. Black voters supported Hooker because of his association with the late President John Kennedy and his brother Robert Kennedy. Hooker projected the image of the young, progressive Democrat who was liberal in viewpoint and strong on civil rights. On primary day, Shelby County Blacks supported Hooker, and he narrowly won Shelby County. However, he lost in the remainder of the urban and rural areas. Most of the rural votes identified with the traditional Southern Democrat which Ellington represented. Hooker even lost Davidson, his home county. Ellington won the primary with 413,950 votes to 360,105 for Hooker.

In 1966 Senator Ross Bass was vulnerable. His ties to Lyndon Johnson did not help, nor did his win in the 1964 Democratic Senate primary over Frank Clement, which had caused some lingering ill will among Clement supporters. Those still loyal to Clement would not support Bass. State law prohibited Clement from succeeding himself as governor, so in light of Bass's political problems, Clement decided to oppose him again in the Democratic Senate primary. The Tennessee Voters Council—the Black Democratic voters' organization—and organized labor held fast with Bass. However, Bass was tagged a Johnson liberal, and Clement made him carry Johnson's baggage into the election. The negative challenge worked. The old East Tennessee political coalition, consisting of Republican J. Will Taylor and Democrat Herbert Walters, supported Clement in hopes of toppling incumbent Senator Bass, thus paving the way for Howard Baker. The primary election ended as the East Tennessee political coalition had hoped and planned, with Clement polling 384,322 votes (51 percent)

BUFORD ELLINGTON was born on June 27, 1907, in Holmes County, Mississippi, to A. E. and Cora Ellington. After his early education in Goodman, Mississippi, he studied religion at Millsaps College in Jackson, Mississippi. While editing a newspaper in Durant, Mississippi, he met and married Catherine Cheek, daughter of James and Fannie Bell Cheek of Marshall County, Tennessee. After ten years of marriage he moved his family to Verona, Marshall County, Tennessee, where he bought a general store. He then spent eight years as a salesman for International Harvester in Memphis. In 1942 he bought a farm and traveled the state for the Farm Bureau Insurance System.

Ellington entered politics by working for Jim Nance McCord in his races for U.S. representative and governor, and serving as Marshall County campaign manager for Joe Evins in 1946. In 1948 Ellington was elected to the state legislature, representing Marshall County. In 1952 he led Frank Clement's campaign to defeat incumbent Governor Gordon Browning. After Clement was elected, Ellington became commissioner of agriculture. When Clement could not succeed himself as governor in 1958 Ellington ran, preserving the Clement-Ellington political coalition. He was elected, took office in 1959, and served until 1963. During the 1960 Democratic primaries for president, Ellington supported Lyndon Johnson and served as the chairman of the 1960 Democratic National Convention. After his four-year term as governor, he sat out the 1962 race as required by the state constitution, and once again Frank Clement was elected governor. Ellington served as vice president of the Louisville-Nashville Railroad until he took a position in President Johnson's civil rights program. He was reelected governor in 1966 and served from 1967 until 1971.

During his second term, Ellington changed his former segregationist stance and embraced civil rights. He appointed Tennessee's first black cabinet officer and created the Tennessee Human Relations Commission. He supported a raise in teachers' pay, and reorganized state government. His tenure saw the repeal of the Anti-Evolution Law of 1925 and a failed effort to amend the 1939 laws for liquor regulation. Ellington served as a trustee for Peabody College, the University of Tennessee, and Rust College in Holly Springs, Mississippi. He was a director of the Millsaps College Alumni Association and a thirty-third degree Scottish Rite Mason. Shortly after leaving the governor's office, Ellington died while playing golf in Florida on April 3, 1972. He was buried in Lone Oak Cemetery in Lewisburg, Tennessee. (Photograph courtesy of TSLA)

to 366,078 for Bass. Clement won Shelby, Davidson, and Hamilton Counties.

Republican Howard Baker Jr., who lost to Democrat Senator Ross Bass two years prior, now faced Democrat Governor Frank Clement for the Senate seat. Many factors conspired against Clement. Senator Bass and his close associates were angry with Clement. Additionally, the relationship between Buford Ellington and Frank Clement had deteriorated and Democrat gubernatorial nominee Ellington refused to support Clement. The antimachine attitude of some Democrats as well as Clement's tie to President Johnson and his liberal policies alienated some traditional Southern White Democratic support. Baker only needed to make it easy for Middle and West Tennessee Democrats to cross over to the Republican column on the ballot. He implored voters to do the right thing rather than follow tradition. He appealed to Black voters and worked the Black community, while enticing the traditional Southern Democrat White voters who did not like Lyndon Johnson's civil rights actions.

Clement had never received the enthusiastic support of organized labor, so he could not count on being carried by the unions. He did have the endorsement of the *Nashville Tennessean*, the *Nashville Banner*, and the *Memphis Commercial Appeal*. He used all the powers and influence of state government to his advantage. Baker continued to attack Clement, linking him to Johnson and playing on the fear of a tax increase. Baker was not radical in his appeal to voters and became acceptable to those who had been alarmed at the perception of extremism in the presidential 1964 election. Minority Leader of the House Gerald Ford came to Tennessee to support Baker as did former Vice President Richard Nixon.

Clement thought that his defeat of Senator Bass in the Democratic primary was tantamount to victory. After all, Democrat was the tradition in Tennessee. Additional confidence came from the fact that Baker had won only 122,617 votes in the Republican Senate primary. But, the people of Tennessee felt some resistance toward Clement's continued hold on public office. A long stay incurs resentment, and indeed Clement had been governor for ten years. His one time protégé, Buford Ellington, had been governor for four years and was headed for his own second term. In all, the Clement-Ellington coalition dominated state politics for eighteen years. The three-time governor of Tennessee overestimated his power. In fact, he was stunned. The people felt a Republican pull in the 1966 U.S. Senate race and did not give Clement the support he needed. East Tennessee, which had aided Clement in past elections, went with Baker. Clement won Davidson County, but Baker won West Tennessee. Clement received 383,843 votes but Baker polled 483,063, becoming the first popularly elected Republican U.S. senator (Class 2) in Tennessee history. (He took office on January 3, 1967, was reelected in 1972 and 1978, and served until January 2, 1985.) However, the people of Tennessee did not totally swing to the Republican column. The Democratic Party still was their heritage and their inclination. They reelected Democrat Buford Ellington governor.

It was extremely unusual that West Tennessee, a Democratic stronghold, went Republican, thus making Baker the first Republican to carry West Tennessee since Reconstruction. Local politics held fast to the Democratic faith; the Seventh, Eighth, and Ninth District U.S. Representative seats in West Tennessee were all won by Democrats (including Ray Blanton, first elected to office by defeating Democratic incumbent Congressman Tom Murray in 1966). Baker's election marked a change in tradition. Now Tennesseans would consider Republicans as viable candidates in races for statewide office. The basis for the philosophical change in Southern Democratic voter attitudes came mainly because of the civil rights movement. Democrats Robert Kennedy, John Kennedy, and Lyndon Johnson had championed civil rights, which attracted more Black voters but alienated some Southern White voters.

With a Republican now holding statewide office, Tennessee held the possibility of a real two-party system. Republicans throughout Tennessee were excited and encouraged by the thought that they might win other seats. Suddenly, a new crew of budding politicians visualized the realization of their ambitions through the Republican Party.

While the civil rights movement helped the Republicans gain White voters, it also helped the Democrats gain Black voters. However, if Democratic candidates were to truly benefit from the civil rights movement, Black voters had to be able to vote and Black candidates had to be able to run for office. While some Southern states used closed primaries and/or literacy tests to eliminate Black votes, Tennessee did not. In past years, Democrats and Republicans held conventions to select their candidates. This of course precluded many from the opportunity of running for office, since those who controlled the party controlled who was nominated. Now both parties held open primaries and Blacks could enter races. Thus, 1966 saw a more involved Black constituency, with an increase in the number of Black voters and even more significant, an increase in the number of Black candidates. Six Black representatives were elected to the Tennessee legislature, including Dorothy Lavinia Brown, the first female Black surgeon in the U.S. and the first Black woman to serve in the Tennessee General Assembly.

With Baker's election to the U.S. Senate in 1966, Republicans were not simply inspired but also competitive, and as a result various Republican groups vied for power. Prior to this election, Republican power was controlled by East Tennessee Republican congressmen. Now Baker was building a statewide organization which threatened the old order. Although they had all worked together, Republican leaders had to face the potential of intraparty threats to their own separate ambitions. By 1967 Republicans were battling each other at all levels across the state. Senator Howard Baker and Congressman Bill Brock split the party into two distinct camps, each with loyalists on the State Republican Executive Committee representing their respective interests. Although there were no outright wars, there was posturing and positioning as each group tried to ensure a solid position within the state party.

By now the Vietnam conflict had polarized the electorate against Lyndon Johnson, and he found himself under intense criticism and pressure. Antiwar protests were commonplace, and the president was the hate target for demonstrators. His outlook for reelection dimmed. From an historical perspective alone, no president who had succeeded to office upon the death of his predecessor and then been elected on his own right had ever been reelected for a second term. Johnson was a determined politician and had always done what was necessary to win, but he now faced the real possibility that he might not be able to overcome his greatest obstacle—public opinion over his Vietnam policies. Early in his presidency he had achieved the height of popularity. Now at a low point, he was concerned about how historians would remember him, and he did not want to go down in defeat, possibly in his own party's nomination process. Pragmatic as well as crafty, he chose not to run for reelection in 1968. For him, it was a wise decision. National unrest over the war only worsened. Martin Luther King Jr. was assassinated on April 4, 1968, in Memphis, Tennessee, and two months later, on June 5, 1968, Democratic presidential hopeful Senator Robert F. Kennedy was shot on the campaign trail in Los Angeles, dying the next day. National disorder forewarned a chaotic election year.

Not only would the antiwar movement affect the 1968 elections, but procivil rights and anticivil rights forces would all gain momentum. Southern Democrats were suffering from an intraparty revolt against the national Democratic procivil rights movement. George Wallace, the Alabama political king, organized his campaign for president, on an anticivil rights platform. He hoped to pull Republicans, Democrats, and Independents who agreed with his die-hard segregationist philosophy. No independent had won before. However, by Wallace's calculations, he could win enough votes to throw the election into the House of Representatives. His campaign spilled over into congressional races, and Tennessee was not excluded.

The August 1968 Democratic National Convention was a disaster. Vietnam War protestors descended on Chicago, interfering with the plans of the Democratic Party bosses and setting off a violent reaction. The demonstrators were clubbed by Chicago policemen and national guardsmen. The entire nation witnessed the violence on television. Democrats were shaken by the disturbance, but the convention mangaged to complete the voting. Vice President Hubert Humphrey received the nomination for president, and Maine Senator Edmund Muskie was chosen as the vice presidential nominee. The Democrats came out of the convention appearing disorganized and divided. Many of their party leaders disagreed over the management and continuation of America's involvement in Vietnam. During the worst of the bloodshed, Johnson was president and the Democrats controlled both the U.S. House and Senate. The Democratic Party could not avoid some association with the war, its death and destruction, and its seemingly chaotic progression.

Tennessee Black voters were now almost totally Democratic in loyalty. Only those who remembered the days when Black Republicans dominated the West Tennessee organization continued to tarry with the Republican Party. Now, George Lee and his group complained that the West Tennessee (Lily White) Republicans, who were now in control, had excluded them from delegate seats at the 1964 Republican National Convention. But the Lily Whites knew that Lee had not only supported Democrats in local U.S. Representative and statewide races in 1964 and 1966, but he had done this many times in the past. Shelby County Blacks had abandoned the Republican Party, and George Lee had little ability to actually produce any Republican votes. Howard Baker, however, was trying to break the racial barrier and win Blacks back to the Republican Party. It was an uphill battle. Baker, the Republican leader in Tennessee, was able to secure only one delegate spot for a Black Republican, Sarah Moore Greene, at the 1968 Republican National Convention.

When the convention met in Miami, Richard Nixon was nominated for president on the first ballot. Spiro Agnew, governor of Maryland, was selected as the vice presidential nominee.

Former Governor George Wallace of Alabama ran for president as the American Independent Party candidate. Retired Air Force General Curtis LeMay was the vice presidential nominee. They sought the anti-civil rights vote.

Tennessee Democrats were in disarray over the presidential election. Hubert Humphrey appeared to be a nice man, but to most Tennesseans he looked too much like another liberal. Many Democrats considered voting for Independent George Wallace rather than vote Republican. Republicans, on the other hand, were solidly behind Nixon, and Senator Howard Baker and Congressman Bill Brock worked the state for him.

The Democratic Party's fracture helped the Republicans. In previously solid Democratic West Tennessee, the Ninth

Congressional District broke the long-standing party barrier when Republican Dan Kuykendall was elected. (Lon Scott was elected Republican U.S. representative in the Seventh District in the late 1920s. The Whigs had also occasionally held this seat prior to the Civil War.) The election was also a success for Republicans in the state legislature. They picked up seats in both the state house and senate. With support from an Independent representative, Republicans gained narrow control of the state house.

The presidential election was close, but on November 5, 1968, Richard M. Nixon was elected thirty-seventh president with 31,785,480 popular votes to 31,275,165 for Hubert Humphrey, and 9,906,473 for George Wallace (301, 191, 46 electoral votes). Nixon took Tennessee with 38 percent of the vote, Wallace finished second, and Democrat Humphrey finished third.

Tennessee Republicans were looking stronger. There was a Republican president. They had one of Tennessee's U.S. Senate seats. They broke into the West Tennessee Democratic stronghold by picking up the Ninth Congressional District seat, and now they had control of the Tennessee house for the first time since Reconstruction.

By 1970 the pendulum of voter mood was in full swing, and this became a pivotal year for Tennessee Republicans. The national mood was still turning against the liberal agenda. Tennessee Democrat U.S. Senator Al Gore Sr. promoted some unpopular causes. He opposed an aggressive war policy and voted for gun control. He either misread the views of most Tennesseans or in good conscience could not vote against what he felt was best for his nation. To other Tennessee Democrats as well as to Republicans, he looked vulnerable. He was challenged in the Democratic primary by Hudley Crockett of Nashville. At first, Crockett did not appear to be a real threat, but he won the Sixth, Seventh, Eighth, and Ninth Districts. Gore narrowly won the primary.

Nineteen seventy was also a gubernatorial election year. Former Governor Frank Clement had died in an automobile accident in 1969, and Governor Ellington could not succeed himself. John J. Hooker, a well-known Tennessee businessman surfaced as the major candidate for the Democrats. He was opposed by West Tennessean Robert L. Taylor, a Tennessee Court of Appeals justice and the grandson of former Governor and Senator Robert Taylor; Mary Anderson, Nashville school teacher and businesswoman; and state Senator Stanley T. Snodgrass of Nashville. Hooker appeared to be the strongest candidate in the Democratic field. However, his company's stock had recently fallen from sixty-nine dollars to two dollars and many Tennessee stockholders questioned so precipitous a loss. The people of Tennessee were also concerned with the issues of school prayer, crime, drugs, gun control, pornography, and busing. Liberal Democrats had voted for or espoused positions on some of these issues in a way that proved philosophically contrary to the views of many Tennessee voters. Hooker's close ties to the Kennedys helped solidify his liberal identity. Traditional Southern Democrats, opposed to civil rights and racial integration, were not quite sure what to think about the possibility of putting a liberal in the governor's seat.

Baker's win in 1966 encouraged several Republicans to run for governor in 1970. Republican businessman Maxey Jarman of Nashville, House Speaker Bill Jenkins of Knoxville, past state Republican Party Chairman Claude Robertson, and a newcomer named Winfield Dunn all wanted to become governor. Dunn was a practicing Memphis dentist who had political interests and a family history of public service. His father had served as a U.S. representative from Mississippi. Dunn had moved to Memphis to attend the University of Tennessee Dental School and later settled in Memphis. He had been active in the local party since the take-over by the new guard and had recently served as Shelby County Republican Party chairman for four years.

The Republican field was crowded and many thought Dunn did not have a chance in the primary. Nevertheless, he ran a hard and dedicated campaign, and was popular in the high population area of Shelby County. His many Shelby County supporters, his appeal in other parts of the state, and the vote split among the other candidates (he outdistanced Jarman by just ten thousand votes) won Dunn the Republican nomination. John Jay Hooker

WINFIELD C. DUNN was born on July 1, 1927, in Meridian, Mississippi, to Albert C. and Dorothy Crum Dunn. He received his early education in local Mississippi schools, then at age seventeen volunteered for the U.S. Navy and served as a pharmacist's mate in World War II. He was overseas from 1945 to 1946. After the end of the war, Dunn returned home and attended the University of Mississippi. He met Betty Jane Pritchard, the daughter of Dr. Frank and Ruby Howell Pritchard, while at the university, and they were married in 1950. The couple had three children. Dunn's father-in-law was a dentist in Memphis. Dunn's father had served as a U.S. representative from Mississippi and there was some consideration by young Winfield to enter law. However, after he obtained a degree in banking and finance at Ole Miss, he worked for a short while in the insurance business. Later, he and Betty moved to Memphis where Winfield enrolled in the University of Tennessee School of Dentistry. After graduation he practiced dentistry in Memphis and was active in Memphis civic affairs and served for four years as chairman of the Shelby County Republican Party.

In 1970 Dunn was elected governor of Tennessee and served four years. While governor he was elected to the Executive Committee of the National Governors Conference and chairman of the Republican Governors Association. He worked for improved education and instituted a statewide kindergarten system. He made strides with the state's mental health hospitals, a regional prison system, and the highway construction program. He began a primary health care program through the Department of Health and created the Department of Economic and Community Development. Tennessee law at that time prohibited a sitting governor from succeeding himself. After completing his tenure, he went to work in Nashville for Hospital Corporation of America as vice president of public relations. In 1986 he was the Republican candidate for governor again, but lost to Ned Ray McWherter, Democrat speaker of the Tennessee house of representatives. Dunn continues to support Republican candidates and remains a leading citizen and activist in Tennessee. He chaired the Education Commission of the States, and served on the University of Tennessee Board of Trustees, the Tennessee Tombigbee Waterway Development Authority, and the Tennessee Board of Regents. Currently on the boards of several corporations, Dunn is a Mason and Shriner and a member of the American Legion and the Methodist Church. He and his wife reside in Nashville. (Photograph courtesy of TSLA) easily won the Democratic primary.

Republicans also fielded candidates for the U.S. Senate race. In the Republican primary, Third District Republican U.S. Representative William E. Brock of Chattanooga, actor and singer Tex Ritter, and others tested the political temperature of the Republican voters. Ritter tried to paint himself as the mainstream Republican and Brock as a right-wing extremist. However, Brock had worked the state for years, had a proven record of moderation, and had established an organizational support base. He solidly won the primary with 75 percent of the vote.

Democrats Gore and Hooker had to deal with the liberal image of their party. In 1970 this was a great obstacle for a Tennessee candidate. The people of Tennessee were tired of most of the liberal social, foreign, and economic policies of the national Democrats. Brock and Dunn drove the issues home. Additionally, Governor Buford Ellington did not agree with the political ideaology of Hooker, who had opposed and lost to Ellington in the 1966 Democratic primary. Ellington was a rural Southern conservative Democrat who quietly supported Winfield Dunn in his quest for the rural vote. Many traditional Tennessee Democrats sat on their hands rather than support Hooker. Dunn's populist-conservative approach won favor with the voters. He received 557,024 votes to 498,757 for Hooker, winning the First, Second, Third, Seventh, and Ninth Congressional Districts. He was the first Republican governor of Tennessee since Alf Taylor was elected in 1920—the first in fifty years.

The Republican momentum made the Senate race difficult for Albert Gore Sr., although Brock's victory was not a foregone conclusion. Brock glued the liberal image to Gore by calling him the "third Senator from Massachusetts," but this was not always seen negatively. Gore had worked to increase Social Security benefits and veterans' benefits. He was regarded as the father of Medicare and the architect of the Interstate Highway system. Substantial allegiance existed for him. The election looked close until Senator Howard Baker submitted an amendment on October 13, 1970 to the Equal Rights Amendment which linked school prayer to the passage. When Gore supported the separation of church and state by voting "no," Brock attacked Gore's antiprayer vote. This was too much for Senator Gore. Brock was elected U.S. senator with 52 percent of the vote. He carried the First, Second, and Third Districts and won by small margins in the Seventh, Eighth, and Ninth Districts. Republican Lamar Baker was elected to fill Brock's seat in the Third Congressional District.

Tennessee Republicans now held both U.S. Senate seats and the governor's seat. This was the first time since 1871—Reconstruction—that both Tennessee U.S. senators were Republican and the first time ever that Republicans held all three positions due to an open election. Nationally, however, they did not have control of either house of Congress. Likewise, the statewide appeal of Republicans did not translate into a local political power shift. Democrats regained control of the state house of representatives, which Republicans had won in 1968, and still held the municipal power, especially in communities that did not hold local county primaries. Many of the Democrats in these communities maintained power not only because of ingrained tradition but by avoiding the negatives associated with identification of their party affiliation on election ballots. In those counties in which local races were officially nonpartisan, party affiliation was not divulged. Many local

WILLIAM EMERSON BROCK III was born on November 23, 1930, in Chattanooga, Hamilton County, Tennessee to William E. Brock II and Myra Kruesi Brock. He was the grandson of former U.S. Senator William Emerson Brock. Brock attended the schools of Chattanooga and Lookout Mountain. Later he received his higher education at Washington and Lee University in Lexington, Virginia, graduating in 1953. He then joined the navy and served from 1953 until 1956. After returning home, he went to work at his family's Brock Candy Company. He was married, on January 11, 1957, to Laura "Muffet" Handly, from Lookout Mountain, Tennessee. They had three sons and one daughter. In 1962 he ran for U.S. representative in the Third Congressional District of Tennessee. He was elected and reelected three times, serving from January 3, 1963, until January 3, 1971. In 1970 he ran for the U.S. Senate and defeated incumbent Senator Albert Gore Sr. He served one term from January 3, 1971, until January 3, 1977. He lost reelection in 1976, along with many other Republicans who suffered from the voter revolt over the Watergate and Agnew scandals.

Brock served as chairman of the Republican National Committee from 1977 until 1981. He served as United States trade representative under President Ronald Reagan from 1981 until 1985 and as Reagan's secretary of labor from 1985 until 1987. After leaving office, he worked as a Washington-based consultant. Laura Brock died on December 30, 1985, and Brock remarried about one year later. In 1994 he ran, unsuccessfully, for the U.S. Senate in Maryland. Former Senator Brock and his wife, Sandy, currently live in Annapolis, Maryland. (Photograph courtesy of SHO)

Democrats avoided the spillover of damage suffered by federal officeholders.

Winfield Dunn was not only the first Republican governor in fifty years, he was only the third Republican governor since the turn of the century, and the sixth in Tennessee's 176-year history. The state awaited to see what the young Republican would do when he took office. Although many Democratic state legislators worked with the Republican governor, some worked to undermine him. In 1971 urban legislator James McKinney, from Davidson County, was elected to be speaker of the Tennessee house. Under his speakership, continual effort was made to embarrass Governor Dunn. Nonetheless, Dunn worked diligently to foster communication and cooperation with the Democrats. He asked the Democratic commissioner of finance, Harlan Mathews, to stay on in his administration. Although Mathews declined and took a job with the AMCON Company in Memphis, this kind of bipartisan effort served to foster a cooperative atmosphere for a Republican governor in a Democratic state capitol. (Two years later a soft-spoken rural legislator from Dresden, Tennessee, Ned Ray McWherter, would be elected as speaker of the Tennessee house. He slowed down the level of animosity from Democrats toward the Republican governor.)

Dunn proposed providing statewide kindergartens, increasing the pay of state employees, improving mental health programs, and reducing state costs. He proposed ninety-five million dollars in taxes to pay for his plans. The legislature reduced the planned outlay and then enacted a 0.6 percent sales tax increase. During Dunn's term, the state legislature ratified the Twenty-sixth Amendment, which lowered the voting age to eighteen, and agreed to a presidential preference primary, which would first occur in 1972. Dunn's kindergarten program plan was delayed, due to a funding shortfall.

From 1970 until 1972 there were no statewide elections in Tennessee. During this time Tennesseans, like most Americans, were caught up in the ongoing drama of the Vietnam War. This was a period of national student unrest. Much of the revolt had started under President Johnson and gathered momentum through Nixon's first term as president. The American people were confused and angry over the apparent lack of progress with the conflict which was costing thousands of American lives. Peace talks produced little progress. A plan was implemented for the progressive substitution of South Vietnamese soldiers for U.S. troops, but the war continued playing out through the lens of the evening news. Continual reports of loss of life struck every American community. Friends, neighbors, brothers, sisters, fathers, and mothers all watched in horror as reports continued to arrive of someone known or loved who had died in the war.

It was a war that many Americans thought was being fought for no truly justifiable reason. It was a war set up for disaster, caught up in the politics of the day. The politicians bickered over whether or not the United States should even be in the war and how the war should be fought. The American people remained confused and divided. Civil instability worsened.

President Nixon, a talented international diplomatic leader, worked to bring an end to the war. Progress was marred, however, by international and national political realities as the war became a tool for candidates seeking office. Meanwhile, Nixon had enjoyed phenomenal diplomatic success with the Soviet Union and China by opening talks and establishing agreements with both. Under these conditions Nixon began to campaign for the upcoming election of 1972.

The Democrats, having enjoyed domination of the White House for twenty-eight out the previous forty years and control of both houses of Congress for thirty-six out of forty years, saw an opportunity to win back power, but the Democratic contenders for president ran rancorous primary campaigns. At the July 1972 Miami, Democratic National Convention, in the liberal wing controlled the outcome of the convention. South Dakota Senator George S. McGovern won the nomination as the Democratic candidate for president. Missouri Senator Thomas F. Eagleton was selected as the vice presidential candidate. Soon afterward, the media disclosed that Eagleton had been hospitalized in the past for a possible psychiatric condition. Eagleton was asked to withdraw, and Sargent Shriver Jr., who was a brother-in-law of late President Kennedy, was chosen as the new Democratic vice presidential candidate.

In August, the Republicans also held their national convention in Miami and renominated President Nixon and Vice President Agnew.

In the Tennessee primary elections of 1972, Democrats elected Seventh District Congressman Ray Blanton, who served three terms in the U.S. House of Representatives, as the Democratic Senate candidate. Republicans reelected Howard Baker, who won 97 percent of the vote in the GOP primary.

As senator, Howard Baker had continued to push for "revenue sharing," which would give the states more federal money. The act required for the added revenue was finally passed and signed into law by President Nixon in October 1972. This effort won Baker a great deal of appreciation from Tennessee state and local officials. He had also promoted the reduction in the voting age to eighteen and an all-volunteer army. Both issues won Baker votes among the eighteen through twenty-four age group. But Black votes were more difficult for the young Republican to attract. He received little Black support in his 1964 loss and his 1966 victory. However, he was finally beginning to gain Black voter approval through his legislative actions. He took a risk on the issue of busing, feeling that this method of integrating schools would worsen tensions and that desegregation should occur through other means rather than through a controversial law.

Baker voted for the extension of the Voting Rights Act and increased funding for the civil rights office in the office of education. He worked to have President Nixon name Judge Benjamin Hooks to the Federal Communications Commission. The fact that Baker faced Ray Blanton in the general election also gained him support with Black voters. Blanton drew from the George Wallace type of reactionary segregationist. He had voted against the extension of the Voters Rights Act, the eighteen-year voting age, and revenue sharing. This did not help his cause with Black voters, young voters, or state and local officials. His Democratic base was split and he had lost the support that Baker had so carefully cultivated. Baker had even won favor with many of the Wallace Democrats by voting against busing and for voluntary school prayer. He was also able to tag Blanton as a liberal because of his listing on the ballot with Democratic presidential nominee George McGovern. Baker, on the other hand, spoke highly of his association and friendship with President Nixon and reminded his crowds of Nixon's plan to end the war in Vietnam.

While Baker campaigned, President Nixon worried over his own campaign. He had narrowly lost the 1960 election and narrowly won the 1968 election. He knew the Democrats, their determination, and their advantage over Republicans from their years of dominance in local political networks throughout the nation. He was well aware of the extent to which political opponents might reach in order to win. He needed only to remember his evidence of election tampering in Illinois and Texas in 1960 to convince him to be extra cautious in the 1972 election. As a result, the "Committee to Re-elect the President" was organized. The committee raised over sixty million dollars for Nixon's campaign.

The Democratic National Headquarters was located in the Watergate office-hotel complex in Washington, D.C. The Committee to Re-elect the President sent five men to plant phone wire-tapping and observation camera equipment in the Democratic National Committee office on June 17, 1972. The attempt was botched, and the burglars were caught and arrested. Newspapers soon began to report evidence that linked the break-in with the Committee to Re-elect the President. When the media, which had been negative toward the Nixon presidency all along, began linking the White House to the Watergate break-in, Republicans considered the coverage a smear campaign against President Nixon.

In late October, the administration announced that peace in Vietnam was imminent. Nixon gained support for his excellent progress in foreign relations. The Democrats were severely disadvantaged running ultraliberal George McGovern as their presidential nominee, and the party squabbled internally over its official idealogy. Many Democratic politicians, aware that the public was generally weary of liberal philosophies, tried to distance themselves from their candidate. President Nixon was reelected in a political landslide with 60.7 percent of the vote. He won 47,169,911 popular votes to 29,170,383 for McGovern and 1,098,482 for John G.

HOWARD HENRY BAKER JR. was born on November 15, 1925, in Scott County, Huntsville, Tennessee. His immigrant ancestors originally settled in Virginia and North Carolina. Around 1811, the Baker settlers came to Campbell County, just east of Scott County. Baker's Forge was named after Howard's great-grandfather, George Washington Baker. His maternal great-grandfather, Alderson T. Keen, along with George Baker, enlisted in the Union army and eventually became majors. After the Civil War both became supporters of the Unionist Party and later the Republican Party.

George Baker's son, James Francis Baker, set up a law office in Huntsville and married Helen Keen from Hustonville, Kentucky in the 1890s. The couple lived in Kentucky and their first son, Howard, was born on January 12, 1902, in Somerset, Kentucky. In 1909 the Baker family moved to Huntsville, Tennessee. In 1918 Howard Baker entered the University of Tennessee, graduating in 1922 and going on to law school. Two years later he completed his study and married Dora Ladd, who was from Roane County. The couple moved to Huntsville, where Baker went into practice with his father. Their first child was Howard Henry Baker Jr.

In 1928 Baker Sr. was elected to the Tennessee General Assembly. Four years later, he began serving as Scott County Republican chairman, serving for sixteen years. In 1934 he was elected as Nineteenth Judicial District attorney general. Unfortunately his wife died just before he was elected to this post, when Howard Jr. was eight years old and sister, Mary, was two. The children's maternal grandfather, John Christopher Ladd, had also recently died, leaving a vacancy in the sheriff's office of Roane County. The spot was filled by their maternal grandmother, Lillie Ladd, who moved in with the Bakers to help with her grandchildren while she also carried out her responsibilities as the first female sheriff of Tennessee.

Baker Jr. received his early education in Huntsville, Tennessee, schools. He received an early political education traveling as a ten-year-old boy with his father, who campaigned throughout Tennessee for the Landon/Knox Republican presidential campaign in 1936. He learned from his father's unsuccessful run as the Republican nominee for governor in 1938 against Democrat Prentice Cooper. In 1940, Howard Baker Sr. was the Republican nominee for U.S. senator, but lost to Democrat Kenneth McKellar with less than 30 percent of the vote.

Baker Sr. married Irene Bailey, a widow, in 1936. Baker Jr. was educated at McCallie Military School in Chattanooga, Tennessee, and graduated as a private in 1943. He was then sent by the navy to the University of the South at Sewanee in 1943 to study electrical engineering. After one year he transferred to Tulane University, in New Orleans, where he completed his undergraduate study.

Schmitz (American Independent candidate). This resulted in an electoral vote of 520 to 17 to 0.

The national mood favored Republicans and the party continued to gain strength in Tennessee. In fact, the state actually went Republican in this election. Nixon carried Tennessee 813,147 to 357,293 and Howard Baker won his U.S. Senate reelection by 716,534 votes to 440,599 for Blanton. Nixon outpolled fellow Republican Baker by 6.2 percent statewide. The senator won 5 percent more than the president in the Ninth Congressional District in Memphis by carrying a greater share of the large Black voter base.

He served in the navy from 1943 until 1946, then returned to Tennessee and began law school at the University of Tennessee at Knoxville in 1946. He graduated and was admitted to the bar in 1949, and then joined his father's law practice.

In 1948 Howard Sr. chaired the Tennessee Republican delegation to the Republican National Convention. Most Tennessee Republicans supported Robert A. Taft for the presidential nomination. However, Republican Second District Tennessee Congressman John Jennings Jr. supported Thomas Dewey. When Dewey won the Republican nomination, he chose Jennings to run his Tennessee campaign. This choice insulted Guy Lincoln Smith, a longtime Republican leader in Tennessee and publisher of the *Knoxville Journal*, and B. Carroll Reece, a twelve-term Republican congressman from the First District, chairman of the Republican National Committee, and the Republican nominee for the U.S. Senate. Jennings campaigned for Dewey on a pledge to put an end to the Tennessee coalition between East Tennessee Republicans, specifically Reece and Democratic Boss Crump of Shelby County. Reece dropped out of the Senate race to campaign for his congressional seat. Guy Smith withdrew his paper's support for Jennings's reelection.

All the infighting created an opportunity for Howard Baker Sr. He ran for Congress against Jennings in the Second District Republican primary. Although Jennings had succeeded the well-known J. Will Taylor and served from 1939 until 1949, Baker won almost two to one in the Republican primary. He then went on to win the general election, in a race with divided Republican support, with only 52.4 percent. (Tennessee's Second District is the only district in the United States to have never gone Democrat since the Civil War).

Howard Baker Jr. helped run his father's campaign and organize his Washington office. While in Washington he met Joy Dirksen, a friend of his sister, and the daughter of Illinois U.S. Senator Everett McKinley Dirksen. They were married December 22, 1951, and had a son and a daughter.

Howard Baker Sr. died on January 7, 1964. Howard Jr. opted not to run for his father's seat. Instead, stepmother, Irene Baker, was elected to complete the congressional term. Baker Jr. had his sights on the U.S. Senate and ran as the Republican nominee against Ross Bass in the 1964 election to fill the unexpired term of the late Estes Kefauver. He lost, but in 1966 he ran in the general election against Frank Clement and became the first Republican popularly elected to the U.S. Senate in Tennessee history. He was reelected in 1972 and 1978, serving from January 3, 1967, until January 3, 1985; as minority leader in the Senate from 1977 to 1979; and as majority leader in the Senate from 1980 to 1985. After leaving the Senate, he practiced law in Washington. From 1987 to 1988 he served as chief of staff for President Ronald Reagan, resigning early to be with his wife Joy, who died on April 24, 1993, of cancer. On December 7, 1996 he married former Kansas U.S. Senator Nancy Kassebaum. Baker lives part of the year in Washington, D.C., and part in Huntsville, Tennessee. (Photograph courtesy of SHO)

Both Nixon and Baker carried all the remaining eight congressional districts in Tennessee. Republican Robin Beard was elected to the U.S. Seventh Congressional District seat, formerly held by Democrat Ray Blanton. Republicans now held five of nine congressional seats in Tennessee (First, Second, Third, Seventh, and Ninth Districts). This political reversal in Tennessee had not been seen since Reconstruction. The Republican Party was now at a new pinnacle. It controlled federal and statewide offices in Tennessee. However, the Republicans did not dominate local politics. The Democrats still controlled offices at local levels in Middle and West Tennessee, and were not without some power statewide. Democrat Bob Clement, former Governor Frank Clement's son, was elected to the Public Service Commission, becoming the youngest statewide elected officeholder in Tennessee history.

Republicans Self-Destruct

Tennessee was the first state in the South to actually move Republican. Winfield Dunn, a Republican, was governor of Tennessee. Both of Tennessee's U.S. senators, Bill Brock and Howard Baker, were Republicans. It looked as if the Democratic tidal wave begun under Franklin Roosevelt and empowered by forty years of patronage was about to lose strength. The strong Republican momentum, fueled by the antiliberal mood of the electorate, could only be halted by some powerful turn of events.

Three days after Nixon's inauguration, on January 23, 1972, the president announced "peace with honor" in Vietnam. The treaty was signed on January 27, 1973, in Paris, France. America felt that perhaps the Vietnam nightmare was almost over. However, the subdued joy of ending this relentless war began to be overshadowed by reports and leaked information linking the Committee to Re-elect the President to the Watergate break-in. Congress launched an investigation, chaired by North Carolina Democratic Senator Sam Ervin. Televised Senate hearings began on May 17, 1973. The Watergate break-in was unquestionably illegal. The question was whether or not the White House had anything to do with it. Republicans were forced to go on the defensive.

In the political backlash, Republicans nationally suffered severe credibility damage. Across Tennessee, local Republican political organizations lost their momentum.

Then, in August 1973, newspapers reported that Vice President Agnew was being investigated by the U.S. attorney's office for charges that he had accepted payments from contractors while governor of Maryland. Agnew initially denied the charges, but when former associates were called to testify in September 1973, information began to surface concerning payments made to him from contractors who were bidding to obtain construction contracts with the state of Maryland. Some payments were alleged to have been made even after he became vice president. On October 10, 1973, Agnew suddenly resigned as vice president of the United States. He stated that he was not guilty but that he was resigning to protect the president. He was later convicted and sentenced to three years probation and a ten-thousand-dollar fine.

On October 12, 1973, Nixon appointed Michigan Republican Congressman Gerald R. Ford, the minority party leader of the House of Representatives, as vice president. After House and Senate investigation hearings, Ford was confirmed and sworn in on December 6, 1973.

The battle over Watergate raged on throughout the Agnew fiasco. Continuous newspaper accounts, the televised Senate investigation, and a stalemate between Watergate investigators and the president over access to secret White House tapes, turned the issue into an enormous national media frenzy. On October 20, 1973, the president ordered special Watergate prosecutor Archibald Cox to drop efforts to obtain the White House tapes. When Cox refused, Nixon ordered Attorney General Elliott Richardson to fire Cox. Richardson and his assistant, William D. Ruckelshaus, resigned. Robert H. Bork was appointed acting attorney general, and he fired Cox. These actions, perceived as the president using his office to stall the investigation, caused public opinion to turn fiercely against President Nixon. The economy was slowing down, the Watergate investigation was picking up, and the GOP was beginning to take on a taint of dishonesty.

Leon Jaworski became the new special prosecutor in November 1973, and he continued to apply pressure to obtain the White House tapes. President Nixon claimed executive privilege precluded him from supplying the tapes. Nevertheless, he turned some of them in—but not all. Jaworski was not satisfied and continued to request the remainder of the tapes.

President Nixon came to Memphis to speak at the Republican Governor's Conference. The conference was hosted by Tennessee Governor Winfield Dunn and was held at the Rivermont Hotel on November 18–20, 1973. Ten thousand people, including hundreds of high school and junior high school students, gathered in front of the Rivermont Hotel to attend a rally for President Nixon and show their support. At the governor's conference the beleaguered president announced an eighteen-minute gap in the White House tapes.

Whatever the president did to shore up his image had little impact. The media pounded him by publishing charges of tax evasion, use of campaign funds for personal purposes, and the indictment of former Nixon officials, such as Treasury Secretary John Connally, for bribery. Nixon, in the meantime, was battling Congress over the military process of ending the Vietnam War. Although a cease-fire was in effect, communist troops in Cambodia continued to fight. The president ordered the bombing of these forces, but the Democratic Congress, beginning to "see the necessity to limit a President" (Nixon 1978), voted to halt funding of troops and then passed a law limiting presidential war powers. To make matters worse for Nixon and the nation, another Arab-Israeli war broke out. When the United States sent supplies to aid Israel, Arab nations embargoed oil shipments to the United States, resulting in a gasoline shortage in the winter of 1973–1974.

On March 1, 1974, former Nixon aides H. R. Haldeman, John Mitchell, and John Ehrlichman, were indicted on charges of conspiracy, obstruction of justice, and perjury. The president decided to release edited transcripts of the White House tapes that had been turned over to the special prosecutor, hoping to turn public opinion, but it was too late. On June 6, 1974, the president was named a coconspirator in the cover-up.

The Watergate scandal was different from previous political scandals because personal greed did not play a role. Rather,

Watergate, because it included burglary, wiretapping, and the attempted use of government agencies to harm political opponents, represented an attack on free and open elections. On July 24, 1974, the Supreme Court unanimously ruled eight to zero that the president could not use executive privilege to withhold the White House tapes. On the same day, the House Judiciary Committee began televised public debate on the articles of impeachment of the president. On July 27, 1974, the committee voted twenty-seven to eleven for one article of impeachment for obstructing justice. Six Republicans voted with twenty-one Democrats for the decision. Two other articles, abuse of power and illegally withholding evidence of Congress, were also approved.

Nixon knew that with the House of Representatives controlled by Democrats impeachment was imminent. He relented and released additional transcripts of the tapes. They revealed evidence that Nixon had authorized the Watergate cover-up at least as early as six days after the break in. Nixon immediately lost almost all his remaining support in Congress and Republican leaders advised him of impending impeachment by the House and conviction by the Senate. On August 9, 1974, Richard M. Nixon became the first American president to resign from office. Without admitting guilt, he stated that he did not have the support in Congress necessary to conduct the affairs of the office of president. On the same day, the vice president, Gerald R. Ford, became the thirty-eighth president of the United States.

President Ford's first and immediate duty was to select a vice president. Tennesseans were in the thick of the competition. Senator Howard Baker had hopes of winning the spot. Governor Winfield Dunn and Congressman Jimmy Duncan publicly urged Ford to select Baker. Other Tennessee political leaders such as Seventh District Congressman Robin Beard, Ninth District Congressman Dan Kuykendall, and First District Congressman Jimmy Quillen "privately urged Ford to take the same course" (Annis 1995). However, other states had politicians with strong interest in the nation's second highest office. On August 20, 1974, President Ford selected New York's Nelson Rockefeller. He would now have to go through the process of congressional hearings which would last for the next four months (throughout the elections) until December.

On Sunday, September 8, 1974, President Ford granted former President Nixon a full pardon in order to save him the possibility of criminal indictment, trial, and possible conviction. Richard Nixon dealt with many complex issues during his presidency—Russia, China, the Middle East conflict, the oil embargo, the Vietnam War, taxes, and a slowdown of the economy. Nevertheless, the enormity of the political scandal of Watergate overwhelmed his political achievements and brought down his presidency. After Nixon's pardon, he admitted that he was mistaken in his handling of the affair and that he should have quickly and more forthrightly responded.

Tennessee Republicans had only recently enjoyed gains which had taken a full one hundred years to achieve. Now, because of Agnew, Watergate, and Nixon's resignation and subsequent pardon, their energies were totally monopolized by damage control. Local Republican spokesmen from counties across Tennessee, instead of being on the offensive, were on the defensive. Unfortunately, there was little they could defend. The state Republican Party and its elected leaders holding federal office were damaged, and they prepared for political casualties in the next election. Democrats, once on the run for their liberal policies, antiwar voting, and support of civil rights, no longer had to defend these issues. The Republicans had diverted the nation's attention to the Watergate scandal and the Democrats did not hesitate to make the best of their opportunity. The Republican image was tarnished, and the Democrats attacked.

President Ford was accused of making a deal with Nixon. He maintained that the pardon was an honest attempt to put Watergate behind and heal the nation.

Most Republicans suffered guilt by association. Two *Washington Post* reporters, Bob Woodward and Carl Bernstein, had achieved national prominence through their investigative reporting of Watergate. Their success brought a new surge of power to the print media, and other reporters, inspired by their fame, may have gone beyond the bounds of fairness writing about Republican politicians.

In spite of the press, many Tennessee Republicans felt there was a chance to follow Dunn to the governor's mansion in the 1974 gubernatorial election. They felt that since Tennessee had gone for Nixon in 1972, a Republican trend among voters might overcome the stigma of Watergate in a state election. Dr. Nat Taylor Winston, a descendent of Governors Alf and Robert Taylor, ran for governor in the Republican primary. He was opposed by Dortch Oldham and Lamar Alexander. Oldham was a wealthy businessman and publisher. Alexander was a protégé of Howard Baker's, had managed Dunn's 1970 gubernatorial campaign, and had worked in the Nixon White House. He beat Winston and Oldham in the Republican primary.

Ray Blanton had entered the Democratic primary early. He had statewide name recognition, not only from his terms as congressman, but from having previously run unsuccessfully for the U.S. Senate seat against Senator Howard Baker. David Pack, Stanley Snodgrass, Ross Bass, Jake Butcher, Franklin Haney, Hudley Crockett, and others all sought the Democratic nomination for governor. Blanton won over eleven other candidates with under 25 percent of the vote. He went into the general election, with a strong West Tennessee home base, against East Tennessean Lamar Alexander.

The national scandals deeply impacted the electorate. The name Republican was now tainted, and even though most Americans had recently voted more conservatively, they were scandal-weary and ready to return to the Democrats. Every Republican who ran for office was tarnished and had to answer questions about Agnew, Watergate, and Ford's pardon of Nixon. Of course the reasons for victory or defeat of the candidates were many and not all were related to Watergate, but its impact was profound.

On election day, November 4, 1974, Ray Blanton defeated Lamar Alexander for governor of Tennessee 576,833 votes to 455,467. Alexander carried the First, Second, and Third Congressional Districts. Blanton carried all the rest. Marilyn Lloyd defeated incumbent Republican U.S. Representative Lamar Baker in the Third District. Dan Kuykendall lost his Ninth District seat to Democratic state legislator Harold Ford Sr.—67,715 to 67,141 votes. Ford became the first Black congressman in Tennessee history. The rejection of Republican candidates by the electorate was a nationwide occurrence. Democrats hammered Republicans by gaining forty-nine seats in the U.S. House and four seats in the U.S. Senate

RAY BLANTON was born on April 10, 1930, in Hardin County, Tennessee, to Leonard and Ova Delaney Blanton. He was raised on a farm and received his early education in county schools. After graduating from Shiloh High School, he began working in a grocery store to help defray college costs while he attended the University of Tennessee. While in college he married Betty Littlefield of Adamsville, Tennessee. After graduation from college with a degree in agriculture and chemistry, he taught a year of school in Indiana. Then he returned to Tennessee and joined in the construction business with his brother and father, who was a former mayor of Adamsville. Shortly thereafter, he was elected to the state legislature in 1964 (representing McNairy and Chester Counties).

In 1966 Blanton was elected to the U.S. House of Representatives. He was reelected in 1968 and 1970. In 1972 he ran for the U.S. Senate against Republican Howard Baker (who was the incumbent elected in 1966). Up until this race, Blanton had never lost an election. However, in 1972 Blanton was soundly defeated. He then ran for the governor's seat in 1974 and was elected.

Blanton was inaugurated in January 1975. His adminstration worked to revise the state's excise and franchise tax laws. It oversaw revision of the Hall Income Tax to provide relief to citizens over sixty-five years of age, the Restitution Centers Act, and the creation of the Department of Tourism. His administration was tainted by a scandal involving the parole of prisoners in return for payoffs. Although some former members of his administration feel that Blanton was not directly responsible for the activities which led to the charges, he was convicted on two of eleven counts of indictments and imprisoned for two and one-half years. Later he ran for other offices but was defeated. He unsuccessfully attempted to have his conviction overturned. After leaving public life Blanton worked at various jobs until his death in 1996. He was a Methodist, and a member of the Shriners and the Lions Club. He was on the Board of Development of Lambuth College. (Photograph courtesy of TSLA)

(House—Democrats 291 to Republicans 144; Senate—Democrats 60 to Republicans 37 to Independents 2).

During Winfield Dunn's four-year term, he had given additional hope to Tennessee Republicans. He was well liked among the rank-and-file party members as well as among many Democrats, and appeared to have additional political potential. However, toward the end of his tenure, in 1974, he vetoed a bill intended to establish a medical school at East Tennessee State University in Johnson City. First District Republican U.S. Representative Jimmy Quillen was not happy with the opposition to the school. Quillen was an undisputed political leader of the area, and candidates needed his support in order to win statewide office. Without East Tennessee's First and Second Congressional Districts solidly behind a candidate, the margins would be much too weak for any Republican to win a statewide election. Dunn's political relationship with Quillen was damaged.

Governor Rockefeller's confirmation hearings lasted four months. On December 19, 1974, Nelson A. Rockefeller, four-time governor of the state of New York (1958–1973), was sworn in as the forty-first vice president of the United States.

During 1975, on two separate occasions, assassinations were attempted on President Ford. In both instances, a woman was the assailant. The president was undaunted by the attempts on his life or his drop in the polls. In 1975 opinion polls showed he trailed former California Governor Ronald Reagan as the preferred 1976 Republican presidential candidate.

For the Democrats, the relatively unknown former governor of Georgia, Jimmy Carter, emerged as the front-runner for the Democratic nomination for president. By the time of the July 1975 Democratic National Convention in New York City, Carter had the nomination locked up on the first ballot. He received 2,238.5 votes. The other candidates split the 1,100 remaining votes. Senator Walter Mondale of Minnesota was the vice presidential nominee.

During 1976, President Ford ran a close presidential primary race with former California Governor Ronald Reagan. Although Howard Baker had lost out to Ford in Nixon's selection of a replacement vice president and to Rockefeller as Ford's selection of a vice president, he served as Ford's honorary chairman of the campaign in Tennessee. Congressmen Beard and Quillen and former Governor Dunn ran as delegates for Ford. In the Tennessee Republican presidential preference primary, Ford carried the state by a narrow 2,170 votes over Ronald Reagan. However, of the forty-three total delegate allotment, twenty-two went to Reagan due to district apportionment. By the August 1976 Republican National Convention in Kansas City, the suspense in the delegate battle between Ford and Reagan was high. The president narrowly won the nomination on the first ballot 1,187 to 1,070 votes, and attention quickly turned to the selection of the vice presidential nominee.

Again, Howard Baker wanted the vice presidential slot. While the Tennessee delegation to the Republican convention worked delegates for support of their favorite son, Baker quietly pursued it in a nonpublic way. He was interviewed by the Ford team, and gave a keynote speech at the convention, further increasing his visibility and acceptance as a party leader. Although he began the vice presidential selection process with broad support, his role in the Watergate hearings hurt him among some Republicans. He also had earned the opposition of Mississippi Republicans who remembered that he and Bill Brock had blocked the nomination of Mississippian William Hooper to the Tennessee Valley Authority Board of Directors. Regardless of the opposition, the Tennessee delegation stood by him and worked for his nomination.

Senator Bob Dole also wanted the vice presidential nomination. He was well liked by many Republican leaders and enjoyed substantial support. He was acceptable to Northeasterners and, as a Kansan, could possibly help Ford pacify farmers from the Great Plains states who were perturbed over the 1975 Soviet grain embargo. In addition, Dole had helped persuade three representatives who were close to him to support Ford for Republican House leader in 1965. Ford's loyalty to Dole, combined with Dole's general acceptance, sealed the deal. Kansas Senator Robert J. Dole was selected by Ford and nominated for vice president.

When Baker lost the nod for the nomination, the Tennessee delegation at the Republican National Convention held a large delegate/alternate meeting. It was an emotional event. The entire delegation felt let down. Baker had enjoyed a strong and united support by his Tennessee friends, and they had held great hope and enthusiasm for his nomination.

Tennessee geared up for a Senate race as well as a presidential race. Under ordinary circumstances, an incumbent U.S. senator would hold an advantage for reelection. However, in 1976, the electorate was poised to reject Republicans, especially in Democratic states like Tennessee. Remembering Watergate and the ultraconservative rhetoric of the Goldwater campaign, many voters were inclined to vote Democrat. Jimmy Carter, who was Southern and Baptist, appealed to both conservative and moderate Southerners as well as his Democratic party base.

Jim Sasser entered the Democratic primary for the nomination in the U.S. Senate race. He was relatively unknown to the voting public, although he had served as state Democratic Party chairman. He lacked money and support when he opposed John J. Hooker and several others in the primary, yet he won the primary with 44 percent of the vote. After his victory, Democrats coalesced behind him and Sasser was now positioned to take advantage of the public's desire for a clean sweep. Sasser ran last-minute campaign ads questioning the fact that Brock, although financially well-off, had legally paid very little federal income tax in 1975. Additionally, questions arose about Brock taking an illegal campaign contribution from the Gulf Oil Company. Although he denied this allegation, he repaid the company in hopes of settling the matter. These charges combined with Jimmy Carter's pull on the average Tennessee voter, leveled the playing field for the incumbent senator and his challenger.

The election of 1976 turned into a voter revolt. U.S. Senator Bill Brock lost his seat (Class 1) to James R. Sasser. (Sasser was sworn into office on January 3, 1977, and served until January 2, 1995.)

Although the results of the Tennessee senate race were clear-cut, the results of the presidential contest were too close to call. On election night, no one could predict the winner. The next day Carter emerged victorious, with 40,825,839 popular votes to 39,147,770 for Ford and 680,390 for Eugene J. McCarthy (297 to 240 electoral votes). Considered a Washington outsider, his open and earnest manner proved irresistible to a scandal-weary but hopeful electorate.

Whether Howard Baker as a running mate could have helped Ford over the narrow margin to victory is pure speculation. Carter won a great deal of the conservative vote, which Baker may or may not have affected. In Tennessee, Baker's home state, Ford managed only 43 percent of the vote. Carter won ten Southern states, though not by significant margins except for Georgia and Arkansas.

The 1976 elections brought restoration for former U.S. Senator Al Gore, who saw the man who had defeated him in 1970 be defeated by Jim Sasser. A more positive and personal delight for the former senator was seeing his son, Albert Gore Jr., move onto the political scene. Congressman Joe L. Evins, who had served in Congress for thirty years, retired in 1976. Gore Jr. ran for the Fourth District seat and won the Democratic primary and the general election.

Overall, Democrats slightly increased their numbers in the U.S. House (Democrats 292 to Republicans 143) and U.S. Senate (Democrats 61 to Republicans 38 to Independents 1), and again controlled the White House, the U.S. Senate and the U.S. House. In Tennessee,

JAMES RALPH SASSER was born September 30, 1936, in Memphis, Shelby County, Tennessee, to Joseph Ralph and Mary Nell Sasser. He obtained his early education in Nashville public schools. In 1954 he began college at the University of Tennessee, stayed for a year, then transferred to Vanderbilt University, graduating in 1958. He attended Vanderbilt University School of Law, graduated in 1961, and was admitted to the bar and began practice in Nashville the same year. In 1962 he married the former Mary Gorman of Louisville, Kentucky, and they had two children, Elizabeth and James. He served in the reserves of the U.S. Marines from 1957 until 1963. In 1976 Sasser ran as a Democrat for the U.S. Senate. He had been serving as chairman of the Tennessee Democratic Party and was little known outside Democratic circles. His campaign benefitted from the anger of an electorate disappointed over the Watergate scandal. Sasser won the general election defeating U.S. Senator Bill Brock. Twice reelected, in 1982 and 1988, he served in the U.S. Senate from January 3, 1977, until January 3, 1995. While in the Senate he served as chairman of the Budget Committee. In 1994 he was defeated for reelection by Republican Bill Frist. Sasser then became a fellow at the John F. Kennedy School of Government at Harvard University in 1995. President Bill Clinton appointed Sasser as ambassador to the People's Republic of China on September 22, 1996. He was confirmed by the U.S. Senate on December 14, 1996, and served until June 30, 1999. (Photograph courtesy of SHO)

Democrat Ray Blanton was in the governor's seat and Jim Sasser was a senator. The turnover was not limited to federal offices. The tide of 1976 brought down six Republican members of the Tennessee state legislature. With the Democrats in total control, they could exert their will without any threat of a Republican stalemate. Democrats, once temporarily in decline, were now politically omnipotent. With the advantage of total control, however, comes the disadvantage of instant blame for any mishandling of the issues.

The remaining statewide Republican officeholder in Tennessee, Senator Howard Baker, now capitalized on his opportunities in Washington. Even though the U.S. Senate was made up of a strong Democratic majority, the minority party still had to have a senate leader. Baker, having twice before lost the leadership bid, contemplated his chances, fearing a third loss would injure future presidential chances. He could run for governor of Tennessee in 1978 and from there prepare to run for president. He had defeated Governor Blanton in his Senate reelection in 1972 and felt confident that he could defeat him in a gubernatorial matchup, especially since Blanton's administration was now under investigation. However, without a Republican president or a Republican majority in the House and Senate, a tremendous opportunity existed to become "the" Republican spokesman as U.S. Senate minority leader. Thirty-eight Republican Senators would elect their leader. Baker and the Senate minority leader under President Ford, Robert Griffin, squared off in the contest. If Ford had been reelected, Griffin would be a shoo-in, but now the contest hinged on the vote of the

ALBERT ARNOLD GORE JR. was born to Albert Sr. and Pauline Gore on March 31, 1948, in Washington, D.C., while his father served Tennessee as a Democrat in the U.S. House of Representatives. Al Gore Jr. went to elementary school in Carthage, Smith County, Tennessee. He graduated from St. Albans High School in Washington, D.C., in 1965, and then from Harvard University in 1969. He subsequently volunteered for the U.S. Army serving from 1969 until 1971, and was assigned to the press corps in Vietnam. Following his army discharge, he became an investigative reporter for the *Nashville Tennessean* from 1971 until 1976. He also enrolled in Vanderbilt Univeristy's School of Religion in Nashville in 1971 until 1972, and then in Vanderbilt's School of Law from 1974 through 1976.

Gore married Mary Elizabeth "Tipper" Aitcheson, whom he met at St. Albans. They have four children—Karenna, Kristen, Sarah, and Albert III.

In 1976 Gore jumped into a crowded field for retiring Joe L. Evin's Fourth District congressional seat (later reconfigured the Sixth District) and emerged with the Democratic nomination. He won the general election and was reelected for three more terms, serving from January 3, 1977, until January 3, 1985. In 1984 he ran successfully for the U.S. Senate seat vacated by retiring Senator Howard Baker Jr., but was unsuccessful in his bid for the 1988 Democratic presidential nomination. He was reelected to the Senate in 1990 and served from January 3, 1985, until he resigned to become vice president of the United States on January 2, 1993, under President Bill Clinton. Vice President Gore was reelected in 1996. He is currently campaigning for nomination as the presidential Democratic candidate for election year 2000. (Photograph courtesy of SHO)

eight newcomers to the Republican Senate. Baker walked into the January 4, 1977, Republican Senate caucus promised only seventeen votes. However, when the votes were counted Baker had eighteen and Griffin seventeen. In 1966, Tennessee Republicans' only hold on political survival was Howard Baker's Senate position. Their inspiration now was his stature as Senate minority leader.

During 1977, the first year of Jimmy Carter's term as president, another potential scandal surfaced, but this time it was within the Democratic Party. Bert Lance was selected by Carter to head the Office of Management and Budget. Lance, a banker, had been a close aide to Carter when he was governor of Georgia and had himself once run for governor, unsuccessfully. The national spotlight, fresh off Watergate, searched and found evidence of illegal activities concerning a $3.4 million loan Lance received to buy bank stock. As the investigation continued, Illinois U.S. Senator Charles Percy and Connecticut U.S. Senator Abraham Ribicoff, leaders of the committee conducting the investigation, told President Carter that there was evidence of wrongdoing and that Lance should resign. Chicago newspapers then revealed that White House press secretary Jody Powell had tried to get them to carry stories smearing Senator Percy to punish him for the investigation. An embarrassed president accepted Lance's resignation on September 21, 1977.

President Carter worked for and signed a treaty on September 7, 1977, which turned over control of the Panama Canal to Panama in 1999. Some Americans resented giving up the canal, which was built and controlled by the United States since the presidency of Teddy Roosevelt. The unpopular political move would become part of a trend of negative public perception problems for the president.

In 1977, Governor Blanton proposed a state income tax in order to pay for state programs. The legislature knew that the people of Tennessee would revolt if the income tax was created. Instead, the sales tax was increased. Blanton traveled extensively, including overseas, to recruit foreign investment. He emphasized economic development and international trade and emphasized equality for women and minorities. His administration created the Department of Tourism, the first in the nation, and changed the state constitution in 1978 to allow a governor to succeed himself for a second term.

President Carter, who had been an honest and forthright governor, was not used to the maneuvers and stroking processes of Washington. Since he had competed for the Democratic presidential nomination against several congressional members, and his assistance had not been required for the election or reelection of many Democratic congressmen, he commanded little allegiance and was somewhat disregarded by them. The relationship between the president and Congress deteriorated to an embarrassing level of uncooperativeness.

The national economy faltered. Carter first proposed income tax cuts for low-income families, then another income tax cut for those in middle income brackets. A plan was passed in November 1978, but it was too late. Inflation was running double digit, and the tax cuts were of little help to households who were pushed into higher tax brackets by inflation.

President Carter adopted a strong human rights' campaign directed toward other nations. But some nations, including the Soviet Union, viewed this program as a campaign to discredit them, and resented the criticism. His mediation in the Middle East peace process was more successful. Carter worked closely with Egyptian President Anwar el-Sadat and Israeli Prime Minister Menachem Begin, and in March 1979, the Camp David Peace Accords were signed. From this breakthrough achievement, the president gained general approval for his negotiating ability.

Although 1978 found Howard Baker solidly positioned as the Senate Republican leader, it was also an election year and nothing was a certainty for a Republican in Tennessee, particularly after Watergate. Only two years had passed since the people put the Democrats back in office. By May 17, Baker was ready to announce his reelection campaign. Carter's presidency was supplying the target for Baker to direct his campaign attacks. In addition to an anti-Carter, anti-Democratic national feeling, at home in Tennessee the electorate was turning against the Democrats. Governor Ray Blanton's administration was surrounded by charges of corruption involving briberies for criminal pardons and paroles. Blanton did not run for reelection.

In the 1978 Democratic primary for governor, six candidates entered the race. The two strongest, Knoxville banker Jake Butcher and Public Service Commissioner Bob Clement, soon took the lead. Butcher spent two million dollars on the race and gained 41 percent of the vote, while Clement received 37 percent, and Nashville Mayor Richard Fulton received 16 percent.

In the Democratic U.S. Senate primary, Nashvillian and Democratic activist Jane Eskind defeated four other candidates, including state Senator Bill Bruce of

Memphis and former chairman of the 1978 state constitutional convention, J. D. Lee of Madisonville, to earn the right to oppose Senator Howard Baker. She was the first Tennessee woman to win nomination for a statewide office.

In 1978, Baker protégé Lamar Alexander, who lost the governor's race to Ray Blanton in 1974, ran again for the Republican nomination for governor. He defeated five other Republicans and took the nomination with 86 percent of the vote. Alexander was now set to oppose Democrat Jake Butcher in the general election. Baker had considered running for governor but opted for the Senate Republican leadership in hopes of setting up a 1980 presidential bid. Baker won the 1978 Republican primary handily. Harvey Howard was the best of the challengers, but he managed only 8.8 percent of the vote. Baker now faced Democrat Eskind in November.

Eskind could not defeat the incumbent Republican. Howard Baker was reelected to the U.S. Senate in 1978 with 645,771 votes to Eskind's 464,756. Baker received 55.5 percent of the vote, Independent Tom Anderson won 4.4 percent, and Eskind the remainder.

Thirty-eight-year-old Lamar Alexander ran an ambitious campaign for governor in which he staged a 1,022- mile walk across Tennessee. His trademark red-checked flannel shirt, his well-run and supported campaign, and widespread anti-Blanton sentiment carried him well. Alexander was elected governor over Jake Butcher, with 665,847 (56 percent) votes to 523,013 for Butcher. Alexander won in spite of the three million dollars spent by Butcher on

LAMAR ALEXANDER was born in Blount County, Tennessee, on July 3, 1940. His parents were Flo and Andrew Alexander, both teachers; his father was also a principal. Alexander attended public schools and graduated from Maryville High School in 1958. He attended Vanderbilt University, then received his law degree from New York University in 1965. Alexander returned to Tennessee and began practicing law in Knoxville. Soon he became a clerk in the court of Fifth Circuit Court of Appeals under Judge John Minor Wisdom. By 1966 he worked as an aide to Howard Baker during his election to the U.S. Senate, then became Baker's legislative assistant. In 1969 he became executive assistant to President Nixon's congressional relations advisor, Bryce Harlow. On January 4, 1969, he married a former aide to U.S. Senator John Tower, Leslee Kathryn "Honey" Buhler. They eventually had four children—Drew, Will, Kathryn, and Leslee. In 1970 he returned to Tennessee to run the gubernatorial campaign of Republican Winfield Dunn, who was elected.

After the campaign Alexander returned to the practice of law until he ran for governor of Tennessee in 1974 at the age of thirty-four. He won the Republican primary against several other opponents but lost to Democrat Ray Blanton. He then went to work, in 1977, for U.S. Senator and Republican minority leader Howard Baker as special counsel. In 1978, Alexander ran again for governor of Tennessee. He easily won the Republican primary, defeated Democrat Jake Butcher in the general election, and was inaugurated on January 18, 1979. During his tenure, state employees received a 7 percent pay raise. The legal drinking age was raised from the campaign. Alexander and Baker took all congressional districts in Tennessee except the Ninth, where new political kingpin, Congressman Harold Ford, oversaw a strong Black voter coalition.

Tennessee Democrats, who had held power since Reconstruction, temporarily lost it in 1970, and regained it almost totally in 1976, now had their confidence shaken again. Republicans, meanwhile, basked in the glory of a return to some state power. They held two of the state's top three seats and, ever confident, began to promote Senator Baker in a presidential bid. Bill Brock, who had recently been defeated for reelection to his U.S. Senate seat, became chairman of the Republican National Committee.

On January 15, 1979, six days before Governor-Elect Lamar Alexander was to take office, Governor Blanton released fifty-two prisoners, twenty of whom had been imprisoned for murder. State law provided that the governor-elect could take office anytime after midnight January 15, 1979. Governor-elect Alexander, at the urging of the FBI and with the agreement of Tennessee's Lieutenant Governor John Wilder and Speaker of the House Ned Ray McWherter, immediately moved to take office and two days later was sworn in. Blanton was later convicted, though not for receiving payments for pardons, and served time for conspiracy, mail fraud, and extortion for selling liquor licenses.

While Tennesseans had been occupied with state elections, an international incident was brewing which would initiate significant political ramifications for both

---

eighteen to nineteen, and the legislature approved the state sales tax for another year at 4.5 percent.

In 1982 Alexander ran for reelection, defeating mayor of Knoxville, Democrat Randy Tyree. He was the first governor to serve two consecutive four-year terms. During his second term, he pushed for school teacher salary increases, more funding for supplies for students, and the addition of computer equipment for students. The additional cost to support his school program required more funding, and a 7.75 percent state sales tax was passed. With this increase, Tennessee had the highest sales tax in the nation. (Tennessee had no state income tax). As governor, Alexander developed a Better Schools program which rewarded teachers through a merit system and provided incentive pay increases. During his tenure, the state maintained its financial integrity but the budget deficit doubled from $80 million to $150 million. Alexander served as chairman of the National Governor's Association in 1985 and 1986.

Nineteen eighty-six was his last full year in office. He considered opposing Senator Jim Sasser in his 1988 campaign for reelection or vying for the vice presidential spot on the ticket with George Bush. However, neither proved to be viable options. On July 1, 1988, he was appointed president of the University of Tennessee, stirring criticism from educators since he had no academic credentials or experience in education. He served in that capacity until appointed secretary of education under President Bush in 1989.

After President Bush was defeated for reelection by Democrat Bill Clinton in 1992, Alexander's tenure as secretary of education ended. He ran in the Republican presidential primary of 1996 but soon trailed other candidates and was forced to drop out of the race. Alexander and his wife live in Nashville. (Photograph courtesy of TSLA) parties. The shah of Iran, Mohammed Reza Pahlavi, aligned himself with the United States, buying arms from and selling oil to the U.S. government. As a dictator, however, his human-rights record was abysmal, much to the consternation of President Carter. In February 1979, the Iranian people, under the leadership of the Islamic leader, Ayatollah Khomeini, overthrew the government of the Shah. In October Carter allowed the Shah to enter the United States for medical treatment. In response Iranian militants took over the American embassy in Teheran, seized over seventy embassy employees, and held them as hostages, threatening to execute them unless the Shah was returned to Iran.

In December 1979 the Soviet Union invaded Afghanistan. This action plunged Soviet-American relations to its lowest level in years, and caused the United States and other nations, at Carter's urging, to boycott the 1980 Summer Olympics in Moscow.

President Carter worked to improve relations with Cuba. Between March and September 1980, he allowed over one hundred thousand Cuban refugees to emigrate to America. When it became apparent that many of those released from Cuba were criminals, the president's administration faced another national embarrassment. Many of the refugees were held at detention centers, where they rioted, which only worsened the publicity.

But the hostage crisis in Iran was the biggest issue of the day. The Iranians held fast to their prisoners, stirring Muslims throughout the world, and showing how a small nation could embarrass the most powerful nation on earth. Carter decided to resolve the situation by taking bold action. He authorized a secret military rescue. During the maneuver, the plan had to be aborted. When the force changed course, a helicopter and a transport plane collided, killing eight men and injuring others. On April 25, 1980, the president informed the nation. Secretary of State Cyrus R. Vance, who had opposed the ill-fated mission, resigned.

While international issues continued to plague Carter's presidency, the time neared for another presidential election. In the Democratic presidential primaries, Massachusetts Senator Edward Kennedy challenged Carter. Most conservative and moderate Democrats continued to give their support to Carter, until the failed April rescue attempt of the American hostages in Iran. After the military failure, Kennedy won primaries in states with large numbers of delegates. However, at the August 1980 New York Democratic National Convention many leading Democrats tried to convince Carter to withdraw. He refused. Kennedy attempted to obtain an open convention in order to free up delegates. This failed 1,936 to 1,390 votes. Carter had enough delegates to gain renomination on the first ballot by 2,123 votes to 1,150 votes for Kennedy. Walter Mondale was renominated as vice president.

During the Republican presidential primaries Ronald Reagan, George Bush, Robert Dole, John Anderson, Phil Crane, John Connally, Howard Baker, and others competed. At the first major stop on the primary trail, George Bush stunned the Reagan campaign by winning Iowa. However, Reagan won in New Hampshire, and from there on took the lead.

After New Hampshire, Massachusetts, and Vermont, Howard Baker's presidential aspirations faltered. Trailing in fourth place behind Bush, Reagan, and Anderson and one million dollars in campaign debt, he dropped his presidential bid. Meanwhile, Reagan kept gaining ground.

By the time the July 1980 Republican National Convention in Detroit convened, the nomination for Reagan was only a formality. He won the nomination with 1,939 votes, while only 55 votes were allotted for other candidates. The only real question of the convention was who would be the vice presidential nominee. Reagan, the outsider, needed an old-guard Republican to solidify the party. Howard Baker, George Bush, and former President Gerald Ford were all considered. Reagan held talks with Ford, but his choice as the Republican vice presidential nominee was George Bush.

U.S. Representative John B. Anderson of Illinois ran as an independent candidate, with former Governor Patrick J. Lucey of Wisconsin as his running mate. During the campaign Carter attempted to paint Reagan as a radical. Reagan was calm, polite, and focused on the issues throughout the campaign. He simply asked the voters if they were better off than they were in 1976 and referred to the weak economy, high interest rates, high inflation, weakened defense, and global aggression of communist countries, while pointing out who was in charge.

Just two days prior to the U.S. presidential election, Khomeini announced his rather harsh terms for Iran's release of the American hostages. President Carter stood only to suffer from the announcement of the terms so close to the election.

The polls showed that the election was too close to call. Ronald Reagan continued to point out that America, with all the disasters, fiascoes, and failures was "losing faith in itself" (Reagan 1990) and wanted a change in direction. The media continued to downplay the mood of the electorate. When the votes were counted, the media and the polls would be shown to be off the mark with both their prediction and their reading of the polls. On November 4, 1980, Reagan received 43,898,770 popular votes to 35,480,948 for Carter and 5,719,222 for Independent John Anderson (489 to 49 electoral votes).

The national vote swing also affected the Senate. With Ronald Reagan's victory came a Republican majority. Senate Minority Leader Howard Baker now had the opportunity to become majority leader. Baker quickly made congratulatory calls to his victorious peers and newly elected Republican Senators, seeking assurances of support for his position as leader. Dan Quayle, James Abdnor, and Charles Grassley were some of the recent victors who were eager to help Baker. In short order the Senate caucus confirmed Baker as Republican Senate majority leader.

On January 20, 1981, the day President Carter left office and Ronald Reagan was sworn in as president, Khomeini released the hostages. Reagan appointed the former president as envoy to receive the fifty-two American hostages when they landed in West Germany.

On the home front in Tennessee, Democrats still controlled the state house and senate and the congressional delegation by a six to three margin. The U.S. Senate was split between Republican Howard Baker and Democrat Jim Sasser. Although Republicans held the presidency and the governor's mansion, the Democratic legislature still had a strong hold on power. The governor could do little within Tennessee without the cooperation of the Democrats.

Governor Alexander worked with Democrat state senate leader Lieutenant Governor John Wilder and state Speaker of the House Ned Ray McWherter for mutual cooperation. He carefully positioned himself for the next gubernatorial election, working for some of the issues which would win support from voters who did not traditionally support Republicans. During his early tenure, state employees received a pay raise and the state sales tax was raised. The legal drinking age was raised from eighteen to nineteen. During 1981, there were no gubernatorial or U.S. Senate elections to cloud a relatively calm political year. Howard Baker, as Senate majority leader, was the official dispenser of President Reagan's patronage and the Republican leader of his home state. He and Alexander totally dominated and controlled the Republican political scene, including the state Republican Party.

In 1982, the governor's seat and a U.S. Senate seat were up for grabs again in Tennessee. Alexander, who was now forty-two, fully intended to run for reelection and had directed his political strategy of the past four years to that end. With his distant goal set on the presidency, he had to remain visible and hold high office. Reelection as governor was the surest route. The Senate was a possibility, but Sasser was by now well entrenched and would be difficult to unseat.

Howard Baker, U.S. Senator and White House Chief of Staff for President Reagan. (Courtesy of Baker, Donelson, Bearman and Caldwell Law Offices, Huntsville, Tennessee)

Robin Beard, the Republican Seventh District U.S. representative, decided to run for U.S. Senate against Democrat Jim Sasser. Although Beard and some of his advisors felt Sasser's support was weak, many of his friends advised him against this move, not sensing any public mood in Tennessee against the Democrats or Senator Sasser. When word got out that Congressman Beard was going to announce for the Senate, political hopefuls began to buzz over the opportunity to take his spot. Former campaign aide to Howard Baker, Don Sundquist decided to run for Beard's seat. Governor Alexander did not feel that Sundquist was strong enough to win the spot and sent an aide to Memphis to look for another candidate. Alexander wanted State Republican Party Chairman Tom Beasley to run against Sundquist, but by the time of the Republican primary, Sundquist was unopposed. However, the Democrats began to line up for the seat as well. Although the Seventh District had previously elected Republican Beard, the district was by no means a Republican stronghold, and, in fact, Democrats had dominated the spot for decades. Ultimately, Sundquist's opponent would be Bob Clement, the son of the late Democratic governor, Frank Clement. Bob Clement had been elected to the State Public Service Commission in 1972, but had resigned to run in an unsuccessful bid for governor against Jake Butcher in the Democratic primary of 1978. Clement, who was well-known and supported, was heavily favored to win the congressional seat.

Also in 1982, the twenty-six-year-old daughter of Senator Howard Baker, Cissy Baker, ran for Congress in a newly configured congressional district created by the census of 1980—the Fourth District. Albert Gore Jr. was first elected, in 1976, to the Fourth District seat. In 1982, the congressional redistricting moved Gore to the Sixth District. This Fourth District spanned from the southwest tip of Virginia to the Alabama border, was four hundred miles long, and included twenty-three counties. Baker was opposed by Marianna Frost in the Republican primary. Frost attacked Baker for supporting abortion, the Equal Rights Amendment, and lesbian rights at the 1977 National Women's Conference. Baker defeated Frost in the Republican primary and now faced Jim Cooper, son of former Governor Prentice Cooper, in the November general election.

The electorate did not want to make any significant changes in 1982. Knoxville Mayor Democrat Randy Tyree opposed Alexander in the gubernatorial general election and tried to make the state budget deficit an issue. He also tried to tie Alexander to Reagan's supply-side economic plan, and the high unemployment rate. However, the electorate felt that the positives of Reagan outweighed the negatives and that many of Reagan's negatives were residual from the Carter administration. Tyree could not muster the necessary support, even in Democratic ranks, against a governor who had gained many Democratic allies. Alexander was reelected governor with 737,963 votes to 500,937 for Randy Tyree. He would now become the first governor to serve two consecutive four-year terms.

Jim Sasser was reelected by defeating U.S. Representative Robin Beard. This ended the political career of the veteran congressman, but opened the career of another. Don Sundquist's run for the Seventh Congressional seat against Bob Clement was a close race, but one with long-range implications. Sundquist narrowly won by less than one vote per precinct, 1,450 votes.

Republican Fourth Congressional District candidate Cissy Baker had the backing of her father, Governor Alexander, and current State Republican Party Chairman Charles Overby. Jim Cooper, a Harvard-educated Nashville attorney, was determined to win the seat and "willing to mortgage his family's farm to make his campaign competitive" (Annis 1995). The Fourth District, essentially rural, held no community with a population over twenty thousand. The rural voters did not feel the enthusiasm for the daughter that they had for the father. Jim Cooper defeated Cissy Baker and won the right to represent the Fourth District. The Republicans held on to their First, Second, and Seventh District U.S. Representative seats, and the Democrats maintained control of the Tennessee congressional delegation by holding seats in the Third, Fourth, Fifth, Sixth, Eighth, and Ninth Districts.

Nineteen eighty-three was quiet politically. No statewide offices were in contest. Republican Alexander was governor. The Senate seats were occupied by Democrat Sasser and Republican Baker, while the U.S. congressional representation from Tennessee and the state house and state senate remained solidly Democrat. The only political skirmishes were local or within political party organizations, as grassroots party supporters jockeyed for positions which would make them likely patronage recipients should their party win the presidency in 1984.

The lull in activity would not last for long. Party activists throughout Tennessee began to prepare themselves to win positions for the upcoming national presidential conventions. As spring turned to summer, the 1984 national convention committees made preparations to meet. The Republican National Convention, with Tennessee Senator Howard Baker as temporary chairman, took place in Dallas, Texas. President Reagan received the Republican Party nomination and George Bush was renominated as the vice presidential contender.

The Democratic National Convention was held in San Francisco. Former Vice President Walter Mondale received the Democratic nomination to run for president. U.S. Representative Geraldine Ferraro of New York was selected as the vice presidential nominee.

The campaign soon became heated. Mondale aggressively attacked Reagan, campaigning on improving efficiency in government and solving an alleged economic crisis. Reagan campaigned on continuing the economic expansion begun during his first term. By the time of the campaign unemployment was down, interest rates were down 4.6 percent, inflation was down, and the Reagan adminstration had demonstrated leadership in world affairs. Mondale's campaign team tried to make Reagan's age an issue. During the presidential debates, a member of the media asked the seventy-three-year-old president if he could hold up under the rigors of the presidency. Reagan replied that he would not only hold up but that he would not stoop to making age an issue by exploiting the youth and inexperience of his opponent.

In 1984 Howard Baker did not run for reelection to the U.S. Senate, surprising state Republicans, many of whom viewed Baker as the one individual who could keep Republicans in the winners' column. Baker had in fact built a strong enduring political network and showed that Republicans could win in Tennessee and break the omnipotent Democratic hold on statewide elective office. Many Republicans felt that he was risking giving the seat back to the Democrats, and their concerns were well justified.

A host of individuals dreamed of taking the U.S. Senate seat, including Albert Gore Jr., the son of former U.S. Senator Albert Gore Sr. Gore, a Democrat, wasted little time entering the race. Republican contenders included Memphian Ed McEteer, a well-known Republican activist for conservative religious causes, and Victor Ashe, mayor of Knoxville. After McEteer realized that the Republican Party apparatus favored Ashe, he ran as an Independent.

During the fall elections of 1984, the voters did not feel any great need to change presidents. President Reagan was extremely popular and the voters gave him 59 percent of the ballots and forty-nine of fifty states' electoral votes in the November 1984 election.

In Tennessee, the voters returned to their traditional Democratic base. Albert Gore Jr. won the Senate seat. The U.S. Representative seats remained unchanged with the Democrats holding the majority. Republicans Jimmy Quillen, John Duncan, and Don Sundquist won reelection to the First, Second, and Seventh Districts, respectively. The Democrats were reelected to their district seats: Marilyn Lloyd, Third; Jim Cooper, Fourth; Bill Boner, Fifth; Ed Jones, Eighth; and Harold Ford, Ninth. Bart Gordon was elected to the Sixth District seat. The Tennessee congressional delegation remained six Democrats to three Republicans. Republican Lamar Alexander was in the midst of his second term as governor and did not have to stand for election in 1984. Now Republicans held only the governership as a statewide office, while both U.S. Senate seats were in the Democratic column.

January 1985 marked the beginning of the return of Tennessee Democrats to political dominance. As Albert Gore Jr. was sworn in as Tennessee's second Democratic U.S. senator, his fellow Democrats began preparations to take back the governorship. Governor Alexander was now on the downside of his second term and could not run for reelection. As 1985 passed into 1986 several Democrats began to test the gubernatorial waters.

The Republicans had learned by the elections of Winfield Dunn and Lamar Alexander that the voters of Tennessee were receptive to having a Republican governor, but in truth, this had only cccurred during periods of Democratic disorganization, scandals, or intraparty bickering. Party activists sought someone who would be a popular choice in 1986—someone who might have support across party lines. Former Governor Dunn felt the call to return to office. After his term ended in 1975, he could not constitutionally succeed himself. The law was amended under Blanton in 1978 to allow a sitting governor to serve two consecutive terms. This change was followed by the two Alexander terms, from 1979 until the present election. Dunn and his supporters felt that since he had been the one to break the fifty-year Democratic grip on the governor's seat, he still possessed enough popularity to win again. Within Republican inner circles, he was the virtual choice for the Republican nomination for governor, but he faced an imposing obstacle in the general election.

During Dunn's tenure as governor, he had opposed the creation of the medical school in Johnson City. It was destined to be Tennessee's fourth medical school—the other three existing schools were the University of Tennessee-Memphis, Vanderbilt University, and Meharry. The existing schools had the capability of increasing class size and graduating more students. Dunn viewed another school as a duplication of educational services and more costs for the state. However, in 1974 state legislators passed legislation which would establish the medical school in East Tennessee. Governor Dunn vetoed the legislation, but the school's proponents would not give up. Memphis Mayor Henry Loeb went to the state capitol to convince legislators that the school was not needed. Both he and Dunn tried to persuade the speaker of the house, Ned Ray McWherter, to halt efforts to establish the school. The legislature overrode the governor's veto, and the school was approved. Dunn's opposition won him the enmity of Republican U.S. Representative Jimmy Quillen, for whom the school was eventually named.

Quillen, the founder and publisher of the *Johnson City Times,* had first began his public service to Tennessee as a representative in the state house in 1954. From 1959 to 1960 he served as minority leader. In 1962 he won his first election as U.S. representative of the First Congressional District. Eventually, Quillen would serve seventeen terms, until 1997, and hold the Tennessee record for the longest continuous service in the U.S. House of Representatives. The big question of the 1986 Tennessee elections was whether or not Quillen's bitterness against Dunn remained. East Tennessee support was generally led by Quillen and his ally, James Duncan. John James Duncan Sr. served as mayor of Knoxville from 1959 until 1965 and as Second District U.S. Representative since 1965. The support of both Duncan and Quillen was a political requirement for Dunn. No Republican could win a statewide race without this East Tennessee support.

By August Dunn received the Republican nomination, easily defeating challengers Hubert Patty and Charles Vick—222,458 votes to 7,660 and 5,954 respectively. Dunn was a popular choice for the Republicans, but party unity was not as good as it was in 1970 and there was no Democratic Party disruption or scandal.

The Democrats had several candidates vying for the gubernatorial primary nod. Ned Ray McWherter, speaker of the Tennessee house of representatives, was opposed by Nashville Democratic activist Jane Eskind, Nashville Mayor Richard Fulton, Joseph Crichton, and Bill Jacox. They ran strong races in the primary. McWherter was a conservative Democrat who had developed a tight political network throughout Tennessee. He had friends in every nook and cranny of public service and industry. His image of a common man with a folksy touch complimented his personal business prowess and political influence. In the end his strong statewide political organization was much more powerful than his opponents suspected, and he won the August primary for the Democratic nomination for governor. The primary vote was McWherter 314,449, Eskind 225,551, Fulton, 190,016, Crichton 6,582, and Jacox 3,817.

The general election matchup between Republican Dunn and Democrat McWherter looked at first to be a competitive contest. Republican Dunn had tremendous popular name recognition from his service as governor from 1971 until 1975. He was supposed to have all the power of the Republican Party behind him, as well as former and current Republican Tennessee officeholders. However, this unified support did not materialize for Dunn. In fact, some suspected that key Republicans were not supporting Dunn.

To the average Tennessean, McWherter was the common man—a rural Tennessean from Dresden who was a self-made farmer and businessman who had worked his way up to speaker of the house of Tennessee's legislature. His campaign slogan was, "I'm one of you." McWherter had done favors for many people during his years of public service. A great number of Tennessee legislators had benefited from the friendship and cooperation of the speaker. When McWherter decided to run for governor, he called in his favors. His support crossed party lines, as exemplified by the difference between the votes for the Republican congressmen in the First and Second Districts and the Republican candidate for governor. First District Republican U.S. Representative Jimmy Quillen won his race 80,289 to 36,278 for Democratic challenger John Russell. In contrast, Dunn only managed 57,766 votes while McWherter took the district with 64,154. In the Second District, U.S. Representative John Duncan polled 96,396 to Democratic challenger John Bowen's 30,088, while Dunn scored only 74,844 to McWherter's 57,476.

While the East Tennessee Republican vote did not come through for Dunn, Middle and West Tennessee voted for McWherter, even giving him Dunn's old home base of Shelby County 102,762 votes to 92,776. McWherter took every county in West Tennessee except Henderson County, which he lost by only 118 votes, and he won all but a handful of the counties in Middle Tennessee. He defeated Dunn 656,602 votes to 553,449. Had the First and Second U.S. Representative Districts polled as many votes for Dunn as they did for their Republican congressmen, the results would have been close. Had Dunn won Shelby County and East Tennessee, the result would have been different. But the Republican organization did not produce enough votes for Dunn, and McWherter's Democratic organization was so strong that the added momentum defeated the former governor.

NED RAY McWHERTER was born October 15, 1930, in Palmersville, Weakley County, Tennessee, to Harmon Ray McWherter and Lucille Golden Smith McWherter, who were sharecroppers. McWherter was educated in Weakley County schools and graduated from Dresden High School in 1948. His first job was on the assembly line of a local shoe factory. He later worked as a shoe salesman for a shoe manufacturing company. In 1953 he married Bette Jean Beck and they had two children—Michael Ray and Linda. His business ventures began in 1964 with the purchase of a beer distributorship, and in 1966 he opened a nursing home with two other partners. In 1972 he developed a trucking company.

As a successful Dresden, Tennessee, businessman, McWherter became active in local Democratic politics. In 1968 he decided to run for the state legislature. He was elected and served in the state house from 1969 until 1987, earning the respect of his colleagues and successive Republican governors for his integrity and political acumen. In 1973 his wife died. That same year he was elected speaker of the Tennessee house of representatives, serving until 1986 for a total of fourteen years—seven consecutive terms as speaker was a record for the state of Tennessee. In 1986 he ran for governor against several challengers in the Democratic primary, pledging to improve transportation, the employment rate, healthcare, and education. McWherter won the primary and went on to defeat former Governor Winfield Dunn in the general election in 1986. He was reelected in 1990.

A commonsense governor, McWherter worked for improved roads, a mandatory seat-belt law, improved health care for the indigent, salary increases for state employees, and improved prisons, education, and mental health. During his administration, the basic education revenue sharing formula was changed in order to assure that poorer counties received the adequate amount of funding required to meet standard educational needs. McWherter also implemented the Twenty-first Century Schools program which was designed to ensure that schools received improvements such as reduction in the student-teacher ratio and advanced educational tools such as computers. Additionally, McWherter made Tennessee the first state in the nation to receive a waiver from the federal government for the Medicaid program. He created TennCare, which was designed to provide health care coverage for indigent as well as for those who worked but either could not afford coverage or were too sick to obtain insurance.

After retiring from office, McWherter returned to Dresden, where he continues as a farmer, investor, and businessman. He served as an advisor to President Clinton from 1994 through Clinton's 1996 reelection. He was then appointed by President Clinton as a member of the Board of Governors of the United States Postal Service. (Photograph courtesy of TSLA)

Democrats now totally controlled Tennessee. They held both U.S. Senate seats with Sasser and Gore Jr.; McWherter was governor. They held six of nine U.S. House of Representative seats, as well as control of the state house and state senate. Democrat representatives were Marilyn Lloyd in the Third District, Jim Cooper in the Fourth District, Bill Boner in the Fifth District, Bart Gordon in the Sixth District, Ed Jones in the Eighth District, and Harold Ford Sr. in the Ninth District. Jimmy Quillen and John Duncan, Republican U.S. representatives from the First and Second Districts in East Tennessee, held the power of patronage with President Reagan. Sundquist, in the Seventh District, was the junior member of the shrinking Republican leadership in Tennessee.

Republicans thought 1986 was a year they would retain some statewide leadership position. The gubernatorial campaign was the hope of the grassroots party faithful, and the loss of the seat, held by them for the last eight years, was a

HAROLD EUGENE FORD SR. was born May 20, 1945 in the family home in Shelby County, Tennessee. His grandfather, Lewis Ford, served on the Shelby county court during Reconstruction. His parents, Newton Jackson Ford and Vera (Davis) Ford, had a total of fifteen children. His father was a mortician and ran the family funeral home business. Ford received his education at Geeter Elementary, Junior High and High School, graduating in 1963. He attended college in Nashville at Tennessee State University, graduating in 1967, then attended the John Gupton College of Mortuary Science, receiving his degree in 1968. After his training he returned to Memphis to work in N. J. Ford and Sons funeral home. He married Dorothy Bowles in Memphis in 1969, and the couple had three sons.

Ford first ran for office in 1970, when he challenged incumbent James I. Taylor, a Black Democrat, for the state house of representatives District 86. He won and was elected to a subsequent term. During his tenure as a state representative, he helped broker the trade-off of Black state representative votes for the proposed East Tennessee medical school, in exchange for the configuration of a Ninth U.S. House of Representatives District which held potential for the election of a Black U.S. House member. In 1974 Ford challenged incumbent Republican U.S. House of Representative Dan Kuykendall. Ford won by less than 600 votes, becoming the first Black congressman in Tennessee's history. Early in his congressional career, Ford attended Howard University in Washington, D.C., and obtained a Masters of Business Administration degree. He was reelected to ten additional terms, serving until January 1997, when his son, Harold Ford Jr. took office.

During Ford's congressional tenure, he served on the House Ways and Means Committee and was instrumental in creating legislation that provided the tax breaks and aircraft use which aided the development of Federal Express Corporation in Memphis. Ford also supported welfare reform and child support legislation. He proved to be a strong and influential Democratic party supporter and organizer, helping several Democratic candidates. After Ford's retirement from the U.S. House of Representatives, he developed the Harold Ford Company, LLC, specializing in health care consulting. He currently resides in Memphis, Tennessee, and is a member of Mt. Moriah East Baptist Church. (Photograph courtesy of TSLA) crippling blow to their morale and their future. Sixteen years earlier the state had two Republican senators and a governor. Nineteen seventy had been what many Republicans thought was the dawn of a new political era. Now they had no statewide offices and were shaken to their political core. All across Tennessee, Republicans felt that their party was decimated and that the dominance of the Democrats would be difficult to overcome. The situation of the Republican Party was so desperate that it prompted feelings like those expressed in a Republican Party newsletter, which called for new leadership.

> The loss of the governor's seat in this election cycle would set the Republican Party back to where it was in 1964. It is essential that we learn from this loss . . . that we recognize the difference between platitude and ability, and that we seek new leaders. . . . If we are lucky some may take a long, hard look at our party and our direction and seek out the Republican worker who can give us the leadership we so sorely need. (Tubb November 1986)

The Democratic control of all statewide offices, including the Public Service Commission, exemplified not only the strength of the Democrats throughout Tennessee but the basic weakness of the Republican Party as well. Once again it was proven that without a crisis such as war, Prohibition, or state debt to trigger an unusual voter reaction, the tradition of the voters of Tennessee was Democrat. Over the next two years weakened Republicans had little to cheer them. One positive note, however, was that former Senator Howard Baker was soon selected as White House chief of staff.

Nineteen eighty-eight was a presidential election year. Ronald Reagan was ending his terms as one of the most popular sitting presidents in history. In the Republican presidential primary Bob Dole and George Bush were the two major candidates. Tennessee U.S. Senator Al Gore Jr. entered the Democratic primary. By the time of the March 1988 Super Tuesday election in the Southern states, the fields had narrowed. Soon it became apparent that George Bush would be the Republican nominee. On the Democratic side, Michael Dukakis, governor of Massachusetts, took the lead. Gore dropped out of the race, but gained significant national exposure.

At the Republican National Convention Bush was nominated for president and Dan Quayle, senator from Indiana, was nominated for vice president. The Democrats nominated Dukakis for president and Texas U.S. Senator Lloyd Bentsen for vice president.

In addition to the presidential election, one of Tennessee's U.S. Senate seats was up for election in 1988. Senator Jim Sasser, elected in 1976 over incumbent Bill Brock, reelected in 1982 over Congressman Robin Beard, had by now proven his political tenacity. No major Republican figure dared challenge him. A young lawyer from East Tennessee, Bill Andersen, ran against Sasser, but his chances appeared bleak.

In the presidential election Dukakis made an unsuccessful attempt to convince voters that the nation was ailing and that Reagan's presidency was a failure. Vice President George Bush's campaign continued to gain momentum, and in the November general election he was voted the forty-first president of the United States. His victory, nevertheless, did not translate into Republican votes for Tennessee's Senate race. The Tennessee electorate was not in the mood to unseat an incumbent in order to elect an unknown candidate. Sasser crushed his challenger scoring 1,020,061 votes, defeating Andersen nearly two to one. Independent candidate Khalil Ullah Al Muhaymin received 6,042 votes. With Sasser keeping the Senate seat in the Democratic column, the political makeup of Tennessee remained unchanged; the governor and both senators were Democrat. The congressional delegation remained six Democrats to three Republicans, and both the state house and state senate remained under Democratic control. Most Republican presidential patronage was dispensed by the senior member of the Republican congressional delegation, Jimmy Quillen. In the previous June of 1988, Quillen's good friend and political partner, Second District Congressman John James Duncan Sr. died in office. Duncan was the ranking Republican on the House Ways and Means Committee. He was one of the first members of Congress to endorse Richard Nixon for the presidential nomination in 1967; he helped Howard Baker Jr. in the 1966 Senate race; and he endorsed Winfield Dunn for governor in 1970. Duncan's son John James Duncan Jr. (Jimmy), a criminal court judge, resigned his position and ran for the seat which had been held by his father and won it with 56.3 percent of the vote. The Second Congressional District is the only seat in the United States which has remained Republican since the party was founded.

The next major election cycle would occur in 1990, when Tennessee would elect a governor and U.S. senator. Tennessee's incumbent Governor McWherter and U.S. Senator Al Gore Jr. both maintained strong political connections and popular support. Neither looked defeatable in their reelection bids. Nevertheless, in the November elections Republican state Representative Dwight Henry challenged the incumbent governor, giving up a safe state assembly seat in what proved to be a futile effort. Democratic Governor Ned McWherter trounced Henry 479,990 to 288,904. Independent W. C. Jacox received 10,980 votes, and 9,094 votes were cast for Independent D. B. Shepard. In the U.S. Senate race, Democrat Al Gore Jr. won with unprecedented margins in all ninety-five counties, defeating William Hawkins, Bill Jacox, and Charles G. Vick—529,914 to 233,324 to 11,172 to 7,995 votes respectively. The U.S. representative makeup for Tennessee did not change in the 1990 elections and remained three Republicans and six Democrats.

Republican Revival and Big Shelby Revolt

Republican George Bush may have reigned as president, but Democrats continued to dominate Tennessee. The organizational machinations of the Republican Party now almost appeared to be an exercise in futility. The GOP did continue to control the First and Second U.S. Representative Districts in East Tennessee, but Middle and West Tennessee were decidedly Democrat. Middle Tennessee, Democratic since the days of Andrew Jackson, was generally expected to continue supporting Democratic candidates in statewide elections. However, West Tennessee, also heavily influenced by the traditional Democratic vote in the past, was now beginning to show signs of political evolution. The now Republican Seventh U.S. Representative District, stretched from a conservative base in the eastern end of Tennessee's largest county of Shelby well out into rural West and Middle Tennessee, East Shelby County was undergoing significant population increase outside the voting districts of the city of Memphis. Many of the new voters in the eastern part of Shelby County had moved from other states, and held Republican economic and social viewpoints.

Since Shelby County's founding, it had elected its county officeholders in nonpartisan elections. Candidates running for county administrative offices or county commission seats did not have to declare their party affiliation on election ballots.

In statewide elections, candidates for high office—governor or U.S. senator—depended upon these local county elected officials to assist them in creating their base of support for successful statewide campaigns. Some Republican activists from Shelby County suspected that nearly all of their officeholders—mayor, county commissioners, various court clerks, property assessor, etc.—who had run as nonpartisan candidates were, in fact, Democrats. Indeed, once these nonpartisan candidates were elected, they often supported Democratic candidates in statewide and federal elections and history shows that some eventually ran for higher offices as Democrats. Thus Republican voters were, in effect, empowering the campaigns of Democrats who ran for statewide offices by allowing nonpartisan races to continue. The nonprimary system made it easy for the Democrats to control Shelby County, from city mayor and county mayor through council, commission, and nearly all administrative offices.

After an intraparty battle between Memphis Republicans who had controlled the local Republican Party for the past decade and many newcomer Republicans, Phillip Langsdon was elected chairman of the Shelby County Republican Party. He represented the new Republicans who were determined to ensure that the voters in Shelby County clearly understood the party label of the candidates they would vote for in future elections. Wasting little time, Langsdon's administration voted to implement a Republican primary system.

Shelby County was the largest county in the state populationwise and had dramatically impacted elections in years past, especially during the Crump era from the early part of the century until the mid-1950s. Beginning in the 1970s, U.S. Representative Harold Ford, Tennessee's only Black congressman, rallied Shelby County Black votes for Democratic candidates running for local or statewide office. No apparatus existed that could counter Democratic unity. When the local Republican administration went public with their proposal for a primary, they were met with an immediate and forceful negative response. Elected officials, the news media, and political power brokers castigated and applied great pressure on the Shelby County Republican Party and Langsdon in an effort to prevent implementation of a Republican primary, which so threatened the status quo. Democratic legislators even attempted to pass a law designed to limit the right of Shelby County to hold a primary. Langsdon fought this legislative maneuvering. Since all counties in Tennessee had the constitutional right to hold primaries, several legislators from other counties in Tennessee became suspicious of the legislative maneuvering by the Shelby County Democrats to single out and limit Shelby County; legislation was halted and the Shelby County Republican Party moved to implement the primary.

The first-ever Shelby County Republican primary for nonstate or federal offices took place in conjunction with the spring 1992 presidential primary, and in the face of continued opposition from the Memphis media, which predicted only negative results. As a first, the primary did not attract a high number of well-known Republican candidates. Nevertheless, the three races produced three Republican nominees. In the August general election a Republican defeated the incumbent county property assessor. The election of the first official Republican countywide officeholder in the history of Shelby County sent political shock waves through the political community. It also inspired the local party to persist in the upcoming 1994 election cycle, even in the face of continued opposition to the process by the media and elected officials. The Republicans' determination would ultimately have far-reaching implications.

Meanwhile, Tennesseans followed the presidential nominating conventions. Republicans renominated President George Bush and Vice President Dan Quayle. Democrats nominated Arkansas Governor Bill Clinton as their presidential nominee and Tennessee's Senator Albert Gore Jr. as their vice presidential nominee.

On a state level, quickly after the August county elections, attention turned to the November 1992 general elections. Tennessee's governor and senators were not up for election, but the legislative races presented real problems for Tennessee Republicans since the Democrats controlled the 1990 state redistricting process. Twelve Republican state legislators were placed into six districts across the state, effectively guaranteeing the automatic reduction of six Republican seats in the General Assembly. Democrats also reconfigured U.S. Republican Representative Don Sundquist's Seventh District in an effort to weaken his chances for reelection. They reduced some of his precincts in the heavily Republican areas along the eastern outskirts of Shelby County and added traditionally Democratic rural West and Middle Tennessee precincts, stretching his district two hundred miles to Maury County. Sundquist was able to organize in the new areas placed in his district, and he won reelection.

President Bush's approval ratings had been extremely high after the Persian Gulf War, but as the election neared, Clinton reminded voters of Bush's 1988 election campaign slogan, "Read my lips, no new taxes," which he abandoned after being elected. This reversal lost him the loyalty of many Reagan supporters, and this, coupled with the vote split caused by Independent Ross Perot's candidacy, spelled opportunity for the Democrats and disaster for Republicans. In the November 1992 election Bill Clinton was elected the forty-second president, with less than a majority of the vote. His vice president was Tennessee's U.S. Senator Al Gore Jr.

With Gore's move to vice president came a vacancy in his Senate seat. By Tennessee law, the governor would appoint someone to fill the vacancy. Several Tennessee Democrats were interested in appointment. With four years remaining in the term, the appointee would serve until the 1994 elections and then have to stand in a special election to complete the remaining two years of the term. Governor McWherter discussed the vacancy with Nashville Democratic activist Jane Eskind, a former Tennessee public service commissioner and the first woman elected to statewide office in Tennessee, in 1980. Congressman Jim Cooper, son of former Governor Prentice Cooper; Peaches Simpkins (who had served in several appointed positions under former

Albert Gore Jr., Vice President of the United States. (Courtesy of The Vice President Press Office, Official White House Photo/Callie Shell)

Governor Lamar Alexander and current Governor McWherter), wife of the owner of the *Nashville Banner*, Irby Simpkins; James Hall, policy and issues advisor to the governor; and of Memphis Judge D'Army Bailey indicated an interest in and discussed the possible appointment with Governor McWherter. He faced no shortage of contenders interested in the appointment, and the decision was difficult. He offered the Senate seat to Eighth District Congressman John Tanner, but he declined. Harlan Mathews was deputy to the governor and secretary of the state cabinet, and was extremely knowledgeable about Tennessee state issues. Mathews was close to Governor McWherter and was well versed and connected in Democratic politics. He had never run for office and had devoted a career to serving his state and fellow Democrats. The governor wanted to honor Mathews with the appointment, but the other candidates pointed out that their elective experience might be an advantage in holding the office for the Democrats during the 1994 election. The issue was settled when Mathews announced he would not run for election in 1994, thus freeing up the seat for his Democratic peers.

Governor McWherter appointed Harlan Mathews, a Democrat, to fill the unexpired U.S. Senate term (Class 2 seat) of Al Gore Jr., who assumed the office of vice president of the United States on January 3, 1993. Mathews took office on the same day, and served until his successor took office on December 2, 1994.

Tennessee's political scene was fairly calm from early 1993 through the remainder of the year. Most political

HARLAN MATHEWS was born to John William and Lillian Young Mathews on January 17, 1927, in Sumiton, Alabama. He attended public schools in Alabama, then college at Jacksonville State College in Jacksonville, Alabama, where he graduated in 1949. After obtaining a graduate degree in political science with a major in public administration from Vanderbilt University in 1950, he went to law school, graduating from the Nashville School of Law in 1962.

A dedicated public servant, Mathews served Tennessee Governor Gordon Browning on his planning staff from 1950 until 1954, Governor Frank Clement on his budget staff from 1954 until 1961, and as commissioner of finance and administration for the state of Tennessee from 1961 until 1971. He worked as senior vice president of Amcon International, Inc. in Memphis, Tennessee, from 1971 until 1973, and as legislative assistant to State Comptroller William Snodgrass from 1973 until 1974. In 1974 he was elected state treasurer and served through January 1987. When Ned McWherter became governor of Tennessee in 1987, Mathews was made deputy to the governor and secretary of the cabinet. He served until January 3, 1993, when McWherter appointed him to the vacated seat of Al Gore Jr., who had become vice president of the United States. Mathews served as a Tennessee U.S. senator, by appointment, from January 3, 1993, until December 1, 1994, and did not run for election for the remainder of the unexpired term. After serving in the U.S. Senate, Mathews returned to the practice of law. He has three grown sons and resides in Nashville with his wife, Pat Jones Mathews. (Photograph courtesy of SHO) activity focused on preparations for the various campaigns that would take place in 1994. During this period of time the mood of the electorate took a decided turn. Bill Clinton had won the presidency with promises of a "New Covenant" for the people. Early in his presidency, however, his administration's image was damaged by the appointment of several controversial individuals to high federal offices who did not reflect the moderate attitude of most Americans. In addition, First Lady Hillary Rodham Clinton attempted to form policy by taking an aggressive role in the national agenda, pushing an extremely controversial national health care plan.

Then questions arose about the connection of the president's inner circle to Hilary Clinton's Little Rock, Arkansas, law firm. A scandal involving her law partner, former Little Rock Mayor Webster Hubbell who was now a Clinton administration associate U.S. attorney general, developed into the "Whitewater" investigation and resulted in Hubbell pleading guilty to mail fraud and tax evasion. Furthermore, a former president of the Perry County (Arkansas) Bank was implicated, and later indicted, for concealing the "withdrawal of large amounts of U.S. currency by the 1990 Clinton campaign" (*Commercial Appeal* 1 March 1995; *Fournier* 1994).

Clinton's initial decisions, appointments, and associations began to cast serious doubt on the new president. His positions on issues often did not match what the majority of voters had expected, and it would not be long until they responded.

Nineteen ninety-four was scheduled for one of the largest elections in Tennessee's history. County administrative offices, county commission seats, and state and federal elections were to be held. It was a rare year in which the governor's seat and both senate seats were to be filled (because of Gore's unexpired term).

In the west end of the state, Chairman Langsdon and the Shelby County Republican Party once again opted to hold a Republican primary—a move designed not only to aid the Republican effort in county elections in 1994 but also to prepare the state's largest voter base for the November federal and state elections of a new governor and two U.S. senators. There were many races on the ballot and no shortage of candidates for the 1994 primary on May 3. An open field of candidates vied for a nomination in nearly every county office. The results of the county offices primary produced seventeen formidable Republican nominees. After the primary, campaign activity on the part of the nominees, press conferences, and events put on by the Shelby County Republican Party, and the party's sample Republican ballot mailed to thousands of Republican households combined to create an unusually high public awareness of who the Republican nominees were by the time the county general election day rolled around.

The Democratic Party Executive Committee could not reach a consensus on holding their own primary to compete with the Republican primary. They decided to respond to the Republicans by "endorsing" their own candidates rather than holding an open primary. Otis Higgs was nominated by the Democratic Executive Committee as their candidate for Shelby County mayor. Democratic Congressman Harold Ford Sr. endorsed White city councilman Jack Sammons as an Independent candidate for Shelby County mayor. Memphis City Mayor Willie Herenton stayed neutral. As a result, a huge split developed in the Democratic Party and Democrat Higgs was left with little support.

An outright and public feud developed between Higgs and Congressman Ford, and between City Mayor Herenton and Congressman Ford. The Shelby County Democratic Party was in an upheaval and the party's chairman, Sidney Chism, "characterized the county elections as 'total confusion'" (Keeter 23 January 1994).

On election day for the August county general election, nearly the entire Republican slate for Shelby County offices won with clear and dominant majorities in races for county mayor, county administrative offices, and county commission. Republicans now controlled the Shelby County government, a first in the history of the county since its founding in 1819 except for the period of martial law under Governor Brownlow's Reconstructionist government. Republicans won fifteen out of seventeen races in 1994 and with the inclusion of the 1992 victory of the county assessor's office placed Shelby County Republicans in a position of dominance they had never before enjoyed. This Republican county landslide brightened the prospects for the Republican U.S. Senate and gubernatorial campaigns coming up in November, and represented the most successful local county Republican victory, not just in Tennessee, but in the entire nation. It was also a vindication of the Shelby County Republican Party administration, whose efforts to improve a process had been severely attacked and criticized, but had now borne fruit.

During the August 1994 election cycle, statewide party primaries were held in contested races for both U.S. Senate seats and the governor's seat. Nashville Mayor Phil Bredesen ran in the Democratic gubernatorial primary against former Shelby County Mayor Bill Morris, Richard Chesteen Sr., Frank Cochran, Steve Cohen, Mike Fugate, Steve Hewlett, Jim Lewis, Virginia Nyabongo, and Carl Wallace. Republican Seventh District U.S. Representative Don Sundquist ran in the Republican gubernatorial primary against state Representative David Copeland of Chattanooga and Hubert Patty. Bill Frist, of Nashville, ran in the Republican Senate primary for the full-term Senate seat, occupied by Senator Jim Sasser, over a large field of candidates including Andrew Benedict III, Byron Bush, Bob Corker, Harold Sterling, and Steve Wilson. In the short-term Senate race to fill Al Gore Jr.'s seat, occupied by Harlan Mathews, Fred Thompson faced some opposition for the Republican nomination from John Baker. Democratic U.S. Representative Jim Cooper appeared headed for the nomination for the short-term Senate seat by his party without opposition.

When the political dust cleared from the statewide primaries, Sundquist was the Republican nominee and Bredesen the Democratic nominee for the gubernatorial race. Republican Frist won the right to face Senator Sasser, and Republican Thompson won the nomination to face Democratic Cooper for the short-term Senate seat. The stage was set for the November general elections.

The missteps of President Clinton during his first two years of office had polarized many voters. West Tennessee Republicans hoped to capitalize on this polarization with plans to ensure a high Republican voter turnout in the November general election.

East Tennessee still played a key role in any statewide victory, but since it took at least two grand divisions of Tennessee to win a race, the outcomes would depend upon the results in Middle or West Tennessee. The fact that Shelby Countians

WILLIAM FRIST, was born on February 22, 1952, to Dorothy Harrison Cate and Thomas Fearn Frist Sr., M.D., in Nashville, Tennessee. He received his early education at Woodmont Grammar School and Montgomery Bell Academy in Nashville, then obtained his college education from Princeton University, graduating in 1974. He graduated from Harvard Medical School in 1978, then three years later married Karyn McLaughlin on March 14, 1981, in Lubbock, Texas. They subsequently had three sons—Harrison, Jonathan, and Bryan. Frist trained in general surgery at Massachusetts General Hospital, followed by a fellowship in Cardiothoracic Surgery at the same institution. He completed his medical training by serving as a Fellow in Transplant Surgery at Stanford University.

After his training, Frist returned to Nashville and helped found and was named director of the Vanderbilt Transplant Center. Governor McWherter named him chairman of the Tennessee Medicaid Reform Task Force. In 1994 he ran as a Republican for the U.S. Senate against incumbent Democrat Jim Sasser. He was elected on November 8, 1994, becoming the first practicing physician elected to the U.S. Senate since 1928.

While in the Senate, Frist worked on many health care related bills, as well as small business and disability legislation. He and his family are members of Westminster Presbyterian Church. He is a Fellow of the American College of Surgeons and a member of the Board of Regents of the Smithsonian Museum, the Board of Trustees of Princeton University, and the Board of Trustees of the National Museum of Natural History. (Photograph courtesy of SHO)

voted overwhelmingly for Republicans in the August county general election only served to encourage the Republican momentum and aid voter turnout.

Most observers did not think Senator Sasser could be defeated. He had an experienced political and campaign staff, was chairman of the powerful banking committee, and had plenty of campaign money. However, Frist was a significant stockholder, and his brother and father were founders and major stockholders in Hospital Corporation of America. He loaned his campaign $3.7 million, an amount even Sasser's war chest could not match. Frist constantly reminded the voters that Sasser was tightly tied to President Clinton and liberal U.S. Senator Ted Kennedy, from Massachusetts. By late October, polls indicated that Sasser was in trouble.

Frist, on the other hand, was hard for Sasser to target, especially since he had no congressional voting record to criticize. However, there were some gaps in Frist's newly minted political armor. Beside the fact that he was running mostly on his own money, there was some evidence that he had not even registered to vote until 1988, and Sasser used this fact to contrast his own political service with that of someone who had not even bothered to vote. "Late in the campaign, Frist gaffes gave Sasser forces some last-minute hope. He admitted he wasn't familiar with TVA issues or who the chairman of the TVA is. He admitted he didn't know the specifics of the 1994 Crime Bill in spite of the fact he'd been criticizing Sasser's support of the measure for months" (Rogers 23 September 1994).

> Frist then sent out letters signed by former [Republican primary] opponent Steve Wilson pledging that he would "vote to end abortion except in cases of rape, incest, and when the life of the mother is in danger"—a direct contradiction of the prochoice stand Frist has taken on the campaign trail.
>
> Then in the final weeks, the Frist campaign was damaged by other Republicans. A supporter on his campaign bus made a remark seen as racist, sparking anger in black communities statewide. And, less than a week before election day, First Congressional District Congressman Rep. Jimmy Quillen made public appearances with Sasser praising their work as a team for Upper East Tennessee. The remarks were taken by some as a sign that Quillen's support for Frist was lukewarm at best. (Wade 9 November 1994)

Fred Thompson, the other Republican senatorial candidate, for the short-term seat, actually held a head start over Congressman Cooper, although he had never held elective office. Thompson had not only served on the Watergate Committee's legal staff under Senator Howard Baker, but he had enjoyed subsequent visibility by playing roles in twenty-three movies, some of which were highly successful. During the campaign, Thompson played up a folksy Southern image by traveling around Tennessee in a red pickup truck, wearing work shirts. Congressman Cooper held the support of the staunch Democrats, and had served for twelve years as U.S. representative in the Fourth Congressional District, but he did not enjoy the type of statewide political network available to Thompson. Thompson's campaign was supported by former Senator Howard Baker, strengthened by the anti-Democratic momentum, and aided by his authority-figure roles from his movies.

In the gubernatorial race, Democratic Phil Bredesen and Republican Don Sundquist ran a tough, costly, and bitter campaign against each other. The two candidates spent a combined amount totaling over $15 million. Sundquist spent over $6.5 million and set a record for fund-raising. Bredesen, who was independently wealthy, spent $8.7 million, $6.2 million of which came from his personal loans to his campaign. His campaign was focused and direct. His television and radio ads attacked Sundquist for voting against minimum wage increases and opposing civil rights legislation. He attacked him for supporting congressional pay raises, accepting speaking fees, and free trips. Sundquist's ads accused Bredesen of "flip-flopping on issues such as public funding for abortion and school privatization" (Branson 9 November 1994).

Sundquist had built a strong network across Tennessee during his twelve years in the U.S. House of Representatives. He had worked for Howard Baker many times in the past and even chaired Baker's unavailing campaign for president in 1980. However, he was concerned about the East Tennessee vote. Without it, he would not win. The Second District seemed well prepared to help since U.S. Representative Jimmy Duncan and Sundquist were friends. The big question among Republican insiders was whether or not First District Republican U.S. Representative Jimmy Quillen would support Sundquist. It was believed that the two had a falling-out of sorts over the appointment of a federal judge during George Bush's presidency. Insiders felt Sundquist had managed to heal the breach with Quillen.

On general election day, November 9, 1994, Tennessee Republicans won all three

FRED THOMPSON was born to Fletcher S. Thompson and Ruth Bradley Thompson in Sheffield, Alabama, on August 19, 1942. His family subsequently moved to Lawrenceburg, Tennessee, where his father worked as a used car salesman. Thompson was educated in public schools in Lawerenceburg, graduating from Lawrence County High School in 1960. He went to Florence State College from the fall of 1960 until the fall of 1961 and entered Memphis State University in 1962, graduating in 1964. He graduated from Vanderbilt University School of Law in 1967. The following year he managed the losing congressional campaign of John T. Williams, who ran against Democrat Ray Blanton. After returning to Lawrenceburg to practice law, he was named assistant U.S. attorney for Middle Tennessee in 1969 and moved to Nashville. There he met Lamar Alexander, who introduced him to U.S. Senator Howard Baker, and in 1972 he served as Middle Tennessee campaign manager for Baker's reelection. Thompson married Sarah Lindsey. Together they had three children—Tony, Betsy, and Daniel. The Thompsons later divorced.

In 1973 Senator Baker appointed Thompson as minority counsel on the Senate Select Committee on presidential Campaign Activity, better known as the Watergate Committee. Thompson later served as special counsel on two other Senate committees, and began practicing law in Washington. In 1977 he represented Marie Ragghianti in her lawsuit against the administration of Governor Ray Blanton, who had fired her as chairperson of the Tennessee Board of Pardons and Paroles. Ragghianti had informed the FBI of her suspicions of payoffs being made in exchange for paroles in Tennessee. Thompson and Ragghianti exposed the cash-for-clemency scandal. In 1985, Thompson played himself in the movie *Marie*, which was based on a book about the scandal.

Over the next few years Thompson played authority figures in over twenty movies and television episodes. He simultaneously maintained his law practice in both Washington and Nashville. In 1994 he ran for the unexpired term of the U.S. Senate seat vacated by Al Gore Jr. occupied by Harlan Mathews by appointment. He was elected with 61 percent of the vote over Congressman Jim Cooper and took office December 2, 1994. He was reelected to a full term in 1996, receiving more votes than any candidate for office in Tennessee history. Thompson was elected chairman of the Governmental Affairs Committee in 1997 and conducted investigations into the activities of the 1996 campaigns. (Photograph courtesy of the Office of Senator Thompson)

major statewide races, representing the most dramatic shift in Tennessee's history. William Frist defeated Jim Sasser 834,226 votes to 623,164, while Independent candidates Hooker, Johnson, and Kienlen received 13,244, 6,631, and 3,087 respectively. Frist was thus elected as U.S. senator in the full-term election (Class 1).

Fred Thompson defeated Jim Cooper for the short-term U.S. Senate seat (Class 2) vacated by Al Gore Jr. and temporarily filled by the appointment of Harlan Mathews. Thompson won with 885,998 votes, winning eighty-three of ninety-five counties. Cooper tallied 565,930 votes and seven Independent candidates, Hancock, Lumpkin, Lytle, Martin, Moore, Schneller, and Walls received 4,169, 1,184, 1,934, 1,719, 2,219, 1,150, and 1,532 respectively.

Don Sundquist defeated Phil Bredesen to become governor. Sundquist received 807,104 votes to Bredesen's 664,252, to

Independents Holt's 9,981, Moffett's 2,347, and Smith's 3,365.

In each major statewide race of 1994, the Republicans won East Tennessee. (Quillen's First District and Duncan's Second District). In past elections, when Republican candidates lost either the First or Second Congressional Districts or failed to do as well as the congressmen from these districts, they lost the statewide race. Sundquist, Frist, and Thompson won these two U.S. Representative districts, along with Hamilton and Knox Counties.

Both Frist and Thompson did well in Middle Tennessee, taking Davidson County. However, Sundquist lost Bredesen's home base 62,653 to 93,411. In Shelby County, Sundquist, Frist, and Thompson all broke the traditional 100,000 county vote barrier needed to win a statewide election, going well beyond the 125,000 mark, and achieved this in a non-presidential election year. In years past, only Democrats had ever done so well. By a combination of factors, the Republican momentum was present in Shelby County for the three Republican candidates in 1994.

In the U.S. Representative races in Tennessee, incumbent Republican James Quillen was reelected in the First District for a seventeenth term. Incumbent Republican James Duncan was reelected in the Second District. Republican Zach Wamp was elected to the Third District in an open race. In the Fourth District, the seat which Democrat Jim Cooper had given up to run for the Senate, was won by Republican Van Hillary. Incumbent Democrat Bob Clement was reelected in the Fifth District and incumbent Democrat U.S. Representative Bart Gordon was reelected in the Sixth District. Republican Ed Bryant was elected to the Seventh Congressional District, which Sundquist had given up in order to run for governor. Incumbent U.S. Representative John Tanner was reelected Democratic congressman for the Eighth District, and Harold Ford Sr. was reelected Democratic congressman for the Ninth District. Republicans now held five of the nine U.S. House of Representative seats in Tennessee. The year 1994 marked a historic point for Tennessee Republicans. They took the governor's seat, both U.S. Senate seats, and held the majority (five out of nine) of Tennessee's U.S. House of Representative seats. The solid Democratic base of Shelby County had reversed to Republican, partially as a result of the implementation of the Republican primaries of 1992 and 1994.

Nationwide, in 1994 Republicans gained control. Democrats lost thirteen governors while Republicans gained ten, moving from twenty to thirty. The U.S. House of Representatives also changed. Democrats went from control at 256 seats, down to 204, while Republicans gained 52 seats and control, moving from 178 to 230. In the U.S. Senate, Democrats also dropped from a majority of 56 to 47, while Republicans went from 44 to 53, gaining nine seats, two of which were from Tennessee, and control. Both the House and Senate were now under Republican control, ending forty straight years of Democrat monopoly.

Republican Don Sundquist was inaugurated Tennessee's forty-seventh governor on January 21, 1995. Senator Fred Thompson, who was filling the unexpired term, took office December 2, 1994, while Senator Bill Frist was sworn in on January 3, 1995. Soon after taking office, Thompson was selected by Senate Majority Leader Bob Dole to give the Republican response to a presidential address on December 15, 1994.

Former Congressman Cooper returned to the practice of law. Phil Bredesen continued to serve as mayor of Nashville

DON SUNDQUIST was born on March 15, 1936, in Moline, Rock Island County, Illinois to Louise H. Rohren Sundquist and Kenneth Maynard Sundquist. His mother's grandfather came to America from Germany. His father's family came from Sweden. Sundquist was educated in public schools and graduated from Moline High School at age seventeen, in 1953. He attended Augustana College and obtained a B.A. degree in business administration in 1957. He next served on active duty in the navy from 1957 until 1959, then went to work in the industrial engineer training program with the John Deere Company in September 1959. He married Martha Swanson in 1959, and the couple had three children—Tania, Andrea, and Deke. In 1961 Sundquist went to work for the Jostens Company, serving in the company plants, first in Princeton, Illinois, then in Owatonna, Minnesota. The company transferred him to the Shelbyville, Tennessee, plant in 1962 then back to Minnesota in 1970.

In 1972 Sundquist left Jostens and returned to Tennessee, moving to Memphis, to become part of Graphic Sales of America, a print and ad firm. His first politically active role was as Tennessee Young Republican chairman, then in 1971–1973 he served as National Young Republican chairman. From 1975 through 1977 Sundquist chaired the Shelby County Republican Party. In 1982 he ran for Congress against Bob Clement in the Seventh Congressional District, narrowly winning the race. Serving twelve years, he was reelected five times.

In 1994 Sundquist ran successfully for governor against Nashville Mayor Phil Bredesen, and was inaugurated in January 1995. During his term he worked to improve Tennessee's health care for the poor, the education system, and the state's infrastructure. He successfully put an end to Tennessee's Public Service Commission, which had been implicated in controversial fund-raising activities for many years. Sundquist was reelected in 1988. (Photograph courtesy of TSLA)

and was soon reelected to another term. President Bill Clinton did not allow Jim Sasser to remain outside the political arena for long. He appointed him as ambassador to the People's Republic of China on September 22, 1995. Sasser was confirmed by the U.S. Senate on December 14, 1995.

During this time President Clinton's liberal policies moved to a moderate center more in tune with the preferences of the voters. Along with the change in policy, his approval ratings improved. Nineteen ninety-six was a presidential election year. Former Governor Lamar Alexander campaigned for the Republican nomination. However, Senate Majority Leader Bob Dole of Kansas easily won the honor. The Republican vice presidential nominee was Jack Kemp. President Bill Clinton was able to stem competition within his own party and retain the nomination without much effort. Vice President Al Gore Jr. was also renominated.

In 1996 Bill Clinton and Al Gore Jr. defeated the Republicans and retained the White House. Seven of Tennessee's incumbent congressmen were reelected. One exception was in the First District where Republican Congressman Quillen retired. Republican Bill Jenkins won a narrow primary victory against ten other candidates, proceeding to win the general election by a wide margin. The other change occurred in the Ninth District where U.S. Representative Democrat Harold Ford Sr. was succeeded by his son, Harold Ford Jr.

Nineteen ninety-six was also the time for completion of the senatorial term originally begun by Al Gore Jr. in 1990. Senator Thompson, having only run two years earlier, faced reelection to a full six-year term. In the general election he defeated Democrat Houston Gordon 1,091,544 votes to 654,937, scoring more votes in his victory than any candidate in the history of Tennessee.

In 1998 the biggest newsmaker was President Bill Clinton. A series of sexual misconduct charges dating back to his years as Arkansas governor and charges of misconduct and obstruction of justice related to an affair with a young White House intern led to his investigation by Independent Counsel Kenneth Starr. The scope of the media coverage was unprecedented.

The only statewide race in Tennessee in 1998 was the gubernatorial race. Republican Don Sundquist ran for reelection and was challenged in the Republican primary by Shirley Beck-Vosse; Sundquist won the August 5 primary 258,786 to 28,951 votes. Several Democrats ran in their primary, which was won by John Jay Hooker with 123,384 votes.

In the November 3 general election Sundquist defeated Hooker by more than two to one, a Tennessee record margin of 69 percent to 29 percent. Sundquist received 669,973 votes to 287,790 for Hooker.

In 1998 the Tennessee U.S. House of Representative makeup remained unchanged. Nationally, Democrats made slight gains in the U.S. House and Senate and the governorships. The slight move toward the Democrats was not enough to remove control from the Republicans. They maintained majorities in all three categories and made Republican history by holding the U.S. House majority for their party for three successive congresses for the first time in three quarters of a century. However, the shift in the U.S. House and Senate was a relief to President Clinton. The narrowed majorities virtually assured that there would not be enough Republican votes in the U.S. Senate to remove him from office. The U.S. House soon passed two articles of impeachment against the president, making him the second president in U.S. history to be impeached, removing the distinction of being the only president to be impeached from Tennessee's Andrew Johnson. The U.S. Senate acquitted Clinton of both charges (55 for and 45 against on the count of perjury, and 50 for and 50 against on the count of obstruction of justice) on February 12, 1999.

In 1999 Tennessee Republicans still held the governor's seat and both U.S. Senate seats, as well as five of the nine U.S. House of Representative seats. The state house and senate, however, remained in the hands of the Democrats. Additional security for Democrats may come with the redistricting process due to take place in the new millennium.

Afterword

When Tennessee was first settled, it was considered a "Western" territory, an outsider region of a new nation whose politics was rooted in the East Coast. The West was looked upon by the Eastern establishment as a society of anti-Federalist and nonaristocratic ruffians. Though the territory's people, as a whole, sided with the likes of Thomas Jefferson and the Democrat-Republicans prior to statehood, political factional infighting was a fact of life within Tennessee from its beginnings. The factional divisions continued, even to the present day, while the state evolved in its national political character.

As the Western territories became populated, a new political party developed to retaliate against the continued domination of the elite group of politicians from the East. Andrew Jackson led political campaigns which resulted in the development of the Democratic Party and a new system of nominating, as well as electing presidential candidates. The Democrats took control in Tennessee. As Jackson's own political influence spread, it took on a powerful character of domination which resulted in a consolidation of factions against his organization. These anti-Jackson factions coalesced into the Whig Party, both nationally and in Tennessee.

The Whig Party grew in power and became a national force. Tennessee politics teetered back and forth between Whig and Democrat, from the time of the election of Newton Cannon as Whig governor in 1835 until the Civil War. Faced with Radical Republican Reconstruction domination from the North and Northeast during and after the war, Tennesseans retreated into the Democratic Party, replacing any anti-Jackson feelings with those of a unified political retrenchment. The post-Civil War Reconstructionist government solidified Democratic politics in Tennessee as well as the rest of the South. Even the very word "Republican" became distasteful to most Tennesseans.

Democrats dominated Tennessee politics from the immediate post-Civil War era until modern times. The only interruptions occurred in times of great controversy, such as the era of Prohibition, which divided Democratic Party ranks. However, from the time of the Civil War, East Tennessee—U.S. Representative Districts One and Two—remained Republican, along with small pockets in West Tennessee made up of a few Black Republican voters. East Tennessee provided a consistent albeit minority Republican vote for over a century. In the 1960s the Democratic Party embraced civil rights and, Black Tennessee voters, who had basically been disenfranchised up until this time, swung to the Democratic Party. Simultaneously, Democratic Party monopoly of White voters began to weaken. Republicans began to win some of the White, previously Democratic vote in Tennessee, which became the first Southern state to move Republican in the late 1960s and early 1970s.

Just as Republicans took control in Tennessee, the Watergate break-in orchestrated by President Nixon's reelection committee was exposed. The scandal resulted in damage to the character of the Republican Party. The setback took the party a quarter of a century to fully recover from. By 1994 Republicans were back in power in Tennessee. Other Southern states experienced a similar trend.

Whatever political drama occurs or has occurred, Tennessee has played a central role in American politics. This is a state painted with colorful characters and national leaders. It boasts three presidents and the current vice president. Through the campaigns of Andrew Jackson, it played a central role in changing the way we hold national political conventions and elect presidents, in the development of the Democratic Party, and indirectly in the development of the Whig Party as a response to Jackson's domination. One of Tennessee's presidents, Andrew Johnson, held the post-Civil War Radical Republican senators and representatives in check, playing a vital role in restoring the South and preventing total domination and destruction, albeit at the expense of his own career. Another president, James K. Polk, oversaw the greatest landmass expansion in American history. One governor, Sam Houston, led efforts to win independence for Texas and then saw it become a part of the United States, serving as commander and chief of the Texas army, the president of the territory, and later governor and senator of that state. Tennessee also played a central role, casting the final and crucial vote, in allowing women the right to vote.

Whatever happens in the future of the Volunteer State, its past did make an indelible mark on the history of this great nation. As we begin the new millenium, there is little indication that Tennessee is losing its political fervor.

Bibliography

Adams, Null. "Political Notebook." *Memphis Press-Scimitar,* 19 September 1966; 7 October 1966.

Allen, Hester Stewart. Notarized statement on 3 March 1954, in the possession of Mr. and Mrs. Lewis Donelson.

Anderson, Judith I. *William Howard Taft: An Intimate History.* New York: W. W. Norton & Company.

Annis, James Lee. *Howard Baker: Conciliator in an Age of Crisis.* New York: Madison Books, 1995.

Associated Press. "Former Bank Chief Indicted for Clinton Campaign Withdrawal." *Memphis Commercial Appeal,* 1 March 1995.

Associated Press Wire Story. "State GOP Delegation Wins Seating Dispute." *Maryville-Alcoa Times,* 14 June 1964.

Biographical Directory of the U.S. Congress, 1774–1989.

Branson, R. "Governor-elect Offers Thanks, Cooperation." *Memphis Commercial Appeal,* 9 November 1994.

Buchignani, Leo, Jan Donelson, and Harry Wellford. "Dear Delegate: Letter in Support of Bob James." 8 October 1963.

Burt, Jesse C. *Nashville: Its Life and Times.* Nashville, Tenn.: Tennessee Book Company, 1959.

Canton, B., R. M. Ketchum, S. W. Sears, J. L. Gardner, M. S. Parson, M. Di Crocco, S. D. Carr, I. Glusker, S. E. Robinson, and D. Greenspan. *The Civil War.* New York: American Heritage/Bonanza Books, 1960, 1982.

Capers, Gerald M. *The Biography of a River Town: Memphis, Its Heroic Age.* New Orleans: Published by author, 1966.

Caro, R. A. *The Years of Lyndon Johnson: The Path to Power.* New York: Alfred A. Knopf Co., 1982.

Chattanooga Times, 18 April 1900, in Isaac, P. "Tennessee Republicans in the Progressive Era, 1896–1916." Nonpublished manuscript loaned to author in November 1995.

Church, Annette E., and Roberta Church. *The Robert R. Churches of Memphis: A Father and Son Who Achieved in Spite of Race.* Ann Arbor, Mich.: Edwards Brothers, 1974.

Cook, K. W. "Brenner Dispute Triggered Rift." *Memphis Commercial Appeal,* 3 May 1963.

———. "Lonely Voice of Protest Sounds Through GOP Rift." *Memphis Commercial Appeal,* 3 May 1963.

Coppock, Paul R. "Mid-South Memoirs—In the Days of Grand Hotels." *Commercial Appeal,* 10 March 1974.

Corlew, R. E. *Tennessee: A Short History.* Knoxville, Tenn.: University of Tennessee Press, 1989.

———. *Tennessee: A Short History,* 2nd edition. Knoxville, Tenn.: University of Tennessee Press, 1990.

Covington, J. "GOP Primary Lacks Competition for Clerk, Judge, Assessor Posts." *Memphis Commercial Appeal,* 10 January 1992.

Craddock, Jack. Personal communication with author, 22 September 1995.

Crawford, Carl. "Brock Shocks Gathering with Blunt Words." *Memphis Commercial Appeal,* 26 May 1963.

———. "West State Bid Made by GOP." *Memphis Commercial Appeal,* 26 May 1963.

Creekmore, Betsey B. *Knoxville.* Knoxville, Tenn.: The University of Tennessee Press, 1958.

Creson, Jayne. "A Brief History of the Shelby County Republican Party." 27 February 1988.

Crockett, D. "The Life of David Crockett," *Heroes of History.* New York: Perkins Book Co., n.d.

Dann, Alex, Warner Hodges, Judge Harry Wellford, Winfield Dunn, and Lewis Donelson. Personal communication with the author, 1995, 1996, and 1997.

Davis, James. "Letter to the Editor." *Raleigh-Bartlett Star,* 27 September 1963.

Donelson, L. R., R. B. James, et al. Answer of the Delegates and Alternates to the Republican National Convention from the 9th Congressional District of Tennessee to a Contest Filed by George W. Lee, 24 June 1964.

Donelson, Lewis. Letter to Brice Harlow, 16 March 1956.

———. Personal communication with the author, 25 August 1997.

Donelson, Lewis and Jan Donelson. Personal communication with the author, 20 August 1995.

Donelson, Lewis, Harry Wellford, and Alec Dann. Bonus Delegate Committee Report to the Shelby County Republican Party Chairman, 28 February 1956.

"Donelson Faction Is Winner as Raleigh GOP Club Splits." *Memphis Commercial Appeal*, 10 May 1963.

Duffy, J. "Elders Going Back to Post at Arkansas Med School." *Memphis Commercial Appeal*, 13 December 1994.

Duncan, John James, Jr. Personal communication with the author, 1996.

Dunn, Winfield, and associates. Personal communication with the author, 1995, 1996, 1997.

Durhan, Walter. "How Say You, Senator Fowler?" *Tennessee Historical Quarterly* 42, Spring 1983.

Dykeman, Wilma. *Tennessee: A Bicentennial History*. New York: W. W. Norton and Company, 1975.

Edmundson, Charles. "Negroes Give Key Support to Cliff Davis." *Memphis Commercial Appeal*, date unclear.

———. "Shelby's GOP Face May Split." *Memphis Commercial Appeal*, 18 February 1963.

"Effort Seen to Make GOP in South All White," 23 August 1962.

Farris, William. Personal communication with author, 7 July 1997.

Ford, Harold Eugene, Sr. Interview with the author, 11 January 1999.

Foscue, Lillian, and Elton Whisenhunt. "New Guard Takes Command; Night Was Cold but Voters Burned." *Memphis Press-Scimitar*, 3 March 1954.

Fournier, Ron. "Hubbell to Plead Guilty, Source Says." *Commercial Appeal*, 2 December 1994.

Fred Thompson biography courtesy of Thompson's Senate office, received 6 February 1996, and May 1998.

"GOP Women Told by Leader of JFK Tactics." *Memphis Commercial Appeal*, 3 May 1962.

Gregory, Neal. "Only Building's Cool as GOP Meets." *Memphis Commercial Appeal*, 27 November 1962.

Hicks, John H. "Congressional Career of B. Carroll Reece, 1920–1948." Master's thesis, East Tennessee State University, 1968.

Hill, K. S., and N. C. Rae. "The Continuing Decline of the Southern White Democrats in the House: 1992–1996" in Southern Political Report #430. Miami, Fla.: Department of Political Science, Florida International University, 31 March 1988.

Hobbs, Nate. "Chism Seeks Party Session to Unify after Loss at Polls." *Memphis Commercial Appeal*, 9 August 1994.

Isaac, Paul E. "Tennessee Republicans in the Progressive Era, 1896–1916." Nonpublished manuscript loaned to author in November 1995.

James, Robert. Personal communication with the author, 20 August 1995.

Keating, J. M. *History of Memphis*. Syracuse: D. Mason & Co., 1888.

Keeter, Terry. "Democrats Plan to Pick Nominees Draws Flak." *Memphis Commercial Appeal*, 21 January 1994.

———. "Democrats Require Oath in Local Races." *Memphis Commercial Appeal*, 23 January 1994.

———. "Partisan Primary Needless, Says Peete." *Memphis Commercial Appeal*, 9 August 1992.

———. Personal communication with author, February 1991.

———. "Shelby Democrats to Meet on Candidate Selection." *Commercial Appeal*, 19 January 1994.

Kitchens, Allen Hampton. "Political Upheaval in Tennessee, Boss Crump and the Senatorial Election of 1948." Master's thesis, George Washington University, 1962.

Knoxville Journal and Tribune, 26 September 1912.

Kuykendall, Dan, et al. "To All Members Shelby County Republican Party," 18 September 1963.

Lewis, G. T. "Democrats Should Resist Pressures for Primary." *Memphis Commercial Appeal*, 6 December 1991.

Locker, R. "Winner Thompson Will Soon Be 'Senior' Senator." *Memphis Commercial Appeal*, 9 November 1994.

Marquis, James. *The Raven: A Biography of Sam Houston*. Indianapolis, Ind.: The Bobbs-Merrill Company, 1929.

Mathews, Harlan. Personal communication with the author, 27 January 1997.

———. Personal communication with the author, February 1997.

Mays, Paul. Information from the office of Congressman James Quillen, 9 January 1996.

McBride, R. M. and D. M. Robison. *Biographical Dictionary of the Tennessee General Assembly, Volume 1, 1796–1861*. Nashville, Tenn.: Tennessee State Library and Archives and the Tennessee Historical Commisssion, 1975.

McKee, Margaret. "Fitzhugh Files Protest with State Group; Calls GOP Meet 'Illegal, Rump,'" May 1963.

McKellar, Kenneth. *Tennessee Senators, As Seen by One of Their Successors*. Kingsport, Tenn.: Southern Publishers, Inc., 1942.

McWherter, Governor Ned Ray. Personal communcation with the author, 15 August 1997.

———. Resume faxed to author from Governor McWherter's home office in Dresden, Tennessee, 1996.

Means, John. "Vote 'Instructors' Paid for 16 Days, Some Worked 4." *Memphis Commercial Appeal*. 18 February 1964.

———. "Lincoln League Election Use Is Long Tradition, Says Lee." *Memphis Commercial Appeal*, 19 February 1964.

Memphis Commercial Appeal, 23 April 1900, in Isaac, P. "Tennessee Republicans in the Progressive Era, 1896–1916."

Memphis Commercial Appeal, 21 March 1906; 27 April 1910; 1 September 1910; 14 October 1910; 17 October 1910; 27 July 1928; 30 July 1928; 10 November 1994.

Memphis Commercial Appeal, 21 March 1906.

Memphis News-Scimitar, 9 June 1920.

Miller, Nathan. *Theodore Roosevelt, A Life*. New York: William Morrow & Co., Inc., 1992.

Miller, William D. *Mr. Crump of Memphis*. Baton Rouge, La.: LSU Press, 1964.

Milton, George Fort. *The Age of Hate*. n.p., n.d.

Morristown *Republican*, 23 June 1900, in Isaac, P. "Tennessee Republicans in the Progressive Era, 1896–1916."

Murdock, Lillie. *A Brief History of the Republican Party*. RNC Information Services, March 1993.

Nashville Banner, 10 February 1906; 13 April 1910; 27 April 1910; 18 August 1910; 26 August 1910; 27 August 1910; 3 September 1910; 10 September 1910; 21 March 1913; 29 March 1913; 5 April 1913.

Nashville Banner, 18 April 1910; 26 April 1910, in Shahan, Joe Michael. *Reform and Politics in Tennessee*. Ann Arbor, Mich.: UMI Dissertation Services, 1993.

"Negroes Walk Out of GOP Meeting—Dunn Is Elected." *Memphis Press-Scimitar*, circa. 1964.

"Negro Leaders Are Lukewarm." *Memphis Commercial Appeal*, 4 November 1962.

Nixon, Richard. *The Memoirs of Richard Nixon*. New York: Grosset and Dunlap, 1978.

Parks, J. H. and S. J. Folmsbee. *The Story of Tennessee*. Norman, Okla.: Harlow Publishing Co., 1973.

Phillips, Margaret I. *The Governors of Tennessee*. Gretna, La.: Pelican Pub. Co., 1978.

Pollard, David. "Old Guard Favored for Election Hiring, Investigation Reveals." *Memphis Commercial Appeal*, 19 February 1964.

Porteous, Clark. "Lincoln League Drafts Atty. Briggs to Run for Congress in GOP Primary." *Memphis Press-Scimitar*, circa 1962.

———. "Shelby GOP Widely Split—Each Side Blames Other." *Memphis Press-Scimitar*, 10 March 1956.

Press-Scimitar, 24 January 1931.

Pruden, Wesley, Jr. "GOP Organizes for Congress Race." *Memphis Commercial Appeal*, 12 April 1962.

Rand, Clayton. *Sons of the South*. New York: Hold, Rinehart, & Winston, 1961.

Reagan, Ronald. *An American Life*. New York: Simon & Schuster, 1990.

Remini, Robert V. *Andrew Jackson and the Course of American Democracy, 1833–1845,* Volume III. New York: Harper & Row Pub., 1984.

———. *Andrew Jackson and the Course of American Empire, 1767–1821,* Volume I. New York: Harper & Row Pub., 1977.

———. *Andrew Jackson and the Course of American Freedom, 1822–1832,* Volume II. New York: Harper & Row Pub., 1981.

———. *The Life of Andrew Jackson.* New York: Harper & Row Pub., 1997.

Richardson, Randal. Personal communication with the author, 1994.

Rogers, D. "Senate Races in Tennessee May Prove Pivotal to GOP Hopes of Regaining Control Next Year." *Wall Street Journal*, 23 September 1994.

Roper, J. *The Founding of Memphis 1818–1820*, published under the auspices of the Memphis Sesquicentennial, Inc., 1970.

Roske, Ralph J. "The Seven Martyrs?" *American Historical Review* 64, January 1959.

Sandburg, Carl. *Abraham Lincoln, The Prairie Years and the War Years.* New York: Galahad Books, 1993.

Schneider, Charles, et al. "Parties and Local Elections." *Memphis Press-Scimitar*, 24 November 1962.

Scott, J. "Partisan Primary Grabs Spotlight in County Election." *Memphis Business Journal*, July 27–31, 1992.

Sefton, J. *Andrew Johnson and the Uses of Constitutional Power.* Boston, Mass. and Toronto, Canada: Little, Brown, & Co., 1980.

Shahan, Joe Michael. "Reform and Politics in Tennessee." Ann Arbor, Mich.: UMI Dissertation Services, 1993.

Sigafoos, Robert A. *Cotton Row to Beale Street.* Memphis, Tenn.: Memphis State University Press, 1979.

Smith, Guy. Form letter to the *Shelby County Republican* addressed, 27 March 1956.

Spence, John. "An All-Democrat Shelby Delegation Again Goes to the Legislature." *Memphis Press-Scimitar*, 4 November 1964.

———. "Hinds' Aid Given Pay of $1800." *Memphis Press-Scimitar*, 18 March 1964.

———. "Payroll Case Is Active on 3 Fronts." *Memphis Press-Scimitar*, 18 February 1964.

Squires, James D. *The Secrets of the Hopewell Box: Stolen Election, Southern Politics, and a City's Coming of Age.* New York: Times Books, 1996.

Street, William. "POLITICS This Morning." *Memphis Commercial Appeal*, 22 October 1967.

———. "POLITICS This Morning." *Memphis Commercial Appeal*, 24 October 1967.

Sundquist, Governor Don. Personal communication with the author, May 1995.

Tennessee Blue Book, 1987–1988.

Tennessee Blue Book, Bicentennial Edition, 1796–1996.

Thomas, Benjamin. *Abraham Lincoln, A Biography*. New York: Random House, Inc., 1982.

"Three Contend without Issues Amid 'Apathy'" *Memphis Commercial Appeal,* 22 July 1996.

Topp, Edward. "Battle in District 2 for Endorsements." *Memphis Press-Scimitar*, 16 October 1967.

Tubb, Jerry. "Thundering Hurd." *INTROSPECTION-3 A.M.* 5 November 1986.

Tucker, D. *Lieutenant Lee of Beale Street.* Nashville, Tenn.: Vanderbilt University Press, 1971.

"21,714 Was Paid for Publishing Notices." *Memphis Press-Scimitar*, 17 February 1964.

U.S. Senate History Office.

Wade, P. "Frist Ends Long Reign of Sasser." *Memphis Commercial Appeal*, 9 November 1994.

Wade, P. "Jackson Joins Fray as Legislators Seek Accord on Remap." *Commercial Appeal*, 19 January 1994.

Wellford, Honorable Harry. Letter to the editor of the *Commercial Appeal*, 15 March 1956.

———. Personal communication with the author, 20 August 1995.

Wellford, Walker. Letter to Leonard Hall, chairman of the Republican National Committee, 9 April 1956.

White, John. "New Question Marks Arise." *Memphis Press Scimitar*, 27 February 1964.

Whitney, David. *The American Presidents*. Garden City, N.Y.: Doubleday & Company, Inc., 1982.

Williams, John T. Personal communication with the author, 1993–1996.

Wilson, George. State Republican Party chairman notice to reorganize, 3 October 1963.

Governors of Tennessee

Name	Birth Year	Birth State	Death Year	Date Inaugurated	Occupation	Politics
*William Blount	1749	NC	1800	Sept. 20, 1790	Soldier	Dem.-Rep.
John Sevier	1745	VA	1815	Mar. 30, 1796	Soldier, pioneer	Dem.-Rep.
Archibald Roane	1759	PA	1819	Sept. 23, 1801	Lawyer	Dem.-Rep.
John Sevier	1745	VA	1815	Sept. 23, 1803	Soldier, pioneer	Dem.-Rep.
Willie Blount	1768	NC	1835	Sept. 20, 1809	Lawyer, planter	Dem.-Rep.
Joseph McMinn	1758	PA	1824	Sept. 27, 1815	Merchant	Dem.-Rep.
William Carroll	1788	PA	1844	Oct. 1, 1821	Merchant, soldier	Dem.-Rep.
Sam Houston	1793	VA	1863	Oct. 1, 1827	Lawyer	Dem.-Rep.
William Hall	1775	NC	1856	Apr. 16, 1829	Planter, soldier	Dem.-Rep.
William Carroll	1788	PA	1844	Oct. 1, 1829	Merchant, soldier	Dem.-Rep.
Newton Cannon	1781	NC	1841	Oct. 12, 1835	Planter	Whig
James K. Polk	1795	NC	1849	Oct. 14, 1839	Lawyer	Dem.
James C. Jones	1809	TN	1859	Oct. 15, 1841	Lawyer	Whig
Aaron V. Brown	1795	VA	1859	Oct. 14, 1845	Lawyer	Dem.
Neill S. Brown	1810	TN	1886	Oct. 17, 1847	Lawyer	Whig
William Trousdale	1790	NC	1872	Oct. 16, 1849	Lawyer	Dem.
William B. Campbell	1807	TN	1867	Oct. 16, 1851	Lawyer	Whig
Andrew Johnson	1808	NC	1875	Oct. 17, 1853	Tailor, President	Dem.
Isham G. Harris	1818	TN	1897	Nov. 3, 1857	Lawyer, U.S. Senator	Dem.
**Andrew Johnson	1808	NC	1875	1862	Tailor, President	Union
William G. Brownlow	1805	VA	1877	Apr. 5, 1865	Editor, preacher	Whig-Rep.
DeWitt C. Senter	1830	TN	1898	Feb. 25, 1869	Lawyer	Rep.
John C. Brown	1827	TN	1889	Oct. 10, 1871	Lawyer	Dem.
James D. Porter	1828	TN	1912	Jan. 18, 1875	Lawyer, educator	Dem.
Albert S. Marks	1836	KY	1891	Feb. 16, 1879	Lawyer, chancellor	Dem.
Alvin Hawkins	1821	KY	1905	Jan. 17, 1881	Lawyer, judge	Rep.
William B. Bate	1826	TN	1905	Jan. 15, 1883	Lawyer, U.S. Senator	Dem.
Robert Love Taylor	1850	TN	1912	Jan. 17, 1887	Lawyer, U.S. Senator	Dem.
John P. Buchanan	1847	TN	1930	Jan. 19, 1891	Farmer	Dem.
Peter Turney	1827	TN	1903	Jan. 16, 1893	Lawyer, judge	Dem.
Robert Love Taylor	1850	TN	1912	Jan. 21, 1897	Lawyer, U.S. Senator	Dem.
Benton McMillin	1845	KY	1933	Jan. 16, 1899	Lawyer, diplomat	Dem.
James B. Frazier	1856	TN	1937	Jan. 19, 1903	Lawyer, U.S. Senator	Dem.
John I. Cox	1857	TN	1946	Mar. 21, 1905	Lawyer	Dem.
Malcolm R. Patterson	1861	AL	1935	Jan. 17, 1907	Lawyer, judge	Dem.
Ben W. Hooper	1870	TN	1957	Jan. 26, 1911	Lawyer	Rep.

* Territorial
** Military

Name	Birth Year	Birth State	Death Year	Date Inaugurated	Occupation	Politics
Tom C. Rye	1863	TN	1953	Jan. 17, 1915	Lawyer, judge	Dem.
**A. H. Roberts	1868	TN	1946	Jan. 15, 1919	Lawyer, judge	Dem.
Alfred A. Taylor	1848	TN	1931	Jan. 15, 1921	Lawyer	Rep.
Austin Peay	1876	KY	1927	Jan. 16,1923	Lawyer	Dem.
Henry H. Horton	1866	AL	1934	Oct. 3, 1927	Lawyer, farmer	Dem.
Hill McAlister	1875	TN	1960	Jan. 17, 1933	Lawyer	Dem.
Gordon Browning	1895	TN	1976	Jan. 15, 1937	Lawyer, judge	Dem.
Prentice Cooper	1895	TN	1969	Jan. 16, 1939	Lawyer	Dem.
Jim McCord	1879	TN	1968	Jan. 16, 1945	Editor	Dem.
Gordon Browning	1895	TN	1976	Jan. 16, 1945	Lawyer, judge	Dem.
Frank G. Clement	1920	TN	1969	Jan. 15, 1953	Lawyer	Dem.
Buford Ellington	1907	MS	1972	Jan. 19, 1959	Farmer	Dem.
Frank G. Clement	1920	TN	1969	Jan. 15, 1963	Lawyer	Dem.
Buford Ellington	1907	MS	1972	Jan. 16, 1967	Farmer	Dem.
Winfield Dunn	1927	MS	Living	Jan. 16, 1971	Dentist	Rep.
Ray Blanton	1930	TN	Living	Jan. 18, 1975	Farmer, businessman	Dem.
Lamar Alexander	1940	TN	Living	Jan. 17, 1979	Lawyer	Rep.
Ned McWherter	1930	TN	Living	Jan. 17, 1987	Businessman	Dem.
Don Sundquist	1936	IL	Living	Jan. 21, 1995	Businessman	Rep.

U.S. Senators of Tennessee

[Throughout, Dem.-Rep. (Democrat-Republicans) also could have been known as Republicans.]

Name	Politics	Congress	Term (Class 1)	Remarks
William Cocke	Dem.-Rep.	4th	Aug. 2, 1796– Mar. 3, 1797	
William Cocke	Dem.-Rep.	5th	Apr. 22, 1797– Sept. 26, 1797	By gov. to fill vac.
Andrew Jackson	Dem.-Rep.	5th–7th	Sept. 26, 1797– Mar. 3, 1803	Res. in Apr. 1798
Daniel Smith	Dem.-Rep.	5th	Oct. 6, 1798– Dec. 12, 1798	By gov. to fill vac.
Joseph Anderson	Dem.-Rep.	5th–10th	Dec. 12, 1798– Mar. 3, 1809	
Joseph Anderson	Dem.-Rep.	11th	Mar. 4, 1809– Apr. 10, 1809	By gov. to fill vac.
Joseph Anderson	Dem.-Rep.	11th–13th	Apr. 11, 1809– Mar. 3, 1815	Vac. Mar. 4– Oct. 10, 1815
George W. Campbell	Dem.-Rep.	14th–16th	Oct. 10, 1815– Mar. 3, 1821	Res. Apr. 20, 1818
John H. Eaton	Dem.-Rep.	15th–16th	Sept. 5, 1818– Oct. 8, 1819	By gov. to fill vac.
John H. Eaton*	Dem.-Rep.	16th–22nd	Oct. 9, 1819– Mar. 3, 1833	Res. Mar. 9, 1829
Felix Grundy	Dem.	21st–25th	Oct. 19, 1829– Mar. 3, 1839	Res. July 4, 1838
Ephraim H. Foster	Whig	25th	Sept. 17, 1838– Mar. 3, 1839	By gov. to fill vac. Vac. Mar. 4– Dec. 14, 1839
Felix Grundy	Dem.	26th–28th	Dec. 14, 1839– Mar. 3, 1845	Died Dec. 19, 1840
Alfred O. P. Nicholson	Dem.	26th–27th	Dec. 25, 1840– Feb. 7, 1842	By gov. to fill vac.
Ephraim H. Foster	Whig	28th	Oct. 17, 1843– Mar. 3, 1845	
Hopkins L. Turney	Dem.	29th–31st	Mar. 4, 1845– Mar. 3, 1851	
James C. Jones	Whig	32nd–34th	Mar. 4, 1851– Mar. 3, 1857	Vac. Mar. 4– Oct. 7, 1857
Andrew Johnson	Dem.	35th–37th	Oct. 8, 1857– Mar. 3, 1863	Res. Mar. 4, 1862 Vac. Mar. 4, 1862– May 4, 1865
David T. Patterson	Unionist	39th–40th	May 4, 1865– Mar. 3, 1869	By leg. to fill vac.

* After Andrew Jackson's 1824 election loss, Eaton became a Jacksonian Democrat.

Name	Politics	Congress	Term (Class 1)	Remarks
William G. Brownlow	Rep.	41st–43rd	Mar. 4, 1869– Mar. 3, 1875	
Andrew Johnson	Dem.	44th–46th	Mar. 4, 1875– Mar. 3, 1881	Died July 31, 1875
David M. Key	Dem.	44th	Aug. 18, 1875– Jan. 19, 1877	By gov. to fill vac.
James E. Bailey	Dem.	44th–46th	Jan. 19, 1877– Mar. 3, 1881	
Howell E. Jackson	Dem.	47th–49th	Mar. 4, 1881– Mar. 3, 1887	Res. Apr. 14, 1886
Washington Whitthorne	Dem.	49th	Apr. 16, 1886– Mar. 3, 1887	By gov. to fill vac.
William B. Bate	Dem.	50th–61st	Mar. 4, 1887– Mar. 3, 1911	Died Mar. 9, 1905
James B. Frazier	Dem.	59th–61st	Mar. 21, 1905– Mar. 3, 1911	
Luke Lea	Dem.	62nd–64th	Mar. 4, 1911– Mar. 3, 1917	
Kenneth D. McKellar	Dem.	65th–82nd	Mar. 4, 1917– Jan. 2, 1953	
Albert Gore Sr.	Dem.	83rd–91st	Jan. 3, 1953– Jan. 2, 1971	
William E. Brock III	Rep.	92nd–94th	Jan. 3, 1971– Jan. 2, 1977	
James R. Sasser	Dem.	95th–103rd	Jan. 3, 1977– Jan. 2, 1995	
William Frist	Rep.	104th	Jan. 3, 1995–	

CLASS 2

William Blount	Dem.-Rep.	4th–5th	Aug. 2, 1796– Mar. 3, 1799	Exp. July 8, 1797
Joseph Anderson	Dem.-Rep.	5th	Sept. 26, 1797– Mar. 3, 1799	
William Cocke	Dem.-Rep.	6th–8th	Mar. 4, 1799– Mar. 3, 1805	
Daniel Smith	Dem.-Rep.	9th–11th	Mar. 4, 1805– Mar. 3, 1811	Res. Mar. 31, 1809
Jenkins Whiteside	Dem.-Rep.	11th–14th	Apr. 11, 1809– Mar. 3, 1817	Res. Oct. 8, 1811
George W. Campbell	Dem.-Rep.	12th–14th	Oct. 8, 1811– Mar. 3, 1817	Res. Feb. 11, 1814
Jesse Wharton	Dem.-Rep.	13th–14th	Mar. 17, 1814– Oct. 10, 1815	By gov. to fill vac.
John Williams	Dem.-Rep.	14th	Oct. 10, 1815– Mar. 3, 1817	

Name	Politics	Congress	Term (Class 2)	Remarks
John Williams	Dem.-Rep.	15th	Mar. 4, 1817– Oct. 1, 1817	By gov. during legislature recess
John Williams	Dem.-Rep.	15th–17th	Oct. 2, 1817– Mar. 3, 1823	
Andrew Jackson	Dem.-Rep.	18th–20th	Mar. 4, 1823– Mar. 3, 1829	Res. Oct. 14, 1825
Hugh Lawson White*	Dem.-Rep.	19th–23rd	Oct. 28, 1825– Mar. 3, 1835	Vac. Mar. 4– Oct. 5, 1835
Hugh Lawson White**	Dem.	24th–26th	Oct. 6, 1835– Mar. 3, 1841	Res. Jan. 13, 1840
Alexander Anderson	Dem.	26th	Jan. 27, 1840– Mar. 3, 1841	Vac. Mar. 4- Oct. 16, 1843
Spencer Jarnagin	Whig	28th–29th	Oct. 17, 1843– Mar. 3, 1847	
John Bell	Whig	30th–32nd	Nov. 22, 1847– Mar. 3, 1853	Vac. Mar. 4, 1841- Oct. 28, 1853
John Bell	Whig	33rd–35th	Oct. 29, 1853– Mar. 3, 1859	
Alfred O. P. Nicholson	Dem.	36th–38th	Mar. 4, 1859– Mar. 3, 1865	Retired Mar. 3, 1861 Vac. Mar. 3, 1861-
Joseph S. Fowler	Unionist	39th–41st	May 4, 1865– Mar. 3, 1871	May 4, 1865
Henry Cooper	Dem.	42nd–44th	Mar. 4, 1871– Mar. 3, 1877	
Isham G. Harris	Dem.	45th–56th	Mar. 4, 1877– Mar. 3, 1901	Died July 8, 1897
Thomas B. Turley	Dem.	55th	July 20, 1897– Feb. 1, 1898	By gov. to fill vac.
Thomas B. Turley	Dem.	55th–56th	Feb. 2, 1898– Mar. 3, 1901	
Edward W. Carmack	Dem.	57th–59th	Mar. 4, 1901– Mar. 3, 1907	
Robert L. Taylor	Dem.	60th–62nd	Mar. 4, 1907– Mar. 3, 1913	Died Mar. 31, 1912
Newell Sanders	Rep.	62nd	Apr. 8, 1912– Jan. 24, 1913	By gov. to fill vac.
William R. Webb	Dem.	62nd	Jan. 24, 1913– Mar. 3, 1913	
John K. Shields	Dem.	63rd–68th	Mar. 4, 1913– Mar. 3, 1925	
Lawrence D. Tyson	Dem.	69th–71st	Mar. 4, 1925– Mar. 3, 1931	Died Aug. 24, 1929
William E. Brock	Dem.	71st	Sept. 2, 1929– Nov. 3, 1930	By gov., to fill vac.
William E. Brock	Dem.	71st	Nov. 4, 1930–	

*White became a Jacksonian Democrat.

**White dropped his affiliation with the Democrats after a dispute with Jackson.

Name	Politics	Congress	Term (Class 2)	Remarks
			Mar. 3, 1931	
Cordell Hull	Dem.	72nd–74th	Mar. 4, 1931– Jan. 2, 1937	Res. Mar. 3, 1933
Nathan L. Bachman	Dem.	73rd	Mar. 4, 1933– Nov. 6, 1934	By gov. to fill vac.
Nathan L. Bachman	Dem.	73rd–77th	Nov. 7, 1934– Jan. 2, 1943	Died Apr. 23, 1937
George L. Berry	Dem.	75th	May 6, 1937– Nov. 8, 1938	By gov., to fill vac. Vac. Nov. 9, 1938-
Tom Stewart	Dem.	75th–80th	Jan. 16, 1939– Jan. 2, 1949	Jan. 15, 1939
Estes Kefauver	Dem.	81st–89th	Jan. 3, 1949– Jan. 2, 1967	Died Aug. 10, 1963
Herbert S. Walters	Dem.	88th	Aug. 20, 1963– Nov. 3, 1964	By gov. to fill vac.
Ross Bass	Dem.	88th–89th	Nov. 4, 1964– Jan. 2, 1967	
Howard H. Baker, Jr	Rep.	90th–98th	Jan. 3, 1967– Jan. 2, 1985	
Albert Gore, Jr.	Dem.	99th–104th	Jan. 3, 1985– Jan. 2, 1997	Res. Jan. 2, 1993 after election as U.S. vice president, Nov. 3, 1992
Harlan Mathews	Dem.	103rd–104th	Jan. 3, 1993– Dec. 1, 1996	By gov. to fill vac.
Fred Thompson	Rep.	104th	Dec. 2, 1996-	

Index